DATE DUE

Brodart Co.   Cat. # 55 137 001   Printed in USA

FOUNDATIONS
of Casualty Actuarial Science

Fourth Edition

Casualty Actuarial Society

The Casualty Actuarial Society acknowledges the cooperation of the Insurance Services Office, Inc. and the National Council on Compensation Insurance for use of their materials.

Casualty Actuarial Society
1100 North Glebe Road, Suite 600
Arlington, VA 22201
(703) 276-3100
www.casact.org

Printed in the United States of America by United Book Press, Inc.

ISBN (cloth) 0-9624762-2-6

Library of Congress Control Number: 2001088378

CONTENTS

Chapter 1   Introduction

Sholom Feldblum

Chapter 2   Risk Theory

Margaret Tiller Sherwood

Chapter 3   Ratemaking

Charles L. McClenahan

Chapter 4   Individual Risk Rating

Margaret Tiller Sherwood

Chapter 5   Loss Reserving

Ronald F. Wiser, revised and updated by
Jo Ellen Cockley and Andrea Gardner

Chapter 6   Risk Classification

Robert J. Finger

Chapter 7   Reinsurance

Gary S. Patrik

Chapter 8   Credibility

Howard C. Mahler and Curtis Gary Dean

Chapter 9   Investment Issues in Property-Liability Insurance

Stephen P. D'Arcy

Chapter 10   Special Issues

*Richard W. Gorvett, John L. Tedeschi, and
Kimberley A. Ward*

PREFACE TO THE FOURTH EDITION

The first edition of the Casualty Actuarial Society's textbook, *Foundations of Casualty Science*, published in 1990, was a landmark effort by the Society to furnish members and students with a comprehensive textbook on basic actuarial topics. Subsequent to publication of the first edition, demand resulted in second and third editions with only limited changes to correct errata. Some of the chapters of that first edition contained material advanced beyond the objective of introductory actuarial concepts. Actuarial science has also progressed substantially since 1990, especially in mathematical modeling of this world in which actuaries labor in predicting the future from evidence of the past.

Thus, in 1998 a task force was charged with the responsibility of evaluating the then existing third edition of the textbook and recommending changes for a fourth. After the task force work was completed, their recommendations were given to the Textbook Rewriting Committee, formed to bring the recommendations into reality. As a result, in the fourth edition, all chapters have now been brought to an introductory level of actuarial science, using updated examples. Further, a new chapter on risk theory is added to cover more completely a topic previously treated as a section in the first edition's final chapter, Special Issues. Risk theory is placed as Chapter 2 to help set the stage for the substantial mathematical-statistical works that follow.

This fourth edition is the result of the dedicated efforts of those willing to share their time, skills, and knowledge. With a few exceptions, authors contributing to the first edition authored this fourth edition. The gratitude of the entire Society go to the authors Stephen P. D'Arcy, Robert J. Finger, Charles L. McClenahan, Margaret Tiller Sherwood, and Gary S. Patrik, all of whom appeared in the first edition and agreed to write chapters for this fourth edition; to Sholom Feldblum, who accepted the challenging task of replacing Matt Rodermund's introductory chapter; to Richard W. Gorvett, who wrote the chapter on special issues with contributions from John L. Tedeschi and Kimberley A. Ward; to Curtis Gary Dean and Howard C. Mahler who coauthored the credibility chapter and are the creators of those challenging exercises; and to Jo Ellen Cockley and Andrea Gardner, who worked together to update Ron Wiser's chapter on loss reserving. Their efforts will benefit students for years.

The fourth edition was guided to print by the Textbook Rewriting Committee, consisting of Stephen P. D'Arcy, Steven J. Groeschen, Farrokh Guiahi, Robert F. Lowe, Donna S. Munt, and Rial R. Simons. The selection of the authors was entirely the responsibility of the committee. After the authors completed their drafts, the chapters were reviewed by members of the Textbook Rewriting Committee, and by the CAS Syllabus and Examination Committees, all of whom offered valuable advice. The Society can be grateful for the time and efforts of all those involved. Thanks also to Elizabeth A. Smith, Publications Production Editor of the CAS office and her staff, for their efforts in bringing this edition to completion.

The hope of the Textbook Rewriting Committee for this fourth edition cannot be stated better than in the preface to the first edition: "It is the sincere hope ... that this textbook will serve its purpose well in the years to come." Expect that this will not be the last revision, and since actuarial science continues evolving to meet complex and changing human society's demands, we repeat again from the prior preface: "Undoubtedly, there will be continuous review, resulting in deletions, additions, and updates." This fourth edition is only one step of "a process which will continue successfully over the years."

Robert F. Lowe
Chairperson, Textbook Rewriting Committee

JO ELLEN COCKLEY is a director and actuary for PMA Reinsurance Company. She is a Fellow of the Casualty Actuarial Society and a Member of the American Academy of Actuaries.

STEPHEN P. D'ARCY, PH.D., professor of finance, is the John C. Brogan Faculty Scholar in Risk Management and Insurance at the University of Illinois at Urbana-Champaign. He has won the Campus Award for Excellence in Undergraduate Teaching and the American Risk and Insurance Association Innovation in Instruction Award. He has served on the Governor's Task Force on Medical Malpractice and published papers on insurance and finance in the *Journal of Risk and Insurance, Risk Management and Insurance Review, Proceedings of the Casualty Actuarial Society, CPCU Journal, Journal of Insurance Regulation*, and *Journal of Business*. He also coauthored *The Financial Theory of Pricing Property-Liability Insurance Contracts*. A Fellow of the Casualty Actuarial Society and a Member of the American Academy of Actuaries, D'Arcy has served as president of the American Risk and Insurance Association and is currently serving on the CAS Board of Directors.

CURTIS GARY DEAN is the Lincoln Financial Group Distinguished Professor of Actuarial Science at Ball State University in Muncie, Indiana. Previously he was vice president and chief actuary for SAFECO's business insurance enterprise. He is a Fellow of the Casualty Actuarial Society and a Member of the American Academy of Actuaries. He has served on several CAS committees, including the Examination Committee on which he served as the chair during the last three years of his eleven-year committee tenure. He was the CAS Vice President–Administration for a three-year term ending November 2000. He has published papers in the *Proceedings of the Casualty Actuarial Society* and the CAS *Forum* and spoken at CAS meetings and seminars.

SHOLOM FELDBLUM is a vice president with the Liberty Mutual Group in Boston. He was graduated from Harvard University in 1978 and spent two years at the Hebrew University in Jerusalem. He is a past member of the CAS Board of Directors, CAS Syllabus Committee, the American Academy of Actuaries' Task Force on Risk-Based Capital, and associate editor of the *Actuarial Review*. He presently serves on the SOA Education Committee for the Advanced Investments and Finance Courses. He is the author of over 100 monographs, papers, reviews, and discussions on ratemaking procedures, reserving techniques, statutory accounting, insurance economics, company valuation, government regulation, and corporate finance. Feldblum received the 1993 Michelbacher Prize for his paper "Professional Ethics and the Actuary," the 1996 DFA Prize Paper for "Financial Modeling of Property-Casualty Insurance Companies," the 1997 Dorweiler Prize for "Automobile Insurance Premiums: An Asset Share Pricing Approach," and the 2000 Brian Hey Prize for "Underwriting Cycles and Business Strategies." He is a Fellow of both the Casualty Actuarial Society and the Society of Actuaries.

ROBERT J. FINGER, a consulting actuary, has written several papers for the *Proceedings of the Casualty Actuarial Society* and Casualty Actuarial Society *Discussion Paper Program*, including papers on ratemaking, reserving, and tax issues. He is a Fellow of the Casualty Actuarial Society, a Member of the American Academy of Actuaries, a Chartered Property and Casualty Underwriter, and member of the State Bar of California.

ANDREA GARDNER, assistant vice president of Reliance Insurance in Philadelphia, is a Fellow of the Casualty Actuarial Society and a Member of the American Academy of Actuaries.

RICHARD W. GORVETT, PH.D., assistant professor of actuarial science at the University of Illinois at Urbana-Champaign, has written papers on a variety of actuarial and financial topics. He won the Michelbacher Prize in 1999 for his paper "Insurance Securitization: The Development of a New Asset Class," and has twice coauthored papers that were awarded a CAS Dynamic Financial Analysis Prize. Prior to earning a Ph.D. in finance, he spent a number of years as a corporate and consulting actuary. He is a Fellow of the Casualty Actuarial Society, a Member of the American Academy of Actuaries, and an Associate in Risk Management.

HOWARD C. MAHLER was for many years the vice president and actuary at the Massachusetts Workers' Compensation Rating Bureau. Currently he teaches actuarial exam seminars. He has published numerous papers in the *Proceedings of the Casualty Actuarial Society* and the CAS *Forum*. In 1987, he won the Dorweiler Prize for his review of Glenn Meyers' paper, "An Analysis of Experience Rating." He served 12 years on the CAS Examination Committee, including 3 years as committee chair. He is a Fellow of the Casualty Actuarial Society and a Member of the American Academy of Actuaries.

CHARLES L. MCCLENAHAN, principal of the actuarial consulting firm William M. Mercer, Inc. in Chicago, has written several papers and articles on various casualty actuarial topics. He is a Fellow of the Casualty Actuarial Society, an Associate of the Society of Actuaries and a Member of the American Academy of Actuaries.

GARY S. PATRIK is currently the chief pricing actuary of Swiss Reinsurance Corporation, Americas Division. He has served the CAS in various functions, including serving on the Board of Directors and chairing the Committee on Theory of Risk, Committee on Reinsurance Research, and the DFA Task Force on Variables. He has also served as the president of the Casualty Actuaries in Reinsurance. He has authored or coauthored many papers, articles, and books for various organizations, including the CAS and the Insurance Institute of America. He is a cowinner of the Michelbacher Prize and the Boleslaw Monic Fund Competition. He is a Fellow of the Casualty Actuarial Society, a Member of the American Academy of Actuaries, a Chartered Property and Casualty Underwriter, and a member of ASTIN.

MARGARET TILLER SHERWOOD is president of Tiller Consulting Group, Inc., an actuarial and environmental risk consulting firm in St. Louis. She is the lead author of the first edition of the textbook, *Essentials of Risk Financing*, and has written many articles in actuarial and risk management publications. She is a Fellow of the Casualty Actuarial Society, an Associate of the Society of Actuaries, a Member of the American Academy of Actuaries, a Fellow of the Conference of Consulting Actuaries, a Chartered Property and Casualty Underwriter, and holds an Insurance Institute of America diploma of Associate in Risk Management. She is also a member of the International Actuarial Association, ASTIN, AFIR, and the International Association of Consulting Actuaries.

JOHN L. TEDESCHI, senior vice president at Guy Carpenter Instrat, has actively participated in the growth of catastrophe simulation models over his career. While the cede reinsurance actuary and risk manager at Royal SunAlliance, he assisted in developing an in-house model and later while with Guy Carpenter, he was a key member of the EQECAT team. He continues to assist large national and multinational insurer and reinsurers with catastrophe reinsurance and securitization issues. He is an Associate of the Casualty Actuarial Society and a Member of the American Academy of Actuaries.

KIMBERLEY A. WARD, chief actuary for the American Association of Insurance Services (AAIS), was the director of environmental and asbestos reserving at CNA prior to her current position at AAIS. At CNA, she developed and implemented the claim department method of evaluating environmental and pollution reserves. In addition, she is a member of the American Academy of Actuaries Environmental Work Group. She is a Fellow of the Casualty Actuarial Society and a Member of the American Academy of Actuaries.

RONALD F. WISER, consulting actuary, Solon Consulting Actuaries, is the author of several papers including "The Cost of Mixing Reinsurance" and "An Algorithm for Premium Adjustment with Scarce Data," both of which were published in the *Proceedings of the Casualty Actuarial Society*. He has received both the Michelbacher and the Dorweiler prizes from the Casualty Actuarial Society. He is a Fellow of the Casualty Actuarial Society and a Member of the American Academy of Actuaries.

2000 Textbook Rewriting Committee

Robert F. Lowe, *Chairperson*
Stephen P. D'Arcy
Steven J. Groeschen
Farrokh Guiahi
Donna S. Munt
Rial R. Simons

CHAPTER 1

INTRODUCTION

SHOLOM FELDBLUM

The new edition of *Foundations of Casualty Actuarial Science* marks another milestone for the CAS, one of the most remarkable professional societies of our time. Born in 1914 as a small group of statisticians setting premium rates for workers compensation, the CAS has emerged as a leading purveyor of actuarial innovation, with rigorous examinations, journals, and seminars, and with expanding employment vistas for its members.

The CAS has matured, and with maturity come new challenges. Actuarial literature has flourished; few actuaries can easily master the entire corpus. The new edition of *Foundations of Casualty Actuarial Science* provides accessible and up-to-date surveys of casualty actuarial science, geared to the new student seeking to join the profession.

The chapters of this textbook, written by some of the leading actuaries of our generation, bring the reader directly into the halls of actuarial science. This introduction provides an overview of this science, along with an understanding of the emerging actuarial trends of our day.

THE SCIENCE

Actuarial science is a blend of academic rigor and business practice. The actuary must justify conclusions with statistical data, never content to rely on intuition alone. The expansion of actuarial science into new domains, such as dynamic financial analysis, testifies to the continuing vitality of the profession.

The actuary must tackle whatever problem confronts him or her. Actuarial science is grounded in business practice. Sound theory generates sound solutions, but theoretical solutions are insufficient. Actuarial solutions must be implemented, or they are not solutions at all.

Credibility

Credibility theory illustrates the actuarial perspective. Credibility theory is the adaptation of theoretical statistics to a variety of daily business problems. Credibility theory was one of the first fruits of actuarial research, and it remains one of the most productive fields of actuarial work. Almost every decade it has been re-invigorated, as actuaries developed new techniques with implications for the pricing and valuation of financial or insurance products. Even now, the theory of credibility has numerous untested uses, beckoning to the next actuary who can adapt the theory to practical problems (see below).

Credibility theory is an exemplar of actuarial science; so well does it epitomize the nature of actuarial science that Matthew Rodermund chose it as the topic for the first introduction to this textbook. The statistician measures confidence intervals, telling us when we may be 95% confident that our estimate is correct. But we are rarely so sure of our results in practice—and when we are so certain, we do not need actuaries. The actuary tells us what to do when we are *not* 95% confident—when we are only 40% confident, or when we don't even know how confident we are. Moreover, the actuary tells us how to join our confidence in the data with other information and with other business considerations.

We return to credibility theory later in this introduction. Let us first address a more fundamental issue: "What is actuarial science?"

Theory and Practice

Actuarial science is the practical application of finance and statistics. Some persons might shun actuarial work, since it is constrained by practice: by the insurance marketplace, by accounting systems, by available data, by management needs. Yet this is the delight of actuarial science: the use of reason and theory to solve business challenges that arise about us. The practicing actuary is not esteemed solely for intellectual skills. The practicing actuary is esteemed for the ability to apply those skills to insurance, financial, and business problems.

One might presume that a textbook titled *Foundations of Casualty Actuarial Science* would lay out the abstract principles that undergird actuarial science. But principles are not the focus of this textbook, and even fewer such principles are to be found among the thousands of practicing actuaries who regularly use the methods described here. The chapters of this textbook do not develop "actuarial theory" from axioms; they do not prove theorems and lemmas.

Actuarial science has borrowed its procedures from a variety of other sources: from economics, from finance, from statistics, and from financial engineering. The theoretical procedures are modified, blended, and transformed; they are merged with underwriting, accounting, and marketing to answer fundamental business questions dealing with property-casualty insurance systems. Sound theory is a prerequisite, but it is insufficient to validate an actuarial procedure. The ultimate judge is the marketplace, whether the marketplace of goods and prices or the marketplace of business practice.

CHARACTERISTICS OF OUR SCIENCE

What are the distinguishing attributes of actuarial science?

1. Actuaries begin with the final problem; they work backwards to devise an optimal solution. The problems range from the determination of adequate rates to the development of accurate reserves or optimal classification plans. Often the problem is vague. There is no single answer to the question: "What makes a classification plan better or worse?" There are multiple manners of proceeding, whether for rate indications or reserve indications or for financial models. The actuary's task is to develop appropriate procedures, to determine what data are needed

for these procedures, and to examine the feasibility and cost of obtaining these data and performing the analyses. The chapter on Risk Classification in this textbook approaches these questions from multiple perspectives, for they are all components of the actuary's work.

2. Actuaries seek optimal solutions, not perfect solutions. Business problems rarely have perfect solutions. There is no perfect classification system, no perfect experience rating plan, no perfect loss reserving method. One classification system may be accurate, but too costly; another system may be less expensive but less accurate. Some procedures work well in one environment, but fare poorly in other environments. The actuary's task is to formulate the best solution to the business problem, not to prove the validity of a particular method.

3. The actuary considers all constraints, whether they seem reasonable or not. The actuary may be asked to devise a classification system within constraints imposed by regulators, or a pricing system within constraints imposed by management, or a capital allocation system with constraints imposed by statutory accounting. Yet the actuary does not hesitate to break the constraining bounds of the environment: to recommend new solvency monitoring systems, new classification dimensions, new pricing and marketing procedures.

4. The marketplace is the ultimate arbiter of the actuary's performance. Pricing procedures are judged by their ability to attract profitable business; reserving procedures are judged by their ability to forecast actual loss emergence.

Because of the emphasis on practical results, actuarial science ever renews itself. As business practice changes, new questions are asked of actuaries and new answers must be provided. Moreover, these changes are not merely at the margin. Many issues that have recently emerged require extensive reworking of our prior paradigms—not because the old ways were wrong, but because new tools, new procedures, and new problems are changing the way in which we analyze our environment.

The Reinsurance chapter in this textbook illustrates the adaptation of actuarial pricing and reserving techniques to various types of reinsurance arrangements for which empirical data are sparse. The extension of trend factors, development factors, and pricing procedures to high layers of loss, often by sophisticated curve fitting techniques that infer the needed relationships from the data that we observe, is testament to the actuaries' ingenuity. Similarly, the chapter on Individual Risk Rating illustrates how actuaries have adapted pricing and credibility techniques to the experience rating and retrospective rating plans that the marketplace produced. Here too, the derivation of insurance charges and excess loss charges for retrospective rating plans by inferences from theoretical loss distributions demonstrates how actuaries used observed data to develop solutions to new business challenges.

Many of the problems that actuaries deal with once seemed insurmountable. For instance, how can one price excess-of-loss casualty reinsurance treaties when the data are sparse or nonexistent? How can one make sense of the myriad cash flows of a large insurance enterprise? Only recently have we been able to provide practical solutions to these problems.

Yet the melding of theory and practice has been the foundation of actuarial success. Theorists may provide impractical advice; business persons may have practical but incorrect recommendations. As the chapters of this textbook testify, actuaries have found sound and practical solutions to myriad business problems.

Actuarial Education

The actuarial education system distinguishes it from other professions. Actuarial science is demanding: actuaries study as they work, spending hours each day for year after year. Most actuaries spend several thousand hours intensely studying a dozen subjects to obtain their Fellowship—often more study time than they spend in their college years. The subjects span an enormous spectrum: mathematics, statistics, economics, finance, modeling, underwriting, ratemaking, reserving, accounting, law, investments, taxes, valuation, financial engineering, and other fields.

The actuarial syllabus is geared to actuarial practice; the value of the education is measured by its ability to enhance the skills of practicing actuaries. But this is not mere on-the-job training. Routine company work is learned from co-workers and supervisors. Actuarial education is considerably more.

The actuarial examination system provides actuaries with the expertise to develop new methods as the company work changes. New actuaries must learn to improvise expertly. A Fellow of the Casualty Actuarial Society must be able to apply actuarially sound solutions to problems never encountered before.

The level of expertise demanded is high. The examinations expect that successful candidates will be experts in these fields; only the most intelligent and studious candidates join the actuarial profession.

The rigorous education system of the actuarial profession is the foundation of actuarial ability. Each new generation of actuaries stands on the shoulders of its predecessors; each new generation of actuaries is also expected to surpass its predecessors. Having mastered the techniques of older actuaries for the problems of the past, we are expected to develop even better techniques for the problems of the future.

This textbook is a portal into the world of actuarial science. Much of the examination syllabus consists of difficult papers or texts that already presume competence in the subject matter. *Foundations of Casualty Actuarial Science* serves as the introduction to the actuarial realm, geared towards the new student or the practicing actuary seeking to gain familiarity with a new area.

Actuarial Research

In some fields, contemporary research deals with the exotica. The foundations were laid generations ago; the fundamental questions have already been examined thousands of times.

Actuarial science is ever reborn. New products continually enter the marketplace, and actuaries are called upon to price them. New technological tools appear—computers, spreadsheets, simulation software—and actuaries use them to address problems that once seemed insurmountable. Actuaries must continually refresh their knowledge and their skills and adapt them to emerging problems.

The continual rebirth of actuarial science is manifest in the chapters of this textbook, many of which have been entirely rewritten for this fourth edition. The chapters are geared to the new student, but they are not mere summaries of received wisdom. The authors of these chapters are among the leading researchers of our day, many of whom have contributed substantially to the subjects they are summarizing.

The vitality of actuarial science is central to actuarial education. The student is not studying these techniques merely to apply them to similar problems. Techniques that are easily replicated are also easily programmed. The laborious actuarial tasks of yesteryear—such as the construction of life insurance mortality tables or automobile insurance rate manuals—are now generated by machine. The actuarial student, in contrast, studies the theory underlying these techniques in order to develop similar methods for new problems. The true actuary is always designing, never just imitating.

Emerging Topics

Sometimes, captivated by the intellectual debates circling financial issues, we come to believe that we venture further than previous actuarial generations. There is truth in this, though we must beware of taking too much credit. Our predecessors were aware of the issues that now confront the actuarial profession, such as quantifying the risks of insurance operations, setting rates in a competitive market, or developing a distribution of future loss payments. They lacked the tools, though, to even address these problems, much less to solve them. Instead, they developed useful simplifications to make the immediate business problems more tractable. Their methods, such as the loss ratio ratemaking procedure, the parallelogram method, or the chain ladder reserving procedure, remain essential components of the actuarial toolkit.

Actuarial science has changed radically in the past few decades, in two ways.

- First, the convergence of financial institutions in the business marketplace has been accompanied by a convergence of disciplines in the intellectual marketplace. No longer can actuaries be content with statistical procedures. Today's actuary must be proficient in modeling, finance, investments, and accounting, in addition to the traditional actuarial topics. Indeed, if actuaries fail to master these disciplines, others will eagerly step in to fill their places.

- Second, the availability of data and the growth of processing power continually outrun our analytical procedures. In the past, we would bemoan the lack of information or the crudeness of our computing facilities. A few years ago, actuaries might have said: *If only we had the financial world at our fingertips, we could price insurance products more accurately!*

Suddenly we have more data than we know what to do with, along with enormous computing power. Actuaries are free to design stochastic financial models, cash flow pricing models, and intricate reserving procedures.

New actuaries entering our profession are arriving amidst a flood of new actuarial paradigms. We are still in the process of moving from formal bureau rates to a wealth of independent pricing techniques and models. Actuarial models are being devised for solvency monitoring and capital allocation; both regulators and company management are turning to actuaries to opine on corporate risk and to recommend operating strategies to safeguard insurance enterprises. Investment theory and corporate finance have become intertwined with actuarial statistics for dealing with insurance issues.

The goal of this textbook—as well as the goal of actuarial education—is not simply to acquaint new students with traditional actuarial techniques. The goal is to produce actuaries who can adapt the knowledge of our predecessors to solve the myriad new problems confronting insurance systems. The faster the world changes around us, the quicker do specific techniques become obsolete, and the more important is a rigorous actuarial education.

INSURANCE

The outsider ever wonders: "What is it that the actuary does?" Upon being told that insurance is the business of risk and that the actuary specializes in the science of risk, the outsider is not satisfied. "After all," the outsider muses, "insurance companies are safe and bland financial institutions, in forty-floor towers of ever circulating paper; why do they need actuaries?"

It is testimony to the success of actuarial science that even in an industry of thin margins and severe competition, where product costs may not be known until years after the sale is complete, the public looks upon insurance as a safe enterprise.

It was not always this way. Before the actuarial societies were established and actuarial theory was accorded the respect it now enjoys, both life insurance and property-casualty insurance enterprises frequently collapsed. The early mutual assessment societies that ignored actuarial reserving theory often failed to pay the promised benefits to all their members. The early fire insurance companies that failed to price their policies adequately and spread their risks broadly often became insolvent after a major conflagration. The losses were borne by the very people that insurance was designed to protect—the dependents of deceased policyholders and families whose homes were destroyed.

This is ancient history, you might think. On the contrary; insurance companies are ever tempted to price policies by intuition and to set claim reserves by speculation. Were it not for the Casualty Actuarial Society, the long-tailed casualty lines of business would probably not be sold by private companies today. Until recently, few countries were willing to place the financial security of their citizens in the hands of a highly competitive industry prone to severe profit cycles. In the United States, we have done so consistently and safely for almost a century.

Risk

> *So what do actuaries do, and why is their specialized education so important?*

This seems like the simplest of questions: "What do actuaries do?" Nevertheless, this question defies consensus. As the insurance industry changes, some roles fade while other roles emerge. Some in the actuarial profession espouse redefining the essence of the actuary into the master of financial risk, and the actuarial syllabus—particularly on the life insurance side—is rapidly being reshaped in accordance with this definition. The emphasis on financial engineering in some actuarial circles similarly reflects this new perspective on actuarial science. Casualty actuaries need to understand the field of financial risk management, but this knowledge cannot replace the expertise in policy forms, underwriting, claims adjusting, marketing, and all the other specialized roles in the insurance industry that has served our society so well.

We return to the new vision of the actuary further below in this introduction. Most of this textbook, though, implicitly takes a traditional view of actuaries. Actuaries are what actuaries do, and most practicing casualty actuaries deal with the pricing and reserving of property-casualty insurance products and the valuation of property-casualty insurance companies. As we review the new challenges facing the casualty actuary, we will see the broadening of actuarial science and we will achieve a finer appreciation of the modern actuary's work.

No other industry has a specialized guild of professionals devoted to pricing their products, setting liabilities, and valuing their companies; what is special about insurance? *Risk is the answer*, we are often told; *actuaries are the specialists of risk, and insurance is the industry of risk.*

There is much truth to this, but the analysis of risk is only a part of the actuary's role and actuaries deal with only certain types of risk. To begin, let us place in perspective the risk of insurance enterprises.

Contrast the automobile manufacturer with the automobile insurer. The automobile manufacturer faces enormous business risk. The manufacturer must build a plant, buy equipment, train a workforce, set up a distribution system, advertise extensively, and commit enormous capital—years before the new auto is produced. If the new auto is successful, the company may double its investment in a few years. If the new auto does not sell well, the company may lose hundreds of millions of dollars.

This is business risk. It is the risk of the commitment of capital for an uncertain return. It is a risk associated particularly with industries that require extensive fixed capital, long research, and rapidly changing products; the pharmaceutical industry is an excellent example. But this is not a risk faced by the automobile insurer, which has almost no "fixed" up-front costs and (relatively) slowly changing products.

The insurer's dilemma is pricing the business, and this is the task of the actuary. The actuary must forecast cash flow payments for years into the future to price the policy sold now. Given the uncertainties of loss fluctuations, of inflation rates, and of interest rates, along with the constant pressure from underwriters and marketing staff for rate discounts to preferred customers, this is a complex balancing act.

The casualty actuary uses mathematical techniques to produce reliable estimates from uncertain projections of future occurrences; these estimates are used in turn for pricing and reserving property-casualty insurance products. The bulk of this textbook deals with methods of producing these estimates: class ratemaking, individual risk ratemaking, reserving, risk classification, credibility theory, financial pricing, and reinsurance pricing. This is an essential but difficult part of an insurer's operations. Many insurance personnel have tried their hand at it, but few have been successful.

Developing estimates from uncertain projections differs from the "science of risk," which—until recently—has been the province of investment analysts. The science of risk deals with the cost of risk itself, as well as the means of quantifying risk and of hedging risk.

The past decade has witnessed the gradual merging of the traditional actuarial tasks with the science of risk, epitomized by the emergence of dynamic financial analysis, which has been added to Chapter 10 of this edition of the *Foundations* textbook. Actuarial science has grown as new and more complex problems have arisen in the insurance industry. Modeling the uncertainty of insurance operations—from loss fluctuations, natural catastrophes, and interest rate changes—has become vital to many companies, and casualty actuaries are being called upon to solve this task.

RATEMAKING

Let us turn to the most fundamental task of the casualty actuary: setting rates for insurance products. The two sides of this task illuminate the ways that actuarial science is now progressing:

1. Determining the expected cost of the insurance product, and

2. Determining the optimal price for the insurance product.

These two tasks are distinct, though they are interrelated. The first task is actuarial. The expected amounts can be determined objectively, and casualty actuaries have excelled at the statistical aspects of this problem.

Charles McClenahan's excellent summary of the actuarial ratemaking procedure in this textbook illustrates the blending of rigor and practicality in actuarial work. Personal automobile insurance is a highly competitive market, and companies must produce new rates each year for hundreds of classifications (class by territory by coverage) in every state. McClenahan shows the structure of the ratemaking procedure; his contribution lies in making even complex tasks seem elementary. Indeed, the simplicity of the actuarial methods has enabled even small companies to price products from uncertain data.

Yet the problem is only partially solved. The more advanced our procedures become, the more opportunities arise to improve the methods. A few examples show the emerging tasks for the next generation of actuaries, even in the fundamentals of actuarial science.

1. Twenty years ago, actuaries used the same procedures for natural catastrophes as they did for routine insurance

losses, though they used longer experience periods and different credibility adjustments. As modeling tools have become more accurate, actuaries have turned to computer simulations of hurricanes and other windstorms to calculate the expected costs of these catastrophes.

Pricing coverage for catastrophic losses requires a blend of meteorological knowledge and modeling expertise. It is a tribute to the versatility of the actuarial profession and the competitiveness of the insurance market that half a dozen different pricing models are already being used in the industry, by small homeowners insurers to large property reinsurers. Above all, this shows the continuing growth of actuarial science, as new techniques allow better solutions to basic business problems.

Catastrophe modeling has progressed rapidly over the past dozen years, beginning with Karen Clark's seminal paper in 1985 and continuing through recent papers by Burger et al., Walters and Morin, and others that deal with ratemaking for windstorm perils. James Stanard and Stephen Lowe have recently created a complete DFA model for simulating excess of loss catastrophe reinsurance treaties. Catastrophe modeling is further discussed in Chapter 10 of this textbook.

2. Loss cost trends are a central part of the actuarial ratemaking procedure. Actuaries often have good knowledge of historical experience, but they must project past costs into future periods.

The economist may speak of random walks and the impossibility of projecting trends. The pricing actuary is not asked to opine on the feasibility of estimating trends; the actuary is asked to price the product. Herein lies the value of the casualty actuary. Although actuaries have had no more luck than economists in projecting future trends, they have succeeded in quantifying the relative effects of loss cost trends on different insurance products, such as low limit primary policies versus high layer excess-of-loss reinsurance treaties. Jeffrey Lange introduced the trend and development problems for higher layers of loss to the actuarial community by 1970, and Robert Miccolis's 1977 *Proceedings* paper on increased limits pricing laid the mathematical foundations that hundreds of pricing actuaries have since followed. The chapters by Charles McClenahan on Ratemaking and by Gary Patrik on Reinsurance discuss these issues in detail.

Financial Pricing

Years ago, actuaries were content with projecting nominal loss costs. Ever since the high interest rate environment of the late 1970s and the early 1980s, actuaries have been developing procedures for discounting losses and for pricing insurance products with return on capital or net present value perspectives.

The work is still in its formative stages. The foundations are now being laid, with continuing questions on the fundamental assumptions: *What is the appropriate rate for discounting future loss payments? How much capital must be held to support insurance operations, and what is the cost of holding this capital? What should be the target rate of return for pricing insurance products?*

These are not idle questions. There is great variety in the actuarial assumptions currently used in the industry, and corresponding variety in the resultant premium rates. D'Arcy's chapter in this textbook reviews several of the more influential pricing models; the interested student may continue with D'Arcy's recent papers in the *Proceedings of the CAS* and with the readings for the "Advanced Ratemaking" actuarial examination. This introductory essay highlights some of the more hotly disputed issues, to give the new candidate a flavor of the current issues in actuarial science.

Discount rates: The pricing of financial products uses present values of future cash payments. For traded securities with sufficiently deep markets, analysts use market determined discount rates. Loss reserves are not traded securities, and market data are not available for determining discount rates.

Actuaries take a variety of opinions. Some casualty actuaries, following one of the common perspectives in life insurance, use current investment yields on the conservative portfolios generally held by insurance enterprises. Other actuaries, such as Richard Woll and Stephen Lowe, have argued forcefully for a risk-free interest rate. Woll demonstrates how to produce "economic" accounting statements from statutory financial statements. As actuaries seek to measure the on-going performance of insurance companies, economic tools are increasingly being used to price insurance products. Lowe shows that the discount rate affects the pattern of income recognition and the division of income between underwriting operations and investment operations. He argues that discounting losses at the risk-free interest rate attributes to underwriting the true gains from the underwriting operations; the additional income from more profitable investment yields should be attributed to the investment operations.

Particularly intriguing—as well as difficult to judge—are the proponents of risk-adjusted discount rates. Beginning in the late 1970s, academics such as Kahane, Hill, Fairley, Myers, and Cohn proposed adaptations of the Capital Asset Pricing Model to insurance pricing, and a "CAPM" risk adjustment has been incorporated into the loss discount rate for some of these models. Although these pricing models have not been adopted by private insurers, the models illustrate the interconnections of corporate finance and modern portfolio theory with insurance pricing. These models are discussed in D'Arcy's chapter, with more extensive treatment in his recent *Proceedings* paper on insurance pricing models and his earlier monograph with Doherty on pricing insurance contracts.

Another approach to loss reserve discount rates and insurance pricing models has been developed by Robert Butsic. Butsic avoids the CAPM approach to loss reserve discount rates, since consistent and meaningful results have been impossible to attain.

Instead, he uses an intuitive and empirical approach to estimate a downward risk adjustment to loss reserve discount rates.

Dozens of other pricing models are being used by private insurers, including investment income offset models, return on capital models, internal rate of return models, and option pricing models. (Several of these models are covered on the "Advanced Ratemaking" examination syllabus.) Actuarial science promises decades of continuing research as actuaries develop more accurate and sophisticated models. New actuarial students, with strong backgrounds in finance and economics, have an opportunity to significantly enhance actuarial science.

Capital Requirements: Consideration of the time value of money is an essential element of financial pricing, particularly for insurance products whose cash flows are widely separated in time. But discounted cash flow models are only a part of property-casualty insurance pricing. Most financial pricing models must also determine a return on invested capital.

For many industries, the theory presents few conceptual problems. If $50 million is needed to build a plant and buy equipment, then the firm must earn a market return on the $50 million of capital, or investors will not be induced to supply the funds.

Insurance is different; no capital seems to be needed. With a typewriter and an office copier, one can hang out a shingle and—*voila!*—one can sell insurance policies. Indeed, one gets the premium before paying the losses. One can start from scratch and build up the business, as though it were a perpetual money machine. Nowhere is capital needed.

Well, perhaps it's not *that* simple. Capital is needed for a variety of reasons: to meet statutory accounting requirements, to guard against adverse scenarios, and to cover initial losses as one builds up a book of business. But no one seems to know how much capital is needed: having more capital may help with demonstrating financial strength to consumers, but having less capital increases the rate of return. Without knowing how much capital is needed to write insurance, one cannot price the insurance policy.

Actuaries generally say that capital is needed as a function of the risk of the enterprise. This seems sensible, though it is not axiomatic, and actuaries have begun quantifying the risk of insurance operations. The task is not easy, since we don't know the distributions of many contingent events and we do not even have a common yardstick to measure the risk of different operations.

Actuarial work in this field is advancing rapidly, since the questions have become paramount among financial institutions. In the 1990s, regulators devised risk-based capital requirements for insurance companies, following the lead taken by the banking industry. As the larger financial institutions spread across industries (banking, insurance, and investments) and across countries, regulators seek more uniform and more justified capital standards.

Actuaries have begun to answer the central questions. Robert Butsic introduced a general risk measure—an expected policyholder deficit ratio—that combines option pricing measures with probability of ruin analysis. Butsic's work has greatly influenced both regulatory solvency requirements and private pricing analyses. Ahead of us lies a vast expanse of actuarial and financial theory, as Butsic's theories join with the work of European actuaries, life actuaries, and investment analysts to develop a true science of risk. There is an abundance of fundamental research questions for the coming generation of actuaries.

CREDIBILITY

Matt Rodermund's introduction to the first edition of this textbook highlighted the development of credibility theory, from the earliest models of classical credibility through the convergence of credibility theory with Bayesian analysis. Credibility theory has continued to advance; recent work on this topic—both by casualty actuaries and by other professionals—testifies to the power of credibility formulas.

- At one time it was presumed that classical credibility and Bayesian–Bühlmann credibility were competing theories, and that the latter would soon replace the former. Gary Venter, in a thorough analysis of credibility in the first edition of this textbook, showed that the two credibility traditions had different objectives: classical credibility sought to minimize rate fluctuations whereas Bayesian–Bühlmann credibility sought to optimize pricing accuracy.

- Credibility theory has undergone some of its most innovative advances in the last decade of the 20th century. Howard Mahler, one of the leading actuarial authors of our generation, showed how credibility varied with the extent to which risk parameters shifted over time. By setting credibility concepts in the world of baseball won-lost statistics, and then providing a complete mathematical framework for large account experience rating, Mahler has authored actuarial papers that are a delight for the layman and a trove of powerful techniques for the practicing actuary.

Mahler has changed many of the previous actuarial notions of credibility. First, the speed at which risk parameters shift is no less important than the volume of business for setting credibility values. Second, Mahler shows that there is a range of optimal or close-to-optimal credibility values, and this range is often quite large. Any credibility value chosen from this range works about equally well for maximizing pricing accuracy. In other words, the difference between 2,000 claims versus 3,000 claims for the full credibility value may be of little significance if both values are within the optimal or close-to-optimal range. However, the pricing actuary should examine the rate at which risk parameters shift to determine whether older experience years have much predictive value for the future.

- Credibility theory was nourished by casualty actuaries, but it is now finding use in other fields. Particularly valuable is its use in financial engineering. Actuaries estimate loss frequency and loss severity; financial engineers estimate betas and volatility. Both sets of professionals use observed data to predict future events. Just as Bayesian–Bühlmann credibility has been used by casualty actuaries to optimize pricing accuracy, financial analysts are beginning to use Bayesian–Bühlmann credibility to optimize their estimates of betas and of stock volatility.

Despite having been studied systematically for 85 years, credibility theory still presents many unexplored fields of study for the next generation of actuaries. The application of actuarial theory to related questions in financial engineering is a particularly promising avenue of research for future actuaries.

RESERVING

Along with ratemaking, loss reserving has traditionally been the actuary's role. The "Reserving" chapter in this textbook introduces the multiplicity of reserving methods, and the "Reinsurance" chapter adds some additional procedures that are especially suitable for the highly volatile reinsurance lines of business.

Loss reserving is particularly important to the Casualty Actuarial Society, since regulatory authorities in North America— both the U.S. and in Canada—require a statement by a certified ("Appointed") actuary opining on the adequacy of loss reserves. In the U.S., certification is generally demonstrated by membership in the CAS, since members of the CAS have passed the actuarial examinations on loss reserving and statutory accounting.

Reserving is a complex task. The actuary's claim to pre-eminence in setting reserves is based upon mastery of a wealth of reserving techniques, many of which are described in Wiser's chapter in this textbook, along with a keen sense of the sensitivity of losses to economic, financial, and operating changes.

The past two decades have witnessed an enormous advance in computing power, along with a proliferation of consulting firms and software packages that efficiently produce reserve indications using all the techniques in Wiser's chapter. Accordingly, the reserving actuary's focus has broadened in recent years, as reserving software has eliminated the time-consuming calculations. Recent actuarial literature suggests many emerging topics, of which we note four that seem especially promising.

1. The traditional actuarial reserving techniques were distinct, both from each other and from classical statistical analysis. Actuaries used chain ladder methods and expected loss methods; statisticians used regression analysis and Bayesian analysis. A masterful synthesis by Dr. J. Eric Brosius, a mathematician and a Fellow of the CAS, combined all four of these analytical methods to produce a more powerful and accurate reserving method.

2. The traditional reserving techniques presume that past history is a model for the future. In particular, these techniques presume that development of losses in "mature" accident years will be repeated in the more recent accident years.

   In the 1980s and 1990s, the insurance industry was faced with estimating its liabilities for asbestos, pollution, and other toxic tort or latent injury exposures. The existing reserving models were of limited usefulness for these claims. For many types of exposure, there was little past claim history. Rather, new medical findings, new legislation, and new environmental concerns caused a sudden emergence of claims from all accident years, even from insurance policies written in the 1950s and 1960s.

The potential liabilities from these new exposures is enormous. Latent disease litigation had already impaired several chemical, manufacturing, and pharmaceutical firms; regulatory authorities feared that some large, commercial lines insurance enterprises might succumb as well. Casualty actuaries developed reserving models to estimate insurer's exposure to these new sources of liability. The writings and presentations of actuaries such as Amy Bouska have helped both the actuarial profession and the insurance industry deal with these new liabilities. The potential liability from these new exposures continues to grow, and actuaries will be called upon more and more frequently to estimate the liabilities of insurance enterprises. Chapter 10 covers some of these issues.

3. As potential loss costs in various lines increase, the reinsurance industry has grown in step. But reserving for high layers of loss is exceedingly complex. The development factors differ so greatly for excess layers that primary company experience cannot be used and reinsurance experience is too sparse to be credible.

Reinsurance actuaries have turned to modeling for both pricing and reserving. Many of the advanced reinsurance pricing techniques are summarized in Gary Patrik's chapter in this textbook. Emanuel Pinto and Daniel Gogol have developed similar modeling and curve fitting techniques to estimate development factors for high layers of loss.

4. Perhaps the most fertile field of new actuarial reserving analysis lies in stochastic simulation. The traditional reserving procedures are deterministic; they indicate "best-estimate" reserves, assuming no change in the insurance

or financial environments. These procedures satisfy accounting needs; they determine the reserve indications for the insurer's balance sheet. But they do not portray the risk of reserve uncertainty, and they do not show the dependence of reserve estimates on interest rates, inflation rates, and various other stochastic variables.

Casualty actuaries, such as James Stanard, Glenn Meyers, Rodney Kreps, and Gary Blumsohn, have begun to meld reserving procedures with estimates of variability, bias, and sensitivities to exogenous factors. For example, in a pair of recent *Proceedings* papers, Dr. Gary Blumsohn has shown that deterministic reserving techniques may vastly underestimate the cost of high retention excess-of-loss reserves, and he has illustrated the use of dynamic financial analysis models to quantify the risk in reserve estimates. James Stanard has used simulation models to demonstrate—much to the astonishment of many reserving actuaries—that the traditional chain ladder loss development techniques are not unbiased. The spread of modeling techniques among casualty actuaries may presage a systematic re-examination of pricing and reserving procedures. Dr. Rodney Kreps has developed a procedure to quantify the parameter risk resulting from estimating loss development link ratios from a limited sample of observation points.

Loss reserving and pricing are the traditional actuarial tasks. The traditional techniques are revised and adapted as new insurance products are sold and as new financial tools are developed. In particular, the emergence of DFA is refashioning the actuary's repertoire; see the section on DFA in Chapter 10 of this textbook.

DFA is more than just another actuarial tool. It is a change in the actuary's perspective. The next generation of actuaries, at ease with computer technology and familiar with financial modeling, have the opportunity to update our existing procedures and perhaps even to rewrite the traditional actuarial techniques.

The following section of this introduction illustrates how the DFA perspective changes one's view of the standard actuarial tasks and opens a new vista of opportunity for the future actuary.

DYNAMIC FINANCIAL ANALYSIS

Dynamic financial analysis is sweeping across the property-casualty insurance landscape, overturning traditional notions of surplus adequacy, and leaving in its wake sophisticated models of financial performance. Ten years ago, dynamic financial analysis was rarely heard of in the casualty insurance industry. Now dynamic financial analysis presentations appear regularly in actuarial conferences—on reserving, ratemaking, and valuation. Ten years ago, there was no mention of dynamic financial analysis in actuarial education. Now it is one of the largest single topics on the casualty actuarial examinations.

New statistical procedures typically grow in obscurity, spending their adolescence in arcane, mathematical papers, reaching adulthood with the passing of generations. How has dynamic financial analysis managed to emerge so suddenly?

Dynamic financial analysis is a perspective, not a statistical tool. It is a manner of viewing the world; it is not a specific model or procedure. Stochastic simulation, scenario testing, financial modeling, risk covariances, sensitivity estimation—all the terms that are associated with dynamic financial analysis—are but handmaidens to the central perspective.

Static versus Dynamic Analysis

To see the power of dynamic financial analysis—and the variety of issues that it addresses—let us contrast dynamic analysis with static analysis. We use casualty loss reserving as our example, as laid out in this textbook.

Until recently, almost all actuarial analysis was static. *Static analysis* assumes that the state of the world will continue unchanged. If inflation is now 5% per annum, and the unemployment rate is 6% of the workforce, static analysis assumes that the same values will continue into the future.

The static assumptions are generally left implicit in the analysis. Inflation, unemployment, investment yields, interest rates, and a host of other variables are assumed to continue unchanged, and no mention is made of them.

Dynamic analysis assumes that various external factors may change in the coming years, and the results of the analysis may depend on these external factors. The assumptions are made explicit, and the relationship between the external factors and the results is quantified.

A Loss Reserving Illustration

The evolution of loss reserve analyses over the past decade illustrates the difference between the static and dynamic perspectives. Static loss reserve analyses are straightforward, and they suffice for most purposes. Dynamic analyses are more complex, but they are essential in turbulent economic times.

Workers compensation insurers have large and volatile loss reserves, whose expected value depends both on medical inflation and on the likelihood of disabled workers returning to work. In turn, how soon disabled workers return to work depends on how many jobs there are, and on how eager employers are to hire more workers. That is, it depends on the rate of unemployment and on the rate of economic expansion.

The static loss reserve analysis assumes no future changes in inflation and no future changes in unemployment. The static analysis produces a "best-estimate" reserve indication. It informs the company of the expected benefit costs—as long as inflation and unemployment do not change.

However, these values do change, sometimes slowly, sometimes abruptly. When medical inflation rises, medical benefit costs rise as well. When unemployment rises, indemnity loss reserves rise in tandem.

Dynamic Analysis

Dynamic analysis links the results of the analysis to the underlying assumptions. The reserving actuary begins with the (static) best-estimate indication as an anchoring point—a point of departure for the dynamic analysis. The major assumptions—such as the expected future inflation rate or the future unemployment rate—are made explicit, and the manner in which they affect the reserve indication is modeled. The actuary then varies each assumption: letting inflation rise by 2% and quantifying the effect on the reserve indication, or letting unemployment fall by 1% and quantifying the effect on the reserve indication.

Static analysis is tantamount to prescient and perfect knowledge of the future state of the world. But the actuary cannot predict the unemployment rates two years hence, much less the inflation rate or interest rates. Instead, the actuary builds a *dynamic* reserve indication: a reserve indication that varies as the inflation rate and the unemployment rate change.

The actuary's results are now more meaningful, but they are also more complex. The actuary no longer presents a single number, since there is no single number that can sum up the variability of future events. The actuary now presents a distribution of results, showing the range of possible outcomes. Some of the variability stems from random loss occurrences, and some of the variability stems from changes in the external factors affecting the insurance industry.

Because of the long duration of many casualty loss reserves, these external factors have major effects. An increase in the future inflation rate of 2% could cause next year's loss payments to rise by 2%, the following years' loss payments to rise by 4%, with larger and larger increases each year. The expected losses to be paid ten years down the road could rise by 22% for a mere 2%

rise in the annual inflation rate. Casualty actuaries refer to this as "inflation-sensitive reserves." These are not actuarial subtleties; these compounding effects of inflation are major management concerns.

Dynamic analysis supplements static analysis; it does not replace it. The static analysis remains the bedrock of loss reserving. It shows the average of future results, and it is readily understood by others. Moreover, it is the ideal figure by which to trace the movement of the reserve indication over time.

Yet this average, this best estimate, tells only a small portion of the story. It tells us nothing about the uncertainty in the reserve estimate, or about the sensitivity of the reserve estimate to other variables. Indeed, dynamic analysis often shows that it is not a best estimate at all; sometimes it is biased upwards or downwards. Dynamic analysis fills in the rest of the loss reserve story, giving us a better view of the changes that the future may hold.

Enterprise Analysis

But we are jumping ahead of ourselves. We will return to scenario testing, sensitivity estimates, stochastic simulation, and the other components of dynamic financial analysis in a few moments. First we look at one of the major developments of dynamic financial analysis: enterprise analysis.

With static analyses, each component of the insurance company's operations was examined separately. Reserving actuaries produced reserve indications, and financial analysts estimated investment returns. In monitoring the company's overall performance, in setting business plans, and in formulating corporate strategy, each component was treated separately.

Rising inflation would raise the reserve indications; rising interest rates would depress the values of fixed income securities, such as bonds, mortgages, and CMOs. Interest rates and inflation

rates often move in tandem; that is, reserving risks and investment risks are interlinked.

This linkage is not unusual. Economic conditions, such as
inflation rates or GNP growth, affect numerous aspects of the
insurance enterprise. Investment returns are intertwined with interest rate risks, and underwriting returns are threatened by inflation risks. But how might one disentangle the various threads?
How does one step back to view the overall effects?

The previous illustration began with the insurance task—loss
reserve estimation—and worked backwards to the external influences. When we step back to view the enterprise as a whole, we
reverse our stance. Dynamic financial analysis generally begins
with the basic financial, economic, and business assumptions.
The dynamic model might say: "If both interest rates and inflation rates rise by 2%, what are the effects on reserve indications,
bond values, and mortgage prepayment rates?"

This perspective is a great advance over static analysis, but
a moment's reflection reveals that the flow of reasoning is still
backwards. Why did we choose to look at changes in interest
rates and inflation rates? Well, we began with reserving risk
and with investment risk, and we searched for the underlying
factors affecting each of them. Some of these factors, such as
interest rates and inflation rates, are interlinked. An analysis of
the enterprise as a whole must examine both risks simultaneously.

But companies do not ask: "How are reserving risk and investment risk interlinked?" Insurance executives do not think solely
in terms of risk correlations and covariance matrices. They think
in terms of economic and business reality.

So dynamic financial analysis inverts the questions, placing
the scenarios first. It asks: "If there is a recession, or if there is
an underwriting cycle downturn, what are the likely effects on

reserves, underwriting, and investments?" Financial models now create the links, breaking recessions or underwriting cycle movements into their component pieces, and examining the effects on insurance operations.

Technical actuarial and financial issues that are meaningful only to the initiated—such as reserve uncertainty and investment returns—metamorphose into fundamental questions of corporate strategy, such as "How might we deal with a recession?" Dynamic financial analysis lifted risk analysis from the actuarial backwaters to the corporate boardroom.

Scenario Testing

There are many forms of dynamic financial analysis, some of which are no less arcane than traditional risk analyses, only with the substitution of Monte Carlo simulations for Poisson distributions. In scenario testing, however, the infiltration of basic business terminology into actuarial analysis is clear. A typical scenario testing dynamic financial analysis might take the following form:

Scenario building: One starts with realistic scenarios, covering a variety of economic, financial, and business conditions, and emphasizing those attributes that have the greatest effect on insurance performance. For example, scenarios might be built for a moderate recession and for a prolonged expansion, so that the differential effects of each on the company's performance is evident. For solvency monitoring, an additional scenario of a severe recession along with an abrupt downturn in financial markets might be used. For each scenario, the attributes of inflation, interest rates, GNP growth, unemployment, and factory production are explicitly modeled.

Relationships: The insurance correlates of these economic attributes are formulated. Some of these relationships are obvious to most insurance personnel. Other relationships seem surprising at first, though they are well known to astute observers of the insurance industry.

For instance, prosperous economic times lead to increased business activity. Less experienced workers are hired, overtime hours increase, and workers compensation claim frequency rises. People purchase new automobiles, and vacation travel increases, leading to more automobile insurance claims. Recessions have the opposite effects on claim frequency in these two lines of business, but they have some unusual effects as well. During recessions, injured workers are reluctant to give up their disability benefits, lest they suddenly find that their old jobs have been eliminated by workforce reductions. Although accompanied by a decline in workers compensation claim frequency, recessions also provoke a lengthening of the time spent on disability by already injured workers.

Sensitivity: The magnitude of the insurance correlates is quantified, either by analytic studies or by business judgment, such as "A 1% drop in the unemployment rate leads to a 1.5% rise in the workers compensation claim frequency." The claims manager of a large workers compensation insurer may have a good feel for the effects of unemployment on claim filing. Other relationships may be taken from economic studies at the Workers Compensation Research Institute, which has produced decades of studies on workers compensation claim filing behavior, or the Insurance Research Council, which has similar analyses of private passenger automobile insurance.

The output of the dynamic financial analysis is not a specific number; it is a future performance of the insurance enterprise. This future performance may be presented as pro-forma financial statements, cash flows of assets and liabilities, or present values of future earnings. The output may be geared to the audience: accountants may prefer the financial statements and investment officers may prefer the cash flows. Dynamic financial analysis extends actuarial analysis to address practical problems in business strategy.

Stochastic Simulation

"Fine," you say, "But what's all this I hear about stochastic simulation and Monte Carlo analyses? Before, the actuaries sounded strange; now they are incomprehensible." The clarity of communication is essential for complex analyses such as the overall corporate sensitivity to multiple external influences. In some early DFA analyses, even the graphs in the final reports seemed like pictures of dense cobwebs—like finger painting in black and white. Indeed, lack of comprehensibility has been the bane of the actuarial profession. Some brilliant actuaries have written brilliant reports that never make it past the waste paper basket. How might something as obscure as stochastic simulation be presented to a business audience?

Static analysis gives a single answer, assuming no changes in the external factors affecting the insurance industry. The result of the analysis might be that a product will give a 12% return on equity. Dynamic analysis gives results that vary with the values of external factors, such as inflation, interest rates, unemployment rates, and claim frequency.

But users were not yet satisfied. These various forces are never known with certainty. Insurance variables, such as claim frequency or claim severity, have always been called uncertain. Now the random walks of interest rates and asset values are added, and the volatile economic environment adds yet another layer of randomness to the results. Single "best estimate" results no longer seem reasonable.

The dynamic analysis rephrases the question. The static analysis predicts a 12% return on equity. The dynamic analysis now asks: "What is the chance that this product will indeed give a 12% return on equity?"

So actuaries have learned to simulate. For static analysis, the actuary predicts; for dynamic analysis, the actuary simulates. In a dynamic financial analysis, the actuary does not predict next year's inflation rate. Rather, the actuary simulates the possible inflation rates in the coming year.

Prediction is difficult, but simulation is twice as hard. Simulation must reflect reality, and scenarios must be internally consistent. Simulated interest rate paths must accord with the expected distribution of these paths. Interest rates, inflation rates, and all other variables in each scenario must be reasonably related to each other.

The dynamic analysis may produce ten thousand simulations, in seven thousand of which the product produces a 12% or better return on equity, but in 500 of which the product actually loses money. The results provide better information. They not only produce the distribution of likely returns, but they also show the sensitivity of the return to the various factors affecting the company.

The multiplicity of variables and the need for thousands of simulations to produce credible results once made such analyses only an actuary's dream. But the power of the microchip is overwhelming. Last generation's mainframe computers now sit on every actuary's desktop. The computers run the simulations; the laborious desk calculator is an actuarial relic. The actuary's task is to build scenarios, to model distributions, and to present the results meaningfully to company personnel.

THE NEXT CENTURY

This textbook is an introduction to actuarial theory. The textbook is appearing at the dawn of the 21st century; where is actuarial theory likely to proceed from here?

Several paths have been outlined above, such as dynamic financial analysis and financial pricing. There are other equally promising areas that young actuaries and actuarial candidates should keep in mind.

Financial modeling is complex; equally complex is market-place pricing. Twenty years go, rating bureaus provided advisory rates, and young actuaries worked with traditional rating formulas. But rating formulas—no matter how complex—are no longer enough to set prices.

Two developments have changed the focus of actuarial pricing. First, bureau ratemaking becomes less important each year, with independent ratemaking taking its place. The elimination of bureau advisory rates, the push for deregulation of commercial lines rate and form filing, and the continuing competitive pressure in the insurance industry should speed the change from statistical rate indications to marketplace pricing. Casualty actuarial science must adapt rapidly to the changing pricing environment by incorporating the marketing and business paradigms essential for competitive pricing recommendations.

Second, the very success of actuaries has led to new roles and new demands. Membership in the CAS has increased rapidly, and our recent graduates are overflowing the bounds of actuarial departments and spilling over into diverse segments of the insurance business. A large number of new actuaries deal with more business-oriented insurance operations, not just with ratemaking or reserving. Their employers demand versatility at marketplace pricing and at general insurance operations, not just at manipulation of figures.

Actuaries must be skilled in a variety of fields: marketing, economics, accounting, and computer technology. Pricing actuaries must deal with underwriting cycles, agent placement, policyholder retention, Internet developments, and consumer demands for better products. These are essential aspects of pricing insurance products, and the successful actuary must be at home with them. There were few studies of these topics in 20th century actuarial research. Yet these are critical issues for the current generation of actuaries. The application of actuarial and financial theory to solve business problems in these areas is an exciting challenge for young actuaries.

CONTINUING EDUCATION

Many persons study hard in their teens and early twenties and then work hard for the rest of their careers. Serious professionals—whether physicians, scientists, or actuaries—cannot afford this dichotomy. Science evolves continuously; education must be equally continuous. The actuarial examinations provide the common knowledge that new actuaries share, but actuarial education cannot cease when Fellowship is earned.

Few professions can afford extensive research and educational programs. The CAS is a particularly small organization, with few members employed full time in research and teaching. Nevertheless, both the quality and the quantity of practical business research by CAS members is astonishing. The CAS publishes half a dozen paper compilations each year, and it sponsors a dozen continuing seminars each year.

This textbook is not entitled *Actuarial Theory*—it is only the *Foundations of Casualty Actuarial Science*. Even the actuarial examinations, despite their extensive scope, provide only the basic education for Fellowship in the Casualty Actuarial Society. But actuarial education is continuous. The reader in whose hands this textbook now lies may soon help strengthen the casualty actuarial society and contribute to new textbooks for future generations of actuaries.

REFERENCES

Blumsohn, Gary, "Levels of Determinism in Workers Compensation Reinsurance Commutations," *Proceedings of the Casualty Actuarial Society*, 1999, 86:1–79.

Blumsohn, et al., "Workers Compensation Reserve Uncertainty," *Proceedings of the Casualty Actuarial Society*, 1999, 86:263–392.

Brosius, Eric, "Loss Development Using Credibility," *CAS Part 7 Examination Study Note*, December 1992.

Burger, George, Beth E. Fitzgerald, Jonathan White, and Patrick B. Woods, "Incorporating a Hurricane Model into Property Ratemaking," *CAS Forum*, Winter 1996, 129–190.

Butsic, Robert P., "Determining the Proper Interest Rate for Loss Reserve Discounting: An Economic Approach," *CAS Discussion Paper Program*, 1988, 147–188.

Butsic, Robert P., "Solvency Measurement for Property-Liability Risk-Based Capital Applications," *Journal of Risk and Insurance*, December 1994, 61, 4:656–690.

Clark, Karen M., "A Formal Approach to Catastrophe Risk Assessment and Management," *CAS Discussion Paper Program*, 1985, 62–103.

D'Arcy, Stephen P., and Michael A. Dyer, "Ratemaking: A Financial Economics Approach," *Proceedings of the Casualty Actuarial Society*, 1997, 84:301–390.

D'Arcy, Stephen P., R. W. Gorvett, J. A. Herbers, T. E. Hettinger, S. G. Lehmann, and M. J. Miller, "Building a Public Access PC-Based DFA Model," *CAS Forum*, Summer 1997, 2:1–40.

D'Arcy, Stephen P., R. W. Gorvett, T. E. Hettinger, and R. J. Walling, "Using the Public Access DFA Model: A Case Study," *CAS Forum*, Summer 1998, 53–118.

Kreps, Rodney E., "Parameter Uncertainty in (Log)normal Distributions," *Proceedings of the Casualty Actuarial Society*, 1997, 84:553–580.

Lange, Jeffrey T., "The Interpretation of Liability Increased Limits Statistics," *Proceedings of the Casualty Actuarial Society*, 1969, 56:163–173; discussion by T. W. Fowler, 1970, 57:88–90; discussion by J. R. Hunter, 90–103.

Lowe, Stephen P., and James N. Standard, "An Integrated Dynamic Financial Analysis and Decision Support System for a Property Casualty Reinsurer," *CAS Forum*, Spring 1996, 89–118.

Lowe, Stephen P., "A New Performance Measure For P/C Insurers," *Emphasis*, Summer 1988, 8–11.

Mahler, Howard C., "A Markov Chain Model of Shifting Risk Parameters," *Proceedings of the Casualty Actuarial Society*, 1997, 84:581–659.

Mahler, Howard C., "An Example of Credibility and Shifting Risk Parameters," *Proceedings of the Casualty Actuarial Society*, 1990, 77:225–308.

Meyers, Glenn G., "Risk Theoretic Issues in Loss Reserving: The Case of Workers Compensation Pension Reserves," *Proceedings of the Casualty Actuarial Society*, 1989, 76:171–192.

Miccolis, Robert S., "On the Theory of Increased Limits and Excess of Loss Pricing," *Proceedings of the Casualty Actuarial Society*, 1977, 64:27–59; discussion by Sheldon Rosenberg, 1977, 60–73.

Pinto, Emanuel, and Daniel F. Gogol, "An Analysis of Excess Loss Development," *Proceedings of the Casualty Actuarial Society*, 1987, 74:227–255; discussion by George M. Levine, 1987, 256–271.

Stanard, J. N., "A Simulation Test of Prediction Errors of Loss Reserve Estimation Techniques," *Proceedings of the Casualty Actuarial Society*, 1985, 72:124–148; discussion by John P. Robertson, 1985, 149–153; discussion by E. F. Peck, 1995, 82:104–120.

Venter, Gary G. Credibility. Chapter 7 in *Foundations of Casualty Actuarial Science*. Second Edition. New York: Casualty Actuarial Society, 1992.

Walters, Michael A., and François Morin, "Homeowners Rate-making Revisited (Use of Computer Models to Estimate Catastrophe Loss Costs)," *Proceedings of the Casualty Actuarial Society*, 1997, 84:1–43.

Woll, Richard G., "Insurance Profits: Keeping Score," *Financial Analysis of Insurance Companies, CAS Discussion Paper Program*, 1987, 446–533.

CHAPTER 2

RISK THEORY
MARGARET TILLER SHERWOOD

INTRODUCTION

Insurance is an obvious and necessary place to apply the theory of risk. The theory of risk will be discussed in this chapter in the broader context of risk management.

The terminology used in this book is contained in an appendix at the end of this chapter.

RISK

Definition of "Risk"

The word "risk" is used in different ways. Traditional dictionaries define "risk" as "exposure to possible loss," as in "to take a risk." A broker or insurer might use the term "risk" to refer to the insured or the property to which an insurance policy relates.

This book is concerned with "risk" as it relates to risk management. The definition used in this book is "the variation in outcomes that could occur over a specified period of time in a given situation."[1]

Types of Risk

There are different ways to categorize risk. The two most common are "objective" versus "subjective" and "pure" versus "speculative."

"Objective risk" is the risk that exists in nature and is the same for all persons or entities facing the same situation. An example is the variation in number of heads in ten coin flips. Sometimes the objective risk can not be determined. For example, to know

---

[1]Williams, C. Arthur, Jr. and Richard M. Heins, *Risk Management and Insurance*, McGraw-Hill Book Company, 1981.

the number of earthquakes of a certain magnitude in a certain area in a certain time period, one would have to know the exact probability distribution for this situation.

"Subjective risk" is each person's or entity's estimate of the objective risk. While the exact probability distribution for number of earthquakes can not be determined, it can be estimated. The estimate of risk using the probability distribution assumed to be correct is a subjective risk estimate.

"Pure risk" exists when there is a chance of loss but no chance of gain. For example, a homeowner has the risk of losing all or part of his home, but no chance of gain, if a fire occurs.

In "speculative risk" there is both the chance of loss and the chance of gain. The same homeowner also has the speculative risk that his property value will increase or decrease over time. The most well-known form of speculative risk is gambling.

Prevalence of Risk

Risk is everywhere. Life is uncertain. Individuals, families, and entities anticipate with pleasure the unexpected gains and fear the unexpected losses.

In speculative risk, there is the possibility of gain or loss. Some speculative risks, such as purchasing real estate for its investment value or purchasing a lottery ticket, may be acceptable.

Other speculative risks, such as large scale gambling, may not be acceptable because the individual can not withstand the financial outcome of the possible loss. In this situation, the individual is not appropriately weighing the small probability of a large gain with the large probability of a large loss. The risk of loss is essentially transferred from the larger asset casino to the smaller asset individual. This type of speculative risk actually increases the chance of loss to an individual.

In pure risk, there is only the possibility of loss. The types of losses from pure risk of concern to risk managers include personnel loss, property loss, net income loss, and legal liability loss. Personnel losses facing an individual include death, poor health, unemployment, and superannuation. The types of losses are discussed in more detail later in this chapter.

Insurance is the primary method individuals, families, and entities use to reduce their economic uncertainty if pure losses do occur. In insurance the financial responsibility for loss is transferred from the smaller asset individual, family, or entity to the larger asset insurance company. Insurance also reduces the uncertainty about the outcome of a loss experienced by individuals, families, or entities even if no loss occurs. Both reductions in uncertainty serve to smooth the functioning of society in general.

Insurance and other risk financing techniques, as well as risk control techniques, for handling pure risk will be discussed in more detail later in this chapter.

RISK THEORY

Definition of "Risk Theory"

"Risk theory" is the use of mathematical models to quantify objective risk as defined above. In other words, it is the determination of subjective risk for a particular person or entity. Risk theory is part of the mathematical subject of stochastic processes that also is applied in the physical sciences and finances.

Use of Risk Theory In Risk Management[2]

The two areas of applications of risk theory to risk management are in statistics and in finances.

---

[2]This section is edited from material in the Risk Theory section of Chapter 9, "Special Issues," that appeared in the first, second, and third editions of *Foundations of Casualty Actuarial Science.* That chapter was written by Stephen P. D'Arcy. Changes were made by Margaret Tiller Sherwood.

Statistics

The statistical area involves using the properties of statistical distributions to model the objective risk. This often involves the use of confidence intervals, which indicate the likelihood that actual outcomes will fall within specified limits.

The two main statistical applications are for ratemaking and for assessing financial solvency. In ratemaking, the use of risk theory allows mathematical determination of an appropriate risk loading. In solvency considerations, risk theory leads to measurement of ruin probability based on particular premium writings and surplus positions.

Finances

The financial area focuses on utility theory and game theory, which apply to individuals, families, and entities retaining and sharing risk, as well as to insurers.

In utility theory, levels of satisfaction or utility are established to correspond with various possible outcomes. As individuals and entities such as corporations are not necessarily twice as satisfied with twice as much money, mathematical functions are assumed to describe the intangible satisfaction levels of the decision-maker. The shape of the describing function corresponds with the individual's or entity's attitude toward risk.

Game theory contemplates the involvement of more than one player, each with a set of strategies. The payoffs of the game are dependent on the intersection of the strategies chosen by the players.

RISK MANAGEMENT

Before giving specific examples of the application of risk theory to risk financing, it is helpful to have the broader context of risk management as a base.

Goals of Risk Management

Risk management is the process of determining how to handle the pure risks to which an individual, family, or entity is exposed with the following goals:

- survive the loss event;

- have peace of mind;

- reduce total risk management costs and, thus, have general higher profits;

- stabilize earnings;

- have little or no interruption in operations;

- have continued growth; and

- help carry out the individual's or entity's sense of social responsibility or desire for a good image.

Types of Loss

"Loss" in the remainder of this chapter primarily refers to loss of assets resulting from pure risk. The types of losses of concern to risk managers include personnel loss, property loss, net income loss, and legal liability loss.

Personnel losses facing an individual include death, poor health, unemployment, and superannuation. These may be handled by the individual and/or the individual's employer.

Personnel losses facing an entity include key-person losses when the key-person does not have an ownership interest, business-discontinuation losses from a person with an ownership interest dying or being disabled, and credit losses due to the death, extended disability, or unemployment of a customer. These losses are usually handled by the entity.

Property is divided into two classes: real and personal. Real property is land and its appurtenant structures or attachments.

Personal property is property that is movable and not attached to land. In a direct property loss, the property itself is damaged or destroyed or disappears. In an indirect property loss, the value of the property is lessened as a result of direct damage to some other property. An example of an indirect property loss is loss of meat in a refrigerator when the refrigerator malfunctions. Both individuals and entities have property that may be the subject of loss.

Net income losses can occur either because income is reduced or because expenses are increased. Net income losses usually are the result of property damage. A loss first affects the entity to which it occurs and then may affect other entities, such as its customers. Revenues may decrease due to loss of rent, interruption in operations, contingent business interruption due to losses by suppliers or customers, and loss of profits on finished goods. Some expenses may continue even when operations are interrupted, there may be additional expenses required to continue operations under loss conditions, and there may be expediting expenses to return the entity to normalcy as soon as possible.

Net income losses occur most often to entities. However, individuals also can suffer net income loss, such as the extra expense for apartment rent when a residence is uninhabitable due to a fire but mortgage payments are due anyway.

Legal liability, or liability, is "any legally enforceable obligation. Within the context of insurance, the obligation to pay a monetary award for injury or damage caused by one's negligent or statutorily prohibited action."[3] Individuals have liability exposures such as general liability if a guest slips and falls in one's home and automobile liability if one causes an automobile accident that injures another person or property of another person. Entities have many liability exposures. The most common are general liability, automobile liability, workers compensation, and products liability.

---

[3]*Glossary of Insurance and Risk Management Terms*, International Risk Management Institute, Inc., Sixth Edition, 1996.

The Risk Management Process

The risk management process encompasses the following five steps:

- identify the exposures to possible loss;

- measure the exposures to possible loss including the probability that they could occur and the impact the losses could have on the financial affairs of the person or entity;

- select the risk management alternatives to best handle the exposures;

- implement the alternatives selected; and

- monitor the alternatives put into practice to see if they are working as expected.

The measurement step usually involves using subjective risk measures, or risk theory, as objective risk measures are not available.

Risk Management Alternatives

The two main types of risk management alternatives are risk control and risk financing. Risk control alternatives are exposure avoidance, loss prevention, loss reduction, segregation of exposure units, and contractual transfer to a non-insurer in which the legal risk is transferred. Risk financing alternatives are risk retention, contractual transfer to a non-insurer in which the legal risk is retained, and insurance. These alternatives will be discussed in detail in the following two sections.

RISK CONTROL

Risk control is "any conscious action (or decision not to act) intended to reduce the frequency, severity, or unpredictability of

accidental losses."[4] Note that risk control deals with the actual
harm, not on the money to restore or compensate for the harm.
The latter are handled through risk financing techniques, which
are discussed in the next section.

Exposure Avoidance

An exposure may be avoided by never undertaking, or aban-
doning, an activity or asset that has an exposure to possible loss.
This reduces to absolute zero the probability of a loss arising
from such an activity or asset.

Exposure avoidance has limited application. Property losses
can be avoided by not owning property. Product liability losses
can be avoided by not manufacturing products. However, not
manufacturing any products will not work for a manufacturer.
There might be certain products that the manufacturer would
decide not to produce because the products liability exposures
are far greater than the benefits (net revenue and public relations)
from manufacturing those products.

Loss Prevention

Loss prevention reduces, but does not completely eliminate,
the probability, or frequency, of a loss. Designing loss prevention measures entails understanding how losses are caused. Steps
that break the chain of events causing the loss should reduce the
frequency of losses from that exposure. An example of loss prevention to prevent fires is to prohibit smoking when pure oxygen
is in use.

Loss Reduction

Loss reduction reduces the size, or severity, of losses that
occur. Loss reduction measures fall into pre-loss and post-loss

---

[4]Head, George L., Editor, *Essentials of Risk Control*, Insurance Institute of America,
1986.

categories. An example of pre-loss loss reduction to reduce the loss from a fire is the use of fire walls to limit the amount of damage from a fire. An example of post-loss loss reduction to reduce the loss from a fire is the installation of sprinklers in buildings to stop or reduce the spread of a fire that has started. Other post-loss loss reduction measures occur after the event has occurred, such as salvaging equipment not damaged by a fire from the fire-damaged building before it is damaged by exposure to the elements.

Segregation of Exposure Units

The purpose of segregation of exposure units is to reduce the size of any one loss by dividing up an entity's exposure into smaller pieces. There are two main types: separation and combination.

Separation is simply taking an entity's existing exposures to possible loss and dividing them into smaller groups that are subject to possible loss. For example, instead of a taxi company keeping all its taxis in one warehouse, it could use four warehouses. Then any loss striking one warehouse would only damage part of the fleet.

Combination increases the entity's number of exposure units, thus making losses more predictable and less likely to affect a significant percentage of the exposures. For example, a taxi company could add to its fleet.

A special example of combination is duplication, in which the number of exposure units is increased but the additional units are not used unless something happens to the original units. For example, a taxi company could maintain more taxis than it normally uses so that there is a greater probability of having enough taxis available if part of the fleet is subject to loss. Additional examples of duplication are cross-training personnel, maintaining duplicates of accounting records, and entering into a mutual aid pact with similar entities.

Contractual Transfer to a Non-Insurer

The final risk control alternative is transferring exposure to possible loss to a non-insurer through a contractual arrangement. Note that the exposure itself is transferred, and the transferor no longer has a legal or financial responsibility for any loss from that exposure. The most common forms of this type of contractual transfer are through lease agreements and subcontracts.

An example is a lease agreement in which the landlord agrees to be responsible for all property damage to the building including that caused by the tenant's negligence. In this situation, the tenant has transferred what would normally be his property exposure to the landlord.

Contractual transfer of exposure to possible loss to a non-insurer is different from exposure avoidance because the exposure to possible loss still exists; it simply has been transferred to someone else. In exposure avoidance, the exposure no longer exists at all because the activity or asset no exists.

Risk control contractual transfers differ from risk financing contractual transfers, which are discussed in more detail later in this chapter. The distinction is that the legal and financial responsibilities are transferred in a risk control transfer, while only the financial responsibility is transferred in a risk financing transfer.

Only property and personnel exposures can be contractually transferred in this manner. Net income and liability exposures can not be transferred because these transfers do not impact the rights of third parties. Risk financing contractual transfers can cover all four types of exposures.

RISK FINANCING

Risk financing is any technique used to obtain funds to restore losses that strike an individual or entity. These techniques fall into three general categories: risk retention, contractual transfer to a non-insurer in which the legal liability is retained, and transfer to an insurer.

Risk Retention

The normal state of events is for an individual or entity to retain its exposures to possible loss. This is risk retention. Sometimes the term "self-insurance" is used. However, this is a misnomer, as "insurance" involves transfer of financial responsibility, and it is not possible to transfer one's own financial responsibility to oneself.

Risk retention can be passive or active. Passive risk retention refers to exposures to possible loss that are retained because they have not been identified or have been forgotten. An entity owning many pieces of real property with buildings may inadvertently forget to purchase property insurance for one of them.

Active risk retention is the preferred state. In active risk retention, the exposures to possible loss have been carefully evaluated, and a conscious decision has been made to retain them. This may be due to some of the advantages of risk retention, such as lower expected cost, or it may be because there is no other choice. An example of the latter is the exposures retained because of the nuclear exclusion found in most property insurance policies.

Risk retention can be partial or total. The nuclear exposures retained because they can not be insured is an example of total risk retention. The losses within a deductible layer are an example of partial retention.

Pooling—A Special Type of Risk Retention

A special type of risk retention is pooling. In pooling, entities get together and share their exposures to possible loss. Thus, an individual entity retains some of its own exposure to possible loss and accepts some of the other pool members' exposures to possible loss. Insurers, particularly reinsurers, often pool the financial exposures they have assumed (this is discussed later in this chapter). Special legislation usually is required for non-insurers to pool exposures.

Pools usually collect contributions in advance of losses occurring and pay for losses from the joint funds. The formulae for contribution collection and loss payment vary. Some pools collect contributions or base surplus distributions at least partly on the individual members' experience. Other pools assume all exposure units have the same risk, and all losses are shared in the same proportion that the individual members' exposures have to the total exposures.

Pooling has the advantage of reducing the variability in losses from what an individual entity would have if its exposures were not pooled with the exposures of others. Pooling has the disadvantage of an entity being responsible, at least partly, for exposures of other entities which may not practice as stringent risk control.

Contractual Transfer to a Non-Insurer

Contractual transfers to a non-insurer as a risk financing technique transfer only the financial, but not the legal, responsibility for losses. This is usually done through provisions in contracts dealing with other matters, often through "hold harmless" clauses.

An example is a lease in which the landlord transfers to the tenant the financial responsibility for damage that occurs while on the premises to third parties' property or selves, such as those due to slips and falls. In other words, the tenant holds the landlord harmless for these losses.

There are many potential problems with this type of transfer. The contractual language often is so complicated that it is difficult to understand what is being transferred and, in fact, it may not accomplish what was meant to be accomplished. And because the transfer provisions can vary widely, there are few precedents for a court to use in interpreting them.

Perhaps most importantly, the transferee, who has the major incentive for risk control, may not have the expertise or authority to practice effective risk control. And the transferor must rely on the good faith and financial security of the transferee to meet its financial obligations, because the transferor still has the legal obligation to meet any financial obligations arising from loss if the transferee is unable or unwilling to do so.

Transfer to an Insurer

It is possible to transfer contractually the financial responsibility for certain exposures to possible loss to a special type of entity whose primary function is to accept these responsibilities for a price, called a premium. From the insured's point of view, this is a risk financing transfer: the insured is protected against financial loss arising from specified occurrences.

The insurer accepts responsibilities from many different individuals and/or entities. From the insurer's point of view, this is the risk control device of combination. By increasing its exposure to possible financial losses, those losses become more predictable, and there is less chance that any one occurrence of loss will be a significant financial problem for the insurer.

Insurance Versus Gambling

The purchase of insurance is not gambling. The insured transfers pure risk. The gambler deals with speculative risk, in which there is the possibility of loss or gain.

Ideally Insurable Exposures

In *Risk Management and Insurance* by C. Arthur Williams, Jr. and Richard M. Heins,[5] the characteristics of an ideally insurable exposure are detailed as follows:

• The exposure transferred should be the subject of pure risk.

• There should be large number of independent entities, all of approximately the same value, with similar exposures and controlled by people interested in insurance protection.

• The insured loss should be definite or determinate in time, place, cause, and amount.

• The expected loss over some reasonable period of time should be estimable.

• The loss should be accidental from the viewpoint of the insured.

Insurers may wish to impose additional criteria for administrative reasons, such as that occurrences of loss should be relatively infrequent and have a large economic impact on the insured. An example of this would be fire coverage on buildings. Automobile physical damage coverage on private passenger automobiles is frequent to the insurer but infrequent to the insured and, depending on the insureds financial situation, may have a large economic impact on the insured. To help assure the infrequency of loss and that there is a large economic impact on the insured, automobile physical damage usually is written with a deductible.

Insurance is available for some exposures that do not meet these standards. Possible reasons for this include because they are close to ideal, because they can be made close to ideal by putting in safeguards, because of societal pressures, because of public policy, or because the exposure is expected to be insurable in the future.

---

[5]Williams, C. Arthur, Jr. and Richard M. Heins, *Risk Management and Insurance*, McGraw-Hill Book Company, 1981.

Damage to houses due to fire is insurable. This is a pure risk. There are large numbers of houses with similar exposures controlled by people interested in purchasing insurance. To maintain independence, insurance may be written on houses that are in significantly different locations. The insured loss is definite in time, place, cause, and amount. The expected loss over some reasonable period of time should be estimable. Losses are accidental from the viewpoint of the insured if arson by the insured is excluded.

Death by suicide is excluded from the first year or two of life insurance policies to maintain the characteristic that losses should be accidental from the viewpoint of the insured. However, most state laws require that death by suicide be covered after that time because society benefits from payments to beneficiaries and suicides are not likely to be contemplated one or two years in advance.

An interesting example of an exposure that is not an ideal insurance exposure is people's health, because sickness is not definite in time and place and is, to some extent, within the control of the insured. However, societal pressures have resulted in the availability and affordability of health insurance being a significant topic of discussion.

Public policy may dictate that insurance be available, such as to drug manufacturers for losses due to problems with vaccinations. Sometimes the insurance dictated by public policy is not acceptable to traditional insurers and must be handled by the government. Examples of this include flood, bank insolvency, and unemployment insurance.

Public policy also may dictate that insurance not be available. It would be against public policy to provide insurance to an individual to cover losses caused by that individual's assault on another person.

When new endeavors are undertaken, insurance often is necessary for them to commence even when no loss information is available. Aviation insurance at the infancy of the aviation industry is an example of this.

What insurers consider insurable constantly evolves. There are two types of insurance that have come into existence in recent years that previously would not have been considered, as the exposures were deemed uninsurable: back-dated liability insurance and retroactive liability insurance. In back-dated liability insurance, the loss its covers has occurred recently and has been reported but its value is unknown. In retroactive liability insurance, the losses covered have not yet been reported. This is used to increase policy limits over what was purchased at the time or to provide coverage where none previously existed.

Societal Benefits of Insurance

There are many benefits to society from insurance. Because insurance contracts tend to be standard, there are fewer problems with interpretation by the insured, the insurer, and the courts.

The insured is indemnified for the specified financial losses. This reduces the insured's uncertainty of the costs of living and/or doing business. The combining of the exposures to financial loss done by the insurer reduces the insurer's uncertainty concerning how much to charge for the transfer.

Insurers have more funds available for investment than would many individuals or entities retaining risk because their costs are more predictable and the constant flow of new funds makes it less likely that they will have to liquidate investments to pay for losses.

Combining Risk Retention and Insurance

Some individuals and entities combine risk retention and insurance. An individual may take a relatively large deductible on her health insurance policy, e.g. $5,000 per person and $10,000 for the family, and choose to insure only the higher medical costs.

Similarly, an entity may decide to retain a substantial portion of its workers compensation exposure, e.g. the first $250,000 per occurrence, and purchase excess insurance above this. Yet another entity may retain the first $5,000 per occurrence of its property exposure, participate in a risk sharing pool for the layer from $5,000 to $1,000,000, and purchase excess insurance above $1,000,000 per occurrence to whatever policy limit is appropriate.

RISK FINANCING OPTIONS FOR AN INSURER

An insurer accepts the financial responsibility for losses arising from exposures to possible loss owned by other entities. It can: choose to retain that responsibility; transfer it to another insurer; pool it with other insurers; or do some combination of these. An example may help.

Suppose an insurer provides a property policy that has a $25,000,000 limit to an entity. This insurer is called the primary insurer. Few insurers could withstand a $25,000,000 loss easily. The insurer might find another insurer, possibly a reinsurer, willing to take the layer from $1,000,000 to $10,000,000 (also called $9,000,000 excess of $1,000,000) for part of the premium originally paid by the insured. Insurers that only accept the financial responsibility for loss from other insurers or from non-insurers that retain a large portion of the financial responsibility for loss are called reinsurers.

The insurer then may put the layer from $10,000,000 to $25,000,000 (also called $15,000,000 excess of $10,000,000) into a pool of similar exposures from other insurers. This will require the contribution of part of the premium originally paid by the insured. Because the risk transfers by the primary insurer are for financial responsibility only, the primary insurer retains the financial responsibility for any obligations the reinsurer and pool are unable to meet.

RISK THEORY—STATISTICAL APPLICATIONS: RATEMAKING AND SOLVENCY[6]

Insurance ratemaking historically has involved use of the expected value for losses and ALAE, ignoring the variability around the mean value. Often, a selected underwriting profit margin is applied to all lines of business without consideration of the degree of volatility of a given line. In this situation, if the expected losses and ALAE for two lines were equal, an insurer would include the same profit loading for lines that have very predictable loss patterns due to the high frequency, low severity nature of losses (e.g., automobile physical damage), as it would for much harder to predict lines that have low frequency but high severity (e.g., occurrence medical malpractice).

Use of risk theory to model these two lines would entail using a distribution with a higher variance for the more volatile line. In choosing a rate level that would be adequate to cover losses and ALAE a specified percentage of the time (e.g., 75% or 95%), the risk loading in the more volatile line would be higher, reflecting the greater variability of the distribution. Differences in variability around the mean value can occur in different coverages within the same line of business, such as occurrence versus claims-made coverages.

Typical applications of risk theory to solvency focus on the total variability of the aggregate loss and ALAE distribution. The larger the variability, the higher the risk loading necessary in rates or the greater the probability of ruin derived in solvency testing.

Two branches of risk theory have evolved: individual and collective. Individual risk theory analyzes individual insurance

---

[6]This section is edited from material in the Risk Theory section of Chapter 9, "Special Issues," that appeared in the first, second, and third editions of *Foundations of Casualty Actuarial Science*. That chapter was written by Stephen P. D'Arcy. Changes were made by Margaret Tiller Sherwood.

policies to measure the likelihood that total costs will exceed premium income. Total company operations are determined by summing the results on individual policies. Collective risk theory disregards individual policies and instead addresses the total gain or loss of the company on the entire book of business.

RISK THEORY—FINANCIAL APPLICATIONS: UTILITY THEORY AND GAME THEORY[7]

Utility Theory

A risk neutral decision-maker would have a utility function that is linear. A risk averse one would have a utility function that increased at progressively lower rates, or had a negative second derivative. A decision-maker who favored risk would have a utility function that increased at progressively faster rates, or had a positive second derivative.

But many individuals both gamble, which is characteristic of a risk-seeker, and insure, which is characteristic of a risk averse entity. Therefore, actual utility functions are likely to be more complex than a simple curve with a consistently signed second derivative.

Utility theory attempts to approximate the actual satisfaction levels of various outcomes to indicate the optimal strategies to follow in risky situations. This area of research has produced recommendations as to the optimal insurance policies to purchase, including deductibles and policy limits, and when to "self-insure," e.g., retain, risks.

---

[7]This section is edited from material in the Risk Theory section of Chapter 9, "Special Issues," that appeared in the first, second, and third editions of *Foundations of Casualty Actuarial Science*. That chapter was written by Stephen P. D'Arcy. Changes were made by Margaret Tiller Sherwood.

Game Theory

In game theory each player selects a strategy and the resulting payoff is determined by the selected strategy in combination with the strategies chosen by the other players. Each person attempts to maximize the utility of his or her own payoffs, but, since the player cannot mandate the choices of the remaining players, the optimal strategy often involves anticipating the choices of others, negotiating the individual selection of strategies, or randomly selecting a strategy to prevent opponents from correctly anticipating one's own selection.

EXAMPLES

Subjective Measures of Objective Risk[8]

Typical applications of risk theory in the statistical area assume that loss frequency and loss severity follow standard statistical distributions. This allows calculations of insurance prices, ruin probabilities, and credibilities. Such families of distributions as the binomial, Poisson, negative binomial, geometric, lognormal, Pareto, Burr, generalized Pareto, gamma, transformed gamma, loggamma, and Weibull have been used to model losses and arrive at specific risk loadings. As the mean, variance, moment-generating functions, and derivatives of these distributions can generally be calculated, quantifiable results can be obtained.

One example of risk theory is included in Chapter 7 of this text, where the Pareto distribution is used to describe reinsurance losses. Another example is illustrated here. An actuary has information about the claim frequency distribution for a book of

[8]This section is edited from material in the Risk Theory section of Chapter 9, "Special Issues," that appeared in the first, second, and third editions of *Foundations of Casualty Actuarial Science*. That chapter was written by Stephen P. D'Arcy. Changes were made by Margaret Tiller Sherwood.

business as follows:

Number of Claims During Year	Number of Policyholders
0	15,100
1	20,708
2	13,182
3	5,727
4	1,685
5	323
6+	0

Each claim is one occurrence. Based on this data, the 56,725 policyholders generated a total of 72,608 claims during the year. If the actuary wanted to know the likelihood of an individual policyholder having three claims in a year, then one method of determining an answer would be to divide the number of policyholders with three claims by the total number of policyholders, or 10.1% (5,727/56,725). Based on this approach, there would be no chance of a policyholder having six or more claims in a year. However, if the data could be fitted to a mathematical function under the assumption that the historical data represent a random sample drawn from a distribution, then perhaps more accurate answers to questions about the chance of a given number of claims could be determined.

One very common function used to fit claim frequency distributions is the Poisson distribution. This function is:

$$\Pr(k) = (e^{-y}(y^{k}))/k!$$

where

$\Pr$ = probability

k = number of claims per year

y = expected number of claims

One of the attractive features of the Poisson distribution is that one parameter describes both the mean and the variance of the distribution. The closeness of fit of the Poisson distribution to the historical data can be checked, generally using the mean of the data set as the expected value for the Poisson distribution. Based on this approach, the value of y in the above example would be 1.28 (72,608/56,725). Comparing the fitted values with the actual data shows:

Number of Claims During Year	Actual Number of Policyholders	Fitted Number of Policyholders
0	15,100	15,772
1	20,708	20,188
2	13,182	12,920
3	5,727	5,513
4	1,685	1,764
5	323	451
6+	0	117

Based on the Poisson distribution, the likelihood of a policyholder having three claims would be 9.7% (5,513/56,725), as opposed to the 10.1% derived directly from the data, and of having six or more claims in a year would be 0.2% (117/56,725), as opposed to zero. In this regard, risk theory leads to slightly different answers than reliance on historical data. The accuracy of the estimate depends on the accuracy of the model used to describe claim frequency.

Utility Theory

Utility theory is a useful way for insurers to analyze whether their insurance has a market at the price it is offered and for potential insureds to evaluate the insurance offered. A simplified example is that of a homeowner evaluating a fire insurance policy. Homeowners usually buy homeowners policies that cover many property and liability perils, but this example is useful to show how utility theory works.

For the insured, there is a one in 1,000 chance that the house will burn to the ground. Partial losses are ignored for the purpose of this example. The value of the house is $200,000. The cost of the fire policy is $285 a year. The insurance has no deductible.

The costs under the different scenarios can be shown in a table as follows:

	No Fire	Fire
Insurance	$285	$ 285
No Insurance	$ 0	$200,000

The expected cost if insurance is purchased is:

$$(\$285 \times (999/1{,}000)) + (\$285 \times (1/1{,}000)) = \$285.$$

The expected cost if insurance is not purchased is:

$$(\$0 \times (999/1{,}000)) + (\$200{,}000 \times (1/1{,}000)) = \$200.$$

If the homeowner makes the decision to insure or not to insure based solely on expected values, the homeowner would not purchase insurance. Making a decision based solely on expected values means that the individual or entity making the decisions is risk neutral, i.e., all dollars have equal value.

However, most homeowners implicitly use utility theory to decide that the risk associated with no insurance and a fire is too big to take and purchase insurance. Explicitly, the reasoning might be as follows:

• The utility value of no expenditure if there is no insurance and no loss is $0.

- The utility value of a $285 expenditure for insurance is small, so it will be assigned a utility value of 1.

- The utility value of a $200,000 expenditure if there is no insurance and a loss is huge. It will be assigned a utility value of 1,000 because the homeowner is risk averse.

The expected utility cost if insurance is purchased is:

$$(\$285 \times (999/1{,}000) \times 1) + (\$285 \times (1/1{,}000) \times 1) = \$285.$$

The expected utility cost if insurance is not purchased is:

$$(\$0 \times (999/1{,}000) \times 0) + (\$200{,}000 \times (1/1{,}000) \times 1{,}000)$$
$$= \$200{,}000.$$

The option with the lower utility cost is, thus, the purchase of insurance.

If the insurer looks at this analysis from its point of view, it will see that fire insurance for a $200,000 home at a $285 per year price should have a viable market.

Solvency

The example just detailed also can be looked at from the insurer's point of view in regards to its solvency. Further assumptions for simplification purposes are as follows:

- The insurer writes only fire coverage for homeowners.

- All policies are for $200,000 homes.

- All occurrences are independent.

- The insurer retains all the financial risk of loss, i.e., there is no reinsurance or pooling.

- The $285 policy premium covers the $200 expected loss, $70 for expected expenses including premium taxes, and $15 for expected profit.

- Expenses do not vary.

- Investment income and income taxes are negligible.

- The insurer has $500,000 of surplus at the beginning of the policy year.

- All policies start on the same date.

If the insurer sells 100 policies, premium income is $28,500. The expected losses are $20,000, the expected expenses are $7,000, and the expected profit is $1,500. One occurrence of a $200,000 loss would mean that there would be an underwriting loss of $178,500 ($28,500 − $200,000 − $7,000). There is sufficient surplus to cover this situation.

If the insurer sells 1,000 policies, premium income is $285,000. The expected losses are $200,000, the expected expenses are $70,000, and the expected profit is $15,000. One occurrence of a $200,000 loss would mean that there would be an underwriting profit of $15,000 ($285,000 − $200,000 − $7,000), as expected. Two occurrences of a $200,000 loss would mean that there would be an underwriting loss of $185,000 ($285,000 − $400,000 − $70,000). There is sufficient surplus to cover this situation. Three occurrences of a $200,000 loss, with the resulting underwriting loss of $385,000, would put the insurer in financial jeopardy.

If the insurer sells 10,000 policies, premium income is $2,850,000. The expected losses are $2,000,000, the expected expenses are $700,000, and the expected profit is $150,000. Ten occurrences of a $200,000 loss would mean that there would be an underwriting profit of $150,000 ($2,850,000 − $2,000,000 − $700,000), as expected. Fourteen occurrences of a $200,000 loss would mean that there would be an underwriting loss of $650,000 ($2,850,000 − $2,800,000 − $700,000). There is not sufficient surplus to cover this situation. Thirteen occurrences of a $200,000 loss, with the resulting underwriting loss of $450,000, would put the insurer in financial jeopardy.

The objective risk of the number of $200,000 occurrences is not known. The insurer can make assumptions about how the number of occurrences is distributed and put together a table that shows the probability of the number of occurrences and expected solvency of the insurer.

If the binomial distribution is used, its function is:

$$\Pr(k) = \binom{N}{k} p^k q^{N-k}$$

where

      Pr = probability

      N = number of possible occurrences

      k = number of occurrences per year

      p = the expected probability of one occurrence

The table for 100 policies is, thus:

Number of Occurrences	Probability	Net Surplus
0	0.9048	$521,500
1	0.0906	321,500
2	0.0045	121,500
3	0.0001	(78,500)

The partial table for 10,000 policies is, thus:

Number of Occurrences	Probability	Net Surplus
0	0.00005	$2,650,000
10	0.12517	650,000
14	0.05207	(150,000)

A complete table would allow the insurer to estimate the probability of ruin by adding up all the probabilities for numbers of occurrences 14 or greater.

The insurer may also wish to consider using a utility theory approach here, once the subjective probabilities have been determined. For example, writing 100 policies may not be worth the administrative burden of state filings. The insurer's utility function should reflect this.

In a more realistic situation, the size of loss varies also. The subjective probability of loss can be determined by computer simulation with probability distributions for the number of occurrences and size of loss.

Other Generalized Examples

There are many other uses of risk theory in risk financing. An entity may need to decide on the excess insurance attachment point and limit for various attachment point and limit options above risk retention. Similarly, an insurer may need to decide on the reinsurance attachment point and limit for various attachment point and limit options above the financial risk it accepted from the insured and retains.

Risk theory also can be used to compare risk control and risk financing options. For example, it could be used to answer the following question: does the expected cost of specialized personnel training in safe equipment use reduce the expected workers compensation costs sufficiently to justify the cost of this training over issuing a general directive to be more careful?

Other Examples from Actuarial Literature[9]

Heckman and Meyers (1983) apply collective risk theory to describe an algorithm that calculates the cumulative probabilities

[9]This section is edited from material in the Risk Theory section of Chapter 9, "Special Issues," that appeared in the first, second, and third editions of *Foundations of Casualty Actuarial Science*. That chapter was written by Stephen P. D'Arcy. Changes were made by Margaret Tiller Sherwood.

and excess pure premiums for a book of insurance policies. This technique, although mathematically complex, can be used to determine the pure premium for a policy with an aggregate limit, the pure premium for an aggregate stop-loss policy and the risk loading for a multiline retrospective rating plan.

Venezian (1981) develops a mathematical model of accident proneness that can be used to demonstrate that an upper bound of classification efficiency exists and is below 100% and that underwriting can serve to offset weaknesses in any classification system. In his model, two types of drivers exist with different accident propensities. Young drivers all initially have a higher loss likelihood, but randomly switch to the lower likelihood category over time. Drivers also can randomly shift from low loss likelihood to the higher category. The constant state of flux in classification, modeled to approximate empirical data, creates the classification problem and allows measurement of classification error.

Hayne (1985) applies risk theory to loss reserving by analyzing the variability of age-to-age and age-to-ultimate loss development patterns. The lognormal distribution is fitted to empirical data. Use of this model provides projections of loss development factors to aid in the standard loss reserving problems facing actuaries. In addition, this model allows the determination of estimates of statistical variability of loss reserves, which are difficult to determine using the current reliance on empirical data.

Dionne and Vanasse (1988) compare a Poisson distribution with a negative binomial distribution to see which provides the closer fit to a sample of automobile insurance experience from Quebec. The negative binomial is shown to be a better fit for this sample.

SUMMARY

Risk management decisions require information about the objective risk of various exposures to possible loss and the costs of handling those exposures in different ways. Risk theory attempts to quantify the objective risk by determining subjective risk. This is done both in terms of the probability of financial losses under different risk retention and transfer scenarios and in terms of the utility of decisions concerning risk control and risk financing options for handling risk.

REFERENCES[10]

Beard, Robert E., Teivo Pentikainen, and Erkki Pesonen, *Risk Theory: The Stochastic Basis of Insurance*, London: Chapman and Hall, 1984.

Borch, Karl H., *The Mathematical Theory of Insurance*, Lexington, Mass: Lexington Books, 1974.

Buhlmann, Hans, *Mathematical Methods in Risk Theory*, New York: Springer-Verlag, 1970.

Dionne, Georges, and Charles Vanasse, *Automobile Insurance Ratemaking in the Presence of Asymmetrical Information*, University of Montréal, Center for Transportation Research, Publication Number 603, 1988.

Gerber, Hans U., *An Introduction to Mathematical Risk Theory*, Homewood, Illinois: Richard D. Irwin, 1979.

Green, Mark R. and Oscar H. Serbein, *Risk Management: Text and Cases*, Reston, Virginia: Reston Publishing Company, Inc., 1978.

Hammond, J. D., *Essays in the Theory of Risk and Insurance*, Glenview, Illinois: Scott Foresman, 1968.

Hayne, Roger M., "An Estimate of Statistical Variation in Development Factor Methods," *Proceedings of the Casualty Actuarial Society*, 1985, 72:25–43.

Head, George L., Editor, *Essentials of Risk Control*, Insurance Institute of America, 1986.

Head, George L. and Stephen Horn II, *Essentials of the Risk Management Process*, Insurance Institute of America, 1986.

Heckman, Philip E., and Glenn G. Meyers, "The Calculation of Aggregate Loss Distributions for Claim Severity and Claim Count Distributions," *Proceedings of the Casualty Actuarial Society*, 1983, 70:22–61.

---

[10]The references listed expand on topics covered in this chapter. Not all of these references are cited in the text.

Hogg, Robert V., and Stuart A. Klugman, *Loss Distributions*, New York: John Wiley and Sons, 1984.

Seal, Hilary L., *Stochastic Methods of a Risk Business*, New York: John Wiley and Sons, 1969.

Tiller, Margaret W., "Risk Financing for Public Entities," *Governmental Risk Management Manual*, Supplement No. 55, 1985.

Venezian, Emilio, "Good and Bad Drivers—A Markov Model of Accident Proneness," *Proceedings of the Casualty Actuarial Society*, 1981, 68:65–85.

Williams Jr., C. Arthur, and Richard M. Heins, *Risk Management and Insurance*, McGraw-Hill Book Company, 1981.

APPENDIX

TERMINOLOGY

The insurance industry is notorious for using words in different ways, even within the same insurer. As the field of risk management grew primarily from an insurance basis, the risk management field has similar terminology problems. It is important to understand in every situation how terms are used, as different usage could produce different results. Some basic terms used in this text are discussed below.

Exposure

The term "exposure" sometimes is used to refer to the state of being subject to loss. It also is used to refer to the rating units on which insurance premium is based or to the units by which the probability and size of loss are measured.

Occurrences and Claims

An "occurrence" is a series of incidents happening over a specified, short period of time that collectively result in a loss, such as from personal injury or property damage. A "claim" is a demand by an individual or other entity to recover for that loss. Note that one occurrence may have multiple claims associated with it. Examples are a hurricane that takes place over several days and generates many claims and an automobile accident in which several people, each of whom files a claim, are injured.

In Chapters 2 and 4 "occurrence" and "claim" are used as defined above. In some situations, "claim" is used when "occurrence" is meant. Additionally, some entities count the different components of a claim as separate claims. For example, a general liability claim with both bodily injury and property damage may be counted as two claims.

"Claim" is often used also to refer to "loss." "Claim" and "occurrence" are indicator words: they indicate either presence or absence and not amount.

In some calculations, losses may be limited. These limits are usually applied to each occurrence. Some formulae for the credibility used in individual risk rating rely on the number of occurrences. This is discussed in Chapter 4.

Loss and Loss Adjustment Expenses

"Loss," when used in relation to a claim, is the amount a claim is worth, not the request for payment. For liability, "loss" includes bodily injury, property damage, and personal damage. For workers compensation, "loss" includes medical, indemnity, and rehabilitation benefits.

Loss adjustment expenses (LAE) are the expenses associated with settling claims. There are two types: allocated loss adjustment expenses (ALAE) and unallocated loss adjustment expenses (ULAE). ALAE are attorneys' fees, investigative fees, and the like associated with settling a particular claim. ULAE are expenses associated with adjusting claims that are not allocated to settlement of a particular claim.

For an insurer, ALAE are usually costs such as outside legal counsel, investigators, expert witnesses, and court costs, and ULAE are usually the costs of the claim department, including office space, salaries and benefits, supplies, etc. However, some insurers use no outside resources to settle claims (and have no ALAE) while other insurers keep time and expense records for the claim department and charge the costs to claims as ALAE (and have no ULAE). Similar situations can occur with nontraditional risk financing mechanisms.

"Loss" sometimes refers to loss only and sometimes to loss and ALAE. "Loss" in the broader risk management context refers to loss of assets from pure risk. "Loss" also is used in a financial context to describe expenses exceeding income.

Time Periods

An accident period is the period in which an occurrence occurs, regardless of when any policies covering it are written, when the occurrence is reported, or when the associated claims are closed and losses and ALAE are paid. A policy period is the period during which an occurrence occurs for policies written during a specified time, regardless of when the associated claims are reported or are closed and losses and ALAE paid.

Not all policies are written to cover accidents occurring during the policy period. Two other options are "claims-made" and "claims-paid." Claims-made policies cover occurrences (or claims, depending on policy definitions) first reported during the policy period, regardless of the occurrence date or when the associated losses and ALAE are paid, provided that the occurrence date is after the retroactive date. Claims-paid policies cover the losses (or losses and ALAE, depending on policy definitions) paid during the policy period, regardless of the associated occurrence or claim report dates if these dates are after the appropriate retroactive dates.

Loss Components

Paid losses are losses that have been paid. Outstanding losses, or case reserves, are estimates by the claim examiner of the remaining amount required to settle particular claims, based on the knowledge about those claims at a particular date. Case reserving involves many subjective judgments, so different examiners may set reserves on the same claim at different amounts.

Case reserves, when added to the payments on open claims, do not necessarily reflect the ultimate settlement amount. Case reserves are based on knowledge at a particular point in time. In general, additional information about a claim tends to reveal that the cost of the claim is higher than previously thought, rather than lower. This means that there is usually an upward development of the payments on open claims plus case reserves for a given group of claims. The difference between the current total of payments on open claims plus case reserves and the ultimate settlement value for a given group of claims is called "case reserve development." Note that occurrence basis and claims-made coverage need a reserve to reflect case reserve development to estimate ultimate costs.

Occurrence-basis coverage will also need a reserve to reflect unreported occurrences to estimate ultimate costs. Claims-made coverage will need a reserve to reflect unreported claims if coverage is provided for occurrences reported during a particular period, since all claims associated with an occurrence may not be reported at the same time. The unreported occurrences/claims reserve is the true "IBNR" (incurred but not reported) reserve. The term "IBNR" is sometimes used to refer to the true unreported occurrences/claims reserve and the case reserve development (see below).

"Reported losses" refers to the sum of payments plus case reserves. "Unreported losses" refers to the case reserve development plus unreported occurrences/claims reserve. "Incurred losses" refers to the sum of reported and unreported losses. Note that unreported losses and incurred losses contain different items for occurrence and claims-made-coverage and may contain different items for different types of claims-made coverage. "Ultimate losses" refers to an estimate of "incurred losses."

"Case reserves" are sometimes used when "reported losses" are meant. Many entities refer to "reported losses" as "incurred losses" and to "unreported losses" as "IBNR." The result is confusion, with incurred losses plus incurred but not reported losses equaling incurred losses.

Exhibit 2.1 illustrates the loss component terminology used in this book. These terms also apply to ALAE. Different rating plans sometimes treat losses and ALAE together, sometimes separately, and sometimes as a mixture. An example of the last is treating paid losses and paid ALAE separately, but setting case

EXHIBIT 2.1

Loss Terminology Illustration

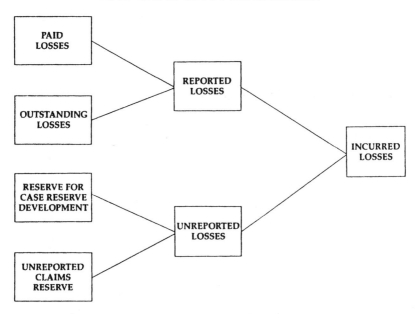

reserves for losses and ALAE combined or for losses only. The treatment of ALAE in this book is specified in each situation in which it appears.

Frequency and Severity

Two other terms that have different usage in different situations and that are used in risk management are "frequency" and "severity." Frequency is the number of occurrences (or claims) per exposure unit. "Frequency" is sometimes incorrectly used to refer to the number of claims or occurrences. Frequency is a relative, not an absolute, measure.

Severity is the average loss per claim (or per occurrence). Note that "loss" may include or exclude ALAE.

CHAPTER 3

RATEMAKING

CHARLES L. McCLENAHAN

INTRODUCTION

The Concept of Manual Ratemaking

From the earliest days of marine insurance, premium charges have been based upon specific characteristics of the individual risk being priced. Lloyd's of London based early hull rates in part upon the design and protection of each specific ship, and the classification assigned to each vessel was written down in a book or **manual** for use by the individual underwriters. Eighteenth century dwelling fire insurance rates in the U.S. were based upon roof type and basic construction. While these early rate manuals were meant to provide general guidance to the underwriters in setting the specific rates, rather than the actual rates to be charged, they contained many of the elements associated with present-day property and liability rate manuals including recognition of differing loss costs between classifications, expense provision, and provision for adverse deviation and profit.

One of the most persistent misconceptions associated with property and liability insurance is the level of accuracy which actuaries are believed to achieve in the assessment of individual loss propensity. Over the years, as the doctrine of *caveat emptor* has been eroded and insurance risks have become increasingly complex, rate manuals have evolved to the point that, for many lines of insurance, they provide the exact premium to be charged for providing a specific coverage to a specific risk for a specific period. It is important, however, not to confuse the level of precision inherent in the rate manual with the level of accuracy. The latter will be judged in the cold light of actual loss experience. No matter how refined the classification and rating process may become, manual rates are still **estimates of average costs** based upon a combination of statistical methods and professional judgment.

This chapter will deal with the basic actuarial methods and assumptions underlying the development of manual rates. While a complete treatment of the subject might well fill several books, the key elements will be covered to such an extent that the reader of this chapter will gain an understanding of the basic actuarial concepts and techniques involved in the review and analysis of manual rates for property and liability coverages.

BASIC TERMINOLOGY

While ratemaking is neither pure science nor pure art, both the scientific and artistic elements of the subject demand the use of precise language. Property and casualty insurance is a complicated business which can be best represented and understood in a technical financial context. Many of the misconceptions about property and liability insurance can be directly attributed to either the failure to use precise terminology, or the failure to understand the terminology in precise terms. This section will introduce some definitions of some of the more important terms used by casualty actuaries.

Exposure

The basic rating unit underlying an insurance premium is called an **exposure**. The unit of exposure will vary based upon the characteristics of the insurance coverage involved. For automobile insurance, one automobile insured for a period of twelve months is a car year. A single policy providing coverage on three automobiles for a six month term would involve 1.5 car years. The most commonly used exposure statistics are **written exposures**, those units of exposures on policies written during the period in question, **earned exposures**, the exposure units actually exposed to loss during the period, and **in-force exposures**, the exposure units exposed to loss at a given point in time. In order to illustrate these three statistics, consider the following four twelve-month, single-car automobile policies:

Effective Date	Written Exposure 1999	Written Exposure 2000	Earned Exposure 1999	Earned Exposure 2000	In-Force Exposure 1/1/2000
1/1/1999	1.00	0.00	1.00	0.00	0.00
4/1/1999	1.00	0.00	0.75	0.25	1.00
7/1/1999	1.00	0.00	0.50	0.50	1.00
10/1/1999	1.00	0.00	0.25	0.75	1.00
Total	4.00	0.00	2.50	1.50	3.00

Note that the in-force exposure counts a full car year for each twelve-month policy in force as of 1/1/2000, regardless of the length of the remaining term.

The specific exposure unit used for a given type of insurance depends upon several factors, including reasonableness, ease of determination, responsiveness to change, and historical practice.

Reasonableness—it is obvious that the exposure unit should be a reasonable measure of the exposure to loss. While every exposure unit definition compromises this principle to some degree—for example a 1999 Rolls Royce and a 1989 Chevrolet might each represent a car year exposure—the selected measure should directly relate to loss potential to the extent possible.

Ease of Determination—the most reasonable and responsive exposure definition is of no use if it cannot be accurately determined. While the most appropriate exposure for products liability insurance might be the number of products currently in use, this number would generally be impossible to determine. If an exposure base is not subject to determination, then an insurer can never be assured of receiving the proper premium for the actual exposure.

Responsiveness to Change—an exposure unit that reflects changes in the exposure to loss is preferable to one which does not. The exposure unit for workers compensation insurance, which provides benefits which are keyed to average wage levels, is payroll. This is obviously preferable to number of employees, for example, as the payroll will change with the prevailing wage levels.

Historical Practice—where a significant body of historical exposure data is available, any change in the exposure base could render the prior history unusable. Since ratemaking generally depends upon the review of past statistical indications, exposure bases are rarely changed once they have been established.

Claim

A **claim** is a demand for payment by an insured or by an allegedly injured third party under the terms and conditions of an insurance contract. The individual making the claim is the **claimant**, and there can be multiple claimants within a single claim. Claim statistics are key elements in the ratemaking process. Generally insurers maintain claim data based upon **accident date**—the date of the occurrence which gave rise to the claim, and **report date**—the date the insurer receives notice of the claim. Claim data can then be aggregated based upon these dates. For example, the total of all claims with accident dates during 2001 is the accident year 2001 claim count.

Frequency

Because the number of claims is directly related to the number of exposures, actuaries express claim incidence in terms of frequency per exposure unit.

$$F_k = \frac{kC}{E} \tag{1}$$

where

F_k = frequency per k exposure units

k = scale factor

C = claim count

E = exposure units

For example, if we earned 32,458 car years of exposure during 2001 and we incur 814 claims with 2001 accident dates, then the 2001 accident year claim frequency per 1,000 earned exposures is 25.08 calculated as follows:

$$F_{1000} = \frac{1,000(814)}{32,458} = 25.08$$

Where the context is established by either data or previous exposition it might be appropriate to refer to this simply as the **frequency**. In general, however, the need for precision would require that the more specific language **accident year frequency per 1,000 earned car years** be used.

Losses and Loss Adjustment Expenses

Amounts paid or payable to claimants under the terms of insurance policies are referred to as **losses**. **Paid losses** are those losses for a particular period that have actually been paid to claimants. Where there is an expectation that a payment will be made in the future, a claim will have an associated **case reserve** representing the estimated amount of that payment. The sum of all paid losses and case reserves for a specific accident year at a specific point in time is known as the **accident year case-incurred losses**. The term **case-incurred** is used to distinguish this statistic from **ultimate incurred losses**, which include losses that have not yet been reported to the insurance company as of the case-incurred evaluation date.

Over time, as more losses are paid and more information becomes available about unpaid claims, accident year case-incurred

FIGURE 3.1

CASE-INCURRED LOSS DEVELOPMENT AUTO LIABILITY

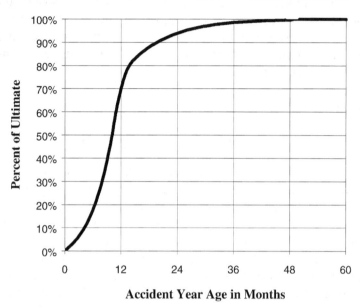

Accident Year Age in Months

losses will tend to approach their ultimate value. Generally, because of the reporting of additional claims that were not included
in earlier evaluations, accident year case-incurred losses tend to
increase over time. In order to keep track of the individual evaluations of case-incurred losses for an accident year, actuaries
use the concept of the **accident year age**. The accident year age
is generally expressed in months. By convention, the accident
year is age 12 months at the end of the last day of the accident
year. Therefore, the 1999 accident year evaluated as of 6/30/2000
would be referred to as the age 18 evaluation of the 1999 accident
year.

Figure 3.1 represents a graphical interpretation of a typical
case-incurred loss development pattern—in this case for automobile liability.

Insurance company expenses associated with the settlement of claims, as distinguished from the marketing, investment, or general administrative operations, are referred to as **loss adjustment expenses**. Those loss adjustment expenses which can be directly related to a specific claim are called **allocated loss adjustment expenses** and those which cannot are called **unallocated loss adjustment expenses**.

Severity

Average loss per claim is called **severity**. Severities can be on a pure loss basis, excluding all loss adjustment expenses, or they can include allocated or total loss adjustment expenses. The loss component can be paid, case-incurred or projected ultimate and the claims component can be reported, paid, closed, or projected ultimate. This profusion of available options again requires that the actuary be precise in the references to the components. Note the differences between **accident year case-incurred loss severity per reported claim** and **report year paid loss and allocated severity per closed claim**. However the loss and claim components are defined, the formula for severity is simply:

$$S = \frac{L}{C} \tag{2}$$

where

$$S = \text{severity}$$
$$L = \text{losses}$$
$$C = \text{claim count}$$

Pure Premium

Another important statistic is the average loss per unit of exposure or the **pure premium**. The reader will by now appreciate the need for precise component definition either in terminology or through context, so the various options will not be recited.

The formula for the pure premium is:

$$P = \frac{L}{E} \tag{3}$$

where

$$P = \text{pure premium}$$
$$L = \text{losses}$$
$$E = \text{exposure units}$$

Note that the pure premium can also be expressed as:

$$P = \frac{C}{E} \times \frac{L}{C}$$

where

$$C = \text{claim count}$$

Or, where frequency is per unit of exposure:

$$P = F_1 \times S \tag{4}$$

In other words, **pure premium equals the product of frequency per unit of exposure and severity.**

Expense, Profit and Contingencies

In order to determine the price for a specific insurance coverage, appropriate provisions must be made for expenses (other than any loss adjustment expenses included in the pure premium) and profit. The profit provision is generally termed the (underwriting) **profit and contingencies provision** reflecting the fact that profits, if any, will be based upon actual results and not expectations or projections. For the purposes of this discussion we will distinguish between fixed expenses per unit of exposure, which do not depend upon premium, and variable expenses which vary directly with price.

This treatment gives rise to the following formula for the rate per unit of exposure:

$$R = \frac{P + F}{1 - V - Q} \qquad (5)$$

where

R = rate per unit of exposure

P = pure premium

F = fixed expense per exposure

V = variable expense factor

Q = profit and contingencies factor

As an example, assume the following:

Loss and loss adjustment expense pure premium	$75.00
Fixed expense per exposure	$12.50
Variable expense factor	17.5%
Profit and contingencies factor	5.0%

The appropriate rate for this example would be calculated as follows:

$$\text{Rate} = \frac{\$75.00 + \$12.50}{1 - .175 - .050} = \$112.90$$

The individual components of the rate would therefore be as follows:

Pure premium	$75.00
Fixed expenses	12.50
Variable expenses ($112.90 × .175)	19.76
Profit and contingencies ($112.90 × .050)	5.64
Total	$112.90

Premium

Application of the rate(s) to the individual exposures to be covered by an insurance policy produces the **premium** for that policy. If, in the above example, the unit of exposure is a commercial vehicle and we are rating a policy for 15 commercial vehicles, the premium would be calculated as follows:

$$\$112.90 \times 15 = \$1,693.50$$

Premium, like exposure, can be either **written, earned**, or **in-force**. If the policy in question was written for a twelve-month term on 7/1/99 then that policy would have contributed the following amounts as of 12/31/99:

Calendar year 1999 written premium	$1,693.50
Calendar year 1999 earned premium	$846.75
12/31/99 premium in-force	$1,693.50

Loss Ratio

Probably the single most widely-used statistic in the analysis of insurance losses is the **loss ratio** or losses divided by premium. Again the need for precision cannot be overemphasized. There is a great difference between a loss ratio based upon paid losses as of accident year age 12 and written premium (termed an **age 12 accident year written-paid pure loss ratio**) and one that is based upon ultimate incurred loss and loss adjustment expenses and earned premium (**ultimate accident year earned-incurred loss and loss adjustment expense ratio**) although either can be properly referred to as a loss ratio.

The Goal of the Manual Ratemaking Process

Broadly stated, the goal of the ratemaking process is to determine rates that will, when applied to the exposures underlying the risks being written, provide sufficient funds to pay expected losses and expenses; maintain an adequate margin for adverse deviation; and produce a reasonable return on (any) funds provided by investors. In addition, manual rates are generally subject to regulatory review and, while detailed discussion of regulatory requirements is beyond the scope of this text, this review is often based upon the regulatory standard that *"rates shall not be inadequate, excessive, or unfairly discriminatory between risks of like kind and quality."*

Internally, there will generally be a review of the competitiveness of the rate levels in the marketplace. While the actuary may be directly involved in both internal and external discussions relating to these reviews, it is the actuary's primary responsibility to recommend rates that can be reasonably expected to be adequate over the period in which they are to be used.

Adequately pricing a line of insurance involves substantial judgment. While actuaries are trained in mathematics and statistics, the actuarial process underlying manual ratemaking also requires substantial understanding of the underwriting, economic, social, and political factors that have in the past impacted the insurance results and will impact those results in the future.

Structure of the Rating Plan

Up to this point the discussion of manual rates has related to the concept of an identified unit of exposure. In practice, manual rates are based upon a number of factors in addition to the basic exposure unit. For example, the elements involved in the rating of a single private passenger automobile insurance policy might include the following:

Age of insured(s)

Gender of insured(s)

Marital status of insured(s)

Prior driving record of insured(s)

Annual mileage driven

Primary use of vehicle(s)

Make and model of vehicle(s)

Age of vehicle(s)

Garaging location of vehicle(s)

The structure of the various elements involved in the manual rating of a specific risk is known as the **rating plan**. Various specific elements are often referred to as **classifications**, **sub-classifications**, or **rating factors**. Rating plans serve to allow the manual rating process to reflect identified differences in loss propensity. Failing to reflect such factors can result in two separate situations. Where a known positive characteristic, i.e., a characteristic tending to be associated with reduced loss propensity, is not reflected in the rating plan, the rate applied to risks possessing that positive characteristic will be too high. This would encourage the insuring of these risks to the partial or total exclusion of risks not possessing the positive characteristic, a practice referred to as **skimming the cream**. On the other hand, the failure to reflect a known negative characteristic will result in the application of a rate that is too low. If other companies are reflecting the negative factor in their rating plans, the result will be a tendency towards insuring risks possessing the negative characteristic, a situation known as **adverse selection**.

Risk characteristics underlying a manual rating plan can be broadly identified as those generally impacting frequency and those generally impacting severity. Prior driving record is an example of a factor that has been demonstrated to correlate with frequency. Individuals with recent automobile accidents and traffic violations have, *as a class*, higher frequencies of future claims than do those individuals with no recent accidents or violations. Individuals driving high-powered sports cars have, *as a class*, higher frequencies than those driving family sedans. Annual mileage driven has an obvious impact on frequency.

On the severity side, some vehicles tend to be more susceptible to damage in collisions than do other vehicles. Repair parts for a Rolls Royce costs more than do those for a Chevrolet. A late model automobile is more valuable than a ten-year-old "clunker" and will therefore, *on average*, have a higher associated severity.

The above examples deal with private passenger automobile insurance, but other lines have identifiable risk characteristics as well. In commercial fire insurance, restaurants generally have a higher frequency than do clothing stores. The presence or absence of a sprinkler system will impact severity as will the value of the building and contents being insured. Workers compensation statistics detail higher frequencies for manufacturing employees than for clerical workers. For every type of property and casualty insurance, there are identifiable factors that impact upon frequency and severity of losses.

The subject of risk classification will be discussed in detail in chapter 6. In addition, the reflection of specific individual risk differences, as opposed to class differences, will be treated in chapter 4. For the purposes of this chapter, it is sufficient to be aware of the existence of and need for rating plans reflecting identifiable risk classification differences.

THE RATEMAKING PROCESS

In this section we will deal with the basic techniques used by casualty actuaries in the development of manual rates. The reader must bear in mind that this discussion will be general in nature—a complete discussion of the elements involved in a single complex line of insurance might require several hundred pages. Nevertheless, the key elements of manual ratemaking will be addressed to such an extent that a good understanding of the actuarial process of manual ratemaking should result.

Basic Manual Ratemaking Methods

There are two basic approaches to addressing the problem of manual ratemaking: the **pure premium method** and the **loss**

ratio method. We will examine the mathematics underlying each method and then develop a relationship between the two.

Pure Premium Method

The pure premium method develops indicated rates—those rates that are expected to provide for the expected losses and expenses and provide the expected profit—based upon formula (5).

$$R = \frac{P + F}{1 - V - Q} \tag{5}$$

where

R = rate per unit of exposure

P = pure premium

F = fixed expense per exposure

V = variable expense factor

Q = profit and contingencies factor

The pure premium used in the formula is based upon **experience losses**, which are trended projected ultimate losses (or losses and loss adjustment expenses) for the experience period under review, and the exposures earned during the experience period. The methods underlying the trending and projection of the losses will be discussed later in this chapter.

Loss Ratio Method

The loss ratio method develops indicated **rate changes** rather than indicated rates. Indicated rates are determined by application of an adjustment factor, the ratio of the **experience loss ratio** to a **target loss ratio**, to the current rates. The experience loss ratio is the ratio of the experience losses to the **on-level earned premium**—the earned premium that would have resulted for the experience period had the current rates been in effect for the entire period. In mathematical terms the loss ratio method works as follows:

$$R = AR_0 \qquad (6)$$

where

R = indicated rate

R_0 = current rate

A = adjustment factor = W/T

W = experience loss ratio

T = target loss ratio

Looking first at the target loss ratio:

$$T = \frac{1 - V - Q}{1 + G} \qquad (7)$$

where

V = premium-related expense factor

Q = profit and contingencies factor

G = ratio of non-premium-related expenses to losses

And then the experience loss ratio:

$$W = \frac{L}{ER_0} \qquad (8)$$

where

L = experience losses

E = experience period earned exposure

R_0 = current rate

Using (6), (7), and (8) we can see:

$$
\begin{aligned}
A &= \frac{L/ER_0}{(1 - V - Q)/(1 + G)} \\
&= \frac{L(1 + G)}{ER_0(1 - V - Q)} \qquad (9)
\end{aligned}
$$

and, substituting (9) into (6):

$$R = \frac{L(1+G)}{E(1-V-Q)} \tag{10}$$

Relationship Between Pure Premium and Loss Ratio Methods

It has been emphasized in this chapter that manual rates are estimates. Nevertheless, they generally represent precise estimates based upon reasonable and consistent assumptions. This being the case, we should be able to demonstrate that the pure premium and loss ratio methods will produce identical rates when applied to identical data and using consistent assumptions. This demonstration is quite simple. It starts with formula (10), the formula for the indicated rate under the loss ratio method:

$$R = \frac{L(1+G)}{E(1-V-Q)} \tag{10}$$

Now, the loss ratio method uses experience losses while the pure premium method is based upon experience pure premium. The relationship between the two comes from (3):

$$P = \frac{L}{E} \tag{3}$$

which can be expressed as:

$$L = EP$$

Also, the loss ratio method relates non-premium-related expenses to losses while the pure premium method uses exposures as the base for these expenses. The relationship can be expressed as follows:

$$G = \frac{EF}{L}$$
$$= \frac{F}{P}$$

Substituting for L and G in formula (10) produces the following:

$$R = \frac{EP[1 + (F/P)]}{E(1 - V - Q)}$$

or

$$R = \frac{P + F}{1 - V - Q} \tag{5}$$

This is the formula for the indicated rate under the pure premium method. The equivalence of the two methods is therefore demonstrated.

Selection of Appropriate Method

Because the two methods can be expected to produce identical results when consistently applied to a common set of data, the question arises as to which approach is the more appropriate for any given situation. Having dealt with the mathematical aspects of the two methods, let us now look at some of the practical differences.

Pure Premium Method	Loss Ratio Method
Based on exposure	Based on premium
Does not require existing rates	Requires existing rates
Does not use on-level premium	Uses on-level premium
Produces indicated rates	Produces indicated rate changes

Noting the above differences, the following guidelines would seem to be reasonable:

- **Pure premium method requires well-defined, responsive exposures**. The pure premium method is based on losses per unit exposure. Where the exposure unit is not available or is not reasonably consistent between risks, as in the case of commercial fire insurance, the pure premium method cannot be used.

- **Loss ratio method cannot be used for a new line**. Because the loss ratio method produces indicated rate changes, its use requires an established rate and premium history. Where manual rates are required for a new line of business, and assuming there are relevant loss statistics available, the pure premium method must be used. Of course, if no statistical data are available, then neither method can be used.

- **Pure premium method is preferable where on-level premium is difficult to calculate**. In some instances, such as commercial lines where individual risk rating adjustments are made to individual policies, it is difficult to determine the on-level earned premium required for the loss ratio method. Where this is the case it is more appropriate to use the pure premium method if possible.

Need for Common Basis

Whichever ratemaking method is selected, the actuary needs to make certain that the experience losses are on a basis consistent with the exposures and premiums being used. This requires that adjustments be made for observed changes in the data. This section will deal with some of the more common sources of change in the underlying data and will discuss methods for dealing with those changes.

Selection of Experience Period

Determination of the loss experience period to be used in the manual ratemaking process involves a combination of statistical and judgmental elements. There is a natural preference for using the most recent incurred loss experience available since it is generally most representative of the current situation. However, this experience will also contain a higher proportion of unpaid losses than will more mature periods and is therefore more subject to loss development projection errors. Where the business involved is subject to catastrophe losses, as in the case of windstorm coverage in hurricane-prone areas, the experience period must be representative of the average catastrophe incidence. Finally, the experience period must contain sufficient loss experience that the resulting indications will have statistical significance or **credibility**.

Reinsurance

Ceded reinsurance, which is discussed in depth in chapter 7, serves to reduce an insurer's exposure to large losses, either individual or in the aggregate, in exchange for a reinsurance premium. While there may be instances in which a reinsurance program represents such a significant transfer of risk that separate and distinct provision for the reinsurance premium is appropriate, such cases are beyond the scope of this chapter. In general, the analysis of manual rates is based upon direct, that is before reflection of reinsurance, premium and loss data. Where reinsurance costs are significant they are often treated as a separate element of the expense provision.

Differences in Coverage

Wherever possible, major coverages within a line of insurance are generally treated separately. For example, liability experience under homeowners policies is often reviewed separately from the property experience. Auto collision data is usually analyzed separately by deductible. Professional liability policies written on a claims-made basis are generally not combined with those written on an occurrence basis for ratemaking purposes. Note that unless the mix has been consistent over the entire experience period these separations will require the segregation of premium and exposure data as well as the loss experience.

Treatment of Increased Limits

Liability coverage rate manuals generally provide rates for a basic limit of liability along with increased limits factors to be applied to these base rates where higher limits are desired. As will be seen in a later section, these increased limits factors tend to change over time. In addition there will be a general movement toward the purchase of higher limits as inflation erodes purchasing power. For these reasons premiums and losses used in the manual ratemaking process should be adjusted to a basic limits basis.

On-Level Premium—Adjusting for Prior Rate Changes

Where, as is the general case, the experience period extends over several years there have typically been changes in manual rate levels between the beginning of the experience period and the date as of which the rates are being reviewed. If the actuary is using the loss ratio method in the development of the indicated rate level changes, the earned premium underlying the loss ratio calculations must be on a current rate level basis.

Where the capability exists, the best method for bringing past premiums to an on-level basis is to re-rate each policy using current rates. Doing this manually is generally far too time-consuming to be practical, but where sufficient detail is available in the computer files and if rating software is available, the resulting on-level premiums will be quite accurate. This method is referred to as the **extension of exposures technique**.

When extension of exposures cannot be used, an alternative, called the **parallelogram method**, is available. This method adjusts calendar year earned premiums to current rate levels based upon simple geometric relationships and an underlying assumption that exposure is uniformly distributed over time.

As an example, assume that the experience period in question consists of the three years 1997, 1998, and 1999. Further assume that each policy has a twelve-month term. Finally, assume that rate increases have been taken as follows:

+ 17.8% effective 7/1/1994

+ 12.5% effective 7/1/1996

+ 10.0% effective 7/1/1998

FIGURE 3.2

DEVELOPMENT OF ON-LINE PREMIUM

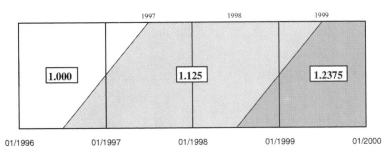

Because we are dealing with twelve-month policies, all of the premium earned during the earliest year of the experience period—1997—was written at either the 7/1/1994 rate level or the 7/1/1996 rate level. If we assign the 7/1/1994 rate level a relative value of 1.000, then the 7/1/1996 rate level has a relative value of 1.125 and the 7/1/1998 rate level has a relative value of (1.125)(1.100) = 1.2375.

Figure 3.2 provides a representation of these data under the parallelogram method. The x-axis represents the date on which a policy is effective, and the y-axis represents the portion of exposure earned.

Each calendar year of earned premium can now be viewed as a unit square one year wide and 100% of exposure high. Figure 3.3 illustrates this treatment of the 1997 year.

As shown in Figure 3.4, we can now use simple geometry to determine the portions of 1997 earned exposure written at the 1.000 and 1.125 relative levels.

According to the parallelogram model, .125 of the 1997 earned exposure arises from policies written at the 1.000 relative

FIGURE 3.3

ON-LEVEL PREMIUM FACTOR

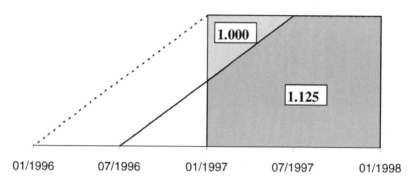

| 01/1996 | 07/1996 | 01/1997 | 07/1997 | 01/1998 |

level and .875 of the exposure was written at a relative level of 1.125. The average 1997 relative earned rate level is therefore [(.125)(1.000) + (.875)(1.125)] = 1.1094. Since the current relative average rate level is 1.2375, the 1997 calendar year earned premium must be multiplied by (1.2375/1.1094) = 1.1155 to reflect current rate levels. The 1.1155 is referred to as the 1997 **on-level factor**.

We can repeat this process for the 1998 and 1999 years to generate the following:

Calendar	Portion of Earned at Relative Level			On-Level
Year	1.0000	1.1250	1.2375	Factor
1997	0.125	0.875	0.000	1.1155
1998	0.000	0.875	0.125	1.0864
1999	0.000	0.125	0.875	1.0115

These on-level factors are then applied to the calendar year earned premiums to generate approximate on-level earned pre-

FIGURE 3.4

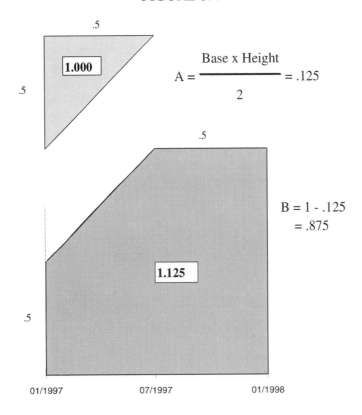

miums. For example:

Calendar Year	Calendar Year Earned Premium	On-Level Factor	Approximate On-Level Earned Premium
1997	$1,926,981	1.1155	$2,149,547
1998	$2,299,865	1.0864	$2,498,573
1999	$2,562,996	1.0115	$2,592,470
Total	$6,789,842		$7,240,590

As noted earlier, the parallelogram method is based upon an assumption that exposures are written uniformly over the calendar period. In cases where material changes in exposure level have occurred over the period, or where there is a non-uniform pattern to the written exposures, the parallelogram method may not produce a reasonable approximation of on-level earned premium. While a discussion of adjustments to the simple model underlying the parallelogram method is beyond the scope of this chapter, Miller and Davis (1976) have proposed an alternative model that reflects actual exposure patterns.

TRENDED, PROJECTED ULTIMATE LOSSES

We are now ready to discuss the method underlying the development of the trended, projected ultimate losses. This element represents the most significant part of any ratemaking analysis and requires both statistical expertise and actuarial judgment. Whether the pure premium method or the loss ratio method is being used, the accuracy with which losses are projected will determine the adequacy of the resulting manual rates.

Inclusion of Loss Adjustment Expenses

The actuary must determine whether to make projections on a pure loss basis, or whether to include allocated loss adjustment expenses with losses. Unallocated loss adjustment data are rarely available in sufficient detail for inclusion with losses and allocated loss adjustment expenses, and are generally treated as part of the expense provision—frequently as a ratio to loss and allocated loss adjustment expenses.

While the decision whether to include allocated loss expense data with losses is generally made based upon data availability, there is one situation in which it is essential that the allocated loss adjustment expenses be combined with the losses. Some liability policies contain limits of liability that apply to both losses and allocated loss adjustment expenses. Where manual rates are being developed for such policies, allocated loss adjustment expenses should be treated as losses.

Projection to Ultimate—the Loss Development Method

A significant portion of the entirety of casualty actuarial literature produced in this century deals with the methods and techniques for projecting unpaid, and often unreported, losses to their ultimate settlement values. Even a casual treatment of the subject is beyond the scope of this chapter. Nevertheless, the general concepts discussed in this section will be based upon the use of projected ultimate losses and claim counts. A thorough understanding of the issues involved in manual ratemaking requires that the context of the problem be clear. At least one technique for projection to ultimate is needed and we will use the most common—the **loss development method**.

The loss development method is based upon the assumption that claims move from unreported to reported-and-unpaid to paid in a pattern that is sufficiently consistent that past experience can be used to predict future development. Claim counts, or losses, are arrayed by accident year (or report year or on some other basis) and accident year age. The resulting data form a triangle of known values. As an example, consider the following accident year reported claim count development data:

Accident Year	Age 12	Age 24	Age 36	Age 48	Age 60	Age 72
1994	1,804	2,173	2,374	2,416	2,416	2,416
1995	1,935	2,379	2,424	2,552	2,552	
1996	2,103	2,384	2,514	2,646		
1997	2,169	2,580	2,722			
1998	2,346	2,783				
1999	2,337					

Remembering the concept of accident year age it can be seen, for example, that as of 12/31/1997 there were 2,424 claims reported for accidents occurring during 1995. By 12/31/1998 this number had developed to 2,552. Horizontal movement to the right represents **development**, vertical movement downward represents **change in exposure level**, and positive-sloped diagonals represent **evaluation dates**. The lower diagonal represents the latest available evaluation—in this case 12/31/1999.

Accident Year	Age 12	Age 24	Age 36	Age 48	Age 60	Age 72
1994						2,416
1995					2,552	
1996				2,646		
1997			2,722			
1998		2,783				
1999	2,337					

The next step in the process is to reflect the development history arithmetically. This involves the division of each evaluation subsequent to the first by the immediately preceding evaluation. The resulting ratio is called an **age-to-age development factor** or, sometimes, a **link ratio**. For example, the accident year 1994 12–24 reported claim count development factor from our example is $2,173/1,804 = 1.2045$.

Accident Year	Age 12	Age 24	Age 36	Age 48	Age 60	Age 72
1994	1,804	2,173	2,374	2,416	2,416	2,416
1995	1,935	2,379	2,424	2,552	2,552	
1996	2,103	2,384	2,514	2,646		
1997	2,169	2,580	2,722			
1998	2,346	2,783				
1999	2,337			$2,173/1,804 = 1.2045$		

We can now produce a second data triangle consisting of age-to-age development factors.

Accident Year	12–24	24–36	36–48	48–60	60–72
1995	1.2045	1.0925	1.0177	1.0000	1.0000
1996	1.2295	1.0189	1.0528	1.0000	
1997	1.1336	1.0545	1.0525		
1998	1.1895	1.0550			
1999	1.1863				

Based upon the observed development factors, age-to-age factors are selected and successively multiplied to generate **age-to-ultimate factors**. These age-to-ultimate factors are then applied to the latest diagonal of the development data to yield projected ultimate values.

Accident Year	Accident Year Age 12/31/1999	Selected Age-to-Age Factor	Age-to Ultimate Factor	Reported Claims 12/31/1999	Projected Ultimate Claims
1994	72	—	1.0000	2,416	2,416
1995	60	1.0000	1.0000	2,552	2,552
1996	48	1.0000	1.0000	2,646	2,646
1997	36	1.0450	1.0450	2,722	2,844
1998	24	1.0550	1.1025	2,783	3,068
1999	12	1.1900	1.3120	2,337	3,066

An identical process can be applied to either paid or case-incurred losses. Generally, case-incurred values are used, especially where the development period extends over several years. Note that losses tend to take longer to develop fully than do reported claims. This is due to the **settlement lag**—the period between loss reporting and loss payment—which affects losses but not reported claims and represents additional development potential beyond the **reporting lag**—the period between loss occurrence and loss reporting—which affects both claims and losses.

An example of the loss development method applied to case-incurred loss and allocated loss adjustment expense data is contained in the Appendix to this chapter.

In some instances, most notably where premiums are subject to audit adjustments, as is often true for workers compensation insurance, premium data requires projection to ultimate in order that the premium being used in the ratemaking calculations properly reflects the actual exposure level that gave rise to the ultimate losses. One method for handling this situation is to aggregate data on a **policy year**, rather than an accident year, basis. Policy year data is based upon the year in which the policy giving rise to exposures, premiums, claims and losses is effective. Another method involves the projection of written premium to ultimate and the recalculation of earned premium, referred to as **exposure year earned premium**, based upon the projected ultimate written premium. In either case, the projection techniques involved are similar to the loss development method.

Identification of Trends

Once claims and losses have been projected to an ultimate basis it is necessary to adjust the data for any underlying trends that are expected to produce changes in indications between the experience period and the period during which the manual rates will be in effect. For example, if rates are being reviewed as of 12/31/1999 based upon 1997 accident year data and the new rates are expected to go into effect on 7/1/2000, the projected ultimate losses for the 1997 accident year are representative of loss exposure as of approximately 7/1/1997 and the indicated rates must cover loss exposure as of approximately 7/1/2001. This is based upon the assumption that the revised rates will be in effect for 12 months, from 7/1/2000 through 6/30/2001. Assuming a one-year policy term, the average policy will therefore run from

1/1/2001 through 12/31/2001 and the midpoint of loss occurrence under that policy will be 7/1/2001. To the extent that there are identifiable trends in the loss data, the impact of those trends must be reflected over the 48 months between the midpoint of the experience period and the average exposure date to which the rates will apply.

The most obvious trend affecting the ratemaking data is the trend in severity. Monetary inflation, increases in jury awards, and increases in medical expenses are examples of factors that cause upward trends in loss severities. Frequency is also subject to trend. Court decisions may open new grounds for litigation that would increase liability frequencies. Legal and social pressures might reduce the incidence of driving under the influence of alcohol, thus reducing automobile insurance frequencies. In workers compensation an amendment in the governing law can cause changes in both severity and frequency of loss.

Some exposure bases also exhibit identifiable trends. Workers compensation uses payroll as an exposure base and products liability coverage might be based upon dollars of sales. Both of these exposures will reflect some degree of trend. Automobile physical damage rates are based upon the value of the automobiles being insured. As automobile prices increase, the physical damage premiums will reflect the change, even though no rate change has been made. When using the loss ratio method for ratemaking it is important that the effect of such trends on premium be properly reflected.

While frequency and severity trends are often analyzed separately, it is sometimes preferable to look at trends in the pure premium, thus combining the impacts of frequency and severity.

Reflection of Trends

Actuaries generally approach the problem of how to reflect observed trends by fitting an appropriate curve to the observed

FIGURE 3.5

SEVERITY TREND THIRD DEGREE POLYNOMIAL FIT

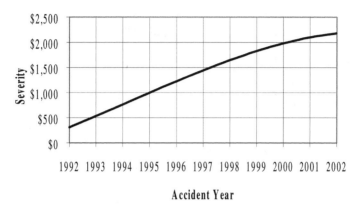

Accident Year

data. The most important word in the preceding sentence is **appropriate**. Consider the following hypothetical projected accident year severity data:

Accident Year	Projected Severity
1992	$ 309
1993	532
1994	763
1995	996
1996	1,225
1997	1,444
1998	1,647
1999	1,828

It so happens that the third-degree polynomial $y = -x^3 + 10x^2 + 200x + 100$ produces a perfect fit to the above data where x is defined as the accident year minus 1991. Figure 3.5 shows the result of this fit graphically.

FIGURE 3.6

Severity Trend Third Degree Polynomial Fit

Accident Year

Based upon the strength of the fit one might be tempted to use the third-degree polynomial to project future severity changes. But is a third-degree polynomial really appropriate for a severity trend model?

If we extend the x axis out through accident year 2010 we see that, regardless of how well it might fit our observations, the third degree polynomial model is not one that is reasonable for projection of severity changes. See Figure 3.6.

While other appropriate models are available, most of the trending models used by casualty actuaries in ratemaking take one of two forms:

Linear $\qquad y = ax + b,\qquad$ or

Exponential $\qquad y = be^{ax}$

Note that the exponential model can be expressed as:

$$\ln(y) = ax + \ln(b)$$

Or, with the substitutions $y' = \ln(y)$ and $b' = \ln(b)$:

$$y' = ax + b'$$

Since either model can therefore be expressed in terms of a linear function, the standard first-degree least-squares regression method can be applied to the observed data to determine the trend model. Note that the linear model will produce a model in which the projection will increase by a constant amount (a) for each unit change in x. The exponential model will produce a constant rate of change of $e^a - 1$, with each value being e^a times the prior value. Drawing an analogy to the mathematics of finance, the linear model is analogous to simple interest while the exponential model is analogous to compound interest.

While either linear or exponential models can be used to reflect increasing trends, where the observed trend is decreasing the use of a linear model will produce negative values at some point in the future. The use of a linear model over an extended period in such cases is generally inappropriate since frequency, severity, pure premium, and exposure must all be greater than or equal to zero.

Exhibits 3.4, 3.5, 3.7, and 3.8 of the Appendix to this chapter provide examples of the application of both linear and exponential trend models using both loss ratio and pure premium methods.

Effects of Limits on Severity Trend

Where the loss experience under review involves the application of limits of liability, it is important that the effects of those limits on severity trend be properly reflected. In order to understand the interaction between limits and severity trend, consider the hypothetical situation in which individual losses can occur for any amount between $1 and $90,000. Assume that insurance coverage against these losses is available at four limits of liability: $10,000 per occurrence, $25,000 per occurrence, $50,000 per occurrence, and $100,000 per occurrence. Note that since losses can only be as great as $90,000, the $100,000 limit coverage is basically unlimited.

In order to analyze the operation of severity trend on the various limits, it will be necessary to look at losses by layer of liability. The following chart illustrates this layering for four different loss amounts.

Distribution of Loss Amount by Layer

Loss Amount	First $10,000	$15,000 excess of $10,000	$25,000 excess of $25,000	$50,000 excess of $50,000
$5,000	$5,000			
$20,000	$10,000	$10,000		
$40,000	$10,000	$15,000	$15,000	
$70,000	$10,000	$15,000	$25,000	$20,000
Total	$35,000	$40,000	$40,000	$20,000

The total line represents the distribution of the $135,000 of losses by layer, assuming that one claim of each amount occurred. Consider now the effect of a constant 10% increase in each claim amount.

Distribution of Loss Amount by Layer

Loss Amount	First $10,000	$15,000 excess of $10,000	$25,000 excess of $25,000	$50,000 excess of $50,000
$5,500	$5,500			
$22,000	$10,000	$12,000		
$44,000	$10,000	$15,000	$19,000	
$77,000	$10,000	$15,000	$25,000	$27,000
Total	$35,500	$42,000	$44,000	$27,000
Increase	1.43%	5.00%	10.00%	35.00%

While the total losses have increased by 10% from $135,000 to $148,500, the rate of increase is not constant across the layers.

FIGURE 3.7

Effect of 10% Severity Trend by Layer

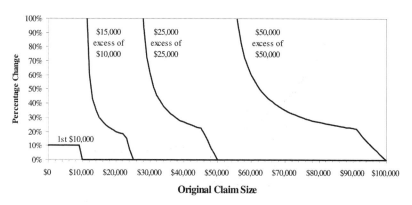

This is due to the fact that the larger claims have already saturated the lower layers, thus reducing the impact of severity increases on these layers. Figure 3.7 provides a graphical representation of this effect by claim size for each of the four layers.

For each layer let us define the following:

$$L = \text{lower bound of layer}$$

$$U = \text{upper bound of layer}$$

$$X = \text{unlimited loss size (before trend)}$$

$$T = \text{severity increase rate (e.g. } 10\% = 0.1)$$

The impact of the severity increase on any given layer can be expressed as:

Original Loss Size	Rate of Increase in Layer
$X \leq L$	*Undefined*
$L < X \leq \dfrac{U}{(1+T)}$	$\dfrac{(1+T)(X)-L}{X-L} - 1 = \dfrac{TX}{X-L}$
$\dfrac{U}{1-T} < X \leq U$	$\dfrac{U-L}{X-L} - 1 = \dfrac{U-X}{X-L}$
$U < X$	0

FIGURE 3.8

THEORETICAL CLAIM DISTRIBUTION

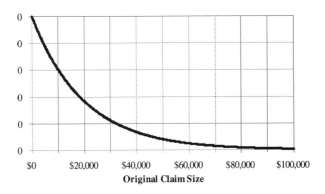

Original Claim Size

FIGURE 3.9

EFFECT OF 10% SEVERITY TREND BY LIMIT

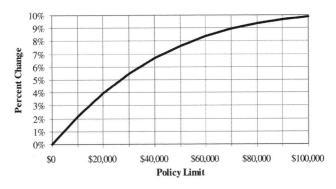

Policy Limit

The four-loss distribution used in the illustration of the impact of policy limit on severity trend is not realistic for most liability lines. In general we see frequency decreasing as loss size increases. If we assume a loss distribution as shown in Figure 3.8, then the impact of a 10% severity increase on each limit will be as shown in Figure 3.9.

Where severity trend has been analyzed based upon unlimited loss data or loss data including limits higher than the basic level, the resulting indicated severity trend must be adjusted before it is applied to basic limits losses. Because such adjustment will require knowledge of the underlying size-of-loss distribution, it is generally preferable to use basic limits data in the severity trend analysis.

Trend Based Upon External Data

Where sufficient loss or claim experience to produce reliable trend indications is not available, the actuary might supplement or supplant the available experience with external data. Insurance trade associations, statistical bureaus, and the U.S. Government produce insurance and general economic data regularly. While the appropriate source for the data will, of course, depend upon the specific ratemaking situation, Masterson (1968) provides a good general reference on the subject. Lommele and Sturgis (1974) provide an interesting example of the application of economic data to the problem of forecasting workers compensation insurance results.

Trend and Loss Development—The "Overlap Fallacy"

It has occasionally been suggested that there is a double-counting of severity trend in the ratemaking process where both loss development factors—which reflect severity changes as development on unpaid claims—and severity trend factors are applied to losses. Cook dealt with this subject in detail, and with elegance, in a 1970 paper. In order to properly understand the relationship between loss development and trend factors, assume a situation in which the experience period is the 1998 accident year and indicated rates are expected to be in effect from 7/1/1999 through 6/30/2000. Now consider a single claim with accident date 7/1/1998 that will settle on 12/31/2000. If a similar claim should occur during the effective period of the indicated rates, say on 7/1/2000, we would expect an equivalent settlement

FIGURE 3.10

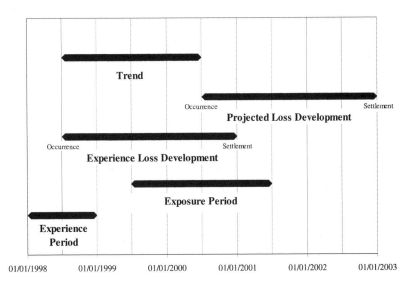

lag and would project that the 7/1/2000 claim would settle on 12/31/2002. Figure 3.10 illustrates the hypothetical situation graphically.

Note that the ratemaking problem, as respects this single hypothetical claim, is to project the ultimate settlement value as of 12/31/2002 based upon the single observed claim, which occurred on 7/1/1998—a total projection period of 54 months. The loss development factor will reflect the underlying severity trend during the 30 months between occurrence on 7/1/2000 and settlement on 12/31/2002. The trend factor will reflect the severity trend between the midpoint of the experience period (7/1/1998) and the midpoint of the exposure period (7/1/2000), which accounts for the remaining 24 months of the projection period. Note that while both trend and loss development factors do reflect underlying severity trends, there is no overlap between the two, and both are required.

Trended Projected Ultimate Losses

The application of loss development and trending techniques to the underlying loss data produces the trended projected ultimate losses, which are the experience losses underlying the application of either the pure premium or the loss ratio methods to produce the indicated rates or rate changes.

EXPENSE PROVISIONS

While a detailed discussion of the reflection of expenses in the ratemaking process is beyond the scope of this chapter, the need for continuity requires at least a limited treatment at this point. For purposes of illustration of the general concepts involved in the reflection of expense provisions in manual rates, assume both that the loss ratio method is being used to develop base rate indications for a line of business, and that allocated loss adjustment expenses are being combined with the experience losses. Suppose that for the latest year the line of business produced the following results on a direct basis:

Written premium	$11,540,000
Earned premium	$10,832,000
Incurred loss and allocated loss adjustment expense	$7,538,000
Incurred unallocated loss adjustment expenses	$484,000
Commissions	$1,731,000
Taxes, licenses & fees	$260,000
Other acquisition expenses	$646,000
General expenses	$737,000
Total loss and expense	$11,396,000

Since our losses and expenses exceeded the earned premium by $564,000 for the year it may be appropriate that we review the adequacy of the underlying rates. Since we are using the loss ratio method we need to develop a target loss ratio. Referring back to formula (7):

$$T = \frac{1 - V - Q}{1 + G} \qquad (7)$$

where

T = target loss ratio

V = premium-related expense factor

Q = profit and contingencies factor

G = ratio of non-premium-related expenses to losses

In order to develop the target loss ratio we therefore need factors for premium-related and for non-premium-related expenses and a profit and contingencies factor. Deferring the discussion of profit and contingencies provisions to the next section, we will look at the expense factors.

Traditional application of the loss ratio method assumes that only the loss adjustment expenses are non-premium-related. Using this approach we can determine the value for G in formula (7) by dividing the unallocated loss adjustment expenses of $484,000 by the loss and allocated loss expense of $7,538,000. G is therefore $(484/7538) = .0642$.

The determination of V in formula (7) is then simply the ratio of the other expenses to premiums. But which premiums—written or earned? Since commissions and premium taxes are generally paid based upon direct written premium, it would seem appropriate to use written premium in the denominator for these expenses. Other acquisition expenses are expended to produce premium, so it might be appropriate to relate those to written premium as well. But the general expenses of the insurance operation involve functions unrelated to the production of premium that could not be immediately eliminated if the company were to cease writing business. For this reason the general expenses are usually related to earned premium.

Based upon the above, we now calculate V as follows:

Ratio of commissions to written	(1,731/11,540)	.1500
Ratio of taxes, licenses & fees to written	(260/11,540)	.0225
Ratio of other acquisition to written	(646/11,540)	.0560
Ratio of general to earned	(737/10,832)	.0680
Total premium-related expense factor		.2965

If, for the moment, we assume that the profit and contingencies factor is zero, we can apply formula (7) and determine our target loss ratio:

$$T = \frac{1 - .2965 - 0}{1 + .0642} = .6611$$

PROFIT AND CONTINGENCIES

While generally among the smaller of the elements in any calculation of indicated manual rates, the profit and contingencies provision represents the essence of insurance in that it is designed to reflect the basic elements of risk and rewards associated with the transaction of the insurance business. While a complete discussion of the topic of appropriate provisions for profit and contingencies are beyond the scope of this chapter, the reader should be aware that there is a distinction between the profit portion, which will generally be based upon some target rate of return, and the contingencies portion, which addresses the potential for adverse deviation.

Sources of Insurance Profit

Highly simplified, the property and casualty insurance operation involves the collection of premium from insureds, the investment of the funds collected, and the payment of expenses and insured losses. If the premiums collected exceed the expenses and losses paid, the insurer makes what is called an **underwriting profit**; if not, there is an **underwriting loss**. In addition, the insurer will generally make an **investment profit** arising out of the investment of funds between premium collection and payment of expenses and losses. In this simplified context, the insurer might be viewed as a leveraged investment operation, with underwriting profits or losses being analogous to negative or positive interest expenses on borrowed funds.

Profit Provisions in Manual Rates

Until the mid-1960s insurance rates would typically include a profit and contingencies provision of approximately 5% of premium. While this practice was rooted more in tradition than in financial analysis, it must be understood that the practice existed in an environment in which property insurance represented a much greater portion of the insurance business than it does today, and in which inflation and interest rates were generally low. In that environment investment income tended to be viewed as a gratuity rather than the major source of income it has become. The 5% provision produced sufficient underwriting profits to support the growth of the industry, and it was not generally viewed as being excessive.

The growth of the liability lines, increased inflation, and higher interest rates resulted in investment profits that dwarfed the underwriting profits. Not only did this change the way insurance management viewed its financial results and plans, but also it focused regulatory attention on the overall rate of return for insurers, rather than on the underwriting results. This regulatory involvement generally took the form of downward adjustments to the traditional 5% profit and contingencies provision to reflect investment income on funds supplied by policyholders. In some jurisdictions, the allowed profit provisions for certain lines became negative.

One of the major problems inherent in the development of a general methodology for the reflection of profit in manual rates is that premium may not be the proper benchmark against which profits should be assessed. Going back to our leveraged investment operation analogy, the specific inclusion of a profit provision based upon premium is the analog to the measurement of profit against borrowed funds—the more you borrow, the more you should earn. If, on the other hand, premiums are viewed in the traditional way, as sales, premium-based profit provisions make more sense.

Unfortunately, the obvious alternative to basing profits on premiums—using return-on-equity as the benchmark—has its own disadvantages. From a regulatory standpoint it both rewards highly leveraged operations and discourages entry to the market, both of which run contrary to regulatory desires. In addition, where rates are made by industry or state rating bureaus, the rates cannot be expected to produce equal return on equity for each company using them.

Risk Elements

A portion of the profit and contingencies provision represents a provision for adverse deviation or a **risk loading**. There are two separate and distinct risk elements inherent in the ratemaking function. These are generally termed **parameter risk** and **process risk**. Parameter risk is simply the risk associated with the selection of the parameters underlying the applicable model of the process. Selecting the wrong loss development factors, resulting in erroneous experience losses, is an example of parameter risk. Process risk, in contrast, is the risk associated with the projection of future contingencies that are inherently variable. Even if we properly evaluate the mean frequency and the mean severity, the actual observed results will generally vary from the underlying means.

From a financial standpoint it is important to understand that the primary protection against adverse deviation is provided by the surplus (equity) of the insurer. If manual rates alone were required to produce sufficient funds to adequately protect the policyholders and claimants from sustaining any economic loss arising out of the policy period in which the rates were in effect, most property and casualty coverages would be unaffordable. It is more proper to view the profit and contingencies provision as providing sufficient funds to offset the economic costs associated with the net borrowings from the insurer's surplus required to offset the adverse deviations.

One method for determination of an appropriate profit and contingencies provision is the ruin theory approach. This method involves the development of a probabilistic model of the insurance operation and then, generally through Monte Carlo simulation, determining the probability of ruin (insolvency) over a fixed period of time. A maximum acceptable probability of ruin is then determined and the rate level assumption underlying the model is adjusted to the minimum rate level producing a ruin probability less than or equal to the acceptable level. The difference between the resultant adjusted rate level assumption and the rate level assumption with no risk margin is then used as the profit and contingencies provision.

OVERALL RATE INDICATIONS

The determination of the overall average indicated rate change will be made on the basis of the experience losses, expense provisions, profit and contingencies provisions and, in the case of the loss ratio method, on-level earned premium. As will be seen, the development of the overall rate change indication is generally only the beginning of the manual ratemaking process, not the end.

For illustrative purposes, assume that the loss ratio method is being applied to the following data:

(1) Experience loss and allocated—accident years 1997–1999 $23,163,751
(2) On-level earned premium—calendar years 1997–1999 $31,811,448
(3) Experience loss and allocated ratio $[(1)/(2)]$ .7282
(4) Target loss and allocated ratio   .6611

The rate change indication follows directly:

(5) Indicated overall rate level change $[(3)/(4)] - 1.0 =$ .1014

Credibility Considerations

The concept of credibility, the weight to be assigned to an indication relative to one or more alternative indications, is the topic of Chapter 8. For the purposes of this chapter, it is only necessary to understand that a statistical indication I_1 has an associated credibility z, between 0 and 1, relative to some other indication I_2. The resulting **credibility-weighted indication** $I_{1,2}$ is determined by the formula:

$$I_{1,2} = z(I_1) + (1 - z)(I_2)$$

If, for example, the credibility associated with our overall rate level indication of +7.28% is .85, and we have an alternative indication, from some source, of +4.50%, the credibility-weighted indication would be 6.86%, determined as follows:

$$(.85)(.0728) + (.15)(.0450) = .0686$$

In the application of credibility weighting, the actuary must be careful to use only reasonable alternative indications. The complement of credibility $(1 - z)$ should be applied to an indication that can be expected to reflect consistent trends in the same general way as the underlying data. For example, where statewide indicated rate changes are less than fully credible, regional or countrywide indications might be a reasonable alternative indication.

CLASSIFICATION RATES

If rate manuals contained a single rate for a given state, the overall rate change indication would be all that was required. But a rate manual will generally contain rates based upon individual classification and sub-classification. In addition, where geographical location of the risk is an important factor, rates may also be shown by rating territory. While classification ratemaking will be discussed in Chapter 6, the basics of the process will be illustrated in this section.

Base Rates

In order to facilitate the process of individual rate determination, especially where rates are computer-generated, classification and territorial rates are generally related to some base rate. The advantages to this system are apparent when one considers that there may be as many as 200 classifications for as many as 50 territories in a private passenger automobile rate manual for a given state. Determination of 250 classification and territorial relativities is obviously less time-consuming, and more reasonable from a statistical standpoint, than is the determination of 10,000 classification and territorial rates.

Indicated Classification Relativities

The relationship between the rate for a given classification (or territory) to the base rate is the classification (or territorial) **relativity**. The determination of indicated classification relativities is similar to the process used in the overall rate level analysis. If the pure premium method is used, the pure premium for the classification is divided by the pure premium for the base classification to generate the indicated relativity.

If the loss ratio method is used, the on-level earned premium for each classification must be adjusted to the base classification level before the experience loss ratios are calculated. Consider the following three-class situation:

(1) Class	(2) Current Relativity to Class 1	(3) On-Level Earned Premium	(4) Class 1 On-Level Earned (3)/(2)	(5) Experience Loss and Allocated	(6) Loss and Allocated Ratio (5)/(4)	(7) Indicated Relativity to Class 1
1	1.0000	$14,370,968	$14,370,968	$11,003,868	0.7657	1.0000
2	1.4500	9,438,017	6,508,977	6,541,840	1.0050	1.3125
3	1.8000	8,002,463	4,445,813	5,618,043	1.2636	1.6503
Total		$31,811,448	$25,325,758	$23,163,751		

In practice, the resulting indicated relativities are generally credibility-weighted with the existing relativities. This protects the relativities for smaller classifications against short-term fluctuations in experience.

Correction for Off-Balance

Assume that the existing base rate is $160. If we have determined that we need a 10.14% increase overall, the indicated base rate is (1.1014)($160) = $176.22. The indicated rate changes by classification are therefore:

Class 1:   [($176.22)(1.0000)/($160)(1.0000)] − 1 = +.1014
Class 2:   [($176.22)(1.3125)/($160)(1.4500)] − 1 = −.0031
Class 3:   [($176.22)(1.6503)/($160)(1.8000)] − 1 = +.0098

Applying these indicated classification rate changes to the on-level earned premium we get the following:

Class 1: $14,370,968 × 1.1014 = $15,828,184
Class 2: $9,438,017 × 0.9969 = $9,408,759
Class 3: $8,002,463 × 1.0098 = $8,080,887

The on-level earned premium at these base rates and classification relativities would be $15,828,184 + $9,408,759 + $8,080,887 = $33,317,830. This represents only a 4.74% increase over the $31,811,448 on-level earned premium at the current rate levels. The difference between this and the 10.14% overall indication is the **off-balance**. The off-balance exists because the indicated classification relativities produce an average classification relativity different from the average classification relativity underlying the current rates. In this case, the Class 1 relativity is unchanged while the relativities for the other two classes are decreased.

We correct for this off-balance by increasing the indicated base rate by an off-balance factor of 1.1014/1.0474 = 1.0516.

The corrected indicated base rate is then (1.0516)($176.22) = $185.31. This will produce the following corrected indicated rate changes by classification:

Class 1:   [($185.31)(1.0000)/($160)(1.0000)] − 1 = +.1582
Class 2:   [($185.31)(1.3125)/($160)(1.4500)] − 1 = +.0484
Class 3:   [($185.31)(1.6503)/($160)(1.8000)] − 1 = +.0619

Applying these corrected indicated classification rate changes to the on-level earned premium, we get the following:

Class 1: $14,370,968 × 1.1582 = $16,644,455
Class 2: $9,438,017 × 1.0484 = $9,894,817
Class 3: $8,002,463 × 1.0619 = $8,497,815

The resulting on-level premium aggregates to $35,037,087 or 10.14% more than the current on-level earned. The corrected base rate of $185.31, in conjunction with the revised classification relativities, now provides the overall level of rate increase indicated.

The Appendix to this chapter contains a more complex example involving both classification and territorial relativities.

Limitation of Rate Changes

Occasionally, due to regulatory requirements or marketing considerations, it is necessary that individual rate changes be limited to a maximum increase or decrease. In the above example, assume that it has been determined that no classification rate may increase or decrease by more than 12.5%. Since the Class 1 rate change indicated is 15.82%, it needs to be limited to 12.50%, or a revised rate of ($160)(1.1250) = $180.00.

Reducing the Class 1 rate to $180.00 has two effects. First, it reduces the indicated on-level earned premium for Class 1 from $16,644,455 to $16,167,339, a reduction of $477,116. If we are to make up for this loss by increasing the rates for the remaining classes, we need an increase of $477,116/($9,894,817 + $8,497,815) or .0259 in Class 2 and Class 3 rates. The second effect of the limitation arises because Class 1 is the base rate. Since the base rate is being reduced, the class relativities must be increased by a factor of $1.1582/1.1250 = 1.0295$ to compensate for the change. The factor necessary to correct for the off-balance due to the limitation is therefore $(1.0259)(1.0295) = 1.0562$. The resulting class relativities are:

Class 2: $(1.3125)(1.0562) = 1.3863$
Class 3: $(1.6503)(1.0562) = 1.7430$

The calculations of the resulting increases by classification and overall increase in on-level premium are left as exercises for the reader.

INCREASED LIMITS

The final topic to be addressed in this chapter is increased-limits ratemaking. While the level of attention to the development of rates for increased limits is sometimes less than that given the development of basic limits rates, the number of increased limits factors that exceed 2.000 should serve to focus attention on this important element of manual ratemaking. In an earlier discussion we saw how the severity trend in excess layers increases as the lower bound of the layer increases. This effect alone is sufficient to produce a general upward movement in increased limits factors. When combined with the effects of our increased litigiousness as a society, the need for regular review of increased limits rate adequacy should be apparent. In this section we will provide brief descriptions of three methods available for the review of increased limits experience.

Trending Individual Losses

This method involves the application of severity trend to a body of individual loss data. Generally, closed claim data are used in order to avoid the problems associated with projecting loss development on individual claims. In order to apply the method, an annual severity trend factor is first determined. This trend factor is then applied to each closed claim for the period from date of closure to the applicable effective period for the indicated increased limits factors. The resulting distribution of trended closed claims is then used to determine the appropriate increased limits factors.

Note that the application of this method requires the use of unlimited losses as the projection base. Since insurers are frequently unaware of the unlimited loss amounts associated with closed claims, this method is often based upon special data surveys.

Loss Development by Layer

Another method that can be used to analyze increased limits experience is to look at loss development patterns by layer. This process involves segregating case-incurred loss data by policy limit and loss layer and then tracking the observed loss development factors in each layer. Generally, the sparsity of data in the upper limits precludes the use of this method.

Fitted Size-of-Loss Distribution

The third method is related to the individual loss trending method. In this method, a theoretical size-of-loss distribution is fitted to existing individual loss data. The resulting distribution can then be used to examine the effects of severity trend on various limits and as a basis for the increased limits factors.

SUMMARY

While this chapter has covered most of what could be considered the basics of manual ratemaking, every line of insurance will have characteristics requiring specialized treatment. For each method illustrated in this chapter, there are situations in which its application would be clearly inappropriate. There is no substitute for informed judgment arising out of a thorough understanding of the characteristics of the insurance coverage being priced. The actuary who becomes a slave to ratemaking methodology rather than a student of the business will, at some point, be led astray.

REFERENCES

Cook, C. F., "Trend and Loss Development Factors," *Proceedings of the Casualty Actuarial Society*, 1970, 57:1–14.

Lommele, J. A., and R. W. Sturgis, "An Econometric Model of Workers' Compensation," *Proceedings of the Casualty Actuarial Society*, 1974, 61:170–189.

Masterson, N. E., "Economic Factors in Liability and Property Insurance Claim Costs, 1935–1967," *Proceedings of the Casualty Actuarial Society*, 1968, 55:61–89.

Miller, D. L., and G. E. Davis, "A Refined Model for Premium Adjustment," *Proceedings of the Casualty Actuarial Society*, 1976, 63:117–124.

RATEMAKING

QUESTIONS FOR DISCUSSION

The Concept of Manual Ratemaking

What is the major difference between the pricing of a manufactured item and property and liability ratemaking?

What other services or products are similar to insurance as far as pricing is concerned?

Basic Terminology

What might be the appropriate exposure base for an insurance product providing coverage against window breakage?

Which of the following would generally be considered as a part of unallocated loss adjustment expenses?

    a. Outside legal expense on a specific claim

    b. Salary of the Claims Vice President

    c. Costs associated with printing the rate manual

Some lines of insurance, for example automobile collision, are characterized as **high frequency—low severity** while others, such as professional liability, are **low frequency—high severity** lines. Which type would generally be expected to exhibit the lower variability of pure premium?

A certain insurer paid losses during the year equal to 10% of the premiums written during the same year. Assuming that expenses amounted to 25% of written premiums, what can be determined about the adequacy of the insurer's rates? What type of loss ratio is the 10%? Is there a more meaningful alternative?

The Goal of the Ratemaking Process

Which of the following are generally reviewed as part of the actuary's primary responsibility in ratemaking?

a. Pure premium

b. Affordability of coverage

c. Desired level of profit

d. What the competition is charging

e. Changes in applicable income tax law

f. Anticipated marketing expenses

g. Relationship between price and demand for coverage

Structure of the Rating Plan

Consider an insurer providing guarantees of individual student loans to undergraduates. What elements might be considered in the rating plan? What might be the result of failure to reflect each element?

Basic Manual Ratemaking Methods

For each of the following, discuss the relative merits of the pure premium and loss ratio methods:

Coverage	Exposure Base
Auto Liability	Car Year
Homeowners	Dwelling Year
Products Liability	Annual Sales

Need for Common Basis

Over the last five years an insurer's loss experience on Florida mobile-homeowners has been better than expected. The Marketing Department has requested that rates be reduced to generate additional business. What consideration might the actuary give to the level of hurricane experience over the past five years? Over the past 100 years?

Given the following rate change history for a level book of 12-month term policies uniformly distributed throughout the experience period, what is the appropriate on-level factor to apply to the 2001 earned premium in order to produce earned premium at the 10/1/2001 rate level? [1.1382]

10/1/1999	+10%
10/1/2000	+15%
10/1/2001	+10%

Trended, Projected Ultimate Losses

Over the past five years a company has experienced exposure growth of 10%, 50%, 25%, 10% and 5% during the first, second, third, fourth and fifth years respectively. Assuming the growth occurred uniformly throughout each year, what impact would the changes in growth rates be expected to have on the age-to-age development factors?

A company has been very successful writing professional liability insurance for college professors with a $50,000 per claim policy limit. Frequency has been stable and severity has been increasing at less than 3% per year and now stands at $41,000 per claim. As a result of good experience, the company has decided to increase the policy limit to $500,000 per claim. How might the pricing actuary project the severity trend for the revised product?

Inflation, which has been running at between 4% and 6% per year, suddenly increases to 15% per year and is expected to remain at that higher level. What impact might this have on the indicated severity trend factors? What impact might it have on expected loss development factors? Is it double-counting to reflect both?

Expense Provisions

Given the following, calculate the target loss and allocated expense ratio assuming a 5% (of premium) profit and contingencies factor. [.5833]

Written premium	$1,000,000
Earned premium	900,000
Incurred losses and allocated loss expenses	500,000
Incurred unallocated loss expenses	40,000
Commissions paid	200,000
Premium taxes paid	20,000
Other acquisition expenses	50,000
General expenses	5,000

Profit and Contingencies

You are the actuary for a rating bureau and have been charged with the responsibility for the recommendation of rates for use by each of the bureau members, regardless of size or financial condition. How might you reflect the profit and contingencies loading in the rates? What problems or opportunities might your selected method create for individual bureau members?

Overall Rate Indication

Your company writes 100% of the market for a certain insurance coverage yet the experience base is so small that it cannot be considered to be fully (100%) credible. What options might be available in developing a credibility-weighted indication?

Classification and Territorial Rates

In a given jurisdiction, rates are not allowed to increase by more than 25% for any given classification. Your indicated rate increase for a classification that represents 60% of total premium volume is +45%. The president of your company wants you to produce rates that are adequate, on average, for the entire jurisdiction. Your major competitor does not provide coverage for risks in your largest classification. How might you treat the off-balance resulting from the 25% capping of rate increases?

Increased Limits

Although your company has never paid a claim greater than $1,000,000 you are concerned about the rate adequacy of your $2,000,000 limit policy. How might you estimate the appropriate additional charge for the $1,000,000 excess of your $1,000,000 basic limit?

APPENDIX

This appendix contains a complete, though simplified, example of a manual rate analysis of private passenger automobile bodily injury. The data are totally fictitious but are meant to be reasonably representative of actual data that might be observed in practice. The appendix consists of 16 exhibits, which are meant to provide an example of the exhibits that might accompany a rate filing with a regulatory body. Following is a brief description of each of these exhibits.

Exhibit 3.1 is meant to represent the existing rate manual, effective 7/1/1998, for the coverage under review. The manual contains basic limits rates for each of three classifications within each of three territories, along with a single increased limits factor to adjust the rates for basic limits of $20,000 per person, $40,000 per occurrence (20/40) upward to limits of $100,000 per person, $300,000 per occurrence (100/300). Territorial and classification rates are keyed to a base rate of $160 for Territory 2, Class 1.

Exhibit 3.2 demonstrates the computation of the on-level earned premium based upon the extension of exposures technique. The experience period is the three years 1997–1999 and the earned exposures, by class and territory, for each of those years are multiplied by the appropriate current rate to yield the on-level earned.

Exhibit 3.3 shows the projection of ultimate loss and allocated loss adjustment expense for accident years 1994–1999, using the case-incurred loss development method.

Exhibit 3.4 contains the projected ultimate claim counts for accident years 1994–1999 based upon the reported count development method.

Exhibit 3.5 details the calculation of the severity trend factor based upon the projected incurred losses and ultimate claims for accident years 1994–1999. The trend factor is based upon a linear least-squares fit.

Exhibit 3.6 addresses the frequency trend factor based upon the earned exposures and projected ultimate claims for accident years 1994–1999, based upon an exponential least-squares fit.

Exhibit 3.7 contains the calculation of the target loss and allocated loss expense ratio. Note that there is no specific provision for profit and contingencies in this example, the assumption being that the investment profits will be sufficient.

Exhibit 3.8 presents the calculation of the indicated statewide rate level change, using the loss ratio method.

Exhibit 3.9 contains projections of trended projected ultimate losses and allocated loss expenses by accident year, classification, and territory for accident years 1997–1999.

Exhibit 3.10 demonstrates the calculation of indicated classification and territorial pure premiums and pure premium relativities.

Exhibit 3.11 shows the calculation of credibility-weighted classification relativities and the selection of relativities to be used.

Exhibit 3.12 shows the calculation of credibility-weighted territorial relativities and the selection of relativities to be used.

Exhibit 3.13 details the correction for off-balance resulting from the selected classification and territorial relativities.

Exhibit 3.14 shows the development of the revised basic limits rates and the calculation of the resulting statewide rate level change.

Exhibit 3.15 describes the calculation of the revised 100/300 increased limits factor using the individual trended loss approach.

Exhibit 3.16 is the proposed rate manual to be effective 7/1/2000.

EXHIBIT 3.1

EXAMPLE AUTO INSURANCE COMPANY

RATE MANUAL—7/1/1998
PRIVATE PASSENGER AUTO BODILY INJURY
20/40 BASIC LIMITS

Territory	Class 1 Adult Drivers, No Youthful Operators	Class 2 Family with Youthful Drivers Not Principal Operators	Class 3 Youthful Owners or Principal Operators
1—Central City	$224	$325	$403
2—Midway Valley	$160	$232	$288
3—Remainder of State	$136	$197	$245

Increased Limits

Limit	Factor
100/300	1.300

EXHIBIT 3.2

EXAMPLE AUTO INSURANCE COMPANY

PRIVATE PASSENGER AUTO BODILY INJURY
BASIC LIMITS
DEVELOPMENT OF INDICATED STATEWIDE RATE LEVEL
CHANGE

A. Earned Premium at Current Rate Level

Year	Territory	Class 1	Class 2	Class 3	Total
		Earned Exposures			
1997	1	7,807	3,877	1,553	13,237
	2	11,659	4,976	3,930	20,565
	3	5,760	2,639	3,030	11,429
	Total	25,226	11,492	8,513	45,231
1998	1	8,539	4,181	1,697	14,417
	2	12,957	5,442	4,262	22,661
	3	5,834	2,614	3,057	11,505
	Total	27,330	12,237	9,016	48,583
1999	1	9,366	4,551	1,870	15,787
	2	14,284	5,939	4,669	24,892
	3	5,961	2,591	3,036	11,588
	Total	29,611	13,081	9,575	52,267

Territory	Class 1	Class 2	Class 3
	Current Rate Level		
1	$224	$325	$403
2	$160	$232	$288
3	$136	$197	$245

Year	Territory	Class 1	Class 2	Class 3	Total
		On-Level Earned Premium			
1997	1	$1,748,768	$1,260,025	$625,859	$3,634,652
	2	$1,865,440	$1,154,432	$1,131,840	$4,151,712
	3	$783,360	$519,883	$742,350	$2,045,593
	Total	$4,397,568	$2,934,340	$2,500,049	$9,831,957
1998	1	$1,912,736	$1,358,825	$683,891	$3,955,452
	2	$2,073,120	$1,262,544	$1,227,456	$4,563,120
	3	$793,424	$514,958	$748,965	$2,057,347
	Total	$4,779,280	$3,136,327	$2,660,312	$10,575,919
1999	1	$2,097,984	$1,479,075	$753,610	$4,330,669
	2	$2,285,440	$1,377,848	$1,344,672	$5,007,960
	3	$810,696	$510,427	$743,820	$2,064,943
	Total	$5,194,120	$3,367,350	$2,842,102	$11,403,572

EXHIBIT 3.3

EXAMPLE AUTO INSURANCE COMPANY

PRIVATE PASSENGER AUTO BODILY INJURY
BASIC LIMITS
DEVELOPMENT OF INDICATED STATEWIDE RATE LEVEL
CHANGE

B. Projected Ultimate Accident Year Losses and Allocated Loss Adjustment Expenses

Accident Year	Cumulative Basic Limits Case-Incurred Losses and Allocated Loss Adjustment Expenses					
	Age 12	Age 24	Age 36	Age 48	Age 60	Age 72
1994	$2,116,135	$3,128,695	$3,543,445	$3,707,375	$3,854,220	$3,928,805
1995	2,315,920	3,527,197	3,992,805	4,182,133	4,338,765	
1996	2,743,657	4,051,950	4,593,472	4,797,194		
1997	3,130,262	4,589,430	5,230,437			
1998	3,625,418	5,380,617				
1999	3,919,522					

Accident Year	Incremental Loss and Allocated Development Factors					
	Age 12	Age 24	Age 36	Age 48	Age 60	Age 72
1994	1.4785	1.1326	1.0463	1.0396	1.0194	1.0000
1995	1.5230	1.1320	1.0474	1.0375		
1996	1.4768	1.1336	1.0444			
1997	1.4661	1.1397				
1999	1.4841					
Selected Ultimate	1.4800	1.1350	1.0450	1.0385	1.0200	1.0000
Factor	1.8595	1.2564	1.1070	1.0593	1.0200	1.0000

Accident Year	Loss and Allocated 12/31/99	Ultimate Factor	Projected Ultimate Loss and Allocated
1994	$3,928,805	1.0000	$3,928,805
1995	4,338,765	1.0200	4,425,540
1996	4,797,194	1.0593	5,081,668
1997	5,230,437	1.1070	5,790,094
1998	5,380,617	1.2564	6,760,207
1999	3,919,522	1.8595	7,288,351

EXHIBIT 3.4

EXAMPLE AUTO INSURANCE COMPANY

PRIVATE PASSENGER AUTO BODILY INJURY
BASIC LIMITS
DEVELOPMENT OF INDICATED STATEWIDE RATE LEVEL
CHANGE

C. Projected Ultimate Accident Year Claim Counts

Accident Year	Cumulative Reported Claims					
	Age 12	Age 24	Age 36	Age 48	Age 60	Age 72
1994	1,804	2,173	2,374	2,416	2,416	2,416
1995	1,935	2,379	2,424	2,552	2,552	
1996	2,103	2,384	2,514	2,646		
1997	2,169	2,580	2,722			
1998	2,346	2,783				
1999	2,337					

Accident Year	Incremental Reported Claim Development Factors					
	Age 12	Age 24	Age 36	Age 48	Age 60	Age 72
1994	1.2045	1.0925	1.0177	1.0000	1.0000	1.0000
1995	1.2295	1.0189	1.0528	1.0000		
1996	1.1336	1.0545	1.0525			
1997	1.1895	1.0550				
1999	1.1863					
Selected Ultimate	1.1900	1.0550	1.0450	1.0000	1.0000	1.0000
Factor	1.3120	1.1025	1.0450	1.0000	1.0000	1.0000

Accident Year	Reported Claims 12/31/99	Ultimate Factor	Projected Ultimate Claims
1994	2,416	1.0000	2,416
1995	2,552	1.0000	2,552
1996	2,646	1.0000	2,646
1997	2,722	1.0450	2,844
1998	2,783	1.1025	3,068
1999	2,337	1.3120	3,066

EXHIBIT 3.5

EXAMPLE AUTO INSURANCE COMPANY

PRIVATE PASSENGER AUTO BODILY INJURY
BASIC LIMITS
DEVELOPMENT OF INDICATED STATEWIDE RATE LEVEL
CHANGE

D. Development of Severity Trend Factor—Basic Limits

Accident Year	Projected Loss and Allocated (Exhibit 3.2)	Projected Ultimate Claims (Exhibit 3.3)	Projected Ultimate Average Severity	Linear Least Squares Fit {Note [1]}
1994	$3,928,805	2,416	$1,626	$1,605.90
1995	$4,425,540	2,552	$1,734	$1,756.68
1996	$5,081,668	2,646	$1,921	$1,907.45
1997	$5,790,094	2,844	$2,036	$2,058.22
1998	$6,760,207	3,068	$2,203	$2,208.99
1999	$7,288,351	3,066	$2,377	$2,359.76
Annual Severity Trend Factor (1999/1998 Least-Squares)				1.0683

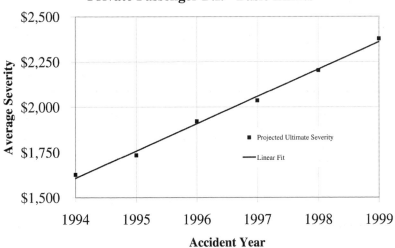

Severity Trend
Private Passenger B.I. - Basic Limits

EXHIBIT 3.6

EXAMPLE AUTO INSURANCE COMPANY

PRIVATE PASSENGER AUTO BODILY INJURY BASIC LIMITS
DEVELOPMENT OF INDICATED STATEWIDE RATE LEVEL
CHANGE

E. Development of Frequency Trend Factor

Accident Year	Projected Ultimate Claims (Exhibit 3.3)	Earned Exposures	Projected Ultimate Frequency	Exponential Least Squares Fit {Note [2]}
1994	2,416	37,846	0.0638	0.0647
1995	2,552	39,771	0.0642	0.0638
1996	2,646	42,135	0.0628	0.0630
1997	2,844	45,231	0.0629	0.0621
1998	3,068	48,583	0.0631	0.0613
1999	3,066	52,267	0.0587	0.0605
Annual Frequency Trend Factor (1999/1998 Least-Squares)				0.9868

$$[2] \quad y = ae^{bx} \text{ where: } x = \text{Accident Year} - 1993$$
$$a = .065562$$
$$b = -.013417$$

Frequency Trend
Private Passenger B.I.

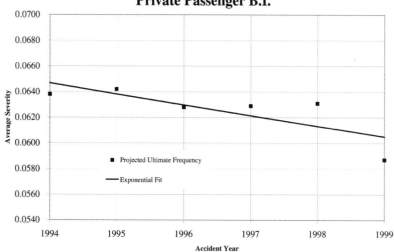

EXHIBIT 3.7

EXAMPLE AUTO INSURANCE COMPANY

PRIVATE PASSENGER AUTO BODILY INJURY
BASIC LIMITS
DEVELOPMENT OF INDICATED STATEWIDE RATE LEVEL
CHANGE

F. Development of Target Loss and Allocated Loss Expense Ratio

---

(1)	Commissions as % of Premium	15.00%
(2)	Taxes, Licenses and Fees as a % of Premium	2.25%
(3)	Other Acquisition Expense as a % of Premium	5.60%
(4)	General Expense as a % of Premium	6.80%
(5)	Premium-Based Expense [(1)+(2)+(3)+(4)]	29.65%
(6)	Unallocated Loss Expense as a % of Loss and Allocated Loss Expense	6.42%
(7)	Target Loss and Allocated Loss Expense Ratio [1.0-(5)]/[1.0+(6)]	66.11%

EXHIBIT 3.8

EXAMPLE AUTO INSURANCE COMPANY

PRIVATE PASSENGER AUTO BODILY INJURY
BASIC LIMITS
DEVELOPMENT OF INDICATED STATEWIDE RATE LEVEL
CHANGE

G. Development of Statewide Indication

[1] Accident Year	[2] Projected Loss and Allocated (Exhibit II)	[3] Midpoint Experience Period	[4] Years to 7/1/01	[5] Severity 1.0683[4]	[6] Frequency .9867[4]
				Trend Factor to 7/1/2001	
1997	$5,790,094	7/1/97	4.0	1.3025	0.9479
1998	6,760,207	7/1/98	3.0	1.2192	0.9606
1999	7,288,351	7/1/99	2.0	1.1413	0.9735

[7] Accident Year	[8] Trended Loss and Allocated [2] × [5] × [6]	[9] On-Level Earned Premium (Exhibit I)	[10] Trended On-Level Loss and Allocated Ratio [8]/[9]	[11] Target Loss & Allocated Ratio (Exhibit VI)	[12] Indicated Statewide Rate Level Change ([10]/[11]) − 1.000
1997	$7,148,680	$9,831,957	72.71%		
1998	7,917,308	10,575,919	74.86%		
1999	8,097,763	11,403,572	71.01%		
Total	$23,163,751	$31,811,448	72.82%	66.11%	10.14%

EXHIBIT 3.9

EXAMPLE AUTO INSURANCE COMPANY

PRIVATE PASSENGER AUTO BODILY INJURY
BASIC LIMITS
DEVELOPMENT OF INDICATED RATE LEVEL CHANGE BY CLASS
AND TERRITORY

H. Development o Trended Loss and Allocated by Class and Territory

Territory	Class	Accident Year	[1] Loss and Allocated 12/31/99	[2] Ultimate Allocated Factor (Exhibit 3.2)	[3] Severity Trend to 7/1/01 (Exhibit 3.7)	[4] Frequency Trend to 7/1/01 (Exhibit 3.8)	[5] Trended Projected Loss and Allocated [1] × [2] × [3] × [4]
1	1	1997	$986,617	1.1070	1.3025	0.9479	$1,348,455
1	1	1998	982,778	1.2564	1.2192	0.9606	1,446,109
1	1	1999	797,650	1.8595	1.1413	0.9735	1,647,951
1	2	1997	680,769	1.1070	1.3025	0.9479	930,438
1	2	1998	703,406	1.2564	1.2192	0.9606	1,035,027
1	2	1999	456,899	1.8595	1.1413	0.9735	943,957
1	3	1997	325,397	1.1070	1.3025	0.9479	444,735
1	3	1998	343,738	1.2564	1.2192	0.9606	505,793
1	3	1999	252,790	1.8595	1.1413	0.9735	522,266
2	1	1997	1,062,395	1.1070	1.3025	0.9479	1,452,024
2	1	1998	1,170,978	1.2564	1.2192	0.9606	1,723,035
2	1	1999	848,551	1.8595	1.1413	0.9735	1,753,113
2	2	1997	597,044	1.1070	1.3025	0.9479	816,008
2	2	1998	575,004	1.2564	1.2192	0.9606	846,090
2	2	1999	449,123	1.8595	1.1413	0.9735	927,892
2	3	1997	557,332	1.1070	1.3025	0.9479	761,731
2	3	1998	650,645	1.2564	1.2192	0.9606	957,391
2	3	1999	469,963	1.8595	1.1413	0.9735	970,947
3	1	1997	401,622	1.1070	1.3025	0.9479	548,915
3	1	1998	394,358	1.2564	1.2192	0.9606	580,278
3	1	1999	243,943	1.8595	1.1413	0.9735	503,988
3	2	1997	252,439	1.1070	1.3025	0.9479	345,020
3	2	1998	228,313	1.2564	1.2192	0.9606	335,951
3	2	1999	174,954	1.8595	1.1413	0.9735	361,456
3	3	1997	366,822	1.1070	1.3025	0.9479	501,353
3	3	1998	331,397	1.2564	1.2192	0.9606	487,634
3	3	1999	225,649	1.8595	1.1413	0.9735	466,193

EXHIBIT 3.10

EXAMPLE AUTO INSURANCE COMPANY

PRIVATE PASSENGER AUTO BODILY INJURY
BASIC LIMITS
DEVELOPMENT OF INDICATED RATE LEVEL CHANGE BY CLASS
AND TERRITORY

I. Development of Trended Pure Premium by Class and Territory

Territory	Class	Accident Year	[1] Trended Projected Loss and Allocated (Exhibit 3.8)	[2] Earned Exposure (Exhibit 3.1)	[3] Trended Pure Premium [1]/[2]	[4] Relativity to Class 1	[5] Relativity to Territory 2
1	1	1997	$1,348,455	7,807	$172.72	1.0000	1.3869
1	1	1998	1,446,109	8,539	169.35	1.0000	1.2735
1	1	1999	1,647,951	9,366	175.95	1.0000	1.4336
1	2	1997	930,438	3,877	239.99	1.3894	1.4634
1	2	1998	1,035,027	4,181	247.55	1.4618	1.5923
1	2	1999	943,957	4,551	207.42	1.1788	1.3276
1	3	1997	444,735	1,553	286.37	1.6580	1.4775
1	3	1998	505,793	1,697	298.05	1.7599	1.3268
1	3	1999	522,266	1,870	279.29	1.5873	1.3430
2	1	1997	1,452,024	11,659	124.54	0.7210	1.0000
2	1	1998	1,723,035	12,957	132.98	0.7852	1.0000
2	1	1999	1,753,113	14,284	122.73	0.6975	1.0000
2	2	1997	816,008	4,976	163.99	0.9494	1.0000
2	2	1998	846,090	5,442	155.47	0.9180	1.0000
2	2	1999	927,892	5,939	156.24	0.8880	1.0000
2	3	1997	761,731	3,930	193.82	1.1222	1.0000
2	3	1998	957,391	4,262	224.63	1.3264	1.0000
2	3	1999	970,947	4,669	207.96	1.1819	1.0000
3	1	1997	548,915	5,760	95.30	0.5517	0.7652
3	1	1998	580,278	5,834	99.46	0.5873	0.7480
3	1	1999	503,988	5,961	84.55	0.4805	0.6889
3	2	1997	345,020	2,639	130.74	0.7569	0.7972
3	2	1998	335,951	2,614	128.52	0.7589	0.8266
3	2	1999	361,456	2,591	139.50	0.7929	0.8929
3	3	1997	501,353	3,030	165.46	0.9580	0.8537
3	3	1998	487,634	3,057	159.51	0.9419	0.7101
3	3	1999	466,193	3,036	153.56	0.8727	0.7384

EXHIBIT 3.11

EXAMPLE AUTO INSURANCE COMPANY

PRIVATE PASSENGER AUTO BODILY INJURY
BASIC LIMITS
DEVELOPMENT OF INDICATED RATE LEVEL CHANGE BY CLASS
AND TERRITORY

J. Development of Indicated Class Relativity to Class 1

Class	Territory	Accident Year	[1] Earned Exposure (Exhibit 3.9)	[2] Relativity to Class 1 (Exhibit 3.9)	[3] Weighted Relativity [1] × [2]
2	1	1997	3,877	1.3894	5,386.70
	1	1998	4,181	1.4618	6,111.79
	1	1999	4,551	1.1788	5,364.72
	2	1997	4,976	1.3167	6,551.90
	2	1998	5,442	1.1691	6,362.24
	2	1999	5,939	1.2730	7,560.35
	3	1997	2,639	1.3719	3,620.44
	3	1998	2,614	1.2921	3,377.55
	3	1999	2,591	1.6500	4,275.15
		Total	36,810	1.3206	48,610.84

Current Class 2 Relativity	1.4500
Credibility $Z = [\text{Exposure}/(\text{Exposure} + 25,000)]$	0.5955
Credibility − Weighted$[Z(\text{indicated}) + (1 − Z)(\text{current})]$	1.3729
Selected Relativity	1.3700

Class	Territory	Accident Year	[1] Earned Exposure (Exhibit 3.9)	[2] Relativity to Class 1 (Exhibit 3.9)	[3] Weighted Relativity [1] × [2]
3	1	1997	1,553	1.6580	2,574.87
	1	1998	1,697	1.7599	2,986.55
	1	1999	1,870	1.5873	2,968.25
	2	1997	3,930	1.5563	6,116.26
	2	1998	4,262	1.6892	7,199.37
	2	1999	4,669	1.6944	7,911.15
	3	1997	3,030	1.7363	5,260.99
	3	1998	3,057	1.6037	4,902.51
	3	1999	3,036	1.8162	5,513.98
		Total	27,104	1.6763	45,433.93

Current Class 3 Relativity	1.8000
Credibility $Z = [\text{Exposure}/(\text{Exposure} + 25,000)]$	0.5202
Credibility − Weighted$[Z(\text{indicated}) + (1 − Z)(\text{current})]$	1.7357
Selected Relativity	1.7400

EXHIBIT 3.12

Example Auto Insurance Company

Private Passenger Auto Bodily Injury
Basic Limits
Development of Indicated Rate Level Change by Class
and Territory

K. Development of Indicated Territorial Relativity to Territory 2

Territory	Class	Accident Year	[1] Earned Exposure (Exhibit 3.9)	[2] Relativity to Territory 2 (Exhibit 3.9)	[3] Weighted Relativity [1] × [2]
1	1	1997	7,807	1.3869	10,827.53
	1	1998	8,539	1.2735	10,874.42
	1	1999	9,366	1.4336	13,427.10
	2	1997	3,877	1.4635	5,673.99
	2	1998	4,181	1.5923	6,657.41
	2	1999	4,551	1.3276	6,041.91
	3	1997	1,553	1.4775	2,294.56
	3	1998	1,697	1.3268	2,251.58
	3	1999	1,870	1.3430	2,511.41
		Total	43,441	1.3941	60,559.91

Current Territory 1 Relativity	1.4000
Credibility Z = [Exposure/(Exposure + 25,000)]	0.6347
Credibility – Weighted[Z(indicated) + $(1 - Z)$(current)]	1.3963
Selected Relativity	1.4000

Territory	Class	Accident Year	[1] Earned Exposure (Exhibit 3.9)	[2] Relativity to Territory 2 (Exhibit 3.9)	[3] Weighted Relativity [1] × [2]
3	1	1997	5,760	0.7652	4,407.55
	1	1998	5,834	0.7480	4,363.83
	1	1999	5,961	0.6889	4,106.53
	2	1997	2,639	0.7972	2,103.81
	2	1998	2,614	0.8266	2,160.73
	2	1999	2,591	0.8929	2,313.50
	3	1997	3,030	0.8537	2,586.71
	3	1998	3,057	0.7101	2,170.78
	3	1999	3,036	0.7384	2,241.78
		Total	34,522	0.7663	26,455.22

Current Territory 3 Relativity	0.8500
Credibility Z = [Exposure/(Exposure + 25,000)]	0.58
Credibility – Weighted[Z(indicated) + $(1 - Z)$(current)]	0.8015
Selected Relativity	0.8000

EXHIBIT 3.13

EXAMPLE AUTO INSURANCE COMPANY

PRIVATE PASSENGER AUTO BODILY INJURY
BASIC LIMITS
DEVELOPMENT OF INDICATED RATE LEVEL CHANGE BY CLASS
AND TERRITORY

L. Adjustment of Base Rate Level Change for Class and Territory Off-Balance

Territory	Class	Accident Year	[1] On-Level Earned Premium (Exhibit 3.1)	[2] Current Class Relativity (Exhibit 3.10)	[3] Current Territorial Relativity (Exhibit 3.11)	[4] Current Relativity to Territory 2 Class 1 [2] × [3]
1	1	1999	$2,097,984	1.0000	1.4000	1.4000
1	2	1999	1,479,075	1.4500	1.4000	2.0300
1	3	1999	753,610	1.8000	1.4000	2.5200
2	1	1999	2,285,440	1.0000	1.0000	1.0000
2	2	1999	1,377,848	1.4500	1.0000	1.4500
2	3	1999	1,344,672	1.8000	1.0000	1.8000
3	1	1999	810,696	1.0000	0.8500	0.8500
3	2	1999	510,427	1.4500	0.8500	1.2325
3	3	1999	743,820	1.8000	0.8500	1.5300
		Total	$11,403,572			

Territory	Class	Accident Year	[5] Proposed Class Relativity (Exhibit 3.10)	[6] Proposed Territorial Relativity (Exhibit 3.11)	[7] Proposed Relativity to Territory 2 Class 1 [5] × [6]	[8] Effect of Relativity Changes [7]/[4] − 1.000	[9] Premium Effect [1] × [8]
1	1	1999	1.0000	1.4000	1.4000	0.00%	$0
1	2	1999	1.3700	1.4000	1.9180	−5.52%	($81,604)
1	3	1999	1.7400	1.4000	2.4360	−3.33%	($25,120)
2	1	1999	1.0000	1.0000	1.0000	0.00%	$0
2	2	1999	1.3700	1.0000	1.3700	−5.52%	($76,019)
2	3	1999	1.7400	1.0000	1.7400	−3.33%	($44,822)
3	1	1999	1.0000	0.8000	0.8000	−5.88%	($47,688)
3	2	1999	1.3700	0.8000	1.0960	−11.08%	($56,530)
3	3	1999	1.7400	0.8000	1.3920	−9.02%	($67,090)
		Total				−3.50%	($398,873)

Indicated Statewide Rate Change (Exhibit VII)	10.14%
Indicated Base Rate Change (1.014/.9650) − 1.0000	14.13%
Current Territory 2, Class 1 Rate	$160
Indicated Territory 2, Class 1 Rate	$183

EXHIBIT 3.14

EXAMPLE AUTO INSURANCE COMPANY

PRIVATE PASSENGER AUTO BODILY INJURY
BASIC LIMITS
DEVELOPMENT OF INDICATED RATE LEVEL CHANGE BY CLASS
AND TERRITORY

M. Development of Basic Limits Rate Changes by Class and Territory

Territory	Class	[1] Class Relativity (Exhibit 3.10)	[2] Territorial Relativity (Exhibit 3.11)	[3] Base Rate (Exhibit 3.12)	[4] Class and Territory Rate [1] × [2] × [3]
1	1	1.0000	1.4000	$183	$256
	2	1.0000	1.0000	183	183
	3	1.0000	0.8000	183	146
2	1	1.3700	1.4000	183	351
	2	1.3700	1.0000	183	251
	3	1.3700	0.8000	183	201
3	1	1.7400	1.4000	183	446
	2	1.7400	1.0000	183	318
	3	1.7400	0.8000	183	255

Territory	Class	[5] 1999 Earned Exposures (Exhibit 3.1)	[6] New Level Earned Premium [4] × [5]	[7] Current Level 1999 Earned Premium (Exhibit 3.1)	[8] Statewide Rate Level Change ([6]/[7]) − 1.000
1	1	9,366	$2,397,696	$2,097,984	
	2	14,284	2,613,972	2,285,440	
	3	5,961	870,306	810,696	
2	1	4,551	1,597,401	1,479,075	
	2	5,939	1,490,689	1,377,848	
	3	2,591	520,791	510,427	
3	1	1,870	834,020	753,610	
	2	4,669	1,484,742	1,344,672	
	3	3,036	774,180	743,820	
Total		52,267	$12,583,797	$11,403,572	10.35%

EXHIBIT 3.15

EXAMPLE AUTO INSURANCE COMPANY

PRIVATE PASSENGER AUTO BODILY INJURY
DEVELOPMENT OF INDICATED 100/300 INCREASED LIMITS
FACTOR

		Distribution of Trended Losses [a]		
Unlimited Loss Amount	Claim Count	Unlimited	20/40	100/300
$1–$20,000	4,249	$17,706,594	$17,706,594	$17,706,594
20,001–30,000	244	5,842,632	5,340,562	5,842,632
30,001–40,000	150	5,102,257	3,884,463	5,102,257
40,001–50,000	107	4,819,591	2,902,869	4,819,591
50,001–60,000	54	2,910,399	1,436,150	2,910,399
60,001–70,000	25	1,641,237	743,278	1,641,237
70,001–80,000	21	1,587,230	611,920	1,587,230
80,001–90,000	20	1,660,283	588,525	1,660,283
90,001–100,000	13	1,268,376	367,077	1,268,376
100,001–200,000	6	681,544	193,968	660,723
200,001–500,000	16	4,354,732	439,906	2,031,077
Total	4,905	$47,574,875	$34,215,312	$45,230,399

[1] Indicated 100/300 Factor ($45,230,399/$34,216,312)   1.3219
[2] 100/300 Factor Indicated as of 12/31/1997   1.2683
[3] Annual Trend $[(1.3219/1.2683).5] - 1.0000$ 2.09%
[4] Projected 7/1/2001 100/300 Factor $[1] \times (1.0000 + [3])1.5$ 1.3636
[5] Selected 100/300 Factor   1.3500

[a] Based upon unlimited claims closed from 1987 through 1999 trended to 12/31/1999 at an annual rate of 8.5%.

EXHIBIT 3.16

EXAMPLE AUTO INSURANCE COMPANY

RATE MANUAL—7/1/2000
PRIVATE PASSENGER AUTO BODILY INJURY
20/40 BASIC LIMITS

Territory	Class 1 Adult Drivers, No Youthful Operators	Class 2 Family with Youthful Drivers Not Principal Operators	Class 3 Youthful Owners or Principal Operators
1—Central City	$256	$351	$446
2—Midway Valley	$183	$251	$318
3—Remainder of State	$146	$201	$255

Increased Limits

Limit	Factor
100/300	1.350

CHAPTER 4
INDIVIDUAL RISK RATING
MARGARET TILLER SHERWOOD

INTRODUCTION

Manual ratemaking determines what rates should be charged average members of groups of entities for specified coverage and entity characteristics. Individual risk rating supplements manual rates by modifying the group rates in whole or in part to reflect an individual entity's experience.

If all entities in all rating groups were truly homogeneous, differences in experience among entities would be fortuitous. While homogeneity is the goal of manual ratemaking, it is not usually possible to achieve. In addition, some entities are large enough that their experience is, to some extent, "credible." Individual risk rating is appropriate when there is a combination of nonhomogeneous rating groups and entities with credible experience.

This chapter discusses individual risk rating in general terms and provides examples from both traditional (insurance) and nontraditional risk financing mechanisms. The latter include risk retention groups, pools, and individual entities retaining risk. In this chapter it is assumed that the manual rates are properly determined, unless otherwise noted.

Goals of Individual Risk Rating

For an insurer, the primary goal of individual risk rating is to price the coverage provided more accurately than if rates were based only on manual rates. Nontraditional risk financing mechanisms also may use individual risk rating techniques to allocate costs.

For groups of entities, such as pools or risk retention groups, the primary goals of individual risk rating (sometimes referred to as cost allocation) are to allocate costs to participants more accurately and to motivate participation in risk control programs. These are also the goals of individual risk rating for individual entities retaining ("self-insuring") all or part of their risks and allocating the associated costs to departments or other units. Individual entities purchasing insurance may similarly wish to allocate the insurance costs to their departments or other units. For individual entities in either situation, the units to which the costs are being allocated take the role of participants or "insureds." Some entities may participate in individual risk rating systems as both allocator and allocatee.

The motivation to participate in risk control programs is a secondary goal of insurers using individual risk rating. Other goals of insurers and other entities using individual risk rating are to balance appropriately risk sharing and risk bearing and to provide information to design or modify risk control programs. For individual entities, the allocation of costs to units allows for more accurate pricing of products and services.

Attributes of Good Individual Risk Rating Systems

Good individual risk rating systems have the following attributes:

- serve the needs of the organization using them,

- appropriately balance risk sharing and risk bearing,

- are not subject to internal or external manipulation,

- are simple to administer,

- are easy to understand, and

- do not subject the affected entities to large fluctuations in costs from one year to the next due to unusual or catastrophic experience.

Some of these attributes may overlap. As practical considerations may override one or more of these attributes, all are listed.

Prior to designing any individual risk rating system, the organization designing it should determine what its needs are. These needs may simply be the goals listed above, or the entity may have different needs that override traditional cost allocation goals. For example, a corporation offering a new product may wish to allocate its product liability insurance costs for the new product to existing products to keep the cost of the new product down until it becomes popular.

An individual risk rating system should appropriately balance risk sharing and risk bearing. The costs for small entities whose experience is not at all credible should be determined solely based on risk sharing. Large entities whose experience is completely credible might have their costs solely based on risk bearing. Entities between these extremes should have their costs based on a weighting of risk sharing and risk bearing.

Individual risk rating systems should not be subject to internal or external manipulation. Manipulation is internal if the entity to which costs are being allocated can influence the cost allocation. An example is the entity to which costs are being allocated setting the case reserves used in the individual risk rating calculation. Manipulation is external if some agency other than the entity to which costs are being allocated can influence the cost allocation. An example is a marketing manager who can override the pricing results of the individual risk rating calculation without additional information to support the override.

As a practical consideration, individual risk rating systems should be simple to administer. If a system proves very complicated to administer, it might not be applied. A system that is simple to administer is also more likely to be easy to understand. Understanding is important particularly in those situations in which participation in risk control programs is one of the goals: the easier a system is to understand, the better will be the motivation to participate, assuming the system is appropriately designed.

A good individual risk rating system does not subject the affected entities to large fluctuations in costs from one year to the next due to unusual experience. An individual risk rating system should reflect an entity's experience only to the extent that it is credible. Unusual experience is not credible because it is not a true reflection of the entity's underlying exposure to loss. An individual risk rating system that reasonably balances risk sharing and risk bearing usually has this attribute of moderating the effect of unusual cost fluctuations. However, a system could have this attribute without reasonably balancing risk sharing and risk bearing.

Overview of Individual Risk Rating

There are two basic types of individual risk rating systems: prospective and retrospective. Prospective systems use past experience to determine costs for the future. Retrospective systems use the actual experience of the period to determine the final costs for that period.

Retrospective systems are more responsive to experience changes than prospective systems. This is an advantage when a primary goal is to motivate participation in risk control programs. This responsiveness also means that retrospective systems result in less stable costs from one time period to the next than do prospective systems. The final cost using a retrospective system is not known until many years after the subject period.

While different systems use different formulae, all individual risk rating systems weight experience and exposure. The weight assigned to the experience component is a reflection of the credibility of the entity's experience as a valid predictor of future costs.

There are practical considerations that affect individual risk rating systems. It may be appropriate to use alternative exposure bases and data if those desired are not readily available. Additionally, if one of the goals is to motivate participation in risk control programs and the results of the individual risk rating calculation do not make a material difference to the entity to which costs are being allocated, there will probably be no such motivation.

For individual entities allocating risk financing costs to units, several additional factors influence how effectively an individual risk rating system will meet its goals. These include variations in tax rates and systems, the ability of units to purchase their own insurance, and whether and how unit managers get the benefits or penalties of the costs allocated to their units.

What is to be Allocated

The second task in designing or understanding an individual risk rating system (after determining goals) is to determine what is to be allocated. For traditional insurance, the answer often is all costs. These include losses, ALAE, ULAE, reinsurance premium, risk control costs, overhead, taxes, miscellaneous expenses, and profit associated with insurance policies of the type being written (e.g., occurrence). (See the appendix to Chapter 2 for definitions.)

Nontraditional risk financing mechanisms and individual entities allocating risk financing costs back to units also may want to allocate all costs associated with the risk financing program. Those costs may include different items, such as excess insurance premium and a risk margin (money for adverse loss and ALAE experience), and exclude others, such as taxes and profit. Nontraditional risk financing mechanisms and individual entities allocating costs back to units and even some insurers may want to allocate only some subset of costs, such as losses, ALAE, and ULAE, with other costs treated in a different manner.

Note that part of the determination of what is to be allocated involves determining the basis on which policies are written or on which funding occurs. This is necessary so that the various components subject to the allocation are appropriately tabulated and adjusted. Also, it is important to understand if the term "loss" includes ALAE in the coverage and in the data available for analysis and how any loss or loss and ALAE limits are to be applied.

PROSPECTIVE SYSTEMS

There are three basic types of prospective individual risk rating systems: schedule rating, experience rating, and some types of composite rating. Schedule rating takes into consideration characteristics that are expected to affect losses and ALAE but that are not reflected in past experience. Experience rating uses an entity's actual experience to modify manual rates (determined by the entity's rating group). Composite rating simplifies the premium calculation for large, complex entities and, in some instances, allows the entities' experience to affect the premium developed from manual rates or to determine the rates regardless of rating group.

Schedule Rating

Schedule rating is the only individual risk rating system that does not directly reflect an entity's claim experience; in theory, it recognizes characteristics that are expected to have a material effect on an entity's experience but that are not actually reflected in that experience. These characteristics could result from recent changes in exposure (such as the addition of a swimming pool in an apartment complex) or risk control programs (such as the recent implementation of a new program). Schedule rating is also used for entities that are too small to qualify for experience rating or composite rating.

Schedule rating systems usually take the form of percentage credits and debits. These credits and debits are sometimes applied before and sometimes after experience rating. There may be a limit to the total debit or credit that an entity can receive.

Note that schedule credits and debits apply only to those characteristics that should affect an entity's loss and ALAE experience. If a characteristic is listed that should not affect a particular entity's loss and ALAE experience, there should be no adjustment to the manual rates for that characteristic for that entity.

Also note that the application of schedule credits and debits may take considerable underwriting judgment. A schedule rating system that is based on objective criteria will result in more consistent treatment of affected entities than a system that relies on subjective evaluation. This is illustrated by the two examples of schedule rating that follow.

Insurance Services Office (ISO) Commercial General Liability Experience and Schedule Rating Plan: Schedule Rating

This section discusses the December, 1997 ISO General Liability Schedule Rating Plan.

For eligible entities, the manual rates may be modified according to the table below in addition to any experience rating modification. The maximum schedule rating modification is 25% up or down. It is applied after experience rating has been applied.

ISO General Liability Schedule Rating Table

A.	Location	
	(i) Exposure Inside Premises	−5% to +5%
	(ii) Exposure Outside Premises	−5% to +5%
B.	Premises—Condition, Care	−10% to +10%
C.	Equipment—Type, Condition, Care	−10% to +10%
D.	Classification Peculiarities	−10% to +10%
E.	Employees—Selection, Training, Supervision, Experience	−6% to +6%
F.	Cooperation	
	(i) Medical Facilities	−2% to +2%
	(ii) Safety Program	−2% to +2%

This plan can be flexibly applied using insurer-specific underwriting guidelines that reflect the insurer's own knowledge and experience and the specific characteristics of the class of insureds to which it is applied. Each insurer's guidelines must be applied consistently and objectively under state insurance laws and regulations. There is some variation possible in the plan in that different insurers might give different schedule credits and debits in identical situations. Underwriters within the same company are expected to apply the same credits or debits in identical situations.

Roller Skating Rink Risk Retention Group Schedule Rating Plan
This schedule rating plan is similar to one developed for a roller skating rink risk retention group offering general liability coverage. All participating entities are eligible. There is no explicit maximum schedule rating modification. The maximum schedule credit is that inherent in the plan (40%). Note that only credits are given. The manual rates are based on experience for rinks in which none of the characteristics in the schedule rating plan were present.

The general credit list is as follows:

A.	Floor supervision	+10%
B.	Premises	+5%
C.	Rental Skates	+5%
D.	Management	+5%
E.	Incident Report	+10%
F.	First Aid	+5%
	Total	+40%

Details of the floor supervision credit follow.

Rink must meet or exceed industry safety standard of one floor supervisor per 200 skaters at all times.

Rink has a written policy or procedure which includes:

• a distinctive uniform or vest for floor supervisors;

- a provision that floor supervisors must be paid employees, owners, or family members of owners;

- a provision that floor supervisors must be at least 18 years of age; and

- a written training program for floor supervisors.

The floor supervisor training program must include the following provisions at a minimum:

- Floor guards should inspect the floor continually for foreign objects.

- During special numbers or events, floor guards should keep unqualified skaters off the floor.

- Floor guards should follow a written policy regarding unruly skaters.

- Floor guards should follow detailed, written instructions in case of an accident, including:

  —not moving the injured skater,

  —diverting skaters from the injured skater,

  —notifying management of an incident, and

  —a procedure for obtaining emergency medical/police/fire assistance.

Floor supervisor training must include a minimum of one safety meeting per calendar quarter.

Floor supervisor training must be recorded and verified by the employee.

ALL OF THE ABOVE MUST BE PRESENT TO EARN THE 10% CREDIT. NO PARTIAL CREDIT WILL BE GIVEN.

The other credits similarly rely on objective criteria that can be verified by audit and/or surprise inspections. All credits encourage activities that should favorably affect loss and ALAE experience. Note that credit is given for activities that a rink has just begun, regardless of its actions in the past.

Because the manual premium is based on experience for rinks in which none of the characteristics in the schedule rating plan were present, there should be no "off-balance," i.e., the premium collected should cover the expected costs. If the manual premium used data for rinks that did have some of the characteristics in the schedule rating plan, the manual rates would need to be corrected for the off-balance resulting from a schedule rating plan that only gives credits.

Experience Rating

All individual risk rating systems are a form of experience rating because they reflect an entity's actual experience or characteristics that should affect the entity's experience. However, the term "experience rating" has come to mean a particular type of prospective system, discussed in this section.

Experience rating is used when the past, with appropriate adjustments, is predictive of the future. Actual losses, and sometimes ALAE, for a prior period are compared to expected losses (and ALAE). The weighting of the actual and expected experience results in the cost to the subject entity for the current period.

To have an "apples to apples" comparison, several different combinations of experience and exposure can be used, including the following:

- actual paid losses (and ALAE) at a particular date and the expected paid losses (and ALAE) at that date, both for the experience period;

- reported losses (and ALAE) at a particular date and the expected reported losses (and ALAE) at that date, both for the experience period;

- projected ultimate losses (and ALAE) and the expected ultimate losses, both for the experience period; and

- projected ultimate losses (and ALAE) for the experience period adjusted to the current exposure and dollar levels and the expected ultimate losses for the current period at the current dollar and exposure levels.

Projected ultimate losses are the expected ultimate settlement value of all subject claims/occurrences. Projected ultimate ALAE are the expected ultimate ALAE costs of all subject claims/occurrences. The expected losses (and ALAE) are based on past or current exposure, as appropriate. The adjustments to current dollar and exposure levels should reflect such items as:

- economic and social inflation;

- changes in the number, size, and type of entities; and

- changes in policy limits.

Social inflation includes such items as changes in litigiousness, judicial decisions, and legislation that directly or indirectly affect the cost of settling claims.

The three components of experience, exposure, and credibility (the weighting factor) and some additional considerations are discussed below.

Experience

The experience component should be related to the exposure component, as detailed above, and to the basis on which policies are written or funding occurs. If the policy to be rated is written on an occurrence basis, any of the four combinations listed above for accidents occurring in the experience period could be used. If the policy to be rated is written on a claims-paid basis, the two best combinations are those using paid losses or projected ultimate losses adjusted to current exposure and dollar levels, both for payments made during the experience period. If the costs to be allocated include ALAE, ALAE usually should be included with losses in the calculation.

The length of the experience rating period usually ranges from two to five years. The shorter the period, the more responsive the plan will be to changes that truly affect loss (and ALAE) experience, such as changes in the risk control program, and the more subject to unusual fluctuations in loss (and ALAE) experience. Conversely, a longer period will result in less responsiveness to changes and to unusual or catastrophic occurrences.

To reduce the effect of unusual or catastrophic occurrences, many experience rating plans place per occurrence limits on the losses (and ALAE) used in the experience rating calculation. These limits sometimes apply to losses only, with ALAE unlimited or treated in a different manner, and sometimes to losses and ALAE combined. Note that if actual losses (and ALAE) are limited, the expected losses (and ALAE) must also be limited to maintain an "apples to apples" comparison. If losses (and ALAE) are limited, the cost of expected losses (and ALAE) above the per occurrence limit must be accounted for in some manner. Annual or other period aggregate limits may also be used.

If projected ultimate losses are to be used in the experience rating calculation, they can be developed in a number of ways similar to those used to develop projected ultimate losses used to determine manual rates. Projected ultimate losses are often based on paid or reported losses at a particular date.

For the last experience combination listed above, projected ultimate losses are adjusted to current exposure and dollar levels. Dollar-level adjustments should include both economic and social inflation.

Exposure adjustments include both converting the experience period to the current period (e.g., dividing by three to go from a three-year experience period to a one-year current period) and adjusting for changes in the magnitude of the exposure. Both can be accomplished at once by dividing the projected ultimate losses for the experience period, adjusted to current dollar level, by the exposure for the experience period, adjusted to current dollar level if appropriate, and applying this "rate" to the exposure for the current period.

Exposure

The expected losses are a function of the past or current exposure, as appropriate. The exposure component should be related to the experience component, as detailed above. For the first three combinations listed-above, past exposure is used; for-the last combination, current exposure is used.

Expected losses are usually estimated as the product of an expected loss rate and the exposure base. The expected loss rate can be based on the manual rates for the prior or current period, adjusted to the appropriate dollar level. For example, to develop expected loss rates for a prior period, the current expected loss rate could be adjusted to the prior period's dollar level, or the prior period's expected loss rates could be used directly. The former approach is usually better if there have been no underlying changes in the nature of the exposure because the current expected loss rate is based on more recent information than the prior period's loss rates.

The exposure base used should reflect the underlying risk of loss and ALAE. It is not always possible to use the theoretically optimal exposure base. In practice, insurers and nontraditional risk financing mechanisms often use whatever exposure base insurers use in their premium calculations.

For general liability, exposure bases often used are sales, payroll, total operating expenditures, and square footage, adjusted for any underlying differences. For workers compensation the exposure base is usually payroll adjusted for differences in payroll type (e.g., a coal miner is expected to have more losses and ALAE per payroll dollar than a secretary, even though both are employed by the same entity). For property, exposure bases often used include actual cash value, stated amount, or replacement cost.

Nontraditional risk financing mechanisms may use different exposure bases for different costs. For example, for a public entity workers compensation pool, the exposure base for all administrative costs may be full-time-equivalent (FTE) employees while the exposure base for losses and ALAE is payroll, with both full-time-equivalent employees and payroll adjusted for differences in payroll type. The use of two exposure bases may be the result of different payroll scales being used by different participants.

Individual entities allocating risk financing costs to units may also use different exposure bases for different costs. And some costs, such as the cost of a policy that applies only to one unit, may be allocated without using the experience rating plan.

Credibility

The actual (experience) and expected (exposure) components of the experience rating calculation are weighted to produce the costs the entity under consideration will pay. The weight assigned to the experience component is called "credibility," and commonly denoted by "Z." The weight assigned to the exposure component is $1 - Z$. This is also called the credibility complement. Credibility reflects the degree of belief that the entity's experience is a valid predictor of future costs. The credibility selected should consider the validity of the component to which the credibility complement is being applied.

Credibility has three criteria that must be met:

1. Credibility must not be less than zero or greater than one.

2. Credibility should increase as the size of risk increases, all else being equal.

3. The percentage change for any loss of a given size should decrease as the size of risk increases.

FIGURE 4.1

GENERAL CREDIBILITY ILLUSTRATION

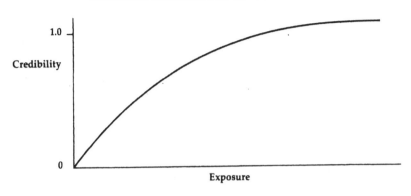

These criteria can also be shown as mathematical relationships. Using Z for credibility and E for size of risk:

1. $0 < Z < 1$

2. $\dfrac{dZ}{dE} > 0$

3. $\dfrac{d}{dE}\left(\dfrac{Z}{E}\right) < 0$

These three criteria are met if credibility follows the curve shown in Figure 4.1. Note that size of risk is represented in the diagram by exposure. Size of risk can also be based on expected losses or expected number of claims. Chapter 8 contains a detailed discussion of credibility.

Other Considerations

Experience rating plans may be designed so that there is a minimum or maximum premium change. These are often based on the prior year's premium adjusted for changes in exposure. For example, the maximum premium change from one year to the next may be the change indicated by any exposure changes plus or minus 25%. This means that if there is an increase of 15%

because of an increase in exposure, the total increase possible after application of the experience rating plan is 44% ((1.15 × 1.25) − 1.00).

The premium collected under experience rating plans may not equal the expected premium in total. This means that the plan has an "off-balance." If this can be anticipated and does not reflect a true difference between experience-rated and nonexperience-rated risks, the experience rating plan can include, as a last step, multiplication by a factor to correct for this off-balance. Alternatively, the manual rates can include an off-balance correction. This latter approach affects non-experience-rated entities also.

ISO Commercial General Liability Experience and Schedule Rating Plan: Experience Rating
The December 1997 ISO Commercial General Liability Experience Rating Plan is illustrated in Tables 4.2 and 4.3. This example is used throughout the following discussion of the plan.

"Company" refers to the insurance company using the experience rating plan. The references to company premium, rates, and expected loss and ALAE ratios reflect that different insurance companies may apply different expected loss and ALAE ratios to the same ISO loss and ALAE costs to arrive at different rates and, thus, different premiums for the same exposures.

This plan may be used for occurrence and claims-made general liability coverages, with a few exceptions, for those entities meeting the eligibility criteria specified in the plan. The coverage in the example is premises/operations and products/completed operations for policy period 7/1/98–99, written on a third-year claims-made basis.

The experience is represented by the projected ultimate losses and ALAE for the experience period. The exposure is represented by the expected losses and ALAE for the experience period. For both the projected ultimate losses and ALAE, and

TABLE 4.2

ISO EXPERIENCE RATING SAMPLE CALCULATION
BASIC CALCULATION

Coverage:	Premises/Operations and Products/Completed Operations	
Policy Being Rated:	7/1/98–99 Third-Year Claims-Made	
Experience Period:	7/1/94–95 Occurrence	
	7/1/95–96 Occurrence	
	7/1/96–97 First-Year Claims-Made	

I. Experience Components

    A. Reported Losses and ALAE at 3/31/98 Limited by Basic Limits and MSL   139,800

    B. Expected Unreported Losses and ALAE at 3/31/98 Limited by Basic Limits and MSL (See Table 4.3)   32,747

    C. Projected Ultimate Losses and ALAE Limited by Basic Limits and MSL ((A) + (B))   172,547

    D. Company Subject Basic Limits Loss and ALAE Costs (See Table 4.3)   156,400

    E. Actual Experience Ratio ((C)/(D))   1.103

II. Exposure Component: Expected Experience Ratio (See Table 4.3)   .888

III. Credibility   0.44

IV. Experience (Credit)/Debit   10.7%
$((((\text{I.E}) - (\text{II}))/(\text{II})) \times (\text{III}))$

Notes: The basic limits apply to losses only. ALAE are unlimited. MSL is the maximum single limit per occurrence, applied to basic limits losses and unlimited ALAE. It is based on the total company subject basic limits loss and unlimited ALAE costs.

The expected experience ratio (II) and the credibility (III) also are based on the total company subject basic limits loss and ALAE costs.

The total company subject basic limits loss and ALAE costs are from Table 4.3.

expected losses and ALAE, the losses are limited to basic limits. The ALAE are unlimited. A maximum single limit per occurrence (MSL) is applied to the basic limited losses and ALAE combined. The basic limits, which also apply to losses and ALAE combined, are as follows:

- $100,000 combined single limit for all bodily injury and property damage liability losses arising from a single occurrence;
- $5,000 per person limit for medical expenses;

TABLE 4.3

ISO EXPERIENCE RATING SAMPLE CALCULATION

EXPECTED UNREPORTED LOSSES AND ALAE AT 3/31/98 AND SUBJECT LOSS COSTS

[1]	[2]	[3]	[4]	[5]	[6]	[7]	[8]	[9]	[10]
		Current Company B/L Loss & ALAE Costs	Policy Adjustment Factors		Detrend Factors	Company Subject B/L Loss & ALAE Costs	Expected Experience Ratio	Expected Percentage B/L Losses & ALAE Unreported at 3/31/98	Expected B/L Losses & ALAE Unreported at 3/31/98
Policy Period	Coverage		Table 13.B	Table 13.C					
7/1/94–95	Prem/Ops	48,750	1.06	1.00	0.804	41,547	0.888	19.2%	7,084
	Products	16,250	1.16	1.00	0.839	15,815	0.888	42.6%	5,983
7/1/95–96	Prem/Ops	48,750	1.06	1.00	0.849	43,872	0.888	30.0%	11,688
	Products	16,250	1.16	1.00	0.876	16,513	0.888	54.5%	7,992
7/1/96–97	Prem/Ops	48,750	1.06	0.67	0.897	31,056	0.888	0.0%	0
	Products	16,250	1.16	0.44	0.916	7,597	0.888	0.0%	0
Total						156,400			32,747

Notes: [3] is for the 7/1/98–99 third-year claims-made policy. It is the company expected loss and ALAE ratio of 0.650 multiplied by the company premium of $75,000 and $25,000 for premises/operations and products, respectively.

[4] adjusts current company basic limits loss and ALAE costs up to an occurrence level.

[5] adjusts for the experience period being claims-made, reflecting claims-made year.

[6] adjusts current company basic limits loss and ALAE costs by the reciprocal of the loss and ALAE trend.

[7] = [3] × [4] × [5] × [6].

[8] is based on the total company subject basic limits loss and ALAE costs in [7].

[9] is from Table 15.

[10] = [7] × [8] × [9].

Tables 13.B, 13.C, and 15 are from the ISO plan.

- $100,000 per person or organizational limit for personal injury or advertising injury; and

- annual aggregate limits of $200,000 for products/completed operations and $200,000 for all other coverages (general aggregate).

For incidental professional liability exposures under commercial general liability, basic limits are $100,000 for all damages on account of each occurrence and, subject to the foregoing limit, a basic annual aggregate limit of $200,000.

The experience period is the three policy periods completed at least six months prior to the rating date. If three policy periods are not available, one or two may be used. Occurrences and loss and ALAE costs associated with tail coverage on claims-made policies are excluded. In the example, the three policy periods are 7/1/94–95, 7/1/95–96, and 7/1/96–97. The older two were written on an occurrence basis; the most recent on a first-year claims-made basis. The evaluation date is 3/31/98.

The projected ultimate losses and ALAE with losses limited by basic limits and with the total limited by the MSL for the experience period are the sum of the reported losses and ALAE at 3/31/98 and the expected unreported losses and ALAE at 3/31/98, both with losses limited by basic limits and the limited losses and unlimited ALAE limited by MSL. The experience component is the actual experience (loss and ALAE) ratio, which is the projected ultimate losses and ALAE with losses limited by basic limits and the total limited by MSL divided by the company subject basic limits loss and unlimited ALAE costs.

The exposure base is company subject basic limits loss and ALAE costs. The exposure component is the expected experience (loss and ALAE) ratio adjusted for the various limits. The actual and expected experience ratios are compared using a credibility factor to arrive at the experience credit (percentage reduction in premium) or debit (percentage increase in premium). This plan has no minimums, maximums, or explicit off-balance correction.

Table 4.2 shows the basic calculation. Table 4.3 shows the calculation of the expected unreported losses and ALAE at 3/31/98 and company subject basic limits loss and ALAE costs. The expected unreported losses and ALAE at 3/31/98 are the product of the company subject basic limits loss and ALAE costs, expected experience ratio, and expected percentage losses and ALAE unreported at 3/31/98. These three quantities reflect the effect of basic limits losses and ALAE and the MSL.

Note that there is no adjustment for unreported losses and ALAE for the claims-made policies, even though there may be case reserve development. This results in a probable understatement of the actual experience ratio and a resulting probable overstatement of any credits or understatement of any debits, if case reserve development is greater than zero.

The company subject basic limits loss and ALAE costs for each year of the experience period are the product of the current company basic limits loss and ALAE costs (for a third-year claims-made policy), two policy adjustment factors, and a detrend factor. The Table 13.B policy adjustment factors adjust current company basic limits loss and ALAE costs to an occurrence level. The Table 13.C policy adjustment factors adjust current company occurrence basic limits loss and ALAE to the respective policy type (occurrence or claims-made) for each year of the experience period. Table 13.C also eliminates basic limits losses and ALAE related to midi-tail coverage. Midi-tail coverage is the coverage associated with the limited automatic extended reporting period. Tables 13.B and 13.C are from the ISO plan.

In 7/1/96–97 in the example, the third-year claims-made company basic limits loss and ALAE costs are adjusted up to an occurrence basis by the Table 13.B factor and down to a first-year claims-made basis (excluding the midi-tail) by the Table 13.C factor because the experience for the 7/1/96–97 period is first-year claims-made. The detrend factors, which are applied to current company basis limits loss and ALAE costs, actually adjust for loss and ALAE trends since the policy period. In other words, the detrend factor is the reciprocal of the loss and ALAE trend. These factors do not adjust for changes in coverage, such as changes in exclusions.

Note that there is an implicit assumption in this example that exposure for the past is the same as the current exposure, except for changes in dollar value. This assumption is not reasonable if there has been growth or decline in the underlying exposure. If this is the case, an alternate calculation that adjusts for the changes in exposure should be used to derive company subject basic limits losses and ALAE. This is done by applying current company rates by subline and the company expected loss and ALAE ratio to the exposures by subline for the experience period to arrive at the current company basic limits loss and ALAE costs.

The calculation performed to determine the experience credit/ (debit) is as follows:

$$CD = \frac{AER - EER}{EER} \times Z$$

where

AER = Actual Experience Ratio

EER = Expected Experience Ratio

Z = Credibility

CD = (Credit)/Debit

This can be rearranged to a more familiar form:

$$M = \frac{[A \times Z] + [E \times (1 - Z)]}{E}$$

where

E = Expected Losses and ALAE Limited by
Basic Limits and MSL

A = Actual Losses and ALAE Limited by
Basic Limits and MSL

Z = Credibility

M = Modification Factor

E and A are calculated as follows:

E = Company Subject Basic Limits Loss and ALAE Costs × *EER*

and

A = Projected Ultimate Losses and ALAE Limited by Basic Limits and MSL

Note that

$$M = 1 + CD$$

For the example:

CD = 10.7% from Table 4.2

$E = 156,400 \times 0.888 = 138,883$

$A = 172,547$

$Z = 0.44$

$M = 1.107 = 1 + 0.107$

The experience credit or debit is applied to the otherwise chargeable premium for the policy being rated. This plan has special rules for treating deductible coverage, company expense variation, situations in which other than basic limits data are readily available, situations in which basic limits premiums are not readily available, and situations in which the claim data are immature due to a change of insurance company. There also is a procedure for converting the plan to a company premium basis.

Workers Compensation Pool Experience Rating Plan

The experience rating plan of a workers compensation pool for fire districts in one state is illustrated in Tables 4.4 through 4.6.

TABLE 4.4

WORKERS COMPENSATION POOL EXPERIENCE RATING SAMPLE CALCULATION
PREMIUM DETERMINATION

[1] Fire District	[2] Minimum Premium	[3] Maximum Premium	[4] A	[5] E	[6] Z	[7] Unadjusted	[8] Premium for 7/1/98–99 Adjusted #1	[9] Adjusted #2
A	93,384	372,825	290,914	280,491	0.59	380,075	376,698	372,825
B	1,494	8,634	821	4,487	0.00	5,980	5,927	5,958
C	18,810	93,623	15,286	56,497	0.12	70,319	69,694	70,063
D	8,409	53,402	6,163	25,257	0.00	33,666	33,367	33,544
E	28,546	171,593	172,188	85,742	0.25	136,014	134,805	135,518
F	38,615	222,414	128,716	115,985	0.33	158,778	157,368	158,200
G	166	1,599	0	499	0.00	664	659	662
H	6,805	41,251	44,007	20,439	0.00	27,243	27,001	27,144
I	13,167	72,625	10,922	39,548	0.09	50,228	49,782	50,045
J	52,999	270,257	121,658	159,188	0.39	197,500	195,745	196,780
K	4,868	28,141	37,010	14,623	0.00	19,491	19,318	19,420
L	1,715	9,593	145	5,151	0.00	6,866	6,805	6,841
M	2,987	15,670	4,105	8,973	0.00	11,960	11,854	11,917
N	5,034	24,623	65	15,121	0.00	20,156	19,977	20,082
Total	277,000	1,386,250	832,000	832,000		1,118,941	1,109,000	1,109,000

Notes: [2] = [6] of Exhibit 4.6.

[3] = [8] of Exhibit 4.6.

[4] = [7] of Exhibit 4.5.

[5] = [3] of Exhibit 4.6.

[6] = [5] of Exhibit 4.6.

[7] = [2] + [4] × [6] + [5] × (1.00 − [6]).

[8] = ([7] × 1,109,000) ÷ Total [7]. 1,109,000 is the recommended contribution for 7/1/98–99.

[9] = [8], adjusted for maximum premiums with amount over maximum premiums reallocated based on [8].

TABLE 4.5

WORKERS COMPENSATION POOL EXPERIENCE RATING SAMPLE CALCULATION
DETERMINATION OF A

[1] Fire District	[2] Reported Limited Losses & ALAE at 6/30/97	[3] FTE Personnel 7/1/94–97	[4] Raw Annual Loss & ALAE Rate ([2]/[3])	[5] FTE Personnel 7/1/98–99	[6] Unadjusted ([4] × [5])	[7] Adjusted
					A	A
A	350,240	463.3	755.97	168.8	127,607	290,914
B	1,000	7.5	133.33	2.7	360	821
C	15,126	76.7	197.21	34.0	6,705	15,286
D	8,892	50.0	177.84	15.2	2,703	6,163
E	193,214	132.0	1,463.74	51.6	75,529	172,188
F	147,865	182.8	808.89	69.8	56,460	128,716
G	0	1.6	0.00	0.3	0	0
H	56,654	36.1	1,569.36	12.3	19,303	44,007
I	13,809	68.6	201.30	23.8	4,791	10,922
J	130,682	234.6	557.04	95.8	53,365	121,658
K	47,965	26.0	1,844.81	8.8	16,234	37,010
L	185	9.0	20.56	3.1	64	145
M	4,768	14.3	333.43	5.4	1,801	4,105
N	63	20.0	3.15	9.1	29	65
Total/Avg.	970,463	1,322.5	733.81	500.7	364,951	832,000

Note: [7] = 832,000 × ([6]/Total[6]). 832,000 is the discounted expected losses and ALAE for 7/1/98–99.

Workers' Compensation Pool Experience Rating Sample Calculation
Determination of E, Z, Minimum Premium, and Maximum Premium

[1]	[2]	[3]	[4]	[5]	[6]	[7]	[8]
	FTE Personnel		FTE Personnel	Credibility	Estimated Discounted Admin. Costs	Contribution	Maximum Premium
Fire District	7/1/98–99	E	7/1/94–97	(Z)	7/1/98–99	7/1/97–98	7/1/98–99
A	168.8	280,491	463.3	0.59	93,384	229,410	372,825
B	2.7	4,487	7.5	0.00	1,494	5,313	8,634
C	34.0	56,497	76.7	0.12	18,810	57,609	93,623
D	15.2	25,257	50.0	0.00	8,409	32,860	53,402
E	51.6	85,742	132.0	0.25	28,546	105,586	171,593
F	69.8	115,985	182.8	0.33	38,615	136,858	222,414
G	0.3	499	1.6	0.00	166	984	1,599
H	12.3	20,439	36.1	0.00	6,805	25,383	41,251
I	23.8	39,548	68.6	0.09	13,167	44,688	72,625
J	95.8	159,188	234.6	0.39	52,999	166,297	270,257
K	8.8	14,623	26.0	0.00	4,868	17,316	28,141
L	3.1	5,151	9.0	0.00	1,715	5,903	9,593
M	5.4	8,973	14.3	0.00	2,987	9,642	15,670
N	9.1	15,121	20.0	0.00	5,034	15,151	24,623
Total	500.7	832,000	1,322.5		277,000	853,000	1,386,250

Notes: [3] is distributed based on [2]. 832,000 is the discounted expected losses and ALAE for 7/1/98–99.

[5] is determined based on [4] as follows:

FTE Personnel Years	Credibility
60 or less	0.00
60–1,199	$\left[\dfrac{\text{FTE personel years} - 60}{1,140}\right]^{1/2}$
1,200 or more	1.00

[6] is distributed based on [2]. This is the minimum premium.

[8] = [7] × (1,109,000/853,000) × 1.25. 1,109,000 is the total recommended contribution for 7/1/98–99.

This example is used throughout the following discussion of the plan.

This plan is used for occurrence workers compensation coverage written on a guaranteed cost basis for all entities participating in the pool. Pool participation has been constant since the pool's inception and is not expected to change for 7/1/98–99, the policy period in question. All policies renew 7/1.

The costs to be allocated using a weighting of experience and exposure are the expected losses and ALAE for 7/1/98–99, discounted for anticipated investment income. The estimated discounted expected expenses other than ALAE for 7/1/98–99 are distributed to participants on the basis of the expected full-time-equivalent (FTE) personnel for 7/1/98–99.

The experience is represented by reported losses and ALAE at 6/30/97 for the experience period, adjusted for changes in FTE personnel. The exposure base is expected FTE employees for the 7/1/98–99 period. The reported losses and ALAE at 6/30/97 are limited to $25,000 per occurrence. The experience period is the latest three complete policy periods, i.e., 7/1/94–95, 7/1/95–96, and 7/1/96–97. Credibility is based on FTE employees for the experience period.

FTE personnel are used rather than payroll as an exposure base, for the credibility base, and to allocate estimated discounted expenses for 7/1/98–99. FTE personnel is a better exposure base than payroll in this instance because of the presence in some of the districts of volunteer firefighters and pay scale discrepancies between districts. Volunteer firefighters are covered by workers compensation law. The nature of workers compensation claims for firefighters (many minor cost claims and a few large cost claims) and the pay-scale discrepancies indicate that some costs and credibility are more closely related to FTE personnel than payroll.

The plan has a built-in minimum: the estimated discounted administrative expenses for 7/1/98–99, as allocated based on expected FTE personnel for 7/1/98–99. The plan also has a maximum for each participant: 25% above the prior year's contribution (for 7/1/97–98 in this example), adjusted for any increase in total recommended contribution but not for any decrease (a 30% increase in this example, from $853,000 to $1,109,000). The total increase allowable in this example is 62.5% $((1.300 \times 1.250) - 1.000)$.

Because pool participation has been and is expected to remain constant, it is possible to calculate the exact off-balance and adjust accordingly so that the total dollars collected are the total recommended contribution for the group. The allocation of the off-balance to districts may need several iterations, depending on the effect of the minimums and maximums.

Table 4.4 shows the premium determination. Table 4.5 shows the determination of A, the discounted expected losses and ALAE for 7/1/98–99 allocated based on experience. Table 4.6 shows the determination of E (the discounted expected losses and ALAE for 7/1/98–99 allocated based on exposure), Z (credibility), minimum premium, and maximum premium.

The premium before adjustment for off-balance, minimums, and maximums is determined as follows:

Unadjusted Premium =

Minimum Premium + $((A \times Z) + [E \times (1.000 - Z)])$.

The unadjusted premium for the example is shown in column (7) of Table 4.4. Column (8) of Table 4.4 shows the premium adjusted for the off-balance. Column (9) of Table 4.4 shows the premium adjusted for maximum premiums combined with an additional off-balance calculation. Note that in the example, no participant's premium was lower than the applicable minimum. Any amounts under minimum premiums would have to be reallocated similarly to the reallocation of the amounts over maximum premiums.

A is the discounted expected losses and ALAE for 7/1/98–99 allocated based on experience (calculated in Table 4.5). The reported losses and ALAE at 6/30/97 for accident period 7/1/94–97 are limited to $25,000 per occurrence. The ratio of these to FTE personnel for 7/1/94–97 results in the raw annual loss and ALAE rate. The raw annual loss and ALAE rate is applied to the expected FTE personnel for 7/1/98–99 to obtain unadjusted A's. The unadjusted A's are adjusted so that the desired total of $832,000 of discounted expected losses and ALAE for 7/1/98–99 would be collected if all participants had credibilities of 1.00.

E is the discounted expected losses and ALAE for 7/1/98–99 allocated based on exposure. The E's are calculated in Table 4.6 by distributing the $832,000 in proportion to the expected FTE personnel for 7/1/98–99. This is what would be collected if all participants had credibility of 0.00. The credibilities (Z) are based on FTE personnel for 7/1/94–97 and the formula in Table 4.6. The minimum and maximum premiums are also calculated in Table 4.6.

National Council on Compensation Insurance (NCCI) Experience Rating Plan

The NCCI Experience Rating Plan has the unique characteristic of dividing the losses for each claim into a primary portion and an excess portion. The expected and actual primary portions are compared using one credibility factor, and the expected and actual excess portions are compared using another credibility factor. The credibility factor applied to the actual primary losses is higher than that applied to the actual excess losses. The formulae for splitting the expected and actual losses and determining the primary and excess credibility factors are discussed in more detail in Chapter 8. A brief summary of the plan is shown below.

The calculation to determine the experience modification is as follows:

$$M = \frac{A_p + B + (A_e \times w) + [(1 - w) \times E_e]}{E_p + B + (E_e \times w) + [(1 - w) \times E_e]}$$

where

M = Experience Modification Factor

A_p = Actual Primary Losses

E_p = Expected Primary Losses

A_e = Actual Excess Losses

E_e = Expected Excess Losses

B = Ballast Value

w = Excess Losses Weighting Factor

Note that the denominator of this formula equals

$$E + B$$

where

$$E = \text{Excess Losses}$$

This formula is also sometimes expressed as follows:

$$M = \frac{A_p + C + (A_e \times w)}{E_p + C + (E_e \times w)}$$

where C is a different stabilizing value than B. C is a function of w, B, and E_e.

Note that $M = 1 + CD$, where CD is the experience rating (credit)/debit.

The experience period is the three complete policy periods at the time the calculation is made. The actual losses are the reported losses evaluated at 18, 30, and 42 months from the beginning of the policy (accident) years.

The expected losses are the actual payroll by class for the experience period years multiplied by the retrospective manual expected loss rates by class for the prospective period. The retrospective expected loss rates reflect the losses expected to be reported at the 18-, 30-, and 42-month evaluations of the latest three available policy periods.

w and C (and, hence, B) result from the specific credibility formulae.

Composite Rating

Composite rating is an administrative tool to facilitate the rating of large, complex risks upon audit. Instead of rating different coverages using different exposure bases, all applicable coverages are rated using one, composite, exposure base.

"Company" refers to the insurance company using the composite rating plan. The references to company loss and ALAE development factors, factors from claims-made to occurrence and vice versa, loss and ALAE trend factors to current year, exposure trend factors, and expected loss and ALAE ratios reflect that different insurance companies may use different factors and ratios. ISO supplies advisory loss and ALAE development factors, factors from claims-made to occurrence and vice versa, loss and ALAE trend factors to current year, and exposure trend factors but does not supply advisory expected loss and ALAE ratios.

The composite rate to be applied to the composite exposure base is determined at the beginning of the policy period under consideration based on historical exposures. Estimated exposures are used if exact exposures are not available. This composite rate is used to determine the deposit premium based on the estimated composite exposure base and the final premium based on the audited composite exposure base. The composite rate may be based on manual rates to which the appropriate experience modification factors have been applied or on the entity's experience. The remainder of this section discusses the latter case, using the loss rating portion of the February, 1999 ISO Composite Rating Plan.

Table 4.7 shows the basic formulae for the ISO Composite Rating Plan loss-rated risks example. Eligibility for loss rating is

TABLE 4.7

PAGE 1

ISO COMPOSITE RATING PLAN LOSS-RATED RISKS EXAMPLE

Types of Losses Covered:	General Liability, Hospital Professional Liability, Commercial Automobile Liability, Commercial Automobile Physical Damage, Glass, and Crime
Experience Period:	Five years beginning between six and five and one-half years prior to the date the composite rate is to be effective. As few as three years, beginning between four and three and one-half years prior to the date the composite rate is to be effective, may be used if that is all that is available.
Experience:	For each type of loss, calculate by accident year and in total the adjusted projected ultimate losses and ALAE as follows:

Reported Limited Losses & ALAE At Latest Evaluation Date	×	Company Loss & ALAE Development Factor	×	Company Conversion Factor From Claims-Made to Occurrence	×	Company Loss & ALAE Trend Factors to Current Year	×	Factors to Reflect Other Changes

Adjusted Composite Exposure for Experience Period:	For the experience period, calculate the adjusted composite exposure as follows:

Composite Exposure for Exper. Period	×	Company Exposure Trend Factors	×	Factors to Reflect Other Changes

based on the reported losses and ALAE at the latest evaluation date, limited to various per occurrence limits, for the same period of time as the experience period to be used in the calculation. Different eligibility requirements apply for different combinations of coverage and limits. The premium charged is based solely on the entity's experience, adjusted for differences in coverage type (occurrence or claims-made year), trends in losses and ALAE and exposure, and other factors which may affect the appropri-

TABLE 4.7

PAGE 2

ISO COMPOSITE RATING PLAN LOSS-RATED RISKS EXAMPLE

Adjusted Premium for Experience Period:	For each type of loss, calculate the loss premium as follows:

<table>
<tr><td></td><td>Company</td><td></td></tr>
<tr><td>Adjusted</td><td>Conversion</td><td>Company</td></tr>
<tr><td>Projected</td><td>Factor</td><td>Expected</td></tr>
<tr><td>Ultimate   ×</td><td>From   ÷</td><td>Loss & ALAE</td></tr>
<tr><td>Losses</td><td>Occurrence to</td><td>Ratio</td></tr>
<tr><td>& ALAE</td><td>Claims-Made</td><td></td></tr>
</table>

Total these to get the total adjusted premium for the experience period.

Composite Rate:	The composite rate is calculated as follows:

<table>
<tr><td></td><td>Adjusted</td></tr>
<tr><td>Adjusted</td><td>Composite</td></tr>
<tr><td>Premium   ÷</td><td>Exposure</td></tr>
<tr><td>for Exper.</td><td>for Exper.</td></tr>
<tr><td>Period</td><td>Period</td></tr>
</table>

Final Premium:	The final premium is calculated as follows:

<table>
<tr><td>Audited</td><td></td></tr>
<tr><td>Exposure   ×</td><td>Composite</td></tr>
<tr><td>for Policy</td><td>Rate</td></tr>
<tr><td>Period</td><td></td></tr>
</table>

Notes: Various per occurrence limits apply to reported losses and ALAE.

For automobile physical damage, exclude ALAE and use unlimited losses.

The following are provided by ISO on an advisory basis:
• loss and ALAE development factors,
• conversion factors from occurrence to claims-made,
• loss & ALAE trend factors,
• exposure trend factors, and
• conversion factors from claims-made to occurrence.

ateness of the composite rate. The entity's experience has an implicit 100% credibility.

The composite rate is the adjusted premium for the experience period divided by the adjusted composite exposure base for the experience period. The adjusted premium for the experience period is the sum of the adjusted projected ultimate losses and ALAE, converted from occurrence to claims-made basis if appropriate, divided by the expected loss and ALAE ratio, for each type of loss. The adjusted composite exposure base for the experience period is the composite exposure base for the experience period, adjusted by exposure trend factors. The projected ultimate losses and ALAE are the reported losses and ALAE at latest evaluation date developed to ultimate, converted from claims-made to occurrence if appropriate, trended to the year for which the composite rate is being calculated, and adjusted for other changes if appropriate.

The reported losses and ALAE used in the calculation are subject to various per occurrence limits. The deposit premium is not subject to experience rating since it is based solely on the entity's experience under the limits used in the calculation. The final premium may be subject to retrospective rating. Both deposit and final premiums may be subject to schedule rating.

RETROSPECTIVE RATING

While experience rating and some forms of composite rating assume that the past, with appropriate adjustments, is predictive of the future, retrospective rating uses the experience during the period to determine the costs for the period. This approach makes costs based on retrospective rating plans more responsive to changes in experience and more subject to unusual fluctuations in experience than is the case with experience rating or composite rating plans. However, retrospective rating is very similar to prospective experience rating in many ways.

As with experience rating, actual losses, and sometimes ALAE, are compared to expected losses (and ALAE), although in this case they are both for the current period. To have an "apples to apples" comparison, several different experience and exposure combinations can be used, including the following:

- actual paid losses (and ALAE) at a particular date and the expected paid losses (and ALAE) at that date, both for the experience period;

- reported losses (and ALAE) at a particular date and the expected reported losses (and ALAE) at that date, both for the experience period; and

- projected ultimate losses (and ALAE) and the expected losses, both for the experience period.

These are the same as the first three combinations listed for experience rating.

As with experience rating, the experience component should be related to the exposure component and to the basis on which policies are written or funding occurs. If the costs to be allocated include ALAE, ALAE should be included with losses in the calculation.

The length of the retrospective rating period is usually one or three years. As with experience rating, the shorter the period, the more responsive the plan will be to changes that truly affect loss and ALAE experience, such as changes in the risk control program, and the more subject to unusual fluctuations in loss and ALAE experience. Conversely, a longer period will result in less responsiveness to changes and to unusual or catastrophic occurrences.

Retrospective rating plans may also limit losses (and ALAE) per occurrence and in aggregate to reduce the effect of unusual or catastrophic occurrences, as may experience rating plans.

If projected ultimate losses are to be used in the retrospective rating calculation, they can be developed in a number of ways similar to those used to develop projected ultimate losses used to determine manual rates. Projected ultimate losses are often based on paid or reported losses at a particular date.

The expected losses are a function of the current exposure. The exposure component should be related to the experience component, as detailed above. As for experience rating, expected losses are usually a product of an expected loss rate and the exposure base.

As is also true for experience rating, the exposure base used should reflect the underlying risk of loss and ALAE. It is not always possible to use the theoretically optimal exposure base. In practice, insurers and nontraditional risk financing mechanisms often use whatever exposure base insurers use in their premium calculations.

Credibility has the same function and is used in the same way for retrospective rating as for experience rating. Retrospective rating plans also may have minimum or maximum premium charges and need to be corrected for off-balance, as with experience rating plans.

Retrospective rating plans require a deposit premium at the beginning of the policy period. The deposit premium is an estimate of the ultimate premium for the policy period and may be determined using an experience rating plan. Retrospective premium adjustments are made periodically after the end of the policy period for a predetermined number of adjustments or until the insurer and insured agree to end the adjustments.

Two examples of retrospective rating plans are discussed below.

NCCI Retrospective Rating Plan

The NCCI Retrospective Rating Plan applies to workers compensation and employer's liability for eligible insureds. An insured must elect to participate in the plan, and the insurer must agree.

The basic formulae are shown in Table 4.8. Losses, some ALAE for workers compensation, and all ALAE for employer's liability are the subject of the allocation. The insured, with the insurer's agreement, may elect to include all ALAE with losses.

TABLE 4.8

PAGE 1

NCCI RETROSPECTIVE RATING PLAN EXAMPLE

Experience Period:	One or Three Years
Deposit Premium:	Experience-Rated Premium
Retrospective Adjustments:	Uses claim data at 18, 30, 42,... months from the beginning of a one-year policy period and claim data at 42, 54, 66,... months from the beginning of a three-year policy period.

Retrospective Rating Formula:

$$\text{Retro. Rating} = \left[\text{Basic Premium} + \text{Converted Losses} \right] \times \text{Tax Multiplier}$$

$$\text{Basic Premium} = \text{Standard Premium} \times \text{Premium Factor}$$

Standard Premium=Manual Premium modified for experience rating, loss constants, and minimum premium excluding premium discount, expense constants, and other items.

$$\text{Converted Losses} = \text{Reported Limited Losses at Eval. Date} \times \text{Loss Conversion Factor}$$

Reported limited losses include: interest on judgments; expenses incurred in obtaining third party recoveries, and ALAE for employer's liability claims; exclude some aircraft-related claims; and have limits on some accidents involving more than one person.

This changes some of the factors used in the retrospective rating calculation. The rating factors are based on first dollar losses. Some aircraft-related claims are excluded and the costs of some accidents involving more than one person are limited. All other costs are collected as a function of the losses, exposure (as represented by the standard premium), or, for taxes only, the retrospective premium before taxes. All policies are written on an occurrence basis.

TABLE 4.8

Page 2

NCCI Retrospective Rating Plan Example

Retrospective Rating Formula With Elective Premium Elements:

$$\begin{array}{l}\text{Retro.}\\\text{Premium}\end{array} = \left[\begin{array}{l}\text{Basic}\\\text{Premium}\end{array} + \begin{array}{l}\text{Converted}\\\text{Losses}\end{array} + \begin{array}{l}\text{Excess}\\\text{Loss}\\\text{Premium}\end{array} + \begin{array}{l}\text{Retro.}\\\text{Devel.}\\\text{Premium}\end{array}\right] \times \begin{array}{l}\text{Tax}\\\text{Multiplier}\end{array}$$

$$\begin{array}{l}\text{Excess}\\\text{Loss}\\\text{Premium}\end{array} = \begin{array}{l}\text{Standard}\\\text{Premium}\end{array} \times \begin{array}{l}\text{Excess}\\\text{Loss}\\\text{Premium}\\\text{Factor}\end{array} \times \begin{array}{l}\text{Loss}\\\text{Conversion}\\\text{Factor}\end{array}$$

$$\begin{array}{l}\text{Retro.}\\\text{Devel.}\\\text{Premium}\end{array} = \begin{array}{l}\text{Standard}\\\text{Premium}\end{array} \times \begin{array}{l}\text{Retro.}\\\text{Devel.}\\\text{Factor}\end{array} \times \begin{array}{l}\text{Loss}\\\text{Conversion}\\\text{Factor}\end{array}$$

Converted losses are calculated as above, but reported limited losses now also have a per accident limit.

Minimum and Maximum Retrospective Premiums:

$$\begin{array}{l}\text{Minimum}\\\text{Retro.}\\\text{Premium}\end{array} = \begin{array}{l}\text{Standard}\\\text{Premium}\end{array} \times \begin{array}{l}\text{Minimum}\\\text{Retro.}\\\text{Premium}\\\text{Factor}\end{array}$$

$$\begin{array}{l}\text{Maximum}\\\text{Retro.}\\\text{Premium}\end{array} = \begin{array}{l}\text{Standard}\\\text{Premium}\end{array} \times \begin{array}{l}\text{Maximum}\\\text{Retro.}\\\text{Premium}\\\text{Factor}\end{array}$$

Notes: The following are provided by the NCCI:
- Formula for Basic Premium Factor,
- Excess Loss Premium Factor,
- Retrospective Development Factor, and
- Tax Multiplier.

The following are selected by the insured in agreement with the insurer:
- Loss Conversion Factor,
- Minimum Retrospective Premium Factor, and
- Maximum Retrospective Premium Factor.

The deposit premium due at the beginning of the period is the experience-rated premium. Retrospective adjustments are made using audited payroll and claim data at 18, 30, 42,… months after the beginning of the policy period, if it is a one-year retrospective period, until insurer and insured agree there will be no more. For a three-year retrospective period, the claim data are evaluated at 42, 54, 66,... months after the beginning of the policy period.

There is no direct application of credibility in this plan. For losses under any applicable limits, the experience is given implicit credibility of 1.000. Losses over any applicable limits are given zero credibility, and money for them is collected based on exposure, as represented by standard premium and the applicable excess loss factor.

The plan allows for selection of minimum and maximum retrospective premiums. Costs above the maximum less those below the minimum are collected from or credited to the insured based on exposure, as represented by standard premium. Various minimum and maximum retrospective premium combinations are possible (including no maximum and minimum equals basic). The choice of minimum and maximum premiums affects the basic premium. The basic premium includes the expenses of the guaranteed cost premium and an insurance charge that reflects the minimum and maximum premiums, so that the average retrospective rating premium is expected to equal the guaranteed cost premium.

The general retrospective rating formula calculates retrospective premium as the sum of basic premium and converted losses, both multiplied by the tax multiplier. The basic premium, which is a function of the standard premium (exposure), provides for the following costs:

- insurer expenses such as acquiring and servicing the insured's account;

- risk control services, premium audit, and general administration of the insurance;

- a net charge for limiting the retrospective premium between the minimum and maximum retrospective premiums; and

- an allowance for the insurer's possible profit or for contingencies.

The converted losses are the reported losses, if any, at the evaluation date limited by the selected limit, and multiplied by the loss conversion factor. The loss conversion factor generally covers the ULAE and ALAE not included with the losses, although there is some flexibility in choice of the loss conversion factor. The tax multiplier covers licenses, fees, assessments, and taxes that the insurer must pay on the premium it collects.

There are two additional elements the insured may elect if the insurer agrees: a loss limitation resulting in an excess loss premium and a retrospective development premium. Both these premiums are subject to the tax multiplier. The retrospective rating formula with these elective premium elements is also shown in Table 4.8.

If the loss limitation is accepted, the reported limited losses at any evaluation are further limited to an agreed-upon amount per accident. The cost of losses above this amount and related ALAE and ULAE are collected through the excess loss premium. It is a function of standard premium (exposure).

The excess loss premium collects for losses and related expenses above the per accident limit; the basic premium collects for losses and related expenses above the maximum limit, some of which are the result of losses above the per accident limit. The excess loss premium factor is calculated to remove any double-counting of losses above the per occurrence limit.

Because reported limited losses tend to develop over time upwards to the ultimate limited losses, the first retrospective adjustment is likely to result in the insurer returning premium to the insured. Successive retrospective adjustments will probably result in most of, if not all of or more than, this amount being returned by the insured to the insurer. To smooth out these back-and-forth payments, some insureds opt to use the retrospective development premium, which attempts to offset this process. The retrospective development premium is a function of standard premium (exposure). It is used only for the first three retrospective adjustments and decreases over time.

Automobile Physical Damage Insurance Retrospective Allocation to Units by Single Entity

Table 4.9 illustrates the retrospective allocation of automobile physical damage insurance premium to units by a single entity. The coverage is actual cash value, written on an occurrence basis for one year.

The deposit premium collected from the units at the beginning of the period is based on the expected cost of insurance, allocated to each unit based on exposure as represented by the expected number of vehicles. There is no distinction for different types of vehicles. This is reasonable if each unit has the same expected cost per vehicle.

There is one retrospective adjustment, made using data at 18 months after the beginning of the policy year. Only one adjustment is made because automobile physical damage claims are reported and settled very quickly and the actual exposure is known shortly after the year ends. The actual cost of the insurance is allocated based on audited exposure (actual number of vehicles) and on reported losses and ALAE. These two allocations are weighted using credibility. Losses and ALAE are unlimited because the cost of any one occurrence is limited by the actual cash value of the vehicle in the accident plus any ALAE, which should be small. All experience is given a credibility of 0.25 regardless of the exposure size to make the plan easier for the unit managers to understand.

The plan has no minimum and maximum retrospective premiums. The plan has no off-balance correction, as none is needed because the credibility factors are the same for all units.

TABLE 4.9

AUTOMOBILE PHYSICAL DAMAGE INSURANCE RETROSPECTIVE ALLOCATION TO UNITS BY SINGLE ENTITY EXAMPLE

	Deposit Premium	
		Expected Cost of Insurance Allocated Based on Exposure
Unit (1)	Expected Number of Vehicle Years (2)	(3)
A	500	50,000
B	1,000	100,000
C	750	75,000
D	500	50,000
E	2,500	250,000
Total	5,250	525,000

Note: (3) is allocated based on (2). (3) is the deposit premium.

		Retrospective Premium				
Unit (1)	Actual Number of Vehicle Years (2)	Actual Cost of Insurance Allocated Based on Exposure (3)	Reported Losses & ALAE at 18 Months (4)	Actual Cost of Insurance Allocated Based on Experience (5)	Credibility (6)	Retro. Premium (7)
A	525	48,659	35,000	52,778	0.25	49,688
B	1,050	97,317	60,000	90,476	0.25	95,607
C	600	55,610	60,000	90,476	0.25	64,326
D	500	46,341	30,000	45,238	0.25	46,066
E	2,450	227,073	130,000	196,032	0.25	219,313
Total	5,125	475,000	315,000	475,000		475,000

Notes: (3) is allocated based on (2).

(5) is allocated based on (4).

$(7) = (3) \times [1.00 - (6)] + [(5) \times (6)]$.

DESIGNING AN INDIVIDUAL RISK RATING SYSTEM

To design an individual risk rating system such as those previously discussed, the following steps should be taken:

1. Determine the goals for the system.

2. Determine what is to be allocated.

3. Determine what kinds of exposure and experience data are available.

4. Decide whether the system will be prospective, retrospective, or a combination.

5. If the system is to be prospective, decide if it will be a schedule rating system, an experience rating system, a composite rating system, or a combination.

6. Design the schedule rating portion of the system.

7. Determine the experience component separately for each remaining portion of the system.

   a. Determine the type of experience to be used.

   b. Determine the experience period.

   c. Decide if there will be any per occurrence or aggregate limits.

8. Determine the exposure component separately for each remaining portion of the system.

   a. Determine the type of exposure to be used.

   b. Determine the exposure period.

9. Determine the credibility component separately for each remaining portion of the system.

10. Consider any other desired plan features such as a minimum or maximum premium charge.

11. Estimate if the system has an off-balance. If so, correct it if indicated.

12. Review the system and determine if it meets the stated goals and attributes of a good individual risk rating system. If not, make changes to the system.

13. Run sample calculations to see if the system functions as expected. If not, make any indicated changes.

14. Collect necessary data and put the system into use.

15. Review the plan at least every three years to be certain that it meets current needs. Needs can change or the situation may change so that the system no longer performs as expected. An example of the latter is that a per occurrence limit selected three years ago may no longer be reasonable because of economic and social inflation.

SUMMARY

Individual risk rating systems supplement the manual rates by modifying the group rates to reflect an individual entity's known or anticipated experience. They can be used by an insurer for all its insureds in one line of coverage, by risk sharing pools to allocate costs among a fixed group of members, or by an individual entity to allocate risk financing costs among its divisions.

Individual risk rating systems should be tailored to the needs of the specific situation in which they will be used. This produces systems with widely varying design, but all should follow the general principles and structures outlined in this chapter.

REFERENCES

Ammeter, H., "Experience Rating—A New Application of the Collective Theory of Risk," *ASTIN Bulletin*, 1962, 2:261–270.

Dorweiler, P., "A Survey of Risk Credibility in Experience Rating," *Proceedings of the Casualty Actuarial Society*, 1934, 21:1–25. Reprinted in *Proceedings of the Casualty Actuarial Society*, 58:90–114.

Fitzgibbon, W. J., Jr., "Reserving for Retrospective Returns," *Proceedings of the Casualty Actuarial Society*, 1965, 52:203–214. See also discussions by F. J. Hope, *Proceedings of the Casualty Actuarial Society*, 1966, 53:185–187, and D. R. Uhthoff, *Proceedings of the Casualty Actuarial Society*, 53:187–189.

Foster, R. B., "The Boiler and Machinery Premium Adjustment Rating Plan," *Proceedings of the Casualty Actuarial Society*, 1954, 41:135–160.

Gillam, W. R., "Retrospective Rating: Excess Loss Factors," *Proceedings of the Casualty Actuarial Society*, 1991, 78:1–42.

Gillam, W. R., "Parametrizing the Workers Compensation Experience Rating Plan," *Proceedings of the Casualty Actuarial Society*, 1992, 79:21–56.

Gillam, W. R., "Workers Compensation Experience Rating: What Every Actuary Should Know," *Proceedings of the Casualty Actuarial Society*, 1992, 79:215–254.

Gillam, W. R., Discussion of D. Skurnick's "The California Table L," *Proceedings of the Casualty Actuarial Society*, 1993, 80:353–365.

Gillam, W. R., Discussion by original author of "Workers Compensation Experience Rating: What Every Actuary Should Know," *Proceedings of the Casualty Actuarial Society*, 1997, 84:766–782.

Gillam, W. R. and J. R. Couret, "Retrospective Rating: 1997 Excess Loss Factors," *Proceedings of the Casualty Actuarial Society*, 1997, 84:450–481.

Harwayne, F., "Accident Limitations for Retrospective Rating," *Proceedings of the Casualty Actuarial Society*, 1976, 63:1–31. See also discussions by D. R. Bradley, *Proceedings of the Casualty Actuarial Society*, 1977, 64:93–95; R. J. Finger, *Proceedings of the Casualty Actuarial Society*, 1976, 63:32–33; and F. Taylor, and F. Lattanzio, *Proceedings of the Casualty Actuarial Society*, 1977, 64:96–102.

Hewitt, C. C., "Loss Ratio Distribution—A Model," *Proceedings of the Casualty Actuarial Society*, 1967, 64:70–88. See also discussion by C. A. Hachemeister, *Proceedings of the Casualty Actuarial Society*, 1967, 54:89–93.

Kulp, C. A., and Hall, J. W. "Individual-Insured Rating Plans," Chapter 22 in *Casualty Insurance*. New York: The Ronald Press Company, 1968.

Insurance Services Office, *Composite Rating Plan*, 1999.

Insurance Services Office, *Commercial General Liability Experience and Schedule Rating Plan*, 1997.

Insurance Services Office, *Retrospective Rating Plan*, 1998.

Lee, Y. S., "The Mathematics of Excess Loss Coverages and Retrospective Rating—A Graphical Approach," *Proceedings of the Casualty Actuarial Society*, 1988, 75:49–77.

Loimaranta, K., "On the Calculation of Variances and Credibilities by Experience Rating," *ASTIN Bulletin*, 1977, 9:203–207.

Mahler, H. C., Discussion of W. R. Gillam's "Parametrizing the Workers Compensation Experience Rating Plan," *Proceedings of the Casualty Actuarial Society*, 1993, 80:148–183.

Mahler, H. C., Discussion of W. R. Gillam's and J. R. Couret's "Retrospective Rating: 1997 Excess Loss Factors," *Proceedings of the Casualty Actuarial Society*, 1998, 85:316–344.

McClure, R. D., "An Actuarial Note on Experience Rating Nuclear Property Insurance," *Proceedings of the Casualty Actuarial Society*, 1972, 59:150–155. See also discussion by R. L. Hurley, *Proceedings of the Casualty Actuarial Society*, 1973, 60:105–111.

Meyers, G., "An Analysis of Retrospective Rating," *Proceedings of the Casualty Actuarial Society*, 1980, 67:110–143. See also discussion by M. E. Fiebrink, *Proceedings of the Casualty Actuarial Society*, 68:113–123, and J. F. Golz, *Discussion Paper Program*, 1980, 355–357.

National Council on Compensation Insurance, Revised 1999, *Experience Rating Plan*, 1984.

National Council on Compensation Insurance, Revised 1999, *Retrospective Rating Plan Manual for Workers' Compensation and Employers' Liability Insurance*, 1984.

Perryman, F. S., "Experience Rating Plan Credibilities," *Proceedings of the Casualty Actuarial Society*, 1937, 24:60–125. Reprinted in *Proceedings of the Casualty Actuarial Society*, 58:143–207.

Skurnick, D., "The California Table L," *Proceedings of the Casualty Actuarial Society*, 1974, 61:117–140. See also discussions by F. Harwayne, *Proceedings of the Casualty Actuarial Society*, 62:16–23 and R. Snader, *Proceedings of the Casualty Actuarial Society*, 62:24–26.

Snader, R. H., "Fundamentals of Individual Risk Rating and Related Topics," *Casualty Actuarial Society* Study Note, 1980.

Stafford, J. R. *Workers' Compensation and Employers' Liability Experience Rating*. Palatine, Illinois: J & M Publications, 1981.

Stafford, J. R. *Retrospective Rating*. Palatine, Illinois: J & M Publications, 1981.

Stanard, J. N., "Experience Rates as Estimators: A Simulation of Their Bias and Variance," *Discussion Paper Program*, 1980, 485–514. See also discussion by J. P. Robertson, *Discussion Paper Program*, 1980, 515–523.

Surety Association of America, *Experience Rating Plan Financial Institutions*, 1976.

Taylor, G. C., "Experience Rating with Credibility Adjustment of the Manual Premium," *ASTIN Bulletin*, 1974, 7:323–336.

Uhthoff, D. R., "The Compensation Experience Rating Plan a Current Review," *Proceedings of the Casualty Actuarial Society*, 1959, 46:285–299. See also discussions by R. M. Marshall, *Proceedings of the Casualty Actuarial Society*, 1960, 47:191–198; R. A. Johnson, *Proceedings of the Casualty Actuarial Society*, 1960, 47:198–200; and E. S. Allen, *Proceedings of the Casualty Actuarial Society*, 1960, 47:200–203.

Valerius, N., "Risk Distributions Underlying Insurance Charges in the Retrospective Rating Plan," *Proceedings of the Casualty Actuarial Society*, 1942, 29:96–121.

Webb, B. L., J. J. Launie, W. P. Rokes, and N. A. Baglini. *1981 Insurance Company Operations, 11(10)*. American Institute of Property and Liability Underwriters.

CHAPTER 5

LOSS RESERVING

RONALD F. WISER

REVISED AND UPDATED BY JO ELLEN COCKLEY AND
ANDREA GARDNER

INTRODUCTION

The financial condition of an insurance company can not be
adequately assessed without sound loss reserve estimates. A loss
reserve is a provision for an insurer's liability for claims. Loss
reserving is the term used to describe the actuarial process of
estimating the amount of an insurance company's liabilities for
loss and loss adjustment expenses. Loss reserving is a major
challenge to the casualty actuary because the estimation process
involves not only complex technical tasks but considerable judgment as well. No formula will provide the correct answer.

The intent of this chapter is to introduce the topic of loss
reserving. We will focus on the purpose, common definitions
and basic principles. Once a common framework has been introduced, we will explore the common techniques used by practicing actuaries in estimating loss reserves. A large number of
numerical examples will be provided to demonstrate the techniques.

The common methods assume that an insurance company's
historical experience can be used to project the future. But in
today's business environment, an insurance company's operations are frequently changing. The loss reserve analyst needs to
recognize and make adjustments for the changes. Based on experience and judgment, an actuary's opinion will always play a
key role in interpreting the results of the numerical techniques.
It is important for an actuary to learn about the organization and
understand the data before embarking on the task of estimating
the loss reserve.

Throughout this chapter, the term **claim** is defined to be the demand for payment by an insured or allegedly injured third party under the terms and conditions of an insurance policy (McClenahan, 1990). We will use the word "claim" and "loss" interchangeably. The term **insurer** represents any risk bearer for property and casualty exposures whether an insurance company, a self-insured entity, a pool or other form of organization.

ACCOUNTING CONCEPTS

To understand the importance of establishing a sound loss reserve estimate, it is helpful to understand the basic accounting principles that apply to insurers. A general reference on accounting principles is Davidson, et al. (1994). Once the basic accounting principles are understood, it will be clearly shown that the loss reserve estimate has a significant impact on the financial strength and stability of an insurance company.

We will focus on two important accounting statements. The balance sheet shows the financial position of a firm. The income statement documents the financial performance of the firm.

The Balance Sheet

The balance sheet reports on the financial position of the firm at a specific point in time. It shows the levels of assets and liabilities, and the status of the shareholders' equity, or surplus, for the insurer. The reporting follows the simple equation:

$$\text{Assets} = \text{Liabilities} + \text{Owners' Equity}$$

An asset is any economic resource that is held by the firm. An asset could be cash, stocks, bonds, real estate, or agents' receivables, for example.

Liabilities are claims on the resources of the firm, to satisfy obligations of the firm. Liabilities could be mortgages, bank debt, bonds issued, premiums received from clients but not yet earned, or benefits payable on behalf of clients due to contractual obligations, for example. Loss and loss expense liabilities are frequently the largest liabilities of an insurer.

Owners' equity is the owners' claim on the assets of the firm. The owners' claim is always subordinate to all other liabilities of the firm. It is actually the balancing item in the equation above. Owners' equity is generally called the surplus of the insurer. For stock companies, the stockholders are the owners, but for mutual insurers, the policyholders are the owners and the surplus belongs to them.

When liabilities exceed assets, the value of the owners' equity is negative, and the firm is insolvent. Another way to write the equation of financial position is then given by:

$$\text{Owners' Equity} = \text{Assets} - \text{Liabilities}$$

The Income Statement

The income statement measures changes in owners' equity during a stated period of time. Owners' equity can be subdivided into the capital contributed by the owners and any retained earnings of the firm from past periods. Thus,

$$\text{Owners' Equity} = \text{Contributed Capital} + \text{Retained Earnings}$$

The income statement measures the firm's performance in the stated period as follows:

$$\text{Income} = \text{Revenue} - \text{Expense}$$

Revenue measures the inflow of assets from providing products or services. Expense measures the outflow of assets that are consumed in providing the firm's products or services.

Income may be either used to increase owners' equity in the firm (i.e., increase retained earnings) or distributed to owners as dividends. This can be written as

$$\text{Income} = \text{Change in Retained Earnings} + \text{Dividends to Owners}$$

This series of equations then defines the relationship between the balance sheet and the income statement. This relationship can be obtained by chaining together the basic accounting equations.

Income = Change in Retained Earnings + Dividends to Owners

but,

Retained Earnings = Owners' Equity – Contributed Capital;

and,

Owners' Equity = Assets – Liabilities.

Thus,

Retained Earnings = Assets – Liabilities – Contributed Capital;

and,

Income = Change in Assets – Change in Liabilities

– Change in Contributed Capital

+ Dividends to Owners.

This formula demonstrates the relationship between the balance sheet and the income statement of a firm. In particular, note that any change in a liability account, such as loss reserves, has a direct impact on insurer's income.

Accrual Accounting

The balance sheet and the income statement of an insurance company are prepared on an accrual basis. A cash basis of accounting simply recognizes revenues when they are received and reports expenses when they are made. The accrual basis does a better job of matching revenues with their associated expenses (Davidson et al., 80–84). Under the accrual basis, revenues are recognized when earned. Costs are reported as expenses in the same period as the revenues giving rise to those costs are recognized. The main sources of an insurer's revenue are earned premium, rather than written premium, and the investment income earned on the assets it holds.

Similarly, policyholder benefits are expenses incurred by the firm, which must be matched to the revenues earned on the policies. It would clearly be inappropriate to count only paid losses and paid loss adjustment expense as expenses. The expenses incurred for policy benefits can be computed through use of the "loss reserve" liability account. The formula is:

Incurred Losses = Paid Losses + Ending Claim Liability

– Beginning Claim Liability

CLAIM DEPARTMENT RESERVING

Before we discuss loss reserving from an actuarial perspective, we will look at the function of a claim department. In its simplest form, an insurance company sells a promise to settle claims that occur from a covered loss. An insurance company incurs a loss liability as soon as the insured incident occurs whether or not the company has even received notice of a loss. A loss liability needs to be established from the time of occurrence to final settlement. For the precise accounting definition of a liability, refer to Appendix A.

After a loss has occurred, an insurance company will receive a report or notice of the claim. Sometimes the delay between the occurrence and the report may be very short such as when a house burns down or a car accident happens. At other times, the delay may be very long. For example, asbestos harmed people many years before any claims were reported to the insurers of the product's manufacturers.

Once a claim has been reported, a claim adjuster establishes an estimate of the settlement amount after taking the facts of the case into consideration. Case reserves are the adjuster's best estimate of the remaining dollars that will eventually be paid on the claim. Taken together, paid loss and case reserves equal the incurred loss value of the claim.

During the process of adjustment, a claims adjuster may revise the case reserve estimate either up or down and make partial payments on the claim. These revisions reflect new information that has been gathered during investigation and settlement of a claim. The term **loss development** is used to describe the changes that take place in the value of a claim over time. Once the claim is settled and no further payments are expected, the claim is closed.

Loss adjustment expenses are also incurred during this process. These expenses include the cost of the claims adjuster and other expenses related to the defense and settlement of a claim. Some claims produce very little loss adjustment expense. For example, the house fire claim may be resolved with a couple of phone calls. Other claims, such as the asbestos example, may revolve around a complex series of issues and involve many interested parties. Frequently, claims of this sort may involve litigation. Attorney's fees and other defense costs may produce very high loss adjustment expenses.

Even after a claim is closed, it is possible for the claim to be reopened if new facts come to light. Also, once an insurer has satisfied its obligation to the policyholder, the company may pursue recoveries from third parties for some part of the indemnity amount paid to the policyholder. This right of recovery is called **subrogation**. An example of subrogation involves the payment of a collision claim by an insurer. If a third party was responsible for the damage, the insurer making the collision coverage payment to its insured has the right to recover the amount of damages from the responsible party.

In addition to subrogation situations, the payment of first party benefits may be accompanied by the insurer's taking of title to the damaged property. This property can often be disposed of for a partial recovery of the amount paid to the policyholder for the loss, and is called **salvage**. An example of a common salvage situation involves an automobile accident in which the insured's vehicle is a total loss. The insurer reimburses the insured for the value of the vehicle and takes title to the vehicle. The auto is then disposed of for any scrap value and the proceeds reduce the amount of loss. Note that both salvage and subrogation serve to reduce the insurer's net payout.

The Claims Inventory

At any point in time, an insurer will have many claims at various stages of development in its claim inventory. A look at the structure of a typical loss reserve case inventory will aid in understanding the processes at work when we observe loss development. For the moment, we'll consider loss development as simply the change in the value of a loss reserve inventory during a specified period of time.

The accompanying table on Case Reserve Activity (see page 204) tracks the types of activity that may occur in a loss reserve inventory during any one time period. Initially, there are 1,015 claims that are open and in the process of adjustment by the insurer's claim department. Losses will enter either as new claims (line 2), reopened claims (line 3), or zero reserves (line 4). A reopened claim is one that has previously been closed, but requires a pending claim file, because further adjusting activity is needed. This must be distinguished from a closed claim that simply requires an additional payment after closure, i.e., a prematurely closed claim (included in line 15). Such a claim is not reopened because no further adjusting effort is expected to be necessary after the single payment.

A particular type of new claim that should be distinguished from others is the precautionary reserve claim or zero reserve claim. This is used to establish a file as a means of monitoring a potential liability situation. No dollar value, or a nominal amount, is put up on the claim file because there is not yet a strong enough fact situation that a liability of the company exists. However, there is potential for liability and the situation must be monitored by the company. The use of these precautionary files is most often found on excess or reinsurance losses. When the primary carrier is another company, there may be very little information in the file initially established, other than the mandatory notice required by the excess policy wording.

Case Reserve Activity

	Counts	Amounts
1. Beginning Outstanding	1,015	$5,673,633
2. New Reserves	80	270,850
3. Reopened Reserves	29	84,472
4. Zero Reserves	2	0
5. Reserve Increases	28	163,995
6. Subtotal: Increases	139	$ 519,317
(2 + 3 + 4 + 5)		
7. Reserve Decreases	81	(57,433)
8. Closed with Payment	30	(713,281)
9. Closed without Payment	71	(147,291)
10. Subtotal: Decreases	182	($ 918,005)
(7 + 8 + 9)		
11. Total Reserve Change	10	($ 398,688)
(Counts 2 + 3 + 4 − 8 − 9)		
(Amounts: 6 + 10)		
12. Final Payments	30	793,180
13. Partial payments	82	60,514
14. Fast Track Payments	8	29,281
15. All Other	51	32,943
16. Total Payments	171	$ 915,918
(12 + 13 + 14 + 15)		
17. Salvage/Subrogation	28	(3,269)
18. Incurred Loss		513,961
(11 + 16 + 17)		
19. Ending Outstanding	1,025	$5,274,945
(1 + 11)		

Many companies also use a "fast track" claim category (line 14). This is simply a claim that is paid without a claim file ever being established. This procedure is often used on small property claims, such as auto physical damage or homeowners.

For reserve analysis purposes, we record only the financial changes that result from the claim adjusters' activities.

Referring to the Case Reserve Activity chart on page 204, we have categorized the types of financial actions we are interested in recording. Reserve increases (line 5) or decreases (line 7) are changes in open claim file valuations, and the file remains open after the change in valuation. These changes in reserve valuation may be accompanied by a loss or expense payment.

Incurred loss is the measure used to calculate the insurance company's liability.

$$\text{Incurred Loss} = \text{Paid Loss} + \text{Ending Loss Reserve}$$

$$- \text{Beginning Loss Reserve}$$

Partial payments may be split into payments with and without incurred effect for the file. A payment may have no incurred effect if the remaining reserve is reduced by the amount of the payment. Thus if the claim adjuster reduces the case reserve by the amount of payment, there is no incurred loss effect. Often, automated claim systems will reduce the case reserve by the amount of the payment. This requires the adjuster to take specific reserve action only if the intent is to change the total valuation of the claim file.

One of the most important statistics to monitor for any claim inventory is the number of claim closings (lines 8 and 9). Note the distinction between claims closed without payment and those closed with some payment of loss or expense. In terms of simple monitoring of reserve activity, the rate of claim closings should be carefully watched. Often, a change in the closing rate can lead the analyst to discover an important operational change in claims administration.

The incurred effect of reserve closings can be calculated from the same formula:

$$\text{Incurred Loss} = \text{Paid Loss} - \text{Beginning Reserve}$$

Note that the ending reserve on a closed claim is zero, hence the formula simplifies as above. For our example, for the 101 closing payments (30 closed with payment, 71 without payment) we can calculate that:

$$\text{Incurred Loss} = \$793{,}180 - \$713{,}281 - \$147{,}291$$

$$\text{Incurred Loss} = (\$67{,}392)$$

Note that for this period, there is actually a savings on claims closed. This can often be the case, especially for lines of business that generate a high proportion of claims closed with no payment. If we only consider claims that close with payment, there is no savings:

$$\text{Incurred Loss} = \$793{,}180 - \$713{,}281 = \$79{,}899$$

In addition to claim payments associated with reserve files, we also can have payments to which no currently open files are attached. Fast Track payments have already been mentioned. There are also other miscellaneous payments, including payments on files already closed.

Note that almost all of the 82 partial claim payments on line 13 are associated with reserve decreases on line 7. This may be a result of the automatic decrease of case reserves to offset the amount of partial payments.

Note how salvage and subrogation serve to reduce the insurer's net payout. Then the total amount paid in the period is

$$\text{Paid loss} = \$915{,}918 - \$3{,}269 = \$912{,}649$$

A more theoretical approach to loss development can be found in Appendix B: An Actuarial Model of Loss Development.

A loss reserving analyst should be familiar with how the claim department of their organization functions. Any changes in how the department operates, such as reorganization, changes in claim handling practices or defense strategies, could affect the claim reserve inventory and loss development. Loss reserve estimates should reflect the impact of such changes. Understanding what a claim adjuster does and frequent communication with the claim department will aid the actuary in this task.

LOSS RESERVE DEFINITIONS

Before we discuss how to estimate loss reserves, we need to define some basic loss reserve terminology. First, a **total loss reserve** consists of 5 elements:

1. Case reserves assigned to specific claims,

2. A provision for future development on known claims,

3. A provision for claims that re-open after they have been closed,

4. A provision for claims that have occurred but have not yet been reported to the insurer, and

5. A provision for claims that have been reported to the insurer but have not yet been recorded.

A loss reserve can be divided into two categories: known claims vs. unknown claims. The reserve for **known claims** represents the amount that will be required for future payments of claims that have already been reported to the insurer (the sum of (1), (2), (3)). This amount includes the case reserves, the aggregate of the individual estimates made by the adjusters. Some case reserves may be set by formula.

The reserve for **unknown claims** is the amount for claims that have been incurred but not reported to the insurer. The reserve for unknown claims is commonly called an IBNR reserve. Often, it is not possible to distinguish between claims in the last two categories. These "pure" IBNR claims (4) and the claims in transit (5) are frequently combined together and called IBNR. This is the strict definition of IBNR, but in practice, future development on known claims, a provision for re-open claims, unreported claims and unrecorded claims are often combined together and called IBNR.

Over time, losses develop and the IBNR claims emerge. One of the reasons loss reserves need to be estimated is due to the delay between when a loss occurs, when it is reported to an insurer, and when it is finally settled. Therefore, dates become very important in the data organization and loss reserve estimation process. The list below defines the five key dates.

1. **Accident Date**—the date on which the loss occurred.

2. **Report Date**—the date on which the loss is first reported to an insurer.

3. **Recorded Date**—the date on which the loss is first recorded in the insurer's statistical information.

4. **Accounting Date**—the date used to define the group of claims to be included in the liability estimate. A loss reserve is an estimate of the liability for unpaid claims as of a given date, called the accounting date. An accounting date may be any date and is generally a date for which a financial statement is prepared such as a month end, quarter end or year end.

5. **Valuation Date**—the date as of which the evaluation of the loss liability is made. The valuation date defines the point in time through which all transactions are to be included for the group of claims. The valuation date can be before, after or the same as the accounting date.

Since the loss reserve liability is always an estimate, and the amount of the estimate will change as of successive valuation dates, we should establish some conventional terminology to discuss the results of the loss reserve process.

The **required loss reserve** as of a given accounting date is the amount that must ultimately be paid to settle all claim liabilities. The value of the required loss reserve can only be known when all claims have been finally settled. Thus, the required loss reserve as of a given accounting date is a fixed number that does not change at different valuation dates. However, the value of the required loss reserve is generally unknown for an extremely long period of time.

The **indicated loss reserve** is the result of the actuarial analysis of a reserve inventory as of a given accounting date conducted as of a certain valuation date. This indicated loss reserve is the analyst's opinion of the amount of the required loss reserve. This estimate will change with successive valuation dates and will converge to the required loss reserve as the time between valuation date and the accounting date of the inventory increases.

The **carried loss reserve** is the amount of unpaid claim liability shown on external or internal financial statements.

The **loss reserve margin** is the difference between the carried reserve and the required reserve. Since the required reserve is an unknown quantity we only have an indicated margin. The indicated loss reserve margin is defined to be the carried loss reserve minus the indicated loss reserve. One should not generally expect the margin to be zero, since for any subset of an entity's business it is unlikely that the carried loss reserve will be identical to either the indicated or required loss reserve.

LOSS RESERVING PRINCIPLES

The Casualty Actuarial Society (CAS) has published a statement of principles regarding property and casualty loss and loss adjustment expense reserves. There are four basic principles. The first principle says that an actuarially sound loss reserve "for a defined group of claims as of a given valuation date is a provision, based on estimates derived from reasonable assumptions and appropriate actuarial methods, for the unpaid amount required to settle all claims, whether reported or not, for which liability exists on a particular accounting date."

The second principle says an actuarially sound loss adjustment expense reserve has the same characteristics except that the liability is for "the unpaid amount required to investigate, defend and effect the settlement of all claims."

The third principle states that since there is inherent uncertainty in the estimation process, a range of reserves can be actuarially sound. The final principle states that the "most appropriate reserve within a range of actuarially sound estimates depends on both the relative likelihood of estimates within the range and the financial reporting context in which the reserve will be presented."

THE LOSS RESERVING PROCESS

Now that we have defined the basic loss reserving terminology and the key loss reserving principles, we are ready to begin the loss reserving process. The loss reserve estimation process can only be properly applied to grouped data. We will be estimating loss reserves in the aggregate as opposed to the claim adjusters' perspective that tends to be on an individual claim basis.

Data Availability

The availability of proper data is essential to the loss reserving process. The actuary is responsible for informing management of the need for sufficiently detailed and quality data to obtain reliable reserve estimates.

Data must be presented that clearly displays the development of losses. One of the most common ways to organize the data is in a loss development triangle. Each row in the triangle represents a given accident year. The data in each row represents a fixed group of claims. The columns keep track of the losses at subsequent evaluations for an individual accident year. Each column represents the age of the accident year. The usual convention is that an accident year is age 12 months at the end of the last day of the accident year.

Groupings other than accident year can be used. In descending order of preference, the rows could represent report year, policy year, or underwriting year (Berquist and Sherman). The rows could also represent quarterly, monthly, or other fixed grouping of data. The columns are typically shown in annual intervals, but quarterly intervals are also common.

To show how a loss development triangle is constructed, we will do an example with paid losses. Suppose the paid losses during calendar year 2000 for a line of business totaled $71,273,000. This information can be readily obtained from an accounting exhibit. It would be useful to know how that amount is split by accident year. In this example, suppose we knew that $11,346,000 of the paid losses came from claims that had accident dates during 2000. Similarly, $16,567,000 of the calendar year 2000 payments were from losses with 1999 dates of loss. By date of loss occurrence, we would find:

	(000 omitted)
Paid on 2000 losses:	$11,346
Paid on 1999 losses:	16,567
Paid on 1998 losses:	19,935
Paid on 1997 losses:	11,956
Paid on 1996 losses:	5,985
Paid on 1995 losses:	3,211
Paid on 1994 losses:	2,274
Total paid loss in 2000	$71,274

Since we now know that \$11,346,000 was paid on 2000 losses during the year 2000, we would like to know the comparable amount paid on 1999 losses during 1999. We can find that a total of \$73,972,000 was paid in 1999 on this line of business, and that \$17,001,000 is for losses that occurred during 1999. Further, the full 1999 paid amount can be split into amounts (in thousands) paid on accidents from different years as was done for 2000 payments:

	(000 omitted)
Paid on 1999 losses:	\$17,001
Paid on 1998 losses:	22,343
Paid on 1997 losses:	13,036
Paid on 1996 losses:	9,098
Paid on 1995 losses:	6,235
Paid on 1994 losses:	4,693
Paid on 1993 losses:	1,566
Total paid loss in 1999	\$73,972

Comparison of these amounts by loss year for several calendar years would quickly become awkward, which is why we construct loss development triangles that facilitate the comparisons we want to make between the accident year components of calendar year paid amounts.

For instance, the incremental payments in thousands, on accident years 1994 through 2000 can be displayed as follows:

Accident Year	Age in months:						
	12	24	36	48	60	72	84
1994	22,603	17,461	14,237	9,813	7,143	4,693	2,274
1995	22,054	21,916	14,767	13,104	6,235	3,211	
1996	20,166	18,981	12,172	9,098	5,985		
1997	19,297	18,058	13,036	11,956			
1998	20,555	22,343	19,935				
1999	17,001	16,567					
2000	11,346						

Now we see that the loss payments of the 2000 calendar year appear on the lowest diagonal of the triangle. Similarly, the 1999 calendar year payments appear on the second lowest diagonal. This data organization greatly facilitates comparison of the development history experienced by an accident year.

While this arrangement shows the amount paid in each 12-month period, it is often convenient to accumulate the payments on a given loss year. This would result in the following triangle of cumulative loss payments:

Accident Year	12	24	36	48	60	72	84
1994	22,603	40,064	54,301	64,114	71,257	75,950	78,224
1995	22,054	43,970	58,737	71,841	78,076	81,287	
1996	20,166	39,147	51,319	60,417	66,402		
1997	19,297	37,355	50,391	62,347			
1998	20,555	42,898	62,832				
1999	17,001	33,568					
2000	11,346						

Age in months:

The cumulative paid loss development triangle shows how the losses in each accident year are developing to their ultimate value. The number of years of development should be great enough so that further developments will be negligible (Berquist and Sherman). A paid loss triangle is only one of several types of triangles that can be constructed. We will discuss other types in the Exploratory Data Analysis section.

Reserve Estimation Strategy

The overall approach to a reserve valuation problem can be broken into four phases:

1. **Exploratory analysis of the data** to identify its key characteristics and possible anomalies. Balancing of data to other verified sources should be undertaken at this point.

2. Application of appropriate **reserve estimation techniques**.

3. **Evaluation** of the conflicting results of the various reserve methods used, with an attempt to reconcile or explain the different outcomes. At this point the proposed reserving ultimate amounts are evaluated in contexts outside their original frame of analysis.

4. **Monitor** projections of reserve development over subsequent calendar periods. Deviations of actual development from projected development of counts or amounts are one of the most useful diagnostic tools in evaluating accuracy of reserve estimates.

PHASE 1: EXPLORATORY DATA ANALYSIS

Considerations

Exploring the data begins by understanding the trends and changes affecting the database. Understanding the data is a prerequisite to estimating sound loss reserves. This exploration will help the analyst select appropriate loss reserving methods and interpret the results of the methods.

Knowledge of the business being evaluated is a key consideration. Changes in the classes of business written or geographical focus may affect the data. Changes in policy provisions such as policy limits and deductibles will impact observed development patterns. Reinsurance purchased by the insurance company will impact net loss development patterns. Changes in the reinsurance limits and attachment points can alter future net development.

Changes that occur in the external environment may impact the data. The legal/social environment can change abruptly. This is a particular concern if the data is concentrated in one state. For example, the introduction of no-fault auto insurance clearly changes the business environment. Changes in the economic environment, such as the inflation rate, may also cause changes in the database.

Operational changes within the company can affect the data over time. The installation of a new computer system may impact the time it takes to process a loss payment. Claims adjusting practices may change because of office consolidation or a new claim management team.

How the data is divided into groups for review is essential if meaningful loss reserve estimates are going to be produced. In order to draw valid conclusions about future loss development, the groups should be homogeneous i.e., display similar characteristics. In loss reserving, the focus is on grouping data that displays similar:

1. loss emergence patterns—the length of time between loss occurrence and report, and

2. loss settlement patterns—the length of time between the loss report and settlement.

Some examples of common divisions include separating data by line of business, coverage type (property or liability), and policy limits. The groupings should be made of business with similar frequency and severity characteristics. Business that produces a high frequency, low severity of losses could mask the development of a low frequency, high severity line.

Actuaries use the term credibility to mean the measure of predictive value given to a block of data. Increasing the homogeneity of the block of data or increasing the volume of data in the block increases credibility. The two means of increasing credibility are conflicting goals and the analyst needs to strike an appropriate balance between the two. If the volume of data is too small to produce meaningful loss development patterns, use of industry development patterns may be necessary.

Issues of credibility and homogeneity for loss reserving should most often be thought of in terms of their impact on loss development patterns. Credibility and homogeneity of data from even the same line of business is greatly enhanced if the policy limits or layers of loss are very similar. For example, loss development data on General Liability excess reinsurance may not be very stable or useful if it is not grouped by underlying limits and layer widths. Similarly, history on a book of basic limits auto liability business is of little value in evaluating a new book with $1 million limits. Aggregate limits of liability or even large losses that are capped at policy limits are very important facts for the loss reserve analyst to take into account in the analysis.

There are many other factors that an analyst should take into consideration when deciding how to group the data. A thorough discussion of the factors can be found in the *CAS Statement of Principles Regarding Property and Casualty Loss and Loss Adjustment Expense Reserves.*

Data Analysis

Before the analyst begins to project immature loss data to ultimate loss estimates, it is important to review the data. The objective of this review is to understand the data in terms of:

1. rate of development,

2. smoothness of development,

3. presence of large losses, and

4. volume of data.

Review of the data will allow the analyst to form conclusions about:

1. appropriate projection methodologies,

2. anomalies in the data, and

3. appropriate questions to ask management concerning issues that manifest themselves in the data, that will further the analyst's understanding of the book of business that generated the data.

Some of the more common data displays that should be reviewed by the loss reserve analyst are discussed here.

Cumulative Incurred Losses: An incurred loss triangle contains the history of combined paid losses and case reserves. The example below is an "accident year triangle," a history of losses incurred organized with losses from the same year of loss in the same row. A review of this incurred loss triangle points to a fluctuating level of losses since 1994. Note that the dip in losses reported on the 1997 accident year as of 12 months did not result in less loss reported through 48 months of development. This should alert the analyst to search for possible processing slowdowns at year-end 1997, or major fluctuations in case reserve adequacy. In light of this, the analyst must consider how to interpret the low level of 2000 accident year incurred losses. Clearly, some measure of exposure is called for—whether earned exposures, earned premiums, or even policies in force. This will help determine whether a level of ultimate incurred losses proportional to the low reported 2000 incurred is reasonable. The situation with loss processing as well as case reserve adequacy needs to be probed in order to decide on the proper 2000 accident year reserve.

Accident Year	\multicolumn{7}{c}{Age in months:}						
	12	24	36	48	60	72	84
1994	58,641	74,804	77,323	77,890	80,728	82,280	82,372
1995	63,732	79,512	83,680	85,366	88,152	87,413	
1996	51,779	68,175	69,802	69,694	70,041		
1997	40,143	67,978	75,144	77,947			
1998	55,665	80,296	87,961				
1999	43,401	57,547					
2000	28,800						

Cumulative Paid Losses: A paid loss triangle contains the history of paid losses. Small variations in paid loss as of 12 months can be seen to be indicative of very large differences in ultimate accident year losses. The low reported incurred on 1997 accident year is also paralleled by a lower paid loss amount on the 1997 accident year. The 20% drop from 1996 to 1997 incurred losses seen above produces only a 5% drop in paid claims from 1996 to 1997 accident years, as of the initial reporting. The large drop in payments in accident year 2000 indicates a much more severe change in claims environment than the drop of 5% in 1997. The analyst would look for evidence of lower 2000 exposure levels to explain the paid losses.

Accident Year	Age in months: 12	24	36	48	60	72	84
1994	22,603	40,064	54,301	64,114	71,257	75,950	78,224
1995	22,054	43,970	58,737	71,841	78,076	81,287	
1996	20,166	39,147	51,319	60,417	66,402		
1997	19,297	37,355	50,391	62,347			
1998	20,555	42,898	62,832				
1999	17,001	33,568					
2000	11,346						

Incremental Incurred Losses: This triangle shows the incremental incurred losses in each successive period. It is useful for the analyst to gauge the reasonability of yearly aggregate loss accumulations on an accident year. Note the "speedup" of incurred losses in 12 to 24-months aging of the 1997 accident year (calendar year 1998), when incurred losses increased $27,835,000. It appears that the second annual development on the 1998 accident year of $24,632,000 is also unusually large when compared to accident years 1996 and prior. Thus, the analyst must suspect that processing problems were also apparent in the organization at year-end 1998. Questions to key managers in Claims and Underwriting should help the analyst gather information to confirm this suspicion.

Accident			Age in months:				
Year	12	24	36	48	60	72	84
1994	58,641	16,163	2,519	567	2,838	1,552	92
1995	63,732	5,779	4,168	1,686	2,786	−739	
1996	51,779	16,396	1,627	−107	347		
1997	40,143	27,835	7,166	2,803			
1998	55,665	24,632	7,665				
1999	43,401	14,147					
2000	28,800						

Incremental Paid Losses: This triangle shows the incremental paid losses in each successive 12-month period. We see immediately that payments during the second annual development period on an accident year are roughly equal to the amount paid in the first annual development period. Thus, we form an expectation that any reasonable projected development to ultimate must yield at least $10–12 million projected paid losses during the 12 to 24-month development on the 2000 accident year.

Accident			Age in months:				
Year	12	24	36	48	60	72	84
1994	22,603	17,461	14,237	9,813	7,143	4,693	2,274
1995	22,054	21,916	14,767	13,104	6,235	3,211	
1996	20,166	18,981	12,172	9,098	5,985		
1997	19,297	18,058	13,036	11,956			
1998	20,555	22,343	19,935				
1999	17,001	16,567					
2000	11,346						

Paid Loss as a Percent of Incurred Loss: This triangle divides paid losses at each development age by reported losses as of the same development age. This statistic tests the consistency of the development of paid and reported losses. It also may give warning of case reserve inadequacies. This statistic clearly flags the 1997 accident year as being inconsistent with history. The high ratio at age 12 indicates that the case reserve portion of the 1997 accident year incurred losses at that age was much weaker than it was historically. One benefit of this statistic is that it appears concurrent with the analysis, and does not rely on hindsight. The crucial 2000 accident year looks normal with regard to case reserves.

Accident	Age in months:						
Year	12	24	36	48	60	72	84
1994	38.5%	53.6%	70.2%	82.3%	88.3%	92.3%	95.0%
1995	34.6%	55.3%	70.2%	84.2%	88.6%	93.0%	
1996	38.9%	57.4%	73.5%	86.7%	94.8%		
1997	48.1%	55.0%	67.1%	80.0%			
1998	36.9%	53.4%	71.4%				
1999	39.2%	58.3%					
2000	39.4%						

Reported Claim Counts: Claim count history is extremely important in any loss reserve analysis. This triangle simply displays all reported claims by development period. We can conclude that for this particular line of business, essentially all claims are reported within 24 months. The 2000 accident year does have a much lower level of reported claims than prior accident years. A radical change in volume, such as 2000 accident year displays, should alert us to possible changes in business mix, reporting patterns or exposures.

Accident	Age in months:						
Year	12	24	36	48	60	72	84
1994	32,751	41,201	41,618	41,755	41,773	41,774	41,774
1995	33,736	39,528	39,926	40,044	40,072	40,072	
1996	27,067	32,740	33,084	33,183	33,209		
1997	24,928	29,796	30,074	30,169			
1998	25,229	31,930	32,281				
1999	17,632	21,801					
2000	15,609						

Closed with Payment Claim Counts: Here, the cumulative number of claims closed with payment are displayed. Note that this does not include all closed claims, as many claims may be closed with no payment. The possible processing problem at the end of 1997 and 1998 also appears in this statistic, which again suggests the need to understand changes in company operations that may have occurred during 1997–1998. The closing counts for 1999 and 2000 support the hypothesis of reduced exposures.

Accident Year	Age in months: 12	24	36	48	60	72	84
1994	23,355	31,940	33,288	33,860	34,091	34,247	34,294
1995	22,662	30,294	31,588	32,129	32,323	32,433	
1996	18,951	25,197	26,214	26,582	26,777		
1997	16,631	22,894	23,806	24,229			
1998	17,381	24,581	25,765				
1999	12,666	16,669					
2000	10,592						

Closed with No Payment Claim Counts: Claims may also be closed without any payment. The claims closed with no payment could easily account for over half or more of all claims reported for some lines such as medical malpractice. In this case, the display does not show any unusual patterns.

Accident Year	Age in months: 12	24	36	48	60	72	84
1994	2,646	6,285	6,935	7,240	7,353	7,393	7,412
1995	3,142	6,529	7,053	7,308	7,411	7,465	
1996	2,752	5,366	5,840	6,050	6,185		
1997	2,343	4,744	5,132	5,400			
1998	2,238	4,666	5,375				
1999	1,749	3,458					
2000	1,246						

Closed Claims as Percent of Reported Claims: Total closed claims can be related to claims reported. This is a monitor on closing activities. We can see a very steady performance of this ratio as of 12 and 24 months of development for accident years 1994 to 1999. Note the slightly lower closing ratio on the 2000 accident year. This should be explored with the claims department. On a property line this could be the result of a catastrophe in December, but in a liability line it indicates potential processing problems.

Accident	Age in months:						
Year	12	24	36	48	60	72	84
1994	79.4%	92.8%	96.6%	98.4%	99.2%	99.7%	99.8%
1995	76.5%	93.2%	96.8%	98.5%	99.2%	99.6%	
1996	80.2%	93.4%	96.9%	98.3%	99.3%		
1997	76.1%	92.8%	96.2%	98.2%			
1998	77.8%	91.6%	96.5%				
1999	81.8%	92.3%					
2000	75.8%						

Open Claim Counts: This triangle displays open claims, i.e., claims reported less all claims closed. Note that there were almost 2,000 fewer claims reported on the 2000 accident year than on the 1998 accident in the initial 12 months of reporting. However, at the end of 2000, there are almost 500 more claims open in the 2000 accident year than the 3,217 claims open on the 1999 accident year at the end of 1999. This could be the result of some very significant changes in the organization.

Accident	Age in months:						
Year	12	24	36	48	60	72	84
1994	6,750	2,976	1,395	655	329	134	68
1995	7,932	2,705	1,285	607	338	174	
1996	5,364	2,177	1,030	551	247		
1997	5,954	2,158	1,136	540			
1998	5,610	2,683	1,141				
1999	3,217	1,674					
2000	3,771						

Average Open Claim Amount: This triangle tracks the average amount reserved on open claims. Note the accident year 2000 average open case reserve has dropped from the prior year's level. This should be investigated with the claim department. Combined with the greater number of 2000 open reserves, a change in case reserving practices or a processing problem should be suspected. Note that the 1997 accident year showed a similar drop in its open reserve amount.

Accident	Age in months:						
Year	12	24	36	48	60	72	84
1994	5,339	11,671	16,499	21,029	28,782	47,240	60,722
1995	5,254	13,137	19,405	22,285	29,820	35,209	
1996	5,894	13,334	17,939	16,832	14,722		
1997	3,501	14,190	21,798	28,896			
1998	6,258	13,941	22,026				
1999	8,206	14,324					
2000	4,629						

Change in Average Open Claim: This triangle charts the change in the average open reserve between accident periods as of each development age. This is useful for determining if case reserves are keeping up with reasonable inflationary increases.

Accident	Age in months:					
Year	12	24	36	48	60	72
1994–95	−1.6%	12.6%	17.6%	6.0%	3.6%	−25.5%
1995–96	12.2%	1.5%	−7.6%	−24.5%	−50.6%	
1996–97	−40.6%	6.4%	21.5%	71.7%		
1997–98	78.7%	−1.8%	1.0%			
1998–99	31.1%	2.7%				
1999–00	−43.6%					
Average	6.0%	4.3%	8.2%	17.7%	−23.5%	−25.5%

Average Closed Claim: This triangle shows paid losses divided by closed with payment counts. Note that these averages are very regular with no reversals across accident years, until 2000 as of 12 months.

Accident			Age in months:				
Year	12	24	36	48	60	72	84
1994	968	1,254	1,631	1,894	2,090	2,218	2,281
1995	973	1,451	1,859	2,236	2,415	2,506	
1996	1,064	1,554	1,958	2,273	2,480		
1997	1,160	1,632	2,117	2,573			
1998	1,183	1,745	2,439				
1999	1,342	2,014					
2000	1,071						

Change in Average Closed Claim: This triangle shows the change in the average paid claim amount between accident years as of identical development periods. The multi-year average increase in closed claim values is also shown. It is useful to compare the annual increases in open case reserves to these increases in closed claim amounts. This allows the analyst to evaluate if the claim department reserves are keeping pace with inflationary increases in settlements. The analyst might suspect a serious backlog in paid claims for the 2000 accident year.

Accident			Age in months:			
Year	12	24	36	48	60	72
1994–95	0.6%	15.7%	14.0%	18.1%	15.6%	13.0%
1995–96	9.3%	7.0%	5.3%	1.6%	2.7%	
1996–97	9.0%	5.0%	8.1%	13.2%		
1997–98	1.9%	7.0%	15.2%			
1998–99	13.5%	15.4%				
1999–00	−20.2%					
Average	2.4%	10.0%	10.7%	11.0%	9.1%	13.0%

Closed Claims as a Percent of Open Claims: The rate of claim closure is one of the most important indicators of the condition of the claim department. This statistic measures the ratio of claims closed in the period to claims open at the beginning of the period. Our example shows some deterioration in claims performance in calendar year 1999. Only 60.2% of the claims occurring in 1997 that were open at 12/31/1998 were closed during the 1999 calendar year. Some level of recovery is evident during calendar year 2000 when 60.8% of 1997 occurrences that were open at 12/31/1999 were closed in the calendar year. However, the analyst might surmise that the closing activity on the 1999 inventory may have slipped in order to allow the catch up activity on the older inventories. These indications of processing problems should be probed with questions for claims management.

Accident Year	Age in months: 12	24	36	48	60	72
1994	181.1%	67.1%	62.9%	52.5%	59.6%	49.3%
1995	138.9%	67.2%	61.9%	48.9%	48.5%	
1996	165.2%	68.5%	56.1%	59.9%		
1997	145.5%	60.2%	60.8%			
1998	171.6%	70.6%				
1999	177.6%					

PHASE 2: LOSS RESERVE ESTIMATION METHODS

There are many methods for the projection of reserves to ultimate values. The most common simply project the growth behavior of the reserve inventory. These methods take little advantage of the fact that we are estimating loss reserves. The methods can equally well be used to project ultimate values of any growth process. Some examples might be the ultimate response rate to a direct mail campaign, or the loan defaults in a loan portfolio. All reserve estimation work must be supplemented with the experience of the reserve analyst.

Triangular Methods

The most common methods used to estimate ultimate loss levels consist of tracking the history of a group of claims with similar definitional groupings. The data for this purpose are arranged in a triangular loss format as discussed above. Each undeveloped loss year is projected to its expected ultimate level based on the assumption that each loss year will be completed in a way that is analogous to prior years. Several of these methods are described below.

Paid Loss Development

Suppose cumulative paid losses are as described by the triangle below.

| Accident Year | Age in months: | | | | | | |
	12	24	36	48	60	72	84
1994	22,603	40,064	54,301	64,114	71,257	75,950	78,224
1995	22,054	43,970	58,737	71,841	78,076	81,287	
1996	20,166	39,147	51,319	60,417	66,402		
1997	19,297	37,355	50,391	62,347			
1998	20,555	42,898	62,832				
1999	17,001	33,568					
2000	11,346						

A review of the data in the first column "as of 12 months" indicates that some rather extreme fluctuations in loss volume seem to have taken place over the last seven years. This should be checked out by a review of the historical claim count triangles, and also the earned exposure history, or earned premiums at a uniform exposure level as a proxy. These concerns are discussed above under the data exploration topics.

These shifts in the volume of losses make it difficult to reach any conclusion about this development. Thus we would like to "normalize" the development history by removing this volume effect. This is accomplished by studying the aging effect within each accident year as follows:

Accident			Age in months:			
Year	12–24	24–36	36–48	48–60	60–72	72–84
1994	1.773	1.355	1.181	1.111	1.066	1.030
1995	1.994	1.336	1.223	1.087	1.041	
1996	1.941	1.311	1.177	1.099		
1997	1.936	1.349	1.237			
1998	2.087	1.465				
1999	1.974					

This triangular display represents the historical development of each accident year. For instance, the development from 12 to 24 months on accident year 1999 is an increase in paid losses of 97.4% ($33,568/$17,001). Now the range of variation is considerably reduced. One can see that 12–24 month development seems to vary from 1.773 to 2.087. The high 1998 development of 2.087 seems to be outside a reasonable range of development factors observed in recent time periods. If we can predict the next 12–24 month development that we expect to see take place during 2001, we would be able to forecast the 2000 accident year paid losses at 24 months of development.

Thus our next task should consist of predicting the 2000 accident year 12–24 month paid loss development factor. One common technique is to inspect several averages of the age-to-age factors. The averages should provide a guide in selecting the next calendar period's development on that accident year.

Accident Year	Age in months:					
	12–24	24–36	36–48	48–60	60–72	72–84
1994	1.773	1.355	1.181	1.111	1.066	1.030
1995	1.994	1.336	1.223	1.087	1.041	
1996	1.941	1.311	1.177	1.099		
1997	1.936	1.349	1.237			
1998	2.087	1.465				
1999	1.974					
Average	1.951	1.363	1.205	1.099	1.053	1.030
Average Last 3	1.999	1.375	1.213	1.099		
Average Last 4	1.985	1.365	1.205			
Avg Exc Hi & Lo	1.961	1.347	1.202	1.099		
Weighted Average	1.948	1.364	1.205	1.099	1.053	1.030
Harmonic Mean	1.949	1.362	1.204	1.099	1.053	1.030

There is a practically unlimited number of ways to average the historical development factors. The key point to remember is that these averages are only guides to selection of the next reasonable development, based on all information that the loss reserve actuary has developed from reviews with management as well as the historical loss development.

Let's review the averages displayed above. The "Average" line is simply the arithmetic average of all historical loss development factors at that stage of development. Similarly, the "Average Last 3" and "Average Last 4" are simple arithmetic averages of the latest 3 and latest 4 development factors respectively at a given point of development. The "Avg Excluding Hi & Lo" is the arithmetic average of the development factors other than the highest and lowest. The "Weighted Average" is weighted by the amount of incurred loss. In this case the weighted average for age 36 to 48 is calculated as follows:

$$\frac{54,301 \times 1.181 + 58,737 \times 1.223 + 51,319 \times 1.177 + 50,391 \times 1.237}{54,301 + 58,737 + 51,319 + 50,391}$$

$$= 1.205$$

The harmonic mean is the nth root of the n historical development factors. Here, the harmonic mean for age 36 to 48 was calculated as follows:

$$(1.181 \times 1.223 \times 1.177 \times 1.237)^{1/4} = 1.204$$

Notice that we are generally interested in examining the averages of the latest few development periods, because any forces that are impacting our current experience are more likely to be seen in the most recent past, rather than in earlier years. Hence we calculate averages of the latest three or four factors. Like many actuarial procedures, the analyst is asked to make a judgment of the most appropriate trade-off between stability (i.e., more development periods in the average computation) and responsiveness (i.e., only include the latest few development periods in the average).

The familiar triangular format also becomes a convenient way to inspect the addition of more development points in the averages. For instance, assume the analyst chose the following development patterns along the right diagonal as the most likely over the next 12 months (in bold).

Accident Year	12–24	24–36	36–48	48–60	60–72	72–84	84–Ult
1994	1.773	1.355	1.181	1.111	1.066	1.030	**1.053**
1995	1.994	1.336	1.223	1.087	1.041	**1.030**	
1996	1.941	1.311	1.177	1.099	**1.060**		
1997	1.936	1.349	1.237	**1.100**			
1998	2.087	1.465	**1.210**				
1999	1.974	**1.350**					
2000	**1.960**						

Often the selected developments are not identical to any of the averages. For instance the 12 to 24 month expected development is 1.960. Review of this history with claims and systems managers indicates that a new claim processing system was installed during 1998 that necessitated a longer installation period than anticipated. Thus the analyst views the 1998 accident year development of 2.087 as an anomaly. This is supported by the recovery of the 1999 accident year 12–24 months development to 1.974, a value that seems to fit with the prior developments. It is extremely important to realize that once the suspected anomalous development pattern on 1998 accident year has been identified, further information must be sought about company operations that may have caused this anomaly. In most cases, this information cannot be acquired through further study of the numbers, but requires the actuary to gather additional information, often of a qualitative nature.

The search for an explanation of recent unusual historical developments is critical to the reserve estimate because the analyst must decide whether the situation causing the abnormal loss development is still a factor that can affect future developments. In this case the new claim processing system has been in place since the end of 1998, and the 1999 accident year shows a return to more normal paid loss development patterns in the 12–24 months development. This leads the analyst to discount the 1998 development from 12 to 24 months as a nonrecurring situation. In general, the analyst should not use averages if the data show a clear trend that makes averaging inappropriate, or if an unusual accident year distorts the average.

On the other hand, suppose the analyst had determined that the unusual development on the 1998 accident year was due to several large losses that required unexpected large payments in 1999. This is clearly a situation that could happen again in any particular year, absent any changes in policy limit profiles or reinsurance retentions, and should receive some weight in future scenarios. In this situation, the averages including the 1998 accident year development from 12 to 24 months should be used as a guide to the 12 to 24 months paid development on the 2000 accident year.

The choice of the next projected development of 24 to 36 months is difficult because of the unusually high development of +46.5% on the 1998 reported paid losses from 24 to 36 months. At this point the analyst must regard the 1998 accident year as very unusual. A note should be made to inspect the projected ultimate on this accident year very carefully once development factors have been selected.

Investigation of events in the 2000 calendar year indicates that several large payments were evident on 1998 accident year cases, but this was on classes of business no longer written by the company. Accordingly the 1998 development cannot be used again in the choice of the 24 to 36 months development on the 2000 accident year.

Once the development factors for calendar year 2001 have been chosen for accident years 1995 through 2000, the analyst must forecast development for the 2002 and subsequent calendar years. The forecasted development for each subsequent calendar year is not necessarily the same as the 2001 calendar year forecast. In the triangle below, initial development factors have been chosen for future periods.

| Accident | Age in months: | | | | | | | Dev to |
Year	12–24	24–36	36–48	48–60	60–72	72–84	84–Ult	Ult
1994	1.773	1.355	1.181	1.111	1.066	1.030	**1.053**	**1.053**
1995	1.994	1.336	1.223	1.087	1.041	**1.030**	**1.053**	**1.085**
1996	1.941	1.311	1.177	1.099	**1.060**	**1.030**	**1.053**	**1.150**
1997	1.936	1.349	1.237	**1.100**	**1.060**	**1.030**	**1.053**	**1.265**
1998	2.087	1.465	**1.210**	**1.100**	**1.060**	**1.030**	**1.053**	**1.622**
1999	1.974	**1.350**	**1.210**	**1.100**	**1.060**	**1.030**	**1.053**	**2.066**
2000	**1.960**	**1.350**	**1.210**	**1.100**	**1.060**	**1.030**	**1.053**	**4.049**

The analyst then learns that the 1998 accident year contained more hazardous classes than the preceding years. These classes were assumed to account for the higher development on the 1998 accident year from 24 to 36 months. After discussions with the

Underwriting Department, the analyst feels that future development will also be higher due to this more hazardous business
mix; however, the amount of the adjustment is in question.

The analyst finds that the 24 to 36 month development on
1998 at 1.465 is higher than the selected development of 1.350
which was based on the observed development in accident years
1994–97. It is also assumed that this differential of 1.085 (the
relativity of the observed 1.465 to the "projected" 1.350) should
dampen back to unity with the passage of time. The analyst de-
cides to reflect this dampening effect by taking the square root
of the differential with the passage of each year. Thus, the differential for the 36 to 48 month development should be the square
root of 1.085 or 1.042. This results in a development from 36 to
48 months of 1.261, given by 1.210 multiplied by 1.042. Carried
out an additional year, the adjusted development factor from 48
to 60 months is the square root of 1.042, or 1.021, times the otherwise selected 1.100. This method of dampening the observed
differential in 1998 accident year development is driven more
by the analyst's experience than a set of mathematical formulae.

In a report on the loss reserve analysis, the analyst should
disclose the assumption that the 1998 year will have higher loss
development due to the more severe business mix.

The final selected development factors can be seen below.

Accident			Age in months:					Dev to
Year	12–24	24–36	36–48	48–60	60–72	72–84	84–Ult	Ult
1994	1.773	1.355	1.181	1.111	1.066	1.030	**1.053**	**1.053**
1995	1.994	1.336	1.223	1.087	1.041	**1.030**	**1.053**	**1.085**
1996	1.941	1.311	1.177	1.099	**1.060**	**1.030**	**1.053**	**1.150**
1997	1.936	1.349	1.237	**1.100**	**1.060**	**1.030**	**1.053**	**1.265**
1998	2.087	1.465	**1.261**	**1.123**	**1.060**	**1.030**	**1.053**	**1.622**
1999	1.974	**1.350**	**1.210**	**1.100**	**1.060**	**1.030**	**1.053**	**2.066**
2000	1.960	**1.350**	**1.210**	**1.100**	**1.060**	**1.030**	**1.053**	**4.049**

As can be seen from the process of selection of development factors the analyst should be able to recognize:

1. normal levels of random fluctuation in developments,

2. aberrations in development patterns and be able to isolate their causes, and determine if they are ongoing or one time changes in development,

3. trends in loss development patterns.

The analyst was also required to make a projection of paid loss from 84 months of age to ultimate settlement. Generally, the historical data should extend back far enough to make the projected development to ultimate, or tail factor as it is often called, very small. The selection of a tail factor is made difficult by two factors:

1. there is generally little relevant data available,

2. the tail factor affects all accident years reserve needs, thus has a disproportionate leverage on the total reserve need.

In this case, the analyst selects a tail factor of 5.3% additional development after 84 months of age, based on a subjective judgment and a review of cases over seven years old that were settled in the last calendar year. In addition to judgment, the analyst should include a review of any available industry data.

This triangle can be then transformed into its dollar equivalents, by successively multiplying the selected development factors by the last actual report of incurred losses.

| Accident | Age in months: | | | | | | | | Paid | |
Year	12	24	36	48	60	72	84	Ultimate	to Date	Reserve
1994	22,603	40,064	54,301	64,114	71,257	75,950	78,224	**82,370**	78,224	4,146
1995	22,054	43,970	58,737	71,841	78,076	81,287	**83,726**	**88,163**	81,287	6,876
1996	20,166	39,147	51,319	60,417	66,402	**70,386**	72,498	**76,340**	66,402	9,938
1997	19,297	37,355	50,391	62,347	**68,582**	72,697	74,878	**78,846**	62,347	16,499
1998	20,555	42,898	62,832	**79,231**	**88,977**	**94,315**	**97,145**	**102,293**	62,832	39,461
1999	17,001	33,568	**45,317**	**54,833**	60,317	63,936	65,854	**69,344**	33,568	35,776
2000	11,346	**22,238**	**30,022**	**36,326**	39,959	42,356	43,627	**45,939**	11,346	34,593

							Total Reserve	147,289

This particular analysis of the paid loss data indicates that a reserve of about $147 million is necessary to provide for unpaid loss reserve liabilities from accident years 1994 through 2000.

While an estimate is available for a reserve need for this book of business, we can note at least two deficiencies in our knowledge at this point. First, we have not made any use of other available information, such as claim counts or case reserve values. Second, we have no means of evaluating prospectively the confidence we should have in this single forecast of the future. Both of these concerns can be addressed by alternative forecasts of the ultimate loss reserve need using other information available to us.

Incurred Loss Development

A triangular development analysis can also be developed using paid losses plus case reserves. Case reserves could be either adjuster determined or set by use of average values. Assume incurred losses and calculated age-to-age development factors as presented below.

Accident Year	Age in months: 12	24	36	48	60	72	84
1994	58,641	74,804	77,323	77,890	80,728	82,280	82,372
1995	63,732	79,512	83,680	85,366	88,152	87,413	
1996	51,779	68,175	69,802	69,694	70,041		
1997	40,143	67,978	75,144	77,947			
1998	55,665	80,296	87,961				
1999	43,401	57,547					
2000	28,800						

	12–24	24–36	36–48	48–60	60–72	72–84
1994	1.276	1.034	1.007	1.036	1.019	1.001
1995	1.248	1.052	1.020	1.033	0.992	
1996	1.317	1.024	0.998	1.005		
1997	1.693	1.105	1.037			
1998	1.443	1.095				
1999	1.326					

| | \multicolumn{6}{c}{Age in months:} | | | | | |
	12–24	24–36	36–48	48–60	60–72	72–84
Average	1.384	1.062	1.016	1.025	1.006	1.001
Average Last 3	1.487	1.075	1.018	1.025		
Average Last 4	1.445	1.069	1.016			
Avg Exc Hi & Lo	1.341	1.060	1.014	1.033		
Weighted Average	1.367	1.062	1.016	1.026	1.005	1.001
Harmonic Mean	1.376	1.062	1.015	1.025	1.005	1.001

Assume the analyst chose the following development patterns as the most likely in future calendar periods:

| Accident | \multicolumn{7}{c}{Age in months:} | | | | | | | Dev to |
Year	12–24	24–36	36–48	48–60	60–72	72–84	84–Ult	Ult
1994	1.276	1.034	1.007	1.036	1.019	1.001	**1.010**	**1.010**
1995	1.248	1.052	1.020	1.033	0.992	**1.000**	**1.010**	**1.010**
1996	1.317	1.024	0.998	1.005	**1.000**	**1.000**	**1.010**	**1.010**
1997	1.693	1.105	1.037	**1.020**	**1.000**	**1.000**	**1.010**	**1.030**
1998	1.442	1.095	**1.020**	**1.020**	**1.000**	**1.000**	**1.010**	**1.051**
1999	1.326	**1.095**	**1.020**	**1.020**	**1.000**	**1.000**	**1.010**	**1.151**
2000	**1.350**	**1.095**	**1.020**	**1.020**	**1.000**	**1.000**	**1.010**	**1.553**

Based on development factors chosen above the complete projection of incurred losses by accident year may be completed.

| Accident | \multicolumn{6}{c}{Age in months:} | | | | | | | \multicolumn{2}{c}{Paid} | |
Year	12	24	36	48	60	72	84	Ultimate	to Date	Reserve
1994	58,641	74,804	77,323	77,890	80,728	82,280	82,372	**83,196**	78,224	4,972
1995	63,732	79,512	83,680	85,366	88,152	87,413	**87,413**	**88,287**	81,287	7,000
1996	51,779	68,175	69,802	69,694	70,041	**70,041**	**70,041**	**70,741**	66,402	4,339
1997	40,143	67,978	75,144	77,947	**79,506**	**79,506**	**79,506**	**80,301**	62,347	17,954
1998	55,665	80,296	87,961	**89,720**	**91,515**	**91,515**	**91,515**	**92,430**	62,832	29,598
1999	43,401	57,547	**63,014**	**64,274**	**65,560**	**65,560**	**65,560**	**66,215**	33,568	32,647
2000	28,800	**38,880**	**42,574**	**43,425**	**44,294**	**44,294**	**44,294**	**44,737**	11,346	33,391
								Total Reserve		129,901

This particular analysis of the incurred loss data indicates that a reserve of about $130 million is necessary to provide for unpaid loss and loss adjustment expenses from accident years 1994 through 2000. This is substantially different from the $147 million reserve estimate obtained through a paid loss projection. Any difference in estimates clearly raises questions that need to be investigated by the analyst in an attempt to reconcile the reserve estimate using two sets of loss data.

Claim Count Development

The pattern of claim reporting should be reviewed in the same fashion. The number of reported claims and calculated development factors are shown below.

Accident Year	Age in months:						
	12	24	36	48	60	72	84
1994	32,751	41,201	41,618	41,755	41,773	41,774	41,774
1995	33,736	39,528	39,926	40,044	40,072	40,072	
1996	27,067	32,740	33,084	33,183	33,209		
1997	24,928	29,796	30,074	30,169			
1998	25,229	31,930	32,281				
1999	17,632	21,801					
2000	13,609						

	12–24	24–36	36–48	48–60	60–72	72–84
1994	1.258	1.010	1.003	1.000	1.000	1.000
1995	1.172	1.010	1.003	1.001	1.000	
1996	1.210	1.011	1.003	1.001		
1997	1.195	1.009	1.003			
1998	1.266	1.011				
1999	1.236					
Average	1.223	1.010	1.003	1.001	1.000	1.000
Average Last 3	1.232	1.010	1.003	1.001		
Average Last 4	1.227	1.010	1.003			
Avg Exc Hi & Lo	1.225	1.010	1.003	1.001		
Weighted Average	1.221	1.010	1.003	1.001	1.000	1.000
Harmonic Mean	1.222	1.010	1.003	1.001	1.000	1.000

Assume the analyst chose the following development patterns as the most likely characterizations of development of total claims on those accident years to their ultimate reported level.

| Accident | Age in months: | | | | | | | Dev to |
Year	12–24	24–36	36–48	48–60	60–72	72–84	84–Ult	Ult
1994	1.258	1.010	1.003	1.000	1.000	1.000	**1.000**	**1.000**
1995	1.172	1.010	1.003	1.001	1.000	**1.000**	**1.000**	**1.000**
1996	1.210	1.011	1.003	1.001	**1.000**	**1.000**	**1.000**	**1.000**
1997	1.195	1.009	1.003	**1.001**	**1.000**	**1.000**	**1.000**	**1.001**
1998	1.266	1.011	**1.003**	**1.001**	**1.000**	**1.000**	**1.000**	**1.004**
1999	1.236	**1.012**	**1.003**	**1.001**	**1.000**	**1.000**	**1.000**	**1.016**
2000	**1.200**	**1.012**	**1.003**	**1.001**	**1.000**	**1.000**	**1.000**	**1.219**

Based on factors chosen above, the complete projection of incurred loss counts by accident year may be completed.

| Accident | Age in months: | | | | | | | | |
Year	12	24	36	48	60	72	84	Ultimate	Reported	Unreported
1994	32,751	41,201	41,618	41,755	41,773	41,774	41,774	**41,774**	41,774	0
1995	33,736	39,528	39,926	40,044	40,072	40,072	**40,072**	**40,072**	40,072	0
1996	27,067	32,740	33,084	33,183	33,209	**33,209**	**33,209**	**33,209**	33,209	0
1997	24,928	29,796	30,074	30,169	**30,199**	**30,199**	**30,199**	**30,199**	30,169	30
1998	25,229	31,930	32,281	**32,378**	**32,410**	**32,410**	**32,410**	**32,410**	32,281	129
1999	17,632	21,801	**22,063**	**22,129**	**22,151**	**22,151**	**22,151**	**22,151**	21,801	350
2000	13,609	**16,331**	**16,527**	**16,576**	**16,593**	**16,593**	**16,593**	**16,593**	13,609	2,984

| | | Total Unreported | 3,493 |

This analysis implies almost 3,500 claims remain to be reported. By itself, this analysis is useful as an indicator of true IBNR reporting. However, the projected ultimate claims may also be used to reduce the paid and incurred triangles to an average basis. Note that these incurred counts include those claims closed without loss payment.

It is possible to project the net claim count after claims closed without payment are excluded. Let the following triangle represent the history of claims reported that are closed with no loss payment (CNP).

Accident Year	Age in months:						
	12	24	36	48	60	72	84
1994	2,646	6,285	6,935	7,240	7,353	7,393	7,412
1995	3,142	6,529	7,053	7,308	7,411	7,465	
1996	2,752	5,366	5,840	6,050	6,185		
1997	2,343	4,744	5,132	5,400			
1998	2,238	4,666	5,375				
1999	1,749	3,458					
2000	1,246						

Below is the percentage of claims without payment relative to total reported claims. For this line of business, it appears about 18% of the claims reported will be closed with no indemnity payment.

Accident Year	Age in months:						
	12	24	36	48	60	72	84
1994	8.1%	15.3%	16.7%	17.3%	17.6%	17.7%	17.7%
1995	9.3%	16.5%	17.7%	18.2%	18.5%	18.6%	
1996	10.2%	16.4%	17.7%	18.2%	18.6%		
1997	9.4%	15.9%	17.1%	17.9%			
1998	8.9%	14.6%	16.7%				
1999	9.9%	15.9%					
2000	9.2%						

This triangular display may be completed to obtain an ultimate estimate of the percent of reported claims closed with no indemnity payment, or alternatively, as shown below, the reported claims could be reduced for the claims closed with no indemnity.

Accident				Age in months:			
Year	12	24	36	48	60	72	84
1994	30,105	34,916	34,683	34,515	34,420	34,381	34,362
1995	30,594	32,999	32,873	32,736	32,661	32,607	
1996	24,315	27,374	27,244	27,133	27,024		
1997	22,585	25,052	24,942	24,769			
1998	22,991	27,264	26,906				
1999	15,883	18,343					
2000	12,363						

Age-to-age development factors may be calculated for the data representing claims reported net of claims closed with no payment.

Accident			Age in months:			
Year	12–24	24–36	36–48	48–60	60–72	72–84
1994	1.160	0.993	0.995	0.997	0.999	0.999
1995	1.079	0.996	0.996	0.998	0.998	
1996	1.126	0.995	0.996	0.996		
1997	1.109	0.996	0.993			
1998	1.186	0.987				
1999	1.155					
Average	1.136	0.993	0.995	0.997	0.999	0.999
Average Last 3	1.150	0.993	0.995	0.997		
Average Last 4	1.144	0.994	0.995			
Avg Exc Hi & Lo	1.138	0.995	0.996	0.997		
Weighted Average	1.133	0.994	0.995	0.997	0.999	0.999
Harmonic Mean	1.135	0.993	0.995	0.997	0.998	0.999

Assume the analyst chose the following development patterns as the most likely to ultimate settlement.

| Accident | | | Age in months: | | | | | Dev to |
Year	12–24	24–36	36–48	48–60	60–72	72–84	84–Ult	Ult
1994	1.160	0.993	0.995	0.997	0.999	0.999	**0.999**	**0.999**
1995	1.079	0.996	0.996	0.998	0.998	**0.999**	**0.999**	**0.998**
1996	1.126	0.995	0.996	0.996	**0.998**	**0.999**	**0.999**	**0.996**
1997	1.109	0.996	0.993	**0.996**	**0.998**	**0.999**	**0.999**	**0.992**
1998	1.186	0.987	**0.994**	**0.996**	**0.998**	**0.999**	**0.999**	**0.986**
1999	1.155	**0.996**	**0.994**	**0.996**	**0.998**	**0.999**	**0.999**	**0.982**
2000	**1.120**	**0.996**	**0.994**	**0.996**	**0.998**	**0.999**	**0.999**	**1.100**

Based on the development factors selected above, the complete projection of the net number of incurred claims by accident year may be obtained.

| Accident | | | Age in months: | | | | | | | |
Year	12	24	36	48	60	72	84	Ultimate	Reported	Unreported
1994	30,105	34,916	34,683	34,515	34,420	34,381	34,362	**34,328**	34,362	−34
1995	30,594	32,999	32,873	32,736	32,661	32,607	**32,574**	**32,542**	32,607	−65
1996	24,315	27,374	27,244	27,133	27,024	**26,970**	**26,943**	**26,916**	27,024	−108
1997	22,585	25,052	24,942	24,769	**24,670**	**24,621**	**24,596**	**24,571**	24,769	−198
1998	22,991	27,264	26,906	**26,745**	**26,638**	**26,584**	**26,558**	**26,531**	26,906	−375
1999	15,883	18,343	**18,270**	**18,160**	**18,087**	**18,051**	**18,033**	**18,015**	18,343	−328
2000	12,363	**13,847**	**13,791**	**13,701**	**13,654**	**13,626**	**13,613**	**13,599**	12,363	1,236

	Total Unreported (Net of CNP)	128

A negative number of unreported claims means the number of reported claims that will eventually close without payment is larger than the gross number of unreported claims. Only accident year 2000 will have a net increase in the number of reported claims net of closed with no payment claims.

Average Paid Claim Projection

A history of average paid claim amounts can be obtained by dividing the paid amounts by the number of claims closed with payments.

| Accident | Age in months: | | | | | | |
Year	12	24	36	48	60	72	84
1994	968	1,254	1,631	1,894	2,090	2,218	2,281
1995	973	1,451	1,859	2,236	2,415	2,506	
1996	1,064	1,554	1,958	2,273	2,480		
1997	1,160	1,632	2,117	2,573			
1998	1,183	1,745	2,439				
1999	1,342	2,014					
2000	1,071						

Note that these average paid amounts will represent both average closing payment, plus any amounts paid on claims before closure. In some lines, such as workers compensation, these interim payments can be substantial. In those cases, this technique may not be as useful as for lines that close with a single payment.

Use the triangular format as a convenient way to inspect the addition of more development points in the averages.

| Accident | Age in months: | | | | | | |
Year	12–24	24–36	36–48	48–60	60–72	72–84	84–Ult
1994	1.296	1.300	1.161	1.104	1.061	1.029	
1995	1.491	1.281	1.203	1.080	1.038		
1996	1.460	1.260	1.161	1.091			
1997	1.406	1.297	1.216				
1998	1.476	1.397					
1999	1.500						
Average	1.438	1.307	1.185	1.092	1.050	1.029	
Average Last 3	1.461	1.318	1.193	1.092			
Average Last 4	1.461	1.309	1.185				
Avg Exc Hi & Lo	1.458	1.293	1.182	1.091			
Weighted Average	1.442	1.310	1.186	1.091	1.048	1.029	
Harmonic Mean	1.436	1.306	1.185	1.092	1.049	1.029	

Assume the analyst chose the following development patterns below. Note that the 12–24 factor on the 2000 year has been chosen to be quite high to compensate for the low average amount of $1,071 paid during 2000.

Accident Year	12–24	24–36	36–48	48–60	60–72	72–84	84–Ult	Dev to Ult
1994	1.296	1.300	1.161	1.104	1.061	1.029	**1.010**	**1.010**
1995	1.491	1.281	1.203	1.080	1.038	**1.020**	**1.010**	**1.030**
1996	1.460	1.260	1.161	1.091	**1.045**	**1.020**	**1.010**	**1.077**
1997	1.406	1.297	1.216	**1.090**	**1.045**	**1.020**	**1.010**	**1.173**
1998	1.476	1.397	**1.200**	**1.090**	**1.045**	**1.020**	**1.010**	**1.408**
1999	1.500	**1.400**	**1.200**	**1.090**	**1.045**	**1.020**	**1.010**	**1.971**
2000	**1.600**	**1.400**	**1.200**	**1.090**	**1.045**	**1.020**	**1.010**	**3.154**

Based on the factors chosen above the complete projection of average paid loss by accident year may be completed.

Accident Year	12	24	36	48	60	72	84	Ultimate Average
1994	968	1,254	1,631	1,894	2,090	2,218	2,281	**2,304**
1995	973	1,451	1,859	2,236	2,415	2,506	**2,556**	**2,582**
1996	1,064	1,554	1,958	2,273	2,480	**2,591**	**2,643**	**2,670**
1997	1,160	1,632	2,117	2,573	**2,805**	**2,931**	**2,990**	**3,020**
1998	1,183	1,745	2,439	**2,926**	**3,190**	**3,333**	**3,400**	**3,434**
1999	1,342	2,014	**2,819**	**3,383**	**3,688**	**3,854**	**3,931**	**3,970**
2000	1,071	**1,714**	**2,399**	**2,879**	**3,138**	**3,280**	**3,345**	**3,379**

Accident Year	Ultimate Average	Ultimate Counts	Ultimate Cost	Paid to Date	Reserve
1994	2,304	34,328	79,092	78,224	868
1995	2,582	32,542	84,023	81,287	2,736
1996	2,670	26,916	71,866	66,402	5,464
1997	3,020	24,571	74,204	62,347	11,857
1998	3,434	26,531	91,107	62,832	28,275
1999	3,970	18,015	71,520	33,568	37,952
2000	3,379	13,599	45,951	11,346	34,605
			Total Reserve		121,757

The 2000 average paid claim at ultimate appears to be completely unreasonable at $3,379 per claim, compared to past values projected. A review of annual increases in the ultimate average paid amount follows:

Accident Year	Ultimate Average	Change
1994	2,304	
1995	2,582	12.1%
1996	2,670	3.4%
1997	3,020	13.1%
1998	3,434	13.7%
1999	3,970	15.6%
2000	3,379	−14.9%

This indicates that a 12% increase from the 1999 value might be more in line with past experience. Using this increase yields an average payment of $4,446 per claim closed.

Accident Year	Ultimate Average	Ultimate Counts	Ultimate Cost	Paid to Date	Reserve
1994	2,304	34,328	79,092	78,224	868
1995	2,582	32,542	84,023	81,287	2,736
1996	2,670	26,916	71,866	66,402	5,464
1997	3,020	24,571	74,204	62,347	11,857
1998	3,434	26,531	91,107	62,832	28,275
1999	3,970	18,015	71,520	33,568	37,952
2000	4,446	13,599	60,461	11,346	49,115
				Total Reserve	136,267

The resulting reserve estimate based on average paid data has allowed us to correct for an obvious aberration in paid claims.

This aberration was not noticeable from the aggregate paid or incurred histories. This provides an example of the necessity of using several methods in investigating reserve needs.

Average Incurred Claim Projection

A similar projection can be made of the average amount of loss incurred per reported claim less claim counts closed with no payment. This amount and calculated development factors are shown below.

| Accident | | | Age in months: | | | | |
Year	12	24	36	48	60	72	84
1994	1,948	2,142	2,229	2,257	2,345	2,393	2,397
1995	2,083	2,410	2,546	2,608	2,699	2,681	
1996	2,130	2,491	2,562	2,569	2,592		
1997	1,777	2,713	3,013	3,147			
1998	2,421	2,945	3,269				
1999	2,733	3,137					
2000	2,330						

	12–24	24–36	36–48	48–60	60–72	72–84
1994	1.100	1.041	1.012	1.039	1.020	1.002
1995	1.157	1.056	1.024	1.035	0.993	
1996	1.170	1.029	1.003	1.009		
1997	1.527	1.110	1.045			
1998	1.216	1.110				
1999	1.148					
Average	1.220	1.069	1.021	1.028	1.007	1.002
Average Last 3	1.297	1.083	1.024	1.028		
Average Last 4	1.265	1.076	1.021			
Avg Exc Hi & Lo	1.173	1.069	1.018	1.035		
Weighted Average	1.210	1.072	1.022	1.027	1.006	1.002
Harmonic Mean	1.212	1.069	1.021	1.028	1.006	1.002

Assume the analyst chose the following development patterns as the most likely outcome.

| Accident | Age in months: | | | | | | | Dev to |
Year	12–24	24–36	36–48	48–60	60–72	72–84	84–Ult	Ult
1994	1.100	1.041	1.012	1.039	1.020	1.002	**1.000**	**1.000**
1995	1.157	1.056	1.024	1.035	0.993	**1.003**	**1.000**	**1.003**
1996	1.170	1.029	1.003	1.009	**1.000**	**1.003**	**1.000**	**1.003**
1997	1.527	1.110	1.045	**1.025**	**1.000**	**1.003**	**1.000**	**1.028**
1998	1.216	1.110	**1.025**	**1.025**	**1.000**	**1.003**	**1.000**	**1.054**
1999	1.148	**1.100**	**1.025**	**1.025**	**1.000**	**1.003**	**1.000**	**1.159**
2000	**1.300**	**1.100**	**1.025**	**1.025**	**1.000**	**1.003**	**1.000**	**1.507**

Based on factors chosen above, the complete projection of average incurred losses by accident year may be completed.

| Accident | Age in months: | | | | | | | Ultimate |
Year	12	24	36	48	60	72	84	Average
1994	1,948	2,142	2,229	2,257	2,345	2,393	2,397	**2,397**
1995	2,083	2,410	2,546	2,608	2,699	2,681	**2,689**	**2,689**
1996	2,130	2,491	2,562	2,569	2,592	**2,592**	**2,600**	**2,600**
1997	1,777	2,713	3,013	3,147	**3,226**	**3,226**	**3,235**	**3,235**
1998	2,421	2,945	3,269	**3,351**	**3,435**	**3,435**	**3,445**	**3,445**
1999	2,733	3,137	**3,451**	**3,537**	**3,626**	**3,626**	**3,637**	**3,637**
2000	2,330	**3,028**	**3,331**	**3,415**	**3,500**	**3,500**	**3,510**	**3,510**

| Accident | Ultimate | Ultimate | Ultimate | Paid | |
Year	Average	Counts	Cost	to Date	Reserve
1994	2,397	34,328	82,284	78,224	4,060
1995	2,689	32,542	87,505	81,287	6,218
1996	2,600	26,916	69,982	66,402	3,580
1997	3,235	24,571	79,487	62,347	17,140
1998	3,445	26,531	91,399	62,832	28,567
1999	3,637	18,015	65,521	33,568	31,953
2000	3,510	13,599	47,732	11,346	36,386
				Total Reserve	127,904

The ultimate reserve estimate resulting from this average incurred history indicates a reserve of $128 million is needed. However, the same problem noted with the 2000 paid claim averages is noted here. The 2000 average ultimate incurred claim of $3,022 does not look realistic based on the steady increases of average incurred losses since 1994.

Year	Average	Change
1994	2,397	
1995	2,681	11.8%
1996	2,600	−3.0%
1997	3,235	24.4%
1998	3,445	6.5%
1999	3,637	5.6%
2000	3,022	−16.9%

Since the average incurred amounts have been increasing at an average rate of 8.7% from 1994 to 1999, this would imply an average incurred of $3,637 multiplied by 1.087 or $3,953. With 13,599 claims at ultimate settlement, the total incurred for 2000 will be $53,757,000, or almost $6 million dollars higher than our original projection. This implies a reserve of $134 million is required to provide for the ultimate disposition of all claims.

Summary of Results

The triangular loss development factor methods applied to the four different loss statistics above yields the following different sets of ultimate accident year incurred losses.

Accident Year	Paid Devel't	Incurred Devel't	Average Paid	Average Incurred
1994	82,370	83,196	79,092	82,284
1995	88,163	88,287	84,023	87,505
1996	76,340	70,741	71,866	69,982
1997	78,846	80,301	74,204	79,487
1998	102,293	92,430	91,107	91,399
1999	69,344	66,215	71,520	65,521
2000	45,939	44,737	60,461	53,757

Note that there is substantial variation from method to method. The analyst must still choose a point estimate in some fashion. This choice will be dependent on the supporting information the analyst has developed concerning company operations as well as further statistical tests discussed below. However, at this point there is strong reason to suspect that both the aggregate paid and incurred loss projection methods have substantially underestimated the 2000 ultimate loss amounts. The final selection of ultimate losses is discussed in detail after additional methods are reviewed.

Reserve Development Methods

The triangular methods have used either paid or incurred data, exclusively, but have not made any use of historical relationships between paid amounts and case reserved amounts. The reserve development method attempts to analyze the adequacy of case reserves based on the history of payments against those case reserves.

Report Year Approach

Report year data are organized by year of report to the company, as opposed to year of loss for accident year. This array freezes the inventory of loss to study only those cases actually reported to a company during a calendar year. Thus, there can be no late reported claims on a report year compilation. This method is discussed in Marker and Mohl (1980) and Mohl (1987).

Case Loss Reserves by Report Year

Report	Age in months						
Year	12	24	36	48	60	72	84
1994	46,770	31,944	18,832	9,559	4,999	2,821	1,693
1995	53,422	36,588	21,214	11,345	8,049	3,701	
1996	41,802	28,899	15,798	9,560	5,403		
1997	40,334	28,266	18,312	8,724			
1998	47,500	35,455	22,225				
1999	42,219	27,221					
2000	30,416						

Incremental Paid by Report Year

Report	Age in months						
Year	12	24	36	48	60	72	84
1994	30,001	16,021	14,144	8,238	5,923	3,119	1,145
1995	29,421	18,081	16,904	10,811	4,942	2,930	
1996	26,601	17,078	13,169	7,522	4,739		
1997	24,981	15,251	12,665	9,465			
1998	27,595	18,196	17,687				
1999	25,886	17,700					
2000	15,220						

The fundamental idea of the reserve development method of reserve evaluation is to track the development of a case reserve amount into subsequent paid losses and remaining reserves. For instance, the $42,219 in reserves from report year 1999 cases has developed into $17,700 of paid loss during 2000, with $27,221 remaining in reserve as of the end of 2000. We are then interested in the amount we expect to be paid on the $27,221 reserve during the next 12 months. The entire liquidation pattern of the report year reserves can then be charted and used to evaluate the ultimate liquidation value of the report year case reserves.

Consider the following ratios of the amounts paid to open reserves in the prior calendar period:

Paid on Reserve Ratio by Report Year

Report	Age in months					
Year	24	36	48	60	72	84
1994	0.343	0.443	0.437	0.620	0.624	0.406
1995	0.338	0.462	0.510	0.436	0.364	
1996	0.409	0.456	0.476	0.496		
1997	0.378	0.448	0.517			
1998	0.383	0.499				
1999	0.419					
Average	0.378	0.461	0.485	0.517	0.494	0.406
Average Last 3	0.393	0.468	0.501	0.517		
Average Last 4	0.397	0.466	0.485			
Avg Exc Hi & Lo	0.378	0.455	0.493	0.496		

The following development patterns were chosen as the most likely to occur for paid on open reserve amounts.

Report			Age in months:				
Year	24	36	48	60	72	84	Ultimate
1994	0.343	0.443	0.437	0.620	0.624	0.406	**1.000**
1995	0.338	0.462	0.510	0.436	0.364	**0.400**	**1.000**
1996	0.409	0.456	0.476	0.496	**0.500**	**0.400**	**1.000**
1997	0.378	0.448	0.517	**0.500**	**0.500**	**0.400**	**1.000**
1998	0.383	0.499	**0.500**	**0.500**	**0.500**	**0.400**	**1.000**
1999	0.419	**0.500**	**0.500**	**0.500**	**0.500**	**0.400**	**1.000**
2000	**0.420**	**0.500**	**0.500**	**0.500**	**0.500**	**0.400**	**1.000**

Likewise, we can create the array of ratios of remaining in reserve compared to the open reserve of the prior calendar period and complete the projection of ultimate reserve outcomes. Note that this statistic is the amount remaining on reserve so that the 84 month to ultimate development must be zero. Thus selection of tail factors is not an issue in this reserve projection method.

Remaining in Reserve Ratio by Report Year

Report			Age in months:			
Year	24	36	48	60	72	84
1994	0.683	0.590	0.508	0.523	0.564	0.600
1995	0.685	0.580	0.535	0.709	0.460	
1996	0.691	0.547	0.605	0.565		
1997	0.701	0.648	0.476			
1998	0.746	0.627				
1999	0.645					
Average	0.692	0.598	0.531	0.599	0.512	0.600
Average Last 3	0.697	0.607	0.539	0.599		
Average Last 4	0.696	0.600	0.531			
Avg Exc Hi & Lo	0.690	0.599	0.521	0.565		

The following development patterns were chosen as the most likely to occur for remaining reserve in reserve amounts.

Report			Age in months:				
Year	24	36	48	60	72	84	Ultimate
1994	0.683	0.590	0.508	0.523	0.564	0.600	**0.000**
1995	0.685	0.580	0.535	0.709	0.460	**0.600**	**0.000**
1996	0.691	0.547	0.605	0.565	**0.500**	**0.600**	**0.000**
1997	0.701	0.648	0.476	**0.600**	**0.500**	**0.600**	**0.000**
1998	0.746	0.627	**0.530**	**0.600**	**0.500**	**0.600**	**0.000**
1999	0.645	**0.635**	**0.530**	**0.600**	**0.500**	**0.600**	**0.000**
2000	**0.690**	**0.635**	**0.530**	**0.600**	**0.500**	**0.600**	**0.000**

The sum of the Paid on Reserve and the Remaining Reserve on Reserve ratios gives a history of the amount developed on open reserves in the prior calendar period.

Incremental Loss Development by Report Year

Report			Age in months				
Year	24	36	48	60	72	84	Ultimate
1994	1.026	1.032	0.945	1.143	1.188	1.006	**1.000**
1995	1.023	1.042	1.044	1.145	0.824	**1.000**	**1.000**
1996	1.100	1.002	1.081	1.061	**1.000**	**1.000**	**1.000**
1997	1.079	1.096	0.993	**1.100**	**1.000**	**1.000**	**1.000**
1998	1.129	1.126	**1.030**	**1.100**	**1.000**	**1.000**	**1.000**
1999	1.064	**1.135**	**1.030**	**1.100**	**1.000**	**1.000**	**1.000**
2000	**1.110**	**1.135**	**1.030**	**1.100**	**1.000**	**1.000**	**1.000**

Once development factor scenarios have been constructed, it is necessary to complete the settlement projections in terms of dollar amounts. An example using the 1998 report year is the most direct illustration of the completion technique.

There are $22.2 million of case reserves outstanding on the 1998 report year as of the end of 2000. The completed development factors indicate that 53% of this reserve will remain in reserve, while 50% of the reserve will be paid out, for a total adverse development of 3% on the 1998 report year cases during 2001.

We can complete the projection of remaining reserves, by using the relationships as above.

Case Loss Reserves by Report Year

Report Year	Age in months							
	12	24	36	48	60	72	84	Ultimate
1994	46,770	31,944	18,832	9,559	4,999	2,821	1,693	0
1995	53,422	36,588	21,214	11,345	8,049	3,701	2,221	0
1996	41,802	28,899	15,798	9,560	5,403	2,702	1,621	0
1997	40,334	28,266	18,312	8,724	5,234	2,617	1,570	0
1998	47,500	35,455	22,225	11,779	7,068	3,534	2,120	0
1999	42,219	27,221	17,285	9,161	5,497	2,748	1,649	0
2000	30,416	20,987	13,327	7,063	4,238	2,119	1,271	0

Based on the amounts remaining in reserve, annual paid amounts by report period can be derived simply by using the selected paid on reserve factors. For instance, on the $22,225 of reserves open at the end of 2000 on 1998 reported claims, 50% will be paid out in 2001. This is $11.1 million of paid claims.

Incremental Paid Losses by Report Year

Report Year	Age in months							
	12	24	36	48	60	72	84	Ultimate
1994	30,001	16,021	14,144	8,238	5,923	3,119	1,145	1,693
1995	29,421	18,081	16,904	10,811	4,942	2,930	1,480	2,221
1996	26,601	17,078	13,169	7,522	4,739	2,702	1,081	1,621
1997	24,981	15,251	12,665	9,465	4,362	2,617	1,047	1,570
1998	27,595	18,196	17,687	11,113	5,890	3,534	1,414	2,120
1999	25,886	17,700	13,611	8,643	4,581	2,748	1,099	1,649
2000	15,220	12,775	10,494	6,663	3,532	2,119	848	1,271

Thus the incremental paid loss projections accumulate to paid losses by report year as shown below.

Cumulative Paid Losses by Report Year

Report Year	12	24	36	48	60	72	84	Ultimate
				Age in Months				
1994	30,001	46,022	60,166	68,404	74,327	77,446	78,591	**80,284**
1995	29,421	47,502	64,406	75,217	80,159	83,089	**84,569**	**86,790**
1996	26,601	43,679	56,848	64,370	69,109	**71,811**	**72,891**	**74,512**
1997	24,981	40,232	52,897	62,362	**66,724**	**69,341**	**70,388**	**71,958**
1998	27,595	45,791	63,478	**74,591**	**80,480**	**84,014**	**85,427**	**87,548**
1999	25,886	43,586	**57,197**	**65,839**	**70,420**	**73,168**	**74,267**	**75,917**
2000	15,220	**27,995**	**38,488**	**45,152**	**48,683**	**50,802**	**51,650**	**52,921**

Report Year	Ultimate	Unpaid	Case Reserve	Case Reserve Development	Case Reserve Adequacy
1994	80,284	1,693	1,693	0	100.0%
1995	86,790	3,701	3,701	0	100.0%
1996	74,512	5,403	5,403	0	100.0%
1997	71,958	9,596	8,724	872	90.9%
1998	87,548	24,070	22,225	1,845	92.3%
1999	75,917	32,331	27,221	5,110	84.2%
2000	52,921	37,701	30,416	7,285	80.7%
	Total Case Reserve Development			15,112	

This analysis indicates a case reserving pattern with case reserves deficient 20% at age 12 months, 15% at age 24 months, and 8–10% at age 36 to 48 months. After 60 months we expect case reserves to be adequate. Note that report year analysis can only evaluate case reserve adequacy. The IBNR liability for this line would require additional analysis.

Accident Year Approach

While the reserve development method is simplest to interpret on report year data, it may also be used on accident period data on an accident year basis. New claims will enter the claim inventory so that the interpretation of paid on open reserve history is made more difficult. In order to apply the method to accident period data one must be able to assume that IBNR claim activity is related consistently to claims already reported. This assumption is a reasonable one for most lines of business that have the bulk of their claims reported in the first accident period to serve as a stable base for IBNR projections.

Assume we take the accident year paid and incurred triangles that were presented above.

Remaining Case Reserves by Accident Year

Accident Year	Age in months:						
	12	24	36	48	60	72	84
1994	36,038	34,740	23,022	13,776	9,471	6,330	4,148
1995	41,678	35,542	24,943	13,525	10,076	6,126	
1996	31,613	29,028	18,483	9,277	3,639		
1997	20,846	30,623	24,753	15,600			
1998	35,110	37,398	25,129				
1999	26,400	23,979					
2000	17,454						

Incremental Paid by Accident Year

Accident Year	Age in months:						
	12	24	36	48	60	72	84
1994	22,603	17,461	14,237	9,813	7,143	4,693	2,274
1995	22,054	21,916	14,767	13,104	6,235	3,211	
1996	20,166	18,981	12,172	9,098	5,985		
1997	19,297	18,058	13,036	11,956			
1998	20,555	22,343	19,934				
1999	17,001	16,567					
2000	11,346						

Consider the following ratios of paid on open reserves.

Paid on Reserve Ratio by Accident Year

Accident Year	Age in months					
	24	36	48	60	72	84
1994	0.485	0.410	0.426	0.519	0.496	0.359
1995	0.526	0.415	0.525	0.461	0.319	
1996	0.600	0.419	0.492	0.645		
1997	0.866	0.426	0.483			
1998	0.636	0.533				
1999	0.628					

Accident			Age in months			
Year	24	36	48	60	72	84
Average	0.623	0.441	0.482	0.542	0.407	0.359
Average Last 3	0.710	0.459	0.500	0.542		
Average Last 4	0.683	0.448	0.482			
Avg Exc Hi & Lo	0.598	0.420	0.488	0.519		

Likewise, we can create the array of ratios of remaining in reserve.

Remaining in Reserve Ratio by Accident Year

Accident			Age in months			
Year	24	36	48	60	72	84
1994	0.964	0.663	0.598	0.688	0.668	0.655
1995	0.853	0.702	0.542	0.745	0.608	
1996	0.918	0.637	0.502	0.392		
1997	1.469	0.808	0.630			
1998	1.065	0.672				
1999	0.908					
Average	1.030	0.696	0.568	0.608	0.638	0.655
Average Last 3	1.147	0.706	0.558	0.608		
Average Last 4	1.090	0.705	0.568			
Avg Exc Hi & Lo	0.964	0.679	0.570	0.688		

Note that the sum of these two ratios, gives a history of the amount developed on reserves, now including IBNR claims.

Accident			Age in months:			
Year	24	36	48	60	72	84
1994	1.448	1.073	1.025	1.206	1.164	1.015
1995	1.379	1.117	1.068	1.206	0.927	
1996	1.519	1.056	0.994	1.037		
1997	2.335	1.234	1.113			
1998	1.702	1.205				
1999	1.536					

In order to complete the projection of ultimate reserve outcomes both the paid on reserve and the remaining reserve on reserve developments must be projected.

Assume the analyst chose the following development patterns as the most likely to be paid as a percent of the reserve over the next 12-month periods.

Accident	Age in months:						
Year	24	36	48	60	72	84	Ultimate
1994	0.485	0.410	0.426	0.519	0.496	0.359	**1.010**
1995	0.526	0.415	0.525	0.461	0.319	**0.430**	**1.010**
1996	0.600	0.419	0.492	0.645	**0.510**	**0.430**	**1.010**
1997	0.866	0.426	0.483	**0.500**	**0.510**	**0.430**	**1.010**
1998	0.636	0.533	**0.495**	**0.500**	**0.510**	**0.430**	**1.010**
1999	0.628	**0.460**	**0.495**	**0.500**	**0.510**	**0.430**	**1.010**
2000	**0.600**	**0.460**	**0.495**	**0.500**	**0.510**	**0.430**	**1.010**

The same exercise must be carried out for the remaining reserve on reserve ratios on an accident year basis. Assume the analyst chose the following development patterns of reserves as a ratio to prior accident period reserves.

Accident	Age in months:						
Year	24	36	48	60	72	84	Ultimate
1994	0.964	0.663	0.598	0.688	0.668	0.655	**0.000**
1995	0.853	0.702	0.542	0.745	0.608	**0.655**	**0.000**
1996	0.918	0.637	0.502	0.392	**0.650**	**0.655**	**0.000**
1997	1.469	0.808	0.630	**0.600**	**0.650**	**0.655**	**0.000**
1998	1.065	0.672	**0.600**	**0.600**	**0.650**	**0.655**	**0.000**
1999	0.908	**0.750**	**0.600**	**0.600**	**0.650**	**0.655**	**0.000**
2000	**1.000**	**0.750**	**0.600**	**0.600**	**0.650**	**0.655**	**0.000**

We can complete the projection of remaining reserves.

Case Loss Reserves by Accident Year

Accident Year	Age in months							
	12	24	36	48	60	72	84	Ultimate
1994	36,038	34,740	23,022	13,776	9,471	6,330	4,148	0
1995	41,678	35,542	24,943	13,525	10,076	6,126	4,013	0
1996	31,613	29,028	18,483	9,277	3,639	2,365	1,549	0
1997	20,846	30,623	24,753	15,600	9,360	6,084	3,985	0
1998	35,110	37,398	25,129	15,077	9,046	5,880	3,852	0
1999	26,400	23,979	17,984	10,791	6,474	4,208	2,756	0
2000	17,454	17,454	13,091	7,854	4,713	3,063	2,006	0

Based on the amounts remaining in reserve, annual paid amounts by accident period can be derived simply by using the selected paid on reserve factors.

Incremental Paid Losses by Accident Year

Accident Year	Age in months							
	12	24	36	48	60	72	84	Ultimate
1994	22,603	17,461	14,237	9,813	7,143	4,693	2,274	4,189
1995	22,054	21,916	14,767	13,104	6,235	3,211	2,634	4,053
1996	20,166	18,981	12,172	9,098	5,985	1,856	1,017	1,565
1997	19,297	18,058	13,036	11,956	7,800	4,774	2,616	4,025
1998	20,555	22,343	19,934	12,439	7,539	4,614	2,528	3,890
1999	17,001	16,567	11,030	8,902	5,395	3,302	1,810	2,784
2000	11,346	10,472	8,029	6,480	3,927	2,403	1,317	2,026

Then the incremental paid loss projections can be accumulated to yield ultimate payment estimates by accident year.

Paid Losses by Accident Year

Accident Year	Age in months									
	12	24	36	48	60	72	84	Ultimate	Paid	Reserve
1994	22,603	40,064	54,301	64,114	71,257	75,950	78,224	82,413	78,224	4,189
1995	22,054	43,970	58,737	71,841	78,076	81,287	83,921	87,974	81,287	6,687
1996	20,166	39,147	51,319	60,417	66,402	68,258	69,275	70,840	66,402	4,438
1997	19,297	37,355	50,391	62,347	70,147	74,921	77,537	81,562	62,347	19,215
1998	20,555	42,898	62,832	75,271	82,810	87,423	89,952	93,842	62,832	31,010
1999	17,001	33,568	44,598	53,501	58,896	62,198	64,007	66,791	33,568	33,223
2000	11,346	21,818	29,847	36,327	40,254	42,658	43,975	46,001	11,346	34,655

| | | | | | | | Total Reserve | | 133,417 |

This analysis results in a total indicated reserve requirement of $133 million. Note this estimate is closest to the $130 million estimate based on the method that used aggregate incurred historical data.

Bornhuetter–Ferguson (BF) Method

There are many cases where relying solely on paid or incurred loss development methods may be inappropriate. The development methods may produce unreliable results for a new line of business with little historical information or a volatile line of business that is subject to very large occasional losses, such as contract bond surety. Also fitting into this category are cases where losses are reported over a long period of time (10 years or longer) and have very little loss reported in the first two to three years such as excess insurance and reinsurance. In situations such as these, a method that offers a blend of stability and responsiveness is more appropriate.

The Bornhuetter–Ferguson (BF) method estimates ultimate loss by adding together actual reported loss with expected future incurred development. Expected future incurred development relies on expected losses and selected loss development factors. Assume we have the following incurred loss data and selected loss development factors by acident year.

| Accident | Age in months: | | | | | | |
Year	12	24	36	48	60	72	84
1994	58,641	74,804	77,323	77,890	80,728	82,280	82,372
1995	63,732	79,512	83,680	85,366	88,152	87,413	
1996	51,779	68,175	69,802	69,694	70,041		
1997	40,143	67,978	75,144	77,947			
1998	55,665	80,296	87,961				
1999	43,401	57,547					
2000	28,800						

| Accident | | | Age in months: | | | | | Dev to |
Year	12–24	24–36	36–48	48–60	60–72	72–84	84–Ult	Ult
1994	1.276	1.034	1.007	1.036	1.019	1.001	**1.010**	**1.010**
1995	1.248	1.052	1.020	1.033	0.992	**1.000**	**1.010**	**1.010**
1996	1.317	1.024	0.998	1.005	**1.000**	**1.000**	**1.010**	**1.010**
1997	1.693	1.105	1.037	**1.020**	**1.000**	**1.000**	**1.010**	**1.030**
1998	1.442	1.095	**1.020**	**1.020**	**1.000**	**1.000**	**1.010**	**1.051**
1999	1.326	**1.095**	**1.020**	**1.020**	**1.000**	**1.000**	**1.010**	**1.151**
2000	**1.350**	**1.095**	**1.020**	**1.020**	**1.000**	**1.000**	**1.010**	**1.553**

In this example, the 1996 accident year is 60 months old. The development from 60 months to ultimate is given by the factor of 1.010. The age to ultimate factor can be interpreted to mean that the accident year is 99% reported as of 60 months. Likewise, the 2000 accident year as of 12 months is expected to be 64.4% or 1/1.553 reported. This implies that the 2000 accident year is 35.6% unreported as of 12/31/2000.

Clearly, if you knew what the 2000 accident year ultimate losses were going to be, you would set aside 35.6% of the ultimate loss estimate as the appropriate IBNR reserve as of 12/31/2000. This is the amount of future incurred loss that has yet to be reported on the 2000 accident year. Although we won't know what the ultimate value of the 2000 accident year will be for many years, we can calculate the expected value by multiplying earned premium by an expected loss ratio (ELR). The expected loss ratio can be estimated by reviewing the pricing assumptions, historical results, or industry results for the line of business.

If the earned premiums and expected loss ratios for each year are given below, we can apply this method to our incurred losses.

Bornhuetter–Ferguson (BF) Method

Accident Year	(1) Earned Premium	(2) ELR	(3) = (1) × (2) Expected Ultimate	(4) Ultimate Develop't	(5) = 1.0− 1.0/(4) Remaining Develop't	(6) = (5) × (3) Expected Unreported	(7) Reported to Date	(8) = (6) + (7) Total Ultimate	(9) Paid to Date	(10) = (8) − (9) Reserve
1994	101,946	80%	81,557	1.010	1.0%	816	82,372	83,188	78,224	4,964
1995	112,068	80%	89,654	1.010	1.0%	897	87,413	88,310	81,287	7,023
1996	97,796	80%	78,237	1.010	1.0%	782	70,041	70,823	66,402	4,421
1997	101,930	78%	79,505	1.030	2.9%	2,306	77,947	80,253	62,347	17,906
1998	107,357	78%	83,738	1.051	4.9%	4,103	87,961	92,064	62,832	29,232
1999	84,531	78%	65,934	1.151	13.1%	8,637	57,547	66,184	33,568	32,616
2000	57,697	78%	45,004	1.553	35.6%	16,021	28,800	44,821	11,346	33,475

Total Reserve 129,637

One advantage of the BF method is that it avoids overreacting to unexpected losses. For illustration, assume that actual losses in accident year 2000 are 35,000 rather than 28,800. The incurred loss development method would produce an ultimate loss estimate of 54,355 ($= 35,000 \times 1.553$) well above the expected loss estimate of 45,004. The Bornhuetter–Ferguson method would produce an estimate of 51,025. This estimate is the weighted result of incurred loss development method and the expected loss estimate where the weights are based on the reciprocal of the age-to-ultimate factor.

$$51,025 = 54,355 \times (1/1.553) + 45,004 \times (1 - 1/1.553)$$

If this had been an older accident year, say 1999, the loss development factor would be 1.151. In this case, 86.9% weight would be given to the loss development method rather than 64.4% weight as shown for accident year 2000. Generally, as an accident year matures, the intial expected incurred loss estimate becomes less important and actual reported loss experience becomes more important. In this fashion, the BF method produces a blend of stability and responsiveness in the loss reserve estimate.

Loss Adjustment Expenses

An extremely important part of the loss reserve evaluation process is the evaluation of loss adjustment expense liabilities. Loss adjustment expenses (LAE) can be split into two components, commonly called allocated loss adjustment expenses (ALAE) and unallocated loss adjustment expenses (ULAE). Until 1998, the determining factor in whether or not a loss expense was considered ALAE or ULAE was whether the expense could be assigned to an individual claim. If an expense could be assigned to a claim, it was considered ALAE.

This approach made it difficult to make comparisons between companies. For example, claim adjuster fees are one type of loss adjustment expense. Claim adjusters are typically either company adjusters or independent adjusters. The distinguishing feature is whether or not the claim adjuster is employed by the company. Company adjuster expenses were typically considered ULAE and independent adjuster expenses were typically considered ALAE. So depending on whether the company uses its own employees or uses outside vendors, the same expense from the same type of activity could be classified in two different ways.

The National Association of Insurance Commissioners (NAIC) introduced new reporting requirements for loss adjustment expenses that became effective 1/1/1998. The goal is to have consistent reporting of expenses among companies. Allocated loss adjustment expenses were deemed by the NAIC to mean expenses, whether internal or external to the company, related to defense, litigation and medical cost containment. Unallocated loss adjustment expenses are considered to be all loss expenses not specifically defined as ALAE. All adjuster fees are considered ULAE. Effective with the 1999 Annual Statement, the NAIC changed the titles of these expenses to match the revised definitions. ALAE became "Defense and Cost Containment" expenses and ULAE became "Adjusting and Other" expenses.

The key in grouping expenses for reserving purposes is still whether or not the expenses are assigned to an individual claim. Significantly more analysis can be completed for those expenses that are assigned to an individual claim (allocated expenses) because more data exists. For instance, the accident date of the claim that generated the expense is known for an allocated expense, but unknown for an unallocated expense.

In evaluating any loss adjustment expense liabilities, the loss reserve analyst needs to know how the data is being defined and, if the definition has changed, how the data is impacted. Once the answers to these questions are known, any necessary adjustments can be made to the liability estimates.

Allocated Loss Adjustment Expenses

One approach to estimating allocated loss adjustment expense liabilities is to combine ALAE with losses and estimate the total liability. Generally, this approach is not desirable because the two development patterns may be quite different. Combining ALAE with losses is often similar to combining two non-homogeneous lines of business. Separate analyses of loss and allocated loss adjustment expense are also necessary to allow for monitoring of actual experience versus projected experience for each component.

The allocated loss adjustment expenses can often be further split into subcategories. The most important subcategory is attorneys' fees and court costs. It will often be conducive to obtaining better estimates of loss adjustment expense to develop legal expense separate from all other allocated expense items.

Case reserve estimates sometimes are not established for allocated loss adjustment expenses. This means that the actuary only has paid allocated loss adjustment expenses to work with. The allocated expense reserve is established on a bulk basis by actuarial estimates, or may be spread to cases by some formula approach. In either case, allocated paid amounts are the only meaningful history available for the analysis.

A common analysis procedure is to compare the allocated expenses paid to the paid losses on the same claims, and follow the development of the relationship of paid allocated expense to paid loss over time.

Assume the same paid loss history from our previous example.

Accident	Age in months:						
Year	12	24	36	48	60	72	84
1994	22,603	40,064	54,301	64,114	71,257	75,950	78,224
1995	22,054	43,970	58,737	71,841	78,076	81,287	
1996	20,166	39,147	51,319	60,417	66,402		
1997	19,297	37,355	50,391	62,347			
1998	20,555	42,898	62,832				
1999	17,001	33,568					
2000	11,346						

We also have available the history of paid allocated loss expense by accident year.

Accident	Age in months:						
Year	12	24	36	48	60	72	84
1994	554	1,110	2,118	3,231	4,211	4,170	5,429
1995	485	1,244	2,256	3,578	4,567	5,202	
1996	446	1,104	1,981	2,973	3,785		
1997	405	953	1,809	2,905			
1998	388	1,025	2,161				
1999	357	843					
2000	216						

The relationship of paid allocated loss expense to paid loss is then derived as follows for this history.

Accident	Age in months:						
Year	12	24	36	48	60	72	84
1994	2.45%	2.77%	3.90%	5.04%	5.91%	5.49%	6.94%
1995	2.20%	2.83%	3.84%	4.98%	5.85%	6.40%	
1996	2.21%	2.82%	3.86%	4.92%	5.70%		
1997	2.10%	2.55%	3.59%	4.66%			
1998	1.89%	2.39%	3.44%				
1999	2.10%	2.51%					
2000	1.90%						

Age-to-age development factors applying to the ratios of paid allocated loss adjustment expense are given below. We are trying to estimate the ultimate ratio of ALAE to loss. Once the ultimate ratio is chosen it can be applied to the estimate of ultimate losses to obtain an estimate of ultimate allocated loss adjustment expense. It often helps to think of these ratios of paid allocated expense to paid loss as the cost to settle $100 of loss. For example, in the 1994 accident year at 12/31/2000, $6.94 of allocated expenses has been paid for every $100 of paid loss.

The development triangle and selected averages of the development factors for these expense amounts are given below.

Accident	Age in months:						
Year	12–24	24–36	36–48	48–60	60–72	72–84	84–Ult
1994	1.130	1.408	1.292	1.173	0.929	1.264	
1995	1.286	1.358	1.297	1.174	1.094		
1996	1.275	1.369	1.275	1.158			
1997	1.216	1.407	1.298				
1998	1.266	1.439					
1999	1.196						
Average	1.228	1.396	1.291	1.168	1.012	1.264	
Average Last 3	1.226	1.405	1.290	1.168			
Average Last 4	1.238	1.393	1.291				
Avg Exc Hi & Lo	1.238	1.395	1.295	1.173			
Weighted Average	1.226	1.394	1.290	1.169	1.011	1.264	
Harmonic Mean	1.227	1.396	1.290	1.168	1.008	1.264	

Assume the analyst chose the following development patterns along the right diagonal as the most likely in the future.

| Accident | | | Age in months: | | | | | Dev to |
Year	12–24	24–36	36–48	48–60	60–72	72–84	84–Ult	Ult
1994	1.130	1.408	1.292	1.173	0.929	1.264	**1.010**	**1.010**
1995	1.286	1.358	1.297	1.174	1.094	**1.010**	**1.010**	**1.020**
1996	1.275	1.369	1.275	1.158	**1.025**	**1.010**	**1.010**	**1.046**
1997	1.216	1.407	1.298	**1.160**	**1.025**	**1.010**	**1.010**	**1.213**
1998	1.266	1.439	**1.295**	**1.160**	**1.025**	**1.010**	**1.010**	**1.571**
1999	1.196	**1.400**	**1.295**	**1.160**	**1.025**	**1.010**	**1.010**	**2.199**
2000	**1.300**	**1.400**	**1.295**	**1.160**	**1.025**	**1.010**	**1.010**	**2.859**

Based on development factors chosen above, paid allocated loss adjustment expense per $100 of loss by accident year may be projected to an ultimate basis.

| Accident | | | Age in months: | | | | | Ultimate |
Year	12	24	36	48	60	72	84	per $100
1994	2.45	2.77	3.90	5.04	5.91	5.49	6.94	**7.01**
1995	2.20	2.83	3.84	4.98	5.85	6.40	**6.46**	**6.53**
1996	2.21	2.82	3.86	4.92	5.70	**5.84**	**5.90**	**5.96**
1997	2.10	2.55	3.59	4.66	**5.40**	**5.54**	**5.60**	**5.65**
1998	1.89	2.39	3.44	**4.45**	**5.17**	**5.30**	**5.35**	**5.40**
1999	2.10	2.51	**3.52**	**4.55**	**5.28**	**5.41**	**5.47**	**5.52**
2000	1.90	**2.47**	**3.46**	**4.49**	**5.20**	**5.33**	**5.39**	**5.44**

| Accident | Ultimate | Ultimate | Ultimate | Paid | ALAE |
Year	per $100	Loss	ALAE	ALAE	Reserve
1994	7.01	83,196	5,832	5,429	403
1995	6.53	88,287	5,764	5,202	562
1996	5.96	70,741	4,216	3,785	431
1997	5.65	80,301	4,538	2,905	1,633
1998	5.40	92,430	4,993	2,161	2,832
1999	5.52	66,215	3,657	843	2,814
2000	5.44	44,821	2,439	216	2,223
				Total Reserve	10,898

This analysis indicates a reserve need of $10.9 million for allocated loss adjustment expenses.

The premise of the above analysis is that the relationship of paid allocated expense to paid loss dollars is usually fairly stable. The premise must be validated by the analyst in discussion with the insurer's management. For example, changes in defense strategies may distort the ratios. Sometimes significant ALAE dollars are spent on claims that will eventually close with no loss payment. One advantage of this method is that it does recognize the relationship of paid loss expense to loss. However, any errors made in estimating ultimate losses will be carried forward into the estimate of allocated loss adjustment expense.

A variation on the above method includes developing the additive increments to the allocated expense to loss ratios in place of multiplicative development of these ratios. If the ratios are very small at early maturities, the additive approach seems to be more stable.

Another common method of estimating the ultimate value of ALAE is to simply develop the paid allocated loss expense history. The drawback of this approach is that the estimate is not related to the ultimate level of losses, hence it could produce widely varying results in terms of allocated expense paid per $100 of claims paid. Clearly, the methods chosen will depend heavily on a review of the data and its characteristics, as well as an understanding of the insurer's operating characteristics with regard to handling of defense and other allocated expenses.

Unallocated Loss Adjustment Expenses
In addition to estimating the liability for allocated loss adjustment expenses, we must also estimate the liability for unallocated loss adjustment expenses. Most ULAE is the expense of operating a claims department and includes such items as claim adjuster fees, office rent, and utilities.

Unallocated loss adjustment expense tends not to be recorded in the same level of detail as allocated loss adjustment expense. Usually some type of internal allocation procedure is used to distribute calendar year ULAE expenses to line of business. This internal allocation procedure should reflect the claim activity that gave rise to the expense such as the number of claims incurred during the year, claims closed during the year, number of claims remaining open during the year, number of days claims are open, or number of payment or reserve transactions during the year. Ideally, standard costs are assigned to each transaction and total claim department costs are allocated in accordance to the distribution of standard costs. The analyst needs to understand how expenses are allocated to line of business and any changes that have occurred in the allocation procedure before meaningful numerical analysis of ULAE can be done.

Once unallocated loss expense payments have been assigned to lines of business, we can begin to estimate the reserve. The most common procedure is to estimate the amount of unallocated loss adjustment expense that is needed per $100 of claims payments.

Suppose the following unallocated loss expense payment history, by calendar year of payment.

Calendar Year	Paid ULAE	Paid Loss	Paid ULAE/ $100 Loss
1994	12,345	91,955	13.43
1995	13,826	100,576	13.75
1996	15,486	111,530	13.89
1997	17,344	130,708	13.27
1998	19,425	145,889	13.31
1999	21,756	164,051	13.26
2000	24,367	171,397	14.22
Total/Avg	124,549	916,106	13.60

These amounts average $13.60 in unallocated loss adjustment expense per $100 of paid loss. It is important to remember that the paid amounts in any calendar year come from a mixture of new claims and claims that were already open.

ULAE expenses are generated throughout the lifetime of a claim. A common simple assumption is that 50% of the total unallocated loss adjustment expense is paid when a new claim is opened and the other 50% over the life of the claim. However, it is preferable to review this assumption with the claim department. Assume that this review indicates that 40% of unallocated loss expense is paid to set up an initial claim. Then the estimated liability for unallocated loss adjustment expense is given by

$$.1360 \times \text{IBNR Reserve} + .1360 \times (1 - .40) \times \text{Case Reserve}$$

If the IBNR reserve required is $90 million and the case reserves total $320 million, then the total ultimate amount of allocated claim expense liability is

$$.1360 \times \$90,000,000 + .1360 \times .60 \times \$320,000,000$$

which totals $38,352,000. Note that the reserve amount needed is higher than the amount paid in any one calendar year. This is because we are estimating the total ULAE liability, not simply how much ULAE will be paid in any given calendar year.

One adjustment that can be made to this method is to split the "pure" IBNR reserve from the remaining broad definition of IBNR. The "pure" IBNR claims would be multiplied by the .1360 factor since no loss adjustment work has yet been done on these claims. The remaining IBNR reserve would be multiplied by $.1360 \times (1 - .4)$ to recognize that some ULAE had already been paid on these claims.

PHASE 3: EVALUATION OF ULTIMATE LOSS ESTIMATES

The application of any particular reserve method to a given body of data will yield a set of estimated ultimate losses. However, each method applied will result in a different set of ultimate losses and an associated reserve estimate. The actuary must still decide on either a best estimate reserve, or a range of possible reserve estimates, or both. Of course, for financial statement purposes, a point estimate of loss reserve requirements must be supplied for the balance sheet.

While a substantial amount of judgment has been an element of the selection and application of each reserving method, the selection of a final reserve estimate is most often a subject of the actuary's experience and judgment. In this section we will present a number of practical tests that will allow one to test a set of estimated ultimate losses for reasonability.

It is important to evaluate the results of each reserving method by attempting to diagnose the reasons the methods vary. The explanation must be the result of the actuary's analysis and experience. The attempt to reconcile a number of different estimates is extremely difficult, but often yields important new insights.

The analysis conducted on the data presented above yielded six different estimates of ultimate losses by accident year. These estimates are the result of different methods that are sensitive to different aspects of the reserve development process. This is to be expected, since each method uses only a limited amount of data about the loss development process. After reviewing the results of the various methods, the analyst makes an initial selection of ultimate loss as follows:

Estimated Ultimate Losses by Accident Year and Method

Accident Year	Paid Devel't	Incurred Devel't	Average Paid	Average Incurred	BF Method	Reserve Devel't	Average	Selected
1994	82,370	83,196	79,092	82,284	83,188	82,413	82,090	83,196
1995	88,163	88,287	84,023	87,505	88,310	87,974	87,377	88,287
1996	76,340	70,741	71,866	69,982	70,823	70,840	71,765	70,741
1997	78,846	80,301	74,204	79,487	80,253	81,562	79,109	80,301
1998	102,293	92,430	91,107	91,399	92,064	93,842	93,856	92,430
1999	69,344	66,215	71,520	65,521	66,184	66,791	67,596	66,215
2000	45,939	44,737	60,461	53,757	44,821	46,001	49,286	44,821

Required Reserve in $1,000's by Method

	Paid Devel't	Incurred Devel't	Average Paid	Average Incurred	BF Method	Reserve Devel't	Average	Selected
All Years	147,289	129,901	136,267	133,929	129,637	133,417	135,073	129,986

The analyst has selected the results of the incurred development method for all years except the most recent. For the most recent year, the BF method has been used because the incurred loss data is still immature. The initial selection of these ultimate loss estimates should be tested for reasonability by comparing them to various loss development history displays.

Comparing these selected ultimate losses to the paid and incurred history yields the following displays of paid and incurred as a percent of ultimate.

Paid Losses as % of Ultimate Losses

Accident	Age in months:						
Year	12	24	36	48	60	72	84
1994	27.2%	48.2%	65.3%	77.1%	85.6%	91.3%	94.0%
1995	25.0%	49.8%	66.5%	81.4%	88.4%	92.1%	
1996	28.5%	55.3%	72.5%	85.4%	93.9%		
1997	24.0%	46.5%	62.8%	77.6%			
1998	22.2%	46.4%	68.0%				
1999	25.7%	50.7%					
2000	25.3%						

Incurred Losses as % of Ultimate Losses

Accident	Age in months:						
Year	12	24	36	48	60	72	84
1994	70.5%	89.9%	92.9%	93.6%	97.0%	98.9%	99.0%
1995	72.2%	90.1%	94.8%	96.7%	99.8%	99.0%	
1996	73.2%	96.4%	98.7%	98.5%	99.0%		
1997	50.0%	84.7%	93.6%	97.1%			
1998	60.2%	86.9%	95.2%				
1999	65.5%	86.9%					
2000	64.2%						

Review of these statistics indicates that the ratios of paid loss to expected ultimate loss in the 1999 and 2000 accident years are somewhat high, at 50.7% and 25.3%, respectively. However the comparison to 1997 and 1998 is difficult because of the anomalous behavior of these two years.

A similar review of the ultimate amounts with respect to carried case reserves is also useful. This display of course is merely the difference between the previous two displays.

Case Reserves as % of Ultimate Losses

Accident	Age in months:						
Year	12	24	36	48	60	72	84
1994	43.3%	41.8%	27.7%	16.6%	11.4%	7.6%	5.0%
1995	47.2%	40.3%	28.3%	15.3%	11.4%	6.9%	
1996	44.7%	41.0%	26.1%	13.1%	5.1%		
1997	26.0%	38.1%	30.8%	19.4%			
1998	38.0%	40.5%	27.2%				
1999	39.9%	36.2%					
2000	38.9%						

Based on the selections, the required reserve is the difference between the paid losses and the ultimate. This required reserve is also a "hindsight" test of the selected ultimate.

Required Reserves as % of Ultimate Losses

Accident	Age in months:						
Year	12	24	36	48	60	72	84
1994	72.8%	51.8%	34.7%	22.9%	14.4%	8.7%	6.0%
1995	75.0%	50.2%	33.5%	18.6%	11.6%	7.9%	
1996	71.5%	44.7%	27.5%	14.6%	6.1%		
1997	76.0%	53.5%	37.2%	22.4%			
1998	77.8%	53.6%	32.0%				
1999	74.3%	49.3%					
2000	74.7%						

It is also useful in some cases to review the ratio of the required reserve to the carried case reserve, as this ratio can be very stable for some lines.

Required Reserves as % of Case Reserves

Accident	Age in months:						
Year	12	24	36	48	60	72	84
1994	168.1%	124.2%	125.5%	138.5%	126.1%	114.5%	119.9%
1995	158.9%	124.7%	118.5%	121.6%	101.3%	114.3%	
1996	160.0%	108.8%	105.1%	111.3%	119.2%		
1997	292.6%	140.2%	120.8%	115.1%			
1998	204.7%	132.4%	117.8%				
1999	186.4%	136.1%					
2000	191.9%						

It is also necessary to compare the ultimate losses to other benchmarks, such as earned premium or exposures. Below the selected ultimate loss is compared to earned premium. The ultimate loss ratio is also compared to the expected loss ratio that was used in the pricing assumptions.

Accident Year	Selected Ultimate	Earned Premium	Loss Ratio	Expected LR
1994	83,196	101,946	81.6%	80.0%
1995	88,287	112,068	78.8%	80.0%
1996	70,741	97,796	72.3%	80.0%
1997	80,301	101,930	78.8%	78.0%
1998	92,430	107,357	86.1%	78.0%
1999	66,215	84,531	78.3%	78.0%
2000	44,832	57,697	77.7%	78.0%

Immediately we see that the loss ratio for the 1998 accident year is higher than the other years. This may be a result of the more hazardous mix of business that was written in that year. The reserving actuary should communicate with the Underwriting Department that results for the 1998 accident year are worse than other years and are significantly higher than expected. In this case, the more hazardous business is no longer written, but the Underwriting Department must get feedback on results from the reserving actuary so appropriate corrective underwriting actions can be taken if they haven't already.

Another benchmark is average ultimate claim size, or severity. Absent any changes in the book of business, we would expect severity to trend with inflation. Below we have compared the selected ultimate losses to the projected number of claims net of claims closed with no payment.

Accident Year	Selected Ultimate	Ultimate Claims	Average Claim	Change in Avg.
1994	83,196	34,328	2,424	
1995	88,287	32,542	2,713	11.9%
1996	70,741	26,916	2,628	−3.1%
1997	80,301	24,571	3,268	24.3%
1998	92,430	26,531	3,484	6.6%
1999	66,215	18,015	3,676	5.5%
2000	44,832	13,599	3,297	−10.3%

History shows that the average claim for this book of business is volatile. However, the 10.3% decrease in severity in the 2000 accident year appears unusual. The actuary should consider whether the ultimate loss selection or the ultimate claim count selection should be modified, or if this change in severity is reasonable.

Claim frequency, which is the number of claims relative to some measure of exposure, can be used as a reasonableness check for the projected number of claims. In this case, we will use earned premium as a proxy for exposure.

Accident Year	Ultimate Claims	Earned Premium	Frequency	Change in Freq.
1994	34,328	101,946	337	
1995	32,542	112,068	290	−13.8%
1996	26,916	97,796	275	−5.2%
1997	24,571	101,930	241	−12.4%
1998	26,531	107,357	247	2.5%
1999	18,015	84,531	213	−13.8%
2000	13,599	57,697	236	10.6%

This exhibit shows that for every $1 million in premium, there were 337 claims in accident year 1994. The frequency for this business is also volatile, and the increase of 10.6% in accident year 2000 is very high.

After discussions with underwriting and claims management, the actuary determines that there has been an increase in the number of reported claims under $1,000. There has been a shift in the portfolio toward high-frequency, low-severity risks. Based on this information, the actuary is comfortable that the 2000 selected ultimate loss is correct. In future reserve reviews, the actuary should watch for possible shifts in loss and allocated loss adjustment expense development patterns that may result from this shifting mix of business.

PHASE 4: MONITORING RESULTS

Once ultimate losses have been selected, it is extremely important for the analyst to be able to derive projections of expected development in the upcoming period. These predictions can be monitored over the next period—month, quarter, or year. If actual loss statistics, such as paid losses, case reserves, IBNR counts, and the number of claims closed with payment actually come in close to the forecast development amount, the analyst can have more confidence in the analysis and understanding of the reserve situation. If results are not as forecast, additional work is required to determine if the differences were random occurrences, or if it is an indication that the projections should be revised.

For example, based on the selected ultimate loss of $44,832,000 for the 2000 accident year, we should expect to see emergence of incurred losses of $10,082,000 during 2001 on the 2000 accident year. The expected loss emergence forecast comes directly from the incurred loss development factors previously selected by the analyst. The selected development factor from age 12 to ultimate of 1.553 implies that 64.4% (= 1/1.553) of losses are unreported at 12 months. The factor of 1.151 for 24 to ultimate implies that 86.9% of the losses are unreported at

24 months. Thus, we can calculate that expected reported losses from 12 to 24 months are 22.5% of ultimate, and 22.5% of the selected ultimate is 10,082,000.

The forecast incurred loss emergence expected in calendar year 2001 is (in $1,000's):

Accident Year	Emergence
1994	0
1995	0
1996	0
1997	1,559
1998	1,759
1999	5,467
2000	10,082
Total	18,867

This indicates a total of $18,867,000 of incurred loss should emerge during 2001 based on the selected loss development factors. The benefit of monitoring the near term forecast is clear. The accuracy of the ultimate estimate on accident year 2000 will take several more years to ascertain, however the accuracy of the development projection for the next calendar year can be measured in only one year. Similar projections can be made for paid loss or loss adjustment expenses.

MISCELLANEOUS TOPICS

Reserve Discounting

In establishing the liabilities for losses and loss adjustment expenses, it is often necessary to recognize the time value of money. We have not taken interest into account in any of the loss reserve estimation procedures reviewed above.

A payout schedule of the liability amount is required to discount the loss reserve liability for the time value of money. If the liability estimate is given by the paid loss development estimate as below, we have an undiscounted liability of $147,289,000. The payment pattern can be deduced from the completed triangle established by the selection of paid loss development factors.

For example, if the paid loss projection is given as follows:

Accident Year	Age in months: 12	24	36	48	60	72	84	Ultimate	Paid to Date	Reserve
1994	22,603	40,064	54,301	64,114	71,257	75,950	78,224	**82,370**	78,224	4,146
1995	22,054	43,970	58,737	71,841	78,076	81,287	**83,726**	**88,163**	81,287	6,876
1996	20,166	39,147	51,319	60,417	66,402	**70,386**	**72,498**	**76,340**	66,402	9,938
1997	19,297	37,355	50,391	62,347	**68,582**	**72,697**	**74,878**	**78,846**	62,347	16,499
1998	20,555	42,898	62,832	**79,231**	**88,977**	**94,315**	**97,145**	**102,293**	62,832	39,461
1999	17,001	33,568	**45,317**	**54,833**	**60,317**	**63,936**	**65,854**	**69,344**	33,568	35,776
2000	11,346	**22,238**	**30,022**	**36,326**	**39,959**	**42,356**	**43,627**	**45,939**	11,346	34,593
										147,289

If we assume that all losses are paid within eight years, we can calculate the forecast of paid amounts by calendar year and accident year. Discount factors are then applied to the payments within each calendar year. Here we have assumed that payment will be made at the mid-point of the calendar year and that interest is earned at an annual rate of 5%.

Accident Year	Calendar Year 2001	2002	2003	2004	2005	2006	2007	Total
1994	4,146	0	0	0	0	0	0	4,146
1995	2,439	4,437	0	0	0	0	0	6,876
1996	3,984	2,112	3,842	0	0	0	0	9,938
1997	6,235	4,115	2,181	3,969	0	0	0	16,499
1998	16,399	9,745	5,339	2,829	5,149	0	0	39,461
1999	11,749	9,517	5,483	3,619	1,918	3,490	0	35,776
2000	10,892	7,783	6,305	3,633	2,398	1,271	2,312	34,593
Total	55,843	37,709	23,150	14,050	9,464	4,761	2,312	147,289
Discount Factor	0.976	0.929	0.885	0.843	0.803	0.765	0.728	
Discounted Reserve	54,498	35,048	20,491	11,844	7,599	3,640	1,684	134,804
						Discount Amount		12,485

The discount of \$12.5 million is about 8.5% of the undiscounted amount. The calculation of discount is very sensitive to the selected interest rate. The analyst should research the type of investments held and the expected return on those investments to determine the appropriate rate of discount.

Reserve Estimate Ranges

Throughout our analyses, we have focused on obtaining point estimates of the loss reserve liability. However, we have also found that it is extremely difficult to obtain one single estimate of the loss reserve liability. Each method results in a different answer. Further, to the extent that we are dealing with the estimation of the mean of a stochastic process, the actual result will almost always differ from the estimate.

Clearly, a range of results and a statement of our confidence that the observed reserve liability at final development will be within the stated range are preferable for this sort of process. However, the insurer's balance sheets will continue to require the analyst to supply a point estimate of the reserve liability.

Working with risk theoretical concepts, it is possible to develop a model of the reserve inventory, in terms of frequency and severity. This model can be used to develop confidence intervals for the development of the reserve. The development of such a risk theory model is outside the scope of this chapter. However, work along these lines has been done (see Hayne [1988]).

CONCLUSION

Accurate loss and loss adjustment reserves are critical to insurance company performance. Although the reserve is a balance sheet item, a change to a liability account on the balance sheet has a direct impact on income. In addition, management must have an accurate picture of results so that appropriate strategic and operational decisions can be made.

A strict formula approach to projecting loss and loss adjustment expense reserves will not work. A number of different projection methods must be used, and the experience and judgment of the analyst is critical. The analyst must be in constant communication with claims and underwriting management so that appropriate methods are used and proper adjustments are made. Of equal importance is communication of the results to management that might lead to improvement in claims processing procedures or development of underwriting initiatives. The reserving actuary should also communicate results to the pricing actuary so that pricing procedures can be modified if required.

In addition, because there is frequently a range of estimates that can be considered reasonable, the analyst should be aware of the context in which the reserve estimates will be used. Different projection techniques may be appropriate if results are to be used to determine the profitability of a specific line of business or if results will be used for statutory reporting of reserves.

Reasonability checks should always be performed after ultimate losses or loss expenses are selected. Revisions to ultimate selections should be considered if results differ significantly from expectations or industry benchmarks. Finally, projections should be frequently monitored and adjustments to ultimate selections should be made when indicated.

REFERENCES

Berquist, J. R., and R. E. Sherman, "Loss Reserve Adequacy Testing: A Comprehensive, Systematic Approach," *Proceedings of the Casualty Actuarial Society*, 1977, 64:123–185.

Bornheutter, R. L., and R. E. Ferguson, "The Actuary and IBNR," *Proceedings of the Casualty Actuarial Society*, 1972, 59:181–195.

Casualty Actuarial Society, Statement of Principles Regarding Property and Casualty Loss and Loss Adjustment Expense Reserves, 1988.

Davidson, S., C. Stickney, and R. Weil, *Financial Accounting: An Introduction to Concepts, Methods, and Uses*, New York: The Dryden Press, 1982.

Degerness, J., "Recognition of Claim Department Impact on Reserving," *1983 Casualty Loss Reserve Seminar Transcript*, 1983, 610–617.

Finger, R. J., "Modeling Loss Reserve Development," *Proceedings of the Casualty Actuarial Society*, 1986, 63:90–106.

Fisher, W., and J. Lange, "Loss Reserve Testing: A Report Year Approach," *Proceedings of the Casualty Actuarial Society*, 1973, 60:189–207.

Hayne, R. M., "Application of Collective Risk Theory to Estimate Variability in Loss Reserves," *CAS Discussion Paper Program*, 1988, 275–300.

Heipler, J. and F. Mele. Losses and Loss Adjustment Expenses. In *Property and Casualty Insurance Accounting*. Seventh Edition. Durham, NC: Insurance Accounting and Systems Association, Inc., 1998, 7:1–29.

Marker, J. O., and F. J. Mohl, "Rating Claims-Made Insurance Policies," *CAS Discussion Paper Program*, 1980, 265–304.

McClenahan, C. L., "A Mathematical Model for Loss Reserve Analysis," *Proceedings of the Casualty Actuarial Society*, 1975, 62:134–153.

McClenahan, C. L. Ratemaking. Chap. 2 in *Foundations of Casualty Actuarial Science*. First Edition. New York: Casualty Actuarial Society, 1990.

McClenahan, C. L., "Liabilities for Extended Reporting Endorsements Guarantees Under Claims-Made Policies," *CAS Discussion Paper Program*, 1988, 345–364.

Mohl, F. J., "Reserving for Claims-Made Policies," *1987 Casualty Loss Reserve Seminar Transcript*, 1987, 384–402.

Nichols, R., and P. Grannan. Estimating Liabilities for Losses and Loss Adjustment Expenses. In *Property and Casualty Insurance Accounting*. Seventh Edition. Durham, NC: Insurance Accounting and Systems Association, Inc., 1998, 3:1–3:42

Philbrick, S. W., "Reserve Review of a Reinsurance Company," *CAS Discussion Paper Program*, 1986, 147–162.

Taylor, G. C., "Separation of Inflation and Other Effects from the Distribution of Non-Life Insurance Claim Delays," *ASTIN Bulletin*, 1977, 9:219–230.

APPENDIX A

THE DEFINITION OF LIABILITY

An obligation satisfies the accounting definition of a liability if it possesses three essential characteristics (Davidson et al., 386–387):

1. The obligation involves a probable future sacrifice of resources at a specified or determinable date;

2. The firm has little or no discretion to avoid the transfer, and

3. The transaction or event giving rise to the obligation has already occurred.

A claim liability of a property and casualty insurer satisfies the second and third characteristics above. The first requirement is not generally satisfied in property and casualty claim situations. For instance, in a workers compensation claim, payments must be made periodically at specified times, often weekly. However, in a third-party liability situation it is not possible to specify the date on which settlement will be made.

A loss reserve is a contingent liability in the sense that each specific claim under adjustment depends on some future contingent event to determine the extent of the insurer's liability. Two tests are proposed by the accounting literature to determine if a contingent liability should be recognized on the company's balance sheet. These are:

1. information at the time of preparation of the financial reports indicates that it is likely that a liability has been incurred, and

2. the amount of the liability can be reasonably estimated.

Clearly, an insurer's loss reserves satisfy both these conditions.

APPENDIX B

AN ACTUARIAL MODEL OF LOSS DEVELOPMENT[1]

Most approaches to loss reserving and financial reporting deal with aggregates over a time period. For example, we may consider all claims that occur, or all claims that are reported, or all amounts that are paid, during one calendar year, quarter, or month. Such approaches usually involve assumptions about how the claims process behaves *within* each year, quarter or month— assumptions that may not be correct. Instead we can create actuarial models that analyze claims continuously, without dividing time into discrete periods. Such models give us more flexibility in dealing with unusual or quickly changing situations.

The basic mathematical form of an actuarial loss development model is outlined below. This model can serve as a conceptual starting point for reserve analysis.

THE LOSS FUNCTION

We begin with a loss function $v(x)$, which represents the rate at which losses are occurring at time x. The ultimate loss for the time period (a,b) is then

$$\int_a^b v(x)\,dx.$$

In practice we cannot observe $v(x)$ directly; we can only observe aggregate loss over a period of time.

Example 1: Losses are occurring at a constant rate of $1,000,000 per year. Find the amount of loss from 1/1/88 to 1/1/91.

Answer: Let $x = 0$ correspond to 1/1/88. and $x = 3$ to 1/1/91. Since $v(x) = \$1,000,000$, we see that

$$\text{Loss} = \int_0^3 \$1,000,000\,dx = \$3,000,000.$$

---

[1] The author thanks Eric Brosius for his efforts in re-drafting the first edition version of this section.

We could have answered this question easily by ordinary multiplication. In most insurance situations, however, $v(x)$ changes over time in response to inflation and other factors.

Example 2: In the previous example, what if the rate of loss were growing exponentially as described by the function $v(x) =$ $\$1,000,000\,e^{0.1x}$?

Answer: This time we compute

$$\text{Loss} = \int_0^3 \$1,000,000e^{0.1x}dx = \$3,498,588.$$

DEVELOPMENT

The function $v(x)$ tells us how losses *occur*. It says nothing about how those losses are reported and paid. To study this question we introduce a development function D. If we are studying loss payments, $D(t)$ will represent the percentage of losses that are paid within t years after occurrence. If we are studying loss reporting, $D(t)$ will represent the percentage of losses that are reported within that period of time. A little thought about the claims process shows us that $D(t) = 0$ for $t < 0$, and that $\lim_{t \to \infty} D(t) = 1$. We sometimes strengthen the second fact by assuming that there is a fixed time T such that $D(t) = 1$ whenever $t > T$. This implies that all development is complete within T years after occurrence.

Example 3: Is it always true that $0 \le D(t) \le 1$?

Answer: This is often true, but not always. For example, if we look at loss payments net of salvage and subrogation, development may exceed 100% for a while before late recoveries bring net paid losses back down to their ultimate value.

By combining the loss function $v(x)$ with the development function $D(t)$ we can describe development as we see it at a particular point in time. The aggregate losses from period (a, b) as developed to time $x = c$ are given by

$$\int_a^b v(x)D(c - x)\,dx.$$

We can understand this integral as follows. Losses that occurred at time $x = a$ have had $c - a$ years to develop, so we multiply these losses by $D(c - a)$. Losses that occurred at time $x = b$ have had only $c - b$ years to develop, and are multiplied by the (usually smaller) value $D(c - b)$.

Example 4: Suppose $v(x) = \$1,000,000$ and $D(t) = 1 - e^{-t}$ for $t \geq 0$. Find the losses from 1/1/1996 to 1/1/1999 as developed to 1/1/2000

Answer: We obtain loss developed to 1/1/2000 as

$$\int_0^3 \$1,000,000(1 - e^{-(4-x)})\,dx \approx \$2,650,436.$$

At 1/1/2000 losses that occurred on 1/1/1996 are 4 years old. They have developed to 98% of ultimate, since $D(4) \approx 0.98$. Losses that occurred on 1/1/1999 are 1 year old, and have developed to only 63% of ultimate ($D(1) \approx 0.63$). What we observe, however, is the entire block of claims that occurred in the period $(0, 3)$. This block has developed to 88% of ultimate ($\$2,650,436/\$3,000,000 \approx 0.88$).

FITTING A MODEL

So far we have used the functions $v(x)$ and $D(t)$ to compute aggregate loss at some stage of development. In practice v and D are unknown to us—we must work backward from aggregate loss observations to determine the underlying functions. As is usual in modeling problems, this process requires some assumptions about what kind of functions v and D might be.

Example 5: Assume that $v(x) = r + sx$ and $D(t) = (1 + t/T)/2$ for $0 \leq t \leq T$. Given the following data,

(a, b)	Reported Loss ($000,000)	
	c = 1	c = 2
(0, 1)	4.5	5.8
(1, 2)	—	6.6

find the ultimate loss for time period $(1, 2)$.

Answer: Reported loss as of time $x = c$ for the period (a, b) is given by

$$\int_a^b (r + sx)D(c - x)\,dx,$$

Our data provides us with three equations:

$$4.5 = \int_0^1 (r + sx)D(1 - x)\,dx,$$

$$5.8 = \int_0^1 (r + sx)D(2 - x)\,dx, \qquad \text{and}$$

$$6.6 = \int_1^2 (r + sx)D(2 - x)\,dx.$$

With some effort we can solve for the model parameters r, s, and T:

$$r = 6.0, \qquad s = 3.6, \qquad T = 3.0.$$

The ultimate loss for time period $(1, 2)$ is then

$$\int_1^2 6.0 + 3.6x\,dx = 11.4,$$

or in actual dollars, \$11,400,000.[2]

PRACTICAL CHALLENGES

Real examples are more complicated. Loss and development functions are usually non-linear; and the resulting equations are much harder to solve than those given above are. Although more data is available, no single development function can describe it all. For one thing, development is subject to random fluctuation; this makes it necessary to estimate model parameters by least-squares type methods.

In addition, the development process itself, and hence the function $D(t)$, can change with time.

---

[2] A fuller treatment of these issues is given in McClenahan, C. L., "Adjusting Loss Development Patterns for Growth," *Proceedings of the Casualty Actuarial Society*, 1987, 74:101–114, and in the discussion by D. P. Gogol on pp. 115–118.

Example 6: A company installs an automated claim handling system. How will this affect the $D(c - x)$ term in the integral?

Answer: If claim reporting speeds up, larger values of $D(c - x)$ will result (and hence larger observed losses.)

Example 7: How does increasing claim litigation affect paid loss development?

Answer: Claims that go to court take longer to settle. As more claims fall into this category, loss payments slow down and the paid loss development function $D(t)$ stretches out.

As these examples show, it may be better to use a family of development functions $Dx(t)$. This allows for changes in loss development patterns, but it adds further complications. It is not usually necessary to solve the resulting equations exactly; solutions can be sought by numerical methods. In particular, the integrals used here can be approximated by finite sums. Even so, few actuaries find these techniques sufficiently tractable for everyday use.

CONCLUSION

One cannot afford to ignore the effects of growth (i.e., changes in $v(x)$) upon loss development. Changes in loss volume can make quite a difference. Actuarial models such as the one described here allow us to correct for these "growth effects" and measure the underlying development patterns.[3]

If these models are to be used regularly, more research into the true form of the loss development functions $D(t)$ will be needed. Such research has only recently begun to take shape.[4]

---

[3]cf. Simon, L. J., "Distortion in IBNR Factors," *Proceedings of the Casualty Actuarial Society*, 1970, 57:64–68, where this problem is studied using graphical methods.

[4]Two recent applications of these ideas may be found in McClenahan, C. L., "Liabilities for Extended Reporting, Endorsement Guarantees Under Claims-Made Policies," *CAS Discussion Paper Program*, 1988, 345–363 and Philbrick, S. W., "Reserve Review of a Reinsurance Company," *CAS Discussion Paper Program*, 1986, 147–162.

CHAPTER 6
RISK CLASSIFICATION
ROBERT J. FINGER

INTRODUCTION

Risk classification involves concepts similar to those in ratemaking (Chapter 3) and individual risk rating (Chapter 4). Actuaries use risk classification primarily in ratemaking when there is not sufficient information to estimate a price for a given individual. In order to derive a price, individuals who are expected to have the same costs are grouped together. The actuary then calculates a price for the group and assumes that the price is applicable to all members of the group. This, in simple terms, is the substance of risk classification.

Relatively recent advances in computer technology and analytical processes allow actuaries to construct complex cost models for individuals. Some examples include multiple regression, neural networks, and global positioning. Even though these models may seem complex, they essentially estimate the average cost for groups of insureds that share the same characteristics.

For purposes of this chapter, we define risk classification as the formulation of different premiums for the same coverage based on group characteristics. These characteristics are called rating variables. For automobile insurance, examples are geography and driver characteristics. Rating variations due to individual claim experience, as well as those due to limits of coverage and deductibles, will not be considered here as part of the classification problem.

Premiums should vary if the underlying costs vary. Costs may vary among groups for all of the elements of insurance cost and income: losses, expenses, investment income, and risk. For losses, as an example, groups may have varying accident frequency or varying average claim costs. Expenses may also differ among groups; in some lines, such as boiler and machinery, inspection expense is a major portion of the premium. Investment income may vary among groups; for example, some insureds may be sued more quickly (emergency physicians versus obstetricians) or claims may be settled more quickly. Finally, risk, defined as variation from the expected, may vary among different types of insureds. For example, more heterogeneous groups are subject to more adverse selection and, hence, more risk. In the remainder of this chapter, the term "costs" will refer to all of the above considerations.

In this chapter, we shall first consider the interaction between classifications and other rating mechanisms, such as exposure bases, marketing, underwriting, and individual risk rating. We shall then review the various criteria (actuarial, operational, social, and legal) for selecting rating variables. We then turn to historical examples of classification systems. Next, we examine measures of classification efficiency. Finally, we shall briefly review problems in and approaches to estimating class relativities. Readers interested in greater detail than provided in this chapter are referred to studies by the Stanford Research Institute (1976) and SRI International (1979).

RELATIONSHIP TO OTHER MECHANISMS

The classification process must be considered within the overall context of marketing, underwriting, and rating. The overall goal is to price an insured properly for a given coverage. This may be accomplished in different ways. Risk classification is one step in a process that makes significant pricing decisions in many ways.

Exposure Base

An important consideration is the exposure base. For personal automobile insurance, the exposure base is an insured car-year. For workers compensation, exposure can be total payroll, hours worked, or limited payroll (i.e., payroll up to some limit for a given time period). Manual premiums are calculated as the exposure times a rate. For example, if payroll is $1 million and the rate is $5 per $100 of payroll, manual premium is $50,000.

Exposure bases should be as closely proportional to costs as possible. For example, consider workers compensation, which has both medical and indemnity benefits. If a worker is injured, the worker's medical costs are paid and the worker receives indemnity payments for time lost from work. Indemnity benefits typically are calculated as two-thirds of wages, subject to a maximum equal to the statewide average wage. For example, assume the maximum benefit is $500 per week. If the worker's wages are $750 or more, the worker receives $500; if the wages are $600, the worker receives $400. The most appropriate exposure base would be hours worked for medical benefits, and limited payroll (limited to $750 per week per employee) for indemnity benefits. These exposure bases would be proportional to costs, assuming that all workers have the same accident frequency per hour worked and that average claim size is a function of wages. (It may be argued that accident frequency, the duration of indemnity benefits, or the total amount of medical expense is related to wages. If so, total payroll could be more accurate than hours worked or limited payroll.)

If all employers pay the same wages, or have proportionately the same number of workers at different wage levels, total payroll is an adequate exposure base. If one employer pays higher wages than another, however, total payroll is not as accurate an exposure base as the combination of hours worked and limited payroll. Because accident frequency or severity varies among different insureds, some element of cost variance remains to be rated by a classification system or other means. For a more complete discussion of exposure bases, see Bouska (1989).

Individual Risk Rating

As mentioned above, the goal in all pricing is to evaluate properly the potential costs. When the individual insured is large enough to have credible claims experience, that claims data can be used to modify the rate that would have been charged by a classification plan alone. If the classification plan is relatively simple, the credibility of the individual claim experience will be greater; if the classification plan is more accurate, the individual risk claim experience will have less credibility. In a simple class plan, there are a larger number of insureds who will receive the same rate(s). It (usually) follows that there will be more cost heterogeneity within each group. Thus, whether or not an individual insured has had a claim, or not had a claim, will be more indicative of whether that individual's actual (unknowable) cost differs from the group average cost. If every insured within the group had exactly the same cost, the actual claims experience would be purely fortuitous and it would have no credibility.

In general, it is better to produce a more accurate classification plan, rather than rely on individual risk rating to improve the overall pricing accuracy. This is because a classification variable effectively has 100% credibility and the credibility of very few individual insureds will approach 100%. For example, if a particular characteristic results in 10% lower costs, incorporating that factor into the class plan will produce a 10% lower premium for every applicable insured. If the factor is not in the class plan, insureds with that characteristic will have 10% lower historical costs, but they will not receive 10% lower premiums if their credibility is less than 100%.

Schedule rating is often part of individual risk rating plans. Underwriters apply judgment to select credits or debits for various items on a schedule. For example, a credit of 0% to 10% might be given for the content and scope of a training/supervision/loss prevention program for workers compensation. Normally, these items are not quantifiable or not includable in a classification or experience rating plan. In some cases, however, it would be possible to measure the impact of various factors on cost. These factors could be included within a classification plan.

Marketing and Underwriting

Insurers may use different strategies for pricing business. As will be pointed out below, many factors that are related to cost potential cannot be objectively defined and rated. Instead of pricing these factors, insurers may adjust their marketing and underwriting practices to account for them.

Two common strategies are: (1) adjust price according to individual cost potential, and (2) accept an individual only if the existing price structure is adequate. (For more detail, see Glendenning and Holtom (1977) and Launie et al. (1976)). The former is more common where premiums are higher. With a larger account, more expense dollars, and more meaningful claims history, an underwriter may feel more comfortable in formulating an individual price.

An alternative to the second strategy is to have several different rate structures within the same insurance group. Due to rate laws, this often requires several different insurance companies. For example, one company in a group may charge standard rates; one charge 20% more; another charges 10% less than standard rates; and a fourth company charges 25% less than standard rates. Using all available information, the underwriter makes a judgment about which rate level is the most appropriate.

In the above case, the underwriter is working with an existing classification plan. Each rate level, presumably, has the level of class detail that can be supported by objective rating variables. The underwriter assesses all other relevant information, including difficult-to quantify data, to fix the charged rate.

In practice, most insurers consider a certain number of insureds to be uninsurable. This can happen when the number of potential insureds with certain characteristics is so small that cost experience will not be credible. Along the same line, the insureds within any given group may be thought to be too heterogeneous. That is, there may be a greater risk in writing certain individuals because the cost may be much higher than the average (or measured) cost for the group. In both cases, the individual insureds are difficult to rate properly because there is not enough experience with analogous types of insureds.

Notwithstanding the above situation, insurers compete on price for larger individual risks and classes of business. An important consideration is the ability and propensity of insureds to shop for the best price. The more insureds shop, the more an insurer must refine its classification plan. Insurers also vary in their ability to select lower cost insureds within a classification through underwriting. More successful insurers are said to be "skimming the cream."

When an insurer receives a disproportionate number of higher cost insureds, relative to its classification plan, it is being adversely selected against. If the adverse selection continues, the insurer must either lose money, change its underwriting criteria, or increase its premiums. Such premium increases may induce the insurer's lower-cost insureds to move to another insurer, creating more adverse selection and producing a need for further premium increases. The insurer can become insolvent, unless it can adequately price its book of business.

In summary, premiums for the same coverage can vary among insureds because of exposure bases, individual risk rating plans, and marketing or underwriting approaches. Classification plans are one aspect, integrated with these others, of accurately pricing individual insureds.

CRITERIA FOR SELECTING RATING VARIABLES

Criteria for selecting variables may be summarized into the following categories: actuarial, operational, social, and legal. Following this discussion, we describe the ramifications of restricting the use of rating variables.

Actuarial Criteria

Actuarial criteria may also be called "statistical" criteria. They include accuracy, homogeneity, credibility, and reliability. Foremost is accuracy. Rating variables should be related to costs. If costs do not differ for different values of a rating variable, the usual methods for estimating rate relativities will produce the same relativity. In that case, the use of a variable adds to administrative expense, and possibly consumer confusion, but does not affect premiums. As an example, most insurers charge the same automobile insurance premiums for drivers between the ages of 30 and 50, not varying the premium by age. Presumably costs do not vary much by age, or cost variances are due to other identifiable factors. As a practical matter, insurers may gather and maintain cost information on a more detailed basis than the pricing structure; data are maintained so that premium differences may be introduced if there actually prove to be cost differences.

Accuracy is important for at least two reasons: the market mechanism and fairness. In a market economy, insurers that price their products more accurately can be more successful. Suppose, for example, that the cost (including a reasonable profit) of insuring Group A is $100 and the cost of insuring Group B is $200. If an insurer charges both groups $150, it is likely to be undersold in Group A by another insurer. The first insurer will tend to insure more people in Group B and, consequently, to lose money. Thus, when insurers can identify costs more accurately, they can compete more successfully. Greater accuracy generally requires more rating variables and a more detailed classification system.

Another reason for the importance of accuracy is fairness. In the example above, it would be fair for Group A members to pay $100 and Group B members to pay $200, because these are the costs of the goods and services provided to them. (Of course, if there are subgroups within Group A whose costs are $50, $150, and $250, it would be fairer to charge those costs to those subgroups). This concept is often called "actuarial fairness" and it is based on the workings of a market economy.

The second actuarial criterion is homogeneity. This means that all members of a group who receive the same rate or premium should have similar expected costs. As a practical matter, it is difficult to know if all group members do have similar costs. The reason for grouping is the lack of credibility of individual experience. Consequently, for many rating groups, subdivisions of the group may not have much more credibility than individual insureds.

The third actuarial criterion, alluded to above, is credibility. A rating group should be large enough to measure costs with sufficient accuracy. There will always be the desire to estimate costs for smaller groups or subdivisions, even down to the individual insured level. Random fluctuations in claims experience may make this difficult, however. There is an inherent trade-off between theoretical accuracy (i.e., the existence of premiums for smaller and smaller groups) and practical accuracy (i.e., consistent premiums over time).

The fourth actuarial criterion is reliability or predictive stability. Based on a given set of loss data, the apparent cost of different groups may be different. The differences, however, may be due to random fluctuations (analogous to the problem discussed under credibility, above). In addition, the cost differences may change over time. For example, historical cost differences between genders may diminish or disappear as societal roles change. Technology may also change relative cost differences.

In summary, actuarial classification criteria are used in an attempt to group individual insureds into groups that: (1) are relatively homogeneous (all group members have similar costs), (2) are sufficiently large to estimate relative cost differences (credibility), and (3) maintain stable mean costs over time (reliability).

Operational Criteria

Actuarial criteria must be tempered by practical or operational considerations. The most important consideration is that the rating variables have an objective definition. There should be little ambiguity, class definitions should be mutually exclusive and exhaustive, and the opportunity for administrative error should be minimized. For example, automobile insurance underwriters often talk of "maturity" and "responsibility" as important criteria for youthful drivers. These are difficult to define objectively and to apply consistently. The actual rating variables, age, gender, and marital status, may be proxies for the underlying sources of cost variation. Maturity might be a more accurate variable, but it is not practical.

Another important practical consideration is administrative expense. The cost of obtaining and verifying information may exceed the value of the additional accuracy. For example, driving mileage may be a very good indicator of cost. It is probably too expensive to obtain and verify, however. Assume that drivers driving under 7,500 miles per year cost 20% less than those who drive 7,501 to 12,000 miles, who in turn cost 20% less than those who drive more than 12,000 miles. Assume also that the middle group costs $100 per year and that it costs $20 per driver to obtain, process, and verify annual mileage data. In a system utilizing mileage, drivers driving under 7,500 would pay $100 (their previous cost of $80 plus $20 for the additional expense), the middle group would pay $120 and the highest cost group, $145. Nobody would pay less than before! Although this example may be extreme, it demonstrates that added expense to classify may not serve insureds (or insurers) any better than not classifying.

Another practical consideration, alluded to above, is verifiability. If insureds know that they can pay lower premiums by lying, some percentage of them will do so. The effect is to cause honest insureds to pay more than they should, to make up for the dishonest insureds that pay less than they should. There are practical trade-offs among verifiability, administrative expense, and accuracy. Few rating variables are free from manipulation by insureds. Insureds supply most insurance rating information and insurers verify it only to a limited extent. At some point, the expense saved by relying upon unverified information is outweighed by its inaccuracy. In practice, variables are added, at a tolerable cost, as long as they result in improved overall accuracy.

There are several other practical considerations in selecting rating variables. The variables should be intuitively related to costs. Age, in life insurance, is intuitively related (i.e., older people are more likely to die). Age in automobile insurance is less so. Younger operators may tend to be more reckless and older operators may tend to be less observant, but the correlation between age and these factors is less precise than with mortality. Intuitive relationships also improve acceptability, which will be discussed below.

When faced with the cost-verifiability issue, it is often better to use measures that are available for another purpose. If the variable is used only for insurance rating, it is more likely to be manipulated and it may be more difficult to verify. Payroll and sales records, for example, are kept for other purposes, such as taxation. These may be manipulated for those purposes, as well as insurance purposes, but such manipulation may be discouraged by the risk of criminal penalties or adverse relations with suppliers or bankers.

Still another practical consideration is the avoidance of extreme discontinuities. If Group A's rate is $100 and Group B's rate is $300, a Group B insured may obtain a significant premium reduction by qualifying for Group A rates. Thus the incentive to cheat and the expense to verify will be higher if there are fewer classes, with larger differences in premiums. It may be difficult in practice, however, to construct gradual changes in rates because there may be very small numbers of very high-cost insureds. Thus, for credibility purposes, there may be fewer classes, with widely differing rates.

Social Criteria

So far in this section we have discussed the actuarial goals of classification and some of the operational difficulties. Another limitation on classification is "social acceptability" or social considerations. A number of key issues, such as "causality," "controllability," and "affordability" have been the subject of public debate. We shall now briefly describe some of the public concerns.

Privacy is an important concern. People often are reluctant to disclose personal information. This affects accuracy of classification, verifiability, and administrative cost. In automobile insurance, for example, a psychological or behavioral profile might be strongly correlated with claims cost. (It might also be expensive to obtain.) Many people might resist this intrusiveness, however. Although Insurer A might achieve a more accurate rating system by using a psychological profile, the company might not obtain a sufficient amount of business. Insureds may choose to pay more to avoid disclosing personal information.

"Causality" implies an intuitive relationship to insurance costs. Assume there is some rating variable, X, which divides insureds into Groups A, B, C, etc. The rating variable is correlated with costs if the mean costs for the various groups are significantly different. There may be other variables for which there are similar correlations. The "real" reason for the differences in costs may be some entirely different variable or combination of variables. Nevertheless, X is correlated to the cost of providing insurance. X may be a proxy for the "real" cost difference.

"Causality" implies a closer relationship to costs than correlation. (See, for example, the study by the Massachusetts Division of Insurance (1978), p.22.) Mileage in automobile insurance might be considered a causal variable; the more miles a driver drives, the higher the cost of insurance should be (other things being equal). Loss costs can be divided into claim frequency and average claim cost. "Causal" variables, then, could be considered to be directly related to claim frequency or average claim cost. Automobile mileage, presumably, is proportional to claim frequency. Proximity to fire protection, in fire insurance, may be inversely proportional to the average claim cost.

Unfortunately, however, the categorization of variables as "causal" or "noncausal" is ambiguous. With automobile insurance, for example, where and when one drives may be more relevant to costs than mileage. Driving in a large city, with more vehicles, more intersections, and more distractions is probably more hazardous than driving in rural areas. Driving at night or when tired or drunk may be more hazardous than driving in daytime or when fully rested or sober. From an actuarial point of view, correlated variables provide more accurate premiums and are thus more desirable in a competitive market place. Eliminating correlated noncausal variables may produce a less accurate rating system and cause certain market corrections. Those will be discussed later.

"Controllability" may be a desirable rating-variable characteristic. A controllable variable is one that is under the control of the insured. If the insured moderates behavior in a certain way, premiums will be reduced. For example, by installing burglar alarms, the insured reduces claims cost potential and should receive some discount. The use of controllable rating variables encourages accident prevention.

From a practical viewpoint, there may not be very many useful controllable variables. The make and model of automobile in physical damage insurance is controllable. Geographical location is controllable in a broad sense, but not very useful in making day-to-day or short-term decisions. Moving a warehouse or petroleum refinery is not practical; nevertheless, the decision to locate a structure is controllable and insurance costs may be a factor in the decision. Driver-training course credits for automobile insurance are also controllable, but most people may qualify for them, reducing the effect of this variable on rate variations.

Controllable variables may increase administrative costs. If the insured has control over premium costs, the insured can manipulate the rating system and insurers may require verification. As with "causality," "controllability" is a useful concept but there is a shortage of usable rating variables that may apply.

Another social consideration is "affordability." In the context of risk classification, it usually arises where classification schemes are more refined, with the attendant spreading of rates. Thus, high rates are often seen as causing affordability problems (even if, for example, the high rate is generated by a youthful operator driving a Corvette in New York City). Another example is the correlation of incomes and insurance rates. In automobile insurance, rates are often highest in urban areas, where, allegedly, most poor people live. In reality, wealthy people also live in urban areas and poor people live in rural areas; youthful drivers that can afford any car or a high-priced car probably are not poor. Thus both high rates, per se, and higher rates for lower-income groups pose an affordability concern.

Another aspect of the affordability issue is the necessity of insurance. Many states require automobile liability insurance. Most mortgagors require property insurance. Of course, owning a car or a house is optional. Still another aspect of affordability is availability. If rates are arbitrarily leveled or reduced below cost, the market may not voluntarily provide coverage. Thus rates may be "affordable" but insurers may be very reluctant to insure people at those rates.

Except for the affordability issue, these social issues are based on accuracy arguments. The basic limitations on accuracy are the competitiveness of the insurance industry and the credibility of the cost information. These factors are related in some cases. As long as the insurance industry is competitive, there are incentives (profitability, solvency) to price individual insureds accurately. These incentives may be minimal, however, for small groups of heterogeneous insureds. Restrictions on competition are unlikely to produce a more accurate rating system. The ramifications of restrictions will be discussed after a brief review of legal considerations.

Legal Criteria

We have now considered actuarial, practical, and social considerations. We now turn to the legal context of risk classifications. The following discussion is necessarily brief, but it provides an overview. The circumstances of each particular case (e.g., rating variable, line of insurance, state statutes, and constitutions) will determine its outcome. The following is based on general concepts and principles.

Risk classification may be affected by constitutions (state and federal), statutes, and regulations. Generally, constitutions govern statutes and statutes govern regulations. Constitutions are usually very general, statutes are more specific, and regulations may be the most specific.

Both federal and state constitutions may apply to a risk classification situation. There must, however, be a specific phrase or section that is applicable. The federal constitution is quite broad and vague. The "equal protection clause" (EPC) might be applicable. Other clauses probably are not. State constitutions are often more specific. Gender discrimination, for example, is specifically mentioned in many state constitutions.

The federal equal protection clause, in the 14th Amendment to the Constitution, reads: "No State shall make or enforce any law which shall...deny to any person within its jurisdiction the equal protection of the laws." This points to two requirements: (1) state or governmental action and (2) unequal treatment. "State action" generally means that the state has acted, either on its own or by officially sanctioning the conduct of private individuals. Purely private discrimination is usually not actionable under the EPC. With insurance, the requisite state action is probably the promulgation of rates; the mere approval of or acquiescence in rates probably is not state action. If rates are not regulated at all, rating classifications are probably exempt from the EPC.

Unequal treatment is also a requirement under the EPC. Arguably, basing premium differences on demonstrable cost differences is not unequal treatment.

Because of the requirement of governmental action, constitutional challenges to insurance rating classifications are unlikely to succeed. Statutes, however, can impose restrictions on insurers. In this case, it is the insurers who will try to invoke constitutional provisions to invalidate the statutes. Several other clauses of the U.S. Constitution, such as "due process," "takings," and "contracts" may be applicable. As a general rule, however, courts have been very deferential towards legislatures in their regulation of businesses. Most likely, any statutory restriction on rating variables would be constitutional.

Finally, regulations issued by state insurance departments may affect classifications. Under a constitutional theory (known as the "delegation doctrine") only the legislature may promulgate substantive law; the executive branch merely carries out the will of the legislature. Although states vary considerably, broad discretionary grants of power to executive agencies may be found unconstitutional. Thus insurance commissioners may only be able to act within guidelines provided by legislatures.

In summary, constitutional provisions, statutes, and insurance department regulations all potentially may affect the freedom of insurers to select and use rating variables. As this brief discussion indicates, constitutional provisions are probably not applicable; statutes are practically invulnerable; and regulations may or may not be subject to challenge by insurers.

Ramifications of Restrictions

Legislatures may abolish the use of certain rating variables or rate variations may be restricted. The consequence will be similar for each, although more extreme for abolition. The discussion below deals with abolition. Insurers can react in three ways: pricing, marketing, and underwriting. In pricing, they can try to find replacement variables. As stated above, there may not be many variables that are suitable, given the above actuarial, operational, and social criteria. Insurers do have incentives to create better variables; they thus may consider the current ones to be the best available. If no replacement variables are found, rates will be leveled and subsidies created. For example, if Group A's cost is $50 and Group B's cost is $150, but the distinction between them cannot be used in rating, both groups may pay $100. Group A would be overcharged by $50 and Group B would be subsidized by $50.

The effect of abolishing rating variables in a competitive market is to create availability problems, unless there are suitable replacement variables. Insurers may withdraw from marketing the coverage to certain groups or refuse to insure them. This will produce, most likely, a larger residual market. Residual markets, such as assigned risk plans in automobile insurance, exist to provide insurance to those not voluntarily insured. Abolition of variables may also affect insurer profitability and solvency. If an insurer, in the above example, has a large percentage of Group B business, it will need to raise its rates or else it will be unprofitable. If it raises its rates, it may drive more of its better business to competitors who have lower rates; this will further increase its costs and require a further rate increase. Eventually, solvency may be threatened.

Abolition of rating variables has social consequences, as well. To some extent, abolition will create subsidies. Insurers may voluntarily insure underpriced groups. Otherwise, residual markets will expand; since most residual markets are subsidized by the voluntary market, subsidies will be created. Such subsidies, deriving from legislation, are a tax-in-kind. Certain insureds pay more for insurance than they otherwise would have, while others pay less. There is a redistribution of income from the disfavored group to the favored group.

In addition to the subsidies, abolition of rating variables can reduce accident prevention incentives. That is, to the extent accurate pricing promotes accident prevention, less accurate pricing reduces it.

Thus the abolition of rating variables probably will reduce the accuracy of the rating system, which either creates subsidies or else produces availability problems. In either case, accident prevention incentives are reduced.

EXAMPLES OF CLASSIFICATION SYSTEMS

So far in this chapter, we have discussed the general principles for developing classification systems. In this section, specific systems, with particular emphasis on automobile insurance, will be discussed. To be concrete, some assumptions will be made that may not be widely accepted within either the actuarial profession or the insurance industry. The objective is not to specify all of the relevant factors and only relevant factors, but to present an approach that a knowledgeable actuary may follow. Risk classification is a difficult subject area. In theory, not enough is known about either the underlying causes of loss or the variations in costs between insureds. In practice, there is never enough data for formulating and testing hypotheses. More research needs to be done.

Forces Affecting Classification Systems

Classification systems vary over time. Automobile liability originally had only one classification. By World War II there were three classes (adult, youthful operator, and business use). These became refined into nine classes by subdividing the youthful class and adding more use categories. In 1965, the National Bureau of Casualty Underwriters (a rating bureau, the predecessor to today's Insurance Services Office) introduced a plan that had 260 classifications. In 1970, the number of classes was reduced to 217. Most of the classifications were for youthful operators. The number of geographical rating territories within a state also generally increased over the above time period.

Many forces, chiefly those related to competition, influence classification plans. Generally, the more competitive the marketplace, the more classifications there will be. Assume one insurer charges the same rate, $100, to Groups A and B, but their costs are different, $50 for A and $150 for B. Another insurer could charge Group A $50 and still be profitable. Thus, to the extent insurers can actually identify cost differences, they will tend to make price differentials. Not to do so affects their profitability and, ultimately, their solvency

Classification systems may also become more refined as coverage becomes more expensive. From the buyer's side, shopping for favorable prices is encouraged when coverage is more expensive. From the insurer's side, more expense dollars may be available to classify and underwrite; in addition, the cost of making mistakes, or of not having as refined a system, is higher when premiums are higher. For example, towing coverage may be priced the same for all automobiles, even though older cars may be more likely to break down and towing costs may be higher in rural areas; at a low premium (e.g., $10 per year), it may not be cost effective to have rate differentials.

Classification systems usually are more refined for larger markets. Considering the credibility of available cost data, more classifications can be supported by larger amounts of insured exposure.

Finally, classification systems have probably become more refined as information technology has progressed. More information can be handled more cost effectively today than in the past. Let us now turn to automobile insurance classifications.

Automobile Liability Insurance Classifications

Automobile liability insurance classifications can be categorized into the following types of variables: (1) age-gender-marital status, (2) use, (3) geography, and (4) others. Classification plans vary significantly among insurers. (See SRI 1976.) Certain types of factors are widely used; many factors are used by only a few insurers.

Age-gender-marital status primarily distinguishes among youthful operators, although most insurers have a separate class for drivers over 65. Youthful operators generally are those under 25, although most insurers separate single males under 30. Some insurers have separate classes for each age; some group ages, such as 17 to 20 and 21 to 24. Most insurers distinguish between single male principal operators (using the automobile 50% or more) and occasional operators. Many insurers distinguish between single and married female operators, and between principal and other operators for females and married males.

Use categories typically are: pleasure, drive to work (sometimes over or under a given number of miles, one-way, such as 10), business, and farm. Added to this may be annual driving mileage over or under a given amount (such as 7,500). Use categories may vary between adult and youthful operators.

Geographical territories are commonly used in classification plans. Contiguous areas, often delineated by city or county boundaries, are the most common. Some insurers use zip codes, sometimes combining adjacent areas or using some other criteria (such as population density). Territories are the same for all age-gender-marital status classes and all use classes. Territories sometimes vary by coverage. For example, there may be fewer claims for uninsured motorist coverage, so there are fewer separate rating territories.

Several other rating variables are in common use. These include good student and driver training discounts for youthful operators; multiple-car discounts; accident and violation surcharges, and sports car surcharges.

In addition to the above variables, several other variables are used for automobile physical damage insurance. These generally relate to the value of the automobile, its crashworthiness, and its age. Most insurers use the make and model of the car; various makes and models are combined into a series of different rate groups.

Cost Variation in Automobile Insurance

Above are the classification variables that are commonly used in automobile insurance. Some are "causal"-type variables; others are correlated to costs. Below, we will discuss potential reasons for cost differences. Some of these are incorporated into rating variables, while others are used only in underwriting (i.e., risk selection or rejection).

Cost differences can be classified into four broad categories: (1) use of the automobile, (2) driving ability, (3) interaction with the claims mechanism, and (4) the extent of damages. In many of these areas, the available evidence is more subjective than objective. What is presented is thought to be relevant to costs, even though concrete data may be elusive.

Different uses of the automobile contribute to varying cost potential. More driving should produce more exposure to liability and collision claims. Driving conditions (time of day, traffic density, weather) are also important. Automobile theft is a significant factor for comprehensive coverage, therefore location of the car in higher crime neighborhoods is relevant for that coverage.

Mileage may be used directly in rating, although commonly the only distinctions are annual mileage over or under a given amount and mileage to work. Indirectly, mileage may be correlated with multiple-car discounts and some age-gender-marital status classifications. For example, over 65 drivers may drive less or under more favorable conditions; females may drive less than males; married males may drive less than single males. Driving conditions are taken into account, at least indirectly, in geographical territories. The territory is usually defined by the principal garage, which may differ, of course, from where the car is usually operated. Driving conditions are considered more directly in the use variables.

Cost differences may be due to differences in driving ability, arising from familiarity with the driving conditions, experience and training, reaction time, eyesight and hearing, concentration, condition of the automobile, and driving style. Some classification variables are related indirectly to these cost differences. For example, youthful operators have less familiarity and less experience; over-65 drivers may have poorer eyesight or hearing; discounts for driver training are available. Admittedly, individual performance varies greatly within the given rating classes.

Cost differences may also arise from interactions with the claims mechanism. Some people are more claims-conscious than others are. This affects the physical damage, personal injury protection, and medical payments coverages for the insured. Geographical differences may be more apparent for liability coverages. Some people may be treated more or less sympathetically by a jury. Some people may press dishonest claims. Some people may be more cooperative in submitting claims or in helping to defend claims. Most of these differences are quite subjective and difficult to quantify in a rating variable. Where higher costs can be discerned, it is more likely that insurers would refuse to insure an individual, rather than try to determine an accurate rate.

Finally, cost differences may result from the extent of damages, given that an accident has occurred. Crashworthiness of the automobile is an obvious rating variable. The same type of accident may produce $100 of damage in one car and $1000 of damage in another. The speed with which a car is driven will also affect damages. The use of safety devices, such as air bags or seat belts, will affect costs. Physical impairments may produce higher loss costs. Some of these differences may only be relevant to certain coverages.

To some extent, existing rating variables consider these differences in costs. Sports cars are often surcharged, presumably because they are driven at higher speeds, are prone to greater damage, cause greater damage, or are more prone to trigger lawsuits.

In summary, a variety of factors have been presented that affect claims costs. Some of these are more objective and lend themselves more readily to becoming rating variables. Many factors, however, are quite subjective, very difficult to measure, and almost infeasible as rating variables; underwriters tend to use these factors to decline coverage or assign to a higher-rated company in the group.

To conclude this section, we briefly mention other lines of business. Most lines of business use geographical rating. Workers compensation classes are mostly based on occupations or industries. There are some 600 different classes used by the National Council on Compensation Insurance in one or more states. Medical malpractice classes are based on specialties, with particular attention to the type of surgery performed, if any. Boiler and machinery rates vary by type of object, because inspection costs are a significant element of the premium. Products liability classes are defined by the type of product. Premises liability is defined by the character of the operation or activity. Homeowners and dwelling fire rating variables include the number of units in the structure and the age and type of the structure. Fire insurance rates are based on the type of construction, type of occupancy, protection features, and special exposure to loss.

MEASURES OF EFFICIENCY

We define "efficiency" as a measure of the accuracy of the classification system. This concept is important to the public debate concerning restrictions on the use of classification variables. It is also important to actuaries, in order to understand how well classification systems are working and to determine if and how they may be improved.

This chapter has discussed how and why costs might vary among insureds. This section turns to the question of how we can measure variations in the costs among the insured population. We may know that members of Group A, on average, cost twice as much to insure as members of Group B (at least, in the past). But we do not know how much cost variation there may be among individual members of groups A and B.

Introduction to Efficiency

The reason for classification systems is the variability in costs from one insured to another. The key to measuring efficiency is understanding this variability. Costs vary because claim frequency varies and because claim sizes vary. A perfect classification system would produce the same variability as the insured population (as well as having all insureds properly classified). Conversely, a classification system that has less variability than the insured population cannot be perfect, because two insureds may receive the same rate when their costs are actually different.

A complicating factor is the fortuitous nature of insurance. Costs are unknown. When measurements are made of cost variability, it is after certain events have already happened. The same events probably will not happen again. It is uncertain whether the actual events that occurred are representative of what will occur in the future. The future may have more or less variability than the past.

Most existing measures of classification efficiency use the statistical measure of variance or some related measure. Other measures are possible, including the average deviation and the average absolute deviation. Variance has the advantage of being widely used in many types of statistical applications (e.g., regression analysis and analysis of variance). This section will use variance concepts as an operational measure of efficiency, but other measures could be used. Specifically, this chapter uses the concept of the coefficient of variation, or *CV*, which is the standard deviation divided by the mean.

There are many possible formulas for efficiency. The measure most commonly used compares the variance explained by the classification system to the total variance underlying the insured population. (See SRI (1976) and Woll (1979).) If the classification system were perfect, the efficiency would be 100%. If the classifications had no predictive value (i.e., were random with respect to potential costs), the efficiency would be 0%. The square of the *CV* can be used to measure efficiency in terms of variance. (It is assumed that both the class plan costs and the underlying population costs have the same mean; if not, adjustments can be made.)

This formula requires the calculation of two items: (1) the variance of the classification system and (2) the variance of the insured population. The former is relatively easy to calculate; the latter is unknowable. Each will be discussed in turn.

Variation in the Classification System

To determine the variability of the class plan, one needs the class relativities and the percentage of exposures by class. It is assumed that the class relativities are the expected values of actual cost differences; if not, the latter should be used instead.

For a numerical example, see Table 6.1.

The coefficient of variation is the standard deviation (.975) divided by the mean (1.5), or 0.65. This numerical example points out several truisms. First, high efficiencies necessarily require extreme rates. Almost two-thirds of the variance is due to the highest cost 5% of insureds. Second, the key to designing highly efficient systems is to find variables that can isolate the highest and lowest cost individuals. Many insured populations seem to have a coefficient of variation of about 1.0. [See SRI (1976).]

TABLE 6.1

VARIATION IN THE CLASSIFICATION SYSTEM

Relativity	Percentage of Exposure	Mean (Extension)	Deviation from Mean	Deviation Squared	Variance (Extension)
0.5	10%	0.05	−1.0	1.00	0.1000
1.0	40%	0.40	−0.5	0.25	0.1000
1.5	30%	0.45	0.0	0.00	0.0000
2.0	10%	0.20	0.5	0.25	0.0250
3.0	5%	0.15	1.5	2.25	0.1125
5.0	5%	0.25	3.5	12.25	0.6125
Total	100%	1.50			0.9500

If this is true for the numerical example above, the efficiency would be about 42% $(0.65^2/1^2)$.

The basic difficulty in computing efficiency is determining the variability of the insured population. Because costs depend upon fortuitous events, the variability is unknowable. It is possible to apply concepts of risk theory, however, to develop some plausible estimates.

Modeling Concepts (for the Variance of the Insured Population)

We can treat observed data as a sample outcome of a hypothetical risk process. We can model that process in various ways. For this chapter, we will assume that claim costs for an **individual policy** can be described by a compound-Poisson process, which is a common model in casualty actuarial practice. Specifically, let

N be the number of claims during the policy period,

S be the amount of any given claim, and

T be the total cost the policy.

We will assume that N is Poisson-distributed with a mean λ. The mean of T, $E(T)$, is the product of the expected claim count, λ, and the average claim size, $E(S)$.

If the number of claims and the amount of each claim are independent, then the variance of the total cost can be determined from the following formula:

$$\text{Var}(T) = E(N)\text{Var}(S) + \text{Var}(N)E^2(S)$$

For the Poisson distribution, the mean is equal to the variance. Here, $E(N) = \text{Var}(N) = \lambda$.

For any variable,

$$\text{Var}(S) = E(S^2) - E^2(S)$$

Since the CV is the ratio of the standard deviation to the mean, the $CV^2(S)$ is $E(S^2)/E^2(S) - 1$.

We can derive the CV of the total claims cost from the above relationships, as follows:

$$CV^2(T) = \frac{\text{Var}(T)}{E^2(T)} = \frac{E(S^2)}{\lambda E^2(S)} = \frac{1 + CV^2(S)}{\lambda}$$

From this equation we can see that the CV of costs will be smaller for higher frequencies (larger λ) and larger for claim size distributions with larger CV's.

The above relationships hold for individual policies. The situation that we need to study, however, is one where the claim costs vary from policy to policy. The variance of the total claim costs for a book of business will consist of the above variance (which we can call the "process variance") and the variance of the insured population (which we can call the "structure variance" or the "variance of the hypothetical means"). Our general procedure will be to (1) measure the total variance, (2) hypothesize and measure the process variance, and (3) calculate the structure variance by subtracting (2) from (1).

Obviously, the validity of our conclusions will depend upon many factors. First, our sample data must be representative of the structure we wish to measure. Is the data sufficiently numerous, consistent, and reliable? Do we expect future conditions to be different from the past? Second, is our model of the process variance sufficiently accurate? Are the assumptions, such as independence between claim counts and claim amounts valid?

Frequency Example

We will begin with a simplified model that uses only claim counts (or frequency). We assume that frequency varies within the insured population according to a variable χ. Without loss of generalization we can assume that the mean of χ is 1. We assume that the variance of χ is β, the structure variance (or variance of the hypothetical means). We also assume that the average frequency for the entire population is λ.

From the fundamental theorem of conditional probabilities, the total population variance of the claim counts will be:

$$\text{Var}(N) = E_\chi[\text{Var}(N/\chi)] + \text{Var}_\chi E(N/\chi)$$

For any given insured, the mean frequency will be $\lambda\chi$. If we assume that the claims are Poisson-distributed, the variance is equal to the mean. $\text{Var}(N/\chi) = \lambda\chi$. Substituting into the above formula, we have:

$$\text{Var}(N) = E_\chi[\lambda\chi)] + \text{Var}_\chi E(\lambda\chi)$$

Since we know that $E(\chi) = 1$ and $\text{Var}(\chi) = \beta$, we have $\text{Var}(N) = \lambda + \beta\lambda^2$. This follows because λ is a scalar with respect to integration over χ.

This formula has been called the "excess variance" formula. If the claim frequency varies among insureds, the total variance of the claim counts will be higher than the average claim frequency for the population, λ, (which would apply to a Poisson process). The excess variance is related to the structure variance. This formula also demonstrates the point made above, that the total variance in costs will consist of two parts, a process variance (λ) and a structure variance ($\beta\lambda^2$). It should be noted that the resulting claim count distribution is a negative binomial distribution with parameters λ and β.

TABLE 6.2

VARIATION IN CLAIM FREQUENCY

Claims per Insured	Insureds	Claims	Deviation From Mean	Deviation Squared	Variance (Extension)
0	793	0	−0.267	0.07129	56.53
1	147	147	+0.733	0.53729	78.98
2	60	120	+1.733	3.00329	180.20
Total	1000	267			315.70

We can construct a numerical example to demonstrate the above formulas (see Table 6.2).

The average frequency is 0.2670. The average variance per insured is 0.3157. The excess variance is the difference, 0.0487. The CV of the insured population is 0.827 ($= \sqrt{(0.0487)}/0.267$).

Relationship to Credibility

The process variance and the structure variance also play an important role in credibility theory. The most general formula for credibility, Z, is:

$$Z = \frac{\tau^2}{\tau^2 + \sigma^2}$$

Where τ^2 ($= \text{Var}(\chi)$) is the structure variance and σ^2 is the (average) process variance. The denominator is also the total variance.

We can also derive this general formula in another significant way. Let us suppose that we have the claims experience for individual policies in two different time periods. Without loss of generalization, we can normalize the loss experience by dividing by the average cost. Let x_i be the (relative) cost in the first time period and y_i be the relative cost in the second time period, for individual policy i. We want to determine the credibility, Z, to apply to the loss experience in the first period, in order to most accurately predict the loss experience in the second period. In other words,

$$\hat{y}_i = Zx_i + (1 - Z)$$

For example, if the insured's experience in the first period was 25% better than the average (75% relative cost) and the estimated credibility is 40%, the insured's premium for the second period would be 10% less than the average (90% relative premium) $(0.9 = 0.4 * 0.75 + 0.6)$.

We can solve for the optimal credibility using least squares regression. That is, by minimizing the sum of squares of $(\hat{y}_i - y_i)$. If we have data for N insureds and they all have the same credibility, the least-squares credibility formula will be:

$$Z = \frac{[\sum (x_i - 1)(y_i - 1)]/N}{[\sum (x_i - 1)^2]/N}$$

where the summations are over i, the individual insureds.

The numerator is the structure variance. The denominator is the total variance. Since we normalized the loss experience to have a mean of 1, the structure variance calculation produces a CV^2.

We can apply the formula to the above numerical example (see Table 6.3).

The average structure variance per insured is 0.525. The CV of the structure function is $0.724 = (\sqrt{(.525)}/1)$.

Note that the input data for this example was relative costs in two different time periods. Although we used claim count data, the formula will work equally well (in theory) for claim amounts. In practice, individual claim amounts greatly increase the CV of individual insured experience. There will be much more sampling error if we use amounts rather than counts.

TABLE 6.3

CALCULATING THE STRUCTURE VARIANCE

Part 1. Data for the First Period				
First Period Claims	Insureds	Claims	Raw Frequency	Relative Frequency x_i
0	793	0	0.000	0.000
1	147	147	1.000	3.745
2	60	120	2.000	7.491
Total	1000	267	0.267	

Part 2. Data for the Second Period				
First Period Claims	Insureds	Second Pd. Claims	Raw Frequency	Relative Frequency y_i
0	793	42	0.053	0.868
1	147	13	0.088	1.450
2	60	6	0.098	1.612
Total	1000	61	0.061	

Part 3. Structure Variance Calculation				
First Period Claims	$x_i - 1$	$y_i - 1$	Product	Extension
0	−1.000	−0.132	0.132	104.68
1	2.745	0.450	1.235	181.55
2	6.491	0.612	3.972	238.35
Total				524.58

Other Formulas for the Structure Variance

Two other formulas are significant. The first can be developed from the regression formula and the general credibility formula. That is,

$$\tau^2 = Z(\tau^2 + \sigma^2)$$

The credibility also can be estimated from (i.e., is equal to) the "claim-free discount," which is measured by the relative cost in the second period of the insureds with no claims in the first period. For the data above, the claim free discount is 13.2%. That

TABLE 6.4

CALCULATING THE TOTAL VARIANCE

First Period Claims	$x_i - 1$	$(x_i - 1)^2$	Extension
0	−1.000	1.000	793.0
1	2.745	7.535	1107.6
2	6.491	42.133	2528.6
Total			4428.6

is, the relative cost of the first-period claim-free insureds was only 0.868 in the second period, or 13.2% better than average. (When there are no claims, the credibility formula produces a projected second period cost of 1 minus the credibility).

In addition, the total variance $(\tau^2 + \sigma^2)$ can estimated from the above first period data (see Table 6.4).

The average total variance per insured is 4.429. The estimated structure variance is 0.585 ($= 0.132 * 4.429$). The CV of the structure function is 0.765.

The final formula depends on the difference between the relative costs in the second period, of insureds with none and one claims during the first period. This is applicable only to count data and only for a gamma-distributed structure function. The formula is:

$$\tau^2 = \text{Var}(\chi) = \frac{y_1 - y_0}{y_0}$$

For the above data, $\text{Var}(\chi) = (1.450 - 0.868)/0.868 = 0.671$. The estimated CV is 0.819.

Measures of efficiency, even if they can be calculated with accuracy and consistency, do not provide a complete answer. The cost of the classification process itself is ignored, for example. Operational and social criteria also may be important. The availability of a feasible, more accurate system is unknown. Efficiency may be low in any given case, but no better system may be available at a reasonable cost. If efficiency is lower, however, it is an indication that there is a greater potential to introduce better variables.

What are the implications of efficiency measures for the design of classification systems? To produce a higher efficiency there must be a higher percentage of insureds at more extreme relativities. This is necessary to produce a higher variance or *CV*. This process, however, runs counter to much public criticism of the insurance industry. Higher rates mean less affordability. In addition, greater efficiency can be produced by any variable that can accurately refine the classification system. Thus, the preference for causal variables is irrelevant to increased efficiency; correlated variables can be just as efficient if they can distinguish cost potential. Similarly, controllable variables are useless unless they can produce greater efficiency. Indeed, controllability and causality are irrelevant; what is important to efficiency is being correlated with costs.

Risk classification efficiency can be approached from another point of view. Insurers have economic incentives to classify insureds accurately. The classification system should be as good as the market allows. In other words, if a group is too small to have credible experience or poses too great a risk (in that there is too much variability in costs within the group), the group may not be very accurately rated. If the group is large and relatively homogeneous, insurers have an incentive to classify and rate it properly.

In summary, existing efficiency measures are a comparison to an abstract ideal. Although they provide an indication of potential improvement, they do not provide useful information about what specific, practical, cost-effective variables might be utilized.

ESTIMATING CLASS RELATIVITIES

In this final section, we begin by describing two general methods of calculating class relativities: a loss ratio approach and a pure premium approach. This has been covered on a preliminary basis in Chapter 3. We then discuss several actuarial problems involved in estimating classification relativities. These include: 1) whether relativities should be additive or multiplicative, 2) how to obtain more and more reliable data, and 3) how to select the appropriate credibility complement for groups with less than fully credible data. This topic was also discussed earlier.

Insurers typically use relativities for classification variables, rather than pure rates, because of credibility problems. For example, there might be 10 territories and 10 classes for a particular line of business in a given state. If there were a great deal of loss data, it might be possible to estimate each of the 100 separate rates, by individual territory and class. Usually, however, there is not credible data for every combination. Indeed, even aggregating the data for each territory or class, for the entire state, may not yield 100% credibility. Most insurers use a similar class plan and relativities for all (or most) states and estimate territorial relativities by state.

The usual assumption is that the relative costs for each territory will be consistent for all classes, and vice versa. For example, class 1 might be 50% of the cost of class 2 and territory 1 might be 75% of the cost of territory 2. Of course, this assumption may not actually be true in practice.

Data and Approaches

Classification ratemaking uses most of the same steps and concepts as the overall statewide determination. Many of the steps are discussed in Chapter 3 and will not be repeated here. For example, loss experience needs to be trended and developed. Losses may be limited to basic limits. The same increased limits factors may be applied to all classes and territories, or may be applied to groups of classes, territories, or states. The most common expense assumption is that each class and territory has the same percentage of premium expense. This could be modified, if certain expenses are constant by policy.

The usual data used for determining class relativities is earned premium or exposure and incurred losses. Severity and frequency may also be considered in selecting relativities, as will be discussed later. In addition, claim counts are often used to determine credibility. Both premium and claim data must be coded with the required classification detail. Policy year or calendar-accident year data can be used; the latter may require special steps to calculate earned premiums or exposures.

When earned premium is used, the method is usually a "loss ratio" method; when earned exposures are used, the method is usually a "pure premium" approach. The loss ratio method can produce equivalent results if "earned premiums at current rates" (often called "on-level" premiums) are calculated. The most accurate approaches require that premium or exposure data be available down to the level of the variables under review. That is, if class and territorial relativities are going to be adjusted, premium or exposure for every combination of class and territory is needed. In some lines of insurance, there are several independent sets of rating variables. In automobile physical damage, for example, there are separate relativities for class (driver and use), territory, age and make of automobile, and coverage (e.g., deductibles). Indeed, there may be separate relativities within the class structure (e.g., for driver training discounts or use). It would be most accurate to simultaneously adjust each set of relativities.

There are advantages and disadvantages of using the loss ratio and pure premium methods. The loss ratio method may be applicable when there is less detailed data available or when there are many different sets of relativities; earned premiums will reflect the various charges made for different classes, territories, and coverages. If earned premiums correspond to historical rate levels, however, it may be difficult to make adjustments for intervening changes in rate relativities. The pure premium approach is usually more accurate because it requires more information. It also has the advantage of producing frequency and severity relativities, as well as pure premium relativities; the loss ratio method only produces loss ratio and severity relativities. Severity relativities, however, will not be meaningful if the underlying coverage is not consistent (e.g., there are differing deductibles or insured limits).

Loss Ratio Approach

Table 6.5 illustrates a loss ratio approach for territorial rates. The given state has three territories: A, B, and C. We assume that we already have determined an appropriate statewide rate level change (e.g., +6%). Here we want to make adjustments to territorial rates; we also want to maintain the selected overall rate level change.

We assume that the available data is earned premiums and incurred losses (developed and trended), by territory, for two past years that had different territorial relativities. We also assume that we have rate pages for each year, but not earned exposures. We also assume that we know the premium volume by territory, at the current rate level. Finally, we assume that the current rate level is different from either of the historical years. Table 6.5 shows this basic data.

This example will illustrate the following four steps: (1) adjusting premiums to current rates, (2) estimating preliminary adjustments to territorial relativities, (3) making an adjustment for credibility, and (4) balancing the rate change for the credibility adjustment.

The first step is to adjust historical earned premiums to current rates. If we used unadjusted historical earned premiums, we would develop relativity changes to the historical relativities, not to the current relativities. When we have more than one set of relativities in our historical experience, we may have difficulty in determining the appropriate "average" historical relativity. The easiest solution is to estimate earned premiums at current rates. (See column (7) in Table 6.5.)

TABLE 6.5

TERRITORIAL RELATIVITIES—LOSS RATIO APPROACH

	(1) Year 1	(2)	(3) Year 2	(4)	(5) Current Business	(6)	(7) Years 1 & 2
Territory	Actual Premium	Base Rate	Actual Premium	Base Rate	Actual Premium	Base Rate	Premium at Current Rates
A	733,050	100	840,240	120	863,313	125	1,791,563
B	240,180	60	266,560	70	262,570	70	546,770
C	133,178	45	230,725	50	285,060	60	454,441
Total	1,106,408		1,337,525		1,410,943		2,792,773

	(8)	(9) Years 1 & 2	(10)	(11) Experience	(12)	(13)	(14)
Territory	Incurred Losses	Claim Count	Severity	Loss Ratio	Preliminary Adjustment	Credibility	Credible Adjustment
A	1,037,495	1,437	722	57.9%	0.988	1.000	0.988
B	346,122	514	673	63.3%	1.080	0.689	1.055
C	252,909	474	534	55.7%	0.950	0.662	0.967
Total	1,636,526	2,425	675	58.6%	1.000		0.996

	(15)	(16) Balanced	(17)	(18) Current	(19) New
Territory	Extension	Adjustment	Extension	Relativity	Relativity
A	853,169	0.992	856,264	1.000	1.000
B	277,099	1.059	278,104	0.560	0.598
C	275,575	0.970	276,575	0.480	0.470
Total	1,405,843		1,410,943		

Notes: Calculations have been made to more significant digits than shown.

$(7) = (3) * (6)/(4) + (1) * (6)/(2)$.

$(10) = (8)/(9)$.

$(11) = (8)/(7)$.

$(12) = (11)/(11, \text{Total})$.

$(13) = \text{Min}\ (\sqrt{[(9)/1082]}, 1)$.

$(14) = (13) * [(12) - 1] + 1$.

$(15) = (5) * (14)$.

$(14, \text{Total}) = (15, \text{Total})/(5, \text{Total})$.

$(16) = (14)/(14, \text{Total})$.

$(17) = (5) * (16)$.

$(18) = (6)/(6, A)$.

$(19) = (18) * (16)/(16, A)$.

We may not always have a complete record of exposures for all of the different rating variables. This example assumes that we have past rates for a "base" class in each territory (e.g., class 1). We then adjust the historical earned premiums for the territory by the change in the rate for the base class. This adjustment may introduce some error, if nonterritorial relativities changed in the past and each territory does not have the same percentage of exposures for each rating variable.

The second step is the preliminary adjustment to the current relativities. We first calculate loss ratios by territory, as shown in column (11). Note that the statewide rate level change will deal with the overall loss ratio; here we only want to make adjustments by territory that will balance to the same overall rate level change. Thus, we are most interested in column (12), which shows the relative loss ratios by territory.

As a general rule, if the historical loss ratio for a territory has been higher than the average (e.g., a relative loss ratio greater than 1.0), we will want to increase rates in that territory relative to the rates in other territories.

The third step is to adjust for credibility. Often in practice, the amount of data for any given territory (or other rating variable) may be relatively small. We may not want to give "full credibility" to the historical experience. The usual approaches to base credibility on the amount of claim experience (e.g., the claim count or the amount of incurred losses) and to use the current relativity for the complement of the credibility.

In Table 6.5, the "full credibility" standard has been assumed to be 1,082 claims and partial credibilities have been calculated according to the square root rule. Thus, Territory B, with 514 claims, has been assigned a credibility of 68.9% $(= \sqrt{[514/1082]})$.

Also in Table 6.5, we assume that the complement of the credibility applies to the current relativity (as shown in column (18)). We then can calculate the credible adjustment as the credibility times (the preliminary adjustment minus 1.0). For example, the loss ratios indicate a 8.0% increase in the relativity for Territory B, but this is given only 68.9% credibility; thus, the credible adjustment would be a 5.5% (= 8.0% × 0.689) increase in the relativity.

The fourth and final step is to balance the territorial change, so that we retain the same overall rate level change. In practice, the application of credibilities will produce either an increase or decrease in the overall rate level. Thus, we must balance these adjustments. We can calculate the off-balance by multiplying the credible adjustments (column (14)) by the premiums at current rates (column (5)), as shown in column (15). (We use the premiums on current business rather than the historical premiums, because we assume that this is the best estimate of future premium volume by territory.)

We take the total of column (15) and divide it by the total current premiums to determine the off-balance factor, which we show for the total of column (14). The balanced adjustment is the credible adjustment divided by the off-balance factor. As a check, we can calculate column (17) as the premiums on the current business, column (5), times the balanced adjustment, column (16). The sum of column (17) is the same as the sum of column (5), indicating that the territorial adjustment will be revenue neutral.

We assumed that we already determined an overall rate level change, such as a 6% increase. The rate change for Territory A will be +5.2% (= 1.06 × 0.992 − 1.0). The rate change for Territory B will be 12.3% (= 1.06 × 1.059 − 1.0). The rate relativity between territory B and territory A will be 0.598 (= 0.56 × [1.123/1.052]).

Table 6.6 shows the same procedure for classification rate relativities. Historical premiums at current rates are not the same as for territorial relativities, because of the approximation that was used. Credibilities are generally smaller, because there are

TABLE 6.6

PAGE 1

CLASS RELATIVITIES—LOSS RATIO APPROACH

Class	(1) Actual Premium	(2) Base Rate	(3) Actual Premium	(4) Base Rate	(5) Actual Premium	(6) Base Rate	(7) Years 1 & 2 Premium at Current Rates
	Year 1		Year 2		Current Business		
1	171,875	100.0	208,500	120.0	219,800	125.0	432,031
2	59,625	90.0	70,380	108.0	74,700	112.5	147,844
3	94,160	110.0	120,348	138.0	128,168	143.8	248,499
4	148,688	150.0	172,333	174.0	178,780	175.0	346,793
5	138,285	180.0	186,200	228.0	199,690	237.5	376,418
6	95,400	160.0	100,275	180.0	108,965	193.8	223,516
7	122,000	200.0	127,680	228.0	125,985	231.3	270,621
8	125,250	250.0	158,210	312.0	167,505	325.0	327,627
9	151,125	300.0	193,600	384.0	207,350	406.3	409,517
Total	1,106,408		1,337,526		1,410,943		2,782,866

Class	(8) Incurred Losses	(9) Claim Count	(10) Severity	(11) Experience Loss Ratio	(12) Preliminary Adjustment	(13) Credibility	(14) Credible Adjustment
		Years 1 & 2					
1	259,800	361	720	60.1%	1.023	0.578	1.013
2	89,820	114	788	60.8%	1.033	0.325	1.011
3	128,601	199	646	51.8%	0.880	0.429	0.949
4	206,800	278	744	59.6%	1.014	0.507	1.007
5	217,170	278	781	57.7%	0.981	0.507	0.990
6	153,125	231	663	68.5%	1.165	0.462	1.076
7	158,130	246	643	58.4%	0.994	0.477	0.997
8	181,320	308	589	55.3%	0.941	0.534	0.969
9	241,760	410	590	59.0%	1.004	0.616	1.002
Total	1,636,526	2,425	675	58.8%	1.000		1.000

TABLE 6.6

PAGE 2

CLASS RELATIVITIES—LOSS RATIO APPROACH

Class	(15) Extension	(16) Balanced Adjustment	(17) Extension	(18) Current Relativity	(19) New Relativity
1	222,666	1.013	222,732	1.000	1.000
2	75,502	1.011	75,525	0.900	0.898
3	121,573	0.949	121,609	1.150	1.077
4	180,051	1.007	180,105	1.400	1.392
5	197,774	0.991	197,832	1.900	1.858
6	117,270	1.077	117,305	1.550	1.647
7	125,602	0.997	125,639	1.850	1.821
8	162,241	0.969	162,289	2.600	2.486
9	207,845	1.003	207,907	3.250	3.216
Total	1,410,524		1,410,943		

Notes: Calculations have been made to more significant digits than shown.

$(7) = (3) * (6)/(4) + (1) * (6)/(2)$.

$(10) = (8)/(9)$.

$(11) = (8)/(7)$.

$(12) = (11)/(11, \text{Total})$.

$(13) = \text{Min} \left(\sqrt{[(9)/1082]}, 1 \right)$.

$(14) = (13) * [(12) - 1] + 1$.

$(15) = (5) * (14)$.

$(14, \text{Total}) = (15, \text{Total})/(5, \text{Total})$.

$(16) = (14)/(14, \text{Total})$.

$(17) = (5) * (16)$.

$(18) = (6)/(6, 1)$.

$(19) = (18) * (16)/(16, 1)$.

more classes than territories. Otherwise, the procedure is similar to that for territories.

The indicated change (i.e., "balanced adjustment") for Class 1 (column (16)) is a 1.3% increase. The current rate for Territory A, Class 1 is $125. The revised rate would be $133.15 (= 125 × 1.06 × 0.992 × 1.013), reflecting a 6% overall increase, a .8% relative decrease for Territory A, and a 1.3% relative increase for Class 1.

For Territory B, Class 1, the revised rate would be $79.60 (= 70 × 1.06 × 1.059 × 1.013). Thus, the relativity between Territory A and Territory B would be 0.598 (= 79.60/133.15).

For Territory A, Class 2, the revised rate would be $119.60 (= 112.5 × 1.06 × 0.992 × 1.011). Thus, the relativity between Class 1 and Class 2 would be 0.898 (= 119.60/133.15). (Note: some of the numbers have been rounded in the exhibits, resulting in the loss of significant digits.)

Pure Premium Approach

Rate relativities also may be adjusted through a "pure premium" approach. The basic difference between the two methods is that the loss ratio method uses earned premiums and the pure premium method uses earned exposures. If data is available at the same level of detail, and consistent methodology is applied, the two methods should produce the same results.

In practice, the loss ratio method often is used when detailed exposures are not available. Earned premiums at current rates are estimated from overall rate changes (or, possibly, rate changes by territory or class). With full exposure detail, earned premiums at current rates can be calculated by applying the current rates to the historical exposures.

When earned premiums at current rates are estimated, the loss ratio and pure premium methods can produce different results.

For example, assume that there was a previous overall rate increase of 6%. Also assume that the territorial and class relativities remained the same. Finally, assume that there is another rating variable, such as a deductible credit, that did change.

For example, half of the total book of business may have been written at a $100 deductible, where the rates did not change and half may have been written at a $200 deductible, where the rates increased 12%. Applying a 6% premium increase to all classes and territories may not be accurate, if the percentage of $100 deductible business in each cell is not the same.

Table 6.7 shows a pure premium approach for territories, using data similar to Table 6.5. Instead of premiums at current rates, we use "base exposures." Base exposures are calculated as the number of insured exposures (e.g., car months) times the rate relativities for all relevant rating variables. One insured exposure in territory A, class 1, of course, would generate one base exposure. One insured exposure in territory B (relativity 0.56) and class 2 (relativity 0.9) would generate 0.504 base exposures.

The concept of "base exposures" is important for two reasons. First, it adjusts for the differences in costs for different insureds (much the same way that earned premium does). For example, it makes an appropriate adjustment if territory A has a higher proportion of high class relativity insureds than territory B. Second, it facilitates an iterative procedure for producing more accurate relativities (as opposed to stopping after the first iteration). This will be explained in greater detail below.

Table 6.7 proceeds much the same as Table 6.5. Base exposures take the place of premium at current rates. The preliminary adjustment is based on relative pure premiums (instead of relative loss ratios, under the loss ratio approach). The pure premiums are the incurred losses divided by the base exposures. The credibility adjustment is the same as for the loss ratio approach. The balancing adjustment uses base exposures (on current business),

TABLE 6.7

TERRITORIAL RELATIVITIES—PURE PREMIUM APPROACH
FIRST ITERATION

	(1)	(2)	(3)	(4) Years 1 & 2	(5)	(6)	(7)	(8)
Territory	Earned Exposures	Base Exposures	Incurred Losses	Claim Count	Frequency	Severity	Pure Premium	Exposures on Current Business
A	9,000	14,409	1,037,495	1,437	10.0%	722	72.00	6,907
B	5,500	4,356	346,122	514	11.8%	673	79.46	2,101
C	5,000	3,628	252,909	474	13.1%	534	69.71	2,280
Total	19,500	22,393	1,636,526	2,425	10.8%	675	73.08	11,288

	(9) Preliminary Adjustment	(10) Credibility	(11) Credible Adjustment	(12) Extension	(13) Balanced Adjustment	(14) Extension	(15) Current Relativity	(16) New Relativity
Territory								
A	0.985	1.000	0.985	6,805	0.989	6,832	1.000	1.000
B	1.087	0.689	1.060	2,227	1.064	2,236	0.560	0.603
C	0.954	0.662	0.969	2,210	0.973	2,219	0.480	0.472
Total			0.996	11,243		11,288		

Notes: Calculations have been made to more significant digits than shown.
      (2),(8) based on rating factors underlying current rates.
      (5) = (4)/(2).
      (6) = (3)/(4).
      (7) = (3)/(2).
      (9) = (7)/(7, Total).
      (10) = Min ($\sqrt{[(3)/1082]}, 1$).
      (11) = [(9) − 1] ∗ (10) + 1.
      (12) = (8) ∗ (11).
      (11, Total) = (12, Total)/(8, Total).
      (13) = (11)/(11, Total).
      (14) = (8) ∗ (13).
      (16) = (15) ∗ (13)/(13, A).

rather than actual exposures, to make the territorial adjustment revenue neutral.

The results in Table 6.7 are different than those in Table 6.5, due to the approximation technique used to calculate premium at current rates. For this data set, the proportion of insureds by class varied considerably by territory.

Table 6.8 shows a pure premium approach for class relativities, which follows the territorial approach shown in Table 6.7. The total base exposures are the same for territories (Table 6.7) and classes (Table 6.8), because we have used a matrix of exposures. Again, the adjustments by class differ somewhat from the adjustments under the loss ratio approach, because of the approximation used to calculate premium at current rates. Had we used a matrix of earned premiums for the loss ratio approach, the adjustments would have been the same for the loss ratio and pure premium approaches.

An iterative approach can produce more accurate relativities. One iterative approach is described in Bailey (1963); it is similar to the procedure described below.

The balanced adjustments are based on the historical losses and the current relativities, as reflected in the base exposures. If we used the revised relativities to adjust our base exposures, we might produce a new set of indicated adjustments. If we continue this process, normally we will obtain convergence to a more accurate set of relativities. An iterative procedure will produce different relativities than a one-step procedure, when some of the territories (classes) have a disproportionate share of some of the classes (territories).

Table 6.9 shows the final iteration of the pure premium approach for territories; Table 6.10 shows the final iteration for classes. At each iteration, the "current relativity," column (15) has been changed to reflect the "balanced adjustment," column (13) (i.e., it is set equal to the "new relativity," column (16),

TABLE 6.8

CLASS RELATIVITIES—PURE PREMIUM APPROACH
FIRST ITERATION

	(1)	(2)	(3)	(4)	(5)	(6)	(7)	(8)
				Years 1 & 2				Exposures
	Earned	Base	Incurred	Claim			Pure	on Current
Class	Exposures	Exposures	Losses	Count	Frequency	Severity	Premium	Business
1	4,250	3,467	259,800	361	10.4%	720	74.94	1,758
2	2,050	1,181	89,820	114	9.7%	788	76.05	598
3	2,125	2,009	128,601	199	9.9%	646	64.01	1,025
4	3,000	2,800	206,800	278	9.9%	744	73.86	1,430
5	2,575	3,019	217,170	278	9.2%	781	71.93	1,598
6	1,775	1,792	153,125	231	12.9%	663	85.45	872
7	1,425	2,169	158,130	246	11.3%	643	72.90	1,008
8	1,150	2,647	181,320	308	11.6%	589	68.50	1,340
9	1,150	3,309	241,760	410	12.4%	590	73.06	1,659
Total	19,500	22,393	1,636,526	2,425	10.8%	675	73.08	11,288

	(9)	(10)	(11)	(12)	(13)	(14)	(15)	(16)
	Preliminary		Credible		Balanced		Current	New
Class	Adjustment	Credibility	Adjustment	Extension	Adjustment	Extension	Relativity	Relativity
1	1.025	0.578	1.015	1,784	1.015	1,784	1.000	1.000
2	1.041	0.325	1.013	606	1.014	606	0.900	0.899
3	0.876	0.429	0.947	970	0.947	971	1.150	1.073
4	1.011	0.507	1.005	1,438	1.006	1,438	1.400	1.387
5	0.984	0.507	0.992	1,585	0.992	1,586	1.900	1.858
6	1.169	0.462	1.078	940	1.079	941	1.550	1.647
7	0.998	0.477	0.999	1,007	0.999	1,007	1.850	1.821
8	0.937	0.534	0.967	1,295	0.967	1,296	2.600	2.477
9	1.000	0.616	1.000	1,659	1.000	1,659	3.250	3.203
Total			1.000	11,284		11,288		

Notes: Calculations have been made to more significant digits than shown.
(2), (8) based on rating factors underlying current rates.
(5) = (4)/(2).
(6) = (3)/(4).
(7) = (3)/(2).
(9) = (7)/(7, Total).
$(10) = \text{Min}\,(\sqrt{[(3)/1082]}, 1)$.
(11) = [(9) − 1] * (10) + 1.
(12) = (8) * (11).
(11, Total) = (12, Total)/(8, Total).
(13) = (11)/(11, Total).
(14) = (8) * (13).
(16) = (15) * (13)/(13, 1).

TABLE 6.9

TERRITORIAL RELATIVITIES—PURE PREMIUM APPROACH
FINAL ITERATION

	(1)	(2)	(3)	(4) Years 1 & 2	(5)	(6)	(7)	(8)
Territory	Earned Exposures	Base Exposures	Incurred Losses	Claim Count	Frequency	Severity	Pure Premium	Exposures on Current Business
A	9,000	13,935	1,037,495	1,437	10.3%	722	74.45	6,907
B	5,500	4,649	346,122	514	11.1%	673	74.45	2,101
C	5,000	3,397	252,909	474	14.0%	534	74.45	2,280
Total	19,500	21,980	1,636,526	2,425	11.0%	675	74.45	11,288

	(9)	(10)	(11)	(12)	(13)	(14)	(15)	(16)
Territory	Preliminary Adjustment	Credibility	Credible Adjustment	Extension	Balanced Adjustment	Extension	Current Relativity	New Relativity
A	1.000	1.000	1.000	6,907	1.000	6,907	1.000	1.000
B	1.000	0.689	1.000	2,101	1.000	2,101	0.604	0.604
C	1.000	0.662	1.000	2,280	1.000	2,280	0.459	0.459
Total			1.000	11,288		11,288		

Notes: Calculations have been made to more significant digits than shown.
(2) based on rating factors for iteration (see (15)).
(5) = (4)/(2).
(6) = (3)/(4).
(7) = (3)/(2).
(8) based on rating factors underlying current rates.
(9) = (7)/(7, Total).
(10) = Min ($\sqrt{[(3)/1082]}$, 1).
(11) = [(9) − 1] ∗ (10) + 1.
(12) = (8) ∗ (11).
(11, Total) = (12, Total)/(8, Total).
(13) = (11)/(11, Total).
(14) = (8) ∗ (13).
(16) = (15) ∗ (13)/(13, A).

TABLE 6.10

CLASS RELATIVITIES—PURE PREMIUM APPROACH
FINAL ITERATION

Class	(1) Earned Exposures	(2) Base Exposures	(3) Incurred Losses	(4) Claim Count	(5) Frequency	(6) Severity	(7) Pure Premium	(8) Exposures on Current Business
				Years 1 & 2				
1	4,250	3,489	259,800	361	10.3%	720	74.45	1,758
2	2,050	1,206	89,820	114	9.4%	788	74.46	598
3	2,125	1,727	128,601	199	11.5%	646	74.45	1,025
4	3,000	2,778	206,800	278	10.0%	744	74.45	1,430
5	2,575	2,917	217,170	278	9.5%	781	74.45	1,598
6	1,775	2,057	153,125	231	11.2%	663	74.45	872
7	1,425	2,124	158,130	246	11.6%	643	74.45	1,008
8	1,150	2,435	181,320	308	12.6%	589	74.45	1,340
9	1,150	3,247	241,760	410	12.6%	590	74.45	1,659
Total	19,500	21,980	1,636,526	2,425	11.0%	675	74.45	11,288

Class	(9) Preliminary Adjustment	(10) Credibility	(11) Credible Adjustment	(12) Extension	(13) Balanced Adjustment	(14) Extension	(15) Current Relativity	(16) New Relativity
1	1.000	0.578	1.000	1,758	1.000	1,758	1.000	1.000
2	1.000	0.325	1.000	598	1.000	598	0.899	0.899
3	1.000	0.429	1.000	1,025	1.000	1,025	0.989	0.989
4	1.000	0.507	1.000	1,430	1.000	1,430	1.372	1.372
5	1.000	0.507	1.000	1,598	1.000	1,598	1.795	1.795
6	1.000	0.462	1.000	872	1.000	872	1.747	1.747
7	1.000	0.477	1.000	1,008	1.000	1,008	1.800	1.800
8	1.000	0.534	1.000	1,340	1.000	1,340	2.399	2.399
9	1.000	0.616	1.000	1,659	1.000	1,659	3.199	3.199
Total			1.000	11,288		11,288		

Notes: Calculations have been made to more significant digits than shown.

(2) based on rating factors for iteration (see (15)).

$(5) = (4)/(2)$.

$(6) = (3)/(4)$.

$(7) = (3)/(2)$.

(8) based on rating factors underlying current rates.

$(9) = (7)/(7, \text{Total})$.

$(10) = \text{Min} (\sqrt{[(3)/1082]}, 1)$.

$(11) = [(9) - 1] * (10) + 1$.

$(12) = (8) * (11)$.

$(11, \text{Total}) = (12, \text{Total})/(8, \text{Total})$.

$(13) = (11)/(11, \text{Total})$.

$(14) = (8) * (13)$.

$(16) = (15) * (13)/(13, 1)$.

from the prior iteration). The base exposures for the class analysis are recalculated from the new relativities that result from the territorial analysis. This may produce a new set of "balanced adjustments" for classes, which are used to recalculate the base exposures for the territorial analysis. The process alternates between class and territory analysis (or multiple sets of relativities).

The base exposures and pure premiums will change at each iteration, until convergence. At convergence, all of the pure premiums will be essentially the same. When the preliminary adjustments are sufficiently close to 1.0, the balanced adjustments also will be close to 1.0.

An iterative procedure should produce more accurate relativities. For example, on the first iteration, the indicated relativity for class 3 was 1.073 and the indicated relativity for class 6 was 1.647 (see Table 6.8). On the final iteration (Table 6.10), the indicated relativity for class 3 is 0.989 and the indicated relativity for class 6 is 1.746. The results reflect the fact that class 3 has a disproportionately high amount of exposures in territory A, which is the highest rated territory, while class 6 has a disproportionately low exposure in territory A. Without making some adjustment for these disproportionate exposures, erroneous relativities can be produced.

An iterative approach is only possible when there are at least two sets of relativities and we can recalculate the base exposures (or premiums at current rates) for each set of relativities. An iterative approach would also work with a loss ratio approach. The key requirement is to have earned premiums for every cell in the matrix of rating variables.

It is relatively simple to set up an iterative process on a spreadsheet. We assume here that we are using a pure premium approach. At each iteration, for each set of relativities, the base exposures are recalculated, leading to a new set of pure premiums and indicated relativities. The ratio of the indicated pure premium (to base exposures) to the overall pure premium is the indicated adjustment for that step. This adjustment can be credibility-weighted and balanced. The adjustments need to be accumulated, so that one knows the indicated relativity to the base. At each step, the indicated relativity is used to recalculate base exposures. Since the indicated adjustments are based on a formula, the numerical result of the formula must be transferred (e.g., "range valued") at each step. When the adjustments are all approximately 1.000, the process has converged.

Additive or Multiplicative

The above examples used multiplicative relativities. In many, though not most, situations additive relativities are used. For example, a third level of classification could be used in addition to the above territory and class splits. The third level might correspond to automobile use, good-student discount, or driver training discounts.

Philosophically, are the third level differentials additive (i.e., a function of the base rates for a given territory) or multiplicative (i.e., a function of the specific age-gender-marital status and use differentials)? For example, is a good-student discount worth 20% of the base (i.e., adult) rate (additive) or 10% of the actual rate (multiplicative)? The actual rate may be 360% of the base for a 17-year-old male principal operator (multiplicative good student discount equals 36% of base rate) or 150% for a 20-year-old female (multiplicative good student discount equals 15% of base rate). Does "good student" status reduce costs equally for all insureds (additive) or does it affect costs proportionally (multiplicative)?

Unequal Exposure in Underlying Variables

Regardless of which form is chosen for the relativities, estimation is not necessarily straightforward. Certain subdivisions of a rating variable may have a disproportionate share of another rating variable; that is, two rating variables may be highly correlated with each other. For example, assume Group A costs twice

TABLE 6.11

Unequal Exposure Example

	A	B	Total
	Part 1. Exposure Data		
X	40	10	50
Y	10	40	50
Total	50	50	100

	A	B
	Part 2. Pure Premium Data	
X	4	2
Y	2	1

	A	B	Total	Exposures	Pure Prem.	Relativity
	Part 3. Costs					
X	160	20	180	50	3.6	3.0
Y	20	40	60	50	1.2	1.0
Total	180	60	240			
Exposures	50	50				
Pure Prem.	3.6	1.2				
Relativity	3.0	1.0				

Group B and Group X costs twice Group Y Also assume that AX occurs 40% of the time, AY 10%, BX 10%, and BY 40% (see Table 6.11).

The empirical cost for X is 3.6, and for Y, 1.2. Thus the empirical relativity is 3.0, when we know the actual cost is only double. This has happened because disproportionate exposure is concentrated in higher and lower cost groups. In determining the relative cost of X and Y, one may expect half of the exposure to be in Group A and half in Group B. Instead, 80% of X's exposure is in high-cost Group A and 80% of Y's exposure is in low-cost Group B. Thus X looks relatively higher in cost than it actually is. Various methods can be used to adjust for unequal distributions of underlying exposures. The iterative method discussed above is one.

Credibility Considerations

Another estimation problem concerns the credibility of the data. Since competition encourages insurers to refine their classification systems, refinement will generally continue to the point where the credibility of the data becomes minimal.

In the context of classification, credibility involves the assessment of the relative meaningfulness of a group's cost versus the meaningfulness of the credibility complement's cost. Assume for example, that the task is to estimate the cost of Group A. If Group A has a large body of data, that experience alone may be sufficient for estimating its cost. As Group A becomes smaller, at some point it will be useful to compare Group A's empirical costs to the cost of some other group. This other group is the credibility complement. Group A's empirical cost may be twice the cost of the complement. Since Group A has less data or less reliable data, the actuary may decide that Group A's true cost is only 60% higher than the complement.

Thus, two credibility related problems emerge: (1) how to obtain more data or more reliable data, and (2) what is the most appropriate credibility complement? Each of these matters can be discussed at length. The purpose here is to provide an overview.

Obtaining more or more reliable data can be done in several ways. Most obviously, more years of data or, possibly, data from several states (or countrywide) can be used. Of course, the threshold question is whether the broader base actually applies. Has there been a change over time? Do countrywide indications apply in each state?

Another method is to give more weight to more stable phenomena. For example, relativities can be based primarily on frequency (by looking only at claim counts or by limiting the size of claims), instead of pure premiums. Partial pure premiums can be calculated. For example, property damage liability costs may be more stable than bodily injury liability; workers compensation

TABLE 6.12

CLASS RATING EXAMPLE

Part 1. Raw Data					
Rating Group	Years	Exposures	Frequency Relativity	Severity Relativity	Pure Premium Relativity
A	89–98	420	4.2	1.15	4.9
	91–98	340	4.6	1.18	5.4
	94–98	193	4.6	1.10	5.1
	96–98	93	4.7	1.36	6.3
B	89–98	846	5.1	1.16	5.9
	91–98	635	5.6	1.22	6.9
	94–98	304	5.2	1.07	5.6
	96–98	147	6.0	1.26	7.6
C	89–98	293	5.9	1.93	11.3
	91–98	233	6.1	1.98	12.1
	94–98	133	4.8	1.72	8.3
	96–98	69	4.5	1.69	7.6
Part 2. Conclusions					
A			4.8	1.25	6.0
B			5.6	1.25	7.0
C			6.0	1.33	8.0

medical costs may be more stable than deaths or permanent disabilities. In determining relativities, more emphasis (credibility) is given to the more stable phenomena.

The choice of credibility complement may be more difficult than obtaining more or more reliable data. It may not be clear which group is most nearly the same as the group in question. National or regional data may be applicable. Related industry group data may be applicable. In most of these cases, adjustments must be made because the level of costs can be quite different for the complement. Often, the percentage change in the complement is considered, rather then the actual value. As a last resort, the complement may be based on the prior year's analysis; this, in effect, takes more years of data into account.

Table 6.12 illustrates some of the credibility issues.

The problem is choosing rate relativities for a group of surgical specialties. At the current time, all specialties shown in Table 6.12 are being charged 8.4 times the base. Data is grouped for various combinations of accident years (all groups ending with 1998). Relativities to the base are shown for claim frequency, severity, and pure premium. The severity relativity for all surgery classifications is about 1.25.

The frequencies seem to be different for the different groups, although Groups B and C could possibly have the same frequency. The severities are much different for Group C, although the number of claims is relatively small (17 for the 10-year period).

Selected relativities were based on judgment rather than a formal credibility formula. Essentially, claim frequency was given high credibility. The overall severity for surgeons (1.25) was used for Groups A and B, although actual data is not much different. The severity for Group C reflects a small upward adjustment to the overall surgeons' relativity (about 15% credibility). The selected pure premium relativities were rounded.

SUMMARY

Risk classification involves the formulation of different premiums for the same coverage based on group characteristics. That is, the task is to price an individual insured, but the available claim data for that individual is insufficient for the purpose. The recourse is to measure group costs and assume that the individual belongs to a certain group. The grouping process may proceed in several dimensions (e.g., class, territory, use).

Premiums should vary because underlying costs vary. Costs may vary due to different claim frequency or average claim size, different administrative expense requirements, different investment income potential, or differing assessments of risk. Risk classification proceeds by identifying variables that distinguish these costs among different insureds. In addition to classification variables, premiums can also vary due to the choice of different exposure bases, individual risk rating methods, and marketing or underwriting strategies.

Various criteria, actuarial, operational, social, and legal, have been suggested for formulating classification variables. Actuarial criteria attempt most accurately to group individual insureds into groups that (1) are relatively homogeneous, (2) are sufficiently large to estimate relative cost differences (credibility), and (3) maintain stable mean costs over time (reliability).

Operational criteria include objective definitions, reasonable administrative expense, and verifiability. Social criteria include privacy, causality, controllability, and affordability.

A competitive market tends to produce more refined classifications and accurate premiums. Competition may be limited, however, when the premium volume for a group is small or where there is significant heterogeneity in costs within the group. Most of the social criteria are based on concepts of accuracy. The abolition of certain rating variables likely will reduce rating accuracy, as well as create subsidies or availability problems. The inaccuracy in the current rating systems is primarily determined by the level of competition and the statistical difficulty of rating small groups of insureds.

The absolute efficiency of current classification systems can be estimated, but the estimates depend upon some measurement of the variability in costs among all insureds (which can never be observed directly). Knowing the absolute efficiency, however, is not particularly useful in determining which specific rating variables would be better than current ones.

REFERENCES

Abraham, Kenneth S., "Efficiency and Fairness in Insurance Risk Classification," *Va. Law Review*, 1985, 71:403.

American Academy of Actuaries, Brief as Amicus Curiae, *Norris v. Arizona Governing Committee*, 1982.

American Academy of Actuaries, Committee on Risk Classification, *Risk Classification Statement of Principles*, 1980.

American Academy of Actuaries, *Report of Academy Task Force on Risk Classification*, 1977.

Bailey, Robert A., "Insurance Rates with Minimum Bias," *Proceedings of the Casualty Actuarial Society*, 1963, 50:4–11.

Bouska, Amy, "Exposure Bases Revisted," *Proceedings of the Casualty Actuarial Society*, 1989, 76:1–23.

Butler, Patrick, Twiss Butler, and Laurie L. Williams, "Sexdivided Mileage, Accident, and Insurance Cost Data Show that Auto Insurers Overcharge Most Women," *Journal of Insurance Regulation*, 1988, 6:243.

Glendenning, G. William, and Robert B. Holtom, *Personal Lines Underwriting*, Malvern, Pa:, Ins. Institute of America, 1977.

Holtom, Robert B., *Restraints on Underwriting: Risk Selection, Discrimination and the Law*, Cincinnati: The National Underwriter Co., 1979.

Launie, J. J., J. Finley Lee, and Norman A. Baglini, *Principles of Property and Liability Underwriting*, Malvern, Pa: Insurance Institute of America, 1976.

Kimball, Spencer L., "Reverse Sex Discrimination: Manhart," *American Bar Foundation Research Journal*, 1979, 83.

Massachusetts Division of Insurance, *Automobile Insurance Risk Classification: Equity and Accuracy*, 1978.

Meyers, Glenn G., "Empirical Bayesian Credibility for Workers' Compensation Classification Ratemaking," *Proceedings of the Casualty Actuarial Society*, 1984, 71:96–121.

National Association of Insurance Commissioners, D-3 Advisory Committee, *Report of the Rates and Rating Procedures Task Force*, 1978.

Skurnick, David, N. Robert Heyer, and G. Ray Funkhouser, "Revising Classification Structure Using Survey Data," *Proceedings of the Casualty Actuarial Society*, 1974, 61:103–115.

SRI International, *Choice of a Regulatory Environment for Automobile Insurance (Final Report)*, 1979.

Stanford Research Institute, *The Role of Risk Classification in Property and Casualty Insurance: A Study of the Risk Assessment Process*, 1976.

Wallace, Frances K., "Unisex Automobile Rating: the Michigan Experience," *Journal of Insurance Regulation*, 1984, 3(2):127.

Walters, Michael A., "Risk Classification Standards," *Proceedings of the Casualty Actuarial Society*, 1981, 68:1–18.

Woll, Richard G,." A Study of Risk Assessment," *Proceedings of the Casualty Actuarial Society*, 1979, 66:84–138.

INTRODUCTION

What is Reinsurance?

Reinsurance is a form of insurance. A reinsurance contract is legally an insurance contract. The *reinsurer* agrees to indemnify the *cedant* insurer for a specified share of specified types of insurance claims paid by the cedant for a single insurance policy or for a specified set of policies. The terminology used is that the reinsurer *assumes* the liability *ceded* on the *subject policies*. The *cession*, or share of claims to be paid by the reinsurer, may be defined on a *proportional share* basis (a specified percentage of each claim) or on an *excess basis* (the part of each claim, or aggregation of claims, above some specified dollar amount).

The nature and purpose of insurance is to reduce the financial cost to individuals, corporations, and other entities arising from the potential occurrence of specified contingent events. An insurance company sells insurance policies guarantying that the insurer will indemnify the policyholders for part of the financial losses stemming from these contingent events. The pooling of liabilities by the insurer makes the total losses more predictable than is the case for each individual insured, thereby reducing the risk relative to the whole. Insurance enables individuals, corporations and other entities to perform riskier operations. This increases innovation, competition, and efficiency in a capitalistic marketplace.

The nature and purpose of reinsurance is to reduce the financial cost to insurance companies arising from the potential occurrence of specified insurance claims, thus further enhancing innovation, competition, and efficiency in the marketplace. The cession of shares of liability spreads risk further throughout the insurance system. Just as an individual or company purchases an insurance policy from an insurer, an insurance company may purchase fairly comprehensive reinsurance from one or more reinsurers. A reinsurer may also reduce its assumed reinsurance risk by purchasing reinsurance coverage from other reinsurers, both domestic and international; such a cession is called a *retrocession*.

Reinsurance companies are of two basic types: *direct writers*, which have their own employed account executives who produce business, and *broker companies* or *brokers*, which receive business through *reinsurance intermediaries*. Some direct writers do receive a part of their business through brokers, and likewise, some broker reinsurers assume some business directly from the ceding companies. It is estimated that more than half of U.S. reinsurance is placed via intermediaries.

The form and wording of reinsurance contracts are not as closely regulated as are insurance contracts, and there is no rate regulation of reinsurance between private companies. A reinsurance contract is often a manuscript contract setting forth the unique agreement between the two parties. Because of the many special cases and exceptions, it is difficult to make correct generalizations about reinsurance. Consequently, as you read this chapter, you should often supply for yourself the phrases "It is generally true that..." and "Usually..." whenever they are not explicitly stated.

This heterogeneity of contract wordings also means that whenever you are accumulating, analyzing, and comparing various reinsurance data, you must be careful that the reinsurance coverages producing the data are reasonably similar. We will be encountering this problem throughout this chapter.

The Functions of Reinsurance

Reinsurance does not change the basic nature of an insurance coverage. On a long-term basis, it cannot be expected to make bad business good. But it does provide the following direct assistance to the cedant.

Capacity

Having reinsurance coverage, a cedant can write higher policy limits while maintaining a manageable risk level. By ceding shares of all policies or just larger policies, the net retained loss exposure per individual policy or in total can be kept in line with the cedant's surplus. Thus smaller insurers can compete with larger insurers, and policies beyond the capacity of any single insurer can be written.

The word "capacity" is sometimes also used in relation to aggregate volume of business. This aspect of capacity is best considered below in the general category of financial results management.

Stabilization

Reinsurance can help stabilize the cedant's underwriting and financial results over time and help protect the cedant's surplus against shocks from large, unpredictable losses. Reinsurance is usually written so that the cedant retains the smaller, predictable claims, but shares the larger, infrequent claims. It can also be written to provide protection against a larger than predicted accumulation of claims, either from one catastrophic event or from many. Thus the underwriting and financial effects of large claims or large accumulations of claims can be spread out over many years. This decreases the cedant's probability of financial ruin.

Financial Results Management

Reinsurance can alter the timing of income, enhance statutory and/or GAAP surplus, and improve various financial ratios by which insurers are judged. An insurance company with a growing book of business whose growth is stressing their surplus can cede part of their liability to a reinsurer to make use of the reinsurer's surplus. This is essentially a loan of surplus from the reinsurer to the cedant until the cedant's surplus is large enough to support the new business. We will see other ways that reinsurance can be used to alter a cedant's financial numbers. As you might expect in a free market, this aspect of reinsurance has led to some abuses in its use. As we discuss the various forms of reinsurance coverage, we will note their financial effects.

Management Advice

Many professional reinsurers have the knowledge and ability to provide an informal consulting service for their cedants. This service can include advice and assistance on underwriting, marketing, pricing, loss prevention, claims handling, reserving, actuarial, investment, and personnel issues. Enlightened self-interest induces the reinsurer to critically review the cedant's operation, and thus be in a position to offer advice. The reinsurer typically has more experience in the pricing of high limits policies and in the handling of large and rare claims. Also, through contact with many similar cedant companies, the reinsurer may be able to provide an overview of general issues and trends. Reinsurance intermediaries may also provide some of these same services for their clients.

The Forms of Reinsurance

Facultative Certificates

A facultative certificate reinsures just one primary policy. Its main function is to provide additional capacity. It is used to cover part of specified large, especially hazardous or unusual exposures to limit their potential impact upon the cedant's net results or to protect the cedant's ongoing ceded treaty results in order to keep treaty costs down. The reinsurer underwrites and accepts each certificate individually; the situation is very similar to primary insurance individual risk underwriting. Because facultative reinsurance usually covers the more hazardous or unusual exposures, the reinsurer must be aware of the potential for antiselection within and among classes of insureds.

Property certificate coverage is sometimes written on a proportional basis; the reinsurer reimburses a fixed percentage of each claim on the subject policy. Most casualty certificate coverage is written on an excess basis; the reinsurer reimburses a share (up to some specified dollar limit) of the part of each claim on the subject policy that lies above some fixed dollar attachment point (net retention).

Facultative Automatic Agreements or Programs

A facultative automatic agreement reinsures many primary policies of a specified type. These policies are usually very similar, so the exposure is very homogeneous. Its main function is to provide additional capacity, but since it covers many policies, it also provides some degree of stabilization. It may be thought of as a collection of facultative certificates underwritten simultaneously. It may cover on either a proportional or excess basis. It is usually written to cover new or special programs marketed by the cedant, and the reinsurer may work closely with the cedant to design the primary underwriting and pricing guidelines. For example, a facultative automatic agreement may cover a 90% share of the cedant's personal umbrella business, in which case the reinsurer will almost certainly provide expert advice and will monitor the cedant's underwriting and pricing very closely.

Facultative automatic agreements are usually written on a fixed cost basis, without the retrospective premium adjustments or variable ceding commissions sometimes used for treaties (as we shall see below).

There are also *non-obligatory* agreements where either the cedant may not be required to cede or the reinsurer may not be required to assume every single policy of the specified type.

Treaties

A treaty reinsures a specified part of the loss exposure for a set of insurance policies for a specified coverage period. For ongoing treaty coverage, the claims covered may be either those occurring during the treaty term or those occurring on policies written during the term. In the case of claims-made coverage, the word "occurring" means those claims made to the ceding company during the term. The premium *subject* to the treaty corresponds to the types of claims covered: it is earned premium arising from policies of the specified type either in force or written during the term of the treaty. The subject exposure is usually defined by Annual Statement line of business or some variant or subsets thereof. Because an ongoing treaty relationship involves a close sharing of much of the insurance exposure, it can create a close working partnership between the parties; the expertise and services of the reinsurer or broker are available to the cedant. This is especially true for treaties written by a direct writer or where there is a strong reinsurer leading a brokered treaty.

Treaty Proportional Covers

A *quota-share* treaty reinsures a fixed percentage of each subject policy. Its main function is financial results management, although it also provides some capacity. The reinsurer usually receives the same share of premium as claims, and pays the cedant a *ceding commission* commensurate with the primary production and handling costs (underwriting, claims, etc.). Quota-share treaties usually assume in-force exposure at inception. The cedant's financial results are managed because the ceding commission on the ceded unearned premium reserve transfers statutory surplus from the reinsurer to the cedant. (We shall see this later.) The cession of premium also reduces the cedant's net-premium-to-surplus ratio.

The ceding commission on quota-share treaties is often defined to vary within some range inversely to the loss ratio. This allows the cedant to retain better-than-expected profits, but protects the reinsurer somewhat from adverse claims experience.

The term quota-share is sometimes (mis-)used when the coverage is a percentage share of an excess layer; we will more properly treat this kind of coverage as being excess.

A *surplus-share* treaty also reinsures a fixed percentage of each subject policy, but the percentage varies by policy according to the relationship between the policy limit and the treaty's specified *net line* retention. Its main function is capacity, but it also provides some stabilization. A surplus-share treaty may also assume in-force exposure at inception, which together with a ceding commission provides some management of financial results. This is typically a property cover; it is rarely used for casualty business.

Treaty Excess Covers

An excess treaty reinsures, up to a limit, a share of the part of each claim that is in excess of some specified *attachment point* (cedant's *retention*). Its main functions are capacity and stabilization. An excess treaty typically covers exposure earned during its term on either a losses-occurring or claims-made basis, but run-off exposure may be added in. The definition of "subject loss" is important.

For a *per-risk excess* treaty, a subject loss is defined to be the sum of all claims arising from one covered loss event or occurrence for a single subject policy. Per-risk excess is mainly used for property exposures. It often provides protection net of facultative coverage, and sometimes also net of proportional treaties. It is used for casualty less often than per-occurrence coverage.

For a *per-occurrence excess* treaty, a subject loss is defined to be the sum of all claims arising from one covered loss event or occurrence for all subject policies. Per-occurrence excess is used for casualty exposures to provide protection all the way up from working cover layers through clash layers.

A *working cover* excess treaty reinsures an excess layer for which claims activity is expected each year. The significant expected claims frequency creates some stability of the aggregate reinsured loss. So working covers are often *retrospectively rated*, with the final reinsurance premium partially determined by the treaty's loss experience.

A *higher exposed layer* excess treaty attaches above the working cover(s), but within policy limits. Thus there is direct single-policy exposure to the treaty.

A *clash treaty* is a casualty treaty that attaches above all policy limits. Thus it may be only exposed by:

1. extra-contractual-obligations (i.e., bad faith claims)

2. excess-of-policy-limit damages (an obligation on the part of the insurer to cover losses above an insurance contract's stated policy limit)

3. catastrophic workers compensation accidents

4. the "clash" of claims arising from one or more loss events involving multiple coverages or policies.

Both higher exposed layers and clash are almost always priced on a fixed cost basis, with no variable commission or additional premium provision.

Catastrophe Covers

A catastrophe cover is a per-occurrence treaty used for property exposure. It is used to protect the net position of the cedant against the accumulation of claims arising from one or more large events. It is usually stipulated that two or more insureds must be involved before coverage attaches. The coverage is typically of the form of a 90% or 95% share of one or more layers (separate treaties) in excess of the maximum retention within which the cedant can comfortably absorb a loss, or for which the cedant can afford the reinsurance prices.

Aggregate Excess, or Stop Loss Covers

For an *aggregate excess* treaty, also sometimes called a *stop loss* cover, a loss is the accumulation of all subject losses during a specified time period, usually one year. It usually covers all or part of the net retention of the cedant and protects net results, providing very strong stabilization. Claims arising from natural catastrophes are often excluded, or there may be a per-occurrence maximum limit.

Finite, or Nontraditional, Reinsurance Covers

Over the past few years, there has been a growing use of reinsurance, especially treaties, whose only or main function is to manage financial results. The word "finite" means that the reinsurer's assumed risk is significantly reduced by various contractual conditions, sometimes called "structure." Of course, the reinsurer's expected margin (expense and profit) is also reduced to reflect this reduced risk transfer. Sometimes these covers are structured to induce a favorable tax treatment for the cedant. Often they are based on the ability of offshore reinsurers to book claims on a discounted basis in anticipation of the future investment income that will be earned from the premium income received before the claims are settled. The reinsurance premium reflects this discounting, thus giving the cedant a statutory and GAAP accounting benefit.

There have been cases where the risk transfer was nonexistent or negligible. In order to stop accounting abuses through reinsurance, the Financial Accounting Standards Board issued FAS 113 in 1992. FAS 113 requires a measurable and significant transfer of risk before a contract can receive the benefit of reinsurance accounting. Although the standard is somewhat ambiguous, it has largely stopped abusive reinsurance practices.

There continues to be debate in the reinsurance community about a workable distinction between the categories: traditional and finite reinsurance. Other than the rather ambiguous FAS 113, there is no clear boundary between traditional reinsurance and finite reinsurance; there is a continuum of risk transfer possibility between full risk transfer and no transfer. Virtually any reinsurance contract can be structured in a way to reduce the risk transfer and become "finite." We shall see this in the following discussion of typical forms for finite reinsurance. Throughout this chapter, we assume that any reinsurance contract under

discussion has sufficient risk transfer to pass FAS 113 requirements.

The first typical form for finite reinsurance is a *financial proportional cover*. As noted above, proportional treaties quite often
have a ceding commission that varies inversely with the losses;
this limits the risk transfer. The degree of variation can be increased to further limit the risk transfer. Also, the loss share
may be defined to decrease somewhat if the losses exceed some
maximum. Quite often, these treaties may also have some kind
of funding mechanism, wherein the aggregate limit of coverage is based upon the fund (net cash position less the reinsurer's
margin) together with some remote risk layer. Whatever the risk-
limiting structure, the contract must be checked with the cedant's
accountants to assure that they will approve the risk transfer for
FAS 113 guidelines.

A *loss portfolio transfer* is also a very prevalent form for finite
reinsurance. This is a retrospective cover, a cession of part of the
cedant's loss liabilities as of a specified accounting date. It may
be a cession of the total liability or, more often, a cession of
some aggregate excess layer of the liability. An aggregate excess
cover attaching at the cedant's carried loss reserve is often called
an *adverse development cover*. It is clear that a loss portfolio
transfer could be a pure risk non-finite cover. To make the risk
transfer finite, it has an aggregate limit and may have sublimits
for various types of claims, and it is priced to be essentially
a present-value funding of liabilities with a substantial upfront
provisional margin for the reinsurer. Part of this margin will be
paid back to the cedant in the form of a profit commission if the
loss experience is favorable.

A *funded aggregate excess cover* is, as you might expect, an
aggregate excess treaty in which the premium is high enough to
fund the loss payments except in extraordinary circumstances.
It is analogous to a funded loss portfolio transfer except that it
covers future occurring claims. In addition to financial results

management, it may provide strong stabilization of the cedant's net results.

A Typical Reinsurance Program

There is no such thing as a typical reinsurance program. Every insurance company is in a unique situation with regard to loss exposure, financial solidity, management culture, future plans, and marketing opportunities. Thus each company needs a unique reinsurance program, a combination of ceded reinsurance covers tailor-made for that company.

Nevertheless, Table 7.1 displays what we might regard as a "typical" reinsurance program for a medium-sized insurance company.

If the company writes surety, fidelity, marine, medical malpractice, or other special business, other similar reinsurance covers would be purchased. If the company were entering a new market (e.g., a new territory or a new type of business), it might purchase a quota-share treaty to lessen the risk of the new business and the financial impact of the new premium volume, and to obtain the reinsurer's assistance. Or it might purchase a proportional facultative automatic agreement for an even closer working relationship with a reinsurer. If the company were exiting a market, it might purchase a loss portfolio transfer, especially an adverse development cover, to cover part of the run-off claims payments.

The Cost of Reinsurance to the Cedant

The Reinsurer's Margin

In pricing a reinsurance cover, the reinsurer charges a margin over and above the ceded loss expectation, commission, and brokerage fee (if any). The margin is usually stated as a percentage of the reinsurance premium. It is theoretically based upon the reinsurer's expenses, the degree of risk transfer, and the magni-

TABLE 7.1

A REINSURANCE PROGRAM
FOR A MEDIUM-SIZED INSURANCE COMPANY

Line of Business	Type of Reinsurance
Fire and Allied Lines HO Section I SMP Section II	1. Proportional and excess facultative certificates to bring each individual policy's net exposure down to $2M
	2. Surplus share of four lines not to exceed $1.6M; maximum cedant retention of $400,000
	3. Per-risk excess working cover of $200k excess of $200k
	4. Catastrophe covers: 4.1. 95% of $5M excess of $5M 4.2. 95% of $10M excess of $10M 4.3. 95% of $10M excess of $20M 4.4. 95% of $10M excess of $30M
Casualty Lines excluding Umbrella	1. Facultative certificates for primary per policy coverage excess of $2M
	2. Working cover $500k excess of $500k
	3. Higher exposed layer $1M excess of $1M
	4. Clash layers: 4.1. $3M excess of $2M 4.2. $5M excess of $5M 4.3. $10M excess of $10M
Personal Umbrellas	1. 90% share facultative automatic program

tude of capacity and financial support, but it is practically influenced by competition in the reinsurance market. Of course, as with most insurance, the actual resulting margin will differ from that anticipated because of the stochasticity of the loss liability and cash flow transferred.

Brokerage Fee

A reinsurance broker charges a brokerage fee for placing the reinsurance coverage and for any other services performed on behalf of the cedant. This fee is incorporated into the reinsurance premium and is paid by the reinsurer. Offsetting this cost is the fact that broker reinsurers usually have lower internal expenses because they don't maintain separate marketing staffs. The brokerage fee is usually a fixed percentage of the reinsurance premium, but on occasion may be defined as either a fixed dollar or as some other variable amount.

Lost Investment Income

For most reinsurance contracts, the premium funds (net of ceding commission) are paid to the broker, if any, who then passes them on (also net of brokerage fee) to the reinsurer. The cedant thus loses the use of those funds, and the reinsurer gains the investment income earned on those funds until returned as loss payments, ceding commission adjustments or other premium adjustments. The price of the reinsurance cover accounts for this investment income.

Some contracts incorporate a *funds withheld* provision, where the cedant pays only a specified margin to the reinsurer, from which the broker, if any, deducts the brokerage fee. The remaining reinsurance premium is "withheld" by the cedant. The cedant then pays reinsurance losses out of the funds withheld until they are exhausted, at which time payments are made directly by the reinsurer. The reinsurance contract may define a mechanism for crediting investment income to the funds withheld. The reinsurer will want a higher profit margin for a funds withheld contract because of the added risk (the credit worthiness of the cedant) and the lost investment income.

Additional Cedant Expenses

The cedant incurs various expenses for ceding reinsurance. These include the cost of negotiation, the cost of a financial analysis of the reinsurer, accounting, and reporting costs, etc. If a broker is involved, the brokerage fee covers some of these services to the cedant. In general, facultative coverage is more expensive than treaty because of individual policy negotiation, accounting, and loss cessions.

Reciprocity

In some cases, in order to cede reinsurance, the cedant may be required to assume some reinsurance from the reinsurer, in this case usually another primary company. If this reciprocal reinsurance assumption is unprofitable, the loss should be considered as part of the cost of reinsurance. Reciprocity is not prevalent in the United States.

Balancing Costs and Benefits

In balancing the costs and benefits of a reinsurance cover or of a whole reinsurance program, the cedant should consider more than just the direct costs versus the benefits of the loss coverage and reinsurance functions discussed previously. A major consideration should be the reinsurer's financial solidity—Will the reinsurer be able to quickly pay claims arising from a natural catastrophe? Will the reinsurer be around to pay late-settled claims many years from now? Also important is the reinsurer's reputation: does the reinsurer pay reasonably presented claims in a reasonable time? Another consideration may be the reinsurer's or broker's services, including possibly underwriting, marketing, pricing, loss prevention, claims handling, reserving, actuarial, investment, and personnel advice and assistance.

Reinsurance Introduction: Final Comments

This introduction is only a brief review of basic reinsurance concepts and terminology. The interested reader will find more extensive discussions in the general reinsurance texts listed in the references.

REINSURANCE PRICING

General Considerations

In general, reinsurance pricing is more uncertain than primary pricing. Coverage terms can be highly individualized, especially for treaties. These terms determine the coverage period, definition of "loss," commission arrangements, premium and loss payment timing, etc. It is often difficult and sometimes impossible to get credible loss experience directly pertaining to the cover being evaluated. Often the claims and exposure data are not as they first seem. So you must continually ask questions in order to discover their true nature. Because of these problems of coverage definition and interpretation of loss and exposure statistics, the degree of risk relative to premium volume is usually much greater for reinsurance than for primary insurance.

Additional risk arises from the low claim frequency and high severity nature of many reinsurance coverages, from the lengthy time delays between the occurrence, reporting, and settlement of many covered loss events, and also from the leveraged effect of inflation upon excess claims. In general, the lower the expected claims frequency, the higher the variance of results relative to expectation, and thus the higher the risk level. In addition, *IBNR* claims emergence and case reserve development are severe problems for casualty excess business. Claims development beyond ten years can be large, highly variant, and extremely difficult to evaluate, as we shall discuss in the Loss Reserving section. Because of this long tail and extreme variability of loss payments, the matching of assets with liabilities is more difficult. Future predictability is also decreased by the greater uncertainty about claims severity inflation above excess cover attachment points. All these elements create a situation where the variance (and higher moments) of the loss process and its estimation are much more important relative to the expected value than is usually the case for primary coverage. For some reinsurance covers, the higher moments (or at least the underwriter/actuary's beliefs regarding uncertainty and fluctuation potential) determine the technical rate.

Reinsurance Pricing Methods

There are many ways to price reinsurance covers. For any given situation, there is no single right way. In this section, we will discuss a few actuarially sound methods. In general, the exposition of pricing methods will begin simply and become more complex as the situation demands and as we ask more questions. In many real situations, you might want to get a quick first evaluation via the simplest methods. Indeed, if you judge the situation to be either fairly predictable by these methods, or if you judge the risk to be small, you may decide to stop there. If not, you may want to pursue your analysis and pricing along the lines presented here. As in most actuarial work, you should try as many reasonable methods as time permits (and also reconcile the answers, if possible).

In this spirit, please note that the simple flat rate pricing formula and the use of the Pareto and Gamma distributions in this chapter are for illustrative purposes. The pricing formula a reinsurance actuary would use depends upon the reinsurer's pricing philosophy, information availability, and complexity of the coverage. The probability models should be selected to describe the actual situation as best as possible given all the real statistical and analytical cost constraints preventing you from obtaining more information. Klugman, Panjer, and Willmot [12], Hogg and Klugman [11], and Patrik [18] all discuss model selection and parameter estimation.

A Flat Rate Reinsurance Pricing Formula

As we get into the formulas, there will be a lot of notation. For clarity, we will preface variables with PC for "primary company" and R for "reinsurer" or "reinsurance." PV will be used in the traditional sense to mean "present value."

A discussion of the pricing formula to be used in this chapter will illustrate certain differences from primary pricing. We will often use the word "technical" to distinguish the actuarially calculated premium, rate, etc. from the actual final premium, rate, etc., agreed to by the cedant and reinsurer. Formula 7.2 calculates the technical reinsurance premium in terms of reinsurance loss cost, external expenses, internal expenses, and target economic return in the simple case where there are no later commission or premium adjustments based upon the actual loss experience. You can see that 7.2 is an "actuarial" formula, based explicitly upon costs.[1]

Formula 7.2: A Flat Rate Reinsurance Pricing Formula

$$RP = \frac{PVRELC}{(1 - RCR - RBF) \times (1 - RIXL) \times (1 - RTER)}$$

where

RP = reinsurance premium

$PVRELC$ = PV of $RELC$

= $RDF \times RELC$

$RELC$ = reinsurer's estimate of the reinsurance expected loss cost, $E[RL]$

RL = reinsurance loss

$E[RL]$ = reinsurance aggregate loss expectation

RDF = reinsurance loss payment discount factor

RCR = reinsurance ceding commission rate (as a percent of RP)

RBF = reinsurance brokerage fee (as a percent of RP)

$RIXL$ = reinsurer's internal expense loading (as a percent of RP net of RCR and RBF)

$RTER$ = reinsurer's target economic return (as a percent of reinsurance pure premium, RP net of RCR, RBF and $RIXL$)

---

[1]Formulas traditionally used by reinsurance underwriters have more often been of the form: undiscounted loss estimate divided by a judgmental loading factor such as 0.85. Of course the problem with this type of formula is that all the information about the expenses, discounting and profit loading are buried in one impenetrable number.

Let's break down this somewhat complicated-looking formula. First, as an actuarial technical pricing formula, we build up the premium starting with the loss cost. The reinsurance pure premium (*RPP*) can be written as follows.

Formula 7.3: Reinsurance Pure Premium

$$RPP = \frac{PVRELC}{1 - RTER}$$

This is the real "risk" premium for the risk transfer. The reinsurer's target economic return, *RTER*, is the reinsurer's charge for profit and risk. It is properly related to *PVRELC* for the contract. By writing the formula this way, the reinsurer's expected profit (present value) is $RTER \times RPP$. In this flat rated case, the reinsurer's expected profit is a simple linear function of the present value of the reinsurance expected loss cost, $RTER/(1 - RTER) \times PVRELC$. A discussion of how to select *RTER*'s for various contracts or lines of business is well beyond the scope of this chapter. The modern actuarial and economic literature derives these profit margins from an overall corporate target return on equity (RoE) and the relative risk level of each particular contract. There is extensive actuarial literature on this topic; see especially Bühlmann [9], Daykin, Pentikäinen and Pesonen [8], and, generally, *The ASTIN Bulletin, The Proceedings of the Casualty Actuarial Society* and any publications connected with the CAS Casualty Actuaries in Reinsurance.

Next, the reinsurer's internal expenses are loaded onto the reinsurance pure premium by dividing it by $1 - RIXL$. Thinking of this from the opposite direction (top down), it may also be thought of as a loading on reinsurance premium less external expenses. It is convenient to think of the loading for the reinsurer's internal expenses this latter way for at least three reasons:

1. This is the reinsurer's actual cash income from the cedant (unless there are funds withheld).

2. It is relatively easy to account for external expenses by reinsurance line of business. Within a line, the reinsurer's

underwriting and claims handling effort, and thus internal expenses, should be similar for each contract, varying only by claims and "risk" volume.

3. Internal expenses by contract should be independent (or almost independent) of commissions or brokerage expenses. Thus the loading should be independent of these expenses.

Together, *RTER* and *RIXL* determine the reinsurer's desired pricing margin for internal expenses and profit (economic return).

Finally, the reinsurance ceding commission rate and brokerage fee are specified in each particular contract; they are almost always stated as percentages of the total reinsurance premium *RP*. There is often no ceding commission on excess coverage; this is very different from primary coverage where commissions almost always exist. Of course, the existence of a reinsurance brokerage fee also depends upon the existence of a reinsurance intermediary for the contract.

An example will help clarify this.

Example 7.4:

PVRELC = $100,000 (calculated by actuarial analysis and formulas)

RTER = 20% (The reinsurer believes this is appropriate to compensate for the uncertainty and risk level of the coverage.)

RIXL = 10% (The reinsurer's allocation for this type of business.)

RCR = 25% (specified in the contract)

RBF = 5% (specified in the contract)

Then

$$RPP = \frac{\$100,000}{0.8} = \$125,000$$

$$RP = \frac{\$125,000}{(1 - .10) \times (1 - .25 - .05)}$$

$$= \$198,413$$

Please note that the reinsurance premium less external expenses is

$$\frac{RPP}{1 - RIXL} = \frac{\$125,000}{0.9}$$

$$= \$138,889$$

$$= 0.7 \times \$198,413$$

$$= (1 - RCR - RBF) \times RP$$

Also, the reinsurer's desired margin for internal expenses and profit is

$$\$138,889 - \$100,000 = \$38,889$$

$$= \$13,889 + \$25,000.$$

Very often the reinsurance premium is not a fixed dollar amount, but is calculated as a rate times a rating basis, quite often *PCP, the primary company (subject) premium.* In our example, if *PCP* was expected to be $5,000,000, the reinsurance rate would most likely be rounded to 0.04 or 4%. Then the expected reinsurance premium would be $200,000 and the expected reinsurance premium less external expenses would be $0.7 \times \$200,000 = \$140,000$, and the expected reinsurance margin would be $\$140,000 - \$100,000 = \$40,000$, greater than the desired margin. So, if the reinsurer's internal expenses were still $13,889, then the reinsurer's expected economic return (profit) would be $\$40,000 - \$13,889 = \$26,111$, greater than the target of $25,000.

Later we will see cases where the commission or premium is dependent upon the actual loss experience on the contract. This leads to a more complicated formula, where in order to obtain a proper actuarial technical premium or rate, you must consider the reinsurer's profit as a more complicated function of the loss experience. But let us start simply.

Thirteen-step Program to Reinsurance Pricing Happiness

In general, when pricing reinsurance, it is desirable to perform both an *exposure rating* and an *experience rating*. An exposure rate is akin to a primary manual rate, using general rating factors independent of the cedant's particular claims experience. An experience rate is akin to a primary loss rate, completely dependent upon the cedant's particular claims experience. The final technical rate will be a weighing together of both of these rates.

The steps in the rating procedure may be abstracted as follows.

1. Gather and reconcile primary exposure, expense and rate information segregated by major rating class groups.

2. Calculate an exposure expected loss cost, *PVRELC*, and, if desirable, a loss cost rate, *PVRELC/PCP*.

3. Gather and reconcile primary claims data segregated by major rating class groups.

4. Filter the major catastrophe claims out of the claims data.

5. Trend the claims data to rating period.

6. Develop the claims data to settlement values.

7. Estimate the catastrophe loss potential.

8. Adjust the historical exposures to the rating period.

9. Estimate an experience expected loss cost, *PVRELC*, and, if desirable, a loss cost rate, *PVRELC/PCP*.

10. Estimate a "credibility" loss cost or loss cost rate from the exposure and experience loss costs or loss cost rates.

11. Estimate the probability distribution of the aggregate reinsurance loss, if desirable, and perhaps other distributions, such as for claims payment timing.

12. Specify values for *RCR*, *RIXL*, and *RTER*.

13. Negotiate, reconcile opinions and estimates, alter terms, and finalize.

Steps 1, 2, and 12 may be considered to be exposure rating, steps 3–9 and 12 to be experience rating, and steps 10–13 to be rate finalization. Step 11 is usually performed only for more complex contracts. We will try to use this same sequence of steps whenever possible. But sometimes the order of the steps will differ depending upon the particular situation. Let us start with the simplest case.

Facultative Certificates

Since a facultative certificate covers a share of a single insurance policy or set of policies covering a single insured, the individual insured can be underwritten and priced. The exposure of the individual insured can be evaluated and manual rates and rating factors can be used to calculate an exposure rate. However, since most facultative certificates are written on larger or more hazardous exposures, manual rates and rating factors may not exist or must often be modified. Thus, the analysis of individual exposure and loss experience, together with a great deal of underwriting judgment, is important.

In contemplating any form of facultative coverage, the underwriter first evaluates the exposure to decide if the risk is acceptable, and may then evaluate the rate used by the cedant to estimate its degree of adequacy. The underwriter also determines if the ceding commission fairly covers the cedant's expenses, but does not put the cedant into a situation significantly more advantageous than that of the reinsurer. That is, except in unusual circumstances, the cedant should not make a significant profit in those circumstances where the reinsurer is losing money, and vice versa.

The Actuary's Role

Historically, actuaries have seldom been directly involved in facultative certificate pricing. But they can be useful in the following ways by:

1. Being sure that the facultative underwriters are provided with, and know how to use, the most current and accurate manual rates and rating factors, e.g., increased limits factors, loss development factors, trend factors, actuarial opinions on rate adequacy by exposure type and by territory (state), etc.

2. Working with the underwriters to design and maintain good pricing methodologies, almost always in the form of interactive computer programs.

3. Working with the underwriters to design and maintain good portfolio monitoring systems for meaningful categories of their business, for relative price level and for the monitoring of claims, underwriting, and bottomline profit experience.

4. Working with the underwriters to evaluate and determine which lines of business and which exposure layers to concentrate upon as market conditions change.

Property Certificates

The evaluation and pricing of property certificate coverage on a proportional share basis usually needs little further actuarial assistance. However, the actuary should be involved in the evaluation of the accumulation of catastrophe exposure, and also in the interpretation of long-term results from a corporate portfolio perspective.

The evaluation and pricing of property certificate coverage on an excess basis is more difficult. Many tables used by underwriters calculate the excess rate as a factor times the primary rate.[2] Instead of relating the excess rate directly to the primary rate, a more actuarially sound method for determining property per-risk excess rating factors expresses the expected excess loss cost for coverage above an attachment point as a percentage of the total expected loss cost. This allows us to use Formula 7.2 to treat expected loss cost, expenses, and profit separately. The curves underlying these factors depend upon the class of business (its claim severity potential) as determined by the most important rating variables: amount insured, *MPL* (maximum possible loss), *PML* (probable maximum loss), construction, occupancy, and protection.

The *MPL*, sometimes called the "amount subject," is a very conservative estimate by the individual underwriter of the maximum loss possible on the policy. For example, it includes the maximum full value of contiguous buildings together with contents, and also reflects maximum time element (e.g., business interruption) coverage. The *PML* is a less conservative estimate of the largest loss, assuming for example, that the sprinkler system works, that the contents are normal, etc. The difference between *MPL* and *PML* is illustrated by considering an office building:

---

[2]Some underwriters use so-called Lloyd's Scales. Underwriters bring these tables with them from job to job; the parentage of the Lloyd's Scales floating around the industry seems to be highly questionable. So, be careful.

Some underwriters also use tables of factors from a 1960 *PCAS* paper by Ruth Salzmann. But these factors were developed for homeowners business. So even if they were adjusted for inflation over the last 40 years, they are of questionable use for the typical commercial property facultative exposure. A paper by Stephen Ludwig [13] uses commercial risk experience to estimate loss curves. ISO and various reinsurance companies have been doing research and developing property loss curves. But so far there are no published, actuarially sound claims severity curves or tables of factors for rating property per-risk excess coverage.

the *MPL* is the total value; the definition of *PML* varies from underwriter to underwriter, but is usually thought to be three to five floors. The *MPL* and *PML* affect the shape of the loss cost curve because you expect, for example, very different loss severity distributions for an insured with a $100,000 *MPL* and *PML* versus an insured with a $10,000,000 *MPL* and $5,000,000 *PML*.

This is illustrated by the accompanying Graph 7.5. An actuary might think of the *MPL* as being essentially the 100th percentile of the probabilistic loss distribution, and the *PML* as being somewhere around the 95th to 99th percentiles. Note that the $10,000,000 *MPL* property has a smaller probability of a total loss. In fact, at every loss level, its graph lies above the graph for the $100,000 *MPL* property, thus having a smaller probability of exceeding each percentage loss level.

Appropriate *RTER*'s and *RIXL*'s could be incorporated into the table or could be recommended as additional loading factors.

An appropriate pricing formula for an excess cover could use Formula 7.2 with (dropping the *PV* for short-tailed property coverage) *RELC* calculated as follows.

Formula 7.6: Reinsurance Expected Loss Cost

$$RELC = ELCF \times PCP \times PCPLR \times RCF$$

where

$ELCF$ = excess loss cost factor
(from the table; as a percent of total loss cost)

PCP = primary company (subject) premium

$PCPLR$ = primary company permissible loss ratio
(including any loss adjustment expenses covered as part of loss)

GRAPH 7.5

EXAMPLES OF PROPERTY CLAIM SEVERITY CUMULATIVE DISTRIBUTION FUNCTIONS

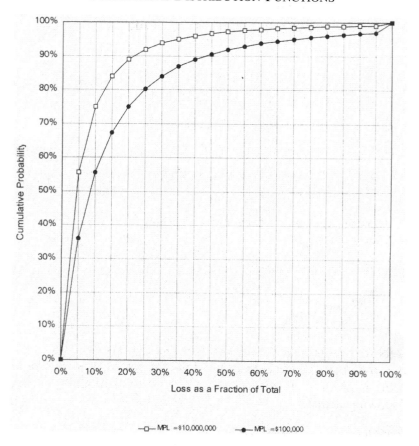

RCF = rate correction factor
(reinsurer's adjustment for the estimated
(in)adequacy of the primary rate)

Again, the reinsurance premium can be translated into a reinsurance rate by dividing it by the primary company premium PCP. An example will help clarify this.

Example 7.7:

$$PCP = \$100,000$$

$$PCPLR = 65\%$$

$$RCF = 1.05 \text{ (estimated 5\% inadequacy)}$$

$$RCR = 30\%$$

$$RBF = 0\% \text{ (no broker)}$$

$$RIXL = 15\%$$

$$MPL = PML = \$10,000,000.$$

$$Attpt = \text{Attachment Point} = \$1,000,000.$$

$$RLim = \text{Reinsurance Limit} = \$4,000,000$$

$$RTER = 10\%$$

Thus the reinsurer believes the total expected loss cost is as follows.

Formula 7.8: Total Expected Loss Cost

$$PCP \times PCPLR \times RCF = \$100,000 \times (.65) \times (1.05)$$
$$= \$68,250$$

Now assume that we believe that the claim severity, including loss adjustment expense, for this class of business and this *MPL*, is given by a censored (at *MPL*) Pareto distribution of the following form.

Formula 7.9: Censored Pareto Model

$$1 - F(x) = \text{Prob}[X > x] = \begin{cases} \dfrac{b}{(b+x)^q} & \text{for} \quad x < 1 \\ 0 & \text{for} \quad x \geq 1 \end{cases}$$

where the claim size X is expressed as a percent of *MPL*.

(Properties of the Pareto distribution are outlined in Appendix A.)

Suppose that the parameters are given by $b = 0.1$ and $q = 2$. We can now verify the following facts.

Formula 7.10: *Expected Claim Severity (as a fraction of MPL)*

$$E[X; 1] = \left\{ \frac{b}{q-1} \right\} \times \left\{ 1 - \left(\frac{b}{b+1} \right)^{q-1} \right\} \quad \text{(Appendix A)}$$

$$= \left\{ \frac{0.1}{2-1} \right\} \times \left\{ 1 - \left(\frac{0.1}{1.1} \right)^{1} \right\}$$

$$= \{0.1\} \times \{1 - 0.91\}$$

$$= 0.0909$$

Thus, if a loss occurs, our estimate of its average size is $0.0909 \times \$10,000,000 = \$909,000$.

We can also calculate the expected claim count.

Formula 7.11: *Expected Claim Count (ground-up)*

$$\text{Expected claim count} = \frac{\text{Total expected loss cost}}{\text{Expected loss severity}}$$

$$= \frac{\$68,250}{\$909,000} = 0.075$$

Formula 7.12: *Expected Claim Severity in the Layer* *[$0, $1,000,000]*

$$E[X; 0.1] = \left\{ \frac{b}{q-1} \right\} \times \left\{ 1 - \left(\frac{b}{b+0.1} \right)^{q-1} \right\}$$

$$= \left\{ \frac{0.1}{2-1} \right\} \times \left\{ 1 - \left(\frac{0.1}{0.1+0.1} \right)^{1} \right\}$$

$$= \{0.1\} \times \{1 - 0.5\}$$

$$= 0.05$$

Thus, if a loss occurs, its average size in the layer [$0, $1,000,000] is $0.05 \times \$10,000,000 = \$500,000$.

Formula 7.13: Expected Claim Severity in the Layer
[$0, $5,000,000]

$$E[X; 0.5] = \left\{ \frac{b}{q-1} \right\} \times \left\{ 1 - \left(\frac{b}{b+0.5} \right)^{q-1} \right\}$$

$$= \left\{ \frac{0.1}{2-1} \right\} \times \left\{ 1 - \left(\frac{0.1}{0.1+0.5} \right)^{1} \right\}$$

$$= \{0.1\} \times \{1 - 0.167\}$$

$$= 0.0833$$

Thus, if a loss occurs, its average size in the layer [$0,$5,000,000] is $0.0833 \times \$10,000,000 = \$833,000$. Therefore, the *ELCF* can be calculated as follows.

Formula 7.14: ELCF (Excess Loss Cost Factor)[3]

$$ELCF = \frac{E[X; 0.5] - E[X; 0.1]}{E[X; 1]}$$

$$= \frac{.0833 - 0.5}{0.0909}$$

$$= 0.367$$

We can now calculate the Reinsurance Expected Loss Cost (*RELC*).

Formula 7.15: Reinsurance Expected Loss Cost

$$RELC = \text{est. } E[RL] = ELCF \times \{\text{Total expected loss cost}\}$$

$$= 0.367 \times \$68,250$$

$$= \$25,028$$

---

[3] The factors in a Lloyd's-type table, mentioned in a previous footnote, would technically be of the following form:

Expected loss cost fraction at limit $c\%$ of total amount insured

$$= \frac{E[X; c]}{E[X; 1]} \qquad \text{for} \quad 0 \le c \le 1$$

Thus the *ELCF* is simply a difference of two of these factors: at the attachment point and at the attachment point plus the limit.

Then we can calculate the technical reinsurance pure premium as

$$RPP = \frac{RELC}{1 - RTER}$$

$$= \frac{\$25,028}{0.9}$$

$$= \$27,808$$

and the technical reinsurance premium as

$$RP = \frac{RPP}{(1 - RIXL) \times (1 - RCR - RBF)}$$

$$= \frac{\$27,808}{(0.85) \times (0.7)}$$

$$= \$46,737.$$

To squeeze out more information about the reinsurance coverage in order to measure the risk transfer, as we will discuss later, we can also estimate the reinsurance expected claim count and severity.

Formula 7.16: Expected Reinsurance Claim Count

Expected excess claim count

$$= \text{Expected claim count (ground-up)} \times \text{Excess probability}$$

$$= 0.075 \times \left(\frac{b}{b + 0.1}\right)^q$$

$$= 0.075 \times \left(\frac{0.1}{0.1 + 0.1}\right)^2$$

$$= 0.075 \times 0.25$$

$$= 0.0188$$

We can then calculate the excess expected claim severity.

Formula 7.17: Expected Claim Severity in the Layer
[$1,000,000, $5,000,000]

Excess expected claim severity

$$= \frac{RELC}{\text{expected reinsurance claim count}}$$

$$= \frac{\$25,028}{0.0188}$$

$$= \$1,333,333.$$

This is the average size (in the layer) of a claim entering the layer. Note that it is one third of the reinsurance limit. Average intra-layer claim sizes for excess layers are typically (but not always) between one quarter to one half of the layer limit.

Further Property Certificate Pricing Considerations

Quite often the pricing situation is much more complicated, with multiple locations and coverages. The underwriter/pricer generally determines a price for each location and each coverage, and then adds them to obtain the total premium.

Instead of working directly with an estimated underlying loss severity distribution like this Pareto, the *ELCF* in Formula 7.14 might be obtained from a Lloyd's-type table. Better yet, a complete pricing procedure such as this can be programmed into an interactive computer package for the underwriters. The package would contain all the appropriate rates and rating factors or underlying loss severity models and parameters to be called upon by the user. It would ask most of the relevant questions of the user and would document the decision trail for each submission seriously contemplated by the underwriter. If desirable, the reinsurer's values for *RIXL*'s and *RTER*'s could be built into the system or as part of the *ELCF*'s.

For facultative certificate property coverage as with any reinsurance business segment, the pricing cycle is very severe. This is mainly due to naive capital flowing into the market because of easy access, but also due to the short-term nature of most peoples' memories. Thus it is very important to monitor the results closely. Renewal pricing and rate competition in the marketplace should be watched monthly; perhaps summaries derived from the aforementioned pricing system would be appropriate. Quarterly updates of underwriting results by accident year in appropriate business segment detail are very important.

Casualty Certificates

The evaluation and pricing of facultative certificate casualty coverage is even trickier than property coverage, due mainly to the additional uncertainty arising from delayed claims reporting and settlement. Because of this increased uncertainty, the actuary's role can be more important in the pricing and in the monitoring and interpretation of results.

As with property excess, a cover may be exposure rated via manual rates and increased limits factors, together with exposure evaluation and underwriting judgement. The same Formula 7.6 may be used to determine $RELC$, except that the $ELCF$ will be based upon increased limit loss cost tables, based upon claim severity curves, and the RCF may be determined both by facts and by judgments regarding the cedant's basic limit rate level and increased limit factors.

Since most companies use Insurance Services Office (ISO) increased limit factors for third party liability pricing (especially for commercial lines), it is very important that the actuaries very closely monitor ISO factors and understand their meaning. Likewise, it is important to monitor and understand information from the National Council on Compensation Insurance (NCCI) regarding workers compensation claim severity. However, you should not use the published excess loss factors (ELF's) for pricing excess loss coverage, since they underestimate per-occurrence excess loss potential.

Allocated Loss Adjustment Expense (ALAE)
ALAE per claim is usually covered on an excess basis either:

• In proportion to the indemnity loss share of the excess cover vis-a-vis the total, or

• by adding the *ALAE* to the indemnity loss before applying the attachment point and limit.

For example, assume the layer $500,000 excess of $500,000 is reinsured. The following claims induce the indicated reinsurance reimbursements.

TABLE 7.18

REINSURANCE PAYMENTS BY *ALAE* SHARE

(1) Indemnity Payment	(2) ALAE	(3) Reinsurer's payment if *ALAE* pro rata	(4) Reinsurer's payment if *ALAE* added
$ 500,000	$ 50,000	$0	$ 50,000
750,000	75,000	275,000	325,000
1,000,000	100,000	550,000	500,000
2,000,000	150,000	537,500	500,000

Increased limits factors published by ISO have no provision for *ALAE* outside of the basic limit. Thus *ELCF*'s based upon these increased limit factors must be adjusted to cover the reinsurer's share of *ALAE*.

Pricing Methods
Since policies subject to facultative coverage are larger than usual, experience rating often comes into play. One method is to first experience rate a lower layer with more credible experience. Then the experience-based loss cost on the lower layer may be used together with the reinsurer's *ELCF* table to extrapolate up to the intended layer of coverage.

For a buffer layer of coverage where the likelihood of loss penetration is significant, it might also be possible to obtain a loss cost estimate directly from a careful analysis of the large loss experience of the insured.

An example should clarify this.

Example 7.19:

- Policy period priced = 2001
- Exposure = General liability premises/operations
- Policy limit = $2,000,000, no aggregate
- *PCP* = $550,000 (estimated for 2001)
- *BLP* (basic limit premium @ $100,000 limit) = $200,000 (estimated for 2001)
- *PCPLR* = 70% (excluding *un*allocated loss adjustment expense from the loss cost)
- *Attpt* (attachment point) = $500,000
- *RLim* (reinsurance limit) = $1,500,000
- *ALAE* is covered pro rata.
- *RCR* (reinsurance commission) = 25%
- *RBF* (reinsurance brokerage fee) = 5%
- *RIXL* (reinsurer's internal expense loading) = 15%
- *RTER* (reinsurer's target economic return) = 20%
- Have exposure and loss experience for policy years 1995 through 1999, consisting of exposures, basic and total limits premiums, current evaluation of basic limits losses and a detailed history for each known claim larger than $100,000

Suppose that the cedant's basic limit premium was determined from a standard experience and schedule rating plan that we believe to be adequate. Also suppose that the cedant uses the appropriate ISO increased limit factors, which we believe also to be adequate, and which include the ISO risk loading but no *ALAE* provision for the layer. Suppose the ISO increased limit factors for this exposure are as follows.

TABLE 7.20

(FICTITIOUS) ISO INCREASED LIMIT FACTORS

(1) Policy limit	(2) Published *ILF*	(3) *ILF* without risk load
$ 100,000	1.00	1.0000
500,000	2.10	1.9077
2,000,000	2.75	2.4264

Suppose that the cedant is offering a manual difference excess premium of $130,000 calculated as follows.

Formula 7.21: Manual Difference Excess Premium

Manual difference excess premium $= \$200,000 \times (2.75 - 2.10)$

$$= \$130,000$$

This is the simplest technical price determination possible. Some reinsurers, after multiplying by a judgment factor to adjust for rate (in)adequacy for this insured or for this type of insured, stop here. However, because there is too much information hidden in this calculation, let us continue onward to calculate an actuarial, technical price based upon the estimated loss cost and the other rating parameters.

Suppose that, based upon a study of the relationship of *ALAE* to claim size for this type of exposure, we believe that an appropriate loading for pro rata *ALAE* is 10% of indemnity loss cost for this layer. Also suppose that we have an estimated expected loss payment pattern for this type of exposure and this layer, and suppose that the corresponding discount factor, using current U.S. Treasury rates (risk-free) timed to the loss payment pattern and reflecting the implications of the current tax law, is .80. Then if we believe the ISO increased limit factors to be adequate for this exposure, the present value reinsurance expected loss cost could be calculated as follows.

Formula 7.22: PVRELC

$$PVRELC = RDF \times RELC$$

$$= RDF \times ELCF \times BLP \times PCPLR \times RCF$$

$$= RDF \times ELCF \times \{\text{basic limit expected loss cost}\}$$

$$= (0.8) \times \{(2.4264 - 1.9077) \times (1.10)\} \times \{\$200,000 \times (0.7) \times (1.00)\}$$

$$= (0.8) \times \{(0.5187) \times (1.10)\} \times \{\$140,000\}$$

$$= 0.8 \times 0.5706 \times \$140,000$$

$$= \$63,904$$

Then the reinsurance premium can be calculated via Formula 7.2.

Formula 7.23: Reinsurance Premium (RP)

$$RP = \frac{PVRELC}{(1 - RCR - RBF) \times (1 - RIXL) \times (1 - RTER)}$$

$$= \frac{\$63,904}{(1 - 0.25 - 0.05) \times (1 - 0.15) \times (1 - 0.2)}$$

$$= \frac{\$63,904}{(0.7) \times (0.85) \times (0.8)}$$

$$= \frac{\$63,904}{0.476}$$

$$= \$134,252$$

Please note that the assumption that ISO increased limit factors appropriately describe the claim severity potential for this insured is a very crucial assumption. Since facultatively reinsured exposures are often more hazardous, the actuary or underwriter may believe that often the claim severity distribution is more dangerous. However, the actuary or underwriter designing a facultative certificate pricing procedure may believe that the increased severity hazard is already reflected in the first $100,000 basic limit price for these insureds. Otherwise, you may wish to adjust ISO claim severity curves accordingly, or allow the certificate pricer to do so on a case-by-case basis.

In this case, the offered $130,000 premium looks reasonably close to our technical premium. So the pricing endeavor usually stops here. But what about the large loss experience? Suppose that for accident years 1995–1999, there are some claims known as of June 30, 2000 whose indemnity values are greater than $100,000. Can any of this insured's large loss information be used to help price the cover, or at least to help form an opinion as to the adequacy of the exposure rate premium?

A recommended rating procedure in this case is to experience rate the layer $400,000 excess of $100,000, and then use the non-risk-loaded increased limit factors to extrapolate upward to a reinsurance loss cost for the layer $1,500,000 excess of $500,000. We will describe a common reinsurance experience rating methodology later in the section on pricing excess treaties.

As with property excess, it is clear that the exposure rating methods can be programmed into an interactive computer package for underwriters. Also, as with property coverage, it is very important to monitor relative rate level and results in appropriate business segment detail. The actuarial evaluations and opinions regarding future case reserve development and *IBNR* emergence should be very important to the underwriters.

Facultative Automatic Programs

These large multi-insured programs are very similar to treaties. One difference, however, is that the reinsurance premium for a facultative automatic excess cover is usually computed on a policy-by-policy basis using agreed-upon excess rates, instead of as a rate times total subject premium, as is usually the case for treaties. Thus the reinsurance premium is more responsive to the individual exposures ceded to the reinsurer. Nevertheless, the risk of anti-selection against the reinsurer on a nonobligatory contract should be evaluated by the underwriter.

The pricing of these agreements is the same or similar to the pricing of excess treaties, discussed below.

Reinsurance Treaties in General

In this discussion the word "treaty" is used interchangeably for both treaties and automatic facultative agreements.

Since a treaty covers a share of a portfolio of insurance policies, insureds are rarely individually underwritten and priced by the reinsurer; many of the policies to be covered may not be written by the cedant until well into the reinsurance coverage period. Instead, the reinsurance underwriter/pricer considers the whole portfolio of potentially subject policies. To do this, the reinsurer evaluates first the management of the potential cedant. What is their management philosophy and ability? Are they honest, fair-dealing? Do they know what they are doing? Is the company financially solid? What are their business plans? Why do they want reinsurance? Why do they need reinsurance?

Once the reinsurer is satisfied that this is a company and these are people we would like to deal with on a long-term basis, we can then evaluate their underwriting, primary pricing, marketing, and claims handling ability. Since individual insureds are not usually underwritten by the reinsurer, we must be generally satisfied with the cedant's underwriting and pricing expertise for the exposure we may assume. For any treaty, we must understand the cedant's insurance exposures, rate level, and policy limits sold. Many reinsurers will send a team of marketing and underwriting people to perform a pre-quote audit, and will also send claims people to review the company's claims handling and reserving practices.

The reinsurer (or the lead reinsurer on a multi-reinsurer brokered treaty) usually reviews the structure of the cedant's reinsurance program to understand how all the reinsurance contracts, facultative and treaty, fit together to provide benefits to the cedant. Lastly, the reinsurer evaluates the particular reinsurance treaties and suggested rates if offered, or creates a program and rates to offer to the cedant company.

Actuaries can provide extremely useful, and often necessary, technical support for treaty business. They can perform the four functions listed at the beginning of the section on facultative certificate pricing. They can also get involved in the technical evaluation and pricing of individual large and/or difficult treaties through many or all of the rating steps. Experience rating is much more important for treaties than for facultative certificates. Consequently, the actuarial tools of data analysis and loss modeling can be critical to a reinsurer's ability to write difficult exposures, especially casualty exposures where long-tail loss development is a significant factor.

Property Proportional Treaties

Proportional treaties are usually priced by evaluating the amount of the commission to be paid ultimately to the cedant. The ultimate commission is comprised of a provisional commission paid at the time of the cession, plus any later adjustments specified by the terms of the treaty.

Property Quota-Share Treaties

A traditional quota-share treaty covers a share of the cedant's net retention after facultative covers. To evaluate the loss exposure, we follow the rating steps outlined before. To facilitate the discussion, we will consider an example using our favorite primary insurer, da Ponte Insurance Company.

Example 7.24:

- Rating period = 2001

- 25% quota share on various property lines

- Risks attaching coverage (primary policy year; reinsurers generally call this *"underwriting year"*)

- Estimated *PCP* (written premium) = $10,000,000

- Estimated unearned premium reserve @ 12/31/01 = $3,000,000

- Per occurrence limit of $7,500,000 for reinsurance losses

- Proposed *RCR* = 35%

- *RBF* = 0% (no broker)

Step 1: Gather and reconcile primary exposure, expense and rate information segregated by major rating class groups.

The grouping may be by Annual Statement line of business, or could be a finer decomposition if the proposed reinsurance coverage is more restricted or if there are any important exposures you may want to evaluate separately. What is meant by the word "exposure" for reinsurance purposes is usually primary subject premiums. The reconciliation should be to publish financial records as much as possible. If there is significant catastrophe potential, we would want the exposure by zip code in order to perform the seventh rating step.

Let us suppose that the proposed treaty is to cover the property exposures in Annual Statement lines 1–5 and 12, net of facultative reinsurance; the liability parts of lines 3–5 are excluded. In this example, the reinsurer would ask for gross written premium by line by year for 1995 through 6/30/00, together with estimates for 2000 and 2001. The expense information could be from the cedant's Insurance Expense Exhibit. The rate information would be contained in the cedant's underwriting line guide. We also want information on average rate deviations.

Step 2: Calculate an exposure expected loss cost, PVRELC, and, if desirable, a loss cost rate, PVRELC/PCP.

For proportional coverage, an exposure loss cost rating is simply an evaluation of the adequacy of the cedant's rates for the exposures to be covered, leading to an estimate of the expected loss ratio. An underwriting review can compare the cedant's rates to those of other primary insurers or to the reinsurer's own database of adequate primary rates.

Many people in the reinsurance business would say that you cannot calculate an exposure rate for proportional coverage, or that you cannot rate the coverage at all; you can only evaluate the ceding commission. The ceding commission should fairly reimburse the cedant's expenses, but should not put the cedant into a position significantly more advantageous than that of the reinsurer. Except in unusual circumstances, the cedant should not make a significant profit while the reinsurer is losing money, and vice versa. The point here is to evaluate the (in)adequacy of the cedant's rates in order to evaluate whether or not the proposed reinsurance commission will work for the reinsurer *and* for the cedant.

Let us suppose that the review indicates that overall, the expected loss ratio for policy year 2001 is 65% including all catastrophe losses. Suppose we estimate that a per occurrence catastrophe limit will only reduce this by a few percent, but less than the amount of the reinsurer's expense and profit loadings, *RIXL* and *RTER*. Thus, it looks as if the reinsurer cannot afford a 35% ceding commission. We will deal with the ceding commission issue further in steps 10–12.

Step 3: Gather and reconcile primary claims data segregated by major rating class groups.

We want the claims data segregated as the exposure data. We usually want *ALAE* separately from indemnity losses. For proportional coverage, the data are usually historical aggregate claims data for the past five to ten policy years, plus individual large claims. We also want some history of claims values (an historical policy year/development year triangle) for step five. The data should be adjusted so that they are approximately on the same basis as our coverage with respect to any other *inuring* reinsurance, that is, reinsurance that applies to the cedant's loss before our coverage.

Suppose we have net aggregate loss development triangles by line for policy years 1995–2000 at evaluation dates 12/31/95, 12/31/96,…,12/31/99, 6/30/00, plus concurrent evaluations by line of all numbered catastrophes occurring during this time period. These are the catastrophes designated by Property Claims Service (PCS). Also suppose that there haven't been significant changes in da Ponte's insurance portfolio or in their reinsurance program during this time. So the data are consistent with the expected 2001 loss exposure.

Step 4: Filter the major catastrophic claims out of the claims data.

This is straightforward. Subtract the numbered catastrophe values by line at each evaluation from the loss development triangles.

Step 5: Trend the claims data to the rating period.

We want to be sure that the historical claims data are adjusted in a manner that makes them reasonably relevant to the rating period. The trending should be for inflation and for other changes in exposure (such as higher policy limits) that might affect the loss potential. For proportional coverage, we may skip this step, and simply look for any apparent trend in the historical loss ratios in step nine.

Step 6: Develop the claims data to settlement values.

Claims development is usually not much of a problem for filtered primary property claims. If we have historical policy year/development year triangles, we can use standard methods to estimate loss development factors and apply these to the filtered data. If we don't have historical triangles, we may be able to use Annual Statement Schedule P accident year data, if they are reasonably reflective of the proposed coverage and if we can filter out major catastrophes, to estimate policy year loss development factors. We also want to compare the development patterns estimated from the cedant's data to what we expect based upon our own historical data for comparable coverages to check for reasonableness.

If the reinsurer believes that the development patterns should be reasonably similar for the various covered lines, we usually estimate the total development from the combined data instead of by line.

Step 7: Estimate the catastrophic loss potential.

This deserves a whole section by itself. The problem is that the historical data, even developed and trended, may not indicate the true potential for catastrophic losses. Reinsurers who have relied entirely upon five to ten years of historical claims to estimate catastrophe potential have often blundered into coverages where the catastrophic events occurring during their coverage period have more than wiped out the "normal" non-catastrophic profits. For example, da Ponte's 1995–1999 experience period does not include such major catastrophes as Hurricane Andrew (1992) and the Northridge earthquake (1994). It also does not include such possibilities as a New Madrid fault earthquake, a Long Island hurricane, etc. If da Ponte's exposures include any potential catastrophe areas, then we must estimate the corresponding catastrophe potential.

We will discuss various methods for this evaluation in the later section on catastrophe covers. If we collected gross written premiums by zip code, we can use these data to parameterize one of the available catastrophe computer models.

Let us assume that our evaluation of this portfolio indicates an expected catastrophic loss ratio to *PCP* of 12% with respect to a $7,500,000 per occurrence limit on reinsurance losses.

Step 8: Adjust the historical exposures to the rating period.

We want to be sure that the historical exposure (premium) data are adjusted in a manner that makes them reasonably relevant to the rating period. The trending should be for primary rate and underwriting changes and for other changes in exposure that might affect the loss potential. For proportional coverage, we only adjust the premiums for significant rate level changes, so that the historical loss ratios in step nine are all consistent with 2001 rate level. The rate adjustments are accomplished using the standard methods.

Step 9: Estimate an experience expected loss cost, PVRELC, and, if desirable, a loss cost rate, PVRELC/PCP.

Suppose that our data and estimates so far are as displayed in Table 7.25.

TABLE 7.25

DA PONTE INSURANCE COMPANY PROPERTY BUSINESS
(IN $1,000's)

(1) Policy Year	(2) Onlevel PCP	(3) Subject Loss	(4) Cat. Loss	(5) Filtered Loss	(6) Loss Devel. Factor	(7) Devel'd Loss $(5) \times (6)$	(8) Loss Ratio $(7) \div (2)$
1995	$ 7,000	$ 3,472	$ 512	$ 2,960	1.00	$ 2,960	42%
1996	7,500	4,116	403	3,713	1.00	3,713	50%
1997	8,000	4,772	188	4,584	1.01	4,630	58%
1998	8,500	4,855	1,286	3,569	1.05	3,747	44%
1999	9,000	4,144	622	3,522	1.20	4,227	47%
2000	4,750	1,000	75	925	n.a.	n.a.	n.a.
Total w/o 2000	$40,000	$21,359	$3,011	$18,348	n.a.	$19,277	48%

Note: Columns 3–5 evaluated @ 6/30/00.

The five-year average filtered loss ratio is 48%. There seems to be no particular trend, and there are no significant rate revisions planned. So we simply take the average to be our estimate of the 2001 loss ratio. According to Step 7, we must add on 12% for catastrophe losses. We thus have a total expected loss ratio of 60%.

Step 10: Estimate a "credibility" loss cost or loss cost rate from the exposure and experience loss costs or loss cost rates.

We must reconcile the experience rating estimate of a 60% loss ratio with our exposure rating estimate of a 65% loss ratio. Remember that the exposure estimate includes unlimited catastrophe losses. The reconciliation is a process of asking questions and judging the relative credibility of the two loss ratio estimates. In the later discussion of treaty working cover excess pricing, we will list some of the questions we should ask.

Let us suppose that our "credibility" estimate of the 2001 expected loss ratio is 62%.

Steps 11–13 are very intertwined. Normally, we would want to perform Step 11 before Step 12, since Step 11 helps us quantify the risk transfer on the contract with respect to the particular contract terms. But sometimes, we have preliminary estimates of *RCR*, *RIXL* and *RTER* which may later be modified. The negotiations with the cedant will often send us back to Step 11 or 12, or even to earlier steps. We will present Steps 11 and 12 simultaneously.

Step 11: Estimate the probability distribution of the aggregate reinsurance loss if desirable, and perhaps other distributions such as for claims payment timing.

Step 12: Specify values for RCR, RIXL, and RTER

Let us start with preliminary values for Step 12. Suppose that a review of the cedant's expenses for the past few years indicates an expense ratio of 33% for this business. Suppose that the cedant will accept a ceding commission of 33%. Does this leave the reinsurer with enough profit?

With a 33% ceding commission, the expected reinsurance premium net of commission is $(1 - RCR) \times RP = 0.67 \times \$2,500,000 = \$1,675,000$. Suppose we determine that the reinsurer's costs for underwriting and accounting for this treaty, plus a general overhead allocation, will be about $50,000. This translates into an *RIXL* of $50,000/$1,675,000 = 3.0\%$ (approx.). The reinsurance risk pure premium with respect to a 33% ceding commission and a 3.0% reinsurer's internal expense loading is as follows.

Formula 7.26: Reinsurance Risk Pure Premium

$$RPP = RP \times (1 - RCR) \times (1 - RIXL)$$
$$= \$2,500,000 \times 0.67 \times 0.97$$
$$= \$1,675,000 \times 0.97$$
$$= \$1,624,750$$

Since the reinsurer's expected loss ratio is 62%, the expected loss is $0.62 \times \$2,500,000 = \$1,550,000$. This leaves a profit of $\$1,624,750 - \$1,550,000 = \$74,750$. Is this enough?

Suppose that the reinsurer generally wants $RTER = 8\%$ for the risk transfer on this type of exposure. With $RPP = \$1,624,750$, the usual 8% profit margin is expected to be $0.08 \times \$1,624,750 = \$129,980$. In addition, since there will be a statutory surplus loan equal to the ceding commission on the unearned premium reserve at year-end, the reinsurer should add some margin for this. Suppose the historical premium data indicate that the average year-end unearned premium reserve is about 40% of written premium. With a 33% ceding commission, the reinsurer will be giving da Ponte an estimated $0.33 \times 0.4 \times 0.25 \times \$10,000,000 = \$330,000$ of surplus relief at the end of 2001 for the 25% quota share. Suppose that an appropriate loan rate would be 7%. Thus,

$0.07 \times \$330,000 = \$23,100$ should be added to the reinsurer's profit margin. Adding \$23,100 to the profit margin produces an overall profit margin of $\$129,980 + \$23,100 = \$153,080$. This is $\$153,080 - \$74,750 = \$78,330$ more than the expected profit.

It is time for us to sharpen our pencil. Do we want to accept this risk below our desired margin? Is this cedant that valuable to us? Do we already have other business with da Ponte whose profit makes up for this reduced margin, or will they cede such business to us? Do we already have or can we build a long-term profitable relationship with da Ponte and a close personal relationship with their president, Yakema Canutt? We also remember that our estimates may have a large random error component. What is the competitive situation?

Perhaps we can interest da Ponte in a more sophisticated contractual alternative involving a variable commission rate, or a loss and profit carryforward to successive years if we believe that primary rates, and thus loss ratios, will improve in the next few years. To evaluate a variable commission rate or a carryforward provision properly, we need an estimate of the ceded aggregate loss distribution. So now we return to Step 11.

There are many ways to estimate the probability distribution of the aggregate reinsurance loss. In a situation like this, where we are not dealing with aggregate deductibles or aggregate limits, it is best to use a simple method. The simplest method is to estimate the first two moments of the aggregate loss distribution from the annual historical aggregate filtered loss data plus a component for the catastrophe exposure. The obvious problem with this is that in this case we have only five data points for the filtered losses, a very small sample.

Considering the filtered loss ratios in column 8 of Table 7.25, the mean of the policy years 1995–1999 is 48% and the standard deviation is 6.1%. We use loss ratios instead of dollars to normalize the distribution, so it can be used for policy year 2001. Since the 6.1% estimate is derived from a small sample, we ask whether or not it is comparable with other standard deviation estimates from similar exposure situations. Let us assume it is.

Suppose our evaluation of the catastrophe loss potential yields the estimated expectation of 12% mentioned previously, and an estimated standard deviation of 13.9% (details in Appendix B). It is appropriate to assume that the filtered loss and catastrophic loss are independent. Under this assumption, their variances are additive. Let us further adjust the expectation of the filtered loss to 50% in order that the expectations add to 62%. Assuming that the reinsurance premium RP is constant, we have the following estimates.

Formula 7.27: First Two Central Moments of the Loss Ratio Distribution

$$\frac{RELC}{RP} = 62\%$$

$$\mathrm{Var}\left[\frac{RL}{RP}\right] = \mathrm{Var}\left[\frac{RL_F}{RP}\right] + \mathrm{Var}\left[\frac{RL_C}{RP}\right]$$

$$= \{(6.1\%)^2 + (13.9\%)^2\} \text{ estimate}$$

$$= 2.29\%$$

where RL_F = filtered reinsurance loss

RL_C = catastrophic reinsurance loss

We thus have an estimate of the standard deviation, $SD[RL/RP]$ = 15.13%. We approximate the loss ratio distribution with a Gamma distribution. This is described and justified in Appendix C, and also in Papush, Patrik and Podgaits [17]. We will later discuss more sophisticated models for approximating the aggregate loss or loss ratio distribution. In our simple case, it is enough to assume that the distribution of L can be represented by a Gamma distribution whose parameters can be estimated by the Method of Moments. We can now evaluate the ceding commission terms with this distribution, and thus estimate the reinsurer's profit.

Let us now finalize Step 12 before negotiations. We will use the values for *RIXL* and *RTER* already obtained. Let us now evaluate a *sliding scale commission* arrangement of the following form in order to specify a formula for *RCR*. Proportional treaties often have sliding-scale or *contingent commissions*. In these cases, the reinsurer pays the cedant a *provisional commission* on the reinsurance gross written premium as it is transferred to the reinsurer. At suitable dates (often quarterly), the cumulative experience on the treaty (usually from the beginning if there is a *deficit carryforward*, or over some period such as three years) is reviewed. If it is profitable, the reinsurer pays the cedant an additional commission; if it is unprofitable, the cedant returns some of the provisional commission to the reinsurer. An example should clarify this.

Formula 7.28: Sliding Scale Commission Arrangement

$$RCR = PRCR - SF \times \left\{ \frac{RL}{RP} - (1 - PRCR - RM) \right\}$$

Subject to $\min RCR \leq RCR \leq \operatorname{Max} RCR$

where $PRCR$ = provisional reinsurance commission rate

$= 33\%$

SF = slide factor = 50%

RM = reinsurer's margin = 5%

in RCR = minimum RCR = 25%

$\operatorname{Max} RCR$ = maximum RCR = 35%

This ceding commission formula varies the commission one half point with each loss ratio point, with a minimum of 25% and a maximum of 35%. Loss development is an issue to be aware of in these types of formulas. If it is not accounted for in the loss evaluation that determines the loss ratio, the formula will compute too high a commission. Thus, the reinsurer will normally be in a position of paying some commission that will eventually be returned. This may usually be a minor point, but it does effect the reinsurer's cash flow, and thus economic profit, on the contract.

If we use the Gamma distribution with the first and second moments estimated in formula 7.27, then the expected reinsurance profit becomes $108,512, as shown in Table 7.29. This is still less than the desired profit margin of $153,080. Many reinsurers who think that the da Ponte Insurance Company is or will be a good client, and thus want to deal with them in the future, will accept these terms. Or the reinsurer may request a change in the commission terms: perhaps a reduction in *PRCR* together with an increase in *RM*.

Please note that the table treats the Gamma as being discreet, and displays probabilities for only selected loss ratios; the computation of the average profit uses the more complete distribution shown in Appendix C. Also note the nonsymmetry of the probabilities in column 2; the skewed right-hand tail is typical of property and casualty aggregate loss distributions.

A more sophisticated evaluation would account for cash flow timing, e.g., when commission adjustments would be made. On the basis of the distribution of the reinsurer's profit displayed in columns 2 and 4, we may specify a different target *RTER*. Suppose this profit distribution is more compact than usual for contracts of this type. This would indicate that there is less risk than usual, thus indicating that a lesser *RTER* value is appropriate. If the profit distribution is more spread than usual, thereby indicating more risk, then a greater value is appropriate.

Step 13: Negotiate, reconcile opinions and estimates, alter terms and finalize

We now have contract terms that meet our underwriting standards and largely meet our profit guidelines. We also believe these terms will be acceptable to da Ponte Insurance Company. Then we meet with them and explain our analysis and evaluation,

TABLE 7.29

AGGREGATE LOSS DISTRIBUTION AND CALCULATION OF REINSURER'S PROFIT

(1) Loss Ratio (selected)	(2) Probability Density (as percent)	(3) Reinsurance Commission	(4) Reinsurer's Profit
20%	0.4%	35.0%	$1,074,750
25%	3.5%	35.0%	949,750
30%	16.1%	35.0%	824,750
35%	47.2%	35.0%	699,750
40%	100.3%	35.0%	574,750
45%	166.2%	35.0%	449,750
50%	226.5%	35.0%	324,750
55%	263.3%	35.0%	199,750
60%	268.5%	34.0%	99,750
65%	245.4%	31.5%	37,250
70%	204.2%	29.0%	(25,250)
75%	156.8%	26.5%	(87,750)
80%	112.2%	25.0%	(175,250)
85%	75.5%	25.0%	(300,250)
90%	48.1%	25.0%	(425,250)
95%	29.2%	25.0%	(550,250)
100%	16.9%	25.0%	(675,250)
105%	9.5%	25.0%	(800,250)
110%	5.1%	25.0%	(925,250)
115%	2.7%	25.0%	(1,050,250)
120%	1.3%	25.0%	(1,175,250)
125%	0.7%	25.0%	(1,300,250)
130%	0.3%	25.0%	(1,425,250)
135%	0.1%	25.0%	(1,550,250)
140%	0.1%	25.0%	(1,675,250)
145%	0.0%	25.0%	(1,800,250)
150%	0.0%	25.0%	(1,925,250)
			$108,512

answer their questions and listen to their counter-arguments and alternative interpretations of information and data. If necessary, we redo the previous steps until we reach a contract structure that satisfies both parties, if possible.

Evaluating an Ongoing Treaty

A reinsurer is in a similar evaluation situation when interpreting the experience on an ongoing treaty. But in addition to evaluating the year 2001 profit potential, we must also evaluate our cumulative experience on the treaty and compare the cumulative profit to our guideline *RTER* (including the charge for year-end statutory surplus loans, if any). The advantage is that we now have our own experience data on the contract for some years, and we also know the cedant and their people better. The questions are similar to the previous pencil-sharpening exercise. How much money do we think we have made, or lost? Do we have other business with this cedant? What is the total account bottomline profit? Is this a good relationship to continue? How credible is our answer?

Property Surplus Share Treaties

A property surplus-share treaty is somewhat more difficult to evaluate. Since the reinsurer does not provide coverage for small insureds, and covers larger insureds in proportion to their size above some fixed retention, the reinsurer must be more concerned with the cedant's pricing of larger insureds. An example should clarify this.

Example 7.30:

- Four line first surplus not to exceed $800,000

- Maximum cedant retention = $200,000

  Then the following statements are true:

- Maximum reinsurance limit per policy = $800,000

- For a policy with limit < $200,000, the reinsurer receives no premium and pays no losses.

- For a policy with limit = $500,000, the reinsurer receives 60% of the policy's premium less ceding commission and brokerage fee, and pays 60% of the policy's losses.

- For a policy with limit = $1,000,000, the reinsurer receives 80% of the policy's premium less ceding commission and brokerage fee, and pays 80% of the policy's losses.

- For a policy with limit = $2,000,000, the reinsurer receives 40% of the policy's premium less ceding commission and brokerage fee, and pays 40% of the policy's losses.

It is easy to see that, given this complicated proportional structure depending upon the limit of each policy, the premium and loss accounting for a surplus-share treaty is somewhat complex. Despite this, surplus-share treaties are popular, because they provide more large loss protection than a quota-share, and are much easier for the reinsurer to evaluate and price (usually only the ceding commission and slide is the subject of negotiations) than an excess treaty.

A surplus-share treaty is generally riskier relative to ceded premium volume than is a simple quota-share. So the reinsurer will charge a correspondingly higher margin for risk assumption.

Casualty Quota-Share Treaties

The pricing or evaluation of a true ground-up net retention quota-share on casualty exposure would be similar to the pricing of a property cover except that the reinsurer would have to be very careful about loss development. The historical catastrophe exposure would be asbestos and pollution clean-up, plus any other mass tort situation that significantly distorts the cedant's claims data patterns. The future catastrophe exposure would be _____ (Fill in the blank: Tobacco? Medical implant devices? Workers compensation claims arising from a major earthquake during working hours? Etc.). The additional uncertainty arising from the longer-tail claims development and trend estimation would add risk to the rate determination, thus tending to increase the reinsurer's *RTER*. But the final evaluation of risk and necessary *RTER* also depends upon the relative catastrophe exposure.

Working Cover Excess Treaties

A working cover is an excess layer where losses are expected. An excess cover is usually riskier than a proportional cover. So the reinsurer will be more mindful of prediction error and fluctuation potential, and will charge a higher *RTER* for assuming this risk. If losses are covered per-occurrence, then the reinsurer is exposed by policy limits below the attachment point because of the "clash" of losses on different policies or coverages arising from the same occurrence.

The reinsurance premium is usually calculated via a reinsurance rate times subject premium. However, for liability coverage, it may be on an increased limits premium collected basis; this is often the premium calculation method used for facultative automatic programs. Here the total reinsurance premium is the sum of the individually calculated reinsurance premiums for each policy.

Working cover treaties are often large enough so that many of the risk parameters can be estimated either directly from the exposure and claims history or by a credibility weighting of the history with more general information. Ideally, the reinsurance pricing consists of both an exposure rating and an experience rating, together with a reconciliation of the two rates. We will illustrate the differences from pricing either facultative certificates or proportional treaties as we deal with an example. We will use a casualty example. Pricing a property per-risk excess working cover would be similar.

Example 7.31:

- da Ponte Insurance Company wants a proposal for a three-year retrospective-rated treaty incepting Jan. 1, 2001

- All liability and workers compensation exposure

- Losses occurring coverage (accident year basis)
- Per-occurrence coverage
- *ALAE* added to indemnity for each claim
- Proposed attachment point AP = $300,000
- Proposed reinsurance limit $RLim$ = $700,000
- $RCR = 0\%$
- $RBF = 0\%$
- Estimated 2001 subject premium PCP = $100,000,000
- Possible reinsurance premium range up to $10,000,000

We will follow the same rating steps we did for Example 7.24.

Step 1: Gather and reconcile primary exposure, expense, and rate information segregated by major rating class groups.

Da Ponte's casualty exposure is as follows.

TABLE 7.32

CASUALTY EXPOSURE CATEGORIES

- Private passenger automobile
- Commercial automobile
- Premises/operations
- Homeowners Section II
- Special Multi-Peril Section II
- Workers compensation
- Personal umbrella

These categories should be further broken down to split the underlying exposure at least according to the most significant applicable increased limit tables and policy limits, or, in the case of workers compensation, by major states and hazard groups. If we cannot get data from da Ponte to do this, we can, as a last resort, use default distributions of premiums by increased limit tables and policy limits for this type of company, that we have estimated from general information.

We should want to start with the information listed in Step 1 for Example 7.24. In addition, we assume that our underwriters have visited da Ponte and have performed an underwriting review. We want to know about deviations from bureau manual rates and average schedule and experience credits. We want historical premiums for at least the last five-and-one-half years 1995 through June 30, 2000 plus predictions for 2001–2003. We also want the names of contact people at da Ponte to talk with, in particular, their pricing actuary.

Step 2: Calculate an exposure expected loss cost, PVRELC, and, if desirable, a loss cost rate, PVRELC/PCP.

Da Ponte writes limits up to $10,000,000, but purchases facultative reinsurance for coverage in excess of $2,000,000. They also purchase facultative coverage above $300,000 for any difficult exposures on the reinsurer's exclusion list, and a 90% facultative automatic cover for their umbrella programs.

Treaty excess exposure rating differs from the facultative certificate excess pricing in Example 7.19 in that the reinsurer deals with broad classes of business by increased limit table or state/hazard group instead of individual insureds. We consider manual rate relativities to bureau rates and/or to other companies writing the same exposure, and evaluate da Ponte's experience and schedule rating plans and pricing abilities. The increased limit factors used by the cedant for liability coverages are especially important. The same Formulas 7.2 and 7.6 can be used. Since the coverage is per-occurrence, we must load the manual difference rate for the clash exposure.

Since *ALAE* is added to each claim in order to determine the reinsurer's excess share, claims from some policy limits below the attachment point will bleed into the excess layer. We may have our own data describing the bivariate distribution of indemnity and *ALAE*, or we may obtain such information from ISO. Using these data, we can construct increased limits tables where *ALAE* is added to loss instead of residing entirely in the basic limits coverage.

Alternatively, and more simplistically, we can adjust the manual increased limits factors to account for the addition of *ALAE* to loss. A simplistic way of doing this is to assume that the *ALAE* for each claim is a deterministic function of indemnity amount for the claim, adding exactly $\gamma\%$ to each claim value for the range of claim sizes that are near the layer of interest. Note that this γ factor is smaller than the overall ratio of *ALAE* to ground-up indemnity loss, because much of the total *ALAE* applies to small claims or claims closed with no indemnity. In our example then, we hypothesize that when *ALAE* is added to loss, every claim with indemnity greater than $\$300,000/(1 + \gamma)$ penetrates the layer $\$700,000$ excess of $\$300,000$, and that the loss amount in the layer reaches $\$700,000$ when the ground-up indemnity reaches $\$1,000,000/(1 + \gamma)$. From this you can see how to modify standard increased limits factors to account for *ALAE* added to loss. In this liability context, Formula 7.6 can be reinterpreted with *PCP* as the basic limit premium and *PC-PLR* as the primary company permissible basic limits loss ratio. Given the clash exposure, suppose we believe that for this type of coverage, an overall loss loading of $\delta\%$ is sufficient to adjust the loss cost for this layer estimated from the stand-alone policies. Then *ELCF* calculates the excess loss in the layer $\$700,000$ excess of $\$300,000$ arising from each policy limit (plus its contribution to clash losses) as a percent of basic limits loss arising from the same policy limit. The formula for *ELCF* evaluated at limit, Lim, is displayed in the following formula.

Formula 7.33: Liability ELCF for ALAE Added To Indemnity Loss

$$ELCF(Lim) = 0$$

$$\text{if} \quad Lim \leq \frac{AP}{1 + \gamma}$$

$$ELCF(Lim) = (1 + \delta) \times (1 + \gamma) \times \left\{ ILF(Lim) - ILF\left(\frac{AP}{1 + \gamma}\right) \right\}$$

$$\text{if} \quad \frac{AP}{1 + \gamma} < Lim \leq \frac{AP + RLim}{1 + \gamma}$$

$$ELCF(Lim) = (1 + \delta) \times (1 + \gamma)$$

$$\times \left\{ ILF\left(\frac{AP + RLim}{1 + \gamma}\right) - ILF\left(\frac{AP}{1 + \gamma}\right) \right\}$$

$$\text{if} \quad \frac{AP + RLim}{1 + \gamma} < Lim$$

where AP = attachment point = \$300,000

$RLim$ = reinsurance limit = \$700,000

δ = clash loading = 5%

γ = excess $ALAE$ loading = 20%

Table 7.34 displays this simplistic method for a part of da Ponte's *GL* exposure using hypothetical increased limits factors (excluding both *ALAE* and risk load) to calculate excess loss cost factors. In Table 7.34, we see that policies with limits \$300,000, \$500,000 and \$1,000,000 and above expose the excess layer.

TABLE 7.34

EXCESS LOSS COST FACTORS WITH *ALAE* ADDED TO INDEMNITY LOSS @ 20% ADD-ON AND A CLASH LOADING OF 5%

(1) Policy Limit	(2) *ILF* w/o risk load and w/o *ALAE*	(3) *ELCF*
\$ 100,000	1.0000	0
250,000	1.2386	0
300,000	1.2842	0.0575
500,000	1.4084	0.2139
833,333	1.5271	0.3635
1,000,000 or more	1.5681	0.3635

Using Formula 7.33, we calculate $ELCF(\$300,000) = 1.05 \times 1.20 \times (1.2842 - 1.2386) = 0.0575$, and $ELCF(\$1,000,000) = 1.05 \times 1.20 \times (1.5271 - 1.2386) = 0.3635$. Back up for Table 7.34 is contained in Appendix D.

Suppose da Ponte's permissible basic limit loss ratio for this exposure is $PCPLR = 65\%$. Suppose our evaluation indicates that their rates and offsets are adequate, so $RCF = 1.00$. Then we can translate Table 7.34 into an exposure rate $RELC$, the reinsurer's estimate of loss cost (undiscounted) in the excess layer as shown in Table 7.35.

TABLE 7.35

$RELC$ (REINSURANCE EXPECTED LOSS COST (UNDISCOUNTED))

(1)	(2) Estimated Subject Premium Year 2000	(3) Manual ILF	(4) Estimated Basic Limit Loss Cost $0.65 \times (2)/(3)$	(5) ELCF from 6.37	(6) RELC $(4) \times (5)$
Policy Limit					
Below $300,000	$1,000,000	1.10 (avg.)	$ 590,909	0	$0
300,000	1,000,000	1.35	481,482	0.0575	27,664
500,000	1,000,000	1.50	433,333	0.2139	92,711
1,000,000 or more	2,000,000	1.75 (avg.)	724,857	0.3635	270,036
Total	$5,000,000	n.a.	$2,248,810	n.a.	$390,411

The estimation of $RELC$ for other categories would be similar. For liability exposure categories where increased limit factors are not published, use judgment to assign appropriate factors. For workers compensation, excess loss cost factor differences would be weighted by estimated subject premium by hazard group, by major state grouping, or the underlying claim severity distributions could be estimated by state, by hazard group. We would then combine these $RELC$ estimates with our estimates of loss discount factors for each exposure in order to calculate $PVRELC$.

A better way of estimating an exposure loss cost is to work directly from probability models of the claim size distributions. This directly gives us claim count and claim severity information to use in our simple risk theoretic model for aggregate loss. Suppose we know that the indemnity loss distribution underlying Table 7.34 is Pareto with $b = 5,000$ and $q = 1.1$. Then our simple model of adding 20% *ALAE* to indemnity per claim (per-occurrence) changes the indemnity Pareto distribution to another Pareto with $b = 5,000 \times 1.20 = 6,000$ and $q = 1.1$. Please note that these parameters are selected simply to make the computations easier for you to check. We then multiply by $1 + \delta = 1.05$ to adjust the layer severity for clash.[4] We can then calculate excess expected claim sizes from each policy limit. Dividing by the *RELC* for each limit yields estimates of expected claim count. This is done in Table 7.36.

TABLE 7.36

EXCESS EXPECTED LOSS, CLAIM SEVERITY, AND COUNT

(1)	(2)	(3)	(4)
Policy Limit	*RELC*	Expected Claim Size (App. E)	Expected Claim Count (2)/(3)
$ 300,000	$ 27,664	$ 57,016	0.485
500,000	92,711	212,210	0.437
1,000,000 or more	270,036	360,517	0.749
Total	$390,411	$233,624	1.671

Dividing *RELC* by the estimate of the total expected claim count, we can back into an estimate of the total excess expected claim size of $233,624 for this exposure. Assuming indepen-

---

[4]One may argue that clash affects the excess claim frequency, not the excess claim severity. The truth is that it affects both. Here, for simplicity, we only adjust the excess claim severity.

dence of claim events across all exposures, we can also add to obtain estimates for the expected claim (occurrence) count and overall excess expected claim (occurrence) size.

Now we turn to experience rating.

Step 3: Gather and reconcile primary claims data segregated by major rating class groups.

As in Example 7.24, we want the claims data segregated as the exposure data, and we want some history of individual large claims. We usually receive information on all claims greater than one-half the proposed attachment point, but, the more data, the better. Suppose a claims review has been performed. In our example, suppose we receive a detailed history for each known claim larger than \$100,000 occurring 1990–2000, evaluated $12/31/90, 12/31/91, \ldots, 12/31/99, 6/30/00$.

Step 4: Filter the major catastrophic claims out of the claims data.

In our example, we want to identify clash claims, if possible, and any significant mass tort claims. By separating out the clash claims, we can estimate their frequency and size relative to non-clash claims, and compare these statistics to values we know from other cedants, thus enabling us to get a better estimate for our δ loading. It should be obvious that the mass tort claims need special treatment.

Step 5: Trend the claims data to the rating period.

As in Example 7.24, the trending should be for inflation and for other changes in exposure (such as higher policy limits) that might affect the loss potential. Unlike proportional coverage, we may not skip this step. The reason is the leveraged effect of inflation upon excess claims: a constant inflation rate increases the aggregate loss above any attachment point faster than the aggregate loss below, because claims grow into the excess layer, while their value below is stopped at the attachment point. We trend each ground-up claim value at each evaluation, including

ALAE, from year of occurrence to 2001. For example, consider the treatment of a 1993 claim in Table 7.37.

TABLE 7.37

TRENDING AN ACCIDENT YEAR 1993 CLAIM

(1) Evaluation Date	(2) Value at Evaluation	(3) Trend Factor	(4) 2001 Level Value	(5) Excess Amount
12/31/93	$0	1.59	$0	$0
12/31/94	0	1.59	0	0
12/31/95	125,000	1.59	198,750	0
12/31/96	125,000	1.59	198,750	0
12/31/97	150,000	1.59	238,500	0
12/31/98	200,000	1.59	318,000	18,000
12/31/99	200,000	1.59	318,000	18,000
6/30/00	200,000	1.59	318,000	18,000

Note the use of a single trend factor. The reasoning here is that the trend affects claim values according to accident date (or year), not by evaluation date. Of course a more sophisticated model for claims inflation could be used. A delicate issue is the trending of policy limits. If a 1993 claim on a policy with limit less than $250,000 inflates to above $300,000 (including *ALAE*), would the policy limit sold in 2001 be greater than $250,000, so to allow this excess claim (including *ALAE* @ 20%)? The da Ponte underwriter and your own marketing people may argue that the policy limit does not change. But, over long time periods, it would appear that the answer is that policy limits do change with inflation. If possible, information on the da Ponte's policy limit distributions over time should be obtained. If this is a real issue, you can try some sensitivity testing on the extreme alternatives:

1. The historical policy limits change with claims inflation.

2. The historical policy limits remain constant.

Then reach some judgmental compromise.

Step 6: Develop the claims data to settlement values.

We want to construct historical accident year/development year triangles from the data produced in column 5 of Table 7.37 for each type of large claim. We would usually combine together all claims by major line of business. Then we can use standard methods to estimate loss development factors and apply these to the excess claims data. We also want to compare the development patterns estimated from da Ponte's data to what we expect based upon our own historical data for comparable coverages, in order to check for reasonableness. This may be a problem, even for filtered claims, if the historical data has insufficient credibility. Consider the claim in Table 7.37: only $18,000 exceeds the attachment point, and only at the fifth development point. Suppose our triangle looks like Table 7.38.

TABLE 7.38

TRENDED HISTORICAL CLAIMS
IN THE LAYER $700,000 EXCESS OF $300,000
(IN $1,000's)

Acc. Year	Age 1	Age 2	Age 3	Development Year ...	Age 9	Age 10	Age 10.5
1990	$0	$80	$254	...	$259	$321	$321
1991	0	0	148	...	743	788	
⋮	⋮	⋮	⋮				
1998	57	117	236				
1999	0	0					
2000	0						
ATA	4.236	1.573	1.076	...	1.239	n.a.	n.a.
ATU	15.026	3.547	2.255	...	1.301	1.050	= tail
Smoothed Lags	10.9%	28.7%	45.7%	...	93.1%	95.3%	96.1%

where   *ATA* = Age-To-Age development factor

ATU = Age-To-Ultimate development factor

Lag(*t*) = percentage of loss reported at time *t*

The tail factor of 1.05 is selected based upon general information about development beyond ten years for this type of exposure.

By switching the point of view from age-to-ultimate factors to their inverse, time lags of claim dollar reporting, as we do later in the Loss Reserving section, we transform the loss reporting view to that of a cumulative distribution function (cdf) whose domain is $[0, \infty)$. This gives us a better view of the loss development pattern. It allows us to consider and measure the average (expected) lag and other moments, which can then be compared to the moments of the loss development patterns from other exposures.

Since excess claims development is almost always extremely chaotic, it is a good idea to employ some kind of smoothing technique, as discussed in the later loss reserving section. If properly estimated, the smoothed factors should yield more credible loss development estimates. They also allow us to unambiguously evaluate the function Lag( ) at any positive time. This is handy, since our latest data evaluation point is 6/30/00, and we want to use these data. The smoothing introduced in the last row of Table 7.38 is based upon a Gamma distribution with mean 4 (years) and standard deviation 3. This model is based upon the data, plus our judgment regarding the general pattern we should expect for loss development, the shape of the cdf. A more sophisticated approach could estimate parameters for the Gamma distribution directly from the development data via the method of Maximum Likelihood Estimation by treating the data for each accident year as a sample truncated at the last age.

Frequently, it is also useful to analyze large claim paid data, if they are available, both to estimate excess claims payment patterns and to supplement the ultimate estimates based only upon the reported (incurred with no *IBNR*) claims used above. It is sometimes true that the paid claims development, although it is of longer duration, is more stable than the reported claims development.

Occasionally, only aggregate excess claims data are available. This would be an historical accident year/development year $700,000 excess of $300,000 aggregate loss triangle. Pricing in a situation like this, with no specific information about large claims, is very risky, but it is sometimes done. Technically, in such a situation, the *RTER* should be higher because of the added risk because of greater (mis-)information uncertainty. But often, the opposite occurs because of marketing pressures.

Step 7: Estimate the catastrophic loss potential.

It should be obvious that mass tort claims need special treatment. Asbestos and pollution clean-up claims, if any, distort the historical data. As is done for property coverage, an analysis of da Ponte's exposures can allow us to guess some suitable loading for future mass tort claim potential.

As we said in Step 4, we want to identify clash claims, if possible. By separating out the clash claims, for each claim, we add its various parts together to apply properly the attachment point and the reinsurance limit to the occurrence loss amount. If we cannot identify the clash claims, then our experience estimate of *RELC* must include a clash loading based upon judgment for the general type of exposure.

Step 8: Adjust the historical exposures to the rating period.

As we did in Example 7.24, we want to be sure that the historical exposure (premium) data are adjusted in a manner that makes them reasonably relevant to the rating period. The trending should be for primary rate and underwriting changes and for other changes in exposure that might affect the loss potential. Table 7.39 shows such a calculation.

Step 9: Estimate an experience expected loss cost, PVRELC, and, if desirable, a loss cost rate, PVRELC/PCP.

Suppose we now have trended and developed excess losses for all classes of da Ponte's casualty exposure. The usual practice is

TABLE 7.39
GL Premium Adjusted to 2001 Level (in $1,000's)

(1) Accident Year	(2) PCP	(3) Rate Change	(4) Deviation from Manual	(5) Exposure Inflation Growth	(6) Written Premium Growth	(7) Earned Premium Growth	(8) Cumulative On-level Factor	(9) Adjusted 2001-level PCP
1990	$ 5,829	3.2%	4.6%	2.9%	101.3%	n.a.	n.a.	n.a.
1991	6,045	2.5%	7.3%	2.8%	103.7%	n.a.	n.a.	n.a.
1992	6,095	1.9%	7.6%	1.9%	107.4%	103.9%	69.8%	$ 8,733
...	...	...	...	...	...	...	...	...
1996	14,484	3.7%	8.3%	1.7%	137.6%	129.4%	86.9%	16,661
1997	16,114	2.6%	9.1%	1.6%	142.2%	137.1%	92.1%	17,488
1998	16,458	1.3%	10.2%	1.4%	144.3%	141.9%	95.3%	17,265
1999	16,810	0.5%	11.4%	1.3%	144.9%	144.1%	96.8%	17,362
2000 (@ 6/30)	8,346	1.0%	11.0%	1.0%	148.5%	145.3%	97.6%	8,549
2001	n.a.	2.0%	10.0%	1.0%	154.7%	148.8%	100.0%	n.a.

Notes:

Col. (6)[199N] = (1 − (4)) × {(1 + (3)[1990] × [1 + (5)[1990]) + (1 + (3)[1991]) × (1 + (5)[1991]) + ⋯

$\quad$ + (1 + (3)[199(N − 1)]) × (1 + (5)[199(N − 1)]) + (1 + (3)[199N] × (1 + (5)[199N])}

Col. (7)[199N] = 0.125 × {(6)[199N] + (6)[199(N − 2)] + 0.75 × (6)[199(N − 1)]

Col. (8)[199N] = $\dfrac{(7)[199N]}{(7)[2001]}$

$\quad$ Col. (9) = $\dfrac{(2)}{(8)}$

to add up the pieces to assemble an exhibit that looks like Table 7.40.

TABLE 7.40

DA PONTE INSURANCE COMPANY CASUALTY BUSINESS
(IN $1,000's)

(1) Accident Year	(2) Onlevel *PCP*	(3) Trended and Developed Loss Excess Loss (Estimated *RELC*)	(4) Estimated Cost Rate (3) ÷ (2)
1992	$ 85,847	$ 3,357	3.91%
1993	87,953	4,644	5.28%
1994	89,076	6,761	7.59%
1995	92,947	5,410	5.82%
1996	94,172	4,567	4.85%
1997	95,674	3,329	3.48%
1998	98,561	4,268	4.33%
1999	99,226	6,420	6.47%
2000	49,750	1,413	2.84%
Total	$793,206	$40,168	5.06%
Total w/o 2000	$743,456	$38,755	5.21%

The eight-year average loss cost rate, eliminating 2000 as being too green (undeveloped), is 5.21%. There seems to be no particular trend from year to year. If there were, we would want to see what its extrapolation to 2001 might be. The standard deviation is 1.37%. These estimates seem to be quite stable. This is not always the case.

Alternative Estimation Methods and Some Potential Problems

Problem: Chaotic excess development

Sometimes the loss development data for the layer $700,000 excess $300,000 for some of the categories of exposure are more chaotic than we have seen in this example, so that we can't estimate model parameters with enough confidence. We have alternatives:

1. We can use our general loss development patterns for these types of exposure, this attachment point.
2. We can experience rate a lower layer, where we may have more stable, more credible development patterns.

For alternative 2, for example, perhaps we would drop down to experience rate the layer $800,000 excess of $200,000, or $300,000 excess of $200,000. We would then calculate the *RELC* for $700,000 excess of $300,000 for each exposure category by an extrapolation employing excess layer relativities derived from claim severity curves.

Problem: Incomplete excess claims sample

If the cumulative trend factor for some exposure for some historical accident year exceeds the ratio of the attachment point divided by the lower bound of the large claims, then we will have an incomplete excess sample extrapolated to the year 2001. Let us illustrate this point with the 1993 accident year. Suppose we were to drop down to experience rate the layer $150,000 excess of $150,000 for 2001. Returning to the claim trending in Table 7.38, since our 1993 trend factor is 1.59, the 2001 values of all the 1993 claims greater than $100,000 will lie above $159,000 = 1.59 × $100,000. So we are missing claims whose 2001 values would be in the interval between $150,000 and $159,000. So our trended claims data from 1993 are representative of the layer $141,000 excess of $159,000, not the layer $150,000 excess of $150,000.

Alternate Estimation Method

With the individual large claims data we have, a more sophisticated methodology would have us look at excess claim count development and excess claim size development separately. If the data give us reasonably stable development indications, we readily obtain claim count and claim size estimates useful for the simple risk theoretic model for excess aggregate loss. With a sufficient number of large claims, we can even estimate excess claim size distribution parameters directly from the data. These can then be compared to general parameters we have to reach credible models for excess claim size.

Problem: Free cover

Also, an analysis that deals with individual claims may un-cover problems buried in the simpler excess aggregate loss esti-mation. One problem may be that of so-called "free cover." This arises when, in our example, the maximum trended historical claim value is $794,826, for instance. Then the experience rate loss cost estimate for the layer $700,000 excess of $300,000 is the same as the experience rate loss cost estimate for the layer $500,000 excess of $300,000. So we would be charging $0 for the layer $200,000 excess of $800,000. It may be the case that there are many claims whose 2001 values are close to $800,000, and it is simply by chance that none of them exceeded $800,000. In this case, you may simply let the experience rate loss cost estimate stand. If this is not the case, then it looks like an insuf-ficient rate is being calculated for coverage excess of $800,000, and consequently a different tactic is called for. We can estimate the loss cost for the layer $200,000 excess of $800,000 via a rel-ative exposure rate extrapolation from the layer $500,000 excess of $300,000. Judgment is important here, together with a review of da Ponte's higher policy limits exposure and a review of the types of historical large claims that might pierce the layer excess of $800,000.

RELC and PVRELC and PVRELC/PCP

Let us complete our estimation of the reinsurance expected loss cost, discounted reinsurance expected loss cost, and the rein-surance loss cost rate. Table 7.40 gives us an experience-based estimate, $RELC/PCP = 5.21\%$. However, this must be loaded for whatever mass tort exposure exists, and also loaded for clash claims if we judge that we had insufficient information on clash claims in the claims data. A more sophisticated approach would add in the catastrophe loss exposure rate, like we did in Example 7.24 for the property catastrophe loss.

Step 10: Estimate a "credibility" loss cost or loss cost rate from the exposure and experience loss costs or loss cost rates.

We must also weigh the experience loss cost rate against the exposure loss cost rate we calculated. If we have more than one answer, and the various answers differ but cannot be further reconciled, final answers for $700,000 excess of $300,000 claim count and severity can be based upon a credibility balancing of the separate estimates. However, all the differences should not be ignored, but should indeed be included in your estimates of parameter (and model) uncertainty, thus giving rise to more realistic measures of variances, etc., and of risk.

Suppose we are in the simple situation, where we are only weighing together the exposure loss cost estimate and the experience loss cost estimate. In Table 7.41 we list six considerations for deciding how much weight to give to the exposure loss cost estimate. You can see that the credibility of the exposure loss cost estimate is decreased if there are problems with any of the six items.

Likewise, in Table 7.42 we list six considerations for deciding how much weight to give to the experience loss cost estimate. You can see that the credibility of the experience loss cost estimate is lessened by problems with any of the six items.

Appendix F has a more detailed discussion of the items in Tables 7.41 and 7.42.

Let us assume that our credibility loss cost rate is $RELC/PCP$ = 5.73%.

For each exposure category, we estimate a loss discount factor. This is based upon the expected loss payment pattern for the

TABLE 7.41

ITEMS TO CONSIDER IN DETERMINING THE CREDIBILITY OF THE
EXPOSURE LOSS COST ESTIMATE

- The accuracy of the estimate of *RCF*, the primary rate correction factor, and thus the accuracy of the primary expected loss cost or loss ratio
- The accuracy of the predicted distribution of subject premium by line of business
- For excess coverage, the accuracy of the predicted distribution of subject premium by increased limits table for liability, by state for workers compensation, or by type of insured for property, within a line of business
- For excess coverage, the accuracy of the predicted distribution of subject premium by policy limit within increased limits table for liability, by hazard group for workers compensation, by amount insured for property
- For excess coverage, the accuracy of the excess loss cost factors for coverage above the attachment point
- For excess coverage, the degree of potential exposure not contemplated by the excess loss cost factors

TABLE 7.42

ITEMS TO CONSIDER IN DETERMINING THE CREDIBILITY OF THE
EXPERIENCE LOSS COST ESTIMATE

- The accuracy of the estimates of claims cost inflation
- The accuracy of the estimates of loss development
- The accuracy of the subject premium on-level factors
- The stability of the loss cost, or loss cost rate, over time
- The possibility of changes in the underlying exposure over time
- For excess coverage, the possibility of changes in the distribution of policy limits over time

exposure in the layer $700,000 excess of $300,000, and upon a selected investment yield. Most actuaries advocate using a risk-free yield, usually U.S. Treasuries for U.S. business, for a maturity approximating the average claim payment lag. Discounting is only significant for longer tail business. So for simplicity, on a practical basis, it's better to use a single, constant fixed rate for a bond maturity between five to ten years. But of course this selection is entirely up to the reinsurer's pricing philosophy.

Let us suppose that the overall discount factor for our loss cost rate of 5.73% is $RDF = 75\%$, giving $PVRELC/PCP = RDF \times RELC/PCP = 0.75 \times 5.73\% = 4.30\%$, or $PVRELC = 4.3\% \times \$100,000,000 = \$4,300,000$.

Note that we will reverse steps 11 and 12.

Step 12: Specify values for RCR, RIXL, and RTER

Suppose our standard guidelines for this type and size of contract and this type of exposure specify $RIXL = 5\%$ and $RTER = 15\%$. We can then calculate the reinsurance pure premium of $RPP = PVRELC/(1 - RTER) = \$4,300,000/0.85 = \$5,058,823$, with an expected profit of $RPP - PVRELC = \$5,058,823 - \$4,300,000 = \$758,823$ for the risk transfer. Since $RCR = 0\%$, we have an indicated technical reinsurance premium of $RP = RPP/(1 - RIXL) = \$5,058,823/0.95 = \$5,325,077$. This technical premium is above the maximum of \$5,000,000 specified by da Ponte. Assuming that there is nothing wrong with our technical calculations, the reinsurer has at least two options:

1. We can accept an expected reinsurance premium of \$5,000,000 at a rate of 5%, with a reduced expected profit (assuming our internal expenses stay at \$5,325,077 − \$5,058,823 = \$266,254) of \$5,000,000 − \$4,300,000 − \$266,254 = \$434,746.

2. We can offer a variable rate contract, where the reinsurance rate varies according to the reinsurance loss experience, in this case a retrospectively rated contract.

Let us select the more interesting second option, especially since, in this example da Ponte is asking for a retrospectively rated contract. In order to construct a balanced and fair rating plan, we need once again to estimate the distribution of the reinsurance aggregate loss. So we proceed with step 11.

Step 11: Estimate the probability distribution of the aggregate reinsurance loss if desirable, and perhaps other distributions such as for claims payment timing.

We will again use a Gamma distribution approximation. But this time, in this lower (excess) claim frequency situation, we will obtain a better approximation of the distribution of aggregate reinsurance loss using the standard risk theoretic model for aggregate losses together with the first two moments of the claim count and claim severity distributions.

The Standard Risk Theoretic Model for the Distribution of Aggregate Loss

The standard model writes the aggregate loss naturally as the sum of the individual claims (or events) as follows.

Formula 7.43: Aggregate Loss

$$L = X_1 + X_2 + \cdots + X_N$$

where $L = rv$ (random variable) for aggregate loss

$N = rv$ for number of claims (occurrences, events)

$X_i = rv$ for the dollar size of the ith claim

Here N and X_i refer to the excess number of claims and the amount of the ith claim respectively. The standard risk theoretic model relates the distributions of L, N and the X_i's, as shown in Appendix G. Under the assumption that the X_i's are independent and identically distributed and also independent of N (reasonable independence assumptions), the kth moment of L is completely determined by the first k moments of N and the X_i's. In particular, we have the following relationships.

Formula 7.44: First Two Central Moments of the Distribution of Aggregate Loss under the Standard Risk Theoretic Model

$$E[L] = E[N] \times E[X]$$

$$\text{Var}[L] = E[N] \times E[X^2] + (\text{Var}[N] - E[N]) \times E[X]^2$$

We start by assuming that $E[L] = RELC = 5.73\% \times$ $\$100,000,000 = \$5,730,000$ (undiscounted). We simplistically assume that the excess claim sizes are independent and identically distributed and are independent of the excess claim (occurrence) count. In most cases this is a reasonable assumption. For our layer $\$700,000$ excess of $\$300,000$, our modeling assumptions and results are shown in Formula 7.45, using the notation in Appendices A and G.

Formula 7.45: da Ponte $\$700,000$ Excess of $\$300,000$ Aggregate Loss Modeling Assumptions and Results

$$N(300) \sim \text{Negative Binomial with}$$

$$E[N(300)] = 24.64$$

$$\text{Var}[N(300)] = 2 \times E[N(300)]$$

$$X(300) \sim \text{Pareto}(350, 2)$$

$$E[X(300); 700] = \$232,543 \text{ censored at } 700$$

$$E[X(300)^2; 700] = 105.308 \times 10^6$$

$$\begin{aligned} E[RL] &= E[N(300)] \times E[X(300); 700] \\ &= 24.64 \times \$232,543 \\ &= \$5,729,860 \end{aligned}$$

$$\begin{aligned} \text{Var}[RL] &= E[N(300)] \times E[X(300)^2; 700] \\ &\quad + \{\text{Var}[N(300)] - E[N(300)]\} \times E[X(300); 700]^2 \\ &= E[N(300)] \times \{E[X(300)^2; 700] + E[X(300); 700]^2\} \\ &= 24.64 \times \{105.308 \times 10^6 + 232.543 \times 10^6\} \\ &= 24.64 \times \{159.384 \times 10^6\} \\ &= 3.9272 \times 10^9 \end{aligned}$$

$$SD[RL] = \$1,981,724$$

$$\frac{SD[RL]}{E[RL]} = 0.346$$

More sophisticated modeling would more explicitly take into account modeling and parameter risks. A good general mathematical reference for "collective risk theory" is Bühlmann [9]. We will continue with our simple model here.

Let us now set up the following retrospective rating plan.

Formula 7.46: Retrospective Rate Plan

$$RP = RC + LF \times RL$$

Subject to $\min RP \leq RP \leq \text{Max} RP$

where RP = final reinsurance premium

PRP = provisional reinsurance premium

= \$4,000,000

RC = reinsurance charge = \$500,000

LF = loss factor = 1.00

$\min RP$ = minimum reinsurance premium

= \$2,000,000

$\text{Max} RP$ = maximum reinsurance premium

= \$8,000,000

RP, PRP, RC, $\min RP$, and $\text{Max} RP$ can also be stated as rates with respect to PCP. Sometimes a loss factor of 1.05 or 1.10 is used. You can see that these are all basic parameters you can play with in order to structure a balanced rating plan.

If we use the Gamma distribution obtained from $E[RL]$ and $\text{Var}[RL]$ in formula 7.45, then the expected reinsurance profit becomes \$745,075, as shown in Table 7.47. This is close enough to the desired profit margin of \$758,823 that any reinsurer will accept these terms.

TABLE 7.47

AGGREGATE LOSS DISTRIBUTION AND CALCULATION OF REINSURER'S PROFIT

(1) Loss Cost Rate (selected)	(2) Probability Density (as percent)	(3) Reinsurance Premium Rate	(4) Reinsurer's Profit
0.0%	0.0%	2.00%	$ 2,984
1.0%	5.2%	2.05%	2,234
2.0%	198.9%	3.10%	1,484
3.0%	914.1%	4.15%	1,109
4.0%	1765.6%	5.20%	1,109
5.0%	2120.8%	6.25%	1,109
6.0%	1886.3%	7.30%	1,109
7.0%	1363.7%	8.00%	734
8.0%	847.0%	8.00%	(16)
9.0%	468.5%	8.00%	(766)
10.0%	236.5%	8.00%	(1,516)
11.0%	110.9%	8.00%	(2,266)
12.0%	48.9%	8.00%	(3,016)
13.0%	20.5%	8.00%	(3,766)
14.0%	8.2%	8.00%	(4,516)
15.0%	3.2%	8.00%	(5,266)
16.0%	1.2%	8.00%	(6,016)
17.0%	0.4%	8.00%	(6,766)
18.0%	0.2%	8.00%	(7,516)
19.0%	0.1%	8.00%	(8,266)
20.0%	0.0%	8.00%	(9,016)
Expected		5.75%	$745,075

The simplified profit formula used in Table 7.47 is as follows.

Formula 7.48: Simplified Profit Formula

Reinsurer's profit $= PRP - RIXL - RDF \times \{PRP - (RP - RL)\}$

where $RIXL = \$266,000$ (in dollars)

This simple formula assumes that the single reinsurance claims payment, RL, and reinsurance premium adjustment, $RP -$

PRP, are simultaneous. A more sophisticated evaluation would account for cash flow timing, e.g., when premium adjustments would be made according to the premium formula timing in the contract.

Step 13: Negotiate, reconcile opinions and estimates, alter terms and finalize

We now have contract terms that meet our underwriting standards and also largely meet our profit guidelines. We also believe these terms will be acceptable to da Ponte Insurance Company. We then meet with da Ponte and explain our analysis and evaluation, answer their questions and listen to their counter-arguments and alternative interpretations of information and data. If necessary, we repeat the previous steps until we reach a contract structure that satisfies both parties, if possible.

If we cannot reach an agreement with da Ponte Insurance Company on the pricing of the layer $700,000 excess of $300,000, then the best bet is to recommend that the attachment point be increased to $350,000 or $400,000. Attachment points should naturally increase over time in an inflationary environment. In this example, the expected excess claim count of 24.64 ($E[N(300)]$) is fairly high for an excess working layer. The standard deviation of about 7 ($SD[N(300)]$) is fairly low relative to the expectation. Perhaps now is the time for an increase so that we and da Ponte aren't simply trading dollars for the more predictable claims just above $300,000.

As with facultative covers, it is clear that much of the above can and should be programmed into an interactive computer package for the underwriters and actuaries. And it is also extremely important to monitor the results of large treaties and groups of treaties. The monitoring of the pricing experience and the monitoring of *IBNR* emergence and the reconciliation of both is important to the reinsurer.

Higher Exposed Excess Layer Treaties

Since there is policy limits exposure on these contracts, an exposure rate may be determined with the same general methodology as for a working cover. The higher the layer, the greater the relative significance of the workers compensation exposure, if any, and the greater the importance of clash and other multiple limit claims' exposure. The clash load δ in Example 7.31, Formula 7.33 must be larger. Since losses are not "expected" for these layers, historical loss data are sparse. And yet the layers have loss potential, or else cedants wouldn't buy reinsurance. An experience loss cost rate on a contract may be calculated by experience rating a working layer below, and using the working cover loss cost estimate as a basis for estimating the higher exposed layer rate via extrapolation using claim size probability distributions or non-risk-loaded increased limit factors.

Since claim frequency is lower than it is for a working layer, the risk transfer is greater relative to premium volume. Thus, *RTER*'s are greater.

Clash Treaties

Since there is no policy limit exposure, the usual exposure rating methodology does not work, except for evaluating workers compensation exposure. Prices for clash covers are usually set by market conditions. The actuarial prices are largely determined by very high *RTER*'s, and may or may not be close to the market-determined prices.

For clash layer pricing, the reinsurer should keep experience statistics on clash covers to see, in general, how often and to what degree these covers are penetrated, and to see if the historical market-determined rates have been reasonable overall, and also the degree to which rating cycles exist. The rates for various clash layers should bear reasonable relationships to one another, depending both upon the underlying exposures and upon the distances of the attachment points from the policy limits sold.

Underwriters sometimes view clash rates with regard to a notion of payback–the premium should cover one loss every m years for some selected m. These kinds of underwriting-judgment rates could be translated into judgmental expected loss cost rates plus *RIXL*'s and *RTER*'s to put them into a consistent actuarial context.

Property Catastrophe Treaties

The price for a catastrophe treaty should depend upon the attachment point, upon the cedant's accumulation of property exposure in localities prone to natural catastrophes, and upon the cedant's net position on each policy after all other reinsurance. Changes in the cedant's noncatastrophe net retentions may have a great effect upon the catastrophe exposure excess of a given attachment point. That is, a reinsurance program can be tricky: a small change here can have a big effect there.

The recent evolution of commercially available, large-scale computer simulation models for natural catastrophe exposures, especially hurricane and earthquake, has greatly increased the accuracy with which these exposures can be evaluated. Of course these models demand much more input information, such as property premium by zip code and information about construction, etc., than was the case for the old underwriter rules-of-thumb. The models are not yet perfect—it seems that after every major catastrophe, the model parameters are re-adjusted to reflect a revised opinion regarding event frequency and severity potential. But they are a significant step forward.

The reinsurer's actuaries should be knowledgeable about and be involved in the use of these models for both pricing reinsurance contracts and for the measurement of the reinsurer's aggregate accumulation of catastrophe exposure. This aggregate exposure, if not properly understood and measured, can have the potential to blow the roof off a reinsurance company, as was demonstrated by Hurricane Andrew in 1992. The reinsurance exposure from every large property contract or portfolio of smaller contracts must be estimated; this would be based upon the cedants' exposed policy limits, locality, and the reinsurance coverage. Then the reinsurer can see where too much catastrophe potential is accumulated, and can then better structure our own catastrophe retrocessional program.

Aggregate Excess, or Stop Loss, Treaties

Stop loss treaties may be used to protect a cedant's net loss ratio. In a sense, this is the ultimate reinsurance cover for protecting a net result. Because of the magnitude of the risk transfer, these covers are quite expensive, and often are not available unless written on a nontraditional basis.

For example, suppose we return briefly to the quota-share Example 7.24. Table 7.29 displays part of the estimated probability distribution for the loss ratio. As an alternative to the quota-share, perhaps da Ponte Insurance Company might be interested in the following stop loss cover.

Formula 7.49: Stop Loss Cover on da Ponte Property Net Retained Exposure

PCP = primary company premium = $10,000,000

AP = attachment point = 70% loss ratio = $7,000,000

$RLim$ = reinsurance limit = 30% loss ratio = $3,000,000

RP = reinsurance premium = $550,000

Suppose that the reinsurer's expected internal expense for this cover is about $50,000. Assuming that we use the same Gamma distribution as before to represent the loss ratio distribution, the profit distribution for the reinsurer is displayed in Table 7.50.

The reinsurer's expected profit of $199,704 looks high in relation to the reinsurer's expected loss of $E[RL]$ = $295,230. But the standard deviation of the reinsurer's loss, $SD[RL]$ = $651,000, is extremely high compared to the expectation, and the probability

TABLE 7.50

Stop Loss Cover on da Ponte Property Exposure

(1) Primary Co. Loss Ratio	(2) Reinsurer's Loss Cost	(3) Probability	(4) Reinsurer's Profit
70% or less	$0	72.17%	$ 500,000
71%	100,000	1.95%	400,000
72%	200,000	1.85%	300,000
73%	300,000	1.76%	200,000
74%	400,000	1.66%	100,000
75%	500,000	1.57%	(0)
76%	600,000	1.47%	(100,000)
77%	700,000	1.38%	(200,000)
78%	800,000	1.29%	(300,000)
79%	900,000	1.21%	(400,000)
80%	1,000,000	1.12%	(500,000)
81%	1,100,000	1.04%	(600,000)
82%	1,200,000	0.96%	(700,000)
83%	1,300,000	0.89%	(800,000)
84%	1,400,000	0.82%	(900,000)
85%	1,500,000	0.75%	(1,000,000)
86%	1,600,000	0.69%	(1,100,000)
87%	1,700,000	0.63%	(1,200,000)
88%	1,800,000	0.58%	(1,300,000)
89%	1,900,000	0.53%	(1,400,000)
90%	2,000,000	0.48%	(1,500,000)
91%	2,100,000	0.44%	(1,600,000)
92%	2,200,000	0.40%	(1,700,000)
93%	2,300,000	0.36%	(1,800,000)
94%	2,400,000	0.32%	(1,900,000)
95%	2,500,000	0.29%	(2,000,000)
96%	2,600,000	0.26%	(2,100,000)
97%	2,700,000	0.24%	(2,200,000)
98%	2,800,000	0.21%	(2,300,000)
99%	2,900,000	0.19%	(2,400,000)
100% or more	3,000,000	1.37%	(2,500,000)
Total	$ 295,230	100%	$ 199,704

that the reinsurer loses money is 19%. This is quite common for stop loss covers. It indicates a very high risk transfer; the reinsurer is getting a relatively small premium to cover part of the more unpredictable tail of da Ponte's aggregate property loss distribution. In relation to the total premium of $10,000,000, the reinsurer's expected profit is only about 2%. Note the shape of the reinsurer's distribution of aggregate loss. It is definitely non-Gamma. It has a positive probability of zero loss, Prob[RL = $0] = 72.17%, and it is stopped (censored) above at 30%, or $3,000,000, with Prob[$RL$ = $3,000,000] = 1.37%.

If we were seriously pricing an aggregate stop loss like this, we would construct our aggregate excess loss model more carefully than we did with an overall Gamma distribution. We might use a Gamma model for the filtered claims, but build up the catastrophe component by modeling event frequency and severity. We would then carefully put the two (or more) pieces together, most likely via simulation. We would also put a lot of effort into sensitivity testing our assumptions and estimates in order to see how wrong we could be and still not get hurt too badly. For example, we would find that if the primary expected loss ratio were 68% instead of 62%, but otherwise with the same standard deviation and also represented by a Gamma distribution, then the reinsurer's expected profit is about $0, or breakeven.

This is a simplified example. More often, to protect an aggregate stop loss from catastrophe shocks, it would either cover only noncatastrophe claims, or there would be a per-occurrence limit.

Aggregate Excess Cover on An Excess Layer

Another form of aggregate excess treaty provides coverage over an aggregate deductible on a per-risk or per-occurrence excess layer. Let us return to Example 7.31, covering da Ponte's casualty exposure $700,000 excess of $300,000. Our previous aggregate loss modeling assumptions for this layer are listed in Formula 7.45. Again, we will simplistically use the Gamma model to price an aggregate deductible and limit. As discussed above, if we were seriously pricing this coverage, we would more carefully construct our aggregate loss model. We would also be very careful to account for our model and parameter uncertainty in order to get a proper spread for the aggregate loss distribution. And we would also perform a lot of sensitivity testing of our modeling assumptions and parameters. In this excess case, with a low claim frequency, the aggregate loss calculations would be most likely performed via simulation or via Panjer recursion as described in Appendix I.

Remember that for the layer $700,000 excess of $300,000 we have the following.

Formula 7.51: $700,000 Excess of $300,000 for da Ponte's Casualty Exposure at a Flat Rate of 5% (Expected RP = $5,000,000)

$$E[RL] = \$5,729,860$$

$$SD[RL] = \$1,981,724$$

$$RDF = \text{reinsurer's loss payment discount factor} = 75\%$$

$$RIXL = 5\% \text{ (or } \$266,254)$$

Reinsurer's expected profit = $434,746

$$RTER = \text{Reinsurer's target economic return (profit)}$$

$$= 15\% \text{(or } \$758,823)$$

Suppose that da Ponte Insurance Company is interested in a cover of the following form.

Formula 7.52: Aggregate Excess Cover on the Layer $700,000 Excess of $300,000 of da Ponte's Casualty Exposure

$$AP = \text{aggregate attachment point} = \$5,000,000$$

$$RLim = \text{aggregate limit} = \$5,000,000$$

$$RP = \text{reinsurance premium} = \$1,200,000$$

Since the loss expectation for the excess layer is $5,729,860, with a $5,000,000 aggregate deductible, da Ponte avoids trading dollars with the reinsurer for fairly predictable loss payments. Keeping the premium for the deductible, da Ponte also keeps the investment income.

Suppose that the reinsurer's expected internal expense for this cover is about $75,000. Also, since the reinsurer is now covering only the tail of the excess claims payments after the first $5,000,000, let us suppose that the reinsurer's loss discount factor decreases from 75% to 60%. Then the reinsurer's profit distribution is displayed in Table 7.53.

Again, the reinsurer's expected profit of $445,041 may look high in relation to the reinsurer's expected loss of $E[RL] = $1,133,265. But the standard deviation of the reinsurer's loss, $SD[RL] = $1,420,620, is again very high compared to the expectation, indicating a high risk transfer. Again, the reinsurer is getting a relatively small premium to cover part of the tail of da Ponte's casualty aggregate excess loss distribution. The reinsurer's expected profit is about the same as the $434,746 for the previous flat-rated whole excess cover, and significantly less than the RTER the reinsurer had wanted for that cover. The reinsurer calculates that there is about a 3% probability that the aggregate excess loss will exceed $AP + RLim = $10,000,000; thus a 3% probability that da Ponte will have to pay claims in this excess tail beyond the reinsurer's coverage. The aggregate limit of $5,000,000 may be acceptable to da Ponte because they believe an excess aggregate loss of $10,000,000 is impossible or, at least, highly improbable.

As mentioned above, these kind of covers are highly sensitive to the assumptions and estimates. The aggregate excess cover in Formula 7.52 becomes unprofitable for the reinsurer if the expected excess loss were really 18% more than calculated, or if the claims were paid out much faster than anticipated. When such a cover is in place, it is important to monitor carefully the develop-

TABLE 7.53

AGGREGATE EXCESS COVER ON THE LAYER $700,000 EXCESS
OF $300,000 OF DA PONTE INSURANCE COMPANY'S CASUALTY
EXPOSURE

(1) Primary Co. Aggregate Loss	(2) Reinsurer's Aggregate Loss	(3) Probability	(4) Reinsurer's Profit
$5,000,000 or less	$0	39.42%	$1,125,000
5,200,000	200,000	4.23%	1,005,000
5,400,000	400,000	4.17%	885,000
5,600,000	600,000	4.07%	765,000
5,800,000	800,000	3.94%	645,000
6,000,000	1,000,000	3.77%	525,000
6,200,000	1,200,000	3.59%	405,000
6,400,000	1,400,000	3.38%	285,000
6,600,000	1,600,000	3.17%	165,000
6,800,000	1,800,000	2.95%	45,000
7,000,000	2,000,000	2.73%	(75,000)
7,200,000	2,200,000	2.51%	(195,000)
7,400,000	2,400,000	2.29%	(315,000)
7,600,000	2,600,000	2.08%	(435,000)
7,800,000	2,800,000	1.88%	(555,000)
8,000,000	3,000,000	1.69%	(675,000)
8,200,000	3,200,000	1.52%	(795,000)
8,400,000	3,400,000	1.35%	(915,000)
8,600,000	3,600,000	1.20%	(1,035,000)
8,800,000	3,800,000	1.06%	(1,155,000)
9,000,000	4,000,000	0.94%	(1,275,000)
9,200,000	4,200,000	0.82%	(1,395,000)
9,400,000	4,400,000	0.72%	(1,515,000)
9,600,000	4,600,000	0.63%	(1,635,000)
9,800,000	4,800,000	0.55%	(1,755,000)
10,000,000 or more	5,000,000	2.98%	(1,875,000)
Total	$1,133,265	100%	$ 445,041

ment of claims payments below the aggregate excess attachment
point to see how the cover is doing. Some reinsurers have been
surprised when an aggregate cover has suddenly blown up when
claims payments reached the attachment point after many years
of no loss to the reinsurer.

Finite, or Nontraditional, Reinsurance Covers

We start with the simplest contract form.

Financial Quota-Share Treaties

The simplest example of a reinsurance cover that might be classified as nontraditional is a financial quota-share. The Example 7.24 quota share could be modified in various ways to emphasize the financial aspects of the cover and decrease the risk transfer, thus decreasing the reinsurer's margin. For example, in Formula 7.28, increasing the slide factor from 50% to 100% and decreasing the minimum commission from 25% to 10%, say, increases the reinsurer's expected profit from $109,000 to $182,000 and decreases the reinsurer's probability of losing money from 34% to 6%. Then the reinsurer can offer a significant profit sharing arrangement for those coverage years that run well. Introducing a loss carryforward from year to year also makes the distribution of the multi-year loss ratio relatively more compact, thus decreasing the risk transfer. Thus the reinsurer can take a lower ultimate margin (after all adjustments).

Da Ponte Insurance Company still gets surplus relief from the provisional commission on the ceded unearned premium reserve, and still decreases their premium-to-surplus ratio. If casualty exposure were covered, the reinsurer would credit da Ponte with some (most) of the investment income earned on the contract's cash balance according to some specified formula. As long as the contract is in a profitable position, this would be returned to da Ponte as an additional commission upon commutation or sooner. On the other hand, there might be a penalty negative commission if da Ponte were to cancel when the ongoing contract were in a deficit position.

Loss Portfolio Transfers

When most insurance people think of nontraditional reinsurance, they think of loss portfolio transfers. A cedant may cede all or part of its liability as of a specified accounting date; this may be for a line of business or territory no longer written, for an impending sale of the company, or for other reasons. Usually, the reinsurance premium is essentially the present value of the transferred estimated liability, plus reinsurer's expense, surplus use, and risk charges. And the cedant can take reinsurance credit for the liability ceded, thus offsetting all or part of the loss reserve previously set up. For a U.S. cedant, this induces a surplus benefit with respect to statutory accounting.

An example may clarify this. Suppose the da Ponte Insurance Company has been told by its domiciliary insurance department that it should increase loss reserves as of December 31, 2000 by 10%. With insurance department approval, da Ponte wishes to purchase a loss portfolio cover for this additional liability. Suppose they would like to minimize the adverse statutory surplus effect as much as possible. Suppose we have the following situation.

Example 7.54: da Ponte Loss Reserves @ 12/31/00

Carried loss reserve 12/31/00 = $300,000,000

Required additional reserve = $30,000,000

Suppose that, based upon a thorough analysis of the da Ponte's financial reports, historical exposure, historical reinsurance program, net loss development, and claim payment distributions by line and in aggregate, we determine that the additional $30,000,000 could easily be funded by a $15,000,000 payment. To get to this point, besides evaluating the adequacy of their loss reserves, we would pay careful attention to the historical claim payment patterns and their fluctuations. Has the recent exposure changed in such a way to cause a significant change in future claims payments? Have there been major changes in da Ponte's claims department or claims processing? A common analytical technique is to study ratios of cumulative loss payment for each accident year divided by ultimate estimates for each category of exposure. A simplified example is displayed in Tables 7.55 and 7.56.

TABLE 7.55

CLAIM PAYMENT DEVELOPMENT FOR NET GL BUSINESS:
CUMULATIVE PAID LOSS AS A RATIO OF ULTIMATE LOSS

Accident Year	Estimated Ultimate Loss (in $1,000's)	Evaluation Year (End of):					
		1	2	3	...	9	10
1990	$60,000	0.150	0.300	0.500	...	0.984	1.000
1991	65,000	0.050	0.370	0.650	...	0.990	
⋮	⋮	⋮	⋮	⋮	⋮		
1997	80,000	0.100	0.380	0.550			
1998	85,000	0.170	0.450				
1999	90,000	0.120					
1. Weighted Average		0.140	0.390	0.570	...	0.987	1.000
2. 3-yr Wtd Average		0.130	0.410	0.520	...	0.987	1.000
3. Maximum		0.170	0.450	0.650	...	0.990	1.000
4. Minimum		0.150	0.300	0.450	...	0.984	1.000
5. Trimmed Average		0.124	0.367	0.589	...	0.987	1.000
6. Selected "Mean"		0.124	0.367	0.589	...	0.987	1.000
7. Selected Extreme		0.170	0.450	0.650	...	1.000	1.000

The ultimate loss in the second column of Table 7.55 is our best estimate obtained by our evaluation. In our case, the trimmed average (weighted average of each column excluding the maximum and minimum) is selected as our "mean" estimate of the claim payment distribution over time. We also select a probable extreme value to use in our sensitivity testing.

The second column of Table 7.56, the "Estimated Liability as % of Total," is simply 1 − "Mean" values from Table 7.55; this is the *expected* tail left to pay for each accident year at 12/31/00. The calendar year columns display the *percent* of the second column expected to be paid in each year; these are stated as percents of the current reserve. For

TABLE 7.56

CUMULATIVE PAID LOSS AS A RATIO
OF NET GL ULTIMATE LOSS: MEAN PAYMENT DISTRIBUTION

| Acc. Year | Estimated Liability as % of Total | Percent of Liability To Be Paid in Year: | | | | | |
		2000	2001	...	2007	2008	2009
1990	0.0%	0.0%	0.0%	...	0.0%	0.0%	0.0%
1991	1.3%	100.0%	0.0%	...	0.0%	0.0%	0.0%
⋮	⋮	⋮	⋮	⋮	⋮	⋮	⋮
1997	41.1%	38.9%	25.6%	...	0.0%	0.0%	0.0%
1998	63.3%	35.1%	25.3%	...	2.1%	0.0%	0.0%
1999	87.6%	27.7%	25.3%	...	1.4%	1.5%	0.0%

| Acc. Year | Estimated Liability | Amount To Be Paid in Year (in $1,000's): | | | | | |
		2000	2001	...	2007	2008	2009
1990	$0	$0	$0	...	$0	$0	$0
1991	650	650	0	...	0	0	0
⋮	⋮	⋮	⋮	⋮	⋮	⋮	⋮
1997	36,000	14,004	9,216	...	0	0	0
1998	46,750	16,409	11,828	...	982	0	0
1999	79,200	21,938	20,038	...	1,109	1,188	0
Total	$202,548	$70,257	$51,666	...	$2,091	$1,188	$0

example, $27.7\% = (87.6\% - 63.3\%)/87.6\%$, $25.3\% = (63.3\% - 41.1\%)/87.6\%$, $1.5\% = 1.3\%/87.6\%$, $35.1\% = (63.3\% - 41.1\%)/63.3\%$, etc. In the lower part of Table 7.56, these percentages are applied to our best estimate loss reserve in the second column to get the expected claim payments in the calendar year columns. The best estimate loss reserves are $650 = (1.000 - 0.990) \times \$650,000$, $\$32,880 = (1.000 - 0.550) \times \$80,000$, etc. Then, $\$12,790 = 0.277 \times \$32,880$, etc. The Total line displays our expected claim payments by calendar year according to our "mean" claim payment distribution. The totals include payments from years not displayed.

We would also produce a Table 7.56 using the "extreme" claim payment distribution from Table 7.55.

The claim payment predictions from all the covered liabilities would be assembled. If a lower risk, lower margin treaty were contemplated, greater care would be taken with the loss discounting: the reinsurer would probably price the claim payment stream via the use of an immunizing asset portfolio. The bond maturities would be selected to allow adequate margin for a possible speed-up of the claim payments.

As mentioned earlier, suppose we determined that a premium payment of $15,000,000 could easily fund an additional $30,000,000 of claims payments, since these claims payments are out in the tail beyond the first $300,000,000 of payments. But we wish to be more clever. To zero out the statutory surplus effect on da Ponte, we would look for an attachment point where the premium payment for the loss portfolio transfer would approximately match the resulting loss reserve takedown. For example, suppose a reinsurance premium of $50,000,000 is sufficient for a cover of $80,000,000 excess of $250,000,000. This transaction would not change da Ponte's beginning statutory surplus (before reserving the additional $30,000,000). Thus, it would have zero initial statutory effect,[5] and da Ponte would be covered for the additional $30,000,000 loss reserve.

To make the loss portfolio transfer into a finite cover, the premium would be more than necessary for a full risk cover, but there would be substantial profit sharing if the cover ran off favorably, and the reinsurer would expect to keep a lower profit margin. A virtual cash fund, sometimes called an *experience account balance*, would keep track of a fund balance, including investment income, usually according to some prescribed calculations. If this experience account balance ended in a positive position, or were in a positive position when the parties agreed

---

[5]The $50,000,000 surplus benefit to da Ponte induced by this treaty would be part of surplus under statutory accounting, but would be designated "restricted surplus."

to commute the treaty some years hence, all or most of it would be returned to da Ponte as profit sharing.

Funded Aggregate Excess Covers

Another example of a nontraditional reinsurance treaty is a funded aggregate excess cover. It is clear that the aggregate excess cover of Formula 7.52 could be transformed into such a cover by increasing the premium and introducing profit sharing. One possible structure for a funded cover would be that the reinsurer takes an initial premium of $2,000,000 instead of $1,200,000. This increases the reinsurer's expected profit by $800,000 from $445,041 to $1,245,041 and decreases the reinsurer's probability of losing money from 26% to 11%. The reinsurer would deduct an expense and profit margin (*RIXL* and *RTER* combined) of perhaps only 5%, instead of the 43% previously, and allocate perhaps 90% of the calculated investment income to the experience account balance. Further, the aggregate limit at any point in time might be equal to the experience account balance plus $1,000,000, up to a maximum of $5,000,000. Loss payments might be made only annually, to allow the fund to grow as large as possible. As with the financial quota-share above, there probably would be a penalty negative commission if da Ponte cancelled in a deficit position.

Double Triggers and Other Such Animals

With the recent advent of financial derivatives and the concept of marketable catastrophe bonds, the area of finite reinsurance is changing rapidly. One concept is a reinsurance coverage that applies only if the primary insurance claims penetrate the reinsurance layer, and also simultaneously some financial index is above or below some designated value. Thus the name "double trigger." The finite reinsurance people and the investment people are busy inventing new forms of reinsurance designed to have very specific financial attributes. This promises to be a real growth area.

Reinsurance Pricing: Final Comments

We have seen some examples of how standard actuarial methods and some not-so-standard actuarial methods apply to reinsurance pricing. We must remember that there is no one right way to price reinsurance. But there are many wrong ways. Common actuarial methods should be used only to the extent they make sense. To avoid major blunders, an underwriter/actuary must always understand as well as possible the underlying primary insurance exposure and must always be aware of the differences between the reinsurance cover contemplated and that primary exposure. The differences usually involve much less specificity of information, longer claim report and settlement timing delays, and often much lower claim frequency together with much larger claim severity, all inducing a distinctly higher risk situation. But with this goes a glorious opportunity for actuaries and other technically sophisticated people to use fully their theoretical mathematical and stochastic modeling abilities and their statistical data analytical abilities.

In the next section, we will see how reinsurance loss reserving differs from primary insurance loss reserving, and we will discuss some simple methods for dealing with these differences.

REINSURANCE LOSS RESERVING

General Considerations

For a reinsurance company, the loss reserve is usually the largest uncertain number in the statement of the company's financial condition. To estimate a loss reserve properly, we must study the run-off of the past business of the company. As a result of this process, we should not only be able to estimate a loss reserve as of a certain point in time. We should also be able to estimate historical loss ratios, loss reporting patterns, and loss settlement patterns by year, by line, and by type of business in enough detail to know whether or not a particular contract or business segment is unprofitable, and if so, when. This information should also be applicable to future pricing and decision-making. The goal is to deliver good management information regarding the company's historical contract portfolio, and also deliver some indications of where the company may be going.

Reinsurance loss reserving has many of the same problems as primary insurance loss reserving, and many of the same methods can be used. But there are also various technical problems that make reinsurance loss reserving somewhat more difficult. First, we will survey some of these problems, and then examine various methods for handling them.

Reinsurance Loss Reserving Problems

There seem to be seven major technical problems that make reinsurance loss reserving somewhat more difficult than loss reserving for a primary company. These technical problems are as follows.

Problem 1: Claim report lags to reinsurers are generally longer, especially for casualty excess losses.

The claim report lag, the time from date of accident until first report to the reinsurer, is exacerbated by the lengthy reporting pipeline. A claim reported to the cedant must first be perceived as being reportable to the reinsurer, then must filter through the cedant's report system to its reinsurance accounting department, then may journey through an intermediary to the reinsurer, then must be booked and finally appear in the reinsurer's claim system. The report lag may also be lengthened by an undervaluation of serious claims by the cedant—for a long time an ultimately serious claim may be valued below the reinsurance reporting threshold (usually one half of an excess contract attachment point). This is not an indictment of primary company claims staffs, but simply an observation that a claims person, faced with insufficient and possibly conflicting information about a potentially serious claim, may tend to reserve to "expectation," which is most likely interpreted by the claims person as the mode of the probability distribution. While this modal reserving may be sufficent for most claims with a certain probable fact pattern, it is those few which blow up above this modal average which will ultimately be covered by the excess reinsurer. Thus these larger claims generally are reported later to the reinsurer than are the smaller claims the cedant carries net.

Also, certain kinds of mass tort claims, such as for asbestosis-related injuries, may have really extreme delays in discovery or in reporting to the cedant, and may have dates of loss specified finally by a court. The extreme report lags of these claims may have a big impact on the reinsurer's experience. Just as we saw these time delays adding greatly to the uncertainty in reinsurance pricing, they also add greatly to the uncertainty in reinsurance loss reserving.

Problem 2: There is a persistent upward development of most claim reserves.

Economic and social inflation cause this development. It may also be caused by a tendency of claims people to reserve at modal values, as noted in Problem 1. Also, there seems to be a tendency to underreserve allocated loss adjustment expenses. Thus, early on, the available information may indicate that a claim will pierce the reinsurance retention, but not yet indicate the ultimate severity.

Problem 3: Claims reporting patterns differ greatly by reinsurance line, by type of contract and specific contract terms, by cedant, and possibly by intermediary.

The exposure assumed by a reinsurance company can be extremely heterogeneous. This is a problem because most loss reserving methods require the existence of large, homogeneous bodies of data. The estimation methods depend upon the working of the so-called law of large numbers; that is, future development *en masse* will duplicate past development because of the sheer volume of data with similar underlying exposure. Reinsurers do not have this theoretical luxury, since many reinsurance contracts are unique. And even when there exist larger aggregates of similar exposure, claim frequency may be so low and report lags so long that there is extreme fluctuation in historical loss data. Thus, normal actuarial loss development methods may not work very well.

As we discussed in the pricing section, a reinsurer knows much less about the specific exposures being covered than does a primary carrier. Also, the heterogeneity of reinsurance coverages and specific contract terms creates a situation where the actuary never has enough information and finds it difficult to comprehend what is being covered and what is the true exposure to loss. This is especially true for a reinsurer writing small shares of brokered business.

Problem 4: Because of the heterogeneity stated in Problem 3, industry statistics are not very useful.

Every two years, the Reinsurance Association of America (RAA) publishes a summary of casualty excess reinsurance loss development statistics in the biannual *Historical Loss Development Study* [34]. These statistics give a very concrete demonstration of the long report and development lags encountered by reinsurers. However, as is noted by the RAA, the heterogeneity of the exposure and reporting differences by company must be considered when using the statistics for particular loss reserving situations.

For any two reinsurers, the Annual Statement Schedule P primary line of business exposure and loss development data are essentially incomparable. The reason for this is that Annual Statement lines of business do not provide a good breakdown of reinsurance exposure into reasonably homogeneous exposure categories useful for loss reserving. And also, most reinsurers' loss reserves are aggregated in one line of business, 30B, excess casualty.

Proper categorization follows the pricing categories we have already seen, and will vary by reinsurance company according to the types of business in which the company specializes. This is a problem because many people who are not expert in reinsurance insist upon evaluating a reinsurer's loss reserves according to Schedule P statistics. For an actuary examining a reinsurer for the purpose of loss reserving, an appropriate exposure categorization for the particular company may not be as apparent or as easily accomplished as for a primary company.

Likewise, ISO loss development statistics by line are not directly applicable to reinsurance loss development without significant adjustments that may greatly increase the indicated growth. This is so because for excess coverage, the lag in reserving or reporting claims grows with the attachment point (see Pinto and Gogol [32]), and also because primary company direct statistics do not reflect the additional delays noted in Problem 1 above. See the Reinsurance Association of America Study [33] for a comparison of reinsurance and primary claims reporting distributions. The RAA Study also has a comparison of loss development patterns by excess attachment point.

Problem 5: The reports the reinsurer receives may be lacking some important information.

Most proportional covers require only summary claims information. Often the data are not even split by accident year or by coverage year, but are reported by calendar year or by underwriting year. An underwriting year is the same as a policy year—all premiums and claims for a contract are assigned to the effective or renewal date of each contract. Calendar year or underwriting year statistics are not sufficient for evaluating loss liabilities by accident year, so various interpretations and adjustments must be made.

Even when there is individual claims reporting, as on excess covers, there often is insufficient information for the reinsurer's claims people to properly evaluate each claim without exerting great effort in pursuing information from the cedant. This is why it is desirable to· have a professional reinsurance claims staff even though the cedant is handling the claims. Also, reinsurance claims people are more accustomed to handling large claims with catastrophic injuries. Thus they are able to advise the cedant's staff (especially in the rehabilitation of seriously injured parties), and sometimes reduce the ultimate payments.

For loss reserving, it is useful to have an exposure measure against which to compare loss estimates. One possible measure is reinsurance premium by year by primary line of business. On most contracts, losses may be coded correctly by primary line, but very often the reinsurance premium is assigned to line according to a percentage breakdown estimate made at the beginning of the contract and based upon the distribution of subject premium by line. To the degree that these percentages do not accurately reflect the reinsurer's loss exposure by primary line, any comparisons of premiums and losses by line may be distorted. This adds to the difficulties noted in Problem 4.

For most treaties, premiums and losses are reported quarterly in arrears; they may not be reported (and paid) until some time in the following quarter. Thus there is an added *IBNR* exposure for both premiums and losses. The actuary must remember that, at year-end, the latest year premiums may be incomplete, so they may not be a complete measure of latest year exposure.

Problem 6: Because of the heterogeneity in coverage and reporting requirements, reinsurers often have data coding and IT systems problems.

All reinsurers have management information systems problems. The business has grown in size and complexity faster, and expectations regarding the necessary level of data detail have also grown faster, than the ability of reinsurers' data systems to handle and produce the reports requested by marketing, underwriting, claims, accounting, and actuarial staffs. This problem may be endemic to the insurance business, but it is even more true for reinsurance.

Problem 7: The size of an adequate loss reserve compared to surplus is greater for a reinsurer.

This is not a purely technical problem. It is more a management problem, and many reinsurance companies have stumbled over it. Problems 1–6 act to increase the size of an adequate loss reserve and also make it more uncertain. Thus, it is difficult for the actuary to overcome the disbelief on the part of management and marketing people, and convince them to allocate adequate resources for loss liabilities. Eventually, claims emerging on old exposure overwhelms this disbelief, at least for those who listen. A cynic might say that many reinsurance managers change jobs often enough to stay ahead of their *IBNR*. Start-up operations in particular have this problem—if there is no concrete claims run-off experience to point to, why believe a "doom-saying" actuary?

So What?

These seven problems imply that uncertainty in measurement and its accompanying financial risk are large factors in reinsurance loss reserving. This became even more important after the U.S. Tax Reform Act of 1986 required the discounting of loss reserves for income tax purposes. This discounting eliminated the implicit margin for adverse deviation that had been built into previous insurance loss reserves simply by not discounting. Insurers lost this implicit risk buffer. Since this buffer then flowed into profits and thus was taxed sooner, assets decreased. This clearly increased insurance companies' risk level. The effect upon reinsurers was even greater.

Components of a Reinsurer's Loss Reserve

The six general components of a reinsurer's statutory loss reserve are as follows.

Component 1: Case reserves reported by the ceding companies

These may be individual case reports or may be reported in bulk, depending upon the loss reporting requirements of each individual contract. Most excess contracts require individual case reports, while most proportional contracts allow summary loss reporting.

Component 2: Reinsurer additional reserves on individual claims

The reinsurer's claims department usually reviews individual case reserve reports and specifies *additional case reserves* (*ACR*) on individual claims as necessary. Additional case reserves may vary considerably by contract and by cedant.

Component 3: Actuarial estimate of future development on Components (1) and (2)

The future development on known case reserves in total is sometimes known is *IBNER*, Incurred (and reported) But Not Enough Reserved.

Component 4: Actuarial estimate of pure IBNR

Most actuaries would prefer that separate estimates be made for Components (3) and (4), the estimate of pure *IBNR*, Incurred But Not Reported. However, because of limitations in their data systems, in practice most reinsurers combine the estimates of Components (3) and (4). Depending upon the reinsurer's mix of business, these together may amount to more than half the total loss reserve.

Unless otherwise noted, the term *IBNR* in this chapter stands for the sum of *IBNER* and pure *IBNR*.

Component 5: Discount for future investment income

Insurance companies are allowed to take statutory accounting credit for future investment income on the assets supporting workers compensation permanent total cases, automobile PIP annuity claims and medical professional liability claims. Some companies do discount these claims reserves, and some don't. And, of course, as mentioned above, the U.S. Tax Reform Act of 1986 requires discounting of loss reserves for income tax purposes.

Component 6: Risk load

The last component of a loss reserve should be the risk loading or adverse deviation loading necessary to keep the reserve at a suitably conservative level, so as not to allow very uncertain income to flow into profits too quickly. Some loss reserving professionals prefer to build this into the reserve implicitly by employing conservative assumptions and methodologies. However, many actuaries would prefer to see it estimated and accounted for explicitly. Because of the long-tailed nature of much of their exposure and its heterogeneity and the uncertainty of their statistics, this component is theoretically more important for reinsurers.

A General Procedure

The four steps involved in a reinsurance loss reserving methodology are as follows.

Step 1: Partition the reinsurance portfolio into reasonably homogeneous exposure groups that are relatively consistent over time with respect to mix of business (exposures).

It is obviously important to segregate the contracts and loss exposure into categories of business on the basis of loss development potential. Combining loss data from nonhomogeneous exposures whose mix has changed over time can increase measurement error rather than decrease it.

Reasonably homogeneous exposure categories for reinsurance loss reserving have been discussed in the actuarial literature and follow closely the categories used for pricing. Table 7.57 lists various important variables for partitioning a reinsurance portfolio. All affect the pattern of claim report lags to the reinsurer and the development of individual case amounts. The listing is meant to be in approximate priority order.

TABLE 7.57

IMPORTANT VARIABLES FOR PARTITIONING A REINSURANCE PORTFOLIO INTO REASONABLY HOMOGENEOUS EXPOSURE CATEGORIES

- Line of business: property, casualty, bonding, ocean marine, etc.
- Type of contract: facultative, treaty, finite (or "financial")
- Type of reinsurance cover: quota share, surplus share, excess per-risk, excess per-occurrence, aggregate excess, catastrophe, loss portfolio transfer, etc.
- Primary line of business—for casualty
- Attachment point—for casualty
- Contract terms: flat-rated, retro-rated, sunset clause, share of loss adjustment expense, claims-made or occurrence coverage, etc.
- Type of cedant: small, large, or E&S company
- Intermediary

Obviously, a partition by all eight variables would split a contract portfolio into numerous pieces, many with too little credibility. However, after partitioning by the first five variables, it may be desirable to recognize the effects of some of the other variables on certain classes of business. For example, whether or not a casualty contract covers on an occurrence or claims-made basis is obviously important. The RAA now requests loss development data for its biannual study to be segregated by specified attachment point ranges. These ranges are a useful guide to any reinsurer wishing to so classify their own claims data and exposure.

Each reinsurer's portfolio is unique and extremely heterogeneous. In order to determine a suitable partition of exposure for reserving and results analysis, we must depend greatly upon the knowledge and expertise of the people writing and underwriting the exposures, the people examining individual claim reports, and the people processing data from the cedants. Their knowledge, together with elementary data analysis (look at simple loss development statistics), help the actuary understand which of the variables are most important.

One possible first-cut partition of assumed reinsurance exposure is shown in Table 7.58. Remember that there is no such thing as a "typical" reinsurance company.

TABLE 7.58

EXAMPLE OF MAJOR EXPOSURE CATEGORIES FOR A
REINSURANCE COMPANY

- Treaty casualty excess
- Treaty casualty proportional
- Treaty property excess
- Treaty property proportional
- Treaty property catastrophe
- Facultative casualty
- Facultative property
- Surety
- Fidelity
- Ocean marine
- Inland marine
- Construction risks
- Aviation
- Finite, or nontraditional, reinsurance
- Miscellaneous special contracts, pools and associations
- Asbestos, pollution, and other health hazard or mass tort claims

The last item in Table 7.58 is not really an exposure category. But anyone in their right mind would advocate that these types of claims should be treated separately for any insurance company, especially a reinsurance company.

Within the major categories, the exposure should be further refined into treaty and facultative, if not already specified. Also, all significant excess exposure should be further segregated by type of retention (per-occurrence excess vs. aggregate excess).

Treaty casualty excess exposure should be further segregated by attachment point range and by primary line (automobile liability, general liability, workers compensation, medical professional liability). Each of these categories would be expected to have distinctly different lags for claims reported to the reinsurer.

Categories for treaty casualty proportional business would be similar. As we have discussed, some contracts classified as proportional are not shares of first dollar primary layers, but rather shares of higher excess layers. Thus, whether the exposure is ground-up or excess is an important classification variable.

Loss reserving categories for facultative casualty would certainly separate out automatic primary programs (pro rata share of ground-up exposure) and automatic nonprimary programs (excess). Certificate exposure should be split by attachment point range, if possible, but at least into buffer versus umbrella layers, and then further by primary line.

Likewise for property and other exposures, the loss reserving categories should correspond closely to the pricing categories.

It will be convenient to discuss steps 2 and 3 together.

Step 2: Analyze the historical development patterns. If possible, consider individual case reserve development and the emergence of IBNR claims separately.

Step 3: Estimate the future development. If possible, estimate the bulk reserves for IBNER and pure IBNR separately.

In our discussion, we will only deal with aggregate claim dollar development of both *IBNER* and pure *IBNR* combined. For certain exposures, especially longer-tail lines, it is often a good idea to deal with them separately. Some techniques for doing so are discussed in the chapter on loss reserving.

For suitably homogeneous categories of exposure, *expected* reinsurance claim development patterns are very stable. However, because of the extreme variability in the year-to-year data, these patterns should be studied using claims data over long time periods, as long as the *expected* patterns are reasonably stable from year-to-year. Usually the longer the time period, the better, in order to obtain accurate estimates of the underlying pattern. This is usually a large, time-consuming analytical job. Because of year-end time pressures, it is almost always a good idea to perform the in-depth analysis of claim development patterns during the third or fourth quarter. The idea is to construct our models and estimate most of the parameters before we get to the year-end crunch. Then, at year-end, and at the end of each quarter, we simply apply our parameterized models to the year-end or quarter-end claims and exposure data to estimate our *IBNR* (remember, here we mean both *IBNER* and pure *IBNR*).

Claim Report and Payment Lags

For analyzing and understanding reinsurance claims development patterns, it is useful to consider the inverse of the usual chainladder age-to-ultimate development factors—we call the factor inverses "*lags*." This view produces a time lag curve, $y = Rlag(t)$, where t measures time, like that shown in Graph 7.59.

As the age goes from 0 years to 10 years, the lag goes from $Rlag(0) = 0\%$ to $Rlag(10) = 99.9\%$. The graph looks like a probability cumulative distribution function (cdf), and, with a bit of imagination, can be interpreted as one. $Rlag(t)$ can be read as the probability that any particular claims dollar will be reported to the reinsurer by time t. This view of the claims reporting process allows us to compute statistics, such as the expected value (in years), by which we can compare one claim report pattern with another. This view also helps us fit smooth curves to the often chaotic tails of claims development data, and compute values at intermediate points. The claims report lag in Graph 7.59 is a Gamma distribution with mean 2.5 years and standard deviation 1.5 years.

The same lag idea applies to claim payment patterns.

GRAPH 7.59

CLAIM REPORT LAG GRAPH

Percentage Claim Dollars Reported

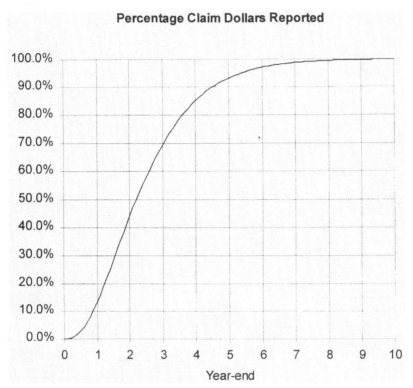

Year-end

It is convenient to discuss the methods to be used for the historical analyses and the estimation methods for the different exposure categories according to the lengths of the average claim dollar report lags.

Methods for Short-tailed Exposure Categories

As is generally true, the best methodologies to use are those that provide reasonable accuracy for least effort and cost. For short-tailed lines of business, such as most property coverage exposure, losses are reported and settled quickly, so loss liabilities are relatively small and run off very quickly. Thus, elaborate loss development estimation machinery is unnecessary.

Reinsurance categories of business that are usually short-tailed are listed in Table 7.60. But, as with any statement about reinsurance, be careful of exceptions.

TABLE 7.60

REINSURANCE CATEGORIES THAT ARE USUALLY SHORT-TAILED (WITH RESPECT TO CLAIM REPORTING AND DEVELOPMENT)

Category	Comments*
Treaty property proportional	Be wary of recent catastrophes
Treaty property catastrophe	Be wary of recent catastrophes
Treaty property excess	Possibly exclude high layers, and be wary of recent catastrophes
Facultative property	Exclude construction risks, and be wary of recent catastrophes
Fidelity proportional	

*Exclude all international exposure, if possible, since there may be significant reporting delays.

Estimation Methods

Many reinsurers reserve property business by setting *IBNR* equal to some percentage of the latest-year earned premium. This is sometimes a reasonable method for non-major-catastrophe "filtered" claims, as defined in the pricing section. It is a good idea to consider major storms and other major catastrophes separately. A recent catastrophe will cause real *IBNR* liability to far exceed the normal reserve. Claims from major catastrophes may not be fully reported and finalized for years, even on proportional covers.

Another simple method used for short-tailed exposure is to reserve up to a selected loss ratio for new lines of business or for other situations where the reinsurer has few or no loss statistics. For short-tailed exposure, provided the selected loss ratio bears some reasonable relationship to past years' experience and provided that it is larger than that computed from already-reported claims, this is a reasonable method for filtered (noncatastrophic) claims.

For some proportional treaties, summary loss reporting may assign claims by underwriting year, according to inception or renewal date of the reinsurance treaty, instead of by accident year. If the reinsurer's claims accounting staff records the reported claims likewise, the loss statistics for each false "accident" year may show great development because of future occurring accidents. In this situation, a more accurate loss development picture and estimation of *IBNR* can be obtained by assigning these "accident" year losses to approximate true accident year by percentage estimates based upon the underwriting year inception date and the general report lag for the type of exposure. Summary claims reported on a calendar (accounting) year basis can likewise be assigned to accident year by percentage estimates, if necessary. For short-tailed lines for which the *IBNR* is estimated as a percentage of premium or reserved up to a selected loss ratio, these re-assignments are unnecessary.

Methods for Medium-Tailed Exposure Categories

Let us consider any exposure for which claims are almost completely settled within five years and with average aggregate dollar claim report lag of one to two years to be medium-tailed for this discussion. Reinsurance categories of business that are usually medium-tailed are listed in Table 7.61.

Even if a property claim is known almost immediately, its ultimate value may not be. Thus it may take longer to penetrate a higher per-risk excess attachment point. This happens more often if time element coverage is involved. The discovery period for construction risk covers may extend years beyond the contract (loss occurrence) period. So for both these exposures, claim report lags may be significantly longer than normal for property business.

TABLE 7.61

REINSURANCE CATEGORIES THAT ARE USUALLY MEDIUM-TAILED (WITH RESPECT TO CLAIM REPORTING AND DEVELOPMENT)

Category	Comments
Treaty property excess higher layers	If it is possible to separate these from working layers
Construction risks	If it is possible to separate these from other property exposure
Surety	
Fidelity excess	
Ocean marine	
Inland marine	
International property	
Non-casualty aggregate excess	Lags are longer than for the underlying exposure

For surety exposure, it is usually a good idea to consider losses gross of salvage and, separately, salvage recoveries. The gross losses are reported fairly quickly, but the salvage recoveries have a longer tail. It is instructive to consider the ratio of salvage to gross loss for mature years. This ratio is fairly stable and may help explain predictions for recent coverage years as long as the underwriters can predict how the salvage ratio may have slowly changed over time.

Estimation Methods

A useful *IBNR* estimation method for medium-tailed lines of business is to use the standard American casualty actuarial *Chain-ladder (CL) Method* of age-to-age factors calculated from cumulative aggregate incurred loss triangles, with or without *ACRs*. This is described fully in the chapter on loss reserving. If accident year data exist, this is good methodology. An advantage of this method is that it strongly correlates future development both with an overall lag pattern and with the claims reported for each accident year. A major disadvantage is simply that the *IBNR* is so heavily correlated with reported claims that, at least for longer-tailed lines, the reported, very random nose wags the extremely large tail estimate for recent, immature years.

It is sometimes true that paid loss development is more stable than reported loss development. If so, then a chainladder estimate of ultimate loss by accident year may be obtained using paid lags. Of course, the problem is that the estimation error may be even greater for immature, recent accident years than it is for reported loss chainladder estimation.

Methods for Long-Tailed Exposure Categories

Just as for pricing, the real problem in loss reserving is long-tailed exposure, especially excess casualty reinsurance. These are the exposures for which the average aggregate claims dollar report lag is over two years and whose claims are not settled for many years. Reinsurance categories of business that are usually long-tailed are listed in Table 7.62.

TABLE 7.62

REINSURANCE CATEGORIES THAT ARE USUALLY LONG-TAILED
(WITH RESPECT TO CLAIM REPORTING AND DEVELOPMENT)

Category	Comments
Treaty casualty excess	Includes the longest lags except for the APH claims listed below
Treaty casualty proportional	Some of this exposure may possibly be medium-tailed
Facultative casualty	
Casualty aggregate excess	Lags are longer than for the underlying exposure
Asbestos, pollution and other health hazard and mass tort claims	May be the longest of the long tails

For most reinsurance companies, this is where most of the loss reserve lies, and almost all the *IBNR*. So it is important for us to spend most of our analytical and estimation effort here. The first step is to separate these exposures into finer, more homogeneous categories. This is, of course, an iterative process. We depend upon our company's marketing, underwriting, claims, and accounting personnel for the first-stage categorization. Further refinements will then depend upon our hypothesis testing and upon our investigation of various comments from the marketing and underwriting people as they receive from us the estimated *IBNR* by major contract or category based upon the latest categorization. Some of the larger, more important contracts are looked upon at least partially on a standalone basis.

Asbestos, Pollution, Other Health Hazard and Other Mass Tort Exposures

We separate out claims arising from asbestosis, pollution clean-up, other health hazard (sometimes collectively known as "*APH*") and other mass tort situations for special consideration. Because of the catastrophic significance of these types of claims (nothing for many years, then suddenly, gigantic totals), they would drastically distort the development statistics if left in the remaining filtered (noncatastrophic) claims data. Also, it is unlikely that the usual actuarial loss development techniques, if used blindly, would yield reasonable answers for these types of claims.

In the past few years, various models have been developed for estimating asbestos and pollution clean-up liabilities. The large actuarial consulting firms have been in the forefront of this development. The models are extremely complex and require very detailed input regarding coverages exposed to these types of claims. Unless we, the reinsurer, have a very large, long, stable and fairly complete claims development history, we judge that it is better that we and our *APH* claims specialists work with one of the actuarial consultants to develop our liability estimates.

Beyond asbestos and pollution clean-up, the question of which exposures or claims should be treated separately or specially is difficult. We should discuss this thoroughly with our claims and underwriting staff. For example, it is desirable to treat claims-made coverages separately from occurrence coverages, if possible. Also, it should be clear that claims from commuted contracts should be excluded from the usual triangles, since their development is artificially truncated (cut off), and thus would distort the noncommuted complete development patterns.

Estimation Methods

The standard *CL* Method is sometimes used for long-tail exposures. But, the problem is that for very long-tailed lags, the resulting *IBNR* estimate for recent, green years is extremely variable, depending upon the few reported or paid claims to date.

An alternative estimation method is the *Bornheutter–Ferguson (BF) Method* (Bornheutter and Ferguson [25]), which is discussed in the chapter on loss reserving. This method uses a selected loss ratio for each coverage year and an aggregate dollar report lag pattern specifying the percentage of ultimate aggregate loss expected to be reported as of any evaluation date. An advantage of this method is that it correlates future development for each year with an exposure measure equal to the reinsurance premium multiplied by a selected loss ratio. Disadvantages with the *BF IBNR* estimate are:

1. It is very dependent upon the selected loss ratio.

2. The estimate for each accident year does not reflect the particular to-date reported losses for that year, unless the selected loss ratio is chosen with this in mind.

Since the loss ratio for a given accident year is strongly correlated with the place of that year in the reinsurance profitability cycle, so is the to-date reported loss. It would seem to be desirable to use this fact in the *IBNR* estimate. As noted before, the reinsurance profitability cycles are more extreme than primary insurance cycles. Thus, when using the *BF* Method, one must select the accident year loss ratios carefully.

Stanard–Bühlmann (Cape Cod) Method

An estimation method that overcomes some of the problems with the *CL* and *BF* Methods was independently derived by James Stanard (described in Patrik [31] and Weissner [36]) and by Hans Bühlmann (internal Swiss Re publications). This *Stanard–Bühlmann (SB) Method* is known to European actuaries as the *Cape Cod Method* because Hans Bühlmann first proposed it at a meeting on Cape Cod. As with the *CL* and *BF* Methods, this method uses an aggregate reported claim dollar lag pattern, which may or may not be estimated via the *CL* Method or via some other method. The key innovation of the *SB* Method is that the ultimate expected loss ratio for all years combined is estimated from the overall reported claims experience, instead of being selected judgmentally, as in the *BF* Method. A problem with the *SB* Method is that the *IBNR* by year is highly dependent upon the rate-level adjusted premium by year. The user must adjust each year's premium to reflect the rate-level cycle on a relative basis. But this is also a problem with the *BF* Method.

A simple example will help explain the *SB* Method.

For a given exposure category, assume that the yearly earned risk pure premiums (net of reinsurance commissions, brokerage fees and internal expenses) can be adjusted to remove any suspected rate-level differences by year. Thus, we believe that each adjusted year has the same expected loss ratio. In primary insurance terminology, assume that the risk pure premiums have been put on-level. This adjustment is difficult and uncertain, but must be done if we are to have a reasonably consistent exposure base. Netting out the commissions and brokerage fees is usually easy, since these are separately coded by contract in our accounting database. Netting out the internal expenses is more difficult, since these are strictly internal numbers, not usually coded to contract. If it is too difficult or impossible to net out the internal expense, we need not bother, since all we need is a relative exposure base, not an absolute one. We study primary business rate levels by considering industrywide Schedule P line loss ratios by year, and work with our underwriters to adjust these rate relativities for our own reinsurance exposure categories. Let *ELR* represent the unknown expected loss ratio to adjusted earned risk pure premium.

Suppose that Table 7.63 displays the current experience for this category. For clarity, to deal with an example with only five years, we use a report lag that reaches 100% at the end of the sixth year.

TABLE 7.63

STANARD–BÜHLMANN (CAPE COD) METHOD
DATA AS OF 12/31/00 (IN 1,000'S)

(1) Calendar/ Accident Year	(2) Earned Risk Pure Premium	(3) Adjusted Premium	(4) Aggregate Reported Loss	(5) Aggregate Loss Report Lag	(6) "Used-Up" Premium (3) × (5)
1996	$ 6,000	$ 8,000	$ 7,000	95%	$ 7,600
1997	7,000	7,000	5,000	85%	5,590
1998	8,000	6,000	3,000	70%	4,200
1999	9,000	7,000	2,000	50%	3,500
2000	10,000	10,000	4,000	30%	3,000
Total	$40,000	$38,000	$21,000	n.a.	$24,250

We will explain column 6 of Table 7.63 in the following discussion.

The *SB ELR* and *IBNR* estimates are given by Formula 7.64.

Formula 7.64: Stanard–Bühlmann (Cape Cod) ELR and IBNR Estimates

$$SBELR = \frac{\Sigma\{RRL(k)\}}{\Sigma\{ARPP(k) \times Rlag(k)\}}$$

$$SBIBNR(k) = SBELR \times ARPP(k) \times (1 - Rlag(k))$$

where   *SBELR* = Stanard–Bühlmann estimate of the *ELR*

   SBIBNR(k) = SB *IBNR* estimate, year *k*

$RRL(k)$ = reported reinsurance loss, year k

$ARPP(k)$ = adjusted risk pure premium, year k

$Rlag(k)$ = aggregate claim dollar report lag, year k

Some *SB* practitioners call the term $ARPP(k) \times Rlag(k)$, the *used-up premium* for year k. You can see that it is that fraction of premium corresponding to the percent of ultimate claims expected to be reported as of the evaluation date. It is the premium earned according to the expected reported claims. Thus *SBELR* is the loss ratio of reported loss divided by used-up premium. So how do we get to these equations?

First of all, simply define $SBIBNR(k)$ to be $SBELR \times ARPP(k) \times (1 - Rlag(k))$. This definition is the same as in the *BF* Method. The only difference is that the *SB* Method will tell us how to estimate *SBELR*. Since the total *IBNR* is the sum of the *IBNR* from each year, then *SBIBNR* can be written as follows.

$$SBIBNR = \Sigma SBIBNR(k)$$
$$= \Sigma \{SBELR \times ARPP(k) \times (1 - Rlag(k))\} \text{ by definition}$$
$$= SBELR \times \Sigma \{ARPP(k) \times (1 - Rlag(k))\}$$

Then, since a loss ratio is simply losses divided by premium, we may write *SBELR* as follows.

$$SBELR = \frac{RRL + SBIBNR}{ARPP}$$
$$= \frac{RRL + SBELR \times \Sigma \{ARPP(k) \times (1 - Rlag(k))\}}{ARPP}$$

Or

$$SBELR \times ARPP = RRL + SBELR \times \Sigma \{ARPP(k) \times (1 - Rlag(k))\}$$
$$= RRL + SBELR \times ARPP$$
$$- SBELR \times \Sigma \{ARPP(k) \times Rlag(k)\}$$

Or, subtracting $SBELR \times ARPP$ from both sides,

$$SBELR \times \Sigma\{ARPP(k) \times Rlag(k)\} = RRL$$

Or

$$SBELR = \frac{RRL}{\Sigma\{ARPP(k) \times Rlag(k)\}}$$

$$= \$21{,}000/(\$8{,}000 \times 0.95 + \$7{,}000 \times 0.85$$
$$+ \$6{,}000 \times 0.70 + \$7{,}000 \times 0.50$$
$$+ \$10{,}000 \times 0.30)$$

$$= \frac{\$21{,}000}{\$24{,}250}$$

$$= 0.866$$

Table 7.65 compares $IBNR$ and estimated ultimate loss ratios for the CL and SB Methods, using the information in Table 7.63 (remember to use the adjusted risk pure premium, $ARPP$, not the original premium, in the SB calculation). The BF Method cannot be compared, since the BF loss ratios are not estimated by formula.

TABLE 7.65

COMPARISON OF CHAINLADDER AND STANARD–BÜHLMANN
METHODS

(1) Cal/Acc. Year	(2) Earned Risk Pure Premium	(3) CL IBNR	(4) CL Loss Ratio	(5) SB IBNR	(6) SB Loss Ratio
1996	$ 6,000	$ 368	123%	$ 346	122%
1997	7,000	882	84%	909	84%
1998	8,000	1,286	54%	1,589	57%
1999	9,000	2,000	44%	3,031	56%
2000	10,000	9,333	133%	6,062	100%
Total	$40,000	$13,870	87%	$11,908	82%

Look at the differences in the 1999 and 2000 loss ratios. As long as the rate relativity adjustments to yearly earned risk pure premium are reasonably accurate, the estimates for recent, immature years and the overall answer are more accurate with the *SB* Method. It is easy to see that the above example would be even more vivid if a real longer-tailed exposure were used.

Credibility IBNR Estimates

For situations where we don't have complete confidence in the year-to-year rate-level premium adjustments, we can calculate a "credibility" *IBNR* estimate by weighing together the *CL* and *SB* estimates. Intuitively, we would want to give more weight to the *SB* estimate for recent, green years, where the *CL* estimate has a high level of variance, and more weight to the *CL* estimate for older years, where we trust the cumulative rate-level adjustments less. One way of doing this is to use some simple, monotonic function of the report lag as the credibility weight for the *CL* estimate. A simple linear function that yields such a credibility estmate as follows.

Formula 7.66: A Simple "Credibility" IBNR Estimate

$\text{Cred}\,IBNR(k) = Z(k) \times CLIBNR(k) + (1 - Z(k)) \times SBIBNR(k)$

where $Z(k) = CF \times Rlag(k)$

and $0 \leq CF$ = credibility factor ≤ 1

$Rlag(k)$ = report lag for year k

$\text{Cred}\,IBNR(k)$ = credibility *IBNR* for year k

$CLIBNR(k)$ = *CL IBNR* for year k

$SBIBNR(k)$ = *SB IBNR* for year k

Using the information in Tables 7.63 and 7.65, we can calculate a credibility *IBNR*, with $CF = 0.5$ for example, in Table 7.67.

TABLE 7.67

CALCULATION OF "CREDIBILITY" *IBNR*

(1)	(2)	(3)	(4)	(5)	(6)
Cal/Acc. Year	Earned Risk Pure Premium	Claim Report Lag	*CL IBNR*	*SB IBNR*	"Credibility" *IBNR*
1996	$ 6,000	95%	$ 368	$ 346	$ 356
1997	7,000	85%	882	909	898
1998	8,000	70%	1,286	1,589	1,483
1999	9,000	50%	2,000	3,031	2,773
2000	10,000	30%	9,333	6,062	6,553
Total	$40,000	n.a.	$13,870	$11,908	$12,063

For example, in Table 7.67, $356 = (0.5) \times (0.95) \times \$368 + (1 - (0.5) \times (0.95)) \times \$346$.

If we were dealing with a real live long-tail example, we would see many more accident years worth of data. Depending upon the length of the claim report and payment lags, we would probably want to be looking at 25 or more years of claims data. We would talk with our marketing people, underwriters, and claims people to see if there are any special contracts, exposures, or types of claims that should be treated separately. We would want to know of any particularly large individual claims which should be censored or otherwise dealt with so as not to have an undue random impact upon either the estimation of the claims report and payment lags or upon the *IBNR* estimation.

Other "Credibility" Procedures

Some reinsurance actuaries also weigh together the *IBNR* estimates obtained separately from reported claims data and paid claims data. A problem with reported claims data is that they include case reserves set up according to the judgments of many claims people, perhaps varying over time. Thus they may lack consistency over time. If we have paid claims data over enough

accident and payment years to capture the long tail, and we believe the data to have a fairly consistent *expected* payment pattern
over the accident years, these data may exhibit more stability than
the reported claims data. Thus they may also be useful for estimating *IBNR* liabilities. The weighing can again be intuitively
simplistic. Perhaps we might decide to use the relative claim report and payment lags for each year as weights.

Some reinsurance actuaries also want to use the information
inherent in the pricing of the exposure. If actuarial pricing techniques similar to those discussed in the pricing section are used,
we automatically have estimates of *ELR* with respect to risk pure
premium for each contract. We may monitor their accuracy and
average them over suitable exposure categories. We may call
these average pricing *ELR*'s our *a priori ELR* estimates and use
them instead of or in conjunction with the *SB ELR*'s. We can use
them as our *BF ELR* estimates and calculate *BF IBNR* with them.
We can then weigh this *a priori IBNR* against the *CL IBNR* to
obtain our final "credibility" *IBNR* estimates. You will find an
interesting discussion of this credibility method in Benktander
[23] and Mack [30].

You can see there are many possibilities, and no single right
method. Any good actuary will want to use as many legiti-
mate methods for which reasonably good information and time
is available, and compare and contrast the estimates from these
methods. As with pricing, it is often informative to see the spread
of estimates derived from different approaches. This helps us understand better the range and distribution of possibilities, and
may give us some idea of the sensitivity of our answers to
varying assumptions and varying estimation methodologies. A
distribution-free method for calculating the variance of chainladder loss reserve estimates is described in Mack [29].

Alternative Estimation Methodologies
Suppose, as above, we have only the summary development
triangles of reported or paid claims. We can obtain maximum

likelihood estimates of the parameters for a continuous lag model (such as the Gamma used above) by treating the increments for each development interval as grouped data, exactly as discussed by Hogg and Klugman [11] for claim severity. The reported claim dollars for each accident year can be considered to be a sample from a truncated model (unknown tail). A slight practical problem here may be negative increments. But for the estimation, the time intervals for the grouping of the data need not necessarily all be one-year periods, so the intervals can always be adjusted to avoid negative increments.

Various statistical and reasonableness tests can then help us decide which lag model best describes the data, and which we believe will best predict future claims development. This model with the fitted parameters can then be used to estimate the probability distribution for the *IBNR*, calculate various statistics such as the expectation and standard deviation, and predict *IBNR* claim emergence.

More advanced models, as discussed in the chapter on loss reserving, could use claim counts and amounts and construct a stochastic model for the whole claims development process. These models are useful for very long-tail exposures. They can give us more information and provide insight we can't get from the simpler models discussed above. But they are very much more complicated, and look to many actuaries like black boxes. A problem with increasingly sophisticated methodologies is that the answers may become less intuitive and may be much more difficult for the actuary to understand and explain to management.

An advantage of using a claim count/claim severity model is that we can contemplate intuitively satisfying models for various lag distributions, such as the time from loss event occurrence until first report and the lag from report until settlement. We can then connect these lags with appropriate models for the dollar reserving and payments on individual claims up through settlement. For surveys of some advanced methodologies, see the chapter on Loss Reserving and various Advanced Techniques sessions in Casualty Loss Reserve Seminar transcripts [26].

Monitoring and Testing Predictions

A loss reserve or an *IBNR* reserve is derived from a hypothesis about future claims settlements for past events. In order to validate our methodology, we must test our predictions against actual future experience. Monitoring and testing quarterly claims run-off against predictions may provide early warning of problems.

For short-tailed and medium-tailed lines, this can be fairly simple. As long as current accident year claims can be reasonably separated from past accident year run-off, the run-off can be compared with the previous year-end reported open and *IBNR* reserves. For long-tailed lines, slightly more sophisticated comparisons are necessary.

Perhaps the best way to describe a simple *IBNR* monitoring methodology is through the use of an example. We will consider *GL* exposure for treaty casualty excess contracts with attachment points in RAA range 4. RAA range 4 currently has attachment points between $1,251,000 to $3,500,000. We, of course, deflate this range back via estimated *GL* ground-up claims severity trend, so that we include the appropriate contracts from earlier years in our database.

Table 7.68 is one possible format. Columns 4 and 5 are a Gamma distribution with mean 5 years and standard deviation 3 years. Column 5 is column 4 adjusted by one half year.

Interpreting Table 7.68 is difficult. Column 8 tells us there was $809,000 more claims emergence in the first half of 2001 than the $2,437,000 = $63,240,000 − $60,803,000 expected. This is about 33% more than expected. Is this purely random? Or does it indicate that the beginning *IBNR* reserve was too small, or the lags too short? We will want to watch these claims emergence

TABLE 7.68

TREATY CASUALTY EXCESS WORKING COVER CLAIMS EMERGENCE TEST
MONITORING 12/31/00 *IBNR* AS OF 6/30/01 (IN $1,000'S)

(1) Acc. Year	(2) Claims @ 12/31/00	(3) IBNR @ 12/31/00	(4) Claim Report Lag @ 12/31/00	(5) Claim Report Lag @ 6/30/01	(6) Predicted Claims @ 6/30/01	(7) Actual Claims @ 6/30/01	(8) Difference (7) − (6)
1981	$ 3,927	$ 3	99.92%	99.94%	$ 3,928	$ 3,927	$ −1
1982	2,743	3	99.88%	99.90%	2,744	2,743	−1
1983	1,052	2	99.80%	99.84%	1,052	1,152	100
1984	5,721	18	99.69%	99.75%	5,725	5,641	−84
1985	2,325	12	99.50%	99.61%	2,327	2,325	−2
...	...	...	...	...	...	...	...
1993	6,167	1,075	85.15%	87.74%	6,354	6,285	−69
1994	2,364	647	78.52%	82.10%	2,472	3,549	1,077
1995	4,642	2,031	69.56%	74.35%	4,962	4,752	−210
1996	2,086	1,512	57.98%	64.11%	2,306	2,201	−105
1997	1,148	1,468	43.89%	51.22%	1,340	1,245	−95
1998	2,359	5,997	28.23%	36.15%	3,021	2,859	−162
1999	542	3,533	13.30%	20.47%	834	1,478	644
2000	0	5,182	2.86%	7.25%	234	0	−234
Total	$60,803	$22,635	5.00 years average	5.00 years average	$63,240	$64,049	$ 809

Notes:

Col. 3 = (Col. 2) × (1.00 − Col. 4)/(Col. 4) except for 2000. For simplicity here, the Col. 3
IBNR is straight chainladder; in practice, it would be our credibility *IBNR*.

Col. 6 = Col. 2 + (Col. 3) × (Col. 5 − Col. 4)/(1.00 − Col. 4) tests each quarter to see if a positive difference persists. This might lead us to decide to lengthen the lags for this exposure.

Reinsurance Loss Reserving: Final Comments

We have seen some examples of how standard actuarial methods and some not-so-standard actuarial methods apply to reinsurance loss reserving. We must remember that there is no one right way to estimate reinsurance loss reserves. But there are many wrong ways. Common actuarial methods should be used only to the extent they make sense. To avoid major blunders, the actuary must always understand as well as possible the types of reinsurance exposure in the reinsurance company's portfolio. The differences from primary company loss reserving mainly involve much less specificity of information, longer report and settlement timing delays, and often much smaller claim frequency together with much larger severity, all inducing a distinctly higher risk situation. But with this goes a glorious opportunity for actuaries to use fully their theoretical mathematical and stochastic modeling abilities and their statistical data analytical abilities.

REFERENCES

Included here are also works in addition to those cited in the text.

References for Introduction

[1] Cass, R. Michael, Peter R. Kensicki, Gary S. Patrik, and Robert C. Reinarz, *Reinsurance Practices* (2nd ed.), Malvern, PA: Insurance Institute of America, 1997.

[2] Elliott, Michael W., Bernard L. Webb, Howard N. Anderson, and Peter R. Kensicki, *Principles of Reinsurance* (2nd ed.), Malvern, PA: Insurance Institute of America, 1997.

[3] Reinarz, Robert C., Janice O. Schloss, Gary S. Patrik, and Peter R. Kensicki, *Reinsurance Practices*, Malvern, PA: Insurance Institute of America, 1990.

[4] Strain, Robert W., *Reinsurance*, New York: The College of Insurance, 1980.

[5] Webb, Bernard L., Howard N. Anderson, John A. Cookman, and Peter R. Kensicki, *Principles of Reinsurance*, Malvern, PA: Insurance Institute of America, 1990.

[6] Webb, Bernard L., Connor M. Harrison, and James J. Markham, *Insurance Company Operations*, Vol. II, Chapters 8 and 9, Malvern, PA: American Institute for Property and Liability Underwriters, 1992.

References for Reinsurance Pricing

[7] Bear, Robert A., and Kenneth J. Nemlick, "Pricing the Impact of Adjustable Features and Loss Sharing Provisions of Reinsurance Treaties," *Proceedings of the Casualty Actuarial Society*, 1990, Vol. 77.

[8] Daykin, C. D., T. Pentikäinen, and M. Pesonen, *Practical Risk theory for Actuaries*, London: Chapman and Hall, 1994.

[9] Bühlmann, Hans, *Mathematical Methods in Risk Theory*, New York: Springer-Verlag, 1970.

[10] Heckman, Philip E., and Glenn G. Meyers, "The Calculation of Aggregate Loss Distributions From Claim Severity and Claim Count Distributions," *Proceedings of the Casualty Actuarial Society*, 1983, 70:22–61; discussion by Gary Venter, 1983, 62–73; exhibits by Heckman and Meyers, 1983, 71:49–66.

[11] Hogg, Robert V., and Stuart A. Klugman, *Loss Distributions*, New York: Wiley, 1984.

[12] Klugman, Stuart A., Harry H. Panjer, and Gordon E. Willmot, *Loss Models: From Data to Decisions*, New York: Wiley, 1998.

[13] Ludwig, Stephen, J., "An Exposure Rating Approach to Pricing Property Excess-of-Loss Reinsurance," *Proceedings of the Casualty Actuarial Society*, 1991, 78:110–145; discussion by Sholom Feldblum, 1993, 80:380–395.

[14] Mashitz, Isaac, and Gary S. Patrik, "Credibility for Treaty Reinsurance Excess Pricing," *CAS Discussion Paper Program*, 1990, 317–368.

[15] Miccolis, Robert S., "On the Theory of Increased Limits and Excess of Loss Pricing," *Proceedings of the Casualty Actuarial Society*, 1977, 64:27–59; discussion by Sheldon Rosenberg, 1977, 60–73.

[16] Panjer, Harry H., "Recursive Evaluation of a Family of Compound Distributions," *ASTIN Bulletin*, 1981, 12, 1:22–26.

[17] Papush, Dmitry, Gary S. Patrik, and Feliks Podgaits, "Approximations of the Aggregate Loss Distribution," *CAS Forum*, Winter 2001, 175–186.

[18] Patrik, Gary S., "Estimating Casualty Insurance Loss Amount Distributions," *Proceedings of the Casualty Actuarial Society*, 1980, 67:57–109.

[19] Patrik, Gary S., and Russell T. John, "Pricing Excess-of-Loss Casualty Working Cover Reinsurance Treaties," *CAS Discussion Paper Program*, 1980, 399–474.

[20] Stanard, James N., and Russell T. John, "Evaluating the Effect of Reinsurance Contract Terms," *Proceedings of the Casualty Actuarial Society*, 1990, 77:1–41.

[21] Steeneck, Lee R., "Loss Portfolios: Financial Reinsurance," *Proceedings of the Casualty Actuarial Society*, 1985, 72:154–167.

[22] Venter, Gary G., "Transformed Beta and Gamma Distributions and Aggregate Losses," *Proceedings of the Casualty Actuarial Society*, 1983, 70:156–193.

References for Reinsurance Loss Reserving

[23] Benktander, Gunnar, "An Approach to Credibility in Calculating IBNR for Casualty Excess Reinsurance," *The Actuarial Review*, 1976, CAS.

[24] Bühlmann, Hans, Rene Schnieper, and Erwin Straub, "Claims Reserves in Casualty Insurance Based Upon a Probabilistic Model," *Bulletin Association of Swiss Actuaries*, 1980.

[25] Bornheutter, Ronald L., and Ronald E. Ferguson, "The Actuary and IBNR," *Proceedings of the Casualty Actuarial Society*, 1972, 59:181–195.

[26] Casualty Loss Reserve Seminar Transcript, CAS, various years, or the CAS Web Site, casact.org.

[27] Hachemeister, Charles A., "A Stochastic Model for Loss Reserving," *International Congress of Actuaries*, 1980.

[28] John, Russell T., "Report Lag Distributions and IBNR," *Casualty Loss Reserve Seminar Transcript*, 1982.

[29] Mack, Thomas, "Distribution-free Calculation of the Standard Error of Chain Ladder Reserve Estimates," *ASTIN Bulletin*, 1993, 23, 2:213–225.

[30] Mack, Thomas, "Credible Claims Reserves: The Benktander Method," *ASTIN Bulletin*, 2000, 30, 2:333–347.

[31] Patrik, Gary S., "An Actuarial Procedure for Estimating a Reinsurance Company's IBNR," *IASA*, 1978.

[32] Patrik, Gary S., "Loss Reserving Problems for New or Small Reinsurers," *Casualty Loss Reserve Seminar Transcript*, 1982.

[33] Pinto, Emanuel, and Daniel F. Gogol, "An Analysis of Excess Loss Development," *Proceedings of the Casualty Actuarial Society*, 1987, 74:227–255.

[34] Reinsurance Association of America, *Historical Loss Development Study*, published bi-annually (odd years).

[35] Weissner, Edward W., "Estimation of Report Lags by the Method of Maximum Likelihood," *Proceedings of the Casualty Actuarial Society*, 1978, 65:1–9.

[36] Weissner, Edward W., "Evaluation of IBNR on a Low Frequency Book Where The Report Development Pattern Is Still Incomplete," *Casualty Loss Reserve Seminar Transcript*, 1981.

APPENDIX A

PARETO DISTRIBUTION

1. Support: $X > 0$

2. Parameters: $b > 0, \ q > 0$

3. C.d.f.:

$$F(x \mid b,q) = 1 - \left(\frac{b}{b+x}\right)^q$$

4. P.d.f.:

$$f(x \mid b,q) = \frac{qb^q}{(b+x)^{q+1}}$$

5. Moments:

$$E[X^k \mid b,q] = \frac{b^k(k!)}{(q-1)(q-2)(q-k)} \qquad \text{for} \quad k < q$$

6.

$$E[X \mid b,q] = \frac{b}{q-1}$$

7.

$$\text{Var}[X \mid b,q] = \frac{qb^2}{(q-2)(q-1)^2}$$

8. Censored (from above) c.d.f.:   (general definition)

$$F(X;c) = \begin{cases} F(x) & \text{for} \quad x < c \\ 1 & \text{otherwise} \end{cases}$$

9. Censored moments: If $q - k$ is not an integer, then

$$E[X^k; c \mid b,q] = \frac{b^k(k!)}{(q-1)(q-2)\ldots(q-k)} - q\left(\frac{b}{(b+c)}\right)^q$$

$$\times \left\{ \frac{(b+c)^k}{q-k} + \cdots + (-1)^i \left(\frac{k!}{(i!)(n-i)!}\right) \right.$$

$$\times \left(\frac{b^i(b+c)^{k-i}}{q-k+i}\right) + \cdots$$

$$\left. + (-1)^k \left(\frac{b^k}{q}\right) - \left(\frac{c^k}{q}\right) \right\}$$

10. Censored expectation:

$$E[X; c \mid b,q] = E[X]\left\{ 1 - \left(\frac{b}{b+c}\right)^{q-1} \right\} \qquad \text{for} \quad q > 1$$

11. Conditional probability:

$$\text{Prob}[X > y \mid X > x] = \left(\frac{b+x}{b+y}\right)^q$$

12. Truncated (from below-conditional) distribution:

Definition: $X(d) = X - d \qquad$ for $\quad X > d$

Then $X(d)$ is Pareto with parameters $b+d, q$:

$$F_{X(d)}(x) = \text{Prob}[X(d) \le x]$$

$$= 1 - \text{Prob}[X(d) > x]$$

$$= 1 - \text{Prob}[X > x + d \mid X > d]$$

$$= 1 - \left(\frac{b+d}{b+(x+d)}\right)^q$$

$$= 1 - \left(\frac{b+d}{(b+d)+x}\right)^q$$

$$= F(x \mid b+d, q)$$

13. Trended distribution:

Definition: $Y = tX$ $t > 0$

Then Y is Pareto with parameters tb, q:

$$F_Y(y) = \text{Prob}[Y \leq y]$$

$$= \text{Prob}\left[X \leq \frac{y}{t}\right]$$

$$= 1 - \left(\frac{b}{b + \left(\dfrac{y}{t}\right)}\right)^q$$

$$= 1 - \left(\frac{tb}{tb + y}\right)^q$$

$$= F(y \mid tb, q)$$

APPENDIX B

CATASTROPHE LOSS MODEL: EXAMPLE 7.24

For simplicity, the catastrophe distribution for Example 7.24, property quota share pricing, is modeled with the following assumptions.

1. N = cat. event count $\sim$ Poisson[3]

   So,

   $$E[N] = 3 = \text{Var}[N]$$

2. X = cat. event severity (as loss ratio) $\sim$ Pareto[8%, 3]

   (see Appendix A)

   So,

   $$E[X] = \frac{8\%}{3-1} = 4\%$$

   $$E[X^2] = \frac{2(0.08)^2}{(3-1)(3-2)} = 0.0064$$

3. L = annual aggregate cat. loss

   Using the standard risk theoretic model described in Appendix G, we have:

   $$E[L] = E[N]E[X]$$
   $$= 3(4\%) = 12\%$$
   $$\text{Var}[L] = E[N]E[X^2]$$
   $$= 3(0.0064) = 0.0192$$
   $$SD[L] = (0.0192)^{1/2} = 13.86\%$$

APPENDIX C

GAMMA DISTRIBUTION

1. Support: $X > 0$

2. Parameters: $\alpha > 0, \ \beta > 0$

3. P.d.f.:

$$f(x \mid \alpha, \beta) = [\beta^{\alpha} \Gamma(\alpha)]^{-1} x^{\alpha-1} \exp\left(\frac{-x}{\beta}\right)$$

$$\text{where} \quad \Gamma(\alpha) = \int_0^{\infty} x^{\alpha-1} e^{-x} dx = (\alpha - 1)\Gamma(\alpha - 1)$$

4. $E[X \mid \alpha, \beta] = \alpha\beta$

5. $\text{Var}[X \mid \alpha, \beta] = \alpha\beta^2$

6. Mode $= \beta(\alpha - 1)$ if $\alpha \geq 1$

7. If $\alpha = 1$, then Exponential distribution.

8. The Gamma distribution is used in the text to model the distribution of aggregate claims. Recent research (Papush, Patrik and Podgaits [17]) has shown that the simple 2-parameter Gamma distribution is a more accurate representation of the aggregate claims distribution induced by the standard risk theoretic model (Appendix G) than is the more commonly used Lognormal distribution. Also, see Venter [22].

APPENDIX D

ELCF CALCULATION: TABLE 7.34

For simplicity, the claim indemnity severity model underlying Table 7.34 is assumed to be Pareto, with parameters $b = 5,000$ and $q = 1.1$. Then Formula 7.33 is used to adjust for *ALAE* added to indemnity loss, with $\gamma = 20\%$, and for a clash loading, $\delta = 5\%$. The following table shows the calculation of the increased limits factors using Appendix A, #10 to compute the censored expectation at each limit.

Pareto[5,000, 1.1] Increased Limits Factors

(1)	(2)	(3)
		ILF w/o risk load
	Pareto	and w/o *ALAE*
Policy Limit	$E[X; PLim \mid 5,000, 1.1]$	$(2) \div (2[\$100,000])$
$100,000	$13,124	1.0000
250,000	16,255	1.2386
300,000	16,854	1.2842
500,000	18,484	1.4084
833,333	20,041	1.5271
1,000,000 or more	20,579	1.5681

APPENDIX E

EXCESS EXPECTED CLAIM SIZE: TABLE 7.36

For simplicity, the claim indemnity severity model underlying Table 7.36 is the Table 7.34 Pareto adjusted to add *ALAE* to indemnity by altering the Pareto b parameter by the $\gamma = 20\%$ *ALAE* loading (new $b = 1.2 \times 5{,}000 = 6{,}000$) and leaving $q = 1.1$. Since the indemnity loss is censored by policy limits, the 20% add-on for *ALAE* is simply modeled by adjusting the combined indemnity-plus-*ALAE* limits upward by 20%. Using Appendix A, #12 (truncated below at \$300,000) and #13 (adding 20% *ALAE* is like trending by 20%), we get the following result.

1. Expected excess claim severity, over attachment point d and subject to reinsurance limit *RLim*, for policy limit λ:

$$(1 + \delta)E[X(d); \; \lambda(1 + \gamma) - d \mid (1 + \gamma)b + d, q]$$

$$\text{for} \quad d(1 + \gamma)^{-1} \leq \lambda \leq (RLim + d)(1 + \gamma)^{-1}$$

$$= (1.05)E[X; (1.2)\lambda - 300{,}000 \mid 306{,}000, 1.1]$$

$$\text{for} \quad 250{,}000 \leq \lambda \leq 833{,}333$$

$$= (1.05)(306{,}000/0.1)$$

$$\times \left\{ 1 - \left(\frac{306{,}000}{6.000 + (1.2)\lambda} \right)^{0.1} \right\}$$

$$= (3{,}213{,}000) \left\{ 1 - \left(\frac{306{,}000}{6.000 + (1.2)\lambda} \right)^{0.1} \right\}$$

2. If $\lambda = 300{,}000$, we computed

$$= (3{,}213{,}000) \left\{ 1 - \left(\frac{306{,}000}{366{,}000} \right)^{0.1} \right\}$$

$$= (3{,}213{,}000)(1 - 0.9823)$$

$$= (3{,}213{,}000)(0.0177)$$

$$= 57{,}016$$

APPENDIX F

CREDIBILITY CONSIDERATIONS FOR EXPOSURE RATING AND EXPERIENCE RATING

We further discuss the items in Tables 7.41 and 7.42.

TABLE 7.41

ITEMS TO CONSIDER IN DETERMINING THE CREDIBILITY OF THE EXPOSURE LOSS COST ESTIMATE

- *The accuracy of the estimate of RCF, the primary rate correction factor, and thus the accuracy of the primary expected loss cost or loss ratio*

The accuracy of the estimate of *RCF* for the rating year, for each line of business, determines the accuracy of the estimate of the primary expected loss cost or loss ratio, $RCF \times PCPLR$. And this estimate is critical because the exposure rating estimate of the excess loss cost for each line of business is proportional to the loss ratio estimate.

- *The accuracy of the predicted distribution of subject premium by line of business*

If this prediction of the mix of business is accurate, and the estimates of loss cost for each line are accurate, then the estimate of the overall loss cost should be accurate. If the cedant has a fairly stable mix of business, and no plans for substantive changes, a fairly accurate prediction can be made of the mix of business for the rating year.

- *For excess coverage, the accuracy of the predicted distribution of subject premium by increased limits table for liability, by state for workers compensation, or by type of insured for property, within a line of business*

Within many liability lines, there are sublines with different increased limits tables, and thus different increased limits factors.

When rating excess coverage, it is clear that the more accurate our estimate of the distribution of primary premium volume by table, the more accurate our exposure rating estimate of loss cost. Since many primary companies do not keep accurate statistics on these distributions, we often use industry statistics, which may not be very accurate for the particular company.

Likewise, for workers compensation, there are large differences in excess exposure by state.

For property, clearly the type of insured (occupancy, construction, protection) are also important in determining excess exposure.

- *For excess coverage, the accuracy of the predicted distribution of subject premium by policy limit within increased limits table for liability, by hazard group for workers compensation, by amount insured for property*

For excess coverage, the policy limit, hazard group or amount insured (or *MPL* or *PML*) clearly affect the amount of exposure to excess claims. Thus, the more accurate these estimates are, the more accurate the overall estimate of excess exposure to loss. Again, since many primary companies do not keep accurate statistics on these distributions, we often use industry statistics, which may not be very accurate for the particular company. If there is a substantial change in the limits written during the rating year, the accuracy of the estimated excess loss cost is reduced.

- *For excess coverage, the accuracy of the excess loss cost factors for coverage above the attachment point*

This is obviously important. If your excess loss cost factors are based upon ISO's increased limits factors or claims severity data, you must recognize that, since ISO's increased limits data are mainly from policies with limits at or below $1,000,000, their increased limits factors may not be very accurate for limits above $1,000,000. Therefore, the higher the attachment point, the less accurate the exposure rating estimate of loss cost. Estimates of property or casualty claims severity above $1,000,000 are subject to great uncertainty.

- *For excess coverage, the degree of potential exposure not contemplated by the excess loss cost factors*

Neither the excess exposure arising from the clash of separate policies or coverages, nor from stacking of limits, are contemplated by bureau increased limits factors. Thus, some adjustment must be made, by using a clash loading factor, to price these additional exposures. Obviously, a great deal of judgment is used. Another part of this problem is the pricing of excess exposure for which there are no bureau increased limits factors, such as umbrella liability, farm owner's liability, or various professional liability lines.

For property coverage, most excess loss cost factors are derived from fire claims severity statistics. There is then the assumption that roughly the same claim severity applies to other perils.

If these other exposures are known to be a minor part of the overall exposure, the same loss cost rates estimated for similar exposures may be used to estimate the loss costs for these minor exposures. This is obviously subject to judgment and uncertainty.

TABLE 7.42

Items to Consider in Determining the Credibility of the Experience Loss Cost Estimate

- *The accuracy of the estimates of claims cost inflation*

This has an obvious effect upon the estimates of ground-up or excess loss cost. Claims cost inflation is usually estimated from broad insurance industry data, because most companies and many individual lines don't have enough claims data in order to make accurate estimates. Historical inflation trends should be modified for anticipated economic and societal changes. There is a lot of judgment involved in these estimates and in the use for particular companies and lines.

- *The accuracy of the estimates of loss development*

Historical claims development statistics for a particular line or company are often chaotic, especially for excess coverage. Thus, we often select claims development lags based upon broader data. These lags may not accurately reflect the development potential of the claims for the exposure being evaluated. And all historical data may not accurately reflect the future claims development potential.

- *The accuracy of the subject premium on-level factors*

As with the estimate of *RCF* for exposure rating, the accuracy of the estimates of the premium on-level factors has a direct effect upon the accuracy of the experience rating estimate of the loss cost. Although most companies have records of their manual rate changes, most do not keep good statistics on their rating plan deviations from manual rates. Therefore, broader insurance data must be used. Also, further rate deviations occur during soft markets when, for competitive reasons, some exposures may be undercounted or more optimistic rate credits are given to retain business.

- *The stability of the loss cost, or loss cost rate, over time*

It should be obvious that the greater the fluctuation in the historical loss cost or loss cost rate from year to year, the greater the sample error in the estimate of the mean, and also the greater the difficulty in measuring any possible trend in the data. This is especially the case for excess experience rating, where there may be few historical claims, so that the so-called process risk generates a high coefficient of variation (see Appendix G).

- *The possibility of changes in the underlying exposure over time*

Experience rating depends upon our ability to adjust past claims and exposure data to future cost level. If there have been significant changes in the book of business of the cedant, such as writing a new line, the experience rate will reflect these changes. Thus it must be adjusted, and this is, of course, subject to error. The less certain you are about the stability of the mix of business over time, the less certain you should be about the experience rate.

- *For excess coverage, the possibility of changes in the distribution of policy limits over time*

It is usually true that policy limits increase over time to keep pace with the inflation in the values being insured, thus with the increase in claim severity. To the extent this is not true, the claim severity data must be adjusted for the slower or faster change in limits.

APPENDIX G

THE STANDARD RISK THEORETIC MODEL

We further discuss Formulas 7.43 and 7.44.

1. Aggregate loss: $L = X_1 + X_2 + \cdots + X_N$

   where

   $L = rv$ (random variable) for aggregate loss

   $N = rv$ for number of claims (occurrences, events)

   $X_i = rv$ for the dollar size of the ith claim

   This formula is true no matter what form the probability models have.

2. Assumptions:

   2.1. The X_i are independent and identically distributed,

   with c.d.f. $F_X(x) = \text{Prob}[X \leq x]$

   2.2. N is independent of the X_i's, and has p.d.f. $p_N(n) = \text{Prob}[N = n]$.

3. Then, the c.d.f. for L has the following form:

   $$F_L(x) = \Sigma_N p_N(n) F_X^{*n}(x)$$

   where $F_X^{*n}(x) = \text{Prob}[X_1 + X_2 + \cdots + X_n \leq x]$
   convolution

4. Thus, each noncentral moment of L can be written:

   $$E[L^k] = \int x^k dF_L(x)$$

   $$= \int x^k d\{\Sigma_N p_N(n) F_X^{*n}(x)\}$$

$$= \Sigma_N \{ p_N(n) \int x^k dF_X^{*n}(x) \}$$

$$= \Sigma_N \{ p_N(n) E[(X_1 + X_2 + \cdots + X_n)^k] \}$$

5. So, in particular:

$$E[L] = \Sigma_N p_N(n) E[X_1 + X_2 + \cdots + X_n]$$
$$= \Sigma_N p_N(n) \{ nE[X] \}$$
$$= E[X] \{ \Sigma_N p_N(n) n \}$$
$$= E[N] E[X]$$

$$E[L^2] = \Sigma_N p_N(n) \{ E[(X_1 + X_2 + \cdots + X_n)^2] \}$$
$$= \Sigma_N p_N(n) \{ E[\Sigma_{i,j}(X_i X_j)] \}$$
$$= \Sigma_N p_N(n) \{ \Sigma_{i,j}(E[X_i X_j]) \}$$
$$= \Sigma_N p_N(n) \{ \Sigma_i E[X_i^2] + \Sigma_{i \neq j}(E[X_i X_j]) \}$$
$$= \Sigma_N p_N(n) \{ nE[X^2] + \Sigma_{i \neq j}(E[X_i] E[X_j]) \}$$
$$= \Sigma_N p_N(n) \{ nE[X^2] + (n-1)nE[X]^2 \}$$
$$= \{ \Sigma_N p_N(n) n \} E[X^2] + \{ \Sigma_N p_N(n) n^2 \} E[X]^2$$
$$\quad - \{ \Sigma_N p_N(n) n \} E[X]^2$$
$$= E[N] \text{Var}[X] + E[N^2] E[X]^2$$

6. Thus, $\text{Var}[L] = E[N] E[X^2] + (\text{Var}[N] - E[N]) E[X]^2$

7. With patience, you can also show that:

$$E[(L - E[L])^3] = E[N] E[(X - E[X])^3]$$
$$+ E[(N - E[N])^3] E[X]$$
$$+ 3 \text{Var}[N] E[X] \text{Var}[X]$$

8. If N is Poisson, then:

$$\text{Var}[L] = E[N]E[X^2]$$
$$E[(L - E[L])^3] = E[N]E[X^3]$$

APPENDIX H

ABBREVIATIONS

- *ACR*   additional case reserve
- *ALAE*   allocated loss adjustment expense
- *BF* Method   Bornheutter–Ferguson method of loss development
- *CL* Method   chainladder method of loss development
- *ELCF*   excess loss cost factor
- *ELR*   expected loss ratio
- $E[X;c]$ expected loss cost up to censor c
- *IBNER*   incurred by not enough reserve
- *L*   random variable for aggregate loss
- *MPL*   maximum possible loss
- *N*   random variable for number of claims
- *PML*   probable maximum loss
- *PCP*   primary company premium
- *PCPLR*   primary company permissible loss ratio
- *PV*   present value
- *RBF*   reinsurance brokerage fee
- *RCF*   rate correction factor
- *RCR*   reinsurance ceding commission rate
- *RDF*   reinsurer's loss discount factor
- *REP*   reinsurer earned premium
- *RELC*   reinsurance expected loss cost
- *RIXL*   reinsurer's internal expense loading
- *RLim*   reinsurance limit
- *RP*   reinsurance premium
- *SB* Method   Stanard–Bühlmann (Cape Cod) method of loss development
- *TER*   target economic return
- *X*   random variable for size of claim
- $X(d)$ random variable X excess of truncation point d

CHAPTER 8

CREDIBILITY

HOWARD C. MAHLER AND CURTIS GARY DEAN

1. INTRODUCTION

Credibility theory provides tools to deal with the randomness of data that is used for predicting future events or costs. For example, an insurance company uses past loss information of an insured or group of insureds to estimate the cost to provide future insurance coverage. But, insurance losses arise from random occurrences. The average annual cost of paying insurance losses in the past few years may be a poor estimate of next year's costs. The expected accuracy of this estimate is a function of the variability in the losses. This data by itself may not be acceptable for calculating insurance rates.

Rather than relying solely on recent observations, better estimates may be obtained by combining this data with other information. For example, suppose that recent experience indicates that carpenters should be charged a rate of $5 (per $100 of payroll) for workers compensation insurance. Assume that the current rate is $10. What should the new rate be? Should it be $5, $10, or somewhere in between? Credibility is used to weight together these two estimates.

The basic formula for calculating credibility weighted estimates is:

Estimate $= Z \times$ [Observation] $+ (1 - Z) \times$ [Other Information],

$$0 \le Z \le 1.$$

Z is called the credibility assigned to the observation. $1 - Z$ is generally referred to as the complement of credibility. If the body of observed data is large and not likely to vary much from one period to another, then Z will be closer to one. On the other hand, if the observation consists of limited data, then Z will be closer to zero and more weight will be given to other information.

The current rate of $10 in the above example is the "Other Information." It represents an estimate or prior hypothesis of a rate to charge in the absence of the recent experience. As recent experience becomes available, then an updated estimate combining the recent experience and the prior hypothesis can be calculated. Thus, the use of credibility involves a linear estimate of the true expectation derived as a result of a compromise between observation and prior hypothesis. The Carpenters' rate for workers compensation insurance is $Z \times \$5 + (1 - Z) \times \$10$ under this model.

Following is another example demonstrating how credibility can help produce better estimates:

Example 1.1: In a large population of automobile drivers, the average driver has one accident every five years or, equivalently, an annual frequency of .20 accidents per year. A driver selected randomly from the population had three accidents during the last five years for a frequency of .60 accidents per year. What is your estimate of the expected future frequency rate for this driver? Is it .20, .60, or something in between?

[*Solution:* If we had no information about the driver other than that he came from the population, we should go with the .20. However, we know that the driver's observed frequency was .60. Should this be our estimate for his future accident frequency? Probably not. There is a correlation between prior accident frequency and future accident frequency, but they are not perfectly correlated. Accidents occur randomly and even good drivers with low expected accident frequencies will have accidents. On the other hand, bad drivers can go several years without an accident. A better answer than either .20 or .60 is most likely something in between: this driver's Expected Future Accident Frequency = $Z \times .60 + (1 - Z) \times .20$.]

The key to finishing the solution for this example is the calculation of Z. How much credibility should be assigned to the information known about the driver? The next two sections explain the calculation of Z.

First, the classical credibility model will be covered in Section 2. It is also referred to as limited fluctuation credibility because it attempts to limit the effect that random fluctuations in the observations will have on the estimates. The credibility Z is a function of the expected variance of the observations versus the selected variance to be allowed in the first term of the credibility formula, $Z \times$ [Observation].

Next, Bühlmann credibility is described in Section 3. This model is also referred to as least squares credibility. The goal with this approach is the minimization of the square of the error between the estimate and the true expected value of the quantity being estimated.

Credibility theory depends upon having prior or collateral information that can be weighted with current observations. Another approach to combining current observations with prior information to produce a better estimate is Bayesian analysis. Bayes Theorem is the foundation for this analysis. This is covered is Section 4. It turns out that Bühlmann credibility estimates are the best linear least squares fits to Bayesian estimates. For this reason Bühlmann credibility is also referred as Bayesian credibility.

In some situations the resulting formulas of a Bayesian analysis exactly match those of Bühlmann credibility estimation; that is, the Bayesian estimate is a linear weighting of current and prior information with weights Z and $(1 - Z)$ where Z is the Bühlmann credibility. In Section 5 this is demonstrated in the important special case of the Gamma-Poisson frequency process.

The last section discusses practical issues in the application of credibility theory including some examples of how to calculate credibility parameters.

The Appendices include basic facts on several frequency and severity distributions and the solutions to the exercises.

2.   CLASSICAL CREDIBILITY

2.1. Introduction

In Classical Credibility, one determines how much data one needs before one will assign to it 100% credibility. This amount of data is referred to as the **Full Credibility Criterion** or the **Standard for Full Credibility**. If one has this much data or more, then $Z = 1.00$; if one has observed less than this amount of data then $0 \leq Z < 1$.

For example, if we observed 1,000 full-time carpenters, then we might assign 100% credibility to their data.[1] Then if we observed 2,000 full-time carpenters we would also assign them 100% credibility. One hundred full-time carpenters might be assigned 32% credibility. In this case the observation has been assigned **partial credibility**, i.e., less than full credibility. Exactly how to determine the amount of credibility assigned to different amounts of data is discussed in the following sections.

There are four basic concepts from Classical Credibility that will be covered:

1. How to determine the criterion for *Full Credibility* when estimating *frequencies*;

2. How to determine the criterion for *Full Credibility* when estimating *severities*;

3. How to determine the criterion for *Full Credibility* when estimating *pure premiums* (loss costs);

4. How to determine the amount of *partial credibility* to assign when one has less data than is needed for full credibility.

---

[1] For workers compensation that data would be dollars of loss and dollars of payroll.

Example 2.1.1: The observed claim frequency is 120. The credibility given to this data is 25%. The complement of credibility is given to the prior estimate of 200. What is the new estimate of the claim frequency?

[*Solution:* $.25 \times 120 + (1 - .25) \times 200 = 180.$]

2.2. Full Credibility for Frequency

Assume we have a Poisson process for claim frequency, with an average of 500 claims per year. Then, the observed numbers of claims will vary from year to year around the mean of 500. The variance of a Poisson process is equal to its mean, in this case 500. This Poisson process can be approximated by a Normal Distribution with a mean of 500 and a variance of 500.

The Normal Approximation can be used to estimate how often the observed results will be far from the mean. For example, how often can one expect to observe more than 550 claims? The standard deviation is $\sqrt{500} = 22.36$. So 550 claims corresponds to about $50/22.36 = 2.24$ standard deviations greater than average. Since $\Phi(2.24) = .9875$, there is approximately a 1.25% chance of observing more than 550 claims.[2]

Thus, there is about a 1.25% chance that the observed number of claims will exceed the expected number of claims by 10% or more. Similarly, the chance of observing fewer than 450 claims is approximately 1.25%. So the chance of observing a number of claims that is outside the range from -10% below to $+10\%$ above the mean number of claims is about 2.5%. In other words, the chance of observing within $\pm 10\%$ of the expected number of claims is 97.5% in this case.

---

[2]More precisely, the probability should be calculated including the continuity correction. The probability of more than 550 claims is approximately $1 - \Phi((550.5 - 500)/\sqrt{500}) = 1 - \Phi(2.258) = 1 - .9880 = 1.20\%$.

More generally, one can write this algebraically. The probability P that observation X is within $\pm k$ of the mean μ is:

$$P = \text{Prob}[\mu - k\mu \le X \le \mu + k\mu]$$

$$= \text{Prob}[-k(\mu/\sigma) \le (X - \mu)/\sigma \le k(\mu/\sigma)] \qquad (2.2.1)$$

The last expression is derived by subtracting through by μ and then dividing through by standard deviation σ. Assuming the Normal Approximation, the quantity $u = (X - \mu)/\sigma$ is normally distributed. For a Poisson distribution with expected number of claims n, then $\mu = n$ and $\sigma = \sqrt{n}$. The probability that the observed number of claims N is within $\pm k$ of the expected number $\mu = n$ is:

$$P = \text{Prob}[-k\sqrt{n} \le u \le k\sqrt{n}]$$

In terms of the cumulative distribution for the unit normal, $\Phi(u)$:

$$P = \Phi(k\sqrt{n}) - \Phi(-k\sqrt{n}) = \Phi(k\sqrt{n}) - (1 - \Phi(k\sqrt{n}))$$

$$= 2\Phi(k\sqrt{n}) - 1$$

Thus, for the Normal Approximation to the Poisson:

$$P = 2\Phi(k\sqrt{n}) - 1 \qquad (2.2.2)$$

Or, equivalently:

$$\Phi(k\sqrt{n}) = (1 + P)/2. \qquad (2.2.3)$$

Example 2.2.1: If the number of claims has a Poisson distribution, compute the probability of being within $\pm 5\%$ of a mean of 100 claims using the Normal Approximation to the Poisson.

[*Solution:* $2\Phi(.05\sqrt{100}) - 1 = 38.29\%$.]

Here is a table showing P, for $k = 10\%$, 5%, 2.5%, 1%, and 0.5%, and for 10, 50, 100, 500, 1,000, 5,000, and 10,000 claims:

Probability of Being Within $\pm k$ of the Mean

Expected # of Claims	$k = 10\%$	$k = 5\%$	$k = 2.5\%$	$k = 1\%$	$k = 0.5\%$
10	24.82%	12.56%	6.30%	2.52%	1.26%
50	52.05%	27.63%	14.03%	5.64%	2.82%
100	68.27%	38.29%	19.74%	7.97%	3.99%
500	97.47%	73.64%	42.39%	17.69%	8.90%
1,000	99.84%	88.62%	57.08%	24.82%	12.56%
5,000	100.00%	99.96%	92.29%	52.05%	27.63%
10,000	100.00%	100.00%	98.76%	68.27%	38.29%

Turning things around, given values of P and k, then one can compute the number of expected claims n_0 such that the chance of being within $\pm k$ of the mean is P. n_0 can be calculated from the formula $\Phi(k\sqrt{n_0}) = (1 + P)/2$. Let y be such that $\Phi(y) = (1 + P)/2$. Then given P, y is determined from a normal table. Solving for n_0 in the relationship $k\sqrt{n_0} = y$ yields $n_0 = (y/k)^2$. If the goal is to be within $\pm k$ of the mean frequency with a probability at least P, then the Standard for Full Credibility is

$$n_0 = y^2/k^2, \qquad (2.2.4)$$

where y is such that

$$\Phi(y) = (1 + P)/2. \qquad (2.2.5)$$

Here are values of y taken from a normal table corresponding to selected values of P:

P	$(1 + P)/2$	y
80.00%	90.00%	1.282
90.00%	95.00%	1.645
95.00%	97.50%	1.960
99.00%	99.50%	2.576
99.90%	99.95%	3.291
99.99%	99.995%	3.891

Example 2.2.2: For $P = 95\%$ and for $k = 5\%$, what is the number of claims required for Full Credibility for estimating the frequency?

[*Solution:* $y = 1.960$ since $\Phi(1.960) = (1 + P)/2 = 97.5\%$. Therefore $n_0 = y^2/k^2 = (1.96/.05)^2 = 1537$.]

Here is a table[3] of values for the Standard for Full Credibility for the frequency n_0, given various values of P and k:

Standards for Full Credibility for Frequency (Claims)

Probability Level P	$k = 30\%$	$k = 20\%$	$k = 10\%$	$k = 7.5\%$	$k = 5\%$	$k = 2.5\%$	$k = 1\%$
80.00%	18	41	164	292	657	2,628	16,424
90.00%	30	68	271	481	**1,082**	4,329	27,055
95.00%	43	96	384	**683**	1,537	6,146	38,415
96.00%	47	105	422	750	1,687	6,749	42,179
97.00%	52	118	471	837	1,884	7,535	47,093
98.00%	60	135	541	962	2,165	8,659	54,119
99.00%	74	166	664	1,180	2,654	10,616	66,349
99.90%	120	271	1,083	1,925	4,331	17,324	108,276
99.99%	168	378	1,514	2,691	6,055	24,219	151,367

The value 1,082 claims corresponding to $P = 90\%$ and $k = 5\%$ is commonly used in applications. For $P = 90\%$ we want to have a 90% chance of being within $\pm k$ of the mean, so we are willing to have a 5% probability outside on either tail, for a total of 10% probability of being outside the acceptable range. Thus, $\Phi(y) = .95$ or $y = 1.645$. Thus, $n_0 = y^2/k^2 = (1.645/.05)^2 = 1,082$ claims.

In practical applications appropriate values of P and k have to be selected.[4] While there is clearly judgment involved in the

---

[3] See the Table in Longley-Cook's "An Introduction to Credibility Theory" (1962) or "Some Notes on Credibility" by Perryman, *PCAS*, 1932. Tables of Full Credibility standards have been available and used by actuaries for many years.

[4] For situations that come up repeatedly, the choice of P and k may have been made several decades ago, but nevertheless the choice was made at some point in time.

choice of P and k, the Standards for Full Credibility for a given application are generally chosen within a similar range. This same type of judgment is involved in the choice of error bars around a statistical estimate of a quantity. Often ± 2 standard deviations (corresponding to about a 95% confidence interval) will be chosen, but that is not necessarily better than choosing ± 1.5 or ± 2.5 standard deviations. So while Classical Credibility involves somewhat arbitrary judgments, that has not stood in the way of its being very useful for decades in many applications.

Subsequent sections deal with estimating severities or pure premiums rather than frequencies. As will be seen, in order to calculate a Standard for Full Credibility for severities or the pure premium, generally one first calculates a Standard for Full Credibility for the frequency.

Variations from the Poisson Assumptions

If one desires that the chance of being within $\pm k$ of the mean frequency to be at least P, then the Standard for Full Credibility is $n_0 = y^2/k^2$, where y is such that $\Phi(y) = (1 + P)/2$.

However, this depended on the following assumptions:

1. One is trying to estimate frequency;

2. Frequency is given by a Poisson process (so that the variance is equal to the mean);

3. There are enough expected claims to use the Normal Approximation to the Poisson process.

Occasionally, a Binomial or Negative Binomial Distribution will be substituted for a Poisson distribution, in which case the difference in the derivation is that the variance is not equal to the mean.

For example, assume one has a Binomial Distribution with parameters $n = 1,000$ and $p = .3$. The mean is 300 and the variance is $(1,000)(.3)(.7) = 210$. So the chance of being within $\pm 5\%$ of the expected value is approximately:

$$\Phi((.05)(300)/210^{.5}) - \Phi((-.05)(300)/210^{.5})$$

$$\simeq \Phi(1.035) - \Phi(-1.035) \simeq .8496 - .1504 \simeq 69.9\%.$$

So, in the case of a Binomial with parameter .3, the Standard for Full Credibility with $P = 70\%$ and $k = \pm 5\%$ is about 1,000 exposures or 300 expected claims.

If instead a Negative Binomial Distribution had been assumed, then the variance would have been greater than the mean. This would have resulted in a standard for Full Credibility greater than in the Poisson situation.

One can derive a more general formula when the Poisson assumption does not apply. The Standard for Full Credibility for Frequency is:[5]

$$\{y^2/k^2\}(\sigma_f^2/\mu_f) \tag{2.2.6}$$

There is an "extra" factor of the variance of the frequency divided by its mean. This reduces to the Poisson case when $\sigma_f^2/\mu_f = 1$.

Exposures vs. Claims

Standards for Full Credibility are calculated in terms of the expected number of claims. It is common to translate these into a number of exposures by dividing by the (approximate) expected claim frequency. So for example, if the Standard for Full Credibility is 1,082 claims ($P = 90\%$, $k = 5\%$) and the expected claim frequency in Homeowners Insurance were .04 claims per house-year, then $1,082/.04 \simeq 27,000$ house-years would be a corresponding Standard for Full Credibility in terms of exposures.

Example 2.2.3: E represents the number of homogeneous exposures in an insurance portfolio. The claim frequency *rate* per exposure is a random variable with mean $= 0.025$ and variance $=$

---

[5]A derivation of this formula can be found in Mayerson, et al. "The Credibility of the Pure Premium."

0.0025. A full credibility standard is devised that requires the observed sample frequency *rate* per exposure to be within 5% of the expected population frequency rate per exposure 90% of the time. Determine the value of E needed to produce full credibility for the portfolio's experience.

[*Solution:* First calculate the number of claims for full credibility when the mean does not equal the variance of the frequency: $\{1.645^2/(.05)^2\}\{.0025/.025\} = 108.241$. Then, convert this into exposures by dividing by the claim frequency rate per exposure: $108.241/.025 = 4,330$ exposures.]

2.2. Exercises

2.2.1. How many claims are required for Full Credibility if one requires that there be a 99% chance of the estimated frequency being within $\pm2.5\%$ of the true value?

2.2.2. How many claims are required for Full Credibility if one requires that there be a 98% chance of the estimated frequency being within $\pm7.5\%$ of the true value?

2.2.3. The full credibility standard for a company is set so that the total number of claims is to be within 6% of the true value with probability P. This full credibility standard is calculated to be 900 claims. What is the value of P?

2.2.4. Y represents the number of independent homogeneous *exposures* in an insurance portfolio. The claim frequency *rate* per exposure is a random variable with mean = 0.05 and variance = 0.09. A full credibility standard is devised that requires the observed sample frequency *rate* per exposure to be within 2% of the expected population frequency rate per exposure 94% of the time. Determine the value of Y needed to produce full credibility for the portfolio's experience.

2.2.5. Assume you are conducting a poll relating to a single question and that each respondent will answer either yes or no. You pick a random sample of respondents out of a very large population. Assume that the true percentage of yes responses in the total population is between 20% and 80%. How many respondents do you need, in order to require that there be a 95% chance that the results of the poll are within ±7% of the true answer?

2.2.6. A Standard for Full Credibility has been established for frequency assuming that the frequency is Poisson. If instead the frequency is assumed to follow a Negative Binomial with parameters $k = 12$ and $p = .7$, what is the ratio of the revised Standard for Full Credibility to the original one? (For a Negative Binomial, mean $= k(1 - p)/p$ and variance $= k(1 - p)/p^2$.)

2.2.7. Let X be the number of claims needed for full credibility, if the estimate is to be within 5% of the true value with a 90% probability. Let Y be the similar number using 10% rather than 5%. What is the ratio of X divided by Y?

2.3. Full Credibility for Severity

The Classical Credibility ideas also can be applied to estimating claim severity, the average size of a claim.

Suppose a sample of N claims, $X_1, X_2, \ldots X_N$, are each independently drawn from a loss distribution with mean μ_s and variance σ_s^2. The severity, i.e. the mean of the distribution, can be estimated by $(X_1 + X_2 + \cdots + X_N)/N$. The variance of the observed severity is $\text{Var}(\sum X_i/N) = (1/N^2)\sum \text{Var}(X_i) = \sigma_s^2/N$. Therefore, the standard deviation for the observed severity is $\sigma_s/\sqrt{N}$.

The probability that the observed severity S is within $\pm k$ of the mean μ_s is:

$$P = \text{Prob}[\mu_s - k\mu_s \leq S \leq \mu_s + k\mu_s]$$

Subtracting through by the mean μ_s, dividing by the standard deviation $\sigma_s/\sqrt{N}$, and substituting u in for $(S - \mu_s)/(\sigma_s/\sqrt{N})$ yields:

$$P = \text{Prob}[-k\sqrt{N}(\mu_s/\sigma_s) \leq u \leq k\sqrt{N}(\mu_s/\sigma_s)]$$

This is identical to the frequency formula in Section 2.2 except for the additional factor of (μ_s/σ_s).

According to the Central Limit Theorem, the distribution of observed severity $(X_1 + X_2 + \cdots + X_N)/N$ can be approximated by a normal distribution for large N. Assume that the Normal Approximation applies and, as before with frequency, define y such that $\Phi(y) = (1 + P)/2$. In order to have probability P that the observed severity will differ from the true severity by less than $\pm k\mu_s$, we want $y = k\sqrt{N}(\mu_s/\sigma_s)$. Solving for N:

$$N = (y/k)^2(\sigma_s/\mu_s)^2 \qquad (2.3.1)$$

The ratio of the standard deviation to the mean, $(\sigma_s/\mu_s) = CV_S$, is the coefficient of variation of the claim size distribution. Letting n_0 be the full credibility standard for frequency given P and k produces:

$$N = n_0 CV_S^2 \qquad (2.3.2)$$

This is the **Standard for Full Credibility for Severity.**

Example 2.3.1: The coefficient of variation of the severity is 3. For $P = 95\%$ and $k = 5\%$, what is the number of claims required for Full Credibility for estimating the severity?

[*Solution:* From Example 2.2.2, $n_0 = 1537$. Therefore, $N = 1537(3)^2 = 13{,}833$ claims.]

2.3. Exercises

2.3.1. The claim amount distribution has mean 1,000 and variance 6,000,000. Find the number of claims required for full credibility if you require that there will be a 90% chance that the estimate of severity is correct within $\pm 1\%$.

2.3.2. The Standard for Full Credibility for Severity for claim distribution A is N claims for a given P and k. Claim distribution B has the same mean as distribution A, but a standard deviation that is twice as large as A's. Given the same P and k, what is the Standard for Full Credibility for Severity for distribution B?

2.4. Process Variance of Aggregate Losses, Pure Premiums, and Loss Ratios

Suppose that N claims of sizes $X_1, X_2, \ldots, X_N$ occur during the observation period. The following quantities are useful in analyzing the cost of insuring a risk or group of risks:

Aggregate Losses : $L = (X_1 + X_2 + \cdots + X_N)$

Pure Premium : $PP = (X_1 + X_2 + \cdots + X_N)/\text{Exposures}$

Loss Ratio : $LR = (X_1 + X_2 + \cdots + X_N)/\text{Earned Premium}$

We'll work with the Pure Premium in this section, but the development applies to the other two as well.

Pure Premiums are defined as losses divided by exposures.[6] For example, if 200 cars generate claims that total to $80,000 during a year, then the observed Pure Premium is $80,000/200 or $400 per car-year. Pure premiums are the product of frequency and severity. **Pure Premium = Losses/Exposures = (Number of Claims/Exposures) (Losses/Number of Claims) = (Frequency)(Severity).** Since they depend on both the number of claims and the size of claims, pure premiums have more reasons to vary than do either frequency or severity individually.

Random fluctuation occurs when one rolls dice, spins spinners, picks balls from urns, etc. The observed result varies from time period to time period due to random chance. This is also true for the pure premium observed for a collection of insureds or for an individual insured.[7] The variance of the observed pure premiums for a given risk that occurs due to random fluctuation

---

[6]The definition of exposures varies by line of insurance. Examples include car-years, house-years, sales, payrolls, etc.

[7]In fact this is the fundamental reason for the existence of insurance.

is referred to as the **process variance**. That is what will be discussed here.[8]

Example 2.4.1: [Frequency and Severity are *not* independent]

Assume the following:

- For a given risk, the number of claims for a single exposure period will be either 0, 1, or 2

Number of Claims	Probability
0	60%
1	30%
2	10%

- If only one claim is incurred, the size of the claim will be 50 with probability 80% or 100 with probability 20%

- If two claims are incurred, the size of each claim, independent of the other, will be 50 with probability 50% or 100 with probability 50%

What is the variance of the pure premium for this risk?

[*Solution:* First list the possible pure premiums and probability of each of the possible outcomes. If there is no claim (60% chance) then the pure premium is zero. If there is one claim, then the pure premium is either 50 with (30%)(80%) = 24% chance or 100 with (30%)(20%) = 6% chance. If there are two claims then there are three possibilities.

Next, the first and second moments can be calculated by listing the pure premiums for all the possible outcomes and taking the weighted average using the probabilities as weights of either the pure premium or its square.

---

[8]The process variance is distinguished from the variance of the hypothetical pure premiums as discussed in Bühlmann Credibility.

Situation	Probability	Pure Premium	Square of P.P.
0 claims	60.0%	0	0
1 claim @ 50	24.0%	50	2,500
1 claim @ 100	6.0%	100	10,000
2 claims @ 50 each	2.5%	100	10,000
2 claims: 1 @ 50 & 1 @ 100	5.0%	150	22,500
2 claims @ 100 each	2.5%	200	40,000
Overall	100.0%	33	3,575

The average Pure Premium is 33. The second moment of the Pure Premium is 3,575. Therefore, the variance of the pure premium is: $3,575 - 33^2 = 2,486$.]

Note that the frequency and severity are *not* independent in this example. Rather the severity distribution depends on the number of claims. For example, the average severity is 60 if there is one claim, while the average severity is 75 if there are two claims.

Here is a similar example with independent frequency and severity.

Example 2.4.2: [Frequency and Severity are independent]

Assume the following:

- For a given risk, the number of claims for a single exposure period is given by a binomial distribution with $p = .3$ and $n = 2$.

- The size of a claim will be 50, with probability 80%, or 100, with probability 20%.

- Frequency and severity are independent.

Determine the variance of the pure premium for this risk.

[*Solution:*   List the possibilities and compute the first two moments:

Situation	Probability	Pure Premium	Square of P.P.
0	49.00%	0	
1 claim @ 50	33.60%	50	2,500
1 claim @ 100	8.40%	100	10,000
2 claims @ 50 each	5.76%	100	10,000
2 claims: 1 @ 50 & 1 @ 100	2.88%	150	22,500
2 claims @ 100 each	0.36%	200	40,000
Overall	100.0%	36	3,048

Therefore, the variance of the pure premium is: $3,048 - 36^2 = 1,752.$]

In this second example, since frequency and severity are independent one can make use of the following formula:

Process Variance of Pure Premium =

(Mean Freq.)(Variance of Severity)

+ (Mean Severity)^2(Variance of Freq.)

$$\sigma_{PP}^2 = \mu_f \sigma_S^2 + \mu_S^2 \sigma_f^2 \tag{2.4.1}$$

Note that each of the two terms has a mean and a variance, one from frequency and one from severity. Each term is in dollars squared; that is one way to remember that the mean severity (which is in dollars) enters as a square while that for mean frequency (which is not in dollars) does not.

Example 2.4.3: Calculate the variance of the pure premium for the risk described in Example 2.4.2 using formula (2.4.1).

[*Solution:* The mean frequency is $np = .6$ and the variance of the frequency is $npq = (2)(.3)(.7) = .42$. The average severity is 60 and the variance of the severity is $(.8)(10^2) + (.2)(40^2) =$

400. Therefore the process variance of the pure premium is $(.6)(400) + (60^2)(.42) = 1,752.$]

Formula (2.4.1) can also be used to compute the process variance of the aggregate losses and the loss ratio when frequency and severity are independent.

Derivation of Formula (2.4.1)

The above formula for the process variance of the pure premium is a special case of the formula that also underlies analysis of variance:[9]

$$\text{Var}(Y) = E_X[\text{Var}_Y(Y \mid X)] + \text{Var}_X(E_Y[Y \mid X]),$$

$$\text{where } X \text{ and } Y \text{ are random variables.} \quad (2.4.2)$$

Letting Y be the pure premium PP and X be the number of claims N in the above formula gives:

$$\text{Var}(PP) = E_N[\text{Var}_{PP}(PP \mid N)] + \text{Var}_N(E_{PP}[PP \mid N])$$

$$= E_N[N\sigma_S^2] + \text{Var}_N(\mu_S N) = E_N[N]\sigma_S^2 + \mu_S^2 \text{Var}_N(N)$$

$$= \mu_f \sigma_S^2 + \mu_S^2 \sigma_f^2$$

Where we have used the assumption that the frequency and severity are independent and the facts:

- For a fixed number of claims N, the variance of the pure premium is the variance of the sum of N independent identically distributed variables each with variance σ_S^2. (Since frequency and severity are assumed independent, σ_S^2 is the same for each value of N.) Such variances add so that $\text{Var}_{PP}(PP \mid N) = N\sigma_S^2$.

- For a fixed number of claims N with frequency and severity independent, the expected value of the pure premium is N times the mean severity: $E_{PP}[PP \mid N] = N\mu_S$.

---

[9]The total variance = expected value of the process variance + the variation of the hypothetical means.

- Since with respect to N the variance of the severity acts as a constant:

$$E_N[N\sigma_S^2] = \sigma_S^2 E_N[N] = \mu_f \sigma_S^2$$

- Since with respect to N the mean of the severity acts as a constant:

$$\text{Var}_N(\mu_S N) = \mu_S^2 \text{Var}_N(N) = \mu_S^2 \sigma_f^2$$

Poisson Frequency

In the case of a Poisson Frequency with independent frequency and severity the formula for the process variance of the pure premium simplifies. Since $\mu_f = \sigma_f^2$:

$$\sigma_{PP}^2 = \mu_f \sigma_S^2 + \mu_S^2 \sigma_f^2$$
$$= \mu_f(\sigma_S^2 + \mu_S^2) = \mu_f(\text{2nd moment of the severity})$$
$$(2.4.3)$$

Example 2.4.4: Assume the following:

- For a given large risk, the number of claims for a single exposure period is Poisson with mean 3,645.

- The severity distribution is LogNormal with parameters $\mu = 5$ and $\sigma = 1.5$.

- Frequency and severity are independent.

Determine the variance of the pure premium for this risk.

[*Solution:* The second moment of the severity = $\exp(2\mu + 2\sigma^2)$ = $\exp(14.5) = 1{,}982{,}759.264$. (See Appendix.) Thus, $\sigma_{PP}^2 = \mu_f$(2nd moment of the severity) = $(3{,}645)(1{,}982{,}759) = 7.22716 \times 10^9$.]

Normal Approximation:

For large numbers of expected claims, the observed pure premiums are approximately normally distributed.[10] For ex-

---

[10]The more skewed the severity distribution, the higher the frequency has to be for the Normal Approximation to produce worthwhile results.

ample, continuing the example above, mean severity = $\exp(\mu +$ $.5\sigma^2)$ = exp(6.125) = 457.14. Thus, the mean pure premium is $(3,645)(457.14) = 1,666,292$. One could ask what the chance is of the observed pure premiums being between 1.4997 million and 1.8329 million. Since the variance is 7.22716×10^9, the standard deviation of the pure premium is 85,013. Thus, this probability of the observed pure premiums being within ±10% of 1.6663 million is

$$\simeq \Phi((1.8329 \text{ million} - 1.6663 \text{ million})/85,013)$$

$$- \Phi((1.4997 \text{ million} - 1.6663 \text{ million})/85,013)$$

$$= \Phi(1.96) - \Phi(-1.96) = .975 - (1 - .975) = 95\%.$$

Thus, in this case with an expected number of claims equal to 3,645, there is about a 95% chance that the observed pure premium will be within ±10% of the expected value. One could turn this around and ask how many claims one would need in order to have a 95% chance that the observed pure premium will be within ±10% of the expected value. The answer of 3,645 claims could be taken as a Standard for Full Credibility for the Pure Premium.[11]

2.4. Exercises

2.4.1. Assume the following for a given risk:

- Mean frequency = 13; Variance of the frequency = 37
- Mean severity = 300; Variance of the severity = 200,000
- Frequency and severity are independent

What is the variance of the pure premium for this risk?

2.4.2. A six-sided die is used to determine whether or not there is a claim. Each side of the die is marked with either a 0 or a 1, where 0 represents no claim and 1 represents a

---

[11]As discussed in a subsequent section.

claim. Two sides are marked with a zero and four sides with a 1. In addition, there is a spinner representing claim severity. The spinner has three areas marked 2, 5, and 14. The probabilities for each claim size are:

Claim Size	Probability
2	20%
5	50%
14	30%

The die is rolled and if a claim occurs, the spinner is spun. What is the variance for a single trial of this risk process?

2.4.3. You are given the following:

- For a given risk, the number of claims for a single exposure period will be 1, with probability 4/5; or 2, with probability 1/5.

- If only one claim is incurred, the size of the claim will be 50, with probability 3/4; or 200, with probability 1/4.

- If two claims are incurred, the size of each claim, independent of the other, will be 50, with probability 60%; or 150, with probability 40%.

Determine the variance of the pure premium for this risk.

2.4.4. You are given the following:

- Number of claims for a single insured follows a Poisson distribution with mean .25

- The amount of a single claim has a uniform distribution on [0, 5,000]

- Number of claims and claim severity are independent.

Determine the pure premium's process variance for a single insured.

2.4.5. Assume the following:

- For the state of West Dakota, the number of claims for a single year is Poisson with mean 8,200

- The severity distribution is LogNormal with parameters $\mu = 4$ and $\sigma = 0.8$

- Frequency and severity are independent

Determine the expected aggregate losses. Determine the variance of the aggregate losses.

2.4.6. The frequency distribution follows the Poisson process with mean 0.5. The second moment about the origin for the severity distribution is 1,000. What is the process variance of the aggregate claim amount?

2.4.7. The probability function of claims per year for an individual risk is Poisson with a mean of 0.10. There are four types of claims. The number of claims has a Poisson distribution for each type of claim. The table below describes the characteristics of the four types of claims.

| Type of Claim | Mean Frequency | Severity | |
		Mean	Variance
W	.02	200	2,500
X	.03	1,000	1,000,000
Y	.04	100	0
Z	.01	1,500	2,000,000

Calculate the variance of the pure premium.

2.5. Full Credibility for Aggregate Losses, Pure Premiums, and Loss Ratios

Since they depend on both the number of claims and the size of claims, aggregate losses, pure premiums, and loss ratios have more reasons to vary than either frequency or severity. Because they are more difficult to estimate than frequencies, all other things being equal, the Standard for Full Credibility is larger than that for frequencies.

In Section 2.4 formulas for the variance of the pure premium were calculated:

General case: $\qquad \sigma_{PP}^2 = \mu_f \sigma_S^2 + \mu_S^2 \sigma_f^2$ $\qquad$ (2.5.1)

Poisson frequency: $\qquad \sigma_{PP}^2 = \mu_f(\sigma_S^2 + \mu_S^2) =$

$\qquad\qquad\qquad\qquad \mu_f(\text{2nd moment of the severity})$

$\qquad\qquad\qquad\qquad\qquad\qquad\qquad\qquad\qquad$ (2.5.2)

The subscripts indicate the means and variances of the frequency (f) and severity (S). Assuming the Normal Approximation, full credibility standards can be calculated following the same steps as in Sections 2.2 and 2.3.

The probability that the observed pure premium PP is within $\pm k$ of the mean μ_{PP} is:

$$P = \text{Prob}[\mu_{PP} - k\mu_{PP} \leq PP \leq \mu_{PP} + k\mu_{PP}]$$
$$= \text{Prob}[-k(\mu_{PP}/\sigma_{PP}) \leq u \leq k(\mu_{PP}/\sigma_{PP})],$$

where $u = (PP - \mu_{PP})/\sigma_{PP}$ is a unit normal variable, assuming the Normal Approximation.

Define y such that $\Phi(y) = (1 + P)/2$. (See Section 2.2 for more details.) Then, in order to have probability P that the observed pure premium will differ from the true pure premium by less than $\pm k\mu_{PP}$:

$$y = k(\mu_{PP}/\sigma_{PP}) \qquad (2.5.3)$$

To proceed further with formula (2.5.1) we need to know something about the frequency distribution function.

Suppose that frequency is a Poisson process and that n_F is the expected number of claims required for Full Credibility of the Pure Premium. Given n_F is the expected number of claims, then $\mu_f = \sigma_f^2 = n_F$ and, assuming frequency and severity are independent:

$$\mu_{PP} = \mu_f \mu_S = n_F \mu_S$$

and,

$$\sigma_{PP}^2 = \mu_f(\sigma_S^2 + \mu_S^2) = n_F(\sigma_S^2 + \mu_S^2).$$

Substituting for μ_{PP} and σ_{PP} in formula (2.5.3) gives:

$$y = k(n_F \mu_S / (n_F(\sigma_S^2 + \mu_S^2))^{1/2}).$$

Solving for n_F:

$$n_F = (y/k)^2[1 + (\sigma_S^2/\mu_S^2)] = n_0(1 + CV_S^2) \qquad (2.5.4)$$

This is the **Standard for Full Credibility of the Pure Premium.** $n_0 = (y/k)^2$ is the Standard for Full Credibility of Frequency that was derived in Section 2.2. $CV_S = (\sigma_S/\mu_S)$ is the coefficient of variation of the severity. Formula (2.5.4) can also be written as $n_F = n_0(\mu_S^2 + \sigma_S^2)/\mu_S^2$ where $(\mu_S^2 + \sigma_S^2)$ is the second moment of the severity distribution.

Example 2.5.1: The number of claims has a Poisson distribution. The mean of the severity distribution is 2,000 and the standard deviation is 4,000. For $P = 90\%$ and $k = 5\%$, what is the Standard for Full Credibility of the Pure Premium?

[*Solution:* From section 2.2, $n_0 = 1{,}082$ claims. The coefficient of variation is $CV = 4{,}000/2{,}000 = 2$. So, $n_F = 1{,}082$ $(1 + 2^2) = 5{,}410$ claims.]

It is interesting to note that the Standard for Full Credibility of the Pure Premium is the sum of the standards for frequency and severity:

$$n_F = n_0(1 + CV_S^2) = n_0 + n_0 CV_S^2$$

$$= \text{Standard for Full Credibility of Frequency}$$

$$+ \text{Standard for Full Credibility of Severity}$$

Note that if one limits the size of claims, then the coefficient of variation is smaller. Therefore, the criterion for full credibility for basic limits losses is less than that for total losses. It is a common practice in ratemaking to cap losses in order to increase the credibility assigned to the data.

The pure premiums are often approximately Normal; generally the greater the expected number of claims or the shorter tailed the frequency and severity distributions, the better the Normal Approximation. It is assumed that one has enough claims that the aggregate losses approximate a Normal Distribution. While it is possible to derive formulas that don't depend on the Normal Approximation, they're not covered here.[12]

Variations from the Poisson Assumption

As with the Standard for Full Credibility of Frequency, one can derive a more general formula when the Poisson assumption does not apply. The Standard for Full Credibility is:[13]

$$n_F = \{y^2/k^2\}(\sigma_f^2/\mu_f + \sigma_S^2/\mu_S^2), \qquad (2.5.5)$$

which reduces to the Poisson case when $\sigma_f^2/\mu_f = 1$. If the severity is constant then σ_S^2 is zero and (2.5.5) reduces to (2.2.6).

2.5. Exercises

[Assume that frequency and severity are independent in the following problems.]

---

[12]One can, for example, use the Normal Power Approximation, which takes into account more than the first two moments. See for example, "Limited Fluctuation Credibility with the Normal Power Approximation" by Gary Venter. This usually has little practical effect.

[13]A derivation can be found in Mayerson, et al, "The Credibility of the Pure Premium."

2.5.1. You are given the following information:

- The number of claims is Poisson.

- The severity distribution is LogNormal with parameters $\mu = 4$ and $\sigma = 0.8$.

- Full credibility is defined as having a 90% probability of being within plus or minus 2.5% of the true pure premium.

What is the minimum number of expected claims that will be given full credibility?

2.5.2. Given the following information, what is the minimum number of *policies* that will be given full credibility?

- Mean claim frequency $= .04$ claims per policy. (Assume Poisson.)

- Mean claim severity $= \$1,000$.

- Variance of the claim severity $= \$2$ million.

- Full credibility is defined as having a 99% probability of being within plus or minus 10% of the true pure premium.

2.5.3. The full credibility standard for a company is set so that the total number of claims is to be within 2.5% of the true value with probability P. This full credibility standard is calculated to be 5,000 claims. The standard is altered so that the total *cost* of claims is to be within 9% of the true value with probability P. The claim frequency has a Poisson distribution and the claim severity has the following distribution:

$$f(x) = .0008(50 - x), \qquad 0 \le x \le 50.$$

What is the expected number of claims necessary to obtain full credibility under the new standard?

2.5.4. You are given the following information:

- A standard for full credibility of 2,000 claims has been selected so that the actual pure premium would be within 10% of the expected pure premium 99% of the time.

- The number of claims follows a Poisson distribution.

Using the classical credibility concepts determine the co-efficient of variation of the severity distribution underlying the full credibility standard.

2.5.5. You are given the following:

- The number of claims is Poisson distributed.

- Claim severity has the following distribution:

Claim Size	Probability
10	.50
20	.30
50	.20

Determine the number of claims needed so that the total cost of claims is within 20% of the expected cost with 95% probability.

2.5.6. You are given the following:

- The number of claims has a *negative binomial* distribution with a variance that is twice as large as the mean.

- Claim severity has the following distribution:

Claim Size	Probability
10	.50
20	.30
50	.20

Determine the number of claims needed so that the total cost of claims is within 20% of the expected cost with 95% probability. Compare your answer to that of exercise 2.5.5.

2.5.7. A full credibility standard is determined so that the total *number* of claims is within 2.5% of the expected number with probability 98%. If the same expected number of claims for full credibility is applied to the total *cost* of claims, the actual total cost would be within $100k\%$ of the expected cost with 90% probability. The coefficient of variation of the severity is 3.5. The frequency is Poisson. Using the normal approximation of the aggregate loss distribution, determine k.

2.5.8. The ABC Insurance Company has decided to use Classical Credibility methods to establish its credibility requirements for an individual state rate filing. The full credibility standard is to be set so that the observed total cost of claims underlying the rate filing should be within 5% of the true value with probability 0.95. The claim frequency follows a Poisson distribution and the claim severity is distributed according to the following distribution:

$$f(x) = 1/100,000 \quad \text{for} \quad 0 \le x \le 100,000$$

What is the expected number of claims, N_F necessary to obtain full credibility?

2.5.9. A full credibility standard of 1,200 expected claims has been established for aggregate claim costs. Determine the number of expected claims that would be required for full credibility if the coefficient of variation of the claim size distribution were changed from 2 to 4 and the range parameter, k, were doubled.

2.6. Partial Credibility

When one has at least the number of claims needed for Full Credibility, then one assigns 100% credibility to the observa-

GRAPH 8.1

CLASSICAL CREDIBILITY

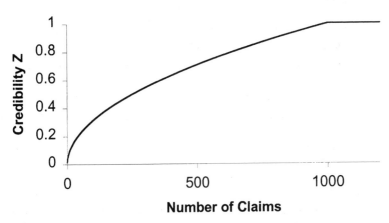

Number of Claims

tions. However, when there is less data than is needed for full credibility, less that 100% credibility is assigned.

Let n be the (expected) number of claims for the volume of data, and n_F be the standard for Full Credibility. Then the partial credibility assigned is $Z = \sqrt{n/n_F}$. If $n \geq n_F$, then $Z =$ 1.00. Use the square root rule for partial credibility for either frequency, severity or pure premiums.

For example if 1,000 claims are needed for full credibility, then Graph 8.1 displays the credibilities that would be assigned.

Example 2.6.1: The Standard for Full Credibility is 683 claims and one has observed 300 claims.[14] How much credibility is assigned to this data?

---

[14]Ideally, n in the formula $Z = \sqrt{n/n_F}$ should be the expected number of claims. However, this is often not known and the observed number of claims is used as an approximation. If the number of exposures is known along with an expected claims frequency, then the expected number of claims can be calculated by (number of exposures) × (expected claims frequency).

[*Solution:* $\sqrt{300/683} = 66.3\%$.]

Limiting Fluctuations

The square root rule for partial credibility is designed so that the standard deviation of the contribution of the data to the new estimate retains the value corresponding to the standard for full credibility. We will demonstrate why the square root rule accomplishes that goal. One does not need to follow the derivation in order to apply the simple square root rule.

Let X_{partial} be a value calculated from partially credible data; for example, X_{partial} might be the claim frequency calculated from the data. Assume X_{full} is calculated from data that just meets the full credibility standard. For the full credibility data, *Estimate* = X_{full}, while the partially credible data enters the estimate with a weight Z in front of it: *Estimate* = $ZX_{\text{partial}} + (1 - Z)[Other Information]$. The credibility Z is calculated so that the expected variation in ZX_{partial} is limited to the variation allowed in a full credibility estimate X_{full}. The variance of ZX_{partial} can be reduced by choosing a Z less than one.

Suppose you are trying to estimate frequency (number of claims per exposure), pure premium, or loss ratio, with estimates X_{partial} and X_{full} based on different size samples of a population. Then, they will have the same expected value μ. But, since it is based on a smaller sample size, X_{partial} will have a larger standard deviation σ_{partial} than the standard deviation σ_{full} of the full credibility estimate X_{full}. The goal is to limit the fluctuation in the term ZX_{partial} to that allowed for X_{full}. This can be written as:[15]

$$\text{Prob}[\mu - k\mu \le X_{\text{full}} \le \mu + k\mu]$$

$$= \text{Prob}[Z\mu - k\mu \le ZX_{\text{partial}} \le Z\mu + k\mu]$$

---

[15]Note that in both cases fluctuations are limited to $\pm k\mu$ of the mean.

Subtracting through by the means and dividing by the standard deviations gives:

$$\text{Prob}[-k\mu/\sigma_{\text{full}} \leq (X_{\text{full}} - \mu)/\sigma_{\text{full}} \leq k\mu/\sigma_{\text{full}}]$$

$$= \text{Prob}[-k\mu/Z\sigma_{\text{partial}} \leq (ZX_{\text{partial}} - Z\mu)/$$

$$Z\sigma_{\text{partial}} \leq k\mu/Z\sigma_{\text{partial}}]^{16}$$

Assuming the Normal Approximation, $(X_{\text{full}} - \mu)/\sigma_{\text{full}}$ and $(ZX_{\text{partial}} - Z\mu)/Z\sigma_{\text{partial}}$ are unit normal variables. Then, the two sides of the equation are equal if:

$$k\mu/\sigma_{\text{full}} = k\mu/Z\sigma_{\text{partial}}$$

Solving for Z yields:

$$Z = \sigma_{\text{full}}/\sigma_{\text{partial}}. \tag{2.6.1}$$

Thus, the partial credibility Z will be inversely proportional to the standard deviation of the partially credible data.

Assume we are trying to estimate the average number of accidents μ in a year per driver for a homogeneous population. For a sample of M drivers, $\mu_M = \sum_{i=1}^{M} m_i/M$ is an estimate of the frequency μ where m_i is the number of accidents for the ith driver. Assuming that the numbers of claims per driver are independent of each other, then the variance of μ_M is $\sigma_M^2 = \text{Var}[\sum_{i=1}^{M} m_i/M] = (1/M^2)\sum_{i=1}^{M} \text{Var}(m_i)$. If each insured has a Poisson frequency with the same mean $\mu = \text{Var}(m_i)$, then $\sigma_M^2 = (1/M^2)\sum_{i=1}^{M} \mu = M\mu/M^2 = \mu/M$.

If a sample of size M is expected to produce n claims, then since $M\mu = n$, it follows that $M = n/\mu$. So, the variance is $\sigma_M^2 = \mu/M = \mu/(n/\mu) = \mu^2/n$, and the standard deviation is:

$$\sigma_M = \mu/\sqrt{n}. \tag{2.6.2}$$

Example 2.6.2: A sample with 1,000 expected claims is used to estimate frequency μ. Assuming frequency is Poisson, what

---

[16]Note that the mean of ZX_{partial} is $Z\mu$ and the standard deviation is $Z\sigma_{\text{partial}}$.

are the variance and standard deviation of the estimated frequency?

[*Solution:* The variance is $\mu^2/1000$ and the standard deviation is $\mu/\sqrt{1,000} = .032\mu$.]

A fully credible sample with an expected number of claims n_0, will have a standard deviation $\sigma_{full} = \mu/\sqrt{n_0}$. A partially credible sample with expected number of claims n will have $\sigma_{partial} = \mu/\sqrt{n}$. Using formula (2.6.1), the credibility for the smaller sample is: $Z = (\mu/\sqrt{n_0})/(\mu/\sqrt{n}) = \sqrt{n/n_0}$. So,

$$Z = \sqrt{n/n_0} \qquad (2.6.3)$$

Equation 2.6.3 is the important square root rule for partial credibility. Note that the Normal Approximation and Poisson claims distribution were assumed along the way. A similar derivation of the square root formula also applies to credibility for severity and the pure premium.[17]

2.6. Exercises

2.6.1. The Standard for Full Credibility is 2,000 claims. How much credibility is assigned to 300 claims?

2.6.2. Using the square root rule for partial credibility, a certain volume of data is assigned credibility of .36. How much credibility would be assigned to ten times that volume of data?

2.6.3. Assume a Standard for Full Credibility for *severity* of 2,500 claims. For the class of Salespersons one has observed 803 claims totaling $9,771,000. Assume the av-

---

[17]The square root formula for partial credibility also applies in the calculation of aggregate losses and total number of claims although equation (2.6.1) needs to be revised. For estimates of aggregate losses and total number of claims, a larger sample will have a larger standard deviation. Letting $L = X_1 + X_2 + \cdots + X_N$ represent aggregate losses, then the standard deviation of L increases as the number of expected claims increases, but the ratio of the standard deviation of L to the expected value of L decreases. Equation (2.6.1) will work if the standard deviations are replaced by coefficients of variation.

erage cost per claim for all similar classes is \$10,300. Calculate a credibility-weighted estimate of the average cost per claim for the Salespersons' class.

2.6.4. The Standard for Full Credibility is 3,300 claims. The expected claim frequency is 6% per house-year. How much credibility is assigned to 2,000 house-years of data?

2.6.5. You are given the following information:

- Frequency is Poisson.

- Severity follows a Gamma Distribution with $\alpha = 1.5$.

- Frequency and severity are independent.

- Full credibility is defined as having a 97% probability of being within plus or minus 4% of the true pure premium.

What credibility is assigned to 150 claims?

2.6.6. The 1984 pure premium underlying the rate equals \$1,000. The loss experience is such that the observed pure premium for that year equals \$1,200 and the number of claims equals 600. If 5,400 claims are needed for full credibility and the square root rule for partial credibility is used, estimate the pure premium underlying the rate in 1985. (Assume no change in the pure premium due to inflation.)

2.6.7. Assume the random variable N, representing the number of claims for a given insurance portfolio during a one-year period, has a Poisson distribution with a mean of n. Also assume $X_1, X_2 \ldots, X_N$ are N independent, identically distributed random variables with X_i representing the size of the ith claim. Let $C = X_1 + X_2 + \cdots X_n$ represent the total cost of claims during a year. We want to use the observed value of C as an estimate of future costs. We are willing to assign full credibility to C provided it is within

10.0% of its expected value with probability 0.96. If the claim size distribution has a coefficient of variation of 0.60, what credibility should we assign to the experience if 213 claims occur?

2.6.8. The Slippery Rock Insurance Company is reviewing their rates. The expected number of claims necessary for full credibility is to be determined so that the observed total cost of claims should be within 5% of the true value 90% of the time. Based on independent studies, they have estimated that individual claims are independently and identically distributed as follows:

$$f(x) = 1/200,000, \qquad 0 \le x \le 200,000.$$

Assume that the number of claims follows a Poisson distribution. What is the credibility Z to be assigned to the most recent experience given that it contains 1,082 claims?

2.6.9. You are given the following information for a group of insureds:

- Prior estimate of expected total losses $20,000,000

- Observed total losses $25,000,000

- Observed number of claims   10,000

- Required number of claims for full credibility 17,500

Calculate a credibility weighted estimate of the group's expected total losses.

2.6.10. 2,000 expected claims are needed for full credibility. Determine the number of expected claims needed for 60% credibility.

2.6.11. The full credibility standard has been selected so that the actual *number of claims* will be within 5% of the expected *number of claims* 90% of the time. Determine the credibility to be given to the experience if 500 claims are expected.

3. LEAST SQUARES CREDIBILITY

The second form of credibility covered in this chapter is called Least Squares or Bühlmann Credibility. It is also referred as greatest accuracy credibility. As will be discussed, the credibility is given by the formula: $Z = N/(N + K)$. As the number of observations N increases, the credibility Z approaches 1.

In order to apply Bühlmann Credibility to various real-world situations, one is typically required to calculate or estimate the so-called Bühlmann Credibility Parameter K. This involves being able to apply analysis of variance: the calculation of the expected value of the process variance and the variance of the hypothetical means.

Therefore, in this section we will first cover the calculation of the expected value of the process variance and the variance of the hypothetical means. This will be followed by applications of Bühlmann Credibility to various simplified situations. Finally, we will illustrate the ideas covered via the excellent Philbrick Target Shooting Example.

3.1. Analysis of Variance

Let's start with an example involving multi-sided dice:

There are a total of 100 multi-sided dice of which 60 are 4-sided, 30 are 6-sided and 10 are 8-sided. The multi-sided dice with 4 sides have 1, 2, 3, and 4 on them. The multi-sided dice with the usual 6 sides have numbers 1 through 6 on them. The multi-sided dice with 8 sides have numbers 1 through 8 on them. For a given die each side has an equal chance of being rolled; i.e., the die is fair.

Your friend picked at random a multi-sided die. He then rolled the die and told you the result. You are to estimate the result when he rolls that same die again.

The next section will demonstrate how to apply Bühlmann Credibility to this problem. In order to apply Bühlmann Credibility one will first have to calculate the items that would be used in "analysis of variance." One needs to compute the Expected Value of the Process Variance and the Variance of the Hypothetical Means, which together sum to the total variance.

Expected Value of the Process Variance:

For each type of die we can compute the mean and the (process) variance. For example, for a 6-sided die one need only list all the possibilities:

A	B	C	D
Roll of Die	A Priori Probability	Column A× Column B	Square of Column A ×Column B
1	0.16667	0.16667	0.16667
2	0.16667	0.33333	0.66667
3	0.16667	0.50000	1.50000
4	0.16667	0.66667	2.66667
5	0.16667	0.83333	4.16667
6	0.16667	1.00000	6.00000
Sum	1	3.5	15.16667

Thus, the mean is 3.5 and the variance is $15.16667 - 3.5^2 = 2.91667 = 35/12$. Thus, the conditional variance if a 6-sided die is picked is: $\text{Var}[X \mid 6\text{-sided}] = 35/12$.

Example 3.1.1: What is the mean and variance of a 4-sided die?

[*Solution:* The mean is 2.5 and the variance is $15/12$.]

Example 3.1.2: What is the mean and variance of an 8-sided die?

[*Solution:* The mean is 4.5 and the variance is $63/12$.]

One computes the **Expected Value of the Process Variance (EPV)** by weighting together the process variances for each type of risk using as weights the chance of having each type of risk.[18] In this case the Expected Value of the Process Variance is: $(60\%)(15/12) + (30\%)(35/12) + (10\%)(63/12) = 25.8/12 = 2.15$. In symbols this sum is: P(4-sided)Var[X | 4-sided] + P(6-sided)Var[X | 6-sided] + P(8-sided)Var[X | 8-sided]. Note that this is the Expected Value of the Process Variance for *one* observation of the risk process; i.e., one roll of a die.

Variance of the Hypothetical Means

The hypothetical means are 2.5, 3.5, and 4.5 for the 4-sided, 6-sided, and 8-sided die, respectively. One can compute the **Variance of the Hypothetical Means (VHM)** by the usual technique; compute the first and second moments of the hypothetical means.

Type of Die	A Priori[19] Chance of this Type of Die	Mean for this Type of Die	Square of Mean of this Type of Die
4-sided	0.6	2.5	6.25
6-sided	0.3	3.5	12.25
8-sided	0.1	4.5	20.25
Average		3	9.45

The Variance of the Hypothetical Means is the second moment minus the square of the (overall) mean = $9.45 - 3^2 = .45$. Note

---

[18]In situations where the types of risks are parametrized by a continuous distribution, as for example in the Gamma-Poisson frequency process, one will take an integral rather than a sum.

[19]According to the dictionary, a priori means "relating to or derived by reasoning from self-evident propositions." This usage applies here since we can derive the probabilities from the statement of the problem. After we observe rolls of the die, we may calculate new probabilities that recognize both the a priori values and the observations. This is covered in detail in section 4.

that this is the variance for a single observation, i.e., one roll of a die.

Total Variance

One can compute the total variance of the observed results if one were to do this experiment repeatedly. One needs merely compute the chance of each possible outcome.

In this case there is a $60\% \times (1/4) = 15\%$ chance that a 4-sided die will be picked and then a 1 will be rolled. Similarly, there is a $30\% \times (1/6) = 5\%$ chance that a 6-sided die will be selected and then a 1 will be rolled. There is a $10\% \times (1/8) = 1.25\%$ chance that an 8-sided die will be selected and then a 1 will be rolled. The total chance of a 1 is therefore:

$$15\% + 5\% + 1.25\% = 21.25\%.$$

A	B	C	D	E	F	G
Roll of Die	Probability due to 4-sided die	Probability due to 6-sided die	Probability due to 8-sided die	A Priori Probability $= B + C + D$	Column A ×Column E	Square of Column A ×Column E
1	0.15	0.05	0.0125	0.2125	0.2125	0.2125
2	0.15	0.05	0.0125	0.2125	0.4250	0.8500
3	0.15	0.05	0.0125	0.2125	0.6375	1.9125
4	0.15	0.05	0.0125	0.2125	0.8500	3.4000
5		0.05	0.0125	0.0625	0.3125	1.5625
6		0.05	0.0125	0.0625	0.3750	2.2500
7			0.0125	0.0125	0.0875	0.6125
8			0.0125	0.0125	0.1000	0.8000
Sum	0.6	0.3	0.1	1	3	11.6

The mean is 3 (the same as computed above) and the second moment is 11.6. Therefore, the total variance is $11.6 - 3^2 = 2.6$. Note that Expected Value of the Process Variance + Variance of the Hypothetical Means = 2.15 + .45 = 2.6 = Total Variance. Thus, the total variance has been split into two pieces. This is true in general.

Expected Value of the Process Variance

+ Variance of the Hypothetical Means = Total Variance

$$(3.1.1)$$

While the two pieces of the total variance seem similar, the order of operations in their computation is different. In the case of the Expected Value of the Process Variance, EPV, first one separately computes the process variance for each of the types of risks and then one takes the expected value over all types of risks. Symbolically, the **EPV** $= E_\theta[\text{Var}[X \mid \theta]]$.

In the case of the Variance of the Hypothetical Means, VHM, first one computes the expected value for each type of risk and then one takes their variance over all types of risks. Symbolically, the **VHM** $= \text{Var}_\theta[E[X \mid \theta]]$.

Multiple Die Rolls

So far we have computed variances in the case of a single roll of a die. One can also compute variances when one is rolling more than one die.[20] There are a number of somewhat different situations that lead to different variances, which lead in turn to different credibilities.

Example 3.1.3: Each actuary attending a CAS Meeting rolls two multi-sided dice. One die is 4-sided and the other is 6-sided. Each actuary rolls his two dice and reports the sum. What is the expected variance of the results reported by the actuaries?

[*Solution:* The variance is the sum of that for a 4-sided and 6-sided die. Variance $= (15/12) + (35/12) = 50/12 = 4.167$.]

One has to distinguish the situation in example 3.1.3 where the types of dice rolled are known, from one where each actuary is selecting dice at random. The latter introduces an additional source of random variation, as shown in the following exercise.

---

[20]These dice examples can help one to think about insurance situations where one has more than one observation or insureds of different sizes.

Example 3.1.4: Each actuary attending a CAS Meeting independently selects two multi-sided dice. For each actuary his two
multi-sided dice are selected *independently* of each other, with
each die having a 60% chance of being 4-sided, a 30% chance
of being 6-sided, and a 10% chance of being 8-sided. Each actuary rolls his two dice and reports the sum. What is the expected
variance of the results reported by the actuaries?

[*Solution:* The total variance is the sum of the EPV and VHM.
For each actuary let his two dice be A and B. Let the parameter
(number of sides) for A be θ and that for B be ψ. Note that A
only depends on θ, while B only depends on ψ, since the two dice
were selected independently. Then EPV $= E_{\theta,\psi}[\mathrm{Var}[A + B \mid \theta, \psi]]$
$= E_{\theta,\psi}[\mathrm{Var}[A \mid \theta, \psi]] + E_{\theta,\psi}[\mathrm{Var}[B \mid \theta, \psi]] = E_{\theta}[\mathrm{Var}[A \mid \theta]] +$
$E_{\psi}[\mathrm{Var}[B \mid \psi]] = 2.15 + 2.15 = (2)(2.15) = 4.30.$ The VHM $=$
$\mathrm{Var}_{\theta,\psi}[E[A + B \mid \theta, \psi]] = \mathrm{Var}_{\theta,\psi}[E[A \mid \theta, \psi] + E[B \mid \theta, \psi]] =$
$\mathrm{Var}_{\theta}[E[A \mid \theta]] + \mathrm{Var}_{\psi}[E[B \mid \psi]] = (2)(.45) = .90.$ Where we have
used the fact that $E[A \mid \theta]$ and $E[B \mid \psi]$ are independent and thus,
their variances add. Total variance $=$ EPV $+$ VHM $= 4.3 + .9 = 5.2.$]

Example 3.1.4 is subtly different from a situation where the
two dice selected by a given actuary are always of the same type,
as in example 3.1.5.

Example 3.1.5: Each actuary attending a CAS Meeting selects
two multi-sided dice both of the same type. For each actuary,
his multi-sided dice have a 60% chance of being 4-sided, a 30%
chance of being 6-sided, and a 10% chance of being 8-sided.
Each actuary rolls his dice and reports the sum. What is the
expected variance of the results reported by the actuaries?

[*Solution:* The total variance is the sum of the EPV and VHM.
For each actuary let his two die rolls be A and B. Let the
parameter (number of sides) for his dice be θ, the same
for both dice. Then EPV $= E_{\theta}[\mathrm{Var}[A + B \mid \theta]] = E_{\theta}[\mathrm{Var}[A \mid \theta]] +$
$E_{\theta}[\mathrm{Var}[B \mid \theta]] = E_{\theta}[\mathrm{Var}[A \mid \theta]] + E_{\theta}[\mathrm{Var}[B \mid \theta]] = 2.15 + 2.15 =$
$(2)(2.15) = 4.30.$ The VHM $= \mathrm{Var}_{\theta}[E[A + B \mid \theta]] = \mathrm{Var}_{\theta}[2E[A \mid \theta]]$
$= (2^2)\mathrm{Var}_{\theta}[E[A \mid \theta]] = (4)(.45) = 1.80.$ Where we have used the

fact that $E[A \mid \theta]$ and $E[B \mid \theta]$ are the same. So, Total Variance = EPV + VHM = 4.3 + 1.8 = 6.1. Alternately, Total Variance = (N)(EPV for one observation) + (N^2)(VHM for one observation) = $(2)(2.15) + (2^2)(.45) = 6.1.$]

Note that example 3.1.5 is the same mathematically as if each actuary chose a single die and reported the sum of rolling his die twice. Contrast this with previous example 3.1.4 in which each actuary chose two dice, with the type of each die independent of the other.

In example 3.1.5: Total Variance = (2)(EPV single die roll) + (2^2)(VHM single die roll).

The VHM has increased in proportion to N^2, the square of the number of observations, while the EPV goes up only as N:

$$\text{Total Variance} = N(\text{EPV for one observation})$$

$$+ (N^2)(\text{VHM for one observation}) \qquad (3.1.2)$$

This is the assumption behind the Bühlmann Credibility formula: $Z = N/(N + K)$. The Bühlmann Credibility parameter K is the ratio of the EPV to the VHM for a *single* die. The formula automatically adjusts the credibility for the number of observations N.

Total Variance = EPV + VHM

One can demonstrate that in general:

$$\text{Var}[X] = E_\theta[\text{Var}[X \mid \theta]] + \text{Var}_\theta[E[X \mid \theta]]$$

First one can rewrite the EPV: $E_\theta[\text{Var}[X \mid \theta]] = E_\theta[E[X^2 \mid \theta] - E[X \mid \theta]^2] = E_\theta[E[X^2 \mid \theta]] - E_\theta[E[X \mid \theta]^2] = E[X^2] - E_\theta[E[X \mid \theta]^2].$

Second, one can rewrite the VHM: $\text{Var}_\theta[E[X \mid \theta]] = E_\theta[E[X \mid \theta]^2] - E_\theta[E[X \mid \theta]]^2 = E_\theta[E[X \mid \theta]^2] - E[X]^2 = E_\theta[E[X \mid \theta]^2] - E[X]^2.$

Putting together the first two steps: EPV + VHM = $E_\theta[\text{Var}[X \mid \theta]]$ + $\text{Var}_\theta[E[X \mid \theta]] = E[X^2] - E_\theta[E[X \mid \theta]^2] + E_\theta[E[X \mid \theta]^2] - E[X]^2$ = $E[X^2] - E[X]^2 = \text{Var}[X] = $ Total Variance of X.

In the case of the single die: $2.15 + .45 = (11.6 - 9.45) + (9.45 - 9) = 11.6 - 9 = 2.6$. In order to split the total variance of 2.6 into two pieces we've added and subtracted the expected value of the squares of the hypothetical means: 9.45.

A Series of Examples

The following information will be used in a series of examples involving the frequency, severity, and pure premium:

Type	Portion of Risks in this Type	Bernoulli (Annual) Frequency Distribution[21]	Gamma Severity Distribution[22]
1	50%	$p = 40\%$	$\alpha = 4, \ \lambda = .01$
2	30%	$p = 70\%$	$\alpha = 3, \ \lambda = .01$
3	20%	$p = 80\%$	$\alpha = 2, \ \lambda = .01$

We assume that the types are homogeneous; i.e., every insured of a given type has the same frequency and severity process. Assume that for an individual insured, frequency and severity are independent.[23]

We will show how to compute the Expected Value of the Process Variance and the Variance of the Hypothetical Means in each case. In general, the simplest case involves the frequency, followed by the severity, with the pure premium being the most complex case.

Expected Value of the Process Variance, Frequency Example

For type 1, the process variance of the Bernoulli frequency is $pq = (.4)(1 - .4) = .24$. Similarly, for type 2 the process variance

---

[21] With a Bernoulli frequency distribution, the probability of exactly one claim is p and the probability of no claims is $(1 - p)$. The mean of the distribution is p and the variance is pq where $q = (1 - p)$.

[22] For the Gamma distribution, the mean is α/λ and the variance is α/λ^2. See the Appendix on claim frequency and severity distributions.

[23] Across types, the frequency and severity are not independent. In this example, types with higher average frequency have lower average severity.

for the frequency is $(.7)(1 - .7) = .21$. For type 3 the process variance for the frequency is $(.8)(1 - .8) = .16$.

The expected value of the process variance is the weighted average of the process variances for the individual types, using the a priori probabilities as the weights. The EPV of the frequency $= (50\%)(.24) + (30\%)(.21) + (20\%)(.16) = .215$.

Note that to compute the EPV one first computes variances and then computes the expected value. In contrast, in order to compute the VHM, one first computes expected values and then computes the variance.

Variance of the Hypothetical Mean Frequencies

For type 1, the mean of the Bernoulli frequency is $p = .4$. Similarly for type 2 the mean frequency is $.7$. For type 3 the mean frequency is $.8$.

The variance of the hypothetical mean frequencies is computed the same way any other variance is. First one computes the first moment: $(50\%)(.4) + (30\%)(.7) + (20\%)(.8) = .57$. Then one computes the second moment: $(50\%)(.4^2) + (30\%)(.7^2) + (20\%)(.8^2) = .355$. Then the VHM $= .355 - .57^2 = .0301$.

Expected Value of the Process Variance, Severity Example

The computation of the EPV for severity is similar to that for frequency with one important difference. One has to weight together the process variances of the severities for the individual types using the chance that a claim came from each type.[24] The chance that a claim came from an individual of a given type is proportional to the product of the a priori chance of an insured being of that type and the mean frequency for that type.

---

[24]Each claim is one observation of the severity process. The denominator for severity is number of claims. In contrast, the denominator for frequency (as well as pure premiums) is exposures.

For type 1, the process variance of the Gamma severity is $\alpha/\lambda^2 = 4/.01^2 = 40,000$. Similarly, for type 2 the process variance for the severity is $3/.01^2 = 30,000$. For type 3 the process variance for the severity is $2/.01^2 = 20,000$.

The mean frequencies are: .4, .7, and .8. The a priori chances of each type are: 50%, 30%, and 20%. Thus, the weights to use to compute the EPV of the severity are $(.4)(50\%) = .2$, $(.7)(30\%) = .21$, and $(.8)(20\%) = .16$. The sum of the weights is $.2 + .21 + .16 = .57$. Thus, the probability that a claim came from each class is: .351, .368, and .281. (For example, $.2/.57 = .351$.) The expected value of the process variance of the severity is the weighted average of the process variances for the individual types, using these weights.[25] The EPV of the severity[26] $= \{(.2)(40,000) + (.21)(30,000) + (.16)(20,000)\}/(.2 + .21 + .16) = 30,702$.

This computation can be organized in the form of a spreadsheet:

A	B	C	D	E	F	G	H
			Weights	Probability that a Claim	Gamma Parameters		
	A Priori	Mean	= Col. B	Came from			Process
Class	Probability	Frequency	×Col. C	this Class	α	λ	Variance
1	50%	0.4	0.20	0.351	4	0.01	40,000
2	30%	0.7	0.21	0.368	3	0.01	30,000
3	20%	0.8	0.16	0.281	2	0.01	20,000
Average			0.57	1.000			**30,702**

---

[25] Note that while in this case with discrete possibilities we take a sum, in the continuous case we would take an integral.

[26] Note that this result differs from what one would get by using the a priori probabilities as weights. The latter *incorrect* method would result in: $(50\%)(40,000) + (30\%)(30,000) + (20\%)(20,000) = 33,000 \neq 30,702$.

Variance of the Hypothetical Mean Severities

In computing the moments one again has to use for each individual type the chance that a claim came from that type.[27]

For type 1, the mean of the Gamma severity is $\alpha/\lambda = 4/.01 = 400$. Similarly for type 2 the mean severity is $3/.01 = 300$. For type 3 the mean severity is $2/.01 = 200$.

The mean frequencies are: .4, .7, and .8. The a priori chances of each type are: 50%, 30%, and 20%. Thus, the weights to use to compute the moments of the severity are $(.4)(50\%) = .2$, $(.7)(30\%) = .21$, and $(.8)(20\%) = .16$.

The variance of the hypothetical mean severities is computed the same way any other variance is. First one computes the first moment: $\{(.2)(400) + (.21)(300) + (.16)(200)\}/(.2 + .21 + .16) = 307.02$. Then one computes the second moment: $\{(.2)(400^2) + (.21)(300^2) + (.16)(200^2)\}/(.2 + .21 + .16) = 100,526$. Then the VHM of the severity = $100,526 - 307.02^2 = 6,265$. This computation can be organized in the form of a spreadsheet:[28]

A	B	C	D	E	F	G	H
			Weights	Gamma			Square
	A Priori	Mean	= Col. B	Parameters		Mean	of Mean
Class	Probability	Frequency	×Col. C	α	λ	Severity	Severity
1	50%	0.4	0.20	4	0.01	400	160,000
2	30%	0.7	0.21	3	0.01	300	90,000
3	20%	0.8	0.16	2	0.01	200	40,000
Average			0.57			307.02	100,526

---

[27]Each claim is one observation of the severity process. The denominator for severity is number of claims. In contrast, the denominator for frequency (as well as pure premiums) is exposures.

[28]After Column D, one could inset another column normalizing the weights by dividing them each by the sum of Column D. In the spreadsheet shown, one has to remember to divide by the sum of Column D when computing each of the moments.

Then the variance of the hypothetical mean severities = $100,526 - 307.02^2 = 6,265$.

Expected Value of the Process Variance, Pure Premium Example

The computation of the EPV for the pure premiums is similar to that for frequency. However, it is more complicated to compute each process variance of the pure premiums.

For type 1, the mean of the Bernoulli frequency is $p = .4$, and the variance of the Bernoulli frequency is $pq = (.4)(1 - .4) = .24$. For type 1, the mean of the Gamma severity is $\alpha/\lambda = 4/.01 = 400$, and the variance of the Gamma severity is $\alpha/\lambda^2 = 4/.01^2 = 40,000$. Thus, since frequency and severity are assumed to be independent, the process variance of the pure premium = (Mean Frequency)(Variance of Severity) + (Mean Severity)^2 (Variance of Frequency) = $(.4)(40,000) + (400)^2(.24) = 54,400$.

Similarly for type 2 the process variance of the pure premium = $(.7)(30,000) + (300)^2(.21) = 39,900$. For type 3 the process variance of the pure premium = $(.8)(20,000) + (200)^2(.16) = 22,400$.

The expected value of the process variance is the weighted average of the process variances for the individual types, using the a priori probabilities as the weights. The EPV of the pure premium = $(50\%)(54,400) + (30\%)(39,900) + (20\%)(22,400) = 43,650$. This computation can be organized in the form of a spreadsheet:

Class	A Priori Probability	Mean Frequency	Variance of Frequency	Mean Severity	Variance of Severity	Process Variance
1	50%	0.4	0.24	400	40,000	54,400
2	30%	0.7	0.21	300	30,000	39,900
3	20%	0.8	0.16	200	20,000	22,400
Average						**43,650**

Variance of the Hypothetical Mean Pure Premiums

The computation of the VHM for the pure premiums is similar to that for frequency. One has to first compute the mean pure premium for each type.

For type 1, the mean of the Bernoulli frequency is $p = .4$, and the mean of the Gamma severity is $\alpha/\lambda = 4/.01 = 400$. Thus, since frequency and severity are assumed to be independent, the mean pure premium = (Mean Frequency)(Mean Severity) = $(.4)(400) = 160$. For type 2, the mean pure premium = $(.7)(300) = 210$. For type 3, the mean pure premium[29] = $(.8)(200) = 160$.

One computes the first and second moments of the mean pure premiums as follows:

Class	A Priori Probability	Mean Frequency	Mean Severity	Mean Pure Premium	Square of Pure Premium
1	50%	0.4	400	160	25,600
2	30%	0.7	300	210	44,100
3	20%	0.8	200	160	25,600
Average				175	31,150

Thus, the variance of the hypothetical mean pure premiums = $31,150 - 175^2 = 525$.

Estimating the Variance of the Hypothetical Means in the Case of Poisson Frequencies

In real-world applications involving Poisson frequencies it is commonly the case that one estimates the Total Variance

---

[29]Note that in this example it turns out that the mean pure premium for type 3 happens to equal that for type 1, even though the two types have different mean frequencies and severities. The mean pure premiums tend to be similar when, as in this example, high frequency is associated with low severity.

and the Expected Value of the Process Variance and then estimates the Variance of the Hypothetical Means via: VHM = Total Variance − EPV.

For example, assume that one observes that the claim count distribution is as follows for a large group of insureds:

Total Claim Count:	0	1	2	3	4	5	> 5
Percentage of Insureds:	60.0%	24.0%	9.8%	3.9%	1.6%	0.7%	0%

One can estimate the total mean as .652 and the total variance as: $1.414 − .652^2 = .989$.

A	B	C	D
Number of Claims	A Priori Probability	Col. A × Col. B	Square of Col. A × Col. B
0	0.60000	0.00000	0.00000
1	0.24000	0.24000	0.24000
2	0.09800	0.19600	0.39200
3	0.03900	0.11700	0.35100
4	0.01600	0.06400	0.25600
5	0.00700	0.03500	0.17500
Sum	1	0.652	1.41400

Assume in addition that the claim count, X, for each individual insured has a Poisson distribution that does not change over time. In other words, each insured's frequency process is given by a Poisson with parameter θ, with θ varying over the group of insureds. Then since the Poisson has its variance equal to its mean, the process variance for each insured is θ; i.e., $Var[X \mid \theta] = \theta$. Thus, the expected value of the process variance is estimated as follows: $E_\theta[Var[X \mid \theta]] = E_\theta[\theta] = $ overall mean = .652.

Thus, we estimate the Variance of the Hypothetical Means as:

Total Variance − EPV = .989 − .652 = .337.

3.1. Exercises

Use the following information for the next two questions:

There are three types of risks. Assume 60% of the risks are of Type A, 25% of the risks are of Type B, and 15% of the risks are of Type C. Each risk has either one or zero claims per year.

Type of Risk	Chance of a Claim	A Priori Chance of Type of Risk
A	20%	60%
B	30%	25%
C	40%	15%

3.1.1. What is the Expected Value of the Process Variance?

3.1.2. What is the Variance of the Hypothetical Means?

Use the following information for the next two questions:

An insured population consists of 9% youthful drivers and 91% adult drivers. Based on experience, we have derived the following probabilities that an individual driver will have n claims in a year's time:

n	Youthful	Adult
0	.80	0.90
1	.15	0.08
2	.04	0.02
3	.01	0.00

3.1.3. What is the Expected Value of the Process Variance?

3.1.4. What is the Variance of the Hypothetical Means?

The following information pertains to the next three questions:

The claim count distribution is as follows for a large sample of insureds:

Total Claim Count	0	1	2	3	4	> 4
Percentage of Insureds	55%	30%	10%	4%	1%	0%

Assume the claim count for each individual insured has a Poisson distribution that does not change over time.

3.1.5. What is the Expected Value of the Process Variance?

3.1.6. What is the Total Variance?

3.1.7. What is the Variance of the Hypothetical Means?

3.1.8. The hypothetical mean frequencies of the members of a class of risks are distributed uniformly on the interval $(0,10]$. The Exponential probability density function for severity, $f(x)$, is defined below, with the r parameter being different for different individuals. r is distributed on $(0,2]$ by the function $g(r)$.

$$f(x) = (1/r)\exp(-x/r) \qquad x \geq 0$$
$$g(r) = r/2 \qquad 0 \leq r \leq 2$$

The frequency and severity are independently distributed. What is the variance of the hypothetical mean pure premiums for this class of risks?

Use the following information for the next six questions:

Two six-sided dice, A_1 and A_2, are used to determine the number of claims. Each side of both dice are marked with either a 0 or a 1, where 0 represents no claim and 1 represents a claim.

The probability of a claim for each die is:

Die	Probability of Claim
A_1	2/6
A_2	3/6

In addition, there are two spinners, B_1 and B_2, representing claim severity. Each spinner has two areas marked 20 and 50. The probabilities for each claim size are:

Spinner	Claim Size 20	Claim Size 50
B_1	.60	.40
B_2	.20	.80

A single observation consists of selecting a die randomly from A_1 and A_2 and a spinner randomly from B_1 and B_2, rolling the selected die, and if there is a claim spinning the selected spinner.

3.1.9. Determine the Expected Value of the Process Variance for the frequency.

3.1.10. Determine the Variance of the Hypothetical Mean frequencies.

3.1.11. Determine the Expected Value of the Process Variance for the severity.

3.1.12. Determine the Variance of the Hypothetical Mean severities.

3.1.13. Determine the Expected Value of the Process Variance for the pure premium.

3.1.14. Determine the Variance of the Hypothetical Mean pure premiums.

Use the following information for the next six questions:

For an individual insured, frequency and severity are independent.

For an individual insured, frequency is given by a Poisson Distribution.

For an individual insured, severity is given by an Exponential Distribution.

Each type is homogeneous; i.e., every insured of a given type has the same frequency process and severity process.

Type	Portion of Insureds in this Type	Mean Frequency	Mean Severity
1	40%	6	100
2	35%	7	125
3	25%	9	200

3.1.15. What is the Expected Value of the Process Variance for the frequency?

3.1.16. What is the Variance of the Hypothetical Mean frequencies?

3.1.17. What is the Expected Value of the Process Variance for the severity?

3.1.18. What is the Variance of the Hypothetical Mean severities?

3.1.19. What is the Expected Value of the Process Variance for the pure premium?

3.1.20. What is the Variance of the Hypothetical Mean pure premiums?

Use the following information for the next two questions:

The probability of y successes in five trials is given by a binomial distribution with parameters 5 and p. The prior distribution of p is uniform on $[0, 1]$.

3.1.21. What is the Expected Value of the Process Variance?

3.1.22. What is the Variance of the Hypothetical Means?

3.2. Bühlmann Credibility

Let's continue along with the simple example involving multi-sided dice:

There are a total of 100 multi-sided dice of which 60 are 4-sided, 30 are 6-sided, and 10 are 8-sided. The multi-sided dice with 4 sides have 1, 2, 3 and 4 on them. The multi-sided dice with the usual 6 sides have numbers 1 through 6 on them. The multi-sided dice with 8 sides have numbers 1 through 8 on them. For a given die each side has an equal chance of being rolled; i.e., the die is fair.

Your friend has picked at random a multi-sided die. He then rolled the die and told you the result. You are to estimate the result when he *rolls that same die again.*

Using Bühlmann Credibility, the new estimate $= Z$(observation) $+ (1 - Z)$(prior mean).

In this example the prior mean is 3. This is the a priori expected value if selecting a die at random and rolling it: $.6(2.5) + .3(3.5) + .1(4.5) = 3.00$. However, since your friend told you additional information about the die he selected, i.e., the value of the first roll, you can come up with a better estimate for the value of the second roll using Bühlmann Credibility.

The prior mean, or a priori expected value, serves as the "other information" to which we apply the complement of credibility. To the extent that our observed data is not credible, we would rely on the prior mean for our estimate. The prior mean reflects what we know about the whole population of dice.

The **Bühlmann Credibility Parameter** is calculated as $K =$ EPV/VHM:

$$K = \text{Expected Value of Process Variance}/$$
$$\text{Variance of Hypothetical Means}, \qquad (3.2.1)$$

where the Expected Value of the Process Variance and the Variance of the Hypothetical Means are each calculated for a *single* observation of the risk process.

In this case[30] $K = \text{EPV}/\text{VHM} = 2.15/.45 = 4.778 = 43/9$.

Then for N observations, the Bühlmann Credibility is:

$$Z = N/(N + K) \qquad (3.2.2)$$

In this case for one observation, $Z = 1/(1 + 4.778) = .1731 = 9/52 = .45/(.45 + 2.15)$. Thus, in this case if we observe a roll of a 5, then the new estimate is: $(.1731)(5) + (1 - .1731)(3) = 3.3462$. The Bühlmann Credibility estimate is a linear function of the observation: $.1731$ (observation) $+ 2.4807$.

Observation	1	2	3	4	5	6	7	8
New Estimate	2.6538	2.8269	3	3.1731	3.3462	3.5193	3.6924	3.8655

Note that if $N = 1$, then $Z = 1/(1 + K) = \text{VHM}/(\text{VHM} + \text{EPV})$ $= \text{VHM}/\text{Total Variance}$.

Number of Observations

It makes sense to assign more credibility to more rolls of the selected die, since as we gather more information we should be able to get a better idea of which type of die has been chosen. If one has N observations of the risk process, one assigns Bühlmann Credibility of $Z = N/(N + K)$. For example, with $K =$

---

[30]The EPV and the VHM were calculated in Section 3.1.

GRAPH 8.2

BÜHLMANN CREDIBILITY

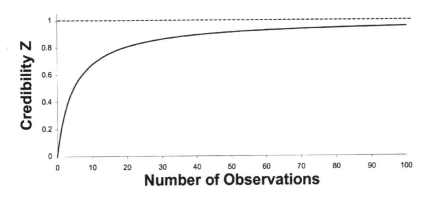

4.778, for three observations we have $Z = 3/(3 + 4.778) = .386$. For the Bühlmann Credibility formula as $N \to \infty$, $Z \to 1$, but Bühlmann Credibility never quite reaches 100%. In this example with $K = 4.778$:

Number of Observations	1	2	3	4	5	10	25	100	1,000	10,000
Credibility	17.3%	29.5%	38.6%	45.6%	51.1%	67.7%	84.0%	95.4%	99.5%	99.95%

Graph 8.2 shows the Bühlmann Credibility. Note that unlike Classical Credibility, Z never reaches 1.00.

If we add up N independent rolls of the same die, the process variances add. So if η^2 is the expected value of the process variance of a single die, then $N\eta^2$ is the expected value of the process variance of the sum of N identical dice. The process variance of one 6-sided die is 35/12, while the process variance of the sum of ten 6-sided dice is 350/12.

In contrast if τ^2 is the variance of the hypothetical means of one die roll, then the variance of the hypothetical means of the sum of N rolls of the *same* die is $N^2\tau^2$. This follows from the fact that each of the means is multiplied by N, and that multiplying by a constant multiplies the variance by the square of that constant.

Thus, as N increases, the variance of the hypothetical means of the sum goes up as N^2 while the process variance goes up only as N. Based on the case with one roll, we expect the credibility to be given by $Z = \text{VHM}/\text{Total Variance} = \text{VHM}/(\text{VHM} + \text{EPV}) = N^2\tau^2/(N^2\tau^2 + N\eta^2) = N/(N + \eta^2/\tau^2) = N/(N + K)$, where $K = \eta^2/\tau^2 = \text{EPV}/\text{VHM}$, with EPV and VHM each for a *single* die.

In general **one computes the EPV and VHM for a single observation and then plugs into the formula for Bühlmann Credibility the number of observations N. If one is estimating claim frequencies or pure premiums then N is in exposures. If one is estimating claim severities then N is in number of claims. (N is in the units of whatever is in the denominator of the quantity one is estimating.[31])**

A Series of Examples

In section 3.1, the following information was used in a series of examples involving the frequency, severity, and pure premium:

Type	Portion of Risks in this Type	Bernoulli (Annual) Frequency Distribution	Gamma Severity Distribution
1	50%	$p = 40\%$	$\alpha = 4, \lambda = .01$
2	30%	$p = 70\%$	$\alpha = 3, \lambda = .01$
3	20%	$p = 80\%$	$\alpha = 2, \lambda = .01$

We assume that the types are homogeneous; i.e., every insured of a given type has the same frequency and severity process. Assume that for an individual insured, frequency and severity are independent.

---

[31]Claim frequency = claims/exposures. Claim severity = losses/claims. Pure Premium = loss/exposures.

Using the Expected Value of the Process Variance and the Variance of the Hypothetical Means computed in the previous section, one can compute the Bühlmann Credibility Parameter in each case.

Suppose that an insured is picked at random and we do not know what type he is.[32] For this randomly selected insured during 4 years one observes 3 claims for a total[33] of $450. Then one can use Bühlmann Credibility to predict the future frequency, severity, or pure premium of this insured.

Frequency Example

As computed in section 3.1, the EPV of the frequency = .215, while the variance of the hypothetical mean frequencies = .0301. Thus, the Bühlmann Credibility parameter is: $K = \text{EPV}/\text{VHM} = .215/.0301 = 7.14$.

Thus, 4 years of experience are given a credibility of $4/(4+K) = 4/11.14 = 35.9\%$. The observed frequency is $3/4 = .75$. The a priori mean frequency is .57. Thus, the estimate of the future frequency for this insured is $(.359)(.75) + (1 - .359)(.57) = .635$.

Severity Example

As computed in section 3.1, the EPV of the severity = 30,702, while the variance of the hypothetical mean severities = 6,265. Thus, the Bühlmann Credibility parameter is $K = \text{EPV}/\text{VHM} = 30,702/6,265 = 4.90$.

Thus, 3 observed claims[34] are given a credibility of $3/(3+K) = 3/7.9 = 38.0\%$. The observed severity is $\$450/3 = \$150$. The

---

[32]The latter is very important. If one knew which type the insured was, one would use the expected value for that type to estimate the future frequency, severity, or pure premium.

[33]Unlike the Bayesian Analysis case to be covered subsequently, even if one were given the separate claim amounts, the Bühlmann Credibility estimate of severity only makes use of the sum of the claim amounts.

[34]Note that the number of observed *claims* is used to determine the Bühlmann Credibility of the severity.

a priori mean severity is \$307. Thus, the estimate of the future severity for this insured is $(.380)(150) + (1 - .380)(307) = \$247.3$.

Pure Premium Example

As computed in section 3.1, the EPV of the pure premium = 43,650, while the variance of the hypothetical mean pure premiums = 525. Thus, the Bühlmann Credibility parameter is $K = \text{EPV}/\text{VHM} = 43{,}650/525 = 83.1$.

Thus, 4 years of experience are given a credibility of $4/(4 + K) = 4/87.1 = 4.6\%$. The observed pure premium is $\$450/4 = \$112.5$. The a priori mean pure premium is \$175. Thus, the estimate of the future pure premium for this insured is: $(.046)(112.5) + (1 - .046)(175) = \$172$.

Note that this estimate of the future pure premium is *not* equal to the product of our previous estimates of the future frequency and severity. $(.635)(\$247.3) = \$157 \neq \$172$. In general one does not get the same result if one uses credibility to make separate estimates of the frequency and severity instead of directly estimating the pure premium.

Assumptions Underlying $Z = N/(N + K)$

There are a number of important assumptions underlying the formula $Z = N/(N + K)$ where $K = \text{EPV}/\text{VHM}$. While these assumptions generally hold in this chapter, they hold in many, but far from every, real-world application.[35] These assumptions are:

1. The complement of credibility is given to the overall mean.

2. The credibility is determined as the slope of the weighted least squares line to the Bayesian Estimates.

---

[35] See for example, Howard Mahler's discussion of Glenn Meyers' "An Analysis of Experience Rating," *PCAS*, 1987.

3. The risk parameters and risk process do not shift over time.[36]

4. The expected value of the process variance of the sum of N observations increases as N. Therefore the expected value of the process variance of the average of N observations decreases as $1/N$.

5. The variance of the hypothetical means of the sum of N observations increases as N^2. Therefore the variance of the hypothetical means of the average of N observations is independent of N.

In addition one must be careful that an insured has been picked at random, that we observe that insured and then we attempt to make an estimate of the future observation of that *same* insured. If instead one goes back and chooses a new insured at random, then the information contained in the observation has been lost.

3.2. Exercises

3.2.1. The Expected Value of the Process Variance is 100. The Variance of the Hypothetical Means is 8. How much Bühlmann Credibility is assigned to 20 observations of this risk process?

3.2.2. If 5 observations are assigned 70% Bühlmann Credibility, what is the value of the Bühlmann Credibility parameter K?

3.2.3. Your friend picked at random one of three multi-sided dice. He then rolled the die and told you the result. You are to estimate the result when he rolls that same die again. One of the three multi-sided dice has 4 sides (with

---

[36] In the Philbrick Target Shooting Example discussed in a subsequent section, we assume the targets are fixed and that the skill of the marksmen does not change over time.

1, 2, 3, and 4 on them), the second die has the usual 6 sides (numbered 1 through 6), and the last die has 8 sides (with numbers 1 through 8). For a given die each side has an equal chance of being rolled, i.e., the die is fair. Assume the first roll was a five. Use Bühlmann Credibility to estimate the next roll of the same die.

Hint: The mean of a die with S sides is: $(S + 1)/2$. The variance of a die with S sides is: $(S^2 - 1)/12$.

Use the following information for the next two questions:

There are three large urns, each filled with so many balls that you can treat it as if there are an infinite number. Urn 1 contains balls with "zero" written on them. Urn 2 has balls with "one" written on them. The final Urn 3 is filled with 50% balls with "zero" and 50% balls with "one." An urn is chosen at random and five balls are selected.

3.2.4. If all five balls have "zero" written on them, use Bühlmann Credibility to estimate the expected value of another ball picked from that urn.

3.2.5. If three balls have "zero" written on them and two balls have "one" written on them, use Bühlmann Credibility to estimate the expected value of another ball picked from that urn.

3.2.6. There are two types of urns, each with many balls labeled $1,000 and $2,000.

Type of Urn	A Priori chance of This Type of Urn	Percentage of $1,000 Balls	Percentage of $2,000 Balls
I	80%	90%	10%
II	20%	70%	30%

An urn is selected at random, and you observe a total of $8,000 on 5 balls drawn from that urn at random. Using Bühlmann Credibility, what is the estimated value of the next ball drawn from that urn?

3.2.7. The aggregate loss distributions for three risks for one exposure period are as follows:

Risk	Aggregate Losses $0	$100	$500
A	0.90	0.07	0.03
B	0.50	0.30	0.20
C	0.30	0.33	0.37

A risk is selected at random and is observed to have $500 of aggregate losses in the first exposure period. Determine the Bühlmann Credibility estimate of the expected value of the aggregate losses for the same risk's second exposure period.

3.2.8. A die is selected at random from an urn that contains four 6-sided dice with the following characteristics:

Number on Face	Number of Faces Die A	Die B	Die C	Die D
1	3	1	1	1
2	1	3	1	1
3	1	1	3	1
4	1	1	1	3

The first five rolls of the selected die yielded the following in sequential order: 2, 3, 1, 2, and 4. Using Bühlmann Credibility, what is the expected value of the next roll of the same die?

Use the following information for the following seven questions:

There are three types of drivers with the following characteristics:

Type	Portion of Drivers of This Type	Poisson Annual Claim Frequency	Pareto Claim Severity*
Good	60%	5%	$\alpha = 5, \lambda = 10{,}000$
Bad	30%	10%	$\alpha = 4, \lambda = 10{,}000$
Ugly	10%	20%	$\alpha = 3, \lambda = 10{,}000$

For any individual driver, frequency, and severity are independent.

3.2.9. A driver is observed to have over a five-year period a single claim. Use Bühlmann Credibility to predict this driver's future annual claim frequency.

3.2.10. What is the expected value of the process variance of the claim severities (for the observation of a single claim)?

3.2.11. What is the variance of the hypothetical mean severities (for the observation of a single claim)?

3.2.12. Over several years, for an individual driver you observe a single claim of size $25,000. Use Bühlmann Credibility to estimate this driver's future average claim severity.

3.2.13. What is the expected value of the process variance of the pure premiums (for the observation of a single exposure)?

3.2.14. What is the variance of the hypothetical mean pure premiums (for the observation of a single exposure)?

3.2.15. A driver is observed to have over a five-year period a total of $25,000 in losses. Use Bühlmann Credibility to predict this driver's future pure premium.

---

*See the Appendix on claim frequency and severity distributions.

3.2.16. There are two classes of insureds in a given population. Each insured has either no claims or exactly one claim in one experience period. For each insured the distribution of the number of claims is binomial. The probability of a claim in one experience period is 0.20 for Class 1 insureds and 0.30 for Class 2. The population consists of 40% Class 1 insureds and 60% for Class 2. An insured is selected at random without knowing the insured's class. What credibility would be given to this insured's experience for five experience periods using Bühlmann's Credibility Formula?

Use the following information for the next two questions:

Class	Number of Claims Mean	Process Variance	Size of Loss Mean	Variance
A	.1667	.1389	4	20
B	.8333	.1389	2	5

Each class is homogeneous with all members of the class having the same mean and process variance. Frequency and severity are independently distributed. Classes A and B have the same number of risks. A risk is randomly selected from one of the two classes and four observations are made of the risk.

3.2.17. Determine the value for the Bühlmann Credibility, Z, that can be applied to the observed pure premium.

3.2.18. The pure premium calculated from the four observations is 0.25. Determine the Bühlmann Credibility estimate for the risk's pure premium.

3.2.19. You are given the following:

• X is a random variable with mean m and variance v.

• m is a random variable with mean 2 and variance 4.

- v is a random variable with mean 8 and variance 32.

Determine the value of the Bühlmann Credibility factor Z, after three observations of X. (m and v are constant during the observation periods.)

3.3. Target Shooting Example

In the classic paper by Stephen Philbrick[37] there is an excellent target shooting example that illustrates the ideas of Bühlmann Credibility. Assume there are four marksmen each shooting at his own target. Each marksman's shots are assumed to be distributed around his target, marked by one of the letters A, B, C, and D, with an expected mean equal to the location of his target. Each marksman is shooting at a different target.

If the targets are arranged as in Figure 8.1, the resulting shots of each marksman would tend to cluster around his own target. The shots of each marksman have been distinguished by a different symbol. So for example the shots of marksman B are shown as triangles. We see that in some cases one would have a hard time deciding which marksman had made a particular shot if we did not have the convenient labels.

The point E represents the average of the four targets A, B, C, and D. Thus, E is the grand mean.[38] If we did not know which marksman was shooting we would estimate that the shot would be at E; the a priori estimate is E.

Once we observe a shot from an unknown marksman,[39] we could be asked to estimate the location of the next shot from

---

[37] "An Examination of Credibility Concepts," *PCAS*, 1981.

[38] In this example, each of the marksmen is equally likely; that is, they fire the same number of shots. Thus, we weight each target equally. As was seen previously, in general one would take a weighted average using the not necessarily equal a priori probabilities as the weights.

[39] Thus, the shot does *not* have one of the convenient labels attached to it. This is analogous to the situation in Auto Insurance, where the drivers in a classification are presumed not to be wearing little labels telling us who are the safer and less safe drivers in the class. We rely on the observed experience to help estimate that.

FIGURE 8.1

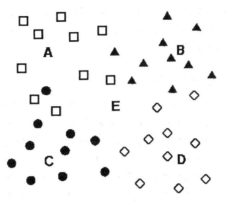

the *same* marksman. Using Bühlmann Credibility our estimate would be between the observation and the a priori mean of E. The larger the credibility assigned to the observation, the closer the estimate is to the observation. The smaller the credibility assigned to the data, the closer the estimate is to E.

There are a number of features of this target shooting example that control how much Bühlmann Credibility is assigned to our observation. We have assumed that the marksmen are not perfect; they do not always hit their target. The amount of spread of their shots around their targets can be measured by the variance. The average spread over the marksmen is the Expected Value of the Process Variance (EPV). The better the marksmen, the smaller the EPV and the more tightly clustered around the targets the shots will be.

The worse the marksmen, the larger the EPV and the less tightly the shots are spread. The better the marksmen, the more information contained in a shot. The worse the marksmen, the more random noise contained in the observation of the location of a shot. Thus, when the marksmen are good, we expect to give more weight to an observation (all other things being equal) than

FIGURE 8.2

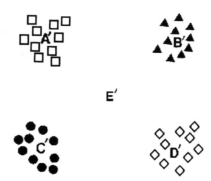

when the marksmen are bad. Thus, the better the marksmen, the higher the credibility:

Marksmen	Clustering of Shots	Expected Value of the Process Variance	Information Content	Credibility Assigned to an Observation
Good	Tight	Small	High	Larger
Bad	Loose	Large	Low	Smaller

The smaller the Expected Value of the Process Variance the larger the credibility. This is illustrated by Figure 8.2. It is assumed in Figure 8.2 that each marksman is better[40] than was the case in Figure 8.1. The EPV is smaller and we assign more credibility to the observation. This makes sense, since in Figure 8.2 it is a lot easier to tell which marksman is likely to have made a particular shot based solely on its location.

Another feature that determines how much credibility to give an observation is how far apart the four targets are placed. As we move the targets further apart (all other things being equal) it is easier to distinguish the shots of the different marksmen. Each

---

[40]Alternatively, the marksmen could be shooting from closer to the targets.

FIGURE 8.3

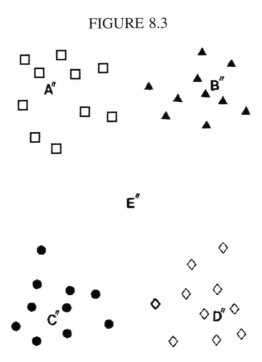

target is a hypothetical mean of one of the marksmen's shots. The spread of the targets can be quantified as the Variance of the Hypothetical Means.

Targets	Variance of the Hypothetical Means	Information Content	Credibility Assigned to an Observation
Closer	Small	Low	Smaller
Further Apart	Large	High	Larger

As illustrated in Figure 8.3, the further apart the targets the more credibility we would assign to our observation. The larger the VHM the larger the credibility. It is easier to distinguish which marksman made a shot based solely on its location in Figure 8.3 than in Figure 8.1.

The third feature that one can vary is the number of shots observed from the *same* unknown marksman. The more shots we observe, the more information we have and thus, the more credibility we would assign to the average of the observations.

Each of the three features discussed is reflected in the formula for Bühlmann Credibility $Z = N/(N + K) = N(\text{VHM})/\{N(\text{VHM}) + \text{EPV}\}$. Thus, as the EPV increases, Z decreases; as VHM increases, Z increases; and as N increases, Z increases.

Feature of Target Shooting Example	Mathematical Quantification	Bühlmann Credibility
Better Marksmen	Smaller EPV	Larger
Targets Further Apart	Larger VHM	Larger
More Shots	Larger N	Larger

Expected Value of the Process Variance vs. Variance of the Hypothetical Means

There are two separate reasons why the observed shots vary. First, the marksmen are not perfect. In other words the Expected Value of the Process Variance is positive. Even if all the targets were in the same place, there would still be a variance in the observed results. This component of the total variance due to the imperfection of the marksmen is quantified by the EPV.

Second, the targets are spread apart. In other words, the Variance of the Hypothetical Means is positive. Even if every marksman were perfect, there would still be a variance in the observed results, when the marksmen shoot at different targets. This component of the total variance due to the spread of the targets is quantified by the VHM.

One needs to understand the distinction between these two sources of variance in the observed results. Also one has to know that the total variance of the observed shots is a sum of these two components: Total Variance = EPV + VHM.

Bühlmann Credibility is a Relative Concept

In Philbrick's target shooting example, we are comparing two estimates of the location of the next shot from the same marksman. One estimate is the average of the observations; the other estimate is the average of the targets, the a priori mean.

When the marksmen are better, there is less random fluctuation in the shots and the average of the observations is a better estimate, relative to the a priori mean. In this case, the weight Z applied to the average of the observations is larger, while $(1 - Z)$ applied to the a priori mean is smaller.

As the targets get closer together, there is less variation of the hypothetical means, and the a priori mean becomes a better estimate, relative to the average of the observations. In this case, the weight Z applied to the average of the observations is smaller, while the complement $(1 - Z)$ applied to the a priori mean is larger.

Bühlmann Credibility measures the usefulness of one estimator, the average of the observations, relative to another estimator, the a priori mean. If $Z = 50\%$, then the two estimators are equally good or equally bad. In general, Bühlmann Credibility is a relative measure of the value of the information contained in the observation versus that in the a priori mean.

A One-Dimensional Target Shooting Example

Assume a one-dimensional example of Philbrick's target shooting model such that the marksmen only miss to the left or right. Assume:

- There are four marksmen.

- The targets for the marksmen are at the points on the number line: 10, 20, 30, and 40.

- The accuracy of each marksman follows a normal distribution with mean equal to his target value and with standard deviation of 12.

Assume a single shot at 18. To use Bühlmann Credibility we need to calculate the Expected Value of the Process Variance and the Variance of the Hypothetical Means. The process variance for every marksman is assumed to be the same and equal to $12^2 = 144$. Thus, the EPV = 144. The overall mean is 25 and the variance is $(1/4)(15^2 + 5^2 + 5^2 + 15^2) = 125$. Thus, the Bühlmann Credibility parameter is K = EPV/VHM = $144/125 = 1.152$. The credibility of a single observation is $Z = 1/(1 + 1.152) = 46.5\%$. Thus, if one observes a single shot at 18, then the Bühlmann Credibility estimate of the next shot is $(18)(46.5\%) + (25)(53.5\%) = 21.7$.

More Shots

What if instead of a single shot at 18 one observed three shots at 18, 26, and 4 from the same unknown marksman?

As calculated above $K = 1.152$. The credibility of 3 observations is $Z = 3/(3 + 1.152) = 72.3\%$. The larger number of observations has increased the credibility. The average of the observations is $(18 + 26 + 4)/3 = 16$. The a priori mean is 25. Thus, the Bühlmann Credibility estimate of the next shot is: $(16)(72.3\%) + (25)(27.7\%) = 18.5$.

Moving the Targets

Assume that the targets were further apart. Assume:

- There are four marksmen.

- The targets for the marksmen are at the points on the number line: 20, 40, 60, and 80.

- The accuracy of each marksman follows a normal distribution with mean equal to his target value and with standard deviation of 12.

Then each shot has more informational content about which marksman produced it. Assume we observe three shots from an unknown marksman at: 38, 46, and 24. The EPV is still 144 while the VHM is now $(4)(125) = 500$, so the Bühlmann Credibility

Parameter $K = \text{EPV}/\text{VHM} = 144/500 = .288$. Thus, the credibility assigned to 3 shots is $3/3.288 = 91.2\%$, larger than before. The larger VHM has increased the credibility.[41] The average of the observations is $(38 + 46 + 24)/3 = 36$. The a priori mean is 50. Thus, the Bühlmann Credibility estimate of the next shot is: $(36)(91.2\%) + (50)(8.8\%) = 37.2$.

Altering the Skill of the Marksmen

Assume that the marksmen are more skilled.[42] Assume:

- There are four marksmen.

- The targets for the marksmen are at the points on the number line: 10, 20, 30, and 40.

- The accuracy of each marksman follows a normal distribution with mean equal to his target value and with standard deviation of 6.

With a smaller process variance, each shot has more informational content about which marksman produced it. Assume we observe three shots from an unknown marksman at: 18, 26, and 4. The EPV is $6^2 = 36$ while the VHM is 125, so the Bühlmann Credibility $K = \text{EPV}/\text{VHM} = 36/125 = .288$. Thus, the credibility assigned to 3 shots is $3/3.288 = 91.2\%$, more than in the original example. The smaller EPV has increased the credibility.[43] The average of the observations is $(18 + 26 + 4)/3 = 16$. The a priori mean is 25. Thus, the Bühlmann Credibility estimate of the next shot is: $(16)(91.2\%) + (25)(8.8\%) = 16.8$.

Limiting Situations and Bühlmann Credibility

As the number of observations approaches infinity, the credibility approaches one. In the target shooting example, as the

---

[41] If instead one had moved the targets closer together, then the credibility assigned to a single shot would have been less. A smaller VHM leads to less credibility.

[42] Alternatively, assume the marksmen are shooting from closer to the targets.

[43] If instead one had less skilled marksmen, then the credibility assigned to a single shot would have been less. A larger EPV leads to less credibility.

number of shots approaches infinity, our Bühlmann Credibility estimate approaches the mean of the observations.

On the other hand, if we have no observations, then the estimate is the a priori mean. We give the a priori mean a weight of 1, so $1 - Z = 1$ or $Z = 0$.

Bühlmann Credibility is given by $Z = N/(N + K)$. In the usual situations where one has a finite number of observations, $0 < N < \infty$, one will have $0 < Z < 1$ provided $0 < K < \infty$. The Bühlmann Credibility is only zero or unity in unusual situations.

The Bühlmann Credibility parameter $K = \text{EPV}/\text{VHM}$. So $K = 0$ if $\text{EPV} = 0$ or $\text{VHM} = \infty$. On the other hand K is infinite if $\text{EPV} = \infty$ or $\text{VHM} = 0$.

The Expected Value of the Process Variance is zero only if one has certainty of results.[44] In the case of the Philbrick Target Shooting Example, if all the marksmen were absolutely perfect, then the expected value of the process variance would be zero. In that situation we assign the observation a credibility of unity; our new estimate is the observation.

The Variance of the Hypothetical Means is infinite if one has little or no knowledge and therefore has a large variation in hypotheses.[45] In the case of the Philbrick Target Shooting Example, as the targets get further and further apart, the variance of the hypothetical means approaches infinity. We assign the observations more and more weight as the targets get further apart. If one target were in Alaska, another in California, another in Maine and the fourth in Florida, we would give the observation virtually 100% credibility. In the limit, our new estimate is the observation; the credibility is one.

---

[44]For example, one could assume that it is certain that the sun will rise tomorrow; there has been no variation of results, the sun has risen every day of which you are aware.
[45]For example, an ancient Greek philosopher might have hypothesized that the universe was more than 3,000 years old with all such ages equally likely.

However, in most applications of Bühlmann Credibility the Expected Value of the Process Variance is positive and the Variance of the Hypothetical Means is finite, so that $K > 0$.

The Expected Value of the Process Variance can be infinite only if the process variance is infinite for at least one of the types of risks. If in an example involving claim severity, one assumed a Pareto distribution with $\alpha \leq 2$, then one would have infinite process variance. In the Philbrick Target Shooting Example, a marksman would have to be infinitely terrible in order to have an infinite process variance. As the marksmen get worse and worse, we give the observation less and less weight. In the limit where the location of the shot is independent of the location of the target we give the observation no weight; the credibility is zero.

The Variance of the Hypothetical Means is zero only if all the types of risks have the same mean. For example, in the Philbrick Target Shooting Example, if all the targets are at the same location (or alternatively each of the marksmen is shooting at the same target) then the VHM = 0. As the targets get closer and closer to each other, we give the observation less and less weight. In the limit, we give the observation no weight; the credibility is zero. In the limit, all the weight is given to the single target.

However, in the usual applications of Bühlmann Credibility there is variation in the hypotheses, and there is a finite expected value of process variance, and therefore K is finite.

Assuming $0 < K < \infty$ and $0 < N < \infty$, then $0 < Z < 1$. **Thus, in ordinary circumstances the Bühlmann Credibility is strictly between zero and one.**

3.3. Exercises

3.3.1. In which of the following should credibility be expected to increase?

1. Larger quantity of observations.

2. Increase in the prior mean.

3. Increase in the variance of hypothetical means.

3.3.2. There are three marksmen, each of whose shots are Normally Distributed (in one dimension) with means and standard deviations:

Risk	Mean	Standard Deviation
A	10	3
B	20	5
C	30	15

A marksman is chosen at random. You observe two shots at 10 and 14. Using Bühlmann Credibility estimate the next shot from the same marksman.

Use the following information to answer the next two questions:

Assume you have two shooters, each of whose shots is given by a (one dimensional) Normal distribution:

Shooter	Mean	Variance
A	+1	1
B	−1	25

Assume a priori that each shooter is equally likely

3.3.3. You observe a single shot at +4. Use Bühlmann Credibility to estimate the location of the next shot.

3.3.4. You observed three shots at 2, 0, 1. Use Bühlmann Credibility to estimate the location of the next shot.

4. BAYESIAN ANALYSIS

Bayesian Analysis is another technique to update a prior hypothesis based on observations, closely related to the use of

Bühlmann Credibility. In fact, the use of Bühlmann Credibility is the least squares linear approximation to Bayesian Analysis.[46] First, some preliminary mathematical ideas related to Bayesian Analysis will be discussed.

4.1. Mathematical Preliminaries

Conditional Distributions

Example 4.1.1: Assume that 14% of actuarial students take exam seminars and that 8% of actuarial students both take exam seminars and pass their exam. What is the chance of a student who has taken an exam seminar passing his/her exam?

[*Solution:* 8%/14% = 57%. (Assume 1,000 total students, of whom 140 take exam seminars. Of these 140 students, 80 pass, for a pass rate of 57%.)]

This is a simple example of a conditional probability.

The conditional probability of an event A given another event B is defined as:

$$P[A \mid B] = P[A \text{ and } B]/P[B] \tag{4.1.1}$$

In the simple example, $A = \{$student passes exam$\}$, $B = \{$student takes exam seminar$\}$, $P[A \text{ and } B] = 8\%$, $P[B] = 14\%$. Thus, $P[A \mid B]$
$= P[A \text{ and } B]/P[B] = 8\%/14\% = 57\%$.

Theorem of Total Probability

Example 4.1.2: Assume that the numbers of students taking an exam by exam center are as follows: Chicago 3,500, Los Angeles 2,000, New York 4,500. The number of students from each exam center passing the exam are: Chicago 2,625, Los Angeles 1,200, New York 3,060. What is the overall passing percentage?

[*Solution:* $(2,625 + 1,200 + 3,060)/(3,500 + 2,000 + 4,500) =$

---

[46] A proof can be found in Bühlmann, "Experience Rating and Credibility" or Klugman, et al., *Loss Models: From Data to Decisions.*

6,885/10,000 = 68.85%.]

If one has a set of mutually disjoint events A_i, then one can write the marginal distribution function $P[B]$ in terms of the conditional distributions $P[B \mid A_i]$ and the probabilities $P[A_i]$:

$$P[B] = \sum_i P[B \mid A_i]P[A_i] \qquad (4.1.2)$$

This theorem follows from $\sum_i P[B \mid A_i]P[A_i] = \sum_i P[B$ and $A_i] = P[B]$, provided that the A_i are disjoint events that cover all possibilities.

Thus, one can compute probabilities of events either directly or by summing a product of terms.

Example 4.1.3: Assume that the percentages of students taking an exam by exam center are as follows: Chicago 35%, Los Angeles 20%, New York 45%. The percentages of students from each exam center passing the exam are: Chicago 75%, Los Angeles 60%, New York 68%. What is the overall passing percentage?

[*Solution:* $\sum_i P[B \mid A_i]P[A_i]$ = (75%)(35%) + (60%)(20%) + (68%)(45%) = 68.85%.]

Note that example 4.1.3 is mathematically the same as example 4.1.2. This is a concrete example of the Theorem of Total Probability, Equation 4.1.2.

Conditional Expectation

In general, in order to compute a conditional expectation, we take the weighted average over all the possibilities x:

$$E[X \mid B] = \sum_x xP[X = x \mid B] \qquad (4.1.3)$$

Example 4.1.4: Let G be the result of rolling a green 6-sided die. Let R be the result of rolling a red 6-sided die. G and R are independent of each other. Let M be the maximum of G and R. What is the expectation of the conditional distribution of M if $G = 3$?

[*Solution:* The conditional distribution of M if $G = 3$ is: $f(3) = 3/6$, $f(4) = 1/6$, $f(5) = 1/6$, and $f(6) = 1/6$. (Note that if $G = 3$, then $M = 3$ if $R = 1$, 2, or 3. So, $f(3) = 3/6$.) Thus, the mean of the conditional distribution of M if $G = 3$ is: $(3)(3/6) + (4)(1/6) + (5)(1/6) + (6)(1/6) = 4$.]

4.1. Exercises

4.1.1. Assume that 5% of men are colorblind, while .25% of women are colorblind. A colorblind person is picked out of a population made up 10% of men and 90% of women. What is the chance the colorblind person is a man?

Use the following information for the next six questions:

A large set of urns contain many black and red balls. There are four types of urns each with differing percentages of black balls. Each type of urn has a differing chance of being picked.

Type of Urn	A Priori Probability	Percentage of Black Balls
I	40%	5%
II	30%	8%
III	20%	13%
IV	10%	18%

4.1.2. An urn is picked and a ball is selected from that urn. What is the chance that the ball is black?

4.1.3. An urn is picked and a ball is selected from that urn. If the ball is black, what is the chance that Urn I was picked?

4.1.4. An urn is picked and a ball is selected from that urn. If the ball is black, what is the chance that Urn II was picked?

4.1.5. An urn is picked and a ball is selected from that urn.
If the ball is black, what is the chance that Urn III was
picked?

4.1.6. An urn is picked and a ball is selected from that urn.
If the ball is black, what is the chance that Urn IV was
picked?

4.1.7. An urn is picked and a ball is selected from that urn. If
the ball is black, what is the chance that the next ball
picked from that same urn will be black?

Use the following information for the next two questions:

V and X are each given by the result of rolling a 6-sided die.
V and X are independent of each other. $Y = V + X$.

4.1.8. What is the probability that $X = 5$ if $Y \geq 9$?

4.1.9. What is the expected value of X if $Y \geq 9$?

Use the following information for the next two questions:

City	Percentage of Total Drivers	Percent of Drivers Accident-Free
Boston	40%	80%
Springfield	25%	85%
Worcester	20%	90%
Pittsfield	15%	95%

4.1.10. A driver is picked at random. If the driver is accident-
free, what is the chance the driver is from Boston?

4.1.11. A driver is picked at random. If the driver has had an
accident, what is the chance the driver is from Pittsfield?

4.1.12. On a multiple choice exam, each question has 5 possible answers, exactly one of which is correct. On those
questions for which he is not certain of the answer, Stu

Dent's strategy for taking the exam is to answer at random from the 5 possible answers. Assume he correctly answers the questions for which he knows the answers. If Stu Dent knows the answers to 62% of the questions, what is the probability that he knew the answer to a question he answered correctly?

4.2. Bayesian Analysis

Take the following simple example. Assume there are two types of risks, each with Bernoulli claim frequencies. One type of risk has a 30% chance of a claim (and a 70% chance for no claims.) The second type of risk has a 50% chance of having a claim. Of the universe of risks, 3/4 are of the first type with a 30% chance of a claim, while 1/4 are of the second type with a 50% chance of having a claim.

Type of Risk	A Priori Probability that a Risk is of this Type	Chance of a Claim Occurring for a Risk of this Type
1	3/4	30%
2	1/4	50%

If a risk is chosen at random, then the chance of having a claim is $(3/4)(30\%) + (1/4)(50\%) = 35\%$. In this simple example, there are two possible outcomes: either we observe 1 claim or no claims. Thus, the chance of no claims is 65%.

Assume we pick a risk at random and observe no claim. Then what is the chance that we have risk Type 1? By the definition of the conditional probability we have: $P(\text{Type} = 1 \mid n = 0)$ $= P(\text{Type} = 1 \text{ and } n = 0)/P(n = 0)$. However, $P(\text{Type} = 1 \text{ and } n = 0) = P(n = 0 \mid \text{Type} = 1)P(\text{Type} = 1) = (.7)(.75)$. Therefore, $P(\text{Type} = 1 \mid n = 0) = P(n = 0 \mid \text{Type} = 1)P(\text{Type} = 1)/P(n = 0)$ $= (.7)(.75)/.65 = .8077$.

This is a special case of **Bayes' Theorem:**

$$P(A \mid B) = P(B \mid A)P(A)/P(B)$$

$$P(\textbf{Risk Type} \mid \textbf{Obser.}) = P(\textbf{Obser.} \mid \textbf{Risk Type}) \quad (4.2.1)$$

$$\times P(\textbf{Risk Type})/P(\textbf{Obser.})$$

Example 4.2.1: Assume we pick a risk at random and observe no claim. Then what is the chance that we have risk Type 2?

[*Solution:* $P(\text{Type} = 2 \mid n = 0) = P(n = 0 \mid \text{Type} = 2)P(\text{Type} = 2)$ $/ P(n = 0) = (.5)(.25)/.65 = .1923.$]

Of course with only two types of risks the chance of a risk being Type 2 is unity minus the chance of being Type 1. The posterior probability that the selected risk is Type 1 is .8077 and the posterior probability that it is Type 2 is .1923.

Posterior Estimates

Now not only do we have probabilities posterior to an observation, but we can use these to estimate the chance of a claim if the same risk is observed again. For example, if we observe no claim the estimated claim frequency for the same risk is: (posterior prob. Type 1)(claim freq. Type 1)+ (posterior prob. Type 2)(claim freq. Type 2) = (.8077)(30%)+ (.1923)(50%) = 33.85%.

Note that the posterior estimate is a weighted average of the hypothetical means for the different types of risks. Thus, the posterior estimate of 33.85% is in the range of the hypotheses, 30% to 50%. This is true in general for Bayesian analysis.

The result of Bayesian Analysis is always within the range of hypotheses.

This is not necessarily true for the results of applying Credibility.

Example 4.2.2: What if a risk is chosen at random and one claim is observed. What is the posterior estimate of the chance of a claim from this same risk?

[*Solution:* $(.6429)(.3) + (.3571)(.5) = 37.14\%$

A	B	C	D	E	F
	A Priori Chance of This Type of Risk	Chance of the Observation	Prob. Weight = Product of Columns B & C	Posterior Chance of This Type of Risk	Mean Annual Freq.
Type of Risk					
1	0.75	0.3	0.225	64.29%[47]	0.30
2	0.25	0.5	0.125	35.71%	0.50
Overall			0.350	1.000	**37.14%**

For example, $P(\text{Type} = 1 \mid n = 1) = P(\text{Type} = 1 \text{ and } n = 1)/P(n = 1) = (.75)(.3)/.35 = .643$, $P(\text{Type} = 2 \mid n = 1) = P(\text{Type} = 2 \text{ and } n = 1)/P(n = 1) = (.25)(.5)/.35 = .357.$]

Note how the estimate posterior to the observation of one claim is 37.14%, greater than the a priori estimate of 35%. The observation has let us infer that it is more likely that the risk is of the high frequency type than it was prior to the observation. Thus, we infer that the future chance of a claim from this risk is higher than it was prior to the observation. Similarly, the estimate posterior to the observation of no claim is 33.85%, less than the a priori estimate of 35%.

We had a 65% chance of observing no claim and a 35% chance of observing a claim. Weighting together the two posterior estimates: $(65\%)(33.85\%) + (35\%)(37.14\%) = 35\%$. The weighted average of the posterior estimates is equal to the overall a priori mean. This is referred to as "the estimates being in balance." If D_i are the possible outcomes, then the Bayesian estimates are $E[X \mid D_i]$. Then $\sum_i P(D_i)E[X \mid D_i] = E[X] =$ the a priori mean.

$$\sum_i P(D_i)E[X \mid D_i] = E[X] \qquad (4.2.2)$$

---

[47] Note that $.6429 = .225/.350$ and $.3571 = .125/.350$. The a priori chance of the observation is .350. Thus, the values in column E are the resluts of applying Bayes Theorem, equation 4.2.1

The estimates that result from Bayesian Analysis are always in balance:

The sum of the products of the a priori chance of each outcome times its posterior Bayesian estimate is equal to the a priori mean.

Multi-Sided Dice Example

Let's illustrate Bayesian Analysis with a simple example involving multi-sided dice:

Assume that there are a total of 100 multi-sided dice of which 60 are 4-sided, 30 are 6-sided and 10 are 8-sided. The multi-sided dice with 4 sides have 1, 2, 3 and 4, on them. The multi-sided dice with the usual 6 sides have numbers 1 through 6 on them. The multi-sided dice with 8 sides have numbers 1 through 8 on them. For a given die each side has an equal chance of being rolled; i.e., the die is fair.

Your friend has picked at random a multi-sided die. (You do not know what sided-die he has picked.) He then rolled the die and told you the result. You are to estimate the result when he rolls that same die again.

If the result is a 3 then the estimate of the next roll of the same die is 2.853:

A	B	C	D	E	F
	A Priori		Prob. Weight =	Posterior	
	Chance of	Chance	Product	Chance of	Mean
Type of	This Type	of the	of Columns	This Type	Die
Die	of Die	Observation	B & C	of Die	Roll
4-sided	0.600	0.250	0.1500	70.6%	2.5
6-sided	0.300	0.167	0.0500	23.5%	3.5
8-sided	0.100	0.125	0.0125	5.9%	4.5
Overall			0.2125	1.000	**2.853**

Example 4.2.3: If instead a 6 is rolled, what is the estimate of the next roll of the same die?

[*Solution:* The estimate of the next roll of the same die is 3.700:

A	B	C	D	E	F
	A Priori		Prob. Weight =	Posterior	
	Chance of	Chance	Product	Chance of	Mean
Type of	This Type	of the	of Columns	This Type	Die
Die	of Die	Observation	B & C	of Die	Roll
4-sided	0.600	0.000	0.0000	0.0%	2.5
6-sided	0.300	0.167	0.0500	80.0%	3.5
8-sided	0.100	0.125	0.0125	20.0%	4.5
Overall			0.0625	1.000	**3.700**

For this example we get the following set of estimates corresponding to each possible observation:

Observation	1	2	3	4	5	6	7	8
Bayesian Estimate	2.853	2.853	2.853	2.853	3.7	3.7	4.5	4.5

Note that while in this simple example the posterior estimates are the same for a number of different observations, this is not usually the case.]

Relation of Bayesian Analysis and Bühlmann Credibility

As discussed in section 3.2 on Bühlmann Credibility, in the multi-sided dice example $K = \text{EPV}/\text{VHM} = 2.15/.45 = 4.778 = 43/9$. For one observation, $Z = 1/(1 + 4.778) = .1731 = 9/52 = .45/(.45 + 2.15)$.

The Bühlmann Credibility estimate is a linear function of the observation:

Observation	1	2	3	4	5	6	7	8
New Estimate	2.6538	2.8269	3	3.1731	3.3462	3.5193	3.6924	3.8655

The above results of applying Bühlmann Credibility differ from those obtained for Bayesian Analysis.

Observation	1	2	3	4	5	6	7	8
Bühlmann Credibility Estimate	2.6538	2.8269	3	3.1731	3.3462	3.5193	3.6924	3.86552
Bayesian Analysis Estimate	2.853	2.853	2.853	2.853	3.7	3.7	4.5	4.5

We note that in this case the line formed by the Bühlmann Credibility estimates seems to approximate the Bayesian Analysis Estimates as shown in Graph 8.3. In general it turns out that the Bühlmann Credibility Estimates are the weighted least squares line fit to the Bayesian Estimates.

GRAPH 8.3

MULTI-SIDED DIE EXAMPLE

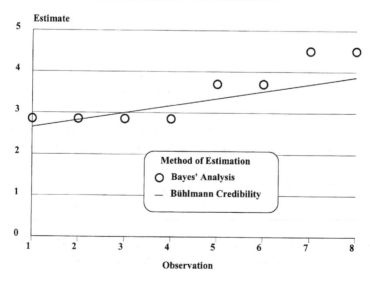

4.2. Exercises

Use the following information for the next seven questions:

There are three types of risks. Assume 60% of the risks are of Type A, 25% of the risks are of Type B, and 15% of the risks are of Type C. Each risk has either one or zero claims per year. A risk is selected at random.

Type of Risk	A Priori Chance of Type of Risk	Chance of a Claim
A	60%	20%
B	25%	30%
C	15%	40%

4.2.1. What is the overall mean annual claim frequency?

4.2.2. You observe no claim in a year. What is the probability that the risk you are observing is of Type A?

4.2.3. You observe no claim in a year. What is the probability that the risk you are observing is of Type B?

4.2.4. You observe no claim in a year. What is the probability that the risk you are observing is of Type C?

4.2.5. You observe no claim in a year. What is the expected annual claim frequency from the same risk?

4.2.6. You observe one claim in a year. What is the expected annual claim frequency from the same risk?

4.2.7. You observe a single risk over five years. You observe 2 claims in 5 years. What is the expected annual claim frequency from the same risk?

4.2.8. Let X_1 be the outcome of a single trial and let $E[X_2 \mid X_1]$ be the expected value of the outcome of a second trial. You are given the following information:

Outcome = T	$P(X_1 = T)$	Bayesian Estimate for $E[X_2 \mid X_1 = T]$
1	5/8	1.4
4	2/8	3.6
16	1/8	—

Determine the Bayesian estimate for $E[X_2 \mid X_1 = 16]$.

Use the following information for the next two questions:

There are two types of urns, each with many balls labeled $1,000 and $2,000.

Type of Urn	A Priori Chance of This Type of Urn	Percentage of $1,000 Balls	Percentage of $2,000 Balls
I	80%	90%	10%
II	20%	70%	30%

4.2.9. You pick an urn at random and pick one ball. If the ball is $2,000, what is the expected value of the next ball picked from that same urn?

4.2.10. You pick an urn at random (80% chance it is of Type I) and pick three balls, returning each ball to the urn before the next pick. If two of the balls were $1,000 and one of the balls was $2,000, what is the expected value of the next ball picked from that same urn?

4.2.11. You are given the following information:

- There are three types of risks

- The types are homogeneous, every risk of a given type has the same Poisson frequency process:

Type	Portion of Risks in This Type	Average (Annual) Claim Frequency
1	70%	.4
2	20%	.6
3	10%	.8

A risk is picked at random and we do not know what type it is. For this randomly selected risk, during one year there are 3 claims. Use Bayesian Analysis to predict the future claim frequency of this same risk.

Use the following information for the next two questions:

There are three marksmen, each of whose shots are Normally Distributed (in one dimension) with means and standard deviations:

Risk	Mean	Standard Deviation
A	10	3
B	20	5
C	30	15

4.2.12. A marksman is chosen at random. If you observe two shots at 10 and 14, what is the chance that it was marksman B?

4.2.13. A marksman is chosen at random. If you observe two shots at 10 and 14, what is the Bayesian Estimate of the next shot from the same marksman?

4.3. Continuous Prior and Posterior Distributions

So far in this section on Bayesian analysis our examples included discrete probability distributions. Now we'll look at continuous distributions.

Let random variables X and Y have the joint p.d.f. (probability density function) $f(x,y)$. The marginal p.d.f. for X is $f_X(x) = \int_{-\infty}^{\infty} f(x,y)dy$ and the marginal p.d.f. for Y is $f_Y(y) = \int_{-\infty}^{\infty} f(x,y)dx$.[48] The conditional p.d.f. for Y given X is:

$$f_Y(y \mid x) = \frac{f(x,y)}{f_X(x)} \qquad (4.3.1)$$

Note the correspondence between this formula and formula (4.1.1): $P[A \mid B] = P[A \text{ and } B]/P[B]$. Formula (4.3.1) applies to both continuous and discrete p.d.f.s, or a combination of the two.

In insurance applications it is common for one of the random variables, call it X, to be a discrete random variable and a second variable, θ, to be continuous. X may be the number of claims.[49] The other random variable, θ, is a parameter of the distribution of X. The conditional p.d.f. of X given θ is denoted $f_X(x \mid \theta)$ and the p.d.f. for θ is $f_\theta(\theta)$. The joint p.d.f. for X and θ is:

$$f(x,\theta) = f_X(x \mid \theta)f_\theta(\theta) \qquad (4.3.2)$$

The p.d.f. $f_\theta(\theta)$ is the **prior distribution** of θ. It may represent our initial guess about the distribution of some characteristic within a population, for example expected claim frequency.

If we select a risk at random from the population and observe the number of claims, x, then we can update our estimate of θ for this risk. Using formula (4.3.1) and replacing the joint p.d.f.

---

[48]If one of the random variables, say Y, is discrete, then the integral is replaced with a summation and the marginal p.d.f. for X becomes: $f_X(x) = \sum_i f(x,y_i)$.

[49]If X represents claim sizes, then X is usually continuously distributed. Examples are given in the Appendix.

of X and θ with (4.3.2) produces:

$$f_\theta(\theta \mid X = x) = f_X(x \mid \theta)f_\theta(\theta)/f_X(x) \qquad (4.3.3)$$

$f_\theta(\theta \mid X = x)$ is the **posterior distribution** of θ for the selected risk. We have used information about the risk to adjust our estimate of the distribution of θ. Equation 4.4.3 is just another form of Bayes Theorem, equation 4.2.1.

Example 4.3.1: The probability of exactly one claim during a year for any insured in a population is θ. The probability of no claims is $(1 - \theta)$. The probability of a claim, θ, varies within the population with a p.d.f. given by a uniform distribution:

$$f_\theta(\theta) = 1 \qquad \text{if} \quad 0 \le \theta \le 1, \quad 0 \text{ otherwise.}$$

An insured, Bob, is selected at random from the population. Bob is observed to have a claim during the next year, i.e. $X = 1$. Calculate the posterior density $f_\theta(\theta \mid X = 1)$ for Bob.

[*Solution:* Calculate the marginal p.d.f. for X evaluated at $X = 1$: $f_X(1) = \int_0^1 f(1,\theta)d\theta = \int_0^1 f_X(1 \mid \theta)f_\theta(\theta)d\theta$. Since $f_X(1 \mid \theta) = \theta$ and $f_\theta(\theta) = 1$ over $[0,1]$, then $f_X(1) = \int_0^1 \theta d\theta = 1/2$. So $f_\theta(\theta \mid X = 1) = f_X(X = 1 \mid \theta)f_\theta(\theta)/f_X(1) = (\theta)(1)/(1/2) = 2\theta$.]

Note that in this example the distribution has shifted from being uniform over the interval $[0,1]$ to one that rises linearly from 0 at the left endpoint to 2 at the right endpoint. The fact that Bob had a claim has shifted the weight of the p.d.f. of θ to the right.

Knowing the conditional p.d.f. allows the calculation of the conditional expectation:

$$E[X \mid Y] = \int_{-\infty}^{\infty} x f_X(x \mid y)dx \qquad (4.3.4)$$

And, the expectation of X is:

$$E[X] = E_Y[E_X[X \mid Y]] = \int_{-\infty}^{\infty} \left\{ \int_{-\infty}^{\infty} x f_X(x \mid y) dx \right\} f_Y(y) dy$$

(4.3.5)

Example 4.3.2: Assuming the information from Example 4.3.1, calculate the following:

1. The expectation for the number of claims in a year for an insured selected at random from the population.

2. The expectation for the number of claims in a year for an insured who was randomly selected from the population and then had one claim during an observation year.

[*Solution:* (1) The distribution of X, the number of claims, is discrete given θ. $E_X[X \mid \theta] = (1)(\theta) + (0)(1 - \theta) = \theta$. Since $f_\theta(\theta) = 1$ for $0 < \theta < 1$, $E[X] = E_\theta[E_X[X \mid \theta]] = E_\theta[\theta] = \int_0^1 \theta f_\theta(\theta) d\theta = \int_0^1 \theta d\theta = 1/2$.

(2) As in (1), $E_X[X \mid \theta] = \theta$. But from example 4.3.1, the posterior p.d.f. of θ given that $X = 1$ is $f_\theta(\theta \mid X = 1) = 2\theta$. So, $E[X] = E_\theta[E_X[X \mid \theta]] = E_\theta[\theta] = \int_0^1 \theta(2\theta) d\theta = 2/3$.]

Bayesian Interval Estimates

By the use of Bayes Theorem one obtains an entire posterior distribution. Rather than just using the mean of that posterior distribution in order to get a point estimate, one can use the posterior density function to estimate the posterior chance that the quantity of interest is in a given interval. This is illustrated in the next example.

Example 4.3.3: Assume the information from example 4.3.1. Given that Bob had one claim in one year, what is the posterior estimate that he has a θ parameter less than .2?

[*Solution:* From example 4.3.1, the posterior density function for θ is: $f_\theta(\theta \mid X = 1) = 2\theta$.

The posterior chance that θ is in the interval $[0, .2]$ is the integral from 0 to .2 of the posterior density:

$$\int_0^{.2} 2\theta\, d\theta = \theta^2 \Big]_{p=0}^{p=.2} = .2^2 = .04.]$$

The idea of a continuous distribution of types of risks is developed for the particular case of the Gamma-Poisson conjugate prior in Section 5.

4.3. Exercises

For the next two problems, assume the following information:

The probability of exactly one claim during a year for any insured in a population is θ. The probability of no claims is $(1 - \theta)$. The probability of a claim, θ, varies within the population with a p.d.f. given by a uniform distribution:

$$f_\theta(\theta) = 1 \quad \text{if} \quad 0 \le \theta \le 1, \quad 0 \text{ otherwise.}$$

An insured, Bob, is selected at random from the population.

4.3.1. Bob is observed for two years after being randomly selected from the population and has a claim in each year. Calculate the posterior density function of θ for Bob.

4.3.2. Bob is observed for three years after being randomly selected from the population and has a claim in each year. Calculate the posterior density function of θ for Bob.

Use the following information for the next two questions:

- The probability of y successes in n trials is given by a Binomial distribution with parameters n and p.

- The prior distribution of p is uniform on $[0, 1]$.

- One success was observed in three trials.

4.3.3. What is the Bayesian estimate for the probability that the unknown parameter p is in the interval $[.3, .4]$?

4.3.4. What is the probability that a success will occur on the fourth trial?

4.3.5. A number x is randomly selected from a uniform distribution on the interval $[0, 1]$. Three independent Bernoulli trials are performed with probability of success x on each trial. All three are successes. What is the posterior probability that x is less than 0.9?

4.3.6. You are given the following:

- The probability that a single insured will produce 0 claims during the next exposure period is $e^{-\theta}$.

- θ varies by insured and follows a distribution with density function

$$f(\theta) = 36\theta e^{-6\theta}, \qquad 0 < \theta < \infty.$$

Determine the probability that a randomly selected insured will produce 0 claims during the next exposure period.

4.3.7. Let N be the random variable that represents the number of claims observed in a one-year period. N is Poisson distributed with a probability density function with parameter θ:

$$P[N = n \mid \theta] = e^{-\theta}\theta^n/n!, \qquad n = 0, 1, 2, \ldots$$

The probability of observing no claims in a year is less than .450. Which of the following describe possible probability distributions for θ?

1. θ is uniformly distributed on $(0, 2)$.

2. The probability density function of θ is $f(\theta) = e^{-\theta}$ for $\theta > 0$.

3. $P[\theta = 1] = 1$ and $P[\theta \neq 1] = 0$.

5. CONJUGATE PRIORS

Conjugate prior distributions have elegant mathematical properties that make them valuable in actuarial applications. The Gamma-Poisson is the most important of these for casualty actuarial work. A study of the Gamma-Poisson model is valuable to the understanding of Bayesian analysis and Bühlmann Credibility.[50]

5.1. Gamma Function and Distribution

The quantity $x^{\alpha-1}e^{-x}$ is finite for $x \geq 0$ and $\alpha \geq 1$. Since it declines quickly to zero as x approaches infinity, its integral from zero to infinity exists. This is the much studied and tabulated (complete) Gamma Function.[51]

$$\Gamma(\alpha) = \int_{t=0}^{\infty} t^{\alpha-1}e^{-t}dt = \lambda^{\alpha}\int_{t=0}^{\infty} t^{\alpha-1}e^{-\lambda t}dt \qquad \text{for} \quad \alpha \geq 0, \quad \lambda \geq 0.$$

(5.1.1)

It can be proven that:[52] $\Gamma(\alpha) = (\alpha-1)\Gamma(\alpha-1)$.

For integral values of α, $\Gamma(\alpha) = (\alpha-1)!$, and $\Gamma(1) = 1$, $\Gamma(2) = 1! = 1, \Gamma(3) = 2! = 2, \Gamma(4) = 3! = 6, \Gamma(5) = 4! = 24$, etc.

Integrals involving e^{-x} and powers of x can be written in terms of the Gamma function:

$$\int_{t=0}^{\infty} t^{\alpha-1}e^{-\lambda t}dt = \Gamma(\alpha)\lambda^{-\alpha}.$$

(5.1.2)

Equation 5.1.2 is very useful for working with anything involving the Gamma distribution, for example the Gamma-Poisson process as will be seen below. (It follows from the definition of the Gamma function and a change of variables.) The probability

---

[50]This is a special case of a general result for conjugate priors of members of "linear exponential families." This general result is beyond the scope of this chapter.
[51]See for example, *Handbook of Mathematical Functions*, Milton Abramowitz, et. al., National Bureau of Standards, 1964.
[52]Use integration by parts: $\int u\,dv = uv - \int v\,du$ with $u = t^{\alpha-1}$ and $dv = e^{-t}dt$.

density of the Gamma Distribution is: $f(x) = \lambda^\alpha x^{\alpha-1} e^{-\lambda x}/\Gamma(\alpha)$. Since the probability density function must integrate to unity, we must have the above relationship. This is a useful way to remember Equation 5.1.2.

Example 5.1.1: In terms of its parameters, α and λ, what is the mean of a Gamma distribution?

[*Solution:* The mean is the expected value of x.

$$\int_0^\infty xf(x)dx = \int_0^\infty xx^{\alpha-1}e^{-\lambda x}dx(\lambda^\alpha/\Gamma(\alpha))$$

$$= \int_0^\infty x^\alpha e^{-\lambda x}dx(\lambda^\alpha/\Gamma(\alpha)) = \{\Gamma(\alpha+1)/\lambda^{\alpha+1}\}\{\lambda^\alpha/\Gamma(\alpha)\}$$

$$= \{\Gamma(\alpha+1)/\Gamma(\alpha)\}/\lambda = \alpha/\lambda.]$$

Example 5.1.2: In terms of its parameters, α and λ, what is the nth moment of a Gamma distribution?

[*Solution:* The nth moment is the expected value of x^n.

$$\int_0^\infty x^n f(x)dx = \int_0^\infty x^n x^{\alpha-1}e^{-\lambda x}dx(\lambda^\alpha/\Gamma(\alpha))$$

$$= \int_0^\infty x^{\alpha+n-1}e^{-\lambda x}dx(\lambda^\alpha/\Gamma(\alpha)) = \{\Gamma(\alpha+n)/\lambda^{\alpha+n}\}\{\lambda^\alpha/\Gamma(\alpha)\}$$

$$= \{\Gamma(\alpha+n)/\Gamma(\alpha)\}/\lambda^n = (\alpha+n-1)(\alpha+n-2)...(\alpha)/\lambda^n.]$$

5.1. Exercises

5.1.1. What is the value of the integral from zero to infinity of $x^5 e^{-8x}$?

5.1.2. What is the density at $x = 8$ of a Gamma distribution with $\alpha = 3$ and $\lambda = .10$?

5.1.3. Using the results of example 5.1.2, show that the variance of the Gamma distribution is α/λ^2.

5.1.4. If $\alpha = 3.0$ and $\lambda = 1.5$, what are the mean and variance of the Gamma distribution?

5.2. The Gamma-Poisson Model

The Gamma-Poisson model has two components: (1) a Poisson distribution that models the number of claims for an insured with a given claims frequency, and (2) a Gamma distribution to model the distribution of claim frequencies within a population of insureds. As in previous sections the goal is to use observations about an insured to infer future expectations.

Poisson Distribution

We'll assume that the number of claims for an insured is Poisson distributed and that the average number of claims in a year is μ. The probability of having n claims in a year is given by:

$$P[n \mid \mu] = \mu^n e^{-\mu}/n!. \qquad (5.2.1)$$

μ is the mean annual number of claims, i.e. $E[n] = \mu$. Any particular insured within the population is assumed to have a μ that remains constant over the time period of interest. However, the estimation of μ is the challenge since μ's may vary from risk to risk. You do not know μ for a risk selected at random.

Example 5.2.1: The number of claims has a Poisson distribution with parameter $\mu = 2$. Calculate the separate probabilities of exactly 0, 1, and 2 claims. Calculate the mean and variance of the distribution.

[*Solution:* $f(n) = \mu^n e^{-\mu}/n!$. Since $\mu = 2.0$, $f(0) = 2^0 e^{-2}/0! = .135$, $f(1) = 2^1 e^{-2}/1! = .271$, and $f(2) = 2^2 e^{-2}/2! = .271$. For the Poisson distribution, mean = variance = $\mu = 2.0$.]

GRAPH 8.4

GAMMA DISTRIBUTION

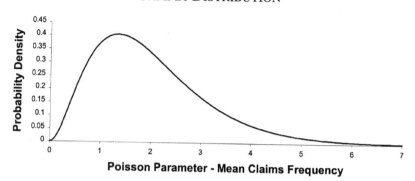

Prior Gamma Distribution

The mean claim frequencies for insureds within the population are assumed to be Gamma distributed with probability density function:

$$f(\mu) = \lambda^\alpha \mu^{\alpha-1} e^{-\lambda\mu}/\Gamma(\alpha), \qquad \text{for} \quad \mu > 0 \quad \text{and} \quad \alpha, \lambda > 0.$$

$$(5.2.2)$$

The random variable is μ and the parameters that determine the shape and scale of the distribution are α and λ. The mean of the distribution is α/λ. So, the average claims frequency across all insureds in the population is α/λ. The variance is α/λ^2. $f(\mu)$ defines the **prior distribution** of the mean claim frequencies.

Let's consider a particular case of the Gamma p.d.f. with parameters $\alpha = 3$, and $\lambda = 1.5$. The p.d.f. for μ is:

$$f(\mu) = 1.5^3 \mu^{3-1} e^{-1.5\mu}/\Gamma(3) = 1.6875\mu^2 e^{-1.5\mu}, \qquad \text{for} \quad \mu > 0.$$

This p.d.f. is shown in Graph 8.4.

Gamma-Poisson Mixed Distribution

Suppose that an insured is selected at random from the population of insureds. What is the distribution of the number of claims for the insured? Or, equivalently, what is the probability that you will see exactly n claims in the next time period?

The probability of exactly n claims for an insured with mean claim frequency μ is $P[n \mid \mu] = \mu^n e^{-\mu}/n!$. But, μ varies across the population. We need to calculate a weighted average of the $P[n \mid \mu]$'s. What weight should we use? Use the p.d.f. (5.2.2), the relative weights of the μ's within the population. After applying weight $f(\mu)$, then we sum over all insureds by taking the integral.

The number of claims for an insured selected at random from the population has a **Gamma-Poisson mixed distribution** defined by the p.d.f.:

$$g(n) = \int_0^\infty P[n \mid \mu] f(\mu) d\mu$$

$$= \int_0^\infty (\mu^n e^{-\mu}/n!) f(\mu) d\mu = \int_0^\infty (\mu^n e^{-\mu}/n!)(\lambda^\alpha \mu^{\alpha-1} e^{-\lambda\mu}/\Gamma(\alpha)) d\mu \tag{5.2.3a}$$

$$= (\lambda^\alpha/n!\Gamma(\alpha)) \int_0^\infty \mu^{n+\alpha-1} e^{-(\lambda+1)\mu} d\mu$$

$$= \{\lambda^\alpha/n!\Gamma(\alpha)\}\{\Gamma(n+\alpha)(\lambda+1)^{-(n+\alpha)}\}^{53}$$

$$= \{\Gamma(n+\alpha)/n!\Gamma(\alpha)\}\{\lambda/(\lambda+1)\}^\alpha\{1/(\lambda+1)\}^n \tag{5.2.3b}$$

$$= \{(n+\alpha-1)!/n!(\alpha-1)!\}\{\lambda/(\lambda+1)\}^\alpha\{1-\lambda/(\lambda+1)\}^n$$

$$= \binom{n+\alpha-1}{n} p^\alpha(1-p)^n \tag{5.2.3c}$$

Note that we have substituted p for $\lambda/(\lambda+1)$ in (5.2.3c).

---

[53]In this derivation we used equation (5.1.2): $\Gamma(\alpha)\lambda^{-\alpha} = \int_0^\infty t^{\alpha-1} e^{-\lambda t} dt$. Through substitution of t for $(\lambda+1)\mu$, it can be shown that $\int_0^\infty \mu^{n+\alpha-1} e^{-(\lambda+1)\mu} d\mu = \Gamma(n+\alpha) (\lambda+1)^{-(n+\alpha)}$.

Thus, the prior mixed distribution is in the form of the Negative Binomial distribution with $k = \alpha$ **and** $p = \lambda/(\lambda + 1)$:

$$\binom{n+k-1}{n} p^k (1-p)^n \qquad (5.2.3d)$$

The Negative Binomial distribution evaluated at n is the probability of seeing exactly n claims in the next year for an insured selected at random from the population. The mean of the negative binomial is $k(1-p)/p$ and the variance is $k(1-p)/p^2$. (See the Appendix.) In terms of α and λ, the mean is α/λ and the variance is $\alpha(\lambda + 1)/\lambda^2$.

Example 5.2.2: The number of claims has a Negative Binomial distribution with parameters $k = \alpha$ and $p = \lambda/(\lambda + 1)$. Assume $\alpha = 3.0$ and $\lambda = 1.5$. Calculate the separate probabilities of exactly 0, 1, and 2 claims. Also calculate the mean and variance of the distribution.

[*Solution:* First, $p = \lambda/(\lambda + 1) = 1.5/(1.5 + 1) = .60$ and $k = \alpha = 3.0$. Next $f(n) = \{(n + \alpha - 1)!/(n!(\alpha - 1)!)\}p^\alpha(1 - p)^n = \{(n + 3 - 1)!/(n!(3 - 1)!)\}(.6^3)(1 - .6)^n$. So, $f(0) = \{(0 + 2)!/(0!(2)!)\} .6^3(.4)^0 = .216$, $f(1) = \{(1 + 2)!/(1!(2)!)\}.6^3(.4)^1 = .259$, and $f(2) = \{(2 + 2)!/(2!(2)!)\}.6^3(.4)^2 = .207$. The mean $= k(1-p)/p = \alpha/\lambda = 2.0$ and variance $= k(1 - p)/p^2 = \alpha(\lambda + 1)/\lambda^2 = 3(1.5 + 1)/1.5^2 = 3.33$.]

Compare example 5.2.2 with example 5.2.1. Even though the two distributions have the same mean 2.0, the variance of the Negative Binomial is larger.[54] The uncertainty introduced by the random selection of an insured from the population has increased the variance.

5.2. Exercises

5.2.1. For an insurance portfolio the distribution of the number of claims a particular policyholder makes in a year

---

[54] For Negative Binomial, variance > mean. For Poisson, variance = mean. For Binomial, variance < mean.

is Poisson with mean μ. The μ-values of the policyholders follow the Gamma distribution, with parameters $\alpha = 4$, and $\lambda = 9$. Determine the probability that a policyholder chosen at random will experience 5 claims over the next year.

5.2.2. The number of claims X for a given insured follows a Poisson distribution, $P[X = x] = \theta^x e^{-\theta}/x!$. Over the population of insureds the expected annual mean of the Poisson distribution follows the distribution $f(\theta) = 9\theta e^{-3\theta}$ over the interval $(0, \infty)$. An insured is selected from the population at random. What are the mean and variance for the number of claims for the selected insured?

5.2.3. Assume that random variable X is distributed according to a Negative Binomial with parameters $k = 2$ and $p = 0.6$. What is the probability that the observed value of X is greater than 2?

5.2.4. Assume the following information:

1. the claim count N for an individual insured has a Poisson distribution with mean λ; and

2. λ is uniformly distributed between 1 and 3.

Find the probability that a randomly selected insured will have no claims.

5.2.5. Prove each of the following:

1. For the Binomial distribution, the mean is greater than or equal to the variance.

2. For the Negative Binomial, the mean is less than or equal to the variance.

If the means are equal for a Binomial distribution, Poisson distribution, and a Negative Binomial distribution, rank the variances by size for the three distributions.

5.3. Bayesian Analysis on the Gamma-Poisson Model

The Gamma p.d.f. $f(\mu)$ defined in section 5.2 is the prior distribution for the mean annual claims frequency μ for a risk selected at random from the population. But, the p.d.f. can be updated using Bayesian analysis after observing the insured. The distribution of μ subsequent to observations is referred to as the **posterior distribution**, as opposed to the prior distribution.

Suppose that the insured generates C claims during a one-year observation period. We want to calculate the posterior distribution for μ given this information: $f(\mu \mid n = C)$. Bayes Theorem stated in terms of probability density functions is:[55]

$$f(\mu \mid n = C) = P[C \mid \mu]f(\mu)/P(C) \qquad (5.3.1)$$

We have all of the pieces on the right hand side. They are formulas (5.2.1), (5.2.2), and (5.2.3b). Putting them all together:

$$f(\mu \mid n = C) = [\mu^C e^{-\mu}/C!][\lambda^\alpha \mu^{\alpha-1} e^{-\lambda\mu}/\Gamma(\alpha)]/$$
$$[\{\Gamma(C + \alpha)/C!\Gamma(\alpha)\}\{\lambda/(\lambda + 1)\}^\alpha\{1/(\lambda + 1)\}^C]$$

Through cancellations and combining terms, this can be simplified to:

$$f(\mu \mid n = C) = (\lambda + 1)^{\alpha+C}\mu^{\alpha+C-1}e^{-(\lambda+1)\mu}/\Gamma(\alpha + C)$$

$$(5.3.2)$$

Substituting $\alpha' = \alpha + C$ **and** $\lambda' = \lambda + 1$, **yields:**

$$f(\mu \mid n = C) = \lambda'^{\alpha'}\mu^{\alpha'-1}e^{-\lambda'\mu}/\Gamma(\alpha') \qquad (5.3.3)$$

This is the posterior distribution for μ and it is also a Gamma distribution.

The fact that the posterior distribution is of the same form as the prior distribution is why the Gamma is called a Conjugate Prior Distribution for the Poisson.

---

[55]See Section 3.3.

Example 5.3.1: The distribution of annual claims frequencies μ within a population of insureds is Gamma with parameters $\alpha = 3.0$ and $\lambda = 1.5$. An insured is selected at random.

1. What is the expected value of μ?

2. If the insured is observed to have a total of 0 claims during a one-year observation period, what is the expected value of μ for the insured?

3. The insured is observed to have a total of 5 claims during a one-year observation period, what is the expected value of μ for the insured?

[*Solution:* (1) $E[\mu] = \alpha/\lambda = 3.0/1.5 = 2.0$. (2) $E[\mu \mid 0$ claims in one year] $= (\alpha + 0)/(\lambda + 1) = (3 + 0)/(1.5 + 1) = 1.2$. (3) $E[\mu \mid 5$ claims in one year] $= (\alpha + 5)/(\lambda + 1) = (3 + 5)/(1.5 + 1) = 3.2$.]

In example 5.3.1, prior to any observations of the insured, our estimate of the expected claim frequency μ is just the population average 2.0 claims per year. If we observe 0 claims in one-year, then we lower our estimate to 1.2 claims per year. On the other hand, if we observe 5 claims in one year, we raise our estimate to 3.2.

Although the distribution of μ remains Gamma as more information is gathered about the risk, the shape of the distribution changes. Graph 8.5 shows as in example 5.3.1, (1) a prior distribution with $\alpha = 3.0$ and $\lambda = 1.5$, (2) the posterior distribution after observing 0 claims in one-year, and (3) the posterior distribution after observing 5 claims in one-year.

Multiple Years of Observation

Suppose we now observe the insured for two years and see C_1 claims in the first year and C_2 claims in the second year. What is the new posterior distribution? The posterior distribution $f(\mu \mid n = C_1)$ after the first observation year becomes the new prior distribution at the start of the second observation year. After observing C_2 claims during the second year, the posterior

GRAPH 8.5

GAMMA DISTRIBUTION

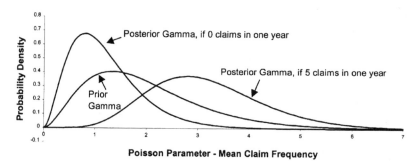

Poisson Parameter - Mean Claim Frequency

distribution is again a Gamma distribution, but with parameters $\alpha'' = \alpha' + C_2 = \alpha + C_1 + C_2$ and $\lambda'' = \lambda' + 1 = \lambda + 1 + 1$. Continuing the observations for a total of Y years and total observed claims of $C = C_1 + C_2 + \cdots + C_Y$ produces a final posterior distribution that is still Gamma but with parameters:

$$\hat{\alpha} = \alpha + C$$
$$\hat{\lambda} = \lambda + Y$$

The mean of the posterior distribution is $(\alpha + C)/(\lambda + Y)$. This is $E[\mu \mid C$ claims in Y years] and the expected value of the annual claims frequency for the insured.

Thus, for the **Gamma-Poisson the posterior density function is also a Gamma. This posterior Gamma has a first parameter equal to the prior first parameter plus the number of claims observed. The second parameter equals the prior second parameter plus the number of exposures (usually years) observed.**

Example 5.3.2: The distribution of annual claims frequencies μ within a population of insureds is Gamma with parameters $\alpha = 3.0$ and $\lambda = 1.5$. An insured is selected at random and then observed for two years. The insured has two claims during the first year and four claims during the second year. What are the parameters of the posterior Gamma distribution for this risk?

[*Solution:* $C = 2 + 4 = 6$ and $Y = 2$, so $\hat{\alpha} = 3 + 6 = 9$ and $\hat{\lambda} = 1.5 + 2 = 3.5$.]

Predictive Distribution

The distribution of the number of claims for the selected insured still follows a Negative Binomial. That's because the posterior distribution is still Gamma. But, in formula (5.2.3c) α is replaced by $\alpha + C$ and p is replaced $p = (\lambda + Y)/(\lambda + 1 + Y)$. This posterior mixed distribution is referred at the **predictive distribution.**

Example 5.3.3: The distribution of annual claims frequencies μ within a population of insureds is Gamma with parameters $\alpha = 3.0$ and $\lambda = 1.5$. An insured is selected at random.

1. Prior to any observations of the insured, what is the probability that the insured will have two or more claims in a year?

Suppose that the insured is observed to have two claims during the first year and four claims during the second year.

2. What is the probability that the insured will have two or more claims in a year?

[*Solution:* (1) With $\alpha = 3.0$ and $\lambda = 1.5$, the parameters for the Negative Binomial distribution are $k = 3$ and $p = 1.5/(1.5 + 1) = .6$. (See formula (5.2.3d).) Then,

$$P[0 \text{ claims}] = \binom{2}{0}.6^3.4^0 = .216 \quad \text{and}$$

$$P[1 \text{ claim}] = \binom{3}{1}.6^3.4^1 = .2592.$$

So, $P[2 \text{ or more claims}] = 1 - .216 - .2592 = .5248$.

(2) The new parameters for the Gamma posterior distribution are $\hat{\alpha} = 3 + 6 = 9$ and $\hat{\lambda} = 1.5 + 2 = 3.5$. The parameters for the predictive Negative Binomial distribution are $k = \hat{\alpha} = 9$ and $p = 3.5/(1 + 3.5) = .778$. Using formula (5.2.3d),

$$P[0 \text{ claims}] = \binom{8}{0} .778^9 .222^0 = .104 \qquad \text{and}$$

$$P[1 \text{ claim}] = \binom{9}{1} .778^9 .222^1 = .209.$$

So, $P[2 \text{ or more claims}] = 1 - .104 - .209 = .687$. The fact that we observed 6 claims in 2 years has raised our estimate of the probability of having two or more claims in a year versus our estimate for someone randomly selected from the population without any additional information.]

The Gamma-Poisson is one example of conjugate prior distributions. There are many other conjugate priors. Examples include the Beta-Bernoulli for frequency and the Normal-Normal for severity.

Figure 8.4 shows the relationships between the Gamma Prior, Gamma Posterior, Negative Binomial mixed distribution, and Negative Binomial predictive distribution for the Gamma-Poisson frequency process.

In this section, the examples have used years Y as the number of exposures: each year represents one unit of exposure. Other exposure bases can be used in the Gamma-Poisson model as shown in Exercises 5.3.4 and 5.3.6. In Figure 8.4, Y can be replaced by an E indicating that we are not limited to using the number of years as the measure of exposure.

5.3. Exercises

5.3.1. The number of claims is distributed according to a Gamma-Poisson mixed distribution. The prior Gamma has parameters $\alpha = 4$ and $\lambda = 2$. Over a three-year period, 5

FIGURE 8.4

GAMMA-POISSON FREQUENCY PROCESS

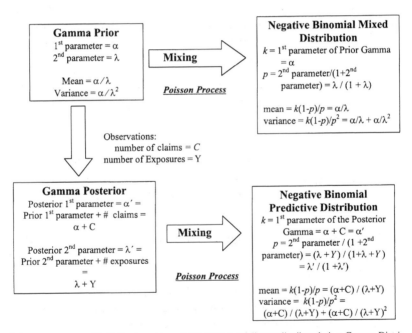

Poisson parameters of individuals making up the entire portfolio are distributed via a Gamma Distribution with parameters α and λ : $f(x) = \lambda^{\alpha} x^{\alpha-1} e^{-\lambda x} / \Gamma(\alpha)$.

claims were observed. Calculate the parameters α' and λ' of the posterior Gamma distribution.

5.3.2. Let the likelihood of a claim be given by a Poisson distribution with parameter θ. The prior density function of θ is given by $f(\theta) = 32\theta^2 e^{-4\theta}$. You observe 1 claim in 2 years. What is the posterior density function of θ?

5.3.3. The number of claims X for a given insured follows a Poisson distribution, $P[X = x] = \theta^x e^{-\theta}/x!$. The expected annual mean of the Poisson distribution over the population of insureds follows the distribution $f(\theta) = e^{-\theta}$ over the interval $(0, \infty)$. An insured is selected from the population at random. Over the last year this particular insured had no claims. What is the posterior density function of θ for the selected insured?

5.3.4. An automobile insurer entering a new territory assumes that each individual car's claim count has a Poisson distribution with parameter μ and that μ is the same for all cars in the territory for the homogeneous class of business that it writes. The insurer also assumes that μ has a gamma distribution with probability density function

$$f(\mu) = \lambda^\alpha \mu^{\alpha-1} e^{-\lambda\mu}/\Gamma(\alpha)$$

Initially, the parameters of the gamma distribution are assumed to be $\alpha = 50$ and $\lambda = 500$. During the subsequent two-year period the insurer covered 750 and 1100 cars for the first and second years, respectively. The insurer incurred 65 and 112 claims in the first and second years, respectively. What is the coefficient of variation of the posterior gamma distribution? (The coefficient of variation is the standard deviation divided by the mean.)

5.3.5. The likelihood of a claim is given by a Poisson distribution with parameter θ. The prior density function of θ is given by $f(\theta) = 32\theta^2 e^{-4\theta}$. A risk is selected from a population and you observe 1 claim in 2 years. What is the probability that the mean claim frequency for this risk falls in the interval $[1, 2]$? (Your answer can be left in integral form.)

5.3.6. You are given the following:

- You are trying to estimate the average number of claims per exposure, μ, for a group of insureds.

- Number of claims follows a Poisson distribution.

- Prior to the first year of coverage, μ is assumed to have the Gamma distribution $f(\mu) = 1000^{150}\mu^{149}e^{-1000\mu}/\Gamma(150)$, $\mu > 0$.

- In the first year, 300 claims are observed on 1,500 exposures.

- In the second year, 525 claims are observed on 2,500 exposures.

After two years, what is the Bayesian probability estimate of $E[\mu]$?

5.4. Bühlmann Credibility in the Gamma-Poisson Model

As in section 5.3, an insured is selected at random from a population with a Gamma distribution of average annual frequencies. Using Bühlmann Credibility we want to estimate the expected annual claims frequency. To do this, we need to calculate the Expected Value of the Process Variance (EPV) and the Variance of the Hypothetical Means (VHM).

Expected Value of the Process Variance
The means μ in the population are distributed according to the Gamma distribution shown in (5.2.2) with parameters α and λ. The mean of the Gamma is α/λ, so $E[\mu] = \alpha/\lambda$. For the Poisson distribution, the means and process variances are equal. So, EPV = E[Process Variance] = E[Mean] = $E[\mu] = \alpha/\lambda$.

Variance of the Hypothetical Means
The means μ in the population are distributed according to the Gamma distribution shown in (5.2.2) with parameters α and λ. The variance of the Gamma is α/λ^2. The μ's are the hypothetical means, so VHM = α/λ^2.

Bühlmann Credibility Parameter

Now we have the K parameter for Bühlmann Credibility in the Gamma-Poisson model: $K = \text{EPV/VHM} = (\alpha/\lambda)/(\alpha/\lambda^2) = \lambda$.

Calculating the Credibility Weighted Estimate

An insured is selected at random from a population of insureds whose average annual claims frequencies follow a Gamma distribution with parameters α and λ. Over the next Y years the insured is observed to have C claims. The credibility-weighted estimate of the average annual claims frequency for the insured is calculated as follows:

1. The observed annual claims frequency is C/Y.

2. The credibility of the Y years of observations is: $Z = Y/(Y + K) = Y/(Y + \lambda)$.

3. The prior hypothesis of the claims frequency is the mean of μ over the population: $E[\mu] = \alpha/\lambda$.

4. The credibility weighted estimate is:

$$Z(C/Y) + (1 - Z)(\alpha/\lambda)$$

$$= \{Y/(Y + \lambda)\}(C/Y) + (1 - \{Y/(Y + \lambda)\})(\alpha/\lambda)$$

$$= \{C/(Y + \lambda)\} + \{\lambda/(Y + \lambda)\}(\alpha/\lambda) = \frac{\alpha + C}{\lambda + Y} \quad (5.4.1)$$

This is exactly equal to the mean of the posterior Gamma distribution. **For the Gamma-Poisson, the estimates from using Bayesian Analysis and Bühlmann Credibility are equal.**[56]

Example 5.4.1: An insured is selected at random from a population whose average annual claims frequency follows a Gamma distribution with $\alpha = 3.0$ and $\lambda = 1.5$. (The insured's number of claims is Poisson distributed.) If the insured is observed to have 9 claims during the next 3 years, calculate the Bühlmann Credibility weighted estimate of the insured's average annual frequency.

---

[56]This is a special case of a general result for conjugate priors of members of "linear exponential families." This general result is beyond the scope of this chapter. In general, the estimates from Bayesian Analysis and Bühlmann Credibility may not be equal.

[*Solution:* This can be calculated directly from formula (5.4.1): $E[\mu \mid 9$ claims in 3 years$] = (3 + 9)/(1.5 + 3) = 2.67$. Alternatively if we want to go through all of the steps, EPV = $3.0/1.5$, VHM = $3.0/1.5^2 = 1.333$, $K = 2/1.333 = 1.5$, and $Z = 3/(3 + 1.5) = 2/3$. The prior estimate of the average annual frequency is $3.0/1.5 = 2$. The observed estimate is $9/3 = 3$. The credibility weighted estimate is $(2/3)(3) + (1/3)(2) = 2.67$.]

5.4. Exercises

5.4.1. An insured is selected at random from a population whose average annual claims frequency follows a Gamma distribution with $\alpha = 2.0$ and $\lambda = 8.0$. The distribution of the number of claims for each insured is Poisson. If the insured is observed to have 4 claims during the next four years, calculate the Bühlmann Credibility weighted estimate of the insured's average annual claims frequency.

5.4.2. You are given the following:

- A portfolio consists of 1,000 identical and independent risks.

- The number of claims for each risk follows a Poisson distribution with mean θ.

- Prior to the latest exposure period, θ is assumed to have a gamma distribution, with parameters $\alpha = 250$ and $\lambda = 2000$.

During the latest exposure period, the following loss experience is observed:

Number of Claims	Number of Risks
0	906
1	89
2	4
3	1
	1,000

Determine the mean of the posterior distribution of θ.

5.4.3. You are given the following:

- Number of claims follows a Poisson distribution with parameter μ.

- Prior to the first year of coverage, μ is assumed to have the Gamma distribution $f(\mu) = 1000^{150}\mu^{149}e^{-1000\mu}/\Gamma(150)$, $\mu > 0$.

- In the first year, 300 claims are observed on 1,500 exposures.

- In the second year, 525 claims are observed on 2,500 exposures.

After two years, what is the Bühlmann probability estimate of $E[\mu]$?

Use the following information for the next three questions:

Each insured has its accident frequency given by a Poisson Process with mean θ. For a portfolio of insureds, θ is distributed uniformly on the interval from 0 to 10.

5.4.4. What is the Expected Value of the Process Variance?

5.4.5. What is the Variance of the Hypothetical Means?

5.4.6. An individual insured from this portfolio is observed to have 7 accidents in a single year. Use Bühlmann Credibility to estimate the future accident frequency of that insured.

6. PRACTICAL ISSUES

This last section covers miscellaneous topics that are important in the application of credibility theory.

6.1. Examples of Choices for the Complement of Credibility

In the Bühlmann Credibility model, observations are made of a risk or group of risks selected from a population. Some characteristic of the risk, for example frequency, is to be estimated.

If the observed frequency of the risk is not fully credible, then it is credibility weighted against the frequency estimate for the whole population.

This is the basic principle underlying experience rating plans that are widely used in calculating insurance premiums for commercial risks. The actual loss experience for an individual insured is used to adjust a "manual rate." (The "manual rate" is the rate from the insurance company's rate manual.) If the insured's experience has little or no credibility, then the insurance company will charge the insured the "manual rate" for the next time period. But, to the extent that the insured's prior experience is credible, the rate will be adjusted downward if the insured has better experience that the average risk to which the rate applies. Or, the rate will be adjusted upward if the insured has worse than average experience.

Credibility theory is used in a variety of situations. In practice, the actuary often uses judgment in the selection of a complement of credibility. The selected complement of credibility should be relatively stable and relevant to the random variable to be estimated.[57]

Example 6.1.1: The Richmond Rodents, your hometown's semi-professional baseball team, recruited a new pitcher, Roger Rocket, at the start of the season. In the first two games of a fifty game season, Roger had three hits in four at bats, a .750 batting average.

You have been asked to forecast Roger's batting average over the whole fifty game season. What complements of credibility would you consider using to make a credibility weighted forecast?

[*Solution:* Some complements of credibility you might consider include: Roger's batting average in high school, the total batting

---

[57]See Boor, "The Complement of Credibility," *Proceedings of the Casualty Actuarial Society* LXXXIII, 1996.

average of the Rodent's pitching staff over the last few years, or last season's batting average for all pitchers in the league.]

The following table lists a quantity to be estimated and a potential complement of credibility:

Value to be Estimated	Potential Complement of Credibility
New rate for carpenters' workers compensation insurance	Last year's rate for carpenters' workers compensation insurance[58]
Percentage increase for automobile rates in Wyoming	Weighted average of the inflation rates for automobile repair costs and medical care
Percentage change in rate for a rating territory in Virginia	Percent that the average statewide rate will change in Virginia
Rate to charge a specific carpenter contracting business for workers compensation insurance	The average workers compensation insurance rate for carpenters

In each case, the complement of credibility should be a reasonable estimate of the quantity of interest.

6.2. Impacts of Differences of Credibility Parameters

Relatively small differences of credibility formula parameters generally do not have big impacts on credibility estimates. In Graph 8.6 we show three credibility curves. The middle curve is a Bühlmann credibility formula $Z = n/(n + 5,000)$ where 5,000 was substituted for the K parameter. The bottom curve shows the results of increasing the K parameter by 25% to $K = 1.25 \times 5,000 = 6,250$. The top curve shows a smaller K value with $K = .75 \times 5,000 = 3,750$. Note that changing the Bühlmann credibility parameter by 25% has a relatively insignificant impact on the credibility.

---

[58] As with all complements of credibility, last year's rate may need to be adjusted for changes since then. For example, one might adjust it by the average rate change for all classes.

GRAPH 8.6

DIFFERENCE IN K PARAMETER

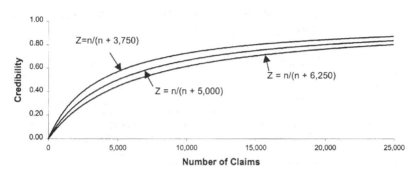

In practice, it is not necessary to determine precisely the best credibility formula parameters.[59] In fact, a good estimate is really the best that one can do.[60] Similar comments apply to Classical Credibility.

6.2. Exercises

6.2.1. The rate for workers compensation insurance for carpenters is currently $18.00 (per $100 of payroll.) The average rate over all classes is indicated to decrease 10%. The indicated rate for carpenters based on recent data is $15.00. This recent data corresponds to $3 million of expected losses. Calculate the proposed rate for carpenters in each following case:

1. Using Bühlmann credibility parameter K = $5 million.

2. Using Bühlmann credibility parameter K = $10 million.

3. Using $60 million of expected losses as the Standard for Full Credibility.

---

[59]Estimating K within a factor of two is usually sufficient. See Mahler's "An Actuarial Note on Credibility Parameters," *Proceedings of the Casualty Actuarial Society* LXXIII, 1986.

[60]Sometimes an actuary will judgmentally select K. Note that K is the volume of data that will be given 50% credibility by the Bühlmann credibility formula.

GRAPH 8.7

CLASSICAL VS. BÜHLMANN CREDIBILITY

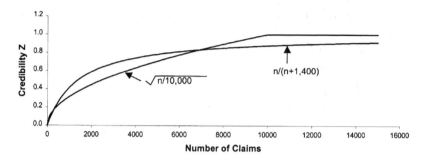

Number of Claims

6.3. Comparison of Classical and Bühlmann Credibility

Although the formulas look very different, Classical Credibility and Bühlmann Credibility can produce very similar results as seen in Graph 8.7.

The most significant difference between the two models is that Bühlmann Credibility never reaches $Z = 1.00$ which is an asymptote of the curve. Either model can be effective at improving the stability and accuracy of estimates.

Classical Credibility and Bühlmann Credibility formulas will produce approximately the same credibility weights if the full credibility standard for Classical Credibility, n_0, is about 7 to 8 times larger than the Bühlmann Credibility parameter K.[61]

Three estimation models were presented in this chapter: (1) Classical Credibility, (2) Bühlmann Credibility, and (3) Bayesian Analysis. For a particular application, the actuary can choose the model appropriate to the goals and data. If the goal is to generate

---

[61] This assumes that the Bühlmann Credibility formula is stated in terms of the number of claims. If it is not, then a conversion needs to be made. Suppose the Bühlmann Credibility formula is $E/(E + K)$ where E is earned premium. Further, assume that \$2,000 in earned premium is expected to generate one claim on average. Then, setting the full credibility standard n_0 equal to 7 or 8 times $K/2,000$ produces similar credibility weights.

the most accurate insurance rates, with least squares as the measure of fit, then Bühlmann Credibility may be the best choice. Bühlmann Credibility forms the basis of most experience rating plans. It is often used to calculate class rates in a classification plan. The use of Bühlmann Credibility requires an estimate of the EPV and VHM.

Classical Credibility might be used if estimates for the EPV and VHM are unknown or difficult to calculate. Classical Credibility is often used in the calculation of overall rate increases. Often it is simpler to work with. Bayesian Analysis may be an option if the actuary has a reasonable estimate of the prior distribution. However, Bayesian Analysis may be complicated to apply and the most difficult of the methods to explain to nonactuaries.

6.4. The Importance of Capping Results

Credibility is a linear process, and thus, extreme cases can present difficulties requiring special attention. A properly chosen cap may not only add stability, but may even make the methodology more accurate by eliminating extremes. A class rating plan may have hundreds, if not thousands, of classifications. Credibility weighting can smooth out the fluctuations as rates or relativities are determined for each class, but with so many different classes, there will be extreme situations.

Suppose one is using a Classical Credibility model and that a full credibility standard has been selected so that the observations should be within 10% of the expected mean 95% of the time. This also means that 5% of the time the estimates will be more than 10% away from the expected mean. If there are 500 classes, then 25 classes on average will fall outside of the range, and some of these may be extreme.

In Classical Credibility, we assume the normal approximation. In practice this may not be a good assumption, particularly for situations where there is a limited volume of data. Insurance claim severities tend to be skewed to the right—in some cases highly skewed.[62] This is particularly true for some types of lia-bility insurance and insurance providing fire coverage for highly valued property. A few large claims can result in very large pure premiums or high loss ratios. As the next section explains, this problem can be addressed by capping individual claims, but there is still the chance that several of these claims can occur during the same time period. Plus, even a capped loss can have a large impact if the volume of data is limited.

Credibility theory assumes that the underlying loss process is random and that events are independent. This may not always be true in the data you are working with. For example, weather events may produce a rash of claims. A spell of bitter cold can lead to many fire losses as people use less safe methods to heat their houses. Or, a couple of days of icy streets can produce many collision losses. The actuary can try to segregate out these special events, but it is not always possible to identify these and make appropriate adjustments.

Capping results is a good supplement to the credibility weight-ing process and makes the estimates more reliable. Users of the estimates may be more willing to accept them knowing that one or two events did not unduly affect the results.

6.4. Exercises

6.4.1. The workers compensation expected loss for crop dusting
    (via airplane) is $20 per $100 of payroll. Angel's Crop
    Dusting had $300,000 of payroll and one claim for $4
    million over the experience period. Predict Angel's fu-
    ture expected losses per $100 of payroll in each of the
    following cases:

    1. You use the losses as reported and a Bühlmann credi-
        bility parameter of $80,000 in expected losses.

---

[62]There is a significant probability that large claims will occur. The means for such distributions can be much larger than the medians.

2. You use the losses limited to $200,000 per claim and a Bühlmann credibility parameter of $50,000 in limited expected losses. Assume that limiting losses to $200,000 per claim reduces them on average to 95% of unlimited losses.

6.5. Capping Data Used in Estimation

A technique commonly used in conjunction with credibility weighting is to cap large losses. Capping large losses can reduce the variance of observed incurred losses allowing more credibility to be assigned to the observations.

Suppose an actuary is calculating automobile insurance rates in a state. The rates will vary by geographic territory within the state. To limit the impact of individual large losses on territorial rates, each individual loss is capped at a selected amount, say $100,000. If a loss is larger than $100,000, then $100,000 is substituted for the actual amount. So, only the first $100,000 of any loss is included in a territory's loss data. The amounts above $100,000 can be pooled and prorated across all territories in the state.

The Classical Credibility standard for full credibility is shown in formula (2.5.4):

$$n_F = n_0(1 + (\sigma_S/\mu_S)^2)$$

n_F is the expected number of claims required for a weight of 100% to be assigned to the data. Capping large losses reduces n_F by reducing the size of the coefficient of variation of the severity, $CV_S = \sigma_S/\mu_S$.

Example 6.5.1: Assume that claim losses can occur in three sizes in the following proportions:

Size of Loss	Proportion of Losses
$1,000	80%
$20,000	15%
$100,000	5%

1. Calculate the coefficient of variation, $CV_S = \sigma_S/\mu_S$, for the severity of uncapped losses.

2. Calculate the coefficient of variation for severity if losses are capped at $50,000.

[*Solution:* (1) Uncapped losses: $\mu_S = .80(1,000) + .15(20,000) + .05(100,000) = 8,800$. And, $\sigma_S = [.80(1,000)^2 + .15(20,000)^2 + .05(100,000)^2 - 8,800^2]^{1/2} = 21,985$. So, $CV_S = \sigma_S/\mu_S = 21,985/8,800 = 2.50$.

(2) Capped losses: $\mu_S = .80(1,000) + .15(20,000) + .05(50,000) = 6,300$. Note that 100,000 has been replaced by 50,000 in the calculation. And, $\sigma_S = [.80(1,000)^2 + .15(20,000)^2 + .05(50,000)^2 - 6,300^2]^{1/2} = 12,088$. So, $CV_S = \sigma_S/\mu_S = 12,088/6,300 = 1.92$.]

Using the results of example 6.5.1, the full credibility standard for uncapped losses is: $n_F = n_0(1 + (2.5)^2) = n_0(7.25)$. The full credibility standard capping losses at $50,000 is: $n_F = n_0(1 + (1.92)^2) = n_0(4.69)$. Comparing these values we note that capping at $50,000 reduced the number of claims required for full credibility by 35%.

Although Classical Credibility has been used as the setting to demonstrate capping, capping is also valuable when using a Bühlmann Credibility model. The process variance is reduced through capping, which in turn usually lowers the K parameter. (Usually the Expected Value of the Process Variance is reduced more by capping than is the Variance of the Hypothetical Means.)

6.6. Estimating Credibility Parameters in Practice

This section discusses a few methods to estimate credibility parameters, but first it should be mentioned that judgment frequently plays a large role in the selection of credibility parameters.

The selection of credibility parameters requires a balancing of responsiveness versus stability. Larger credibility weights put more weight on the observations, which means that the current data has a larger impact on the estimate. The estimates are more responsive to current data. But, this comes at the expense of less stability in the estimates. Credibility parameters often are selected to reflect the actuary's desired balance between responsiveness and stability.

Classical Credibility

With Classical Credibility, P and k values must be chosen where P is the probability that observation X is within $\pm k$ percent of the mean μ. Bigger P's and smaller k's mean more stability but smaller credibility for the observations. A common choice for these values is $P = 90\%$ and $k = 5\%$, but there is no a priori reason why these choices are better than others.

When estimating the expected pure premium or loss ratio, the coefficient of variation of the severity distribution is needed to calculate the full credibility standard (see formula (2.5.4)). In practice this can be estimated from empirical data as demonstrated in the following example.

Example 6.6.1: A sample of 100 claims was distributed as follows:

Size of Claim	Number of Claims
$1,000	85
$5,000	10
$10,000	3
$25,000	2

Estimate the coefficient of variation of the claims severity based on this empirical distribution.

[*Solution:* The sample mean is: $\hat{\mu} = .85(1,000) + .10(5,000) + .03(10,000) + .02(25,000) = 2,150$. The sample standard deviation is: $\hat{\sigma} = \{[1/(100-1)][85(1,000-2,150)^2 + 10(5,000-2,150)^2 + 3(10,000-2,150)^2 + 2(25,000-2,150)^2]\}^{1/2} = 3,791$ where we are dividing by $(n-1)$ to calculate an unbiased estimate. The coefficient of variation is $CV_S = \hat{\sigma}/\hat{\mu} = 3,791/2,150 = 1.76$.]

With $P = 90\%$ and $k = 5\%$, the full credibility standard for frequency is $n_0 = 1082$ claims. The full credibility standard for the pure premium is $n_F = n_0(1 + CV_S^2) = 1,082(1 + 1.76^2) = 4,434$ with the coefficient of variation from example 6.6.1.

Bühlmann Credibility—Estimate EPV and VHM from Data

One way to estimate the K parameter in the formula $Z = N/(N + K)$ is to compute the numerator and denominator of K from empirical data.

Suppose that there are M risks in a population and that they are similar in size. Assume that we tracked the annual frequency year by year for Y years for each of the risks. The frequencies are:

$$\begin{bmatrix} X_{11} & X_{12} & \cdots & X_{1Y} \\ X_{21} & X_{22} & \cdots & X_{2Y} \\ \vdots & \vdots & & \vdots \\ X_{M1} & X_{M2} & \cdots & X_{MY} \end{bmatrix}$$

Each row is a different risk and each column is a different year. So, X_{ij} represents the frequency for the ith risk and j^{th} year.

Our goal is to estimate the expected frequency for any risk selected at random from the population. The credibility $Z = N/(N + K)$ will be assigned to the risk's observed frequency where N represents the number of years of observations. The complement of credibility will be assigned to the mean frequency for the population.

The following table lists estimators:

	Symbol	Estimator
Mean Frequency for Risk i	$\bar{X}_i$	$(1/Y)\sum_{j=1}^{Y} X_{ij}$
Mean Frequency for Population	$\bar{X}$	$(1/M)\sum_{i=1}^{M} \bar{X}_i$
Process Variance for Risk i	$\hat{\sigma}_i^2$	$[1/(Y-1)]\sum_{j=1}^{Y}(X_{ij}-\bar{X}_i)^2$
Expected Value of Process Variance	**EPV**	$(1/M)\sum_{i=1}^{M}\hat{\sigma}_i^2$
Variance of the Hypothetical Means	**VHM**	$[1/(M-1)]\sum_{i=1}^{M}(\bar{X}_i-\bar{X})^2 - EPV/Y$

The estimator for the Expected Value of the Process Variance is just an average of the usual estimators for each risk's process variance. The estimator for the Variance of the Hypothetical Means may not be intuitive, but we will use this result without a rigorous derivation.[63] After making the computations in the above table, we can set $K = EPV/VHM$. If the sample VHM is zero or negative, then the credibility can be assigned a value of 0.

The process variance of risk i, $\hat{\sigma}_i^2$, is the estimated process variance of the *annual* frequency for risk i. Since we have observed the frequency for Y years, we are able to estimate the variance in the annual frequency.

Example 6.6.2: There are two auto drivers in a particular rating class. The first driver was observed to have 2 claims in the first year, 0 in the second, 0 in the third, 1 in the fourth, and 0 in the fifth. The second driver had the following sequence of claims in years 1 through 5: 1, 1, 2, 0, 2. Estimate each of the values in the prior table.

---

[63] See Klugman, et al., *Loss Models: From Data to Decisions* for a more thorough and rigorous treatment of the estimation of Bühlmann credibility parameters.

[*Solution:* For driver #1, $\bar{X}_1 = (2 + 0 + 0 + 1 + 0)/5 = .6$ and $\hat{\sigma}_1^2$
$= [(2 - .6)^2 + (0 - .6)^2 + (0 - .6)^2 + (1 - .6)^2 + (0 - .6)^2]/(5 - 1)$
$= .80$. For driver #2, $\bar{X}_2 = (1 + 1 + 2 + 0 + 2)/5 = 1.2$ and $\hat{\sigma}_2^2$
$= [(1 - 1.2)^2 + (1 - 1.2)^2 + (2 - 1.2)^2 + (0 - 1.2)^2 + (2 - 1.2)^2]/$
$(5 - 1) = .70$.

The population mean annual frequency is estimated to be
$\bar{X} = (\bar{X}_1 + \bar{X}_2)/2 = (.6 + 1.2)/2 = .90$. The expected value of the
process variance is $EPV = (\hat{\sigma}_1^2 + \hat{\sigma}_2^2)/2 = (.8 + .7)/2 = .75$. The
variance of the hypothetical means is $VHM = [(\bar{X}_1 - \bar{X})^2 + (\bar{X}_2 - \bar{X})^2]/(2 - 1) - EPV/5 = [(.6 - .9)^2 + (1.2 - .9)^2]/1 - .75/5 = .03$.]

The K parameter for the data in example 6.6.2 is $K = EPV/VHM = .75/.03 = 25$. The credibility that we would assign five years of experience is $Z = 5/(5 + 25) = 1/6$. Thus,
the estimated future claim frequency for the first driver is
$(1/6)(.6) + (5/6)(.9) = .85$. Similarly, the estimated future claim
frequency for the second driver is $(1/6)(1.2) + (5/6)(.9) = .95$.
While in most practical applications there would be more than
two drivers, this technique would apply in the same manner.
When there are different sizes of insureds, for example commercial automobile fleets, the techniques are modified somewhat,
but this is beyond the scope of this chapter.[64]

In practice there are many techniques used to estimate K. This
was just one example of how to do so. It dealt with the simpler
situation where every insured is of the same size.

Bühlmann Credibility—Estimate K from Best Fit to Data

Experience rating adjusts a policyholder's premium to reflect
the policyholder's prior loss experience. If the policyholder has
generated few insurance losses, then experience rating applies a
credit to adjust the premium downward. And, if the policyholder
has had worse than average loss experience, then debits increase

---

[64] See Klugman, et al., *Loss Models: From Data to Decisions.*

future premiums. A credibility formula of the form $Z = N/ (N + K)$ is usually used to weight the policyholder's experience.[65]

One can estimate K by seeing which values of K would have worked well in the past. The goal is for each policyholder to have the same expected loss ratio after the application of experience rating. Let LR_i be the loss ratio for policyholder i where in the denominator we use the premiums after the application of experience rating.[66] Let LR_{AVE} be the average loss ratio for all policyholders. Then, define $D(K)$ to be:

$$D(K) = \sum_{\text{all } i} (LR_i - LR_{AVE})^2$$

The sum of the squares of the differences is a function of K, the credibility parameter that was used in the experience rating. The goal is to find a K that minimizes $D(K)$. This requires recomputing the premium that each policyholder would have been charged under a different K' value. This generates new LR_i's that are then put into the formula above and $D(K')$ is computed. Using techniques from numerical analysis, a $\hat{K}$ that minimizes $D(K)$ can be found.[67]

Another approach to calculating credibility parameters is linear regression analysis of a policyholder's current frequency, pure premium, etc. compared to prior experience. Suppose that we want to estimate next year's results based on the current year's. Then, using historical data for many policyholders we set up our regression equation:

Observation in year $Y =$

m(Observation in year $(Y - 1)$) + Constant

---

[65] The credibility weighting can be more complex and involve separate credibility factors for primary and excess losses.

[66] The experience modification relies on data from prior years, other than the one being tested, as well as the value of K.

[67] Criteria other than least squares can be used to see which credibilities would have worked well in the past.

The slope m from a least squares fit to the data turns out to be the Bühlmann credibility Z. The "Constant" term is $(1 - Z)$ (Overall Average).[68] After we have calculated the parameters in our model using historical data, then we can estimate future results using the model and recent data. Regression models can also be built using multiple years.

6.6. Exercises

6.6.1. Sue "Too Much Time on her Hands" Smith recorded her commute times to work in the morning while driving her husband's car during the week her sports car was in the shop. She also recorded her times for a week when she got her car back. Here were the results:

Trial	Husband's Car	Her Car
1	30 minutes	30 minutes
2	33 minutes	28 minutes
3	26 minutes	31 minutes
4	31 minutes	27 minutes
5	30 minutes	24 minutes

Using Bühlmann Credibility, Sue wants to estimate her expected commute time to work in her sports car. Calculate EPV, VHM, K, Z, and the credibility weighted estimate.

The next three problems share information and should be worked in order.

6.6.2. You observe the following experience for five insureds during years 1, 2, and 3 combined:

---

[68] See Mahler, "A Graphical Illustration of Experience Rating Credibilities," *Proceedings of the Casualty Actuarial Society* LXXXV, 1998 for more information.

Insured	Premiums (prior to experience mod)	Losses	Loss Ratio
1	1,000	600	60.0
2	500	200	40.0
3	2,000	1,100	55.0
4	1,500	700	46.7
5	3,000	2,200	73.3
Total	8,000	4,800	60.0

You will calculate experience modifications for these insureds using the formulas:

$$Z = P/(P + K), \quad \text{and}$$
$$M = \{(L/P)Z + 60.0(1 - Z)\}/60.0$$

where

Z = credibility, $\quad K$ = Bühlmann credibility parameter

P = premium, $\quad M$ = experience modification

L = losses, $\quad 60.0$ = observed overall loss ratio.

What would the experience modifications be for each insured if you used $K = 1,000$?

6.6.3. You observe the following experience for these same five insureds during year five:

Insured	Premiums (prior to experience mod)	Losses	Loss Ratio
1	400	300	75.0
2	200	100	50.0
3	900	200	22.2
4	500	200	40.0
5	1,000	700	70.0
Total	3,000	1,500	50.0

Experience modifications are calculated using the data from years 1, 2, and 3 with various values of K.

For $K = 1,000$ what is the sum of the squared differences for year five between the modified loss ratios and the overall average loss ratio?

[Note: Modified premiums are calculated by multiplying premiums by modification factors. Modified loss ratios use modified premiums in the denominator.]

6.6.4. For what value of K would the sum of the squared differences in the previous problem be minimized? (Suggestion: use a computer to help you find the solution.)

REFERENCES

H = Historical, B = Basic, I = Intermediate, A = Advanced

H Bailey, Arthur L., "A Generalized Theory of Credibility," *Proceedings of the Casualty Actuarial Society*, 1945, 32:13–20.

H Bailey, Arthur L., "Credibility Procedures, Laplace's Generalization of Bayes' Rule and the Combination of Collateral Knowledge with Observed Data," *Proceedings of the Casualty Actuarial Society*, 1950, 37:7–23.

B Bailey, Robert A., and LeRoy J. Simon, "An Actuarial Note on the Credibility of Experience of a Single Private Passenger Car," *Proceedings of the Casualty Actuarial Society*, 1959, 46:159–164.

I Boor, Joseph A., "Credibility Based on Accuracy," *Proceedings of the Casualty Actuarial Society*, 1992, 79:166–185.

I Boor, Joseph A., "The Complement of Credibility," *Proceedings of the Casualty Actuarial Society*, 1996, 83:1–40.

I Brosius, Eric, "Loss Development Using Credibility." *CAS 2001 Exam 6 Web Notes*, 1993. http://www.casact.org/students/syllabus/2001/6web.htm (1 Oct. 1999).

H Bühlmann, Hans, "Experience Rating and Credibility," *ASTIN Bulletin*, 1967, 4, 3:200–207.

H Bühlmann, Hans and E. Straub, 1970. Glaubwürdigeit für schadensätze (Credibility for loss ratios), English translation, *ARCH*, 1972, 2.

I Conger, Robert F., "The Construction of Automobile Territories in Massachusetts," *Proceedings of the Casualty Actuarial Society*, 1987, 74:1–74.

B Dean, Curtis Gary, "An Introduction to Credibility," *CAS Forum*, Winter 1997, 55–66.

A De Vlyder, F. Etienne, *Advanced Risk Theory—A Self-Contained Introduction*, University of Brussels, Belgium, 1996.

H Dorweiler, Paul, "A Survey of Risk Credibility in Experience Rating," *Proceedings of the Casualty Actuarial Society*, 1971, 58:90–114. First published in *Proceedings of the Casualty Actuarial Society*, 1934, 21:1–25.

I Feldblum, Sholom, Discussion of "The Complement of Credibility," *Proceedings of the Casualty Actuarial Society*, 1998, 85:991–1033.

I Finger, Robert J., "Merit Rating for Doctor Professional Liability Insurance," *Proceedings of the Casualty Actuarial Society*, 1993, 80:291–352.

I Gerber, Hans, "A Teacher's Remark on Exact Credibility," *ASTIN Bulletin*, 1995, 25, 2:189–192.

I Gillam, William R., "Parametrizing the Workers Compensation Experience Rating Plan," *Proceedings of the Casualty Actuarial Society*, 1992, 79:21–56.

I Gillam, William R. and Richard H. Snader, "Fundamentals of Individual Risk Rating." *CAS 2001 Exam 9 Web Notes*, http://www.casact.org/students/syllabus/2001/9web.htm 1992.

I Goulet, Vincent, "On Approximations in Limited Fluctuation Credibility Theory," *Proceedings of the Casualty Actuarial Society*, 1997, 84:533–552.

I Goulet, Vincent, "Principles and Applications of Credibility," *Journal of Actuarial Practice*, 1998, 6:1, 2, 5–62.

I Hachemeister, Charles A., "Credibility for Regression Models with Application to Trend." In *Credibility, Theory and Applications, Proceedings of the Berkeley Actuarial Research Conference on Credibility*, 1975, 129–163, (reprinted with discussion by Al Quirin, in CAS *Forum*, Spring 1992, 307–348.)

I Heckman, Philip E., "Credibility and Solvency," *CAS Discussion Paper Program*, 1980, 116–152.

B Herzog, Thomas N., *An Introduction to Credibility*, Mad River Books, 1996.

B   Hewitt, Charles C., "Credibility for Severity," *Proceedings of the Casualty Actuarial Society*, 1970, 57:148–171.

B   Hewitt, Charles C., Discussion of "A Bayesian View of Credibility," *Proceedings of the Casualty Actuarial Society*, 1965, 52:121–127.

B   Hossack, I. B., J. H. Pollard, and B. Zehnwirth, *Introductory Statistics with Applications in General Insurance*, Cambridge University Press, New York, 1983.

I   Insurance Services Office, *Report of the Credibility Subcommittee: Development and Testing of Empirical Bayes Credibility Procedures for Classification Ratemaking*, ISO, New York, 1980.

A   Jewell, W. S., "Credible Means Are Exact Bayesian for Exponential Families," *ASTIN Bulletin*, 1974, 8, 1:77–90.

A   Jewell, W. S., "The Use of Collateral Data in Credibility Theory: A Hierarchical Model," *Giornale dell'Istituto Italiano degli Attuari*, 1975, 38:1–16.

A   Klugman, Stuart A., "Credibility for Classification Ratemaking Via the Hierarchical Normal Linear Model," *Proceedings of the Casualty Actuarial Society*, 1987, 74:272–321.

I   Klugman, Stuart A., Harry H. Panjer, and Gordon E. Willmot, *Loss Models: From Data to Decisions*, John Wiley and Sons, New York, 1998.

B   Longley-Cook, Lawrence H., "An Introduction to Credibility Theory," *Proceedings of the Casualty Actuarial Society*, 1962, 49:194–221.

B   Mahler, Howard C., "A Graphical Illustration of Experience Rating Credibilities, *Proceedings of the Casualty Actuarial Society*, 1998, 85:654–688.

A   Mahler, Howard C., "A Markov Chain Model for Shifting Risk Parameters," *Proceedings of the Casualty Actuarial Society*, 1997, 84:581–659.

B   Mahler, Howard C., "An Actuarial Note on Credibility Parameters," *Proceedings of the Casualty Actuarial Society*, 1986, 73:1–26.

I   Mahler, Howard C., "An Example of Credibility and Shift-
     ing Risk Parameters," *Proceedings of the Casualty Actuarial
     Society*, 1990, 77:225–308.

B   Mahler, Howard C., "Credibility: Practical Applications,"
     CAS Forum, Fall 1989, 187–199.

A   Mahler, Howard C., "Credibility With Shifting Risk Param-
     eters, Risk Heterogeneity and Parameter Uncertainty," *Pro-
     ceedings of the Casualty Actuarial Society*, 1998, 85:455–653.

A   Mahler, Howard C., Discussion of "An Analysis of Experi-
     ence Rating," *Proceedings of the Casualty Actuarial Society*,
     1987, 74:119–189.

I   Mahler, Howard C., Discussion of "Parametrizing the Work-
     ers Compensation Experience Rating Plan," *Proceedings of
     the Casualty Actuarial Society*, 1993, 80:148–183.

B   Mahler, Howard C., "Introduction to Basic Credibility," *CAS
     Forum*, Winter 1997, 67–103.

A   Mahler, Howard C., "Workers' Compensation Classification
     Relativities," *CAS Forum*, Fall 1999, 425–462.

B   Mayerson, Allen L., "A Bayesian View of Credibility," *Pro-
     ceedings of the Casualty Actuarial Society*, 1964, 51:85–104.

B   Mayerson, Allen L., Donald A. Jones, and Newton Bowers
     Jr., "The Credibility of the Pure Premium," *Proceedings of
     the Casualty Actuarial Society*, 1968, 55:175–185.

A   Meyers, Glenn G., "An Analysis of Experience Rating," *Pro-
     ceedings of the Casualty Actuarial Society*, 1985, 72:278–317.

A   Meyers, Glenn G., "Empirical Bayesian Credibility for
     Workers Compensation Classification Ratemaking," *Pro-
     ceedings of the Casualty Actuarial Society*, 1984, 71:96–121.

H   Michelbacher, Gustav F., "The Practice of Experience Rat-
     ing," *Proceedings of the Casualty Actuarial Society*, 1918,
     4:293–324.

H   Mowbray, A. H., "How Extensive a Payroll Exposure is Nec-
     essary to Give a Dependable Pure Premium?" *Proceedings of
     the Casualty Actuarial Society*, 1914, 1:25–30.

H   Perryman, Francis S., "Experience Rating Plan Credibilities," *Proceedings of the Casualty Actuarial Society*, 1971, 58:143–207. First published in *Proceedings of the Casualty Actuarial Society*, 1937, 24:60–125.

H   Perryman, Francis S., "Some Notes on Credibility," *Proceedings of the Casualty Actuarial Society*, 1932, 19:65–84.

B   Philbrick, Stephen W., "An Examination of Credibility Concepts," *Proceedings of the Casualty Actuarial Society*, 1981, 68:195–219.

I   Robbin, Ira, "A Bayesian Credibility Formula for IBNR Counts," *Proceedings of the Casualty Actuarial Society*, 1986, 73:129–164.

H   Uhthoff, Dunbar R., "The Compensation Experience Rating Plan—A Current Review," *Proceedings of the Casualty Actuarial Society*, 1959, 46:285–299.

I   Van Slyke, E. Oakley, "Credibility-Weighted Trend Factors," *Proceedings of the Casualty Actuarial Society*, 1981, 68:160–171.

B   Van Slyke, E. Oakley, "Credibility for Hiawatha," *CAS Forum*, Fall 1995, 281–298.

I   Venter, Gary G., "Classical Partial Credibility with Application to Trend," *Proceedings of the Casualty Actuarial Society*, 1986, 73:27–51.

I   Venter, Gary G. Credibility. Chap. 7 in *Foundations of Casualty Actuarial Science*. First Edition. New York: Casualty Actuarial Society, 1990.

A   Venter, Gary G., "Structured Credibility in Applications—Hierarchical, Multi-Dimensional and Multivariate Models," *ARCH*, 1985, 2.

I   Waters, H. R., "An Introduction to Credibility Theory," Institute of Actuaries Study Note.

H   Whitney, Albert W., "The Theory of Experience Rating," *Proceedings of the Casualty Actuarial Society*, 1918, 4:274–292.

APPENDIX

FREQUENCY AND LOSS DISTRIBUTIONS

Actuaries commonly use distributions to model the number of claims and sizes of claims. This appendix will give key facts about the most commonly used frequency distributions and some of the more commonly used loss distributions.

Frequency Distributions

Binomial Distribution

Support: $x = 0, 1, 2, 3 \ldots, n$ Parameters: $1 > p > 0$, $n \geq 1$.
Let $q = 1 - p$.

Probability density function: $f(x) = \binom{n}{x} p^x q^{n-x}$

Mean $= np$

Variance $= npq$

Special Case: For $n = 1$ one has a Bernoulli Distribution

Poisson Distribution

Support: $x = 0, 1, 2, 3 \ldots$ Parameters: $\lambda > 0$

Probability density function: $f(x) = \lambda^x e^{-\lambda}/x!$

Mean $= \lambda$

Variance $= \lambda$

Negative Binomial Distribution

Support: $x = 0, 1, 2, 3 \ldots$ Parameters: $k \geq 0$, $0 < p < 1$.
Let $q = 1 - p$

Probability density function: $f(x) = \binom{x + k - 1}{x} p^k q^x$

Mean $= kq/p = k(1 - p)/p$

Variance $= kq/p^2 = k(1-p)/p^2$

Special Case: For $k = 1$ one has a Geometric Distribution

Loss Distributions

Exponential Distribution

Support: $x > 0$ Parameters: $\lambda > 0$

Distribution Function: $F(x) = 1 - e^{-\lambda x}$

Probability density function: $f(x) = \lambda e^{-\lambda x}$

Moments: $E[X^n] = (n!)/\lambda^n$

Mean $= 1/\lambda$

Variance $= 1/\lambda^2$

Gamma Distribution

Support: $x > 0$ Parameters: $\alpha, \lambda > 0$

Distribution Function: $F(x) = \Gamma(\alpha; \lambda x)$

Probability density function: $f(x) = \lambda^\alpha x^{\alpha-1} e^{-\lambda x}/\Gamma(\alpha)$

Moments: $E[X^n] = \prod\limits_{i=0}^{n-1} (\alpha + i)/\lambda^n = \lambda^{-n} \Gamma(\alpha + n)/\Gamma(\alpha)$

Mean $= \alpha/\lambda$

Variance $= \alpha/\lambda^2$

Special Case: For $\alpha = 1$ one has an Exponential Distribution

Weibull Distribution

Support: $x > 0$ Parameters: $c, \tau > 0$

Distribution Function: $F(x) = 1 - \exp(-cx^\tau)$

Probability density function: $f(x) = c\tau x^{\tau-1}\exp(-cx^\tau)$

Moments: $E[X^n] = \Gamma(1 + n/\tau)/c^{n/\tau}$

Special Case: For $\tau = 1$ one has an Exponential Distribution

LogNormal Distribution

Support: $x > 0$

Parameters:
$-\infty < \mu < +\infty, \ \sigma > 0$

Distribution Function: $F(x) = \Phi[\ln(x) - \mu/\sigma]$

Probability density function:
$$f(x) = \exp[-.5(\{\ln(x) - \mu\}/\sigma)^2]/\{x\sigma\sqrt{2\pi}\}$$

Moments: $E[X^n] = \exp[n\mu + .5n^2\sigma^2]$

Mean $= \exp(\mu + .5\sigma^2)$

Variance $= \exp(2\mu + \sigma^2)\{\exp(\sigma^2) - 1\}$

Pareto Distribution

Support: $x > 0$

Parameters: $\alpha, \ \lambda > 0$

Distribution Function:
$$F(x) = 1 - (\lambda/(\lambda + x))^\alpha = 1 - (1 + x/\lambda)^{-\alpha}$$

Probability density function:
$$f(x) = (\alpha\lambda^\alpha)(\lambda + x)^{-(\alpha+1)} = (\alpha/\lambda)(1 + x/\lambda)^{-(\alpha+1)}$$

Moments: $E[X^n] = \lambda^n n! / \prod_{i=1}^{n} (\alpha - i) \qquad \alpha > n$

Mean $= \lambda/(\alpha - 1) \qquad \alpha > 1$

Variance $= \lambda^2\alpha/\{(\alpha - 2)(\alpha - 1)^2\} \qquad \alpha > 2$

SOLUTIONS

Solution 2.2.1: $\Phi(2.576) = .995$, so that $y = 2.576$. $n_0 = y^2/k^2 = (2.576/.025)^2 = $ **10,617**.

Solution 2.2.2: $\Phi(2.326) = .99 = (1 + .98)/2$, so that $y = 2.326$. $n_0 = y^2/k^2 = (2.326/.075)^2 = $ **962**.

Solution 2.2.3: $n_0 = y^2/k^2$. Therefore, $y = k\sqrt{n_0} = .06\sqrt{900} = 1.80$. $P = 2\Phi(y) - 1 = 2\Phi(1.80) - 1 = (2)(.9641) - 1 = $ **.9282**.

Solution 2.2.4: For Y risks the mean is $.05Y$ and variance is $.09Y$. (The means and variances of independent variables each add.) Thus, the $\pm 2\%$ error bars correspond to $\pm(.02)(.05Y)$. The standard deviation is $.3(Y^{.5})$. "94% of the time," corresponds to 1.881 standard deviations, since $\Phi(1.881) = 97\%$. Thus, we set the error bars equal to 1.881 standard deviations: $(1.881)(.3)Y^{.5} = (.02)(.05Y)$. Therefore, $Y = (1.881/.02)^2(.09)/.05^2 = $ **318,434**.

Comment: In terms of claims instead of exposures the full credibility standard would be $318,434 \times .05 = 15,922 = 8,845 \times 1.8 = 8,845$ (variance/mean). If the claim frequency were Poisson, the variance equals the mean and one would get a standard for full credibility of 8,845 claims; in this case since the Poisson assumption does not hold, one must multiply by an additional term of $(.09/.05) = $ variance/mean. Since the variance is larger than the mean, we need more claims to limit the fluctuations than would be the case with a Poisson frequency.

Solution 2.2.5: Let x be the number of respondents and let p be the true percentage of yes respondents in the total population. The result of the poll is a Binomial Distribution with variance $xp(1-p)$. Thus, the variance of the average is $(1/x^2)$ times this or $p(1-p)/x$. Using the Normal Approximation, 95% probability corresponds to ± 1.96 standard deviations of the mean of p. Thus, we want $(.07)(p) = (1.96)\sqrt{(p(1-p)/x)}$. $\sqrt{x} = (1.96)(\sqrt{(1-p)/p})/.07$. $x = 784((1/p) - 1)$. As p gets smaller x approaches infinity. However, we assume $p \geq .2$ so that $x \leq 784(5 - 1) = $ **3,136**.

Comment: The 3,136 respondents are similar to 3,136 exposures. If one has at least a 20% chance of a yes response, then the expected number of yes responses is at least $(3,136)(.2) = 627$. This is similar in concept to 627 expected claims. The general form of the standard for full credibility is in terms of expected claims: $(\sigma_f^2/\mu_f)(y^2/k^2)$. In this case, $k = .07$, $P = 95\%$ and $y = 1.960$. $\sigma_f^2/\mu_f = npq/(np) = q$. Thus, the standard for full credibility in terms of expected claims would be: $q(1.960/.07)^2 = 784q$. In terms of exposures it would be: $784q/p = 784(1/p - 1)$. For p between .2 and .8, this expression is maximized when $p = .2$ and is then $784(5 - 1) = 3,136$ exposures.

Solution 2.2.6: For frequency, the general formula for the Standard for Full Credibility is: $(\sigma_f^2/\mu_f)\{y^2/k^2\}$. Assuming y and k (not the parameter of a Negative Binomial, but rather the tolerance around the true mean frequency) are fixed, then the Standard for Full Credibility is proportional to the ratio of the variance to the mean. For the Poisson this ratio is one. For a Negative Binomial with parameters p and k, this ratio is: $(kq/p^2)/(kq/p) = 1/p$. Thus, the second Standard is $1/p = 1/.7 = 1.429$ times the first standard.

Comment: The Negative Binomial has a larger variance than the Poisson, so there is more random fluctuation, and therefore the standard for Full Credibility is larger. For the Poisson $\sigma_f^2/\mu_f = 1$. For the Negative Binomial the variance is greater than the mean, so $\sigma_f^2/\mu_f > 1$. Thus, for the Negative Binomial the Standard for Full Credibility is larger than the Poisson case, all else equal.

Solution 2.2.7: Since the full credibility standard is inversely proportional to the square of k: $n_0 = y^2/k^2$, $X/Y = (10\%/5\%)^2 = 4$. Alternately, one can compute the values of X and Y assuming one is dealing with the standard for Frequency. For $k = 5\%$ and $P = 90\%$: $\Phi(1.645) = .95 = (1 + .90)/2$, so that $y = 1.645$, $n_0 = y^2/k^2 = (1.645/.05)^2 = 1,082 = X$. For $k = 10\%$ and $P = 90\%$:

$\Phi(1.645) = .95 = (1 + .90)/2$, so that $y = 1.645$, $n_0 = y^2/k^2 = (1.645/.10)^2 = 271 = Y$. Thus, $X/Y = 1,082/271 = $ **4**.

Comment: As the requirement gets less strict, for example $k = 10\%$ rather than 5%, the number of claims needed for Full Credibility decreases. If one is dealing with the standard for pure premiums rather than frequency, then both X and Y have an extra factor of $(1 + CV^2)$, which doesn't effect X/Y.

Solution 2.3.1: $y = 1.645$ since $\Phi(1.645) = .95$. $n_0 = (y/k)^2 = (1.645/.01)^2 = 27060$. For severity, the Standard For Full Credibility is: $n_0 CV^2 = (27,060)(6,000,000/1,000^2) = (27,060)(6) = $ **162,360**.

Solution 2.3.2: $n_0 CV_S^2 = $ Full Credibility Standard for Severity. n_0 is the same for both risks A and B. Since the means of the severity of A and B are the same, but the standard deviation of severity for B is twice as large as A's, then $CV_S^2(B) = 4CV_S^2(A)$. This implies that $n_0 CV_S(B) = 4n_0 CV_S(A) = $ **4N**.

Solution 2.4.1: $\sigma_{PP}^2 = \mu_F \sigma_S^2 + \mu_S^2 \sigma_F^2 = (13)(200,000) + (300)^2(37) = $ **5,930,000**.

Solution 2.4.2: Frequency is Bernoulli with $p = 2/3$, with mean $= 2/3$ and variance $= (2/3)(1/3) = 2/9$. Mean severity $= 7.1$, variance of severity $= 72.1 - 7.1^2 = 21.69$. Thus, $\sigma_{PP}^2 = \mu_F \sigma_S^2 + \mu_S^2 \sigma_F^2 = (2/3)(21.69) + (7.1^2)(2/9) = $ **25.66**.

For the severity the mean and the variance are computed as follows:

Probability	Size of Claim	Square of Size of Claim
20%	2	4
50%	5	25
30%	14	196
Mean	7.1	72.1

Solution 2.4.3: The average Pure Premium is 106. The second moment of the Pure Premium is 16,940. Therefore, the variance = $16,940 - 106^2 = $ **5,704.**

Situation	Probability	Pure Premium	Square of P.P.
1 claim @ 50	60.0%	50	2,500
1 claim @ 200	20.0%	200	40,000
2 claims @ 50 each	7.2%	100	10,000
2 claims: 1 @ 50 & 1 @ 150	9.6%	200	40,000
2 claims @ 150 each	3.2%	300	90,000
Overall	100.0%	106	16,940

For example, the chance of 2 claims with one of size 50 and one of size 150 is the chance of having two claims times the chance given two claims that one will be 50 and the other 150 = $(.2)(2)(.6)(.4) = 9.6\%$. In that case the pure premium is $50 + 150 = 200$. One takes the weighted average over all the possibilities.

Comment: Note that the frequency and severity are *not* independent.

Solution 2.4.4: Since the frequency and severity are independent, the process variance of the Pure Premium = (mean frequency)(variance of severity) + (mean severity)^2 (variance of frequency) = $.25$ [(variance of severity) + (mean severity)^2] = $.25$ (2nd moment of the severity)

$$= (.25/5,000) \int_0^{5000} x^2 dx$$

$$= (.25/5,000)(5,000)^3/3 = \textbf{2,083,333.}$$

Solution 2.4.5: The mean severity = $\exp(\mu + .5\sigma^2) = \exp(4.32) = 75.19$. Thus, the mean aggregate losses is $(8,200)(75.19) = $ **616,547.** The second moment of the severity = $\exp(2\mu + 2\sigma^2) = \exp(9.28) = 10,721$. Thus, since the frequency is Poisson and independent of the severity the variance of the aggregate losses

$= \mu_F$ (2nd moment of the severity) $= (8,200)(10,721) = $ **87.91 million.**

Solution 2.4.6: For a Poisson frequency, with independent frequency and severity, the variance of the aggregate losses $= \mu_F$ (2nd moment of the severity) $= (0.5)(1,000) = 500$.

Solution 2.4.7: Since we have a Poisson Frequency, the Process Variance for each type of claim is given by the mean frequency times the second moment of the severity. For example, for Claim Type Z, the second moment of the severity is $(1,500^2 + 2,000,000) = 4,250,000$. Thus, for Claim Type Z the process variance of the pure premium is: $(.01)(4,250,000) = 42,500$. Then the process variances for each type of claim add to get the total variance, 103,570.

Type of Claim	Mean Frequency	Mean Severity	Square of Mean Severity	Variance of Severity	Process Variance of P.P.
W	0.02	200	40,000	2,500	850
X	0.03	1,000	1,000,000	1,000,000	60,000
Y	0.04	100	10,000	0	400
Z	0.01	1,500	2,250,000	2,000,000	42,500
Sum					**103,750**

Solution 2.5.1: For a LogNormal, the mean severity $= \exp(\mu + .5\sigma^2) = \exp(4.32) = 75.19$. The second moment of the severity $= \exp(2\mu + 2\sigma^2) = \exp(9.28) = 10,721$. Thus, $1 + CV^2 = $ second moment divided by square of the mean $= 10,721/75.19^2 = 1.896$. (Note that for the LogNormal Distribution: $1 + CV^2 = \exp(\sigma^2) = \exp(.8^2) = 1.8965$.) $y = 1.645$ since $\Phi(1.645) = .95 = (1 + .90)/2$. Therefore, $n_0 = y^2/k^2 = (1.645/.025)^2 = 4,330$. Therefore, $n_F = n_0(1 + CV^2) = (4,330)(1.896) = $ **8,210 claims.**

Solution 2.5.2: Square of Coefficient of Variation $= (2 \text{ million})/(1,000^2) = 2$. The Normal distribution has a 99.5% chance of being less than 2.575. Thus, $y = 2.575$. $k = 10\%$. Therefore, in terms of number of claims the full credibility standard is $= y^2(1 + CV^2)/k^2 = (2.575^2)(1 + 2)/10\%^2 = 1989$ claims. This is equivalent to $1989/.04 = $ **49,725 policies**.

Solution 2.5.3: The severity has a mean of 16.67 and a second moment of 416.67:

$$\int_0^{50} xf(x)dx = .0008 \int_0^{50} (50x - x^2)dx$$

$$= .0008(25x^2 - x^3/3) \Big]_0^{50} = 16.67$$

$$\int_0^{50} x^2 f(x)dx = .0008 \int_0^{50} (50x^2 - x^3)dx$$

$$= .0008(50x^3/3 - x^4/4) \Big]_0^{50} = 416.67$$

$$1 + CV^2 = E[X^2]/E^2[X] = 416.67/16.67^2 = 1.5.$$

The standard for Full Credibility for the pure premiums for $k = 2.5\%$ is, therefore, $n_F = n_0(1 + CV^2) = (5,000)(1.5) = 7,500$. For k=9% we need to multiply by $(2.5/9)^2$ since the full credibility standard is inversely proportional to k^2. $7,500(2.5/9)^2 = $ **579**.

Solution 2.5.4: We have $y = 2.576$ since $\Phi(2.576) = .995$. Therefore, $n_0 = (y/k)^2 = (2.576/.10)^2 = 663$. $n_F = n_0(1 + CV^2)$, therefore, $CV = \sqrt{(n_F/n_0) - 1} = \sqrt{(2,000/663) - 1} = $ **1.42**.

Solution 2.5.5: We have $y = 1.960$ since $\Phi(1.960) = .975$. Therefore, $n_0 = (y/k)^2 = (1.960/.20)^2 = 96$. The mean severity is $(10)(.5) + (20)(.3) + (50)(.2) = 21$. The variance of the severity is: $(11^2)(.5) + (1^2)(.3) + (29^2)(.2) = 229$. Thus, the coefficient of variation squared $= 229/21^2 = .519$. $n_F = n_0(1 + CV^2) = 96(1.519) = $ **146**.

Solution 2.5.6: The Poisson assumption does not apply so we use formula [2.5.5]: $n_F = (y^2/k^2)(\sigma_f^2/\mu_f + \sigma_s^2/\mu_s^2)$. We have $y = $

1.960 since $\Phi(1.960) = .975$. Therefore, $(y/k)^2 = (1.960/.20)^2 = 96$. The mean severity is $(10)(.5) + (20)(.3) + (50)(.2) = 21$. The variance of the severity is: $(11^2)(.5) + (1^2)(.3) + (29^2)(.2) = 229$. Therefore, $\sigma_s^2/\mu_s^2 = 229/21^2 = .519$. The variance of the frequency is twice the mean, so $\sigma_f^2/\mu_f = 2$. The answer is: $n_F = (96)(2 + .519) = \mathbf{242}$. Because of the greater variance in frequency relative to the mean, more claims are required for the Negative Binomial frequency than the Poisson frequency in the previous problem.

Solution 2.5.7: $\Phi(2.327) = .99$, so $y = 2.327$. For frequency, the standard for full credibility is $(2.327/.025)^2 = 8,664$. On the other hand, the Standard for Full Credibility for the pure premium: $\Phi(1.645) = .95$, so $y = 1.645$. Thus, $8,664 = n_F = (y^2/k^2)(1 + CV^2) = (1.645^2/k^2)(1 + 3.5^2) = 35.85/k^2$. Thus, $k = \sqrt{(35.85/8,664)} = \mathbf{.064}$.

Solution 2.5.8: The mean of the severity distribution is $100,000 /2 = 50,000$. The Second Moment of the Severity Distribution is the integral from 0 to $100,000$ of $x^2 f(x)$, which is $100,000^3/3(100,000)$. Thus, the variance is $100,000^2/3 - 50,000^2 = 833,333,333$. Thus, the square of the coefficient of variation is $833,333,333/50,000^2 = 1/3$. $k = 5\%$ (within $\pm 5\%$) and since $P = .95$, $y = 1.960$ since $\Phi(1.960) = (1 + P)/2 = .975$.

The Standard for Full Credibility Pure Premium $= (y/k)^2 (1 + CV^2) = (1.96/.05)^2 (1 + 1/3) = 1537 (4/3) = \mathbf{2,049 \text{ claims}}$.

Solution 2.5.9: $n_F = (y/k)^2(1 + CV^2)$. If the CV goes from 2 to 4, and k doubles then the Standard for Full Credibility is multiplied by $\{(1 + 4^2)/(1 + 2^2)\}/2^2 = (17/5)/4$. Thus, the Standard for Full Credibility is altered to: $(1,200)(17/5)/4 = \mathbf{1,020}$.

Solution 2.6.1: $Z = \sqrt{(300/2,000)} = \mathbf{38.7\%}$.

Solution 2.6.2: Since the credibility is proportional to the square root of the number of claims, we get $(36\%)(\sqrt{10}) = 114\%$. However, the credibility is limited to $\mathbf{100\%}$.

Solution 2.6.3: $Z = \sqrt{(803/2,500)} = .567$. Observed average cost per claim is $9,771,000/803 = 12,168$. Thus, the estimated severity $= (.567)(12,168) + (1 - .567)(10,300) = \mathbf{\$11,359}$.

Solution 2.6.4: The expected number of claims is $(.06)(2,000) = 120$. $Z = \sqrt{(120/3,300)} = 19.1\%$.

Comment: The Standard for Full Credibility could be given in terms of house-years rather than claims: for $3,300/.06 = 55,000$ house-years one expects 3,300 claims.

The credibility for 2,000 house years is: $\sqrt{(2,000/55,000)} = 19.1\%$.

Solution 2.6.5: $\Phi(2.17) = .985$, so that $y = 2.17$. $n_0 = y^2/k^2 = (2.17/.04)^2 = 2,943$. For the Gamma Distribution, the mean is α/λ, while the variance is α/λ^2. Thus, the coefficient of variation is $(\text{variance}^{.5})/\text{mean} = \{\alpha/\lambda^2\}^{.5}/\alpha/\lambda = 1/\alpha^{.5}$. So for the given Gamma with $\alpha = 1.5$: $(1 + CV^2) = 1 + 1/1.5 = 1.667$. $n_F = n_0(1 + CV^2) = (2,943)(1.667) = 4,905$. $Z = \sqrt{(150/4,905)} = 17.5\%$.

Solution 2.6.6: The credibility $Z = \sqrt{(600/5,400)} = 1/3$. Thus, the new estimate is: $(1/3)(1,200) + (1 - 1/3)(1,000) = \mathbf{\$1,067}$.

Solution 2.6.7: $(1 + P)/2 = (1.96)/2 = .98$. Thus, $y = 2.054$ since $\Phi(2.054) = .98$. The standard for full credibility is: $(y^2/k^2)(1 + CV^2) = (2.054/.10)^2 (1 + .6^2) = 574$ claims. Thus, we assign credibility of $Z = \sqrt{(213/574)} = \mathbf{60.9\%}$.

Solution 2.6.8: $k = .05$ and $P = .90$. $y = 1.645$, since $\Phi(1.645) = .95 = (1 + P)/2$. $n_0 = y^2/k^2 = (1.645/.05)^2 = 1,082$. The mean of the severity distribution is $100,000$. The second moment of the severity is the integral of $x^2/200,000$ from 0 to 200,000, which is $200,000^2/3$. Thus, the variance is $3,333,333,333$. The square of the coefficient of variation is $\text{variance}/\text{mean}^2 = 3,333,333,333/100,000^2 = .3333$. Thus, $n_F = n_0(1 + CV^2) = (1,082)(1.333) = 1,443$. For 1,082 claims $Z = \sqrt{(1,082/1,443)} = \sqrt{(3/4)} = \mathbf{.866}$.

Solution 2.6.9: $Z = \sqrt{(10,000/17,500)} = 75.6\%$. Thus, the new estimate $= (25 \text{ million})(.756) + (20 \text{ million})(1 - .756) = \textbf{\$23.78 million}$.

Solution 2.6.10: $Z = \sqrt{(n/\text{standard for full credibility})} = \sqrt{(n/2,000)}$. Setting the credibility equal to .6: $.6 = \sqrt{(n/2,000)}$. Therefore, $n = (.6^2)(2,000) = \textbf{720 claims}$.

Solution 2.6.11: We are given $k = 5\%$ and $P = 90\%$, therefore, we have $y = 1.645$ since $\Phi(1.645) = .95 = (1 + P)/2$. Therefore, $n_0 = (y/k)^2 = (1.645/.05)^2 = 1,082$. The partial credibility is given by the square root rule: $Z = \sqrt{(500/1,082)} = \textbf{.68}$.

Solution 3.1.1:

Type of Risk	A Priori Probability	Process Variance
A	0.60	0.16
B	0.25	0.21
C	0.15	0.24
Average		**0.1845**

For a Bernoulli the process variance is *pq*. For example, for Risk Type B, the process variance $= (.3)(.7) = .21$.

Solution 3.1.2:

Type of Risk	A Priori Probability	Mean	Square of Mean
A	0.60	0.2	0.04
B	0.25	0.3	0.09
C	0.15	0.4	0.16
Average		0.2550	0.0705

Thus, the Variance of the Hypothetical Means $= .0705 - .255^2 = \textbf{.0055}$.

Solution 3.1.3:

Number of Claims	Probability for Youthful	n	Square of n
0	0.80	0	0
1	0.15	1	1
2	0.04	2	4
3	0.01	3	9
Average		0.2600	0.4000

Thus, the process variance for the Youthful drivers is $.4 - .26^2 = .3324$.

Number Claims	Probability for Adult	n	Square of n
0	0.90	0	0
1	0.08	1	1
2	0.02	2	4
3	0.00	3	9
Average		0.1200	0.1600

Thus, the process variance for the Adult drivers is $.16 - .12^2 = .1456$.

Thus, the Expected Value of the Process Variance $= (.1456)(91\%) + (.3324)(9\%) = \mathbf{.162}$.

Solution 3.1.4:

Type of Driver	A Priori Probability	Mean	Square of Mean
Youthful	0.0900	0.2600	0.06760
Adult	0.9100	0.1200	0.01440
Average		0.1326	0.01919

Thus, the Variance of the Hypothetical Means $= .01919 - .1326^2 = .00161$.

Solution 3.1.5:

A Number of Claims	B A Priori Probability	C Col. A Times Col. B.	D Square of Col. A. Times Col. B
0	0.55000	0.00000	0.00000
1	0.30000	0.30000	0.30000
2	0.10000	0.20000	0.40000
3	0.04000	0.12000	0.36000
4	0.01000	0.04000	0.16000
Sum	1	0.6600	1.22000

Each insured's frequency process is given by a Poisson with parameter θ, with θ varying over the group of insureds. Then the process variance for each insured is θ. Thus, the expected value of the process variance is estimated as follows:

$$E_\theta[\text{Var}[X \mid \theta]] = E_\theta[\theta] = \text{overall mean} = \textbf{.66}.$$

Solution 3.1.6: Consulting the table in the prior solution, the mean number of claims is .66. The second moment of the distribution of the number of claims is 1.22. So, the Total Variance for the distribution of the number of claims is: $1.220 - .660^2 = \textbf{.784}$.

Solution 3.1.7: Using the solutions to the previous questions, we estimate the Variance of the Hypothetical Means as: Total Variance − EPV = .784 − .66 = **.124**.

Solution 3.1.8: Let m be the mean claim frequency for an insured. Then $h(m) = 1/10$ on $[0, 10]$. The mean severity for a risk is r, since that is the mean for the given exponential distribution. Therefore, for a given insured the mean pure premium is mr. The first moment of the hypothetical mean pure premiums is (since the frequency and severity distributions are independent):

$$\int_{m=0}^{m=10} \int_{r=0}^{r=2} mrg(r)h(m)dr\,dm = \int_{m=0}^{m=10} m/10\,dm \int_{r=0}^{r=2} r(r/2)dr$$

$$= (5)(4/3) = 6.667$$

The second moment of the hypothetical mean pure premiums is (since the frequency and severity distributions are independent):

$$\int_{m=0}^{m=10} \int_{r=0}^{r=2} m^2 r^2 g(r)h(m)dr\,dm = \int_{m=0}^{m=10} m^2/10\,dm \int_{r=0}^{r=2} r^2(r/2)dr$$

$$= (100/3)(2) = 66.667$$

Therefore, the variance of the hypothetical mean pure premiums is $66.667 - 6.667^2 = \mathbf{22.22}$.

Comment: Note that when frequency and severity are independent, the second moment of their product is equal to the product of their second moments. The same is *not* true for variances.

Solution 3.1.9: For a Bernoulli the process variance is $pq = p(1-p)$. For example for Die A_1, the process variance $= (2/6)(1-2/6) = 2/9 = .2222$.

Type of Die	Bernoulli Parameter	A Priori Probability	Process Variance
A1	0.3333	0.50	0.2222
A2	0.5000	0.50	0.2500
Average			**0.2361**

Solution 3.1.10:

Type of Die	A Priori Probability	Mean	Square of Mean
A1	0.50	0.33333	0.11111
A2	0.50	0.50000	0.25000
Average		0.41667	0.18056

Thus, the Variance of the Hypothetical Means= $.18056 - .41667^2$ = **.00695**.

Solution 3.1.11: For spinner B_1 the first moment is $(20)(.6) +$ $(50)(.4) = 32$ and the second moment is $(20^2)(.6) + (50^2)(.4) =$ $1,240$. Thus, the process variance is $1,240 - 32^2 = 216$. For spinner B_2 the first moment is $(20)(.2) + (50)(.8) = 44$ and the second moment is $(20^2)(.2) + (50^2)(.8) = 2,080$. Thus, the process variance is $2,080 - 44^2 = 144$. Therefore, the expected value of the process variance $= (1/2)(216) + (1/2)(144) = $ **180**.

Type of Spinner	A Priori Probability	Mean	Second Moment	Process Variance
B1	0.50	32	1,240	216
B2	0.50	44	2,080	144
Average				180

Solution 3.1.12:

Type of Spinner	A Priori Probability	Mean	Square of Mean
B1	0.50	32	1,024
B2	0.50	44	1,936
Average		38	1,480

Thus, the Variance of the Hypothetical Means= $1,480 - 38^2 = 36$.

Comment: Note that the spinners are chosen independently of the dice, so frequency and severity are independent across risk types. Thus, one can ignore the frequency process in this and the prior question. One can not do so when for example low frequency is associated with low severity.

Solution 3.1.13: For each possible pair of die and spinner use the formula: variance of $p.p. = \mu_f \sigma_s^2 + \mu_s^2 \sigma_f^2$.

Die and Spinner	A Priori Chance of Risk	Mean Freq.	Variance of Freq.	Mean Severity	Variance of Sev.	Process Variance of P.P.
A1, B1	0.250	0.333	0.222	32	216	299.6
A1, B2	0.250	0.333	0.222	44	144	478.2
A2, B1	0.250	0.500	0.250	32	216	364.0
A2, B2	0.250	0.500	0.250	44	144	556.0
Mean						**424.4**

Solution 3.1.14:

Die and Spinner	A Priori Chance of Risk	Mean Freq.	Mean Severity	Mean Pure Premium	Square of Mean P.P.
A1, B1	0.250	0.333	32	10.667	113.778
A1, B2	0.250	0.333	44	14.667	215.111
A2, B1	0.250	0.500	32	16.000	256.000
A2, B2	0.250	0.500	44	22.000	484.000
Mean				15.833	267.222

Thus, the Variance of the Hypothetical Means = 267.222 − 15.833^2 = **16.53**.

Solution 3.1.15: For the Poisson the process variance is the equal to the mean. The expected value of the process variance is the weighted average of the process variances for the individual types, using the a priori probabilities as the weights. The EPV of the frequency = (40%)(6) + (35%)(7) + (25%)(9) = 7.10.

Type	A Priori Probability	Poisson Parameter	Process Variance
1	40%	6	6
2	35%	7	7
3	25%	9	9
Average			**7.10**

Solution 3.1.16: One computes the first and 2nd moments of the mean frequencies as follows:

Type	A Priori Probability	Poisson Parameter	Mean Frequency	Square of Mean Freq.
1	40%	6	6	36
2	35%	7	7	49
3	25%	9	9	81
Average			7.10	51.80

Then the variance of the hypothetical mean frequencies = 51.80 − 7.10² = **1.39**.

Comment: Using the solution to this question and the previous question, as explained in the next section, the Bühlmann Credibility parameter for frequency is K = EPV/VHM = 7.10/1.39 = 5.11. The Bühlmann Credibility applied to the observation of the frequency for E *exposures* would be: $Z = E/(E + 5.11)$.

Solution 3.1.17: One has to weight together the process variances of the severities for the individual types using the chance that a claim came from each type. The chance that a claim came from an individual type is proportional to the product of the a priori chance of an insured being of that type and the mean frequency for that type.

As per the Appendix, parameterize the Exponential with mean $1/\lambda$. For type 1, the process variance of the Exponential severity is $1/\lambda^2 = 1/.01^2 = 10,000$. (For the Exponential Distribution, the variance is the square of the mean.) Similarly for type 2 the process variance for the severity is $1/.008^2 = 15,625$. For type 3 the process variance for the severity is $1/.005^2 = 40,000$.

The mean frequencies are: 6, 7, and 9. The a priori chances of each type are: 40%, 35%, and 25%. Thus, the weights to use to compute the EPV of the severity are (6)(40%), (7)(35%),

(9)(25%) = 2.4, 2.45, 2.25. The expected value of the process variance of the severity is the weighted average of the process variances for the individual types, using these weights. The EPV of the severity = {(2.4)(10,000) + (2.45)(15,625) + (2.25)(40,000)}/(2.4 + 2.45 + 2.25) = 21,448.

A	B	C	D	E	F
Type	A Priori Probability	Mean Frequency	Weights= Col. B × Col. C	Exponential Parameter λ	Process Variance
1	40%	6	2.40	0.01	10,000
2	35%	7	2.45	0.008	15,625
3	25%	9	2.25	0.005	40,000
Average			7.10		**21,448**

Solution 3.1.18: In computing the moments one has to use for each individual type the chance that a claim came from that type. The chance that a claim came from an individual type is proportional to the product of the a priori chance of an insured being of that type and the mean frequency for that type. Thus, the weights to use to compute the moments of the mean severities are: (6)(40%), (7)(35%), (9)(25%) = 2.4, 2.45, 2.25.

A	B	C	D	E	F
Type	A Priori Probability	Mean Frequency	Weights= Col. B × Col. C	Mean Severity	Square of Mean Severity
1	40%	6	2.40	100	10,000
2	35%	7	2.45	125	15,625
3	25%	9	2.25	200	40,000
Average			7.10	140.32	21,448

Then the variance of the hypothetical mean severities = 21,448 − 140.32^2 = **1,758**.

Comment: Using the solution to this question and the previous question, as explained in the next section, the Bühlmann Credibility parameter for severity is $K = \text{EPV}/\text{VHM} = 21,448/1,758 = 12.20$. The Bühlmann Credibility applied to the observation of the mean severity for N *claims* would be: $Z = N/(N + 12.20)$.

Solution 3.1.19: For type 1 the mean frequency is 6 and the variance of the frequency is also 6. As per the Appendix, parameterize the Exponential with mean $1/\lambda$. For type 1 the mean severity is 100. For type 1, the variance of the Exponential severity is $1/\lambda^2 = 1/.01^2 = 10,000$. (For the Exponential Distribution, the variance is the square of the mean.) Thus, since frequency and severity are assumed to be independent, the process variance of the pure premium = (Mean Frequency)(Variance of Severity) + (Mean Severity)^2 (Variance of Frequency) = $(6)(10,000) + (100)^2(6) = 120,000$. Similarly for type 2 the process variance of the pure premium = $(7)(15,625) + (125)^2(7) = 218,750$. For type 3 the process variance of the pure premium = $(9)(40,000) + (200)^2(9) = 720,000$. The expected value of the process variance is the weighted average of the process variances for the individual types, using the a priori probabilities as the weights. The EPV of the pure premium = $(40\%)(120,000) + (35\%)(218,750) + (25\%)(720,000) = \textbf{304,562}$.

Type	A Priori Probability	Mean Frequency	Variance of Frequency	Mean Severity	Variance of Severity	Process Variance
1	40%	6	6	100	10,000	120,000
2	35%	7	7	125	15,625	218,750
3	25%	9	9	200	40,000	720,000
Average						**304,562**

Solution 3.1.20: One has to first compute the mean pure premium for each type. Since frequency and severity are assumed to be independent, the mean pure premium = (Mean Frequency)(Mean

Severity). Then one computes the first and second moments of the mean pure premiums as follows:

Type	A Priori Probability	Mean Frequency	Mean Severity	Mean Pure Premium	Square of Pure Premium
1	40%	6	100	600	360,000
2	35%	7	125	875	765,625
3	25%	9	200	1,800	3,240,000
Average				996.25	1,221,969

Then the variance of the hypothetical mean pure premiums = $1,221,969 - 996.25^2 = \textbf{229,455}$.

Comment: Using the solution to this question and the previous question, as explained in the next section, the Bühlmann Credibility parameter for the pure premium is $K = \text{EPV}/\text{VHM} = 304,562/229,455 = 1.33$. The Bühlmann Credibility applied to the observation of the pure premium for E *exposures* would be: $Z = E/(E + 1.33)$.

Solution 3.1.21: The process variance for a binomial distribution is $npq = 5p(1 - p)$. $\text{EPV} = \int_0^1 5p(1 - p)dp = (5p^2/2 - 5p^3/3)\big|_0^1 = \textbf{5/6}$.

Solution 3.1.22: The mean for the binomial is $\mu = np = 5p$. $\text{VHM} = E[\mu^2] - (E[\mu])^2$. The first moment is $E[5p] = \int_0^1 5p\,dp = 5/2$. The second moment is $E[(5p)^2] = \int_0^1 (5p)^2 dp = 25/3$. So, $\text{VHM} = E[(5p)^2] - (E[5p])^2 = 25/3 - 25/4 = \textbf{25/12}$.

Solution 3.2.1: The Bühlmann Credibility parameter is: $K =$ (The Expected Value of the Process Variance)/(The Variance of the Hypothetical Means) $= 100/8 = 12.5$. $Z = N/(N + K) = 20/(20 + 12.5) = \textbf{61.5\%}$.

Solution 3.2.2: $Z = N/(N + K)$, therefore, $K = N(1/Z) - N = 5(1/.7) - 5 = \textbf{2.14}$.

Solution 3.2.3:

Type of Die	A Priori Chance of This Type of Die	Process Variance	Mean Die Roll	Square of Mean Die Roll
4-sided	0.333	1.250	2.5	6.25
6-sided	0.333	2.917	3.5	12.25
8-sided	0.333	5.250	4.5	20.25
Overall		3.1389	3.50	12.91667

The variance of the hypothetical means $= 12.91667 - 3.5^2 = .6667$. $K = $ EPV/VHM $= 3.1389/.6667 = 4.71$. $Z = (1/1 + 4.71) = .175$. The a priori estimate is 3.5 and the observation is 5, so the new estimate is $(.175)(5) + (.825)(3.5) = \mathbf{3.76}$.

Solution 3.2.4: Expected Value of the Process Variance $= .0833$.

Variance of the Hypothetical Means $= .4167 - .5^2 = .1667$.

Type of Urn	A Priori Probability	Mean for This Type Urn	Square of Mean of This Type Urn	Process Variance
1	0.3333	0	0	0
2	0.3333	1	1	0.00000
3	0.3333	0.5	0.25	0.25000
Average		0.5	0.4167	0.0833

$K = $ EPV/VHM $= .0833/.1667 = .5$ Thus, for $N = 5$, $Z = 5/(5 + .5) = 90.9\%$. The observed mean is 0 and the a priori mean is .5, therefore, the new estimate $= (0)(.909) + (.5)(1 - .909) = \mathbf{.0455}$.

Solution 3.2.5: As computed in the solution to the previous question, for 5 observations $Z = 90.9\%$ and the a priori mean is

.5. Since the observed mean is $2/5 = .4$, the new estimate is: $(.4)(.909) + (.5)(1 - .909) = \mathbf{.4091}$.

Solution 3.2.6: For example, the second moment of Urn II is $(.7)(1{,}000^2) + (.3)(2{,}000^2) = 1{,}900{,}000$. The process variance of Urn II $= 1{,}900{,}000 - 1{,}300^2 = 210{,}000$.

Type of Urn	A Priori Probability	Mean	Square of Mean	Second Moment	Process Variance
I	0.8000	1,100	1,210,000	1,300,000	90,000
II	0.2000	1,300	1,690,000	1,900,000	210,000
Average		1,140	1,306,000		114,000

Thus, the expected value of the process variance $= 114{,}000$, and the variance of the hypothetical means is: $1{,}306{,}000 - 1{,}140^2 = 6{,}400$.

Thus, the Bühlmann Credibility parameter is $K = \text{EPV}/\text{VHM} = 114{,}000/6{,}400 = 17.8$. Thus, for 5 observations $Z = 5/(5 + 17.8) = 21.9\%$. The prior mean is \$1,140 and the observation is $8{,}000/5 = \$1{,}600$.

Thus, the new estimate is: $(.219)(1{,}600) + (1 - .219)(1{,}140) = \mathbf{\$1{,}241}$.

Solution 3.2.7: For Risk A the mean is $(.07)(100) + (.03)(500) = 22$ and the second moment is $(.07)(100^2) + (.03)(500^2) = 8{,}200$. Thus, the process variance for Risk A is $8{,}200 - 22^2 = 7{,}716$. Similarly for Risk B the mean is 130 and the second moment is 53,000. Thus, the process variance for Risk B is $53{,}000 - 130^2 = 36{,}100$. For Risk C the mean is 218 and the second moment is 95,800. Thus, the process variance for Risk C is $95{,}800 - 218^2 = 48{,}276$. Thus, the expected value of the process variance $= (1/3)(7{,}716) + (1/3)(36{,}100) + (1/3)(48{,}276) = 30{,}697$.

Risk	A Priori Chance of Risk	Mean	Square of Mean
A	0.333	22	484
B	0.333	130	16,900
C	0.333	218	47,524
Mean		123.33	21,636

Thus, the Variance of the Hypothetical Means $= 21{,}636 - 123.33^2$
$= 6{,}426$.

Therefore, the Bühlmann Credibility Parameter for pure premium $= K = \text{EPV}/\text{VHM} = 30{,}697/6{,}426 = 4.78$. Thus, the credibility for 1 observation is $1/(1 + K) = 1/5.78 = .173$. The a priori mean is 123.33. The observation is 500. Thus, the estimated aggregate losses are: $(.173)(500) + (1 - .173)(123.33) = \mathbf{188.5}$.

Solution 3.2.8: For Die A the mean is $(1 + 1 + 1 + 2 + 3 + 4)/6 = 2$ and the second moment is $(1 + 1 + 1 + 4 + 9 + 16)/6 = 5.3333$. Thus, the process variance for Die A is $5.3333 - 2^2 = 1.3333$. Similarly for Die B the mean is 2.3333 and the second moment is 6.3333. Thus, the process variance for Die B is $6.333 - 2.333^2 = .889$. The mean of Die C is 2.6667. The process variance for Die C is: $\{(1 - 2.6667)^2 + (2 - 2.6667)^2 + (3)(3 - 2.6667)^2 + (4 - 2.6667)^2\}/6 = .889$, the same as Die B. The mean of Die D is 3. The process variance for Die D is: $\{(1 - 3)^2 + (2 - 3)^2 + (3 - 3)^2 + (3)(4 - 3)^2\}/6 = 1.333$, the same as Die A. Thus, the expected value of the process variance $= (1/4)(1.333) + (1/4)(.889) + (1/4)(.889) + (1/4)(1.333) = 1.111$.

Die	A Priori Chance of Die	Mean	Square of Mean
A	0.250	2.0000	4.0000
B	0.250	2.3333	5.4443
C	0.250	2.6667	7.1113
D	0.250	3.0000	9.0000
Mean		2.5000	6.3889

Thus, the Variance of the Hypothetical Means $= 6.3889 - 2.5^2 = .1389$.

Therefore, the Bühlmann Credibility Parameter $= K = \text{EPV}/\text{VHM} = 1.111/.1389 = 8.0$. Thus, the creibility for 5 observations is $5/(5+K) = 5/13$. The a priori mean is 2.5. The observed mean is $(2 + 3 + 1 + 2 + 4)/5 = 2.4$. Thus, the estimated future die roll is: $(5/13)(2.4) + (1 - 5/13)(2.5) = \mathbf{2.462}$.

Solution 3.2.9: For each Poisson, the process variance is the mean. Therefore, Expected Value of the process variance $= (.6)(.05) + (.3)(.1) + (.1)(.2) = .08 = $ Overall mean frequency. The expected value of the square of the mean frequencies is .0085. Therefore, the Variance of the hypothetical mean frequencies $= .0085 - .08^2 = .0021$. Alternately, Variance of the hypothetical mean frequencies $= (.6)(.03^2) + (.3)(.02^2) + (.1)(.12^2) = .0021$. Therefore, $K = \text{EPV}/\text{VHM} = .08/.0021 = 38.1$. $Z = 5/(5 + 38.1) = 11.6\%$. Estimated frequency $= (11.6\%)(.2) + (88.4\%)(.08) = \mathbf{.0939}$.

Type of Driver	A Priori Chance of This Type of Driver	Mean Annual Claim Frequency	Square of Mean Claim Frequency	Poisson Process Variance
Good	0.6	0.05	0.0025	0.05
Bad	0.3	0.1	0.0100	0.1
Ugly	0.1	0.2	0.0400	0.2
Average		0.080	0.0085	0.080

Solution 3.2.10: One needs to figure out for each type of driver a single observation of the risk process, in other words for the observation of a single claim, the process variance of the average size of a claim. Process variances for the Pareto Distributions are $\lambda^2\alpha/\{(\alpha-1)^2(\alpha-2)\}$, so the process variances are: 10.42, 22.22, and 75 million. The probability weights are the product of claim frequency and the a priori frequency of each type of driver: $(.6)(.05)$, $(.3)(.10)$, $(.1)(.20)$. The probabilities that a claim came

from each of the types of drivers are the probability weights divided by the their sum: .375, .375, .25. Thus, the weighted average process variance of the severity is: (10.42 million)(.375) + (22.22 million)(.375) + (75 million)(.25) = **30.98 million.**

Type of Driver	A Priori Chance of This Type of Driver	Average Claim Frequency	Probability Weight For Claim	Probability For Claim	Alpha	Process Variance Claim Severity
Good	0.6	0.05	0.030	0.375	5	1.042×10^7
Bad	0.3	0.1	0.030	0.375	4	2.222×10^7
Ugly	0.1	0.2	0.020	0.25	3	7.500×10^7
Average			0.080	1.000		$\mathbf{3.098 \times 10^7}$

Comment: A claim is more likely to be from a Good Driver since there are many Good Drivers. On the other hand, a claim is more likely to be from an Ugly Driver, because each such driver produces more claims. Thus, the probability that a claim came from each type of driver is proportional to the product of claim frequency and the a priori frequency of each type of driver. The (process) variances for the Pareto Distribution follow from the moments given in the Appendix.

Solution 3.2.11: Average severities for the Pareto Distributions are: $\lambda/(\alpha - 1) = 2,500, 3,333$ and $5,000$. Probability weights are: $(.60)(.05), (.30)(.10), (.10)(.20)$. The overall average severity is 3437.5. Average of the severity squared is: $(.375)(6.25$ million$) + (.375)(11.11$ million$) + (.25)(25$ million$) = 12.76$ million. Therefore, the variance of the hypothetical mean severities $= (12.76$ million$) - (3437.5^2) = \mathbf{.94}$ **million.**

Type of Driver	A Priori Chance of This Type of Driver	Average Claim Frequency	Probability Weight For Claim	Probability For Claim	Alpha	Average Claim Severity	Square of Average Claim Severity
Good	0.6	0.05	0.030	0.375	5	2,500	6.250×10^6
Bad	0.3	0.1	0.030	0.375	4	3,333	1.111×10^7
Ugly	0.1	0.2	0.020	0.250	3	5,000	2.500×10^7
Average			0.080	1.000		3,437.5	1.276×10^7

Solution 3.2.12: Using the solutions to the previous two questions, $K = \text{EPV}/\text{VHM} = 31/.94 = 32.8$. $Z = 1/(1 + 32.8) = 1/33.8$. New estimate $= (1/33.8)25{,}000 + [1 - (1/33.8)]3{,}437.5 =$ **\$4,075**.

Solution 3.2.13: For each type of driver one uses the formula: variance of $p.p. = \mu_f \sigma_s^2 + \mu_s^2 \sigma_f^2$. In the case of a Poisson frequency $\mu_f = \sigma_f^2$ and: variance of $p.p. = (\text{mean frequency})(\text{the second moment of the severities})$.

For the Pareto, the second moment $= 2\lambda^2/\{(\alpha - 1)(\alpha - 2)\}$.

A	B	C	D	E	F
	A Priori Chance of			Expected Value	Variance of P.P. Product
Type of Driver	This Type of Driver	Claim Frequency	Alpha	of Square of Claim Sizes	of Columns C & E
Good	0.6	0.05	5	1.667e+7	8.333×10^5
Bad	0.3	0.1	4	3.333e+7	3.333×10^6
Ugly	0.1	0.2	3	1.000e+8	2.000×10^7
Average					$\mathbf{3.500 \times 10^6}$

Solution 3.2.14: The overall average pure premium $= (.6)(125) + (.3)(333.3) + (.1)(1{,}000) = 275$. The average of the squares of the hypothetical mean pure premiums is: $(.6)(125^2) + (.3)(333.3^2) + (.1)(1{,}000^2) = 142{,}708$. Therefore, the variance of the hypothetical pure premiums $= 142{,}708 - (275^2) = \mathbf{67{,}083}$.

Type of Driver	A Priori Chance of This Type of Driver	Average Claim Frequency	Alpha	Average Claim Severity	Average Pure Premium	Square of Average Pure Premium
Good	0.6	0.05	5	2,500	125.0	15,625
Bad	0.3	0.1	4	3,333	333.3	111,111
Ugly	0.1	0.2	3	5,000	1,000.0	1,000,000
Average					275.0	142,708

Solution 3.2.15: The observed pure premium is $25,000/5 = $5,000. Using the results of the previous two questions, $K = 3,500,000/67,083 = 52$. $Z = 5/(5 + 52) = 8.8\%$. Estimated pure premium $= (8.8\%)(\$5,000) + (1 - 8.8\%)(\$275) = \textbf{\$691}$.

Solution 3.2.16:

Class	A Priori Probability	Mean for This Class	Square of Mean of This Class	Process Variance
1	0.4000	0.2	0.04	0.16
2	0.6000	0.3	0.09	0.21
Average		0.26	0.0700	0.1900

Expected Value of the Process Variance $= .19$.

Variance of the Hypothetical Means $= .070 - .26^2 = .0024$.

$K = \text{EPV}/\text{VHM} = .19/.0024 = 79.2$ Thus, for $N = 5$, $Z = 5/(5 + 79.2) = \textbf{5.94\%}$.

Solution 3.2.17: The hypothetical mean pure premiums are $(.1667)(4)$ and $(.8333)(2)$; which are $2/3$ and $5/3$. Since the two classes have the same number of risks the overall mean is $7/6$ and the variance of the hypothetical mean pure premiums between classes is: $[(2/3 - 7/6)^2 + (5/3 - 7/6)^2]/2 = 1/4$.

Each class is homogeneous and the stated data are the process variance for a risk from each class. For each type of risk, the process variance of the pure premiums is given by: $\mu_f \sigma_s^2 + \mu_f^2 \sigma_s^2$. For Class A, that is: $(.1667)(20) + (4^2)(.1389) = 5.5564$. For Class B, that is: $(.8333)(5) + (2^2)(.1389) = 4.7221$. Since the classes have the same number of risks, the Expected Value of the Process Variance $= (.5)(5.5564) + (.5)(4.7221) = 5.139$. Thus,
$K = \text{EPV}/\text{VHM} = 5.139/.25 = 20.56$. $Z = N/(N + K) = 4/(4 + 20.56) = \textbf{.163}$.

Solution 3.2.18: The prior estimate is the overall mean of $7/6$. The observation is .25. Thus, the new estimate is $(.163)(.25) + (7/6)(1 - .163) = \mathbf{1.017}$.

Comment: Uses the solution of the previous question.

Solution 3.2.19: Expected Value of the Process Variance = $E[v] = 8$.

Variance of the Hypothetical Means = $\text{Var}[m] = 4$.

$K = \text{EPV}/\text{VHM} = 8/4 = 2$. So, $Z = 3/(3 + K) = 3/(3 + 2) = 3/5 = \mathbf{.6}$.

Solution 3.3.1: 1. True. 2. False. 3. True.

Solution 3.3.2: The expected value of the process variance is 86.333. The variance of the hypothetical means is $466.67 - 20^2 = 66.67$.

Type of Marksman	A Priori Chance of This Type of Marksman	Mean	Square of Mean	Standard Deviation	Process Variance
A	0.333	10	100	3	9
B	0.333	20	400	5	25
C	0.333	30	900	15	225
Average		20.000	466.667		86.333

$K = \text{EPV}/\text{VHM} = 86.333/66.67 = 1.295$.

$Z = N/(N + K) = 2/(2 + 1.295) = .607$. The average observation is $(10 + 14)/2 = 12$. The a priori mean = 20. Thus, the new estimate = $(.607)(12) + (1 - .607)(20) = \mathbf{15.14}$.

Solution 3.3.3: The expected value of the process variance is 13. The variance of the hypothetical means is $1 - 0^2 = 1$. Therefore, $K = \text{EPV}/\text{VHM} = 13/1 = 13$. $Z = 1/(1 + 13) = 1/14$. New Estimate = $(4)(1/14) + (0)(1 - 1/14) = 2/7 = \mathbf{.286}$.

Shooter	A Priori Probability	Process Variance	Mean	Square of Mean
A	0.5	1	1	1
B	0.5	25	−1	1
Average		13	0	1

Solution 3.3.4: The EPV is $(1/2)(1 + 25) = 13$. The VHM is $(1/2)[(1 − 0)^2 + (−1 − 0)^2] = 1$. Therefore, $K = \text{EPV}/\text{VHM} = 13/1 = 13$. Since there are three observations, $n = 3$ and $Z = n/(n + K) = 3/(3 + 13) = 3/16$. The average position of the three shots is $(1/3)(2 + 0 + 1) = 1$. So, Estimate $= (1)(3/16) + (0)(1 − 3/16) = 3/16 = .188$.

Solution 4.1.1: The probability of picking a colorblind person out of this population is $(5\%)(10\%) + (1/4\%)(90\%) = .725\%$. The chance of a person being both colorblind and male is: $(5\%)(10\%) = .5\%$. Thus, the (conditional) probability that the colorblind person is a man is: $.5\%/.725\% = 69.0\%$.

Solution 4.1.2: Taking a weighted average, the a priori chance of a black ball is 8.8%.

A Type	B A Priori Probability	C % Black Balls	D Col. B × Col. C
I	0.4	0.05	0.020
II	0.3	0.08	0.024
III	0.2	0.13	0.026
IV	0.1	0.18	0.018
Sum	1		**0.088**

Solution 4.1.3: $P[\text{Urn} = \text{I} \mid \text{Ball} = \text{Black}] = P[\text{Urn} = \text{I and Ball} = \text{Black}]/P[\text{Ball} = \text{Black}] = .020/.088 = 22.7\%$.

Solution 4.1.4: $P[\text{Urn} = \text{II} \,|\, \text{Ball} = \text{Black}] = P[\text{Urn} = \text{II and Ball} = \text{Black}]/P[\text{Ball} = \text{Black}] = .024/.088 = \textbf{27.3\%}$.

Solution 4.1.5: $P[\text{Urn} = \text{III} \,|\, \text{Ball} = \text{Black}] = P[\text{Urn} = \text{III and Ball} = \text{Black}]/P[\text{Ball} = \text{Black}] = .026/.088 = \textbf{29.5\%}$.

Solution 4.1.6: $P[\text{Urn} = \text{IV} \,|\, \text{Ball} = \text{Black}] = P[\text{Urn} = \text{IV and Ball} = \text{Black}]/P[\text{Ball} = \text{Black}] = .018/.088 = \textbf{20.5\%}$.

Comment: The conditional probabilities of the four types of urns add to unity.

Solution 4.1.7: Using the solutions to the previous problems, one takes a weighted average using the posterior probabilities of each type of urn: $(22.7\%)(.05) + (27.3\%)(.08) + (29.5\%)(.13) + (20.5\%)(.18) = \textbf{.108}$.

Comment: This whole set of problems can be usefully organized into a spreadsheet:

A	B	C	D	E	F
Type	A Priori Probability	% Black Balls	Probability Weights = Col. B × Col. C	Posterior Probability	Col. C × Col. E
I	0.4	0.05	0.0200	0.227	0.011
II	0.3	0.08	0.0240	0.273	0.022
III	0.2	0.13	0.0260	0.295	0.038
IV	0.1	0.18	0.0180	0.205	0.037
Sum			0.0880	1.000	**0.108**

This is a simple example of Bayesian Analysis, which is covered in the next section.

Solution 4.1.8: There are the following 10 equally likely possibilities such that $Y \geq 9$: $(3,6), (4,5), (4,6), (5,4), (5,5), (5,6), (6,3), (6,4), (6,5), (6,6)$. Of these, 3 have $X = 5$, so that $\text{Prob}[X = 5 \,|\, Y \geq 9] = \text{Prob}[X = 5 \text{ and } Y \geq 9]/\text{Prob}[Y \geq 9] = (3/36)/(10/36) = 3/10 = \textbf{.3}$.

Solution 4.1.9: There are the following 10 equally likely possibilities such that $X + V \geq 9$: (3,6), (4,5), (4,6), (5,4), (5,5), (5,6), (6,3), (6,4), (6,5), (6,6). Of these one has $X = 3$, two have $X = 4$, three have $X = 5$, and four have $X = 6$. Therefore, $E[X \,|\, Y \geq 9] = \{(1)(3) + (2)(4) + (3)(5) + (4)(6)\}/10 = $ **5.0**. For those who like diagrams:

X	1	2	3	4	5	6	Possibilities	Conditional Density Function of X given that $X + V \geq 9$
1							0	
2							0	
3						X	1	1/10
4					X	X	2	2/10
5				X	X	X	3	3/10
6			X	X	X	X	4	4/10

$E[X \,|\, Y \geq 9] = \sum i P[X = i \,|\, Y \geq 9] = (1)(0) + (2)(0) + (3)(.1) + (4)(.2) + (5)(.3) + (6)(.4) = 5.0$.

Solution 4.1.10: The chance that a driver accident-free is: $(40\%)(80\%) + (25\%)(85\%) + (20\%)(90\%) + (15\%)(95\%) = 85.5\%$. The chance that a driver is both accident-free and from Boston is $(40\%)(80\%) = 32\%$. Thus, the chance this driver is from Boston is $32\%/85.5\% = $ **37.4%**.

Comment: Some may find it helpful to assume for example a total of 100,000 drivers.

Solution 4.1.11: The chance that a driver has had an accident is: $(40\%)(20\%) + (25\%)(15\%) + (20\%)(10\%) + (15\%)(5\%) = 14.5\%$. The chance that a driver both has had an accident and is from Pittsfield is $(15\%)(5\%) = .75\%$. Thus, the chance this driver is from Pittsfield is: $.75\%/14.5\% = $ **.052**.

Comment: Note that the chances for each of the other cities are: $\{(40\%)(20\%), (25\%)(15\%), (20\%)(10\%)\}/14.5\%$. You should confirm that the conditional probabilities for the four cities sum to 100%.

Solution 4.1.12: If Stu knows the answer, then the chance of observing a correct answer is 100%. If Stu doesn't know the answer to a question then the chance of observing a correct answer is 20%.

A	B	C	D	E
Type of Question	A Priori Chance of This Type of Question	Chance of the Observation	Prob. Weight = Product of Columns B & C	Posterior Chance of This Type of Question
Stu Knows	0.620	1.0000	0.6200	**89.08%**
Stu Doesn't Know	0.380	0.2000	0.0760	10.92%
Overall			0.696	1.000

Solution 4.2.1: $(20\%)(60\%)+(30\%)(25\%)+(40\%)(15\%)=$**25.5%**.

Comment: Since there are only two possible outcomes, the chance of observing no claim is: $1 - .255 = .745$.

Solution 4.2.2: $P(\text{Type A} \mid \text{no claim}) = P(\text{no claim} \mid \text{Type A})$ $P(\text{Type A})/P(\text{no claim}) = (.8)(.6)/.745 = $ **64.43%**.

Solution 4.2.3: $(.7)(.25)/.745 = $ **23.49%**.

Solution 4.2.4: $(.6)(.15)/.745 = $ **12.08%**.

Solution 4.2.5:

A	B	C	D	E	F
Type of Risk	A Priori Chance of This Type of Risk	Chance of the Observation	Prob. Weight = Product of Columns B & C	Posterior Chance of This Type of Risk	Mean Annual Freq.
A	0.6	0.8	0.480	64.43%	0.20
B	0.25	0.7	0.175	23.49%	0.30
C	0.15	0.6	0.090	12.08%	0.40
Overall			0.745	1.000	**24.77%**

Solution 4.2.6:

A	B	C	D	E	F
Type of Risk	A Priori Chance of This Type of Risk	Chance of the Observation	Prob. Weight = Product of Columns B & C	Posterior Chance of This Type of Risk	Mean Annual Freq.
A	0.6	0.2	0.120	47.06%	0.20
B	0.25	0.3	0.075	29.41%	0.30
C	0.15	0.4	0.060	23.53%	0.40
Overall			0.255	1.000	**27.65%**

Solution 4.2.7:

A	B	C	D	E	F
Type of Risk	A Priori Chance of This Type of Risk	Chance of the Observation	Prob. Weight = Product of Columns B & C	Posterior Chance of This Type of Risk	Mean Annual Freq.
A	0.6	0.2048	0.123	48.78%	0.20
B	0.25	0.3087	0.077	30.64%	0.30
C	0.15	0.3456	0.052	20.58%	0.40
Overall			0.252	1.000	**27.18%**

For example, if one has a risk of Type B, the chance of observing 2 claims in 5 years is given by (a Binomial Distribution): $(10)(.3^2)(.7^3) = .3087$.

Solution 4.2.8: Bayesian Estimates are in balance; the sum of the product of the a priori chance of each outcome times its posterior Bayesian estimate is equal to the a priori mean. The a priori mean is $(5/8)(1) + (2/8)(4) + (1/8)(16) = 3.625$. Let $E[X_2 | X_1 = 16] = y$. Then setting the sum of the chance of each outcome times its posterior mean equal to the a priori mean: $(5/8)(1.4) +$ $(2/8)(3.6) + (1/8)(y) = 3.625$. Therefore, $y =$ **14.8**.

Solution 4.2.9:

A	B	C	D	E	F
Type of Urn	A Priori Chance of This Type of Urn	Chance of the Observation	Prob. Weight = Product of Columns B & C	Posterior Chance of This Type of Urn	Mean Draw from Urn
I	0.8000	0.1000	0.0800	0.5714	1100
II	0.2000	0.3000	0.0600	0.4286	1300
Overall			0.140	1.000	**1186**

Solution 4.2.10:

A	B	C	D	E	F
Type of Urn	A Priori Chance of This Type of Urn	Chance of the Observation	Prob. Weight = Product of Columns B & C	Posterior Chance of This Type of Urn	Mean Draw from Urn
I	0.8000	0.2430	0.1944	0.6879	1100
II	0.2000	0.4410	0.0882	0.3121	1300
Overall			0.283	1.000	**1162**

For example, the chance of picking 2 @ \$1,000 and 1 @ \$2,000 from Urn II is given by $f(2)$ for a Binomial Distribution with $n = 3$ and $p = .7$: $(3)(.7^2)(.3) = .4410$.

Solution 4.2.11: The chance of observing 3 claims for a Poisson is $e^{-\theta}\theta^3/3!$ Therefore, for example, the chance of observing 3 claims for a risk of type 1 is: $e^{-.4}(.4^3)/6 = .00715$.

A	B	C	D	E	F
Type	A Priori Probability	Chance of the Observation	Prob. Weight = Product of Columns B & C	Posterior Chance of This Type of Risk	Mean Annual Freq.
1	70%	0.00715	0.005005	39.13%	0.4
2	20%	0.01976	0.003951	30.89%	0.6
3	10%	0.03834	0.003834	29.98%	0.8
Overall			0.012791	1.000	**0.5817**

Solution 4.2.12: The density for a Normal Distribution with mean μ and standard deviation σ is given by $f(x) = \exp(-.5\{(x-\mu)/\sigma\}^2) /\{\sigma(2\pi)^{.5}\}$. Thus, the density function at 14 for Marksman A is $\exp(-.5\{(14-10)/3\}^2)/\{3(2\pi)^{.5}\} = .0547$.

A	B	C	D	E	F	G	H	I
Marks-man	Mean	Standard Deviation	A Priori Chance of This Type of Marksman	Chance of the Observing 10	Chance of the Observing 14	Chance of the Observation	Prob. Weight = Product of Columns D & G	Posterior Chance of This Type of Marksman
A	10	3	0.333	0.1330	0.0547	0.007270	0.002423	92.56%
B	20	5	0.333	0.0108	0.0388	0.000419	0.000140	**5.34%**
C	30	15	0.333	0.0109	0.0151	0.000165	0.000055	2.10%
Overall							0.002618	**1.000**

Reading from the table above, we see that the chance that it was marksman B is **5.34%**.

Solution 4.2.13: Use the results of the previous question to weight together the prior means:

Marksman	Posterior Chance of This Type of Risk	A Priori Mean
A	0.9256	10
B	0.0534	20
C	0.0210	30
Overall		**10.954**

Solution 4.3.1: Use equation [4.3.3]: $f_\theta(\theta \mid X = x) = f_X(x \mid \theta) f_\theta(\theta)/$ $f_X(x)$ where x is the event of a claim in each of two years. The probability of one claim in one year is θ, so the probability of a claim in each of two years given θ is $f_X(x \mid \theta) = \theta^2$. By definition, $f_\theta(\theta) = 1$ for $0 \leq \theta \leq 1$. The last piece is $f_X(x)$ $= \int_0^1 f_X(x \mid \theta) f(\theta) d\theta = \int_0^1 \theta^2 \cdot 1 \, d\theta = \theta^3/3 \mid_0^1 = 1/3$. The answer is: $f_\theta(\theta \mid X = x) = \theta^2 \cdot 1/(1/3) = \mathbf{3\theta^2}$ **for** $\mathbf{0 \leq \theta \leq 1}$.

Solution 4.3.2: Use equation [4.3.3]: $f_\theta(\theta \mid X = x) = f_X(x \mid \theta) f_\theta(\theta)/$ $f_X(x)$ where x the event of a claim in each of three years. The probability of one claim in one year is θ, so the probability of a claim in each of three years given θ is $f_X(x \mid \theta) =$ θ^3. By definition, $f_\theta(\theta) = 1$ for $0 \leq \theta \leq 1$. The last piece is $f_X(x) = \int_0^1 f_X(x \mid \theta) f(\theta) d\theta = \int_0^1 \theta^3 \cdot 1 \, d\theta = \theta^4/4 \mid_0^1 = 1/4$. The answer is: $f_\theta(\theta \mid X = x) = \theta^3 \cdot 1/(1/4) = \mathbf{4\theta^3}$ **for** $\mathbf{0 \leq \theta \leq 1}$.

Solution 4.3.3: Assuming a given value of p, the chance of observing one success in three trials is $3p(1 - p)^2$. The prior distribution of p is: $g(p) = 1, 0 \leq p \leq 1$. By Bayes Theorem, the posterior distribution of p is proportional to the product of the chance of the observation and the prior distribution: $3p(1 - p)^2$. Thus, the posterior distribution of p is proportional to $p - 2p^2 + p^3$. (You can keep the factor of 3 and get the same result working instead with $3p - 6p^2 + 3p^3$.) The integral of $p - 2p^2 + p^3$ from 0 to 1 is $1/2 - 2/3 + 1/4 = 1/12$. Thus, the posterior distribution of p is $12(p - 2p^2 + p^3)$. (The integral of the posterior distribution has to be unity. In this case dividing by $1/12$; i.e., multiplying by 12, will make it so.) The posterior chance of p in $[.3,.4]$ is:

$$12 \int_{p=.3}^{.4} (p - 2p^2 + p^3) dp = 6p^2 - 8p^3 + 3p^4 \, \Big]_{p=.3}^{.4}$$

$$= .42 - .296 + .0525 = \mathbf{.1765}.$$

Solution 4.3.4: From the solution to the prior question, the posterior distribution of p is: $12(p - 2p^2 + p^3)$. The mean of this posterior distribution is:

$$12 \int_{p=0}^{1} (p - 2p^2 + p^3)p\,dp = 4p^3 - 6p^4 + (12/5)p^5 \Big]_{p=0}^{1} = .4.$$

The chance of a success on the fourth trial is $E[p] = $ **.4**.

Solution 4.3.5: Given x, the chance of observing three successes is x^3. The a priori distribution of x is $f(x) = 1$, $0 \leq x \leq 1$. By Bayes Theorem, the posterior density is proportional to the product of the chance of the observation and the a priori density function. Thus, the posterior density is proportional to x^3 for $0 \leq x \leq 1$. Since the integral from zero to one of x^3 is $1/4$, the posterior density is $4x^3$. (The posterior density has to integrate to unity.) Thus, the posterior chance that $x < .9$ is the integral of the posterior density from 0 to .9, which is $.9^4 = $ **.656**. Alternately, by Bayes Theorem (or directly from the definition of a conditional distribution): $\Pr[x < .9 \,|\, 3 \text{ successes}] = \Pr[3 \text{ successes} \,|\, x < .9]\Pr[x < .9]/\Pr[3 \text{ successes}] = \Pr[3 \text{ successes} \text{ and } x < .9]/\Pr[3 \text{ successes}] =$

$$\int_{x=0}^{.9} x^3 f(x)dx \Big/ \int_{x=0}^{1} x^3 f(x)dx = \int_{x=0}^{.9} x^3 dx \Big/ \int_{x=0}^{1} x^3 dx$$

$$= \{(.9^4)/4\}/\{(1^4)/4\} = .656.$$

Solution 4.3.6:

$$\int_0^{\infty} e^{-\theta} f(\theta)d\theta = \int_0^{\infty} e^{-\theta} 36\theta e^{-6\theta} d\theta = 36 \int_0^{\infty} \theta e^{-7\theta} d\theta$$

$$= (36)(\Gamma(2)/7^2) = (36)(1/49) = .735.$$

Comment: Note that $\int_0^{\infty} t^{\alpha-1} e^{-\lambda t} dt = \Gamma(\alpha)\lambda^{-\alpha}$. This follows from the fact that the Gamma Distribution as per the Appendix is in fact a distribution function, so that its density integrates to unity. In this case $\alpha = 2$ and $\lambda = 7$.

Solution 4.3.7:

$$P(Y = 0) = \int P(Y = 0 \,|\, \theta) f(\theta) d\theta = \int e^{-\theta} f(\theta) d\theta.$$

For the first case, $f(\theta) = 1/2$ for $0 \le \theta \le 2$

$$P(Y = 0) = \int_{\theta=0}^{2} e^{-\theta}/2 \, d\theta = (1 - e^{-2})/2 = .432.$$

For the second case, $f(\theta) = e^{-\theta}$ for $\theta > 0$ and

$$P(Y = 0) = \int_{\theta=0}^{\infty} e^{-2\theta} d\theta = 1/2.$$

For the third case, $P(Y = 0) = e^{-1} = .368$.

In the first and third cases $P(Y = 0) < .45$.

Comment: Three separate problems in which you need to calculate $P(Y = 0)$ given $f(\theta)$ and three different conditional distributions $P(Y = y \,|\, \theta)$.

Solution 5.1.1: $\Gamma(5 + 1)/8^{5+1} = 5!/8^6 = \mathbf{4.58 \times 10^{-4}}$.

Solution 5.1.2: $\lambda^{\alpha} x^{a-1} e^{-\lambda x}/\Gamma(\alpha) = (.1^3) 8^2 e^{-.8}/\Gamma(3) = \mathbf{.0144}$.

Solution 5.1.3: Variance $= E[x^2] - (E[x])^2 = (\alpha + 1)(\alpha)/\lambda^2 - (\alpha/\lambda)^2 = \alpha/\lambda^2$.

Solution 5.1.4: Mean $= \alpha/\lambda = 3.0/1.5 = 2.0$. Variance $= \alpha/\lambda^2 = 3.0/(1.5)^2 = \mathbf{1.33}$.

Solution 5.2.1: Gamma-Poisson has a Negative Binomial mixed frequency distribution. The Negative Binomial has parameters $k = \alpha = 4$ and $p = \lambda/(1 + \lambda) = .9$. Thus, the chance of 5 claims is

$$\binom{5 + k - 1}{5} p^k (1 - p)^5 = \binom{8}{5} .9^4 (.1)^5 = (56)(.6561)(.00001)$$

$$= \mathbf{.000367}.$$

Solution 5.2.2: The prior distribution is Gamma with $\alpha = 2.0$ and $\lambda = 3.0$. The number of claims for an insured selected at random is a Negative Binomial with parameters $k = \alpha = 2.0$ and $p =$

$\lambda/(\lambda + 1) = 3/4$. The mean number is $k(1 - p)/p = \alpha/\lambda = \mathbf{2/3}$ and the variance is $k(1 - p)/p^2 = \alpha(\lambda + 1)/\lambda^2 = 2(3 + 1)/3^2 = \mathbf{8/9}$.

Solution 5.2.3:

$$k = 2, \qquad p = 0.6 \qquad \text{and} \qquad f(n) = \binom{n + 2 - 1}{n}(.6)^2.4^n.$$

So,

$$P[X > 2] = 1 - P[X = 0] - P[X = 1] - P[X = 2]$$

$$= 1 - f(0) - f(1) - f(2) = 1 - \binom{1}{0}(.6)^2(.4)^0 - \binom{2}{1}.6^2.4^1$$

$$- \binom{3}{2}.6^2.4^2 = 1 - .36 - .288 - .1728 = \mathbf{.1792}.$$

Solution 5.2.4: The chance of no claims for a Poisson is $e^{-\lambda}$. We average over the possible values of λ:

$$(1/2)\int_1^3 e^{-\lambda}d\lambda = (1/2)(-e^{-\lambda})\Big|_1^3 = (1/2)(e^{-1} - e^{-3})$$

$$= (1/2)(.368 - .050) = \mathbf{.159}.$$

Solution 5.2.5: (1) Binomial: $\mu = np$ and $\sigma^2 = npq$. Then $\mu = np \geq npq = \sigma^2$ for $q \leq 1$. (2) Negative Binomial: $\mu = k(1 - p)/p$ and $\sigma^2 = k(1 - p)/p^2$. Then, $\mu = k(1 - p)/p \leq k(1 - p)/p^2 = \sigma^2$ for $p \leq 1$. Rank for equal means: σ^2 binomial $\leq \sigma^2$ poisson $\leq \sigma^2$ negative binomial.

Solution 5.3.1: The Prior Gamma has parameters $\alpha = 4$ and $\lambda = 2$. The Posterior Gamma has parameters $\alpha' = 4 + 5 = 9$ and $\lambda' = 2 + 3 = 5$.

Solution 5.3.2: For the Gamma-Poisson, if the prior Gamma has parameters $\alpha = 3$, $\lambda = 4$, then the Posterior Gamma has parameters $\alpha = 3 + 1$ and $\lambda = 4 + 2$. Posterior Gamma $= \lambda^{\alpha}\theta^{\alpha-1}e^{-\lambda\theta}/\Gamma(\alpha) = 6^4\theta^3e^{-6\theta}/(3!) = 216\theta^3e^{-6\theta}$.

Solution 5.3.3: The prior Gamma has $\alpha = 1$ (an Exponential Distribution) and $\lambda = 1$. The posterior Gamma has $\alpha' =$ prior $\alpha +$ number of claims $= 1 + 0 = 1$ (an Exponential Distribution) and $\lambda' =$ prior $\lambda +$ number of exposures $= 1 + 1 = 2$. That is, the posterior density function is: $2e^{-2\theta}$.

Comment: Given θ, the chance of observing zero claims is $\theta^0 e^{-\theta}/0! = e^{-\theta}$. The posterior distribution is proportional to product of the chance of observation and the a priori distribution of θ: $(e^{-\theta})(e^{-\theta}) = e^{-2\theta}$. Dividing by the integral of $e^{-2\theta}$ from 0 to ∞ gives the posterior distribution: $e^{-2\theta}/(1/2) = 2e^{-2\theta}$.

Solution 5.3.4: For the Gamma-Poisson, the posterior Gamma has shape parameter $\alpha' =$ prior $\alpha +$ number of claims observed $= 50 + 65 + 112 = 227$. For the Gamma Distribution, the mean is α/λ, while the variance is α/λ^2. Thus, the coefficient of variation is: (variance$^{.5}$)/mean $= \{\alpha/\lambda^2\}^{.5}/\{\alpha/\lambda\} = 1/\alpha^{.5}$. The CV of the posterior Gamma $= 1/\alpha'^{.5} = 1/227^{.5} = $ **.066**.

Solution 5.3.5: The Prior Gamma has parameters $\alpha = 3$ and $\lambda = 4$. The Posterior Gamma has parameters $(3 + 1)$, $(4 + 2)$ $= 4,6$: $f(\theta) = (6^4/(3!))e^{-6\theta}\theta^3 = 216e^{-6\theta}\theta^3$. Thus, the posterior chance that the Poisson parameter, θ, is between 1 and 2 is the integral from 1 to 2 of $f(\theta)$: $\int_1^2 216e^{-6\theta}\theta^3 d\theta$.

Solution 5.3.6: Prior Gamma has (inverse) scale parameter $\lambda = 1000$ and shape parameter $\alpha = 150$. After the first year of observations: the new (inverse) scale parameter $\lambda' = \lambda +$ number of exposures $= 1000 + 1500 = 2500$, and the new shape parameter $\alpha' = \alpha +$ number of claims $= 150 + 300 = 450$. Similarly, after the second year of observations: $\lambda'' = \lambda' + 2,500 = 5,000$ and $\alpha'' = \alpha' + 525 = 975$. The Bayesian estimate $=$ the mean of the posterior Gamma $= \alpha''/\lambda'' = 975/5000 = $ **.195**.

Comment: One can go directly from the prior Gamma to the Gamma posterior of both years of observations, by just adding in the exposures and claims observed over the whole period of time. One would obtain the same result. Note that one could proceed through a sequence of many years of observations in exactly the same manner as shown in this question.

Solution 5.4.1: Using [5.4.1] the credibility weighted estimate is $(\alpha + N)/(\lambda + Y) = (2 + 4)/(8 + 4) = 6/12 = $ **.50**. For an alternative solution, we start with the Bühlmann Credibility parameter $K = \lambda = 8$. Then the credibility for four years is $Z = 4/(4 + 8) = 1/3$. So the credibility estimate is $(1/3)(4/4) + (1 - 1/3)(2/8) = $ **.50**.

Solution 5.4.2: Mean of the posterior distribution of θ is $(\alpha + N)/(\lambda + Y) = (250 + 89(1) + 4(2) + 1(3))/(2000 + 1000) = $ **.117**.

Solution 5.4.3: This is a Gamma-Poisson whose Prior Gamma has (inverse) scale parameter $\lambda = 1000$ and shape parameter $\alpha = 150$. Thus, the Bühlmann Credibility Parameter is $K = \lambda = 1000$. One observes a total of $1500 + 2500 = 4000$ exposures. Therefore, $Z = 4000/(4000 + K) = .8$. The prior estimate is the mean of the prior Gamma, $\alpha/\lambda = .15$. The observed frequency is $825/4000 = .206$. Thus, the new estimate is: $(.8)(.206) + (.2)(.15) = $ **.195**.

Comment: Same result as question 5.3.6. For the Gamma-Poisson, the Bühlmann Credibility estimate is equal to that from Bayesian Analysis.

Solution 5.4.4: EPV = Expected Value of the Poisson Means = overall mean = 5.

Solution 5.4.5: The overall mean is 5. Second moment = $.1 \int_0^{10} x^2\, dx = 100/3$. Therefore, VHM = $33.333 - 5^2 = $ **8.333**.

Comment: For the uniform distribution on the interval (a, b), the Variance = $(b - a)^2/12$. In this case with $a = 0$ and $b = 10$, the variance is $100/12 = 8.333$.

Solution 5.4.6: $K = \text{EPV}/\text{VHM} = .6$. For one year, $Z = 1/(1 + .6) = 5/8$. New estimate is $(7)(5/8) + (5)(3/8) = \mathbf{6.25}$.

Solution 6.2.1: (1) $Z = 3/(3 + 5) = 3/8$. Proposed rate $= (3/8)(15) + (1 - 3/8)[(18)(.9)] = \mathbf{\$15.75}$. (2) $Z = 3/(3 + 10) = 3/13$. Proposed rate $= (3/13)(15) + (1 - 3/13)[(18)(.9)] = \mathbf{\$15.92}$. (3) $Z = \sqrt{3/60} = .224$. Proposed rate $= (.224)(15) + (1 - .224)[(18)(.9)] = \mathbf{\$15.93}$.

Comment: Note how the proposed rates vary much less than the credibility parameters and/or formulas.

Solution 6.4.1: (1) Reported experience $= \$4$ million$/3,000 = \$1,333$ per $\$100$ of payroll. Expected losses $= (\$20)(3,000) = \$60,000$. (Note that $3,000$ represents the number of units of $\$100$ in payroll for Angel.) $Z = 60/(60 + 80) = .429$. So, future expected losses $= (.429)(\$1,333) + (1 - .429)(\$20) = \mathbf{\$583}$ **per $100 of payroll**.

(2) Reported *limited* experience $= \$200,000/3,000 = \$66.67$ per $\$100$ of payroll. Expected *limited* experience $= (\$20)(3000)(.95) = \$57,000$. $Z = 57/(57 + 50) = .533$. Reported limited experience loaded for excess losses $= \$66.67/.95 = \$70.18$. So, future expected losses $= (.533)(\$70.18) + (1 - .533)(\$20) = \mathbf{\$46.75}$ **per $100 of payroll**.

Comment: Using unlimited losses, the prediction is that Angel's future losses will be 29 times average. Using limited losses, the prediction is that Angel's future losses will be 2.3 time average. In an application to small insureds, one might cap even the estimate based on limited losses.

Solution 6.6.1: Husband's car: mean $= (30 + 33 + 26 + 31 + 30)/5 = 30$ and sample variance $= [(30 - 30)^2 + (33 - 30)^2 + (26 - 30)^2 + (31 - 30)^2 + (30 - 30)^2]/(5 - 1) = 6.5$. *Sue's sports car:* mean $= (30 + 28 + 31 + 27 + 24)/5 = 28$ and sample variance $= [(30 - 28)^2 + (28 - 28)^2 + (31 - 28)^2 + (27 - 28)^2 + (24 - 28)^2]/(5 - 1) = 7.5$. The mean time for both cars is $(30 + 28)/2 = 29$. EPV $= (6.5 + 7.5)/2 = \mathbf{7.0}$. VHM $= [(30 - 29)^2 + (28 - 29)^2]/$

$(2-1) - \text{EPV}/5 = 2 - 7/5 = \textbf{.60}$. The Bühlmann K parameter is $\text{EPV}/\text{VHM} = 7.0/.60 = 35/3$. The credibility is $Z = 5/(5 + 35/3) = \textbf{.30}$. Sue's estimated commute time in her sports car is: $(.30)(28) + (1 - .30)(29) = \textbf{28.7 minutes}$.

Solution 6.6.2: **1.000, .889, .944, .867**, and **1.167**.

Solution 6.6.3: $(.5 - .75/1.000)^2 + (.5 - .5/.889)^2 + (.5 - .222/.944)^2 + (.5 - .40/.867)^2 + (.5 - .7/1.167)^2 = \textbf{.1480}$.

Solution 6.6.4: A K value around 800 produces a sum of squared differences that is close to the minimum.

Comment: We want the modified loss ratios to be close to the overall average loss ratio. Based on this limited volume of data, a Bühlmann credibility parameter of about 800 seems like it would have worked well in the past. Actual tests would rely on much more data. This is insufficient data to enable one to distinguish between $K = 800$ and $K = 1,000$. Here is a graph that shows the sum of the squared differences between the modified loss ratios and the overall average loss ratio. Note that there is a range of K values that produce about the same minimum sum of squares.

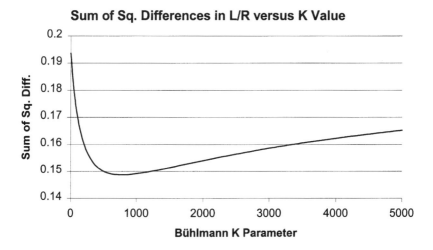

Sum of Sq. Differences in L/R versus K Value

CHAPTER 9

INVESTMENT ISSUES IN PROPERTY-LIABILITY INSURANCE

STEPHEN P. D'ARCY[1]

INVESTMENT INCOME

For the most part, the prior chapters in this text have focused on what is termed the underwriting side of insurance. This aspect of insurance involves estimating the value of losses to be paid, both for coverage that has already been provided and for policies to be written in the future, determining rate levels for various types of coverage, generating classification plans and establishing reinsurance contracts to share losses with other insurers. A more general view of an insurance company would regard the insurer as a financial intermediary, collecting and dispensing revenue. Premiums are collected from policyholders and the money is invested until needed for paying expenses, losses, or taxes. The invested assets generate investment income that is either reinvested or used to satisfy obligations. Under this view of an insurer, the underwriting and investing aspects of an insurer are inextricably interwoven. In this chapter the investment side of insurance will be presented and its relationship with underwriting issues analyzed.

The property-liability insurance industry has traditionally segregated operating divisions and returns into the two components, underwriting and investments. The concentration of most insurance textbooks, allocation of personnel, and management attention, at least until very recently, have been on the underwriting side of operations. In many cases, this emphasis on underwriting has led to neglect of investment operations. Until the 1970s investment income was generally not explicitly considered in

[1]The author would like to acknowledge the assistance of Michael Mielzynski, who updated the tables and provided valuable technical support, and Richard Derrig, who provided helpful comments on the revision of this chapter.

ratemaking. This neglect has produced an investment strategy for insurers that is often inefficient and uncoordinated with underwriting performance. In most insurance companies, investment departments tend to be isolated from the underwriting side of the business.

One reason for the relative neglect of the investment side of property-liability insurance operations was the comparative stability of underwriting profitability and net investment income, the value commonly used by insurers to describe investment performance. Figure 9.1 illustrates the underwriting profit or loss and net investment income for the period 1933 through 1998 for stock property-liability insurers. The net investment income is much less volatile than the underwriting profit or loss value.

The variability of underwriting profitability led to an emphasis on this aspect of insurance operations as insurance managers concluded that close attention to the underwriting aspect of operations could minimize the adverse results and increase the likelihood of favorable results. The rapid growth of investment income that began in the late 1960s, resulting from both higher rates of return and longer loss payout patterns (resulting from a growth in liability coverages and emergence of long-tailed asbestos and environmental exposures), prevented the industry from neglecting investment income any longer. Concurrently with the rapid growth in investment income, some regulatory authorities mandated the inclusion of investment income in the ratemaking methodology. By the mid-1980s investment income had become recognized, by necessity, as an equally important component of insurance operating results as underwriting income. In the 1990s, Dynamic Financial Analysis and Financial Risk Management became important topics for property-liability insurers. These developments drew additional attention to the investment side of the insurance business and highlighted the importance of developing a coordinated approach to underwriting and investment operations.

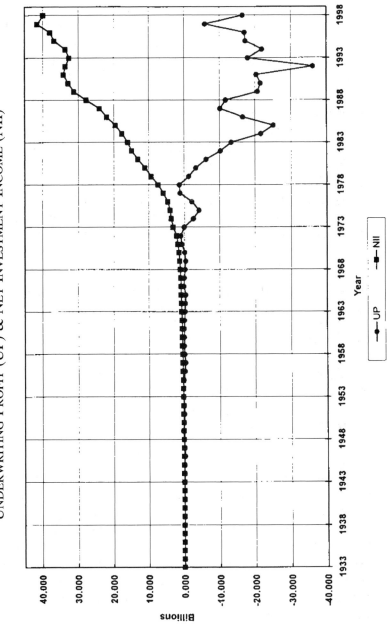

FIGURE 9.1

UNDERWRITING PROFIT (UP) & NET INVESTMENT INCOME (NII)

TABLE 9.2

Distribution of Admitted Assets—1998

Bonds	
U.S. Government	11.1%
State, Municipal, etc.	10.3
Special Revenue	17.8
Industrials	15.1
Other	2.9
Subtotal—Bonds	57.2
Stocks	
Industrials	13.3
Parent, Subs. & Affiliated Co.	4.6
Other	2.8
Preferred	1.3
Subtotal—Stocks	22.0
Real Estate	1.0
Cash & Short-Term Investments	5.1
Mortgages	0.2
Premium Balances	6.7
Other Assets	7.8
Total	100.0

Source: *Best's Aggregates & Averages (Prop./Cas.) 1999*, A. M. Best Co. Inc., page 178.

The purpose of this section is to describe the typical investments of property-liability insurers and define investment terminology. As of the end of 1998, the property-liability insurance industry (excluding state funds) had a total of $909 billion in admitted assets. Admitted assets are those recognized by statutory accounting conventions, which tend to be conservative in valuing assets, with the notable exception being valuing bonds at amortized rather than market value. Invested assets at the end of 1998 comprised approximately $796 billion. The allocation of admitted assets among investment alternatives and other categories for the aggregate of the property-liability insurance industry is displayed in Table 9.2.

Bonds

Bonds, including U.S. government, municipal (state and local government units), and corporate issues, represent the primary investment medium for the property-liability insurance industry. Bond investments have several characteristic attributes. Bonds typically consist of principal (the amount paid to the bondholder at the maturity date) and coupons (the periodic interest payments to the bondholder). However, bonds that have no maturity date (perpetuities) exist, as do bonds that pay no current interest (zero coupon bonds).

In most cases, the principal, maturity date, and coupon rate for bonds are fixed. However, some bonds are convertible, generally to the common stock of the issuing firm but occasionally to a commodity or a general price index. In addition, most corporate and municipal bonds have a call feature that allows the issuer to redeem them at a certain price prior to the maturity date. Frequently, the bonds cannot be called immediately, but only after a certain number of years. These bonds have what is termed a deferred call provision. The call feature would work to the disadvantage of the purchaser in the absence of an interest rate premium. In the case of a decline in interest rates after bonds are issued, the issuer will redeem the bonds after the deferred period, forcing investors to reinvest the proceeds at the then current, lower interest rate. If interest rates rise, the issuer will not redeem the bonds early. Bonds with call features generally command higher rates of interest than bonds of similar risk but without calls; the difference in interest rates is the price of the option to call in the bond. In addition, mortgage-backed bonds also have an indeterminate maturity date, since the mortgage holders have the right to prepay the mortgage, usually without penalty, at any time. Prepayment rates are a function of interest rates, as many homeowners refinance their mortgages when interest rates decline, in the same way that a corporate bond issuer calls bonds when interest rates decline. Finally, variable interest rate bonds are available in which the coupon rate changes in line with current interest rates.

If an investor purchases a bond at issuance, the price is usually close to the principal value. The coupon rate produces an income stream that approximates the current interest rate on investments with similar risk and maturity. Any difference between the coupon rate and market interest rates is reflected in a price differential between the cost and principal. After issuance, changes in interest rates affect the market value of the bond. If interest rates were to rise, an investment yielding the prior, lower rate of interest would not be worth as much as it was previously. Thus, the market value of the bond would decline. Conversely, the market value of outstanding bonds rises as interest rates fall. The market value of any fixed income investment can be determined from the present value formula:

$$PV = \Sigma CF_t / (1 + r)^t \tag{1}$$

where

PV = present value

CF = cash flow from investment (coupon or principal)

r = current rate of return

t = time until cash flow is received

This formula, although commonly used, implicitly assumes a level term structure of interest rates in which the same interest rate applies no matter how long the funds are invested. This is an overly simplistic assumption, but the formula can be revised to reflect a more realistic interest rate pattern.

Insurance accounting uses an amortized value for fixed income investments rather than market value accounting, for bonds that are not held for trading. The amortized value is determined by equation (1) with the rate of return applicable at the time the asset was purchased instead of the current interest rate. Theoretically, equation (1) with the current rate of return as the interest rate would yield the current market value. The amortized value gradually adjusts the value of the bond from the purchase price to the principal over the maturity of the bond. The justification used for this treatment is that it prevents the value of insurers' assets, and therefore surplus, from fluctuating with changes in interest rates. The major drawback of the use of amortized values is that they do not reflect the current price in the market. If an insurer sold bonds, the market value would determine the proceeds. Although insurers frequently hold bonds until maturity, when a catastrophe, insolvency or other need for funds arises and bonds have to be sold, the market value reflects the proceeds that will be received. This distortion also frequently prevents even very solvent insurers from redeeming bonds early for tax considerations or other reallocation needs.

The interest received on corporate and U.S. government bonds is fully taxable under federal income tax regulations. Prior to the Tax Reform Act of 1986 (TRA), interest received on municipal bonds was exempt from federal income taxation. The revised tax law has a "proration" feature that subjects 15% of interest on municipal bonds purchased after August 7, 1986, to regular income taxation. This "proration" feature also applies to other tax-exempt income as well. The Alternative Minimum Tax (discussed later) may increase the taxable portion of municipal bond interest, depending on the interaction of underwriting gains or losses, taxable investment income, tax preference items, and municipal bond interest. Traditionally, property-liability insurers invested heavily in tax-exempt securities because these issues generated a higher after-tax income for insurers. However, during the mid-1980s, insurers' investment portfolios shifted more heavily to taxable issues as statutory underwriting losses served as a tax shield for otherwise taxable investment income. The provisions of TRA added further complexity to the investment allocation strategy for property-liability insurers.

In addition to interest income on bonds, investors may also incur gains or losses on the value of the bond itself. Realized gains or losses on fixed-income investments, which are the difference between the selling price and the purchase price, are fully taxable for all types of bonds in the year the bond is sold or redeemed. This provision provides for tax deferral on changes in the market values of bonds. The market value of bonds moves inversely to interest rate changes. Thus, depending on recent directions of interest rates, insurers may have a substantial amount of unrealized gains or losses that can be sold to maximize after-tax returns. These sales need to be coordinated with expected underwriting results to achieve this objective.

Investors in fixed-income securities are accepting investment risk and, as such, require a return commensurate with the level of risk. Investments in low-risk debtors, such as the U.S. government, generate lower yields than those in more risky debtors. Corporate bonds yield more than U.S. government bonds, and corporations with a low credit rating pay higher interest rates than more solvent firms. Similarly, the length of time until the debt will be redeemed also reflects different levels of risk. Thus, bonds of the same issuer with different maturities will provide different yields. The plot of yields versus time to maturity is known as the yield curve.

Normally, the yield curve is upward sloping, meaning that longer-term securities have higher yields than shorter-term ones. However, occasionally the yield curve is inverted, with shorter-term debt yielding more than longer-term securities. This inverted yield curve usually results from an upward spurt in the rate of inflation that investors expect to subside in the long run, from short-term capital shortages due to an expanding economy, or from the influence of the money supply.

In order to take advantage of the usual higher yields on longer-term issues, the property-liability insurance industry is normally heavily invested in intermediate and long-term debt. The maturity

TABLE 9.3

MATURITY DISTRIBUTION OF BOND INVESTMENTS—1988–1998

Maturity	Allocation		
	1988	1993	1998
1 Year or Less	11.68%	10.43%	12.59%
1 to 5 Years	22.93	26.94	26.92
5 to 10 Years	23.10	27.81	29.61
10 to 20 Years	27.31	23.07	20.73
Over 20 Years	14.98	11.76	10.15

Source: *Best's Aggregates & Averages (Prop./Cas.)* **1989, 1994, 1999**, A. M. Best Co. Inc.

distribution of bond investments for the industry is shown in Table 9.3. The advantage of a long-term investment portfolio is that it locks in current interest rates, making investment income less volatile and usually higher than short-term securities yield. The major disadvantages are that it locks insurers into historic rates of return when interest rates rise, and that the market values of long-term bonds are more volatile than shorter-term securities. In recognition of this greater risk, insurers have been reducing the average maturity of their bond investments over the last decade.

The long-term fixed-income investment strategy highlights one problem with the lack of coordination between underwriting and investments. An unexpected increase in inflation adversely affects underwriting performance by increasing loss costs above the levels anticipated when rates were set. The market values of long-term bonds are reduced by an unexpected increase in inflation, which tends to push interest rates up. Thus, both underwriting and investments are adversely affected by increases in inflation. Conversely, both areas are favorably affected by declines in inflation. An investment strategy that hedged the impact of inflation on underwriting could be implemented, which would reduce the total risk of the insurer. Consideration of such a coordinated strategy by increasing actuaries' awareness of investment operations is one objective of this chapter.

Equities

The second largest component of insurance company investments is in common and preferred stocks, commonly termed equities. Shares of stock represent ownership interests in the firms, as opposed to the debtor-creditor relationship generated by bonds. Common stock is the primary ownership interest in the firm; preferred stock is a hybrid between a direct ownership interest and a fixed-income investment. Preferred stock pays a predetermined dividend rate. The dividend can be omitted or reduced, but, generally, dividends to common stockholders cannot be paid until the preferred stockholders have been paid in full for any back dividends. Some preferred stock is convertible to common stock at a predetermined ratio. Without the convertibility feature, the prices of preferred stock fluctuate in line with bond prices rather than with stock prices. Preferred stock is an outgrowth of tax regulations that exempt a portion of dividends paid to stockholders from corporate income taxation. Prior to TRA this tax-exempt portion was 85%; TRA reduced this value to 80% and subsequent legislation reduced it to 70%. The exemption is reduced further by the proration tax on otherwise tax-exempt income. The current (2000) effective tax rate on stock dividends is 14.5% instead of the marginal 35 percent corporate rate.

Dividends on common stocks are subject to more volatility than those of preferred stocks. These dividends can be raised or lowered, or omitted without any obligation to restore prior levels or pay omitted values. The total return on common stocks consists of the dividends, if any, and price changes. In general, the common-stock investor expects price appreciation to supplement the dividend income and thus produce a total rate of return in excess of bond yields, as common stocks are more risky investments than fixed-income securities. The actual rate of return on common-stock investments has been higher (on average) and more volatile than on fixed-income securities. The average annual rates of return and standard deviations for common stocks

TABLE 9.4

TOTAL ANNUAL RATES OF RETURN: 1926–1998

	Geometric Mean	Arithmetic Mean	Standard Deviation
Large Company Stocks	11.2	13.2	20.3
Small Company Stocks	12.4	17.4	33.9
Long Term Corporate Bonds	5.8	6.1	8.6
Long Term Government Bonds	5.3	5.7	9.2
U.S. Treasury Bills	3.8	3.8	3.2

Source: Stocks, Bonds, Bills, And Inflation 1999 Yearbook, Ibbotson Associates, Chicago, Illinois, 1999, page 33.

and bonds by type are displayed in Table 9.4 for the period 1926 through 1998.

Although bonds are stated at amortized value for statutory accounting purposes, stocks are stated at market value. Thus, changes in stock prices flow directly into statutory surplus. However, unrealized gains or losses have not been subjected to taxation. Thus, if an insurer were to sell appreciated stock and incur taxes, the actual surplus would be less than the statutory value just prior to the realization of the gains. Generally Accepted Accounting Principles (GAAP) does recognize this future tax liability.

Real Estate

Although insurance companies are allowed considerable leeway in real-estate investments, several statutory provisions limit the usefulness of this form of investment. Statutory requirements that vary by state establish upper limits on the amount of real-estate holdings that are allowed as admitted assets. Any excess real-estate investments are nonadmitted, and thus are not included in surplus. Also, real-estate investments are valued at the lower of net book value (cost less depreciation) or market value.

Real estate has traditionally been viewed as an inflation hedge for investors. As insurers are adversely impacted by inflation on underwriting operations, real-estate investments may serve to reduce overall corporate risk. However, the severe valuation and investment restrictions discourage such investments. Under current regulations, the potential benefits from real-estate investments must be weighed against the statutory accounting drawbacks. Regulations that tend to reduce the desirability of holding a fully diversified portfolio reduce investment flexibility and may prevent the use of optimal portfolio choices. More enlightened regulation may be enacted in the future that allows full utilization of all investment possibilities for insurers to manage risk optimally.

Other Investments

A small portion of property-liability insurers' assets is invested in mortgage loans, collateral loans, cash, and miscellaneous assets, including oil and gas production payments, transportation equipment, timber deeds, mineral rights, and motor vehicle trust certificates. Insurers are now allowed to invest in options and futures under regulations in some states. An option represents the right, but not the obligation, to buy or sell a financial asset at a predetermined exercise price within a given time period. Financial futures are obligated transactions that will be consummated at a later date. Although the prices of options and futures are extremely volatile by themselves, investment strategies utilizing options and futures can reduce overall investment risk. Insurers are now beginning to adopt some of these approaches, although in a very limited way [Cummins, Phillips and Smith (1997)].

Investment Income

The total investment income of the insurance industry is segregated into several categories and reported separately in financial reports. Net investment income is reported in Part 1 of the Annual Statement. This value consists of all interest, dividend, and real estate income earned during the year (adjusting for unpaid accruals), less all investment expenses incurred and less any depreciation on real-estate.

Net realized capital gains and losses consist of any difference between the net sale price and the net purchase price of bonds, stocks, or any other investment assets and are determined in Part 1A of the Annual Statement. These gains or losses can be realized as a result of a sale of an asset or upon the maturity of a bond. Net investment gain or loss is the sum of the net investment income and the net realized capital gains or losses. This total is displayed in the Annual Statement on line 9A of the Statement of Income.

Net unrealized capital gains and losses are also determined in Part 1A. These consist of adjustments in book value resulting from market value changes (for equities) or amortized value changes (for bonds) and any gain or loss from changes in the difference between book value and admitted value. Thus, this value is a combination of actual price changes on equities, amortization on bonds, and statutory accounting conventions. The entire net unrealized gain or loss flows directly into the surplus determination as listed on line 19 of the Statement of Income in the Annual Statement. The future tax consequences of the eventual realization of these gains or losses is not taken into account.

When investment income is considered in insurance ratemaking, either formally in the regulatory process or informally in company deliberations, the determination of the rate of return on investments must be established. Generally, one of two measures of investment income is used: the portfolio rate or the new-money rate. The portfolio rate of return is determined by dividing the net investment income earned by the statutory value of investable assets. The value of investable assets is usually determined by averaging the beginning and ending values. This measure ignores capital gains, either realized or unrealized. As statutory, rather than market, values are used for investable assets, this becomes a weighted average of past fixed-income investments and dividends on equities. If market values were used to determine the portfolio rate of return, the value of the investable assets would change in line with changes in interest rates, so the portfolio rate of return would approximate the new-money rate. The portfolio rate should be the net return to reflect the cost of investing.

New-money rates of return reflect the current rates of return available in the market. Frequently, a composite rate is applied that reflects a weighted average rate of different maturities and risk levels in line with the mix commonly followed by the insurer. This rate reflects current market conditions only, ignoring historic returns that the insurer may have locked in by past investments. The new-money rate reflects current market conditions and indicates the rate of return the insurer is likely to obtain on any funds generated for investment purposes by writing policies.

INVESTMENT AND TAX STRATEGIES

In a typical property-liability insurance company, the underwriting and investment operations are frequently run separately. Each area attempts to maximize returns independently of the other. The underwriting area provides the cash flow for investment and generates the need for cash to pay expenses and claims. The investment area produces cash to reinvest from the sale and maturity of assets and generates investment income from the funds invested. Although the two areas are thus inextricably linked operationally, few insurers actively coordinated the two activities prior to the mid-1980s, other than determining the taxable/tax-exempt investment allocation based on anticipated underwriting results. However, the Tax Reform Act of 1986 increased both the importance and the complexity of tax planning for property-liability insurers, which led to some coordination of the two areas. Also, the increasing number of applications of Dynamic Financial Analysis helped to demonstrate the potential advantages, both in increasing expected returns and lowering the risk of insolvency, by developing a coordinated approach. In this section, several strategies that link underwriting and investment operations will be discussed.

Asset-Liability Matching

The investment strategy behind asset-liability matching is to invest funds for exactly as long as they will be held. If a certain amount of funds will be needed in six years to pay claims, then investments would be made that would generate that amount in six years. If longer-term bonds were held, then the insurer might have to sell the bonds when the funds are needed, creating the possibility of a gain or loss on the sale depending on interest-rate fluctuations. A shorter-term investment would require that funds be reinvested upon the earlier maturity of the asset at the then available interest rates, exposing the insurer to interest-rate risk during the interim. By locking in the current rate of return for the applicable holding period, the insurer eliminates interest-rate risk.

Financial institutions such as banks and life insurers utilize asset-liability matching more heavily than property-liability insurers. By matching assets and liabilities, for example, banks avoid the problem of investing long term (fixed-rate mortgages), while borrowing short term (passbook savings accounts and short-term certificates of deposit). If assets and liabilities were not matched, banks would be exposed to interest-rate risk: a rise in interest rates would increase the cost of funds but would not increase the investment income.

If a property-liability insurer were to adopt asset-liability matching, the payout pattern on existing liabilities would be matched by an investment portfolio that produced the cash flow as needed. Changes in interest rates would not affect the availability of cash, as the desired flow would be locked in.

Three arguments are raised against the need for property-liability insurers to adopt asset-liability matching. First, in most situations the cash inflow in a given period from new and renewal policies is adequate to pay all losses and expenses. Even if premium receipts were not enough to pay all losses and expenses, they are predictable enough to avoid the need to generate cash needs from investments. A small margin of liquid assets could prevent an insurer from incurring losses on premature sale of assets. However, paying claims on prior policies with the cash flow on new policies does not reduce the mismatch that is occurring in the pricing of policies; it merely obscures it by spreading it into the future. If interest rates were to rise significantly, then an insurer following this practice would have to forego investing premium income on new policies at the high interest rates in order to meet the cash flow requirements of policies previously issued. This insurer would be at a competitive disadvantage to another insurer that did not face this drain on current cash flow.

The second argument against asset-liability matching revolves around the predictability of payout patterns for property-liability insurers. For banks, the values of liabilities are fixed and the maturity dates of savings accounts are known. For insurers, the loss costs and payout dates are not certain, but must be estimated. Future inflation rates could affect the value of losses. An investment strategy that generates a predetermined amount of cash at a set time may not match the need for cash as the loss payouts develop. A rise in the rate of inflation would most likely increase the cost of losses while, at the same time, increasing interest rates. Thus, a more appropriate hedging strategy for a property-liability insurer might be to invest in maturities shorter than the indicated need for cash in order to reinvest at interest rates that more closely approximate the underlying rate of inflation that affects loss costs.

A final objection raised to asset-liability matching involves its cost. Most liabilities for property-liability insurers have fairly short durations. Estimates of the duration (see below) of loss reserves for property lines run in the range of one half year for

FIGURE 9.5

PRESENT VALUE OF A $1000 10 YEAR 8% ANNUAL COUPON
BOND

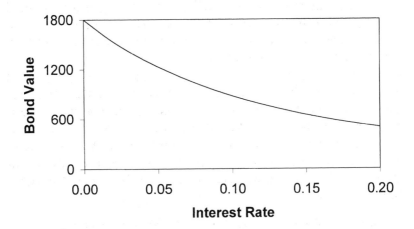

property lines, between one and one and a half years for automobile, and two to five years for general liability and medical
malpractice. An investment strategy that matched the average
durations of liabilities would, under normal yield curve situations, give up two to three percentage points in interest rates
from long-term bonds. Thus, an insurer that invests assets for a
longer period than its liabilities will be earning a higher return,
but is accepting interest rate risk.

Duration

The value of a fixed income investment is sensitive to interest
rate changes. As interest rates rise, the value of a fixed income
bond falls. Conversely, the value rises as interest rates decrease.
Typically, for a noncallable bond, the relationship between the
value of the bond and interest rates is a curve that is convex
to the origin, as illustrated in Figure 9.5. The sensitivity of the
value of a fixed income security to interest rate changes depends

on such factors as the maturity of the bond, the coupon rate and the current interest rate.

The maturity of a bond, although relatively easy to determine, is inappropriate for analyses of interest-rate risk because it considers only the time when the principal will be repaid. However, during the time until maturity, the asset will be generating interest income, which is either used by the asset holder or reinvested at the then current interest rates. The effective yields based on market valuation on two bonds with the same maturity dates but different coupon rates would be the same under stable interest rates but would differ if interest rates change.

Several methods have been developed to estimate the sensitivity of a fixed income security to interest rate changes. Macaulay duration is the weighted average of the length of time until payments will be received by the holder. This duration value can be calculated as shown in equation (2) under the assumption of a flat term structure of interest (level yield curve):

$$D = \frac{\sum_{t=1}^{n} C_t(t)/(1+r)^t}{\sum_{t=1}^{n} C_t/(1+r)^t} \qquad (2)$$

where

C_t = interest or principal payment at time t

t = length of time to payment

n = length of time until maturity

r = yield to maturity

The denominator of the equation is the present value of the fixed income investment. The numerator is the present value of the payments weighted by the length of time until they are paid. The higher the duration, the longer into the future the payments will, on average, be received.

To illustrate the concept of Macaulay duration, two bonds of $1000 face value, each with a remaining maturity of five years and annual coupon payments, will be used. The first bond has a coupon rate of 6% and the second 12%. Each has a yield to maturity of 9%, reflecting current interest rates on five-year bonds. The Macaulay duration of the first bond is calculated by:

$$D_1 = \frac{\dfrac{(60)(1)}{1.09} + \dfrac{(60)(2)}{(1.09)^2} + \dfrac{(60)(3)}{(1.09)^3} + \dfrac{(60)(4)}{(1.09)^4} + \dfrac{(1060)(5)}{(1.09)^5}}{\dfrac{60}{1.09} + \dfrac{60}{(1.09)^2} + \dfrac{60}{(1.09)^3} + \dfrac{60}{(1.09)^4} + \dfrac{1060}{(1.09)^5}}$$

$$D_1 = 3909.70/883.32 = 4.426$$

The duration of the second bond is calculated similarly, except the coupon is 12%, or 120 per year, rather than 60 per year.

$$D_2 = \frac{\dfrac{(120)(1)}{1.09} + \dfrac{(120)(2)}{(1.09)^2} + \dfrac{(120)(3)}{(1.09)^3} + \dfrac{(120)(4)}{(1.09)^4} + \dfrac{(1120)(5)}{(1.09)^5}}{\dfrac{120}{1.09} + \dfrac{120}{(1.09)^2} + \dfrac{120}{(1.09)^3} + \dfrac{120}{(1.09)^4} + \dfrac{1120}{(1.09)^5}}$$

$$D_2 = 4569.74/1116.68 = 4.092$$

The Macaulay duration of the second bond is less than the duration of the first bond because the interim payments are larger. The weighted average of the date of the receipt of cash from the second bond is sooner than that of the first bond. The Macaulay duration is used to approximate the change in value of a fixed income security as shown in equation (3):

$$\Delta P = -(1/(1+r))(D)(\Delta r) \qquad (3)$$

where

P = the price (market value) of the fixed income security

r = current interest rate

D = Macaulay duration

Δ = change operator (shows the change in price corresponding to a change in interest rate)

An alternative but equivalent approach to determining the price sensitivity of a fixed income security is termed modified duration. Modified duration is the negative of the first derivative of the price of the asset with respect to the interest rate, divided by the price. Modified duration is calculated as follows:

$$\text{Modified Duration} = -\frac{\partial P}{\partial r} \times \frac{1}{P} = \sum_{t=1}^{n} \frac{t \times C_t}{(1+r)^{t+1}} \times \frac{1}{P}$$

$$= \frac{1}{(1+r)} \times \text{Macaulay Duration}$$

The use of modified duration to approximate the effect of an interest rate change, is shown in equation (4):

$$\Delta P = -(\text{Modified Duration})(\Delta r) \tag{4}$$

The first derivative provides a reasonable approximation of the change in the value of a fixed income security only for very small changes in interest rates. For a more accurate approximation, the second derivative can be included. This value is termed convexity and is calculated as follows:

$$\text{Convexity} = \frac{\partial^2 P}{\partial r^2} \times \frac{1}{P} = \frac{1}{P} \times \frac{1}{(1+r)^2} \times \sum_{t=1}^{n} \frac{t \times (t+1) \times C_t}{(1+r)^t}$$

The effect of an interest rate change on the value of a fixed income security is approximated using convexity as shown in equation (5):

$$\Delta P = -(\text{Modified Duration})(\Delta r) + (1/2)(\text{Convexity})(\Delta r)^2$$

$$(5)$$

Macaulay and modified duration and convexity are commonly calculated on fixed-income securities in which the maturity, coupon payments and principal are known and do not change as interest rates change. If the cash flows can change based on interest rate changes, for example for callable bonds or mortgage-backed securities, then effective duration and effective convexity measures must be used instead of duration and convexity. Effective duration is calculated by determining the price of the security if interest rates increase slightly and decrease slightly. The formula for effective duration is:

$$\text{Effective Duration} = (P_- - P_+)/(2P_0)(\Delta r) \qquad (6)$$

where

P_0 = current value of the security

P_- = value of the security if interest rates decline by Δi

P_+ = value of the security if interest rates increase by Δi

Δr = a small change in interest rate

The effective convexity is calculated as shown in equation (7):

$$\text{Effective Convexity} = (P_+ + P_- - 2P_0)/(P_0)(\Delta r)^2 \qquad (7)$$

The values for effective duration and effective convexity can be substituted for modified duration and convexity in equations (4) and (5) to determine the approximate price changes for a security.

For property-liability insurers, the duration of liabilities, particularly loss reserves, can also be determined, although not with certainty. In this context the equivalent to the Macaulay duration of liabilities would simply be the weighted average of the length of time until the payments will be made (use equation (2) with the cash flows representing loss payments instead of bond interest or principal payments). The modified duration would be the Macaulay duration divided by 1 plus the interest rate. If the effect of interest rate changes on future loss payments can be estimated, then the effective duration and effective convexity can be measured as well. Since loss payments are likely to increase with inflation, and inflation rates and interest rates are positively related, then the effective duration of loss reserves will be less than the modified duration, which means that liabilities will be less sensitive to interest rate changes than the modified duration would indicate. See D'Arcy and Gorvett (2000) for an expanded analysis of this relationship.

Immunization

Immunization of a portfolio is any strategy that eliminates price risk and coupon reinvestment risk on a fixed-income portfolio. Asset-liability matching is one method of immunization, but it requires an exact balancing of income from investments against cash needs. A less restrictive method of immunization is for the duration of the investment portfolio to equal the duration of the cash flow needs, or the duration of the assets to equal the duration of the liabilities.

On an immunized portfolio, interest-rate changes affect the two investment risks in offsetting ways. A rise in interest rates lowers the market price of outstanding bonds, but allows reinvestment of income to be made at a higher rate, preventing a change in eventual cash flow. A drop in interest rates raises the price of outstanding bonds but reduces the reinvestment rate. Thus, the predicted amount of cash can be available when needed.

The immunization strategy can be thwarted if the yield curve changes shape. If short-term interest rates fall proportionately more than long-term rates, the reinvestment rate will drop more than the price of outstanding issues will increase. Theoretically, the investment portfolio can be adjusted continually to minimize such distortions, but this increases the cost of this strategy. Also, the liabilities of property liability insurers can differ from the original forecast, making even an immunized portfolio inadequate to meet the new cash flow needs.

Taxation

The Tax Reform Act of 1986 (TRA) dramatically changed the income tax regulations for the property-liability insurance industry. The major provisions of TRA will be discussed here, but the reader is urged to refer to more complete and timely sources for a full explanation of this watershed tax legislation.

The stated goal of TRA was to raise significant tax revenue from the property-liability insurance industry starting in 1987. One reason for the concentration on tax revenue is the federal budget deficit, then running in the $150–200 billion level annually. The property-liability insurance industry was the target of such a significant change in tax regulations as a result of the failure of the prior tax code to produce any significant revenue from the industry (Derrig, 1994). In fact, during the five-year period 1982–1986, the property liability insurance industry in aggregate recouped $6.2 billion in taxes previously paid. The sudden shift from recouping an average of $1.2 billion in taxes per year to paying $3–5 billion per year caused distortions and market tightening, as well as led to price increases industry-wide.

In addition to the aggregate negative tax position of the property liability insurance industry, several other situations called attention to the industry during discussion about the 1986 tax legislation. Retroactive insurance was becoming a feasible product, fueled in part by tax subsidies and the differential tax treatment of property-liability insurers. After the MGM Grand Hotel in Las Vegas suffered a major fire loss in 1980, the owners purchased additional liability coverage for less than the expected value of the losses that were incurred. The insurers expected that they could profit from this below cost pricing by immediately establishing loss reserves at the expected loss level and reporting an underwriting loss for tax purposes. This loss generated tax savings which, in addition to the net premium, could be invested until the losses were paid. Thus, the tax code was subsidizing insurers in pricing coverage to the extent that known losses could be covered by insurance more inexpensively than if the noninsurance corporation paid the loss itself. The tax regulations for noninsurance firms allow a tax deduction for losses only when the losses are paid, not when they are incurred. In addition to generating a market for retroactive insurance, this differential contributed to the growth in captive insurance companies as they attempted, unsuccessfully it turned out, to qualify for classification as insurers. This would have allowed the parent firm to utilize the more favorable rules of deducting losses when incurred rather than when paid.

Another aspect of the property-liability insurance industry that caught the tax reformers' attention was the growing practice of loss reserve transfers. Insurers were using this strategy to optimize the use of taxable income and tax loss carrybacks. Under this approach, an insurer with an excess of tax losses would sell loss reserves to another insurer in a tax-paying position through the use of reinsurance. The first insurer would transfer loss reserves to the second insurer and, at the same time, pay the second insurer a premium that was less than the statutory value of the losses, but more than the present value of those losses. The first insurer would immediately book an underwriting gain equal to the difference between the premium and the statutory loss reserve value. The second insurer would book an underwriting loss, which could be used to offset other taxable income.

The primary provision in insurance tax regulations that generated negative tax payments for the prior five years and promoted retroactive insurance, the growth of captives, and loss reserve transfers, was the ability of insurers to deduct the total future value of loss and loss adjustment expense payments on incurred losses as opposed to their economic worth, or present value. Discounting loss reserves at an appropriate rate would alleviate this problem. Although discounting of loss reserves was included in TRA, the mandated discount rate is not necessarily the appropriate rate, and several other, far more onerous, provisions were included in TRA.

For property-liability insurers, the primary provisions of TRA are to:

1. Tax a portion of previously tax-exempt interest and dividends

2. Include a portion of the unearned premium reserve as taxable income

3. Discount loss reserves for tax purposes

4. Apply a strict Alternative Minimum Tax (AMT) to insurers as well as corporations in general

Tax Exempt Interest and Dividends

Municipal bonds have traditionally been exempt from federal income taxation as a subsidy to state and local government units in raising revenue. The property-liability insurance industry has been a heavy investor in such issues. A common investment strategy has been to invest in taxable bond issues to the extent of offsetting any underwriting losses, with the remainder of the investment portfolio invested in municipal bonds. This strategy led to the low nominal tax rates on property-liability insurers during the 1980s.

Common and preferred-stock dividends from domestic corporations have also received favorable tax treatment. In order to reduce double taxation of dividends for corporate investors, an income-tax deduction of 85% of the dividends received was allowed prior to TRA. Under TRA, this deduction was reduced to 80% of dividends received and subsequent legislation further reduced it to 70%. Thus, all municipal bond income and 70% of dividend income is exempt from taxation for corporate investors. However, the proration feature of TRA reduces the deduction of tax-exempt income by 15% of this otherwise tax-free income on any investment acquired after August 7, 1986, in essence taxing 15% of this income.

Unearned Premium Reserve

The unearned premium reserve is the pro rata portion of premiums that reflect unexpired coverage. As expenses tend to be paid at the beginning of the exposure period and losses generated proportionally over the coverage period, the unearned premium reserve includes a well-recognized redundancy to the extent that the reserve still includes a provision for previously paid expenses. Unless the insurer were to cancel a policy mid-term and refund the full portion of the premium that reflects the unexpired coverage period to the policyholder, the amount already paid for expenses will flow back to the insurer as the policy term expires. This redundancy is commonly termed the "equity in the unearned premium reserve." This "equity" varies depending on the individual insurer's expense ratio and expected loss ratio. Accordingly, it would be highest for lines of business and insurers with high expense ratios and lowest for lines and insurers with low expense ratios. This distinction is not recognized under the revised tax regulations. Under TRA, 20% of the change in the unearned premium reserve is included in taxable income. In addition, 20% of the unearned premium reserve as of December 31, 1986, was included in taxable income ratably over the six-year period beginning in 1987 and ending in 1992.

Loss Reserves

Prior to TRA, statutory loss and loss adjustment expense reserves were used to calculate taxable income. These statutory values are intended to be the total undiscounted value of all loss and loss adjustment expense payments to be made in the future for losses that have occurred prior to the evaluation date. By not adjusting for the present value of these payments, a payout to be made in ten years is valued equally with an imminent payout.

TRA requires discounting of loss and loss adjustment expense reserves for determining taxable income. The interest rate to be used for discounting is the five-year moving average of the Applicable Federal Rate (AFR) on three- to nine-year securities. The sixty-month moving average from January 1995 through December 1999 was 6.09%, which would be used for discounting accident year 2000 loss reserves.

The payment pattern for loss and loss adjustment expense reserves can be either the pattern promulgated by the Treasury Department, based on five years of industry experience as reported by A. M. Best, or a company's individual experience. Whichever choice an insurer made for determining 1987 taxable income was binding for five years. The payment pattern determined by the Treasury Department was updated twice since that initial five-year period. An insurer electing to use its own payout pattern must update the values each year, but only with respect to the new accident year. Payout patterns on prior years cannot be changed, even if the actual loss payment differs from the original projection.

Alternative Minimum Tax (AMT)

The more stringent provisions of the corporate Alternative Minimum Tax regulations will result in most property-liability insurers' calculating two indicated tax amounts and paying the higher. The regular tax is calculated on the regular taxable income; the AMT is calculated from the alternative minimum taxable income (AMTI). The AMTI is determined by adding tax-preference items to the regular taxable income. These preference items include:

1. book income versus regular taxable income

2. certain tax-exempt income

3. accelerated depreciation

Book income will normally be the statutory annual statement income after dividends to policyholders but before income taxes. However, if GAAP statements are filed with the Securities and Exchange Commission or audited financial statements used for other purposes, these income values take precedence over annual statement data. The tax-preference item for the years 1987 through 1989 was 50% of the difference between the book income and the AMTI excluding this item. After 1989 the preference item is 75% of the difference between adjusted current earnings and AMTI before this adjustment.

TRA also greatly restricted state and local governments from using their tax-exempt status to issue bonds for the benefit of private parties. A large volume of the special revenue bonds held by insurers now are fully taxable. Any tax-exempt interest on these private activity bonds (e.g., industrial development bonds) issued after August 7, 1986, must be included as a tax-preference item. Also, any depreciation taken in excess of the 150% declining balance method for tangible personal property or over 40-year straight-line depreciation for real property will be included as a preference item.

Tax and Investment Strategies

An entirely new operating strategy for property-liability insurers emerged as a result of TRA. Insurers now pay the larger of the regular tax or the AMT. Net after-tax income is generally maximized when the two taxes are equal. Thus, insurers may manage their investment portfolios by shifting assets between taxable and tax-exempt investments, depending on the relative yields and the company's tax calculations. Projected underwriting losses, based on discounted loss reserves and including part of the unearned premium reserve as income, will indicate the optimal investment mix to minimize taxes. As the final tax liabilities will not be known until after the year is over, this strategy involves forecasting and rebalancing during the year to achieve the optimal after-tax income. In addition, the consequences of misestimation on either side are not equal. The penalty associated with the AMT is more severe in that, starting in 1990, no credit for AMT carry-forward is allowed, so the insurer should aim to err on the side of the regular tax calculation. Considerations of the risk involved with different types of investments and the different treatment of regular tax and AMT carry-forwards complicate the determination of the optimal investment strategy.

The need for coordination between underwriting and investment operations increased as a result of TRA. Actuaries should be involved in developing this tax strategy because underwriting results must be forecast and loss reserves discounted. This new role for actuaries increases the need for actuaries to master investment and tax issues.

RATE OF RETURN MEASURES

In order to quantify the profitability of the property-liability insurance industry users of financial data have developed a number of measures that are relied upon to provide some insight into current and past operating results. Some of these measures are easy to calculate, and others are more complex. Some measures are widely used, whereas others are applied only in the more complex rate-regulatory hearings and in sophisticated company analyses. In this section we will describe several of these measures, discuss the meaning of the values, and analyze the strengths and weaknesses of the measures.

Combined Ratio

The combined ratio is determined in two different ways. It can be calculated as the sum of the loss ratio and the expense ratio, or as this sum plus the policyholders' dividends ratio. The loss ratio is determined by dividing the incurred losses, including all loss adjustment expenses, by the earned premium. The expense ratio is calculated by dividing expenses by the written premium. The policyholders' dividend ratio is determined by dividing dividends by earned premium. The combined ratio thus involves combining ratios with different denominators.

The combined ratio is calculated in the foregoing manner to make an approximate adjustment for the different rates at which losses and expenses tend to be incurred for property-liability insurers. Losses tend to be incurred evenly over the coverage period for most lines of business. If a policy is for an annual term, then, except for slight seasonal patterns, losses are likely to occur evenly over the year. One-twelfth of the losses are expected to occur in the first month the policy is in force, one-half by the middle of the exposure period, and so forth. Therefore, losses that have been incurred are divided by the earned premium to determine the portion of the premium incurred on losses to date.

Conversely, expenses for such items as commissions, premium taxes, policy coding costs, and overhead, tend to be incurred about the time the policy is written. Thus, the expenses are divided by the premium written to determine the portion of premiums that are used to cover expenses.

For an insurer that is writing a constant premium volume, eventually the written and earned premiums will be equal. In this case, the use of the different denominators in the combined ratio will not have any effect. However, most insurers do not write a constant level of premiums. During inflationary periods, even an insurer not writing any increase in exposures will be experiencing an increase in written premium. In general, the written premium exceeds the earned premium when premium income is rising. The combined ratio adjusts the expenditure pattern to reflect the different rates of payouts for losses and expenses for this normal difference, creating a better match between the numerators and the denominators and more accurately reflecting the true underlying experience which will emerge.

The loss ratio included in the combined ratio is generally a calendar-year value. As any changes in reserve adequacy over the year distort calendar-year-loss ratios, the combined ratio will also be affected. An alternative approach is to use accident-year loss ratios, but other drawbacks exist for this measure. Accurate accident-year values would only be available for years long past, when the usefulness for the information is lessened. The accuracy of the accident-year loss ratios for current years depends on the accuracy of the loss reserve estimates and the combined ratios based on accident-year loss ratios for a given year can change over time.

The combined ratio is easy to calculate and widely used within companies and in public discussion of insurance profitability. Figure 9.6 shows the combined ratio including dividends to policyholders for the period 1948 through 1998 for all stock property-liability insurers. This graph shows that the combined ratio fluctuates considerably and the levels during the mid-1980s were unusually high. Many industry publications concentrate on the combined ratio as a measure of financial health of the insurance industry. Levels below 100% indicate that an insurer, or the industry, is paying out less in losses, expenses, and dividends than it is taking in as premium, and therefore is profitable, even ignoring investment income. Levels in excess of 100% indicate that expenditures exceed premium income. Interpretation of the meaning of such values is difficult and often leads to erroneous statements. As the insurance industry receives both premium and investment income, the fact that losses and expenses exceed the premium income does not necessarily mean that the insurance industry is losing money or not achieving an adequate rate of return. Conversely, for coverages that are paid quickly the fact that the combined ratio is below 100% does not mean that it is achieving an adequate profit.

FIGURE 9.6

COMBINED RATIO

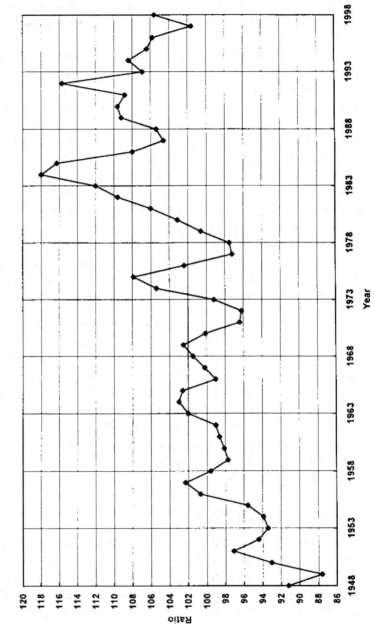

The advantage of the combined ratio as a measure of insurance performance is its simplicity However, this also leads to its major problem. The combined ratio does not include any provision for investment income. As insurers generally pay losses after the premium is received, they earn investment income prior to payment of claims. If the delay between receipt of premium and payment of losses were stable among lines and over time, and the interest rate on invested funds were constant, then the contribution of investment income to insurer profitability would be consistent and an easy adjustment to the combined ratio could be made. Unfortunately, loss payout patterns vary among lines of business and over time, and interest rates have been volatile, especially over the past two decades. Thus, a combined ratio of 110%, for example, could be acceptable if the loss payout pattern is slow, as in liability lines, and interest rates high. Conversely if the loss payout pattern is rapid, as in a property line, and/or interest rates are at the low end of the cycle over the period, then the same 110% combined ratio could indicate a pricing problem.

An example of a combined ratio calculation is shown in Table 9.7, which represents an illustrative insurance company income statement. The combined ratio of 110.1% is determined by adding incurred losses and loss adjustment expenses divided by the net earned premium ($(68 + 10)/95$) to the other underwriting expenses divided by net written premium ($28/100$). This is a calendar-year combined ratio figure. The accident-year combined ratio is 112.2%, based on accident year losses and loss adjustment expenses of $80 million, as shown in the Discounting section of Table 9.7.

Underwriting Profit Margin

The underwriting profit margin is calculated by subtracting the combined ratio from 100%. Conversely, the expected loss ratio is often determined by subtracting the sum of the target underwriting profit margin and the expense ratio from 100%. For the illustration on Table 9.7, the underwriting profit margin

TABLE 9.7

SAMPLE INCOME STATEMENT

COMPETITIVE INSURANCE COMPANY
(DOLLAR FIGURES ARE IN MILLIONS)

Underwriting Income	
Net Written Premium	$100
Net Earned Premium	95
Incurred Losses	68
Loss Adjustment Expense Incurred	10
Other Underwriting Expenses	28
Net Underwriting Gain or Loss	−11
Investment Income	
Net Investment Income Earned	14
Net Realized Capital Gains or Losses	2
Net Investment Gain or Loss	16
Net Income Determination	
Net Income Before Dividends to	
Policyholders and Income Taxes	5
Dividends to Policyholders	2.5
Federal and Foreign Income Taxes Incurred	−1.5
Net Income	4
Capital and Surplus Account	
Beginnning Surplus	57
Gains and Losses in Surplus	
Net Income	4
Net Unrealized Capital Gains or Losses	1
Ending Surplus	62
Average Statutory Surplus	59.5
Rate of Return Measures	
Combined Ratio	
Loss and Loss Adjustment Expense Ratio	82.1%
Expense Ratio	28
Combined Ratio	110.1
Underwriting Profit Margin	
Underwriting Profit Margin	−10.1

Operating Ratio

A) Net Investment Income Earned/Earned Premium	14.7
B) Net Investment Gain or Loss/Earned Premium	16.8
C) Net Investment Gain or Loss Including	17.9
Unrealized Capital Gains or Losses/Earned Premium	
Operating Ratio Based on A	95.4
Operating Ratio Based on B	93.3
Operating Ratio Based on C	92.2

Discounting

Accident Year Experience

Paid Loss and Loss Adjustment Expenses	$35
Undiscounted Loss and LAE Reserves	45*
Discounted Loss and LAE Reserves	36
Loss and LAE Ratio—Undiscounted	84.2%
Accident Year Combined Ratio	112.2
Loss and LAE Ratio—Discounted	74.7
Accident Year Combined Ratio—Discounted	102.7

Return on Equity Measures

Net Income/Average Statutory Surplus	6.7
Net Income plus Unrealized Capital Gains	
or Losses/Average Statutory Surplus	8.4

---

*Note that the calendar year incurred loss and loss adjustment expenses total $78 million but the accident year loss and LAE equal $80 million. This would result if favorable development were experienced on prior years' loss and LAE reserves.

is −10.1%, based on this calculation. The underwriting profit margin suffers from the same basic problem as the combined ratio since the underwriting profit margin is calculated from the same data; investment income is not included. Thus, determining the appropriate underwriting profit margin is difficult.

Historically, the property-liability insurance industry sought to achieve standard underwriting profit margins. The industry standard was 2.5% for workers compensation and 5% for all other lines. These standards were derived from the 1920 era of insurance regulation and had no mathematical or economic support. By achieving a 5% underwriting profit margin, an insurer was, in the long run, retaining 5% of sales, which was considered a reasonable proportion. This measure was not equated to a return-on-equity measure. As investment income was not included, it did not reflect total insurance profitability. Also, as different insurers operated at different premium-to-surplus ratios, total return on equity would vary among insurers with the same underwriting profit margins.

Fluctuations in the underwriting profit margin occur normally as a result of catastrophic losses and other unpredicted developments, as well as varying intensity of competition in the industry. The gradual increasing trend of the combined ratio shown in Figure 9.6 (and therefore the decreasing trend of the underwriting profit margin) is the result of competitive pressures as longer payout patterns and higher interest rates developed. Negative underwriting profit margins occurred in almost each year since 1973, which some industry spokespersons claimed indicated inadequate rates. Although the statement about inadequate rates may have been true, negative underwriting profit margins do not, by themselves, lead to this conclusion.

Operating Ratio

The failure of the combined ratio and the underwriting profit margin to include the effect of investment income has led to the emphasis on the operating ratio as a profitability measure. The operating ratio is calculated by subtracting the ratio of investment income divided by the earned premium from the combined ratio. Thus, investment income is "included" in the profitability measure.

A number of problems still exist in the use of the operating ratio as a measure of profitability. The first problem is the definition of investment income. Some users of financial data include only net investment income earned, which consists of interest and dividends received. Others use the net investment gain or loss value, which includes net realized capital gains and losses as well as investment income. A third possible definition of investment income includes net unrealized capital gains and losses in addition to the other components. Thus, three possible operating ratios can be calculated leading to considerable confusion.

Regardless of which definition of the investment income is used, potential problems result. The most commonly used definition of investment income is net investment income earned. This is not a realistic measure of investment income for any investment other than very short-term debt instruments. Longer-term bonds pay interest and also experience fluctuations in value as interest rates and credit conditions change. Thus, the actual rate of return differs from simply the interest received. For investments in equities, the dividend income is generally only a small portion of the total investment income expected. Capital gains are expected to occur to provide the required rate of return commensurate with the investment risk accepted. Similarly, investments in real estate are also expected to produce capital gains.

An insurer could intentionally generate zero dollars of net investment income earned by investing in zero coupon bonds and common stock in firms that do not pay dividends. Such an investment strategy would produce a high operating ratio that would not reflect the investment income potential of the insurer. Thus, some reflection of capital gains is necessary to produce a reasonable measure of investment income. Therefore, the second operating ratio measure includes net realized capital gains and losses with net investment income, the total of which is termed the net investment gain or loss. This investment income measure is consistent with taxable income, since only realized capital gains are subject to taxation.

The problem with using realized gains and losses to measure investment income is the timing factor involved in this determination. Realized gains and losses occur when an asset is sold, and reflect all the change in value that has occurred since the asset was purchased. If an insurer does not sell any capital assets, then, regardless of the change in values of investments, no capital gains or losses would be recorded. When an asset is sold, though, all of the change in value is reflected in that year, even though all or most of the change may have occurred in prior years. Thus, unless an insurer is experiencing a constant portfolio turnover and consistent appreciation in asset values, the net realized capital gains and losses value will fluctuate considerably and will not necessarily reflect current investment earnings.

The third measure of investment income includes the change in unrealized capital gains and losses in addition to the net investment gain or loss. By including unrealized gains and losses, all investment performance is reflected in this profitability measure. By adding or subtracting the change in unrealized gains and losses to the net realized gains and losses, only the investment gains experienced during the current year are reflected. Changes in asset values that occurred in prior years would not distort the results. This definition of investment income is consistent with the economic or market valuation approaches.

Several problems still exist with this measure of the operating ratio. One problem is the degree of fluctuation that will occur as a result of changes in equity values. A rapidly rising stock market will inflate the investment income measure and reduce the operating ratio. A falling stock market will reduce the investment income value. This increased volatility is a cost of fully reflecting investment income in the operating results of insurance companies.

Another problem is that insurance accounting conventions value bonds at amortized values rather than market values. Thus, unrealized capital gains and losses for bonds are not representative of market values but are based on the values when the assets were purchased and the time left until maturity. In this regard, the investment income value based on reported unrealized capital gains and losses is not a true market measure.

Another major problem with all of the operating ratio measures is the mismatch in the asset base that generated the investment income and the earned premium that is used as the denominator in the calculation. To a large extent, the investable assets currently generating the investment income were produced by premium writings in prior years. The loss reserve outstanding comes from both current and prior years' writings. However, all the investment income is being credited against the current year's experience. This distortion will most significantly affect rapidly growing or declining insurers. However, even insurers with a stable premium volume may experience a change in loss payout patterns so that the operating ratio is distorted.

Calculations of the three different operating ratios are demonstrated in Table 9.7. To determine the first operating ratio, the ratio of net investment income to earned premium (14/95 = 14.7%) is subtracted from the combined ratio of 110.1% to yield 95.4%. For the second operating ratio, the net realized gains and losses are added to the net investment income and the sum divided by earned premium ((2 + 14)/95 = 16.8%). This ratio is then subtracted from the combined ratio to yield an operating ratio of 93.3%. The final operating ratio includes the unrealized gains and losses of $1 million in addition to the net investment income and realized gains and losses ((14 + 2 + 1)/95 = 17.9%). Subtracting this value from the combined ratio yields an operating ratio of 92.2%.

The operating ratios for the insurance industry for the period 1984 through 1998, based on the net investment income earned, net investment gain or loss and the net investment gain or loss including unrealized capital gains or losses, are shown in Table 9.8. These values are calculated from the consolidated industry Annual Statement data published by A. M. Best Company.

Combined Ratio Based on Discounted Losses

The Tax Reform Act of 1986 instituted the discounting of property-liability loss reserves for tax purposes. The effect of discounting loss reserves is to reflect the time value of money in the reserving process, and hence net income. Undiscounted reserves value loss payments in future years equally with current

TABLE 9.8

INDUSTRY OPERATING RATIOS

	1984	1985	1986	1987	1988	1989	1990	1991	1992	1993	1994	1995	1996	1997	1998
Combined Ratio After Dividends	118.0	116.3	108.0	104.6	105.4	109.2	109.6	108.8	115.7	106.9	108.4	106.4	105.8	101.6	105.6
Net Investment Income/EP	15.4	14.6	13.2	12.7	13.9	15.1	15.2	15.4	14.9	13.9	13.8	14.5	14.4	15.3	14.4
Operating Ratio I	102.6	101.7	94.8	91.9	91.5	94.1	94.4	93.4	100.8	93.0	94.6	91.9	91.4	86.3	91.2
Net Investment Gain/EP	18.0	18.7	17.3	14.4	15.2	17.3	16.6	17.6	19.3	18.0	14.5	16.9	17.9	19.3	20.9
Operating Ratio II	100.0	97.6	90.7	90.2	90.2	91.9	93.0	91.2	96.4	88.9	93.9	89.5	87.9	82.3	84.7
Net Investment Gain Including Unrealized Gains & Losses/EP	15.5	22.7	18.5	12.8	16.6	21.2	14.2	23.6	19.3	18.5	13.7	25.4	23.0	29.9	24.6
Operating Ratio III	102.5	93.6	89.5	91.8	88.8	88.0	95.4	85.2	96.4	88.4	94.7	81.0	82.8	71.7	81.0

Source: *Best's Aggregates & Averages (Prop./Cas.)* **1985–1999**, A. M. Best Co. Inc.

loss payments. Statutory reserving requirements currently prohibit discounting loss reserves except in specific circumstances. Tabular reserves (those where the future payment stream is definite as to timing and amount) may be discounted, but this must be disclosed in Notes to Financial Statements. An example of such a claim would be a long-term workers compensation indemnity case where predetermined benefits are paid at a periodic rate for a prescribed duration. Any discounting of nontabular reserves must be disclosed in Schedule P–Part 1 of the Annual Statement. A stated rationale for using undiscounted loss reserves is to instill a level of conservatism into the reported financial position of insurers.

The level of conservatism included by not discounting property-liability loss reserves depends on the loss payout pattern of the line of business, on the general level of interest rates and on the amount of ad hoc discounting performed by insurers who realize the undiscounted loss reserves are excessive and therefore make unreasonably optimistic assumptions about future loss development. As the concentration of the industry moved from property to liability insurance, the loss payout patterns lengthened. Also, over the last several decades the general level of interest rates has increased. Thus, the degree of conservatism engendered by not discounting statutory loss reserves has increased, assuming no change in the reserve adequacy position of the industry. As taxable income was traditionally based on statutory accounting conventions, the federal government's tax receipts from the property-liability insurance industry eroded. Over the period 1976 through 1986, the industry as a whole paid little, if any, federal income taxes as a result of investments in tax-favored assets and underwriting losses that offset taxable investment income. The revenue needs of the federal government led to the adoption of discounting for tax purposes.

Discounting loss reserves at an appropriate rate of interest for the calculation of incurred losses would present the relevant economic value of losses instead of simply the sum of the stream of payments ignoring the time value of money. In addition, loss reserve discounting can be justified based on a desire to match revenues and expenses correctly, if premium rates have been lowered in recognition of the time value of money. Once the loss payout pattern is estimated, the primary problem is the determination of the appropriate discount rate. Rates that have been proposed include:

1. The current risk-free rate as measured by the return on U.S. Treasury bills and bonds;

2. The rate of return earned by the industry over a particular recent time interval;

3. The rate of return achieved by the specific insurer over a particular recent time interval;

4. A selected interest rate based on a specific asset return index over a particular time interval;

5. The current risk-free interest rate adjusted to produce an expected premium for underwriting risk.

No general consensus exists as to the proper discount rate. Basic finance theory suggests that the appropriate discount rate should reflect the relevant risk of the loss payment pattern (Butsic, 1988). The Capital Asset Pricing Model (CAPM), a widely used model for analyzing security returns discussed in some detail in the next section, would determine this rate based on the systematic risk of loss payout patterns (D'Arcy, 1989). Systematic risk is the covariance of returns for a given asset with the returns of the market as a whole scaled by the variance of the market returns. The Arbitrage Pricing Model (APM), a more recent and more general model for determining security returns, would base the discount rate on the results of a factor analysis of historical experience. Under the APM covariance of returns with factors in addition to, or in place of, the market as a whole would affect the relevant risk of an asset. Research in the 1990s points to multiple factors, such as firm size and book-to-market ratios, in addition to market covariation (Fama and French, 1997). The scarcity of market-value information on loss reserves makes the determination of a market-driven discount rate difficult. As insurance prices are affected by current, rather than historical, interest rates, the interest rate achievable by the insurer when the policies are written would be a better measure than the proposals to use moving averages of past interest rates, either general or company-specific. The most commonly used discount rate, for reasons of simplicity rather than technical accuracy, is the current risk-free interest rate.

Use of the current short-term U.S. Treasury bond interest rate to discount the loss payout pattern in the calculation of the incurred loss ratio would have the effect of including the time value of money in the combined ratio. Thus, investment income does not have to be factored in separately, as currently introduced in the operating ratio. The loss payout pattern expected to apply to the current book of business is used. Also, the current market conditions on risk free investments are applied. This measure avoids the distortions caused in the investment income measures when stocks and other risky assets experience marked price movements in a given year.

Woll (1987) applies a similar technique in his paper "Insurance Profits: Keeping Score." The accident-year combined ratio based on discounted loss reserves is also illustrated in Table 9.7. The discounted accident-year combined ratio is the sum of paid losses and LAE and the discounted reserve for future loss and LAE payments divided by the earned premium $[(35 + 36)/95 = 74.7\%]$ plus the expense ratio $(28/100 = 28.0\%)$, which totals 102.7%. This compares with the undiscounted accident-year combined ratio of 112.2%.

Return on Equity

Corporate financial analysis commonly uses a value termed the return on equity (ROE) to measure profitability. This value is calculated by dividing the net profit after taxes available to common stockholders (after deducting preferred dividends and payments to debtholders) by the value of the common equity in the firm. The value of common equity is traditionally a book value either at the beginning of the year or the average of the beginning and ending values. The common equity values are not based on market value, although this may be a more appropriate measure.

Return on equity values can similarly be derived for property-liability insurers, but several adjustments are needed. Initially, a determination of net profit must be made. This value can be either on a statutory or GAAP basis. Neither profit figure includes unrealized capital gains or losses incurred during the period. For an insurer with significant values in this category, the ROE value would be distorted. However, if unrealized gains or losses were to be included, they cannot simply be added (or subtracted) from the net profit value. The present value of future taxes associated with realization of these gains or losses must be accounted for before an adjustment to the net profit figure is made.

The primary advantage of a return on equity measure is that it allows a comparison of insurance profitability with other industries. All prior profitability measures discussed are specific to insurance companies. Return on equity measures for other industries are readily available for comparison purposes. However, the comparison of return on equity values must be done with care. Many industries have recognized distortions either in the net profit figure or the book values. For example, loan loss reserves for banks are often well below the level needed to absorb problem loans. Also, natural resource firms often carry assets at purchase price rather than market price. For the property-liability insurance industry, the distortions in net profits and book value must be recognized in order to interpret the ROE results meaningfully. Among the problems with statutory financial statements are:

1. The equity in the unearned premium reserve is not recognized;

2. Bonds are valued at amortized rather than market value;

3. Loss and loss adjustment expense reserves are carried at the sum of estimated future payments rather than the present value, and the estimates may be inadequate or redundant;

4. Some assets are not included in statutory surplus, such as nonadmitted reinsurance.

Two return-on-equity values are illustrated in Table 9.7. The first divides the statutory net income by the average statutory surplus (average of beginning and ending values) during the year $(4/59.5 = 6.7\%)$. The second includes the effect of unrealized capital gains and losses $[(4 + 1)/59.5 = 8.4\%]$. Neither of these values adjusts the surplus for the cited distortions.

Internal Rate of Return

The internal rate of return of an investment is the mathematically determined discount rate that sets the present value of the total cash flow equal to zero. When discounted at the internal rate of return, the present value of the cash inflows equals the present value of the cash outflows. For standard investment decisions, the initial investment outlay is the cash outflow and the subsequent receipts are the cash inflows. The situation is reversed when the internal rate of return is calculated from the insurer's point of view on an insurance policy. The standard treatment of this transaction is that the insurer receives a cash inflow when the policy is written, pays some expenses immediately and others in future periods, and pays losses in the future as well. In order for a positive internal rate of return to result, expenses and losses must exceed premium. (This would result in a combined ratio in excess of 100%.)

A more realistic description of the cash flows involved for insurance policies would have some expenses incurred prior to writing the policy. These prepaid expenses would include policy development costs and training expenditures. Other expenses would be paid when the policy is actually written. Premium income would be received several months after the policy is written, representing lags in collecting premiums from agents or insureds. Additional expenses and the losses would be paid subsequent to the receipt of premium. Following loss payments, salvage, subrogation, and reinsurance payments might be received.

This more representative cash flow model would thus entail cash outflows preceding and following the cash inflow, with the potential for more cash inflows at the end of the sequence. Solving the discount rate that sets the present value of the cash flows to zero may yield multiple values. Mathematically, the number of discount rates that solve the equation equals the number of sign reversals in the cash flow. Selecting the proper internal rate of return from competing values is occasionally a complex endeavor.

For example, assume that an insurer experiences the following cash flow pattern in writing a policy, based on incurring $10 of expenses associated with the policy five years prior to receiving premium income (training sales force, setting up computer system, etc.), receiving $45 on net premium (premiums less concurrent expenses such as commissions), and then pays a total of $35 in losses over the next four years as indicated:

Year	Cash Flow
0	−10
5	45
6	−10
7	−10
8	−10
9	− 5

The two internal rates of return from this cash flow pattern, resulting from the two changes in sign of the cash flow, are 0% and 13%. The mathematically relevant internal rate of return is 13%. Thus, the insurer writing this business would be receiving a 13% rate of return on this business. In situations such as this, though, the recommended approach is to calculate the Net Present Value (NPV) of the cash flow at the appropriate cost of capital and determine if the cash flow represents a positive NPV opportunity for the insurer. (See D'Arcy and Dyer, 1997, for a more complete explanation.)

Another way around the problem of multiple sign changes is used in the NCCI IRR model that considers the implied cash flows between the owners of an insurance company and the company. At the inception of a policy, the owners provide equity (surplus) to the company and also prepay any expected underwriting losses. These funds, plus the premium net of expenses, are invested, generating investment income. The owners receive an income flow that represents the after tax investment income and a return of the surplus as the losses are paid.

A simplified example, based on Feldblum (1992), has a company writing workers compensation coverage in which the premium is $125 million, the expenses are $25 million and the losses are $120 million. The premiums and expenses are paid in full at the inception of the policy and the losses are paid in full four years later. The owners provide equity equal to one-half of the undiscounted losses plus the entire underwriting loss at the inception of the policy. This capital is returned to the owners when the losses are paid. All the funds, the net premiums and the contributed equity and underwriting loss, are invested in four-year zero coupon bonds that have 10% interest rate. For simplification, there are no taxes.

The cash flow from the owners is $80 million at the inception of the policy ($60 million equity plus the $20 million prefunded underwriting loss). The owners receive $143.54 million after four years, which is the amount that $180 million (the $80 million initial investment plus premiums of $125 million less $25 million expenses) grows to after four years at ten percent interest minus the $120 million loss payment. The internal rate of return on this cash flow is 15.7 percent.

In actual applications of the internal rate of return model, the cash flows occur throughout the policy term and loss development period. For an additional analysis of the internal rate of return approach, see Bingham (1999), Cummins (1990), Robbin (1999), or Taylor (1994).

IMPACT OF INVESTMENT INCOME ON PRICING

Standard Profit Formula

From the promulgation of the 1921 standard profit formula until the mid-1960s, investment income was virtually ignored in insurance ratemaking. In establishing the 5% underwriting profit benchmark, the majority report of the 1921 Fire Insurance Committee of the National Convention of Insurance Commissioners concluded that "no part of the so-called banking profit (or loss) should be considered in arriving at the underwriting profit (or loss)." The model bill for state rate regulation, approved by the National Association of Insurance Commissioners (NAIC) in 1946 in the wake of the McCarran–Ferguson Act's affirmation of the rights of states to regulate insurance, included the provision that "due consideration shall be given...to a reasonable margin for underwriting profit and contingencies...." All but eight states adopted the model bill including this provision. The other eight states excluded the word "underwriting." Despite the different statutory language, by the early 1960s a 5% underwriting profit margin was the normal loading for all lines except workers compensation, where a 2.5% loading was accepted. This lower rate for workers compensation was justified on the basis that the more stringent regulation applicable to this line of business would make it less risky (an arguable point), as well as on the basis that the longer payout pattern on losses would generate more investment income.

In addition to an established profit margin target, provision in insurance rates was made for a contingencies factor. The general concept of a contingencies factor was to provide a cushion in rate levels for events that could not be accurately forecast, such as severe economic conditions, unusual loss occurrences, or other "unpredictable" developments. Thus, the total factor included in the rate level was for a "profit and contingencies" factor. Lehmann (1985) discusses the contingencies factor in some detail. An in-depth discussion of the issues involved in including investment income in ratemaking is provided in the 1984 Investment Income Task Force Report to the NAIC. For a more complete explanation of the different financial pricing models, see D'Arcy and Dyer (1997), D'Arcy and Gorvett (1998), Taylor (1994), and Van Slyke (1999).

New Jersey Remand Decision

During the 1960s, Florida, Maryland, and Virginia began to require the consideration of investment income in ratemaking. A 1969 New Jersey Supreme Court decision ruled that investment income could not be ignored in setting insurance rates and remanded the case for reconsideration by the insurance commissioner. That ruling led to the New Jersey Remand Decision of 1972, which established a fair rate of return for an insurer and reduced that value by the policyholders' share of investment earnings. The policyholders' share of investment earnings is measured by multiplying the insurer's portfolio rate of return by the unearned premium and loss reserves less deductions for prepaid expenses. Considerable controversy has raged in New Jersey over both the determination of the fair rate of return for insurers and the application of the specific formula for arriving at the target underwriting profit provision.

Capital Asset Pricing Model

In 1975, rate regulators in Massachusetts began to require the inclusion of investment income in automobile and workers compensation rates (Derrig in Cummins and Harrington 1987). Protracted hearings led to the introduction of the Capital Asset Pricing Model (CAPM) into insurance ratemaking in 1978. The basic formula of the CAPM is:

$$E(r_A) = r_F + \beta[E(r_M) - r_F]$$

where

r_A = return on an asset

r_F = risk-free rate of return

r_M = return on the market portfolio

β = systematic risk of asset

E = expectation operator (expected value)

Applying the CAPM to insurance pricing leads to the following example. (For the specific derivation see the Fairley paper included in Cummins and Harrington 1987. Fairley does not include expenses, but uses net premiums instead. For consistency with conventional pricing models, the application below has been modified to reflect expenses specifically.)

$$E(r_u) = -k(1 - x)r_F + \beta[E(r_M) - r_F]$$

where

r_u = underwriting profit margin

k = average claim payment lag

x = expense ratio

β = systematic underwriting risk

For example, if claims are paid on average 9 months after the premium is received, the expense ratio is 30%, the systematic underwriting risk has been determined to be 25%, the yield on short-term government bills is 7% and the expected stock market risk premium is 8%, then the indicated underwriting profit margin can be determined as follows:

$$k = .75$$

$$x = .30$$

$$\beta = .25$$

$$r_F = .07$$

$$E(r_M) - r_F = .08$$

$$E(r_u) = -(.75)(1 - .30)(.07) + (.25)(.08) = -.0168$$

The theory behind the CAPM is that the equity markets are controlled by well-diversified investors that are not concerned about the total risk (volatility of price) of an individual asset any more than an insurer is concerned about the risk of an individual policy. The law of large numbers assures that independent volatility (unsystematic risk) will be of no consequence in the total risk of a portfolio of either individual investments or policies. The factor that does concern investors is the systematic risk, or that risk that cannot be diversified away. Based on the assumption that insurers are owned by diversified investors (which may not hold true for mutual insurers), this theory leads to the conclusion that only systematic underwriting risk needs to be considered in pricing insurance products. A more detailed discussion of this approach can be found in the papers by Heinz Muller (1987, 1988), and Andrew Turner (1987).

A number of problems arise in applying the CAPM to insurance pricing. Market values of beta cannot be determined for individual lines since no single line insurer is publicly traded. Instead, accounting data is used to generate an assumed beta by measuring the fluctuations in reported underwriting profitability in line with stock market movements. No known technique demonstrates that accounting data can be used to determine underwriting betas for use in the insurance CAPM. In addition to this problem, the betas calculated from accounting data are not stable over time, so use of a beta determined from historical data is unlikely to be valid for the ratemaking horizon.

Total Rate of Return Model

Other methods for including investment income in ratemaking have also arisen as alternatives to the New Jersey Remand methodology and the CAPM. One method commonly used by insurers is termed the total rate of return model (see Ferrari 1968). The common application of this technique is to select a target rate of return for a given line of insurance, either after analyzing its volatility or by use of a company-wide standard. In some cases, the target rate is allowed to vary to reflect the underwriting cycle, with a lower target during very competitive conditions and a higher target during tight market conditions. The contribution of investment income toward this total return is then projected, usually by multiplying the portfolio rate of return by the expected holding period for premium income, and subtracted from the target total return. The remainder of the target rate needs to be obtained from underwriting, providing a target underwriting profit margin.

An example of the total rate of return model is as follows:

$$TRR = (IA/S)(IRR) + (P/S)(UPM)$$

where

$$TRR = \text{Total Rate of Return}$$

$$IA = \text{Investable Assets}$$

$$S = \text{Surplus}$$

$$IRR = \text{Investment Rate of Return}$$

$$P = \text{Premium}$$

$$UPM = \text{Underwriting Profit Margin}$$

If an insurer with investable assets of two times surplus and a premium-to-surplus ratio of three-to-one wanted to achieve a 15% total rate of return at a time when the investment rate of return equaled 9%, then the appropriate underwriting profit margin would be minus 1%, based on the following solution:

$$.15 = (2)(.09) + (3)(UPM)$$

$$UPM = -.01$$

The major weaknesses of the target rate of return approach are the difficulty in determining the proper target return and the frequent use of portfolio rates of return to determine the investment income contribution. The appropriate target should be adjusted to reflect such economic conditions as the inflation rate and alternative investment returns, and perhaps competitive conditions in insurance markets, as well. The portfolio rate of return does not necessarily reflect what the insurer can earn on the investable funds generated from selling insurance in the current period. Finally, this single period model can only be an approximation to the return on multiperiod insurance cash flows.

Discounted Cash Flow Analysis

Another approach that has been proposed in regulatory hearings is termed discounted cash flow analysis. Under this technique, all of the cash flows emanating from writing a policy are projected, period by period. The cash flows include premium income, expenses, taxes, and loss payments. All cash flows are discounted to the beginning of the policy term by the appropriate discount rate. The primary drawback of this technique is the difficulty of determining the appropriate discount rate. This drawback is avoided if the calculation is made as an internal rate of return determination on cash flows expected between the investor and the insurer. For an explanation and applications of this approach, see Bingham (1999), Cummins (1990 and 1991), D'Arcy and Dyer (1997), and Taylor (1994).

Option Pricing Model

The framework of contingent claims analysis that has been widely used in pricing options and other derivative securities has also been applied to insurance in several theoretical analyses [Cummins (1989), Doherty and Garven (1986), Wacek (1997)]. Empirical tests of the different models indicate that the option pricing model compares well with the other financial models [D'Arcy and Garven (1990), D'Arcy and Gorvett (1998)]. The underlying approach of the option pricing model is to assign claims against the residual value of the insurer, at the end of the contract period, first to the policyholder, who gets the lesser of the value of any losses or the total value of the firm, then to the government, which gets a set share of any gains in the firm's value during the period, and finally to the owners of the insurer, who are entitled to whatever is left, if anything, after paying claims and taxes. Under the option pricing model, the premium is set at a level so that the contingent claim of the owners equals or exceeds the initial value of the firm. The owners would not be willing to write the coverage at any lower-rate level, as that would reduce the firm's value.

Arguments Against Using a Specific Formula

The various methodologies for including investment income in the determination of an allowable underwriting profit margin have the advantage of producing specific indications that can be used to establish rates. However, each method is subject to criticism for ignoring certain circumstances or for requiring a value to be estimated that is difficult or impossible to obtain. An alternative school argues that investment income should be given indirect consideration, rather than be included directly in the ratemaking process. The arguments in favor of this position are:

1. No formula approach is recognized as producing the correct results in all situations;

2. The effect of competition on insurance prices is ignored in ratemaking formulas, but is crucial to the ability of an insurer to charge a particular rate level;

3. If rates in a particular market are producing an excessive rate of return for insurers in total, then new entrants will drive the price down to the proper level;

4. If rate levels are inadequate to produce an acceptable rate of return in total, then insurers will exit from the market until price levels increase to the acceptable level, leading to temporary insurance availability problems;

5. Analysis of the difference in rate levels in prior approval and open competition states indicates that there are no significant differences in profitability over any extended time, although regulatory lag does tend to generate lower profits under prior approval during periods of volatile, but increasing inflation rates.

Value of a Generally Accepted Insurance Pricing Model

The conclusion of these observations is that financial and insurance markets will work to produce the proper total rate of return for insurers, without the need for complicated formula adjustments. Although this may be true in the long run, the well-known underwriting cycle (the consistent pattern of fluctuation between profitability and losses for underwriting results as depicted in Figure 9.1) indicates that severe market distortions are caused as the market moves toward the proper level. Exits and entry take time to affect prices. Thus, the slowness of market adjustments needs to be weighed against the inaccuracies of any rigid formula approach to insurance pricing problems.

Having a generally accepted insurance pricing model is not necessary for the insurance industry to function, just as stocks were traded for a long time before the CAPM arose to explain security returns. Tests of the validity of the CAPM for pricing financial assets are based on how well it explains historical returns for securities (not very well, according to Fama and French 1992). Similarly, the usefulness of any insurance pricing model depends on how well it explains the prices actually charged. Using the model to determine regulated prices should be redundant if competitive forces are at play. If the model is correct, then it would not be necessary to force insurers to charge the indicated price. This restriction would be similar to requiring investors to buy and sell securities at prices determined by a theoretical model and not allowing the market to establish prices independently. The model rests on being able to explain prices, and not on prices being set by the model.

However, having a generally accepted insurance pricing model would be a substantial benefit. Although prices should move toward the proper level in the long run, a usable model would assist insurers to price more accurately in the short run as well. This increase in pricing accuracy would not prevent insurers from periodically undercharging or overcharging the indicated price, and thus would not eliminate the underwriting cycle. Nevertheless, a generally accepted pricing model would allow insurers to determine the appropriate price level and might reduce the degree of fluctuations in results and lower the probability of insurer insolvency.

CONCLUSION

Over the last three decades, the level of attention that casualty actuaries have paid to the investment side of operations has grown from neglect, to incorporating a few investment figures into ratemaking calculations, to an attempt to integrate underwriting and investments in tax planning and dynamic financial analysis applications. Hopefully, this increasing trend will continue and this chapter will be of value in this development. The investment field combines mathematics and risk analysis, two areas in which actuaries have strong skills. Applying actuarial talent to investment issues is likely to provide continued advances in financial theory and practice. Insurance companies are financial institutions and the mathematical specialists in our industry need to be equally well versed in both the underwriting and investment fields in order to provide the greatest value to insurance organizations.

REFERENCES

Actuarial Considerations Regarding Risk and Return in Property-Casualty Insurance Pricing. Edited by E. Oakley Van Slyke. Arlington, Va.: Casualty Actuarial Society, 1999.

Almagro, Manuel, and Thomas L. Ghezzi, "Federal Income Taxes Provisions Affecting Property-Casualty Insurers," *Proceedings of the Casualty Actuarial Society* 1988, 75:95–161.

A. M. Best Company, *Best's Aggregates & Averages*, Oldwick, NJ: A. M. Best Company, various years.

Bingham, Russell E. Cash Flow Models in Ratemaking: A Reformulation of Myers–Cohn NPV and IRR Models for Equivalency. In *Actuarial Considerations Regarding Risk and Return in Property-Casualty Insurance Pricing.* Edited by E. Oakley Van Slyke. Arlington, Va.: Casualty Actuarial Society, 1999.

Butsic, Robert P., "Determining the Proper Interest Rate for Loss Reserve Discounting: An Economic Approach," *CAS Discussion Paper Program*, 1988, 147–188.

Cummins, J. David, "Multi-Period Discounted Cash Flow Models in Property-Liability Insurance," *Journal of Risk and Insurance*, 1990, 57:79–109.

Cummins, J. David, "Statistical and Financial Models of Insurance Pricing and the Insurance Firm," *Journal of Risk and Insurance*, 1991, 58:261–303.

Cummins, J. David, "Risk-Based Premiums for Insurance Guaranty Funds," *Journal of Finance*, 1989, 43:823–839.

Cummins, J. David, and Lena Chang, "An Analysis of the New Jersey Formula for Including Investment Income in Property-Liability Insurance Ratemaking," *Journal of Insurance Regulation*, 1983, 1:555–573.

Cummins, J. David, and Scott A. Harrington, "Property-Liability Insurance Rate Regulation: Estimation of Underwriting Betas Using Quarterly Profit Data," *Journal of Risk and Insurance*, 1985, 52:16–43.

Cummins, J. David, Richard D. Phillips, and Stephen D. Smith, "Corporate Hedging in the Insurance Industry: The Use of Financial Derivatives by U.S. Insurers," *North American Actuarial Journal*, 1997, 1:13–39.

D'Arcy, Stephen P., "Duration-Discussion," *Proceedings of the Casualty Actuarial Society*, 1984, 71:8–25.

D'Arcy, Stephen P., "Use of the CAPM to Discount Property-Liability Loss Reserves," *Journal of Risk and Insurance*, 1989, 55:481–491.

D'Arcy, Stephen P., and Neil A. Doherty, *The Financial Theory of Pricing Property-Liability Insurance Contracts*, Homewood, IL: Richard D. Irwin, 1988.

D'Arcy, Stephen P., and Michael A. Dyer, "Ratemaking: A Financial Economics Approach," *Proceedings of the Casualty Actuarial Society*, 1997, 84:301–390.

D'Arcy, Stephen P., and James R. Garven, "Property-Liability Insurance Pricing Models: An Empirical Evaluation," *Journal of Risk and Insurance*, 1990, 57:391–430.

D'Arcy, Stephen P., and Richard W. Gorvett, "Property-Liability Insurance Pricing Models: A Comparison," *Proceedings of the Casualty Actuarial Society*, 1998, 85:1–88.

D'Arcy, Stephen P., and Richard W. Gorvett, "Measuring the Interest Rate Sensitivity of Loss Reserves," *Proceedings of the Casualty Actuarial Society*, 2000.

Derrig, Richard A., "The Use of Investment Income in Massachusetts Private Passenger Automobile and Workers' Compensation Ratemaking," *Fair Rate of Return in Property-Liability Insurance*, J. David Cummins, Scott Harrington, Eds., Kluwer Academic Publisher, 1987, 119–147.

Derrig, Richard A., "Price Regulation in US Automobile Insurance A Case Study of Massachusetts Private Passenger Automobile Insurance 1978–1990," *The Geneva Papers on Risk and Insurance*, 1993, 67:158–173.

Derrig, Richard A., "Theoretical Considerations on the Effect of Federal Income Taxes on Investment Income in Property-Liability Ratemaking," *Journal of Risk and Insurance*, 1994, 61:691–709.

Derrig, Richard A., and Krysztof M. Ostaszewski, "Managing the Tax Liability of a Property-Liability Insurance Company," *Journal of Risk and Insurance*, 1997, 64:695–711.

Doherty, Neil A, and James R. Garven, "Price Regulation in Property-Liability Insurance: A Contingent Claims Approach," *Journal of Finance*, 1986, 41:1031–1050.

Fama, Eugene F., and Kenneth R. French, "The Cross-Section of Expected Stock Returns," *Journal of Finance*, 1992, 47:427–465.

Fama, Eugene F., and Kenneth R. French, "Industry Costs of Equity," *Journal of Financial Economics*, 1997, 43:153–193.

Feldblum, Sholom, Pricing Insurance Policies: The Internal Rate of Return Model, Part 10A Note, 1992.

Ferguson, Ronald F., "Duration," *Proceedings of the Casualty Actuarial Society*, 1983, 70:265–288.

Ferrari, I. Robert, "The Relationship on Underwriting, Investment, Leverage, and Exposure to Total Return on Owners' Equity," *Proceedings of the Casualty Actuarial Society*, 1968, 55:295–302.

Gleeson, Owen, and Gerald I. Lenrow, "An Analysis of the Impact of the Tax Reform Act on the Property/Casualty Industry," *CAS Discussion Paper Program*, 1987, 119–190.

Harrington, Scott A., "The Impact of Rate Regulation on Prices and Underwriting Results in the Property-Liability Insurance Industry: A Survey," *Journal of Risk and Insurance*, 1984, 51:577–623.

Ibbotson Associates, *Stocks, Bonds, Bills and Inflation 1999 Yearbook*, Chicago: Ibbotson, 1999.

Lehmann, Steven G., "Contingency Margins in Rate Calculations," *CAS Discussion Paper Program*, 1985, 220–242.

Muller, Heinz H., "Economic Premium Principles in Insurance and the Capital Asset Pricing Model," *ASTIN Bulletin*, 1987, 17:141–150.

Muller, Heinz H., "Modern Portfolio Theory: Some Main Results," *ASTIN Bulletin*, 1988, 18:127–145.

National Association of Insurance Commissioners, Measurement of profitability and treatment of investment income in property and liability insurance, *Proceedings of the National Association of Insurance Commissioners*, 1970, 2A:719–894.

National Association of Insurance Commissioners, Report of the investment income task force, *Proceedings of the National Association of Insurance Commissioners*, 1984, 2:719–807.

Panning, William H., "Asset/Liability Management: Beyond Interest Rate Risk," *CAS Discussion Paper Program*, 1987, 322–352.

Robbin, Ira. Theoretical Premiums for Property and Casualty Insurance Coverage—A Risk Sensitive, Total Return Approach. In *Actuarial Considerations Regarding Risk and Return in Property-Casualty Insurance Pricing*. Edited by E. Oakley Van Slyke. Arlington, Va.: Casualty Actuarial Society, 1999.

Smith, Michael L., and Robert C. Witt, "An Economic Analysis of Retroactive Liability Insurance," *Journal of Risk and Insurance*, 1985, 52:379–401.

Strain, Robert W., *Property-Liability Insurance Accounting*, Santa Monica, CA: Merritt, 1988.

Taylor, Gregory, "Fair Premium Rating Methods and the Relations Between Them," *Journal of Risk and Insurance*, 1994, 61:592–616.

Turner, Andrew L. Insurance in an Equilibrium Asset-Pricing Model. Chapter 4 in *Fair Rate of Return in Property-Liability Insurance*, edited by J. David Cummins and Scott A. Harrington. Boston: Kluwer Nijhoff, 1987.

Wacek, Michael G., "Applications of the Option Market Paradigm to the Solution of Insurance Problems," *Proceedings of the Casualty Actuarial Society*, 1997, 89:701–733.

Webb, Bernard L., "Investment Income in Insurance Ratemaking," *Journal of Insurance Regulation*, 1982, 1:46–76.

Woll, Richard C., "Insurance Profits: Keeping Score," *CAS Discussion Paper Program*, 1987, 446–533.

CHAPTER 10
SPECIAL ISSUES
RICHARD W. GORVETT, JOHN L. TEDESCHI,
AND KIMBERLEY A. WARD

With increasing frequency, casualty actuaries are using their skills to perform analyses that extend beyond the traditional actuarial functions associated with ratemaking and loss reserving. An actuary's quantitative expertise, combined with an understanding—obtained through the examination process or experience or both—of an insurance company's operational and financial processes, means that the actuary is often called upon to study and opine on important nontraditional questions and issues. These opportunities for expanded responsibility require familiarity with topics and techniques beyond those previously covered in this book.

This chapter discusses a number of "special issues," that include several recent developments in actuarial science and insurance. Only a brief outline of each topic can be provided in this chapter; it is hoped that these descriptions will encourage the interested reader to pursue the articles referenced in this chapter, along with other relevant material associated with these topics. The first section of this chapter covers the valuation of insurance companies, including accounting principles and the measurement of surplus or net worth, approaches to allocating surplus, and valuation issues involving environmental and catastrophic exposures. The second section considers issues relating to operating an insurance company, including planning and forecasting, dynamic financial analysis, and insurance securitization. The third section discusses the regulation of insurance companies, including solvency issues and risk-based capital. The final section describes data sources that might be useful in support of actuarial analyses.

VALUING AN INSURANCE COMPANY

This section introduces several issues involved in the valuation of an insurance company. A number of different definitions of "value" are described, and the differences between these various value measures are examined. Issues surrounding the allocation of surplus to different operating entities or lines of business or both are also discussed, and accounting and ratemaking considerations related to surplus allocation are examined. Finally, two exposures that can significantly impact insurance company valuation are discussed: environmental liabilities and catastrophic risks.

Measuring Surplus or Net Worth

The determination of an accurate value for the net worth of an insurer is important for operational and regulatory purposes. In addition, the insurance industry—in fact, the entire financial services sector—has periodically been characterized by significant merger, acquisition, and consolidation activity. Such activity entails evaluations of insurers' net worths. Thus, it is critical that actuaries understand how company "value" is determined from many different perspectives. This section defines these perspectives, describes the specific orientations and users of each measure of value, and discusses their attributes and differences.

Statutory Value

Statutory valuation and accounting conventions are peculiar to the insurance industry. The measures and methods used to determine statutory values are promulgated by the regulatory authorities that oversee the insurance industry, and may—and very often do—differ from other valuation conventions (discussed later). Despite the existence of "distortions" in statutory accounting, statutory values are relied upon heavily by regulators.

It is useful to characterize different accounting and valuation conventions according to their overall perspective. Statutory values can be characterized as having the following orientations:

- *Solvency:* The historical development and primary purpose of statutory accounting revolved around helping regulators to evaluate the solvency of insurance companies better.

- *Conservatism:* Statutory valuation is typically oriented toward providing a conservative estimate of a company's value and solvency potential. To that end, assets are sometimes valued below their "fair market" values and liabilities above their economic values. Some of the specific statutory valuation rules are discussed below.

- *Balance sheet:* Consistent with its solvency orientation, statutory accounting often focuses on the balance sheet of the insurance company, in an effort to determine a (conservative) estimate of the value of the company.

- *Liquidation value:* Statutory accounting can be viewed as ultimately providing a value of the company as if it had to be liquidated as of the date of the balance sheet. Such a perspective provides regulators with an indication as to whether or not the various claimholders of a company—especially policyholders—would be satisfied financially in the event of the company's insolvency.

Some of the specific statutory conventions include the following rules. Several of these rules are instrumental in establishing the "conservative" nature of statutory valuation.

- Bonds (those in good standing) are generally valued at "book" value, i.e., amortized value. (Note that this rule may or may not be "conservative," depending upon the relationship between the book and market values of a bond on the valuation date, which in turn depends upon the path that interest rates have taken between the purchase date of the bond and the valuation date.)

- Common stock values are based on market value.

- Certain assets are "nonadmitted"—that is, considered to have no value—such as agents' balances over 90 days past due, reinsurance recoverables over 90 days past due, and furniture and equipment.

- Expenses are recognized on a cash basis.

- Loss reserves are generally not discounted to reflect the time value of money.

An insurer's statutory surplus is equal to its statutory assets minus its statutory liabilities. Thus, the statutory surplus is, in a sense, the regulator's conservative estimate of the net worth of the company, i.e., the value of the owners' interest in the company. For a stock company, the statutory surplus represents the stockholders' value or interest in the insurer; for a mutual company or a reciprocal, it reflects the policyholders' interest.

GAAP Value

"GAAP" accounting stems from Generally Accepted Accounting Principles. GAAP principles are largely based upon rules promulgated by the Financial Accounting Standards Board. One of the primary functions of GAAP accounting is to provide information to the investment community about the performance of companies. Since earnings information is critically important to investors, GAAP tends to have an income statement orientation. Also consistent with this investment perspective, GAAP views the company as a going concern.

GAAP principles tend to be less conservative, and more "realistic," than statutory accounting rules. Some of the GAAP principles include the following.

- Bonds are booked at amortized value only if they are categorized as being "held to maturity." "Trading" and "available for sale" bonds are booked at market value.

- Common stock is booked at market value.

• There are no "nonadmitted assets" under GAAP—all receivable assets are accounted for to the extent that they are reasonably expected to be collectible.

• Expenses associated with the writing of policies are matched against the revenues associated with those policies.

Thus, there are several important differences between GAAP and statutory accounting in terms of asset valuation, nonadmitted assets, and the treatment and timing of policy acquisition expenses. While statutory accounting tends to be the more conservative of the two, this sometimes depends upon specific company or financial conditions.

"Economic" Value

The term "economic value" has been used in a variety of ways. Here, it is intended to reflect the value of an asset, liability, or company by beginning with statutory or GAAP accounting conventions, and then incorporating more "realistic" economic adjustments than allowed for under either statutory or GAAP rules. For example, the economic value of the equity of a property-liability insurer might be considered as an adjustment to statutory surplus:

Economic value of equity = Statutory surplus

+ Equity in the unearned premium reserve

+ Excess of statutory over statement reserves

+ Nonadmitted assets

+ Difference between nominal and time-discounted loss reserves

+ Difference between market value and book value of bonds

− Tax liability on equity in unrealized capital gains

Market Value

If a financial entity or instrument is actively traded, a possible basis for valuation is the price at which it is bought and sold. The market value of a publicly traded insurer is calculated by multiplying the number of outstanding shares of stock of the company by its current stock price. This represents the company value as interpreted by the capital markets. For nonpublicly traded companies, or for insurers that are owned by large publicly traded companies, this process cannot be done directly. It is possible that an indirect method could be used, for example by applying a market value to book value ratio from a "comparable" stock insurer. Since the stock price represents the capital market's assessment of the firm as a whole, using the stock price can, in theory, provide an indication of the *franchise* value of the firm. The franchise value includes certain aspects of an insurer that are difficult to quantify, such as reputation, goodwill, and the value of the existing book of business. Goodwill, for example, can be a significant asset, which is generally not included in either statutory or GAAP valuations (although it might be recognized as an asset when a company is acquired).

In some instances, two or more of the valuation frameworks described above—statutory, GAAP, economic, and/or market values—might result in similar or identical indications of a company's surplus or equity. However, they can often produce significantly different surplus values. The relationships between the values depend upon a company's specific asset distribution, the type of insurance the company is engaged in, general financial and economic conditions, and a variety of other factors.

Allocation of Surplus

It is important that actuaries be comfortable with the underpinnings of each valuation technique described above. While the terms "equity" and "surplus" are frequently used interchangeably and as general labels, there are many instances in which one or another measure of equity described above is required for a specific application—for example, in the allocation of surplus for ratemaking purposes. Depending upon the type of ratemaking formula used, different specifications of "equity" may be necessary. Certain ratemaking formulas require that the amount of capital allocated to the insurance business being priced represents the amount of capital on which a competitive rate of return should be achieved. This "capital attraction" standard recognizes that assets can be redeployed to alternative investments if a competitive rate of return cannot be earned on the insurance business. Other formulas simply require a capital allocation in order to determine a level of investment income, and, in turn, to determine the amount of tax liability incurred on that investment income.

There is no generally accepted approach to allocating surplus. Some of the possibilities include:

- *Premium-to-surplus ratio.* This essentially assumes that surplus is no longer needed to support business after the premium has been written. However, to the extent that surplus exists to provide a safety margin, surplus should be allocated to business as long as there is any potential for future activity and uncertainty relating to that business, for example, until all possible losses have been paid.

- *Loss reserve-to-surplus ratio.*

- *Proportion of total marginal profit.* This approach has its underpinnings in microeconomic theory.

- *Relative "riskiness."* Under this approach, surplus is allocated in such a way that the expected return on equity is the same across all types of business.

Financial Analysis

Regardless of the valuation framework used, the purpose of accounting and accounting rules is to summarize the financial activity of a company. Financial statements that provide these summaries can be utilized by at least four different sets of interested parties: internal decision makers, external investors, regulators, and taxing authorities. Because each of these parties has specific interests and concerns, different sets of accounting rules have been developed for each purpose: management, financial, statutory, and tax accounting, respectively, corresponding to each of the four sets of interested parties.

Financial statements represent sources of financial information, which can be important to evaluating the status of a company for a number of purposes. Some of the more important statements include:

- *Balance sheet:* provides a snapshot of the company's financial position as of a specified date.

- *Income statement:* summarizes the operations of a company over a period of time.

- *Statement of cash flows:* summarizes the sources of cash receipts and payments from the various company activities over a period of time.

- *Letter to shareholders in the annual report:* often provides significant qualitative information about the company's activities, results, and performance, as well as goals for the future.

Whether investigating the financial condition of an insurer or a noninsurance corporation, there are certain quantitative tests that are commonly performed. These tests typically take the form of ratios, with their component elements derived from the financial statements of the company, and they help to identify the company's operating condition. Some examples of important ratios and their purposes include:

- Ratios that measure *liquidity*

  — *Current ratio* = current assets divided by current liabilities ("current" assets and liabilities are those that are expected to mature or be paid in the "short-term," say within one year)

  — *Cash ratio* = cash plus marketable securities, divided by current liabilities

- Ratios that measure *financial leverage* or *capital structure*
  - *Leverage ratio* = debt divided by equity
- Ratios that measure *profitability*
  - *Return on equity* (ROE) = net income divided by equity
  - *Asset turnover* = annual sales divided by assets
- Ratios that reflect *market value*
  - *Market-book ratio* = stock price divided by book value per share
  - *Earnings yield* = earnings per share divided by stock price
  - *Tobin's Q* = market value of the firm divided by its replacement value

These and other ratios can be used to indicate the relative operating position of the company, either with respect to other companies and industry standards, or in relation to the company's own historical performance. In the "Regulating an Insurance Company" section later in this chapter, insurance-specific versions of some of these tests—the Insurance Regulatory Information System (IRIS) tests—are discussed.

Issues in Valuing an Insurance Company: Environmental Liabilities

For many companies, the liabilities arising from asbestos, pollution, and other mass torts (referred to here as "environmental" liabilities) comprise a significant portion of the losses from casualty policies written prior to 1990. This section describes the history and evaluation of these liabilities.

Until recently, environmental liabilities were not believed to be "reasonably estimable" as required by Financial Accounting Statement 5: Accounting for Contingencies. The Securities and Exchange Commission required companies to provide more detail on environmental liabilities in their financial reports starting in June 1993. This was followed by the Financial Accounting Standards Board Issue 93-5 release requiring disclosure of these liabilities. Later, the National Association of Insurance Commissioners required the reporting of five calendar years of incurred loss and reserve history for asbestos and pollution as a note in the Annual Statement. These disclosures helped focus attention on the problem of quantifying environmental losses.

According to A. M. Best (1998), ultimate environmental losses due to asbestos are estimated to be $40 billion, and losses due to pollution are estimated to be $56 billion (both estimates are based upon evaluations made as of December 1997). Net incurred environmental losses caused the industry's combined ratio to increase by 4.1 percentage points in 1995, 2.1 points in 1996, and 0.7 points in 1997.

Companies faced with heavy environmental losses have handled the problem in various ways. Some have formed run-off entities, while others have formed specialized claim units within the company. The 17 (as of this writing) run-off entities are structured so that the environmental losses are not intermingled with their current business. The separation can be total (the losses are transferred to the new entity with supporting surplus and an aggregate reinsurance arrangement), or the separation can be partial (when the insurance group guarantees the solvency of the run-off entity using the group's surplus). Both types heavily depend upon reinsurance recoveries and commutations as important aspects of their solvency considerations.

Asbestos—History

Asbestos is a group of naturally occurring silicates that have been found to be incombustible, flexible, durable, strong, and resistant to heat, corrosion, and wear. Asbestos fibers were used in thousands of products, such as building materials, brake and boiler linings, insulation, and fire-retardant and electrical products. Unfortunately, the characteristics that make the fibers so useful in products make them dangerous to human health. Asbestos becomes dangerous when it becomes airborne and is inhaled into the lungs. Four main diseases either caused or aggravated by asbestos include mesothelioma (a cancer of the lung lining), lung cancer, asbestosis (severe scarring of the lung lining), and other benign pleural plaques. Severity of the resulting illness is directly correlated with the exposure concentration and length of exposure. If smoking is a factor, the chance of serious illness is magnified.

The Environmental Protection Agency (EPA) virtually banned asbestos mining and manufacture in the U.S. in 1989, but not before more than 30 million workers were exposed to asbestos. Since 1950, workers compensation has covered those workers with occupational diseases caused by asbestos. In 1973, the first significant lawsuit, *Borel vs. Fibreboard*, held manufacturers of asbestos responsible for the harm resulting from exposure to their products.

Asbestos—Issues for Insurers
A number of issues related to asbestos exist for insurers. They include:

- Which policies are triggered in the event of an asbestos-related loss?

- How should the litigation burden be handled?

- What is an occurrence?

- What coverage is available?

The most commonly applied trigger of coverage is the continuous trigger. All policies in effect during the time of exposure, through the latency period and including the manifestation of the disease, are deemed to be exposed to loss. Two other less frequently used triggers are the exposure trigger and the manifestation trigger. Under the exposure trigger, only policies in effect during the period of time the individual was exposed to asbestos will respond to the claim. Under the manifestation trigger, response to the claim is determined by the single policy year during which the medical diagnosis was made. Under any trigger, the most vulnerable policies are those with no clear asbestos exclusion.

The number of suits is staggering. There were close to 200,000 suits pending in state courts by 1992. In order to manage and settle so many claims in so many jurisdictions, negotiations between policyholders and insurers establish the applicable trigger, claim handling procedures, expense cost-sharing agreements, and the allocation of loss payments to insurer and year of coverage, to establish a "coverage block." The claims are allocated, as agreed, across the years of the coverage block until the policy's aggregate limit is exhausted. If no aggregate limit exists, the insurer's liability is unlimited.

The majority of asbestos losses have been claimed as product liability losses. There have been a small number of premises/operations claims filed as a result of installation activities of contractors. The coverage issues are enormous, including the lack of an aggregate limit. A major mitigating factor is that liability is not strict and, therefore, negligence must be proven by the claimant.

For ease of evaluation, the defendants of asbestos losses have been classified into tiers. The first and second tiers consist of major and minor manufacturers of asbestos products. Many of these are now bankrupt from the financial burden of asbestos claims. The third tier, also called the second wave, consists of distributors of asbestos products. The next tier, or the third wave, refers to the premises/operations claims.

Asbestos—Risk Factors

The following factors (modified from Cross and Doucette (1997)) may indicate a greater likelihood that the insurer may experience significant liabilities due to asbestos. This list is not intended to be comprehensive.

- Policy years 1975 through 1988

- General liability market share greater than 1.5%

- Incomplete or inconsistent application of the asbestos exclusion

- Insureds that are Fortune 1000 companies

- Insureds in manufacturing/construction industries

- Coverage layers up to $5 million are high risk

- Inconsistent use of aggregate limits

- Policies that cover expenses in addition to limits

Pollution—History

"Pollution" refers to a subset of claims that arise because of pollution activity. For purposes of this discussion, pollution refers to gradual releases of pollution being claimed against general liability policies issued prior to 1987. Pollution sites include waste dumps, landfills, and other places containing hazardous substances.

The EPA was formed in 1960 in response to growing concerns about the level of pollution in U.S. cities and the water supply. The Love Canal disaster in the 1970s led to the passage of the Comprehensive Environment Restoration, Compensation, and Liability Act (CERCLA), commonly known as Superfund. The primary purpose of the Superfund law is to clean up the nation's most hazardous abandoned waste sites. Superfund applies joint and several, strict and retroactive liability to anyone who has contributed to a site, including generators, past or present owners, lenders, and transporters. The worst sites are placed on the National Priority List (NPL). The potentially responsible parties (PRPs) are identified by the EPA and ordered to clean up the site or reimburse the EPA for doing so.

Of the over 40,000 identified sites, 1,211 were listed on the NPL as of July 1999. Only 185 sites have been removed from the NPL, while 63 are currently (as of this writing) being considered for addition to the NPL. As many as 30,000 sites may not require any remediation, and others are being cleaned up by state or local environmental agencies. The estimation of ultimate pollution costs for the non-NPL sites is hampered by a lack of information regarding site characteristics and costs. It is believed that the average clean-up cost is lower for non-NPL sites due to their less hazardous nature and the less stringent clean-up rules.

Pollution—Issues for Insurers

Insurer concerns can be grouped into four major categories:

- Judicial interpretations of coverage issues
- Determination of estimated clean-up costs
- Cost allocation over policy years
- High costs of litigation

In 1966, the Insurance Services Office (ISO) converted the standard general liability policy form from an "accident" basis to an "occurrence" basis, clarifying that the covered event must be "neither expected nor intended from the standpoint of the insured." In 1973, the coverage was further clarified as applying to "sudden and accidental" pollution events, not to gradual releases. Court interpretations about the meaning of "sudden" varied, prompting ISO to clarify the language in 1985, adopting the so-called "absolute" pollution exclusion. Nevertheless, the courts in many states have ordered insurers to cover the pollution losses of their insureds, in spite of the language. Many states have yet to rule on important pollution coverage issues, causing more uncertainty as to the ultimate costs.

Clean-up costs are difficult to estimate due to the evolving nature of clean-up standards. Over the years, the standards have been relaxed—in particular, the future use of the site can be considered in estimating the costs of cleanup.

Like asbestos, the trigger and allocation scheme is negotiated between the PRPs and their insurers. The results of these discussions may not reflect the PRPs' true proportional shares of the damage. Insurers and PRPs have strong incentives to litigate over responsibility, shares, allocations, and other coverage issues or to find other PRPs for a given site. This causes ALAE costs to be high compared to the loss payments made and the number of sites remediated.

Pollution—Risk Factors

The following factors (see Bouska and McIntyre (1994)) indicate an increased likelihood that the insurer may experience significant liabilities due to pollution. This list is not intended to be comprehensive.

- Policy years 1970 through 1985

- Incomplete or inconsistent application of the absolute pollution exclusion

- Insureds that are Fortune 1000 companies

- Primary insurers with limits less than $5 million

- Policies that cover expenses in addition to limits

Mass Torts

Mass tort claims are characterized by the large number of people affected and the latent and/or sustained nature of their injuries. The list of torts considered "mass torts" varies from company to company, but can include blood products, breast implants, chemical exposure, hearing loss, lead paint, and repetitive stress syndrome. There are many unresolved coverage and causation issues causing ALAE cost to be high in relationship to the losses paid.

Methods for Estimating Environmental Losses

There are two primary classes of methodologies for estimating an entity's environmental liabilities: *benchmark* and *ground-up*.

Benchmark methods include the market share method, the aggregate loss development method, and the survival ratio method. Ground-up methods include policy exposure models and the claim department method. This section briefly discusses these techniques. (In the subsequent discussion, the phrase "type of loss" refers to either asbestos or pollution.)

Standard actuarial methods do not work with environmental losses for several reasons. First, judicial and legislative decisions impact all accident years at once, forcing a strong calendar year influence on the loss development triangle. In addition, multiple policies over several layers and policy years are often triggered, blurring the accident-year distinction. Loss dollars are not all equal: for example, some reflect settlements, while others reflect court orders.

Benchmark Methods

Market Share Method: This method is intuitive. Beginning with a range of estimated ultimate industry losses, these losses are allocated to year. Then an insurer's share of the industry losses by year is determined from its share of the GL market premium for the same period. Alternatively, an average market share for the period in question can be used rather than allocating the industry ultimate by year.

Usually several adjustments are made to the market share estimates. Notably, premium on policies without significant exposures, such as medical malpractice, should be removed. The market share estimates can be adjusted for other qualitative factors such as limits written or mix of business. It is common to omit CMP premium, as CMP has not produced significant environmental losses due the smaller insureds written.

Aggregate Loss Development Method: This nontraditional development approach ignores accident-year detail in favor of aggregate cumulative paid losses and case reserves evaluated at a series of successive year-ends. In its simplest form, an incurred-to-ultimate or paid-to-ultimate factor is then applied to the appropriate cumulative value to produce the ultimate losses.

Determining the appropriate factor is complicated and subjective. One way is to project a calendar year payment pattern based on the number and amount of new claims and expected developments on existing claims. Alternatively, a statistical curve, such as the S-curve formula, could be used (see Ollodart, 1997).

Survival Ratio Method: The survival ratio is the carried reserves divided by calendar year payments, thereby measuring the time in years until the reserves are exhausted, providing a rough benchmark statistic. It assumes that future year payments are equal to current calendar year payments.

The survival ratio method works in reverse. Required reserves are estimated using a projected annual payment multiplied by a selected survival ratio. The survival ratio selected is based on the distribution of attachment points, the layers of coverage, and the applicable policy years. It may be higher for excess and umbrella coverage, due to both the relatively low amounts of payments to date and a significant reporting lag.

Ground-Up Methods

While the benchmark methods give basic indications of an insurer's ultimate liabilities, they frequently provide widely divergent results. There may be a need for greater understanding of the types of policies and losses that are contributing to the company's overall position. Methods are needed that allow for the individual characteristics and expert knowledge of the company and provide documentation of the assumptions used in the scenario.

There are two basic types of ground-up methods in use for environmental liabilities. It is important to note that each of these calculates the liabilities on *known* accounts—a provision for *unknown* cases (pure IBNR) will be needed. IBNR is commonly added by estimating the number and cost of new cases or by estimating an IBNR factor.

Policy Exposure Model: Policy exposure models use databases of policy information and loss information to simulate insured losses and apply the policy/reinsurance terms. The process differs for asbestos and pollution, so each is described briefly below.

- *Asbestos:* Insureds are categorized based on a tier structure, as described earlier, to form relatively homogeneous insureds for analysis. The analysis is done on a gross of reinsurance basis, and a range of ceded factors is used to estimate ceded amounts. For the highest tier groups, the insured's policy terms are examined individually, while for the lower tier groups, a small sample group of insureds is used. The policy exposure model projects ground-up loss and ALAE for each insured in the sample and allocates, using the policy terms, the loss and ALAE to policy year in that insured's coverage block. The losses are projected using information about the insured's losses and the actual insured losses. The lower tiers are examined by "burn factors," which represent the percentage of a coverage layer expected to be eroded by asbestos losses.

- *Pollution:* The pollution policy exposure model works similarly. For reported pollution liabilities, the insureds are matched to PRPs on NPL lists or to other known polluters. For PRPs on NPL sites, the site costs are extracted from the NPL site cost database and combined with the PRP's share, policy terms, limits, and other coverage factors. For non-NPL sites, the number and cost of sites are simulated for each insured. Then the insured's policy terms, limits, and other factors are combined to calculate the insured's cost.

Claim Department Method: The claim department method uses the company's environmental claim unit analysts to provide ultimate settlement costs by policy and site for all known exposures. In this way, the analyst can implicitly take into account the coverage issues, the success of litigation relating to the case, the progress of settlement talks with the insured, and the impairment of the limit by nonenvironmental losses. To calculate the net amount, the losses by policy are laid out and the reinsurance terms and limits applied to estimate the ceded.

Issues in Valuing an Insurance Company: Catastrophe Exposures and Modeling

Catastrophe exposures have a huge impact on insurer performance, and thus have generated tremendous attention in the property/casualty insurance industry. The unprecedented economic losses stemming from Hurricane Andrew in 1992 and the Northridge earthquake in 1994 forced the industry to re-examine how to evaluate the impact of natural disasters. The coincidence of these major natural catastrophes with the exponential growth in computing capability has created a niche for catastrophe modelers.

This section discusses recent technology associated with the simulation of natural peril catastrophic risk and the impact that this technology has had on the insurance industry. Specific topics include the evaluation of catastrophic risk, how advanced models are built, what exposure information is required, and how the models are validated. In addition, this section describes the utilization of model results for ratemaking, portfolio management, reinsurance strategies, and marketing purposes, and discusses the impact of catastrophe models on third parties, such as regulators and rating agencies.

The Evolution of Catastrophe Modeling

It is difficult to pinpoint when insurance carriers began to evaluate their losses from natural disasters. Some of the earliest tools were paper maps manufactured by Sanborn Maps Corp., which were used to monitor the density of insured properties in key cities. The intent was to avoid underwriting risks in proximity to existing insureds. The 1960s and 1970s brought about the beginnings of computer-assisted modeling, which motivated insurers to aggregate exposure information. This early methodology applied an approximate damage percentage to the exposures, producing a deterministic loss estimate. This evolution continued with research pioneered by Dr. Don Friedman at the Travelers Insurance Company through their Natural Hazard Research Service (NHRS). Dr. Friedman was the first to compile loss information from hurricanes, and his work continues to be used by modelers.

The deterministic approach was later enhanced by increasing the number of simulated events, and by assigning a probability of occurrence for each event. The first service provider of this technology was Applied Insurance Research (AIR), which provided the results for several thousand events, greatly improving the resolution of analysis. Risk Management Solutions (RMS) followed with a PC-based product for primary insureds. More recent providers, such as EQECAT, have introduced models that simulate many hundreds of thousands of events. These full probabilistic models now allow companies to analyze the impact of changing insurance policy terms and conditions, as well as allow catastrophe claims response teams to handle clients' needs effectively.

Natural Hazards—Modeled and Not Modeled

It is very difficult for models to analyze the full impact of a natural peril. For example, an earthquake model may not include the impact of fire following the quake, or the losses associated with a subsequent tsunami or landslide. While these ancillary perils typically do not generate a major portion of a loss, they need to be considered when estimating a peril's loss potential.

In addition to loss causes that may not be modeled, not all lines of business are handled at this time. For example, losses to mobile assets, such as automobiles, goods in transit, and watercraft, are very difficult to estimate since it is impossible to determine where the assets are located at the time of the event. Workers compensation is another line of business that has not received much attention by the catastrophe modeling industry—and yet, the potential injuries and loss of life from a major earthquake striking a manufacturing facility could be significant.

Exposure Data Requirements

The type of exposure data required by catastrophe models varies. Some require no more than the name of the insurance company, while others can handle over 90 fields of data. Those that simply need the company name rely on A. M. Best premium information to estimate a market share loss. Slightly more sophisticated models rely on insured values by county by line of business. The newest models handle exact street address locations and construction type details. While the examples of data requirements given above seem basic, they do reflect the evolutionary aspect of catastrophe models. Basic data elements are:

- *Geographic location of assets at risk:* address information

- *Structural information of risks:* class of business, type of construction, age of building

- *Values at risk:* total insured value for each coverage type for each location

- *Insurance structure:* deductible and limit information

While the computing technology permits more parameters to be analyzed, the user needs to have confidence that the modeler has the appropriate skill to handle this additional information. The user should also investigate what minimal level of data is appropriate for the company being modeled. A user might find it valuable to experiment with a model by feeding it fictitious data to see whether the model results are intuitive.

Model Analysis

A catastrophe model has three major components:

- *Hazard calculation:* an estimate of the hazard intensity

- *Damage calculation:* an estimate of the ground-up damage, given the hazard

- *Loss calculation:* the loss to the insurer or reinsurer, given the damage estimate

Hazard Module

The hurricane peril will be used as an example, since it receives significant news coverage when an event is forming, and since most individuals can visualize the components of a hurricane. Analogies to other perils will be given as appropriate.

Hurricane models are primarily based on historical records of landfall location and intensity. The historical record used spans roughly one hundred years. While this might appear to be an impressive sample to draw from, the quality of the data is very suspect prior to the 1940s—good information did not become available until the 1960s. Meteorologists developing these models have diligently reviewed the historical data and tried to adjust for any inconsistencies. New information is becoming available from core samples of lake beds, satellites, oceanic recording devices, and aircraft reconnaissance.

The process typically begins by segmenting the coastline of the U.S. into uniformly spaced sections, say 100 miles. These sections are referred to as bins; the size of the bins can vary by modeler. Each historical event is placed into the bin that corresponds to the landfall location. Too small a bin can generate spiking of results as one moves from one bin to a neighboring bin; too large a bin may not reflect the topographical and climatic patterns that influence an area. The meteorological information for each bin is then analyzed to evaluate the range of potential outcomes for that region.

Modelers create a distribution of all the parameters associated with hurricanes in each bin. Distributions for parameters such as forward speed of the hurricane, the radius to maximum winds, and the profile of hurricanes in that area are derived. A stochastic set of hurricanes is then sampled from these distributions. The size of the stochastic set can vary significantly: some modelers use a few thousand events, while others use several hundred thousand.

Hurricane models use these parameters in their meteorological formulas to define the windspeed that exposes a risk. Other factors such as terrain features are modeled to reduce or increase the wind speed. All hurricane models generate a smooth wind field representation of the hurricane. In reality, the chaotic nature of hurricanes generates small tornadoes, which no modeler can currently simulate.

Damage Calculation

Generally speaking, the damage calculation module of a catastrophe model needs two pieces of information: the location of the risk, and the type of structure. The location of the risk is typically referred to as geocoding; the structure description is usually characterized by a vulnerability function. Geocoding will be discussed first, followed by vulnerability.

The location of a risk can be presented in several different ways, such as CRESTA (Catastrophe Risk Evaluating and Standardizing Target Accumulations) zones, counties, zip codes, or street addresses. Geocoding assigns an exact latitude and longitude for the location of the risk. Geocoding is used to determine where the risk is relative to a coastline or earthquake fault, whether it is eligible for a windpool, or to identify what type of soil is beneath the risk.

The damage module also requires information regarding the type of construction for each risk. These construction classes define the vulnerability curves used to estimate the amount of damage at each level of hazard intensity. Vulnerability functions can be derived from three primary sources: empirical claim information, engineering consensus, and engineered simulation.

For some recent catastrophic events, such as the Northridge earthquake or Hurricane Andrew, there is considerable claim data available to modelers. Modelers take the claim information at a given location and overlay the corresponding exposure information in force at the time of the event. It is important that the modeler use all exposure information, and not just the exposure information for those risks that sustained losses. This is necessary in order to capture the portion of risks that might not sustain a loss. The modeler determines what the actual intensity was at the claim location for that event. Estimating the intensity at the location of the claim is very difficult, as there are a limited number of instruments that measure the hazard intensity. Ultimately, the modeler develops a relationship of damage to intensity.

Another approach to developing vulnerability curves is by engineering opinion. For many years, the vulnerability curves used for earthquake were based on Applied Technology Council Report 13 (ATC-13). These vulnerability curves were essentially based on a Delphi method of consensus opinion on the damage likely to be inflicted on a given structure, given the intensity level. This method can be acceptable when there is no actual claim experience. Another approach to developing vulnerability curves, especially for complex commercial structures, is to create computer-aided design (CAD) simulations that analyze the failure mode of a structure given different loads.

Loss Calculation

The final module involves estimating the loss associated with the given level of damage. The commercially available models differ significantly in the variety of insurance and reinsurance structures allowed. Some are very basic and might be too limiting for insurers who underwrite complex commercial risks. The same applies for reinsurance programs: some models do not address reinsurance at all, while others can handle very complex facultative or treaty reinsurance.

Industry-altering events like Northridge and Andrew have spurred the introduction of insurance policies with very high deductibles. For example, the California Earthquake Authority and many other insurers in California now write a policy that requires a 15% deductible. In many hurricane-prone states there now are parametric triggered deductibles that apply once a hurricane reaches a certain windspeed or SSI. These newer policy structures are forcing catastrophe modelers to modify their software to address this evolution.

Model Validation

Due to the rare nature of perils being analyzed, it is virtually impossible to validate a model. A model *can* be reviewed from a scientific perspective to determine whether it has the appropriate components. This is a lengthy and costly exercise with minimal interest to users, since they are not typically interested in whether the model has the latest soil database or the most accurate terrain component, but rather whether the loss estimates are accurate. Models can generate two different types of loss estimates: deterministic and probabilistic. A deterministic analysis involves fixing all the necessary parameters associated with an event and calculating the loss. In this type of analysis, there is no consideration given to the likelihood of the event occurring. A deterministic analysis of an event can be validated—for example, a user can input the exposure that was at risk at the time of Hurricane Andrew, and allow the model to then simulate Hurricane Andrew on that risk portfolio. The typical model output is an expected loss for that event. Models can also provide some confidence bounds around these estimates. A form of validation would then be to compare the actual loss with the modeled loss.

Probabilistic analyses consider many individual events, with each event assigned a likelihood of occurrence. Exceedance probability (EP) curves are derived by aggregating the loss estimates resulting from each event and the likelihood of occurrence. EP curves represent the likelihood that the portfolio will sustain a loss over a certain loss level. For example, if the 1%

exceedance probability for a portfolio is $125 million, this indicates that within the next year, there is only a 1% chance that an event will generate a loss greater then $125 million. It is difficult to validate an EP curve, but it is possible to take actual event losses and compare them with points on the EP curve. If a relatively low severity event generates a loss in excess of high probabilities, then the EP may be understated.

The Florida Commission on Hurricane Loss Projection Methodology (FCHLPM) is the only agency that has undertaken a review of catastrophe models, but it was limited to residential ratemaking for Florida hurricane exposures. The FCHLPM requires that any modeler desiring to have a model considered for ratemaking purposes must provide a comparison of results with respect to the expected annual state-wide loss generated from running all of the historical events that have impacted Florida in the past century. The process begins by inputting a portfolio that represents risks throughout the state. The modelers then run the 57 historical events that have affected Florida in the past 100 years. The average of the expected loss for each event is then compared to the expected loss generated from the probabilistic event set. While this is a fruitful exercise for validating the mean loss, it does not allow for an accurate comparison of the EP curve.

Utilization of Catastrophe Models

Catastrophe models have grown in popularity over the years. Reinsurers and regulators have put pressure on primary insurers to manage and price their risks better. The use of models has evolved from simply being used by corporate risk management departments to becoming a key component in the underwriting process. This evolution includes the expansion of the traditional portfolio management roles to the allocation of capital, reinsurance structuring, claims handling, marketing, dynamic financial analysis, rating agencies, and securitization.

Property lines of business can be greatly enhanced by the use of catastrophe models. If a carrier feels it is necessary to cull risks from a portfolio, models can be used to supplement this decision making process by selecting those risks that generate the highest loss relative to the premium received. In today's merger environment, catastrophe models are incorporated into the decision-making process by determining whether a portfolio under consideration correlates with an existing portfolio.

OPERATING AN INSURANCE COMPANY

Actuaries have had, over time, increasing involvement in various aspects of insurance company operations. Historically, the traditional underwriting function of insurers provided the primary focus of actuarial efforts. Recently, the importance of investment income and asset portfolio management to insurer results has led to actuarial involvement in these areas. Even more recently, other operational developments in the insurance industry have provided opportunities for actuarial input—in some cases, these developments have been spearheaded by actuaries. This section will introduce the reader to several of the issues and recent developments involving the operations of an insurance company. First, some of the types of insurer planning and forecasting processes that casualty actuaries often find useful are described. Next, the process of dynamic financial analysis will be examined. Finally, the evolution and early development of insurance securitization will be discussed.

Planning and Forecasting

This section describes the business planning process, some of the specific forecasting techniques available, and how those techniques might be utilized in the planning effort. Most attention is given to describing several important statistical forecasting techniques—in particular, various types of regression and time series analyses. In addition, scenario analysis and stochastic simulation are described, and their differences discussed.

Planning

"Planning" is the process by which management makes operational and financial decisions that affect the company's future. Ideally, a plan will be responsive to changes in the company's operating environment. Specifically, planning involves the following steps.

- *Determine the corporation's objectives.* A company's short-term and long-term objectives are a function of the firm's particular situation, including its management, products, and operating environment. Objectives may relate to the company's solvency, revenues, profitability, or other measures of performance.

- *Identify possible alternative plans and actions.* A company may entertain a variety of possible plans that are anticipated to satisfy, probably to varying degrees, the objectives of the organization. The strategic impact of each plan is considered and evaluated.

- *Evaluate alternatives and select a plan.* The company's management achieves a consensus regarding which plan is optimal. This step relies on the forecasting process (discussed below) to identify the potential financial consequences of the various courses of action. A variety of metrics that measure the anticipated performance of each alternative plan may be considered. Possible plan outcomes may also be measured against the projected consequences of maintaining the status quo.

- *Implement the plan.* For a plan to be successful, it must be coordinated and carried out at all appropriate levels of the organization.

- *Monitor the effectiveness of the plan.* Appropriate databases and information systems must exist in order for the plan to be adequately monitored and evaluated. Adjustments may be made to the plan as necessary.

Like any other type of business, insurers can improve their decision-making through appropriate planning and forecasting. Because of the need to project the future financial consequences of different action plans, the input of actuaries is important. In some insurance companies, actuaries have significant responsibility for long-range forecasting, and thus they can have a large impact on the planning process. At a minimum, the actuary would provide information about such critical items as loss reserves and rate adequacy.

Lowe (1985) mentions two categories of property/casualty insurance company planning activities: financial planning (typically resulting in a forecast of financial results over a 1- to 5-year time horizon), and operation planning. According to Lowe, the primary goal of insurance company planning is to determine estimates of the insurance cash flows. This requires consideration of, and appropriate data regarding, the insurance, investment, and financial/accounting processes. Analysis involving the interaction of these areas is a cornerstone of, for example, dynamic financial analysis.

One of the corollary benefits of a thorough planning process is the opportunity it presents for the various functional areas and departments within an insurance company to communicate with each other. The development of goals, consideration of alternative courses of action, and implementation of a final plan all potentially involve interaction between several departments and divisions: actuarial, underwriting, marketing, financial, accounting, claims, and information systems.

Forecasting

In order to create and evaluate plans, companies must be able to forecast the potential future consequences of current actions. The development of future financial scenarios and the valuation of contingencies are inherently quantitative processes, and thus might logically be considered to be, at least in part, actuarial functions. There are a variety of mathematical forecasting techniques available to the actuary. One way to categorize these techniques is as either regression or time series approaches. Regression techniques involve the relationships between different variables, and include simple regression and multiple regression. Time series techniques involve characterizing the movement of a variable or variables through time.

Simple Regression

In simple linear regression, two variables have the following functional relationship:

$$y_t = b_0 + b_1 x_1$$

where

y_t = the observation of the "dependent" variable at time t,

x_t = the observation of the "independent" variable at time t,

b_0 = the intercept of the relationship between variables x and y, and

b_1 = the slope of the relationship between variables x and y.

Historical data are used to parameterize the model. Typically, the estimates of the b coefficients are chosen to minimize the sum of the squared differences between the actual and the fitted dependent variable data. This is referred to as a least squares estimate. The formulas for the b coefficients in a simple regression framework, when determined according to least squares, have straightforward forms:

$$b_1 = \frac{\sum (y_i - \bar{y})(x_i - \bar{x})}{\sum (x_i - \bar{x})^2} \quad \text{and} \quad b_0 = \bar{y} - b_1 \bar{x}$$

Determining the "quality" of a regression, i.e., it's "appropriateness," can involve several more or less sophisticated techniques. Two basic and common statistical measures of a regression's appropriateness are the following:

- The coefficient of determination (R^2) indicates the proportion of the overall variability in the dependent variable y, which is explained by the regression relationship. R^2 values range from zero to one. All else equal, an R^2 value closer to 1.0 indicates a better explanatory relationship. R^2 can be calculated according to the following formula:

$$R^2 = \frac{\sum (\hat{y}_i - \bar{y})^2}{\sum (y_i - \bar{y})^2}$$

- The t-statistic of each coefficient in the regression equation indicates the statistical significance of the constant or the independent variable x in explaining the values of the dependent variable. The t-statistic, calculated as the value of the estimated regression coefficient divided by its standard error, identifies the number of standard errors the coefficient value is removed from zero. Relatively high absolute values of the t-statistic suggest greater significance, with the specific "threshold" depending upon the degree of statistical confidence desired.

Multiple Regression

When there are multiple independent or explanatory variables, a linear relationship with the dependent variable might be specified as follows:

$$y_t = b_0 + b_1 x_{1,t} + b_2 x_{2,t} + \cdots + b_n x_{n,t}$$

where

y_t = the observation of the "dependent" variable at time t,

$x_{j,t}$ = the observation of the jth "independent" variable at time t,

b_0 = the intercept of the relationship between the x_j variables and y, and

b_j = the coefficient specifying the relationship between the x_j variable and y.

This framework is referred to as multiple linear regression. Again, the estimates of the *b* coefficients are based on historical data, and are typically chosen to minimize the sum of the squared differences between the actual and the fitted dependent variable data. Approaches similar to those mentioned for simple regression above can also be used to evaluate the appropriateness of any given hypothesized multiple linear regression relationship. However, the analysis is more complex. For example, "multicollinearity," which involves two or more of the independent variables being correlated, can cause difficulties in performing and interpreting a multiple regression analysis. Such problems, once identified, can often be dealt with through more sophisticated statistical techniques or adjustments.

For both simple and multiple regression, transforming the variables prior to implementing the model might provide a better fit. For example, natural logs of variables are sometimes taken prior to fitting a regression. Another adjustment might involve using differences between successive values of variables, instead of the variable values themselves. From this perspective, regression analysis is often art as well as science.

Time Series Methods

Time series techniques are based on the underlying assumption that patterns exist in the historical data of a variable, and those patterns can be analyzed to determine the manner in which they will recur over time. Common versions of such patterns can be categorized (e.g., Wheelwright and Makridakis, 1985) as trend (general increases or decreases over time), horizontal (involving no trend), cyclical, or seasonal patterns. Where there are multiple patterns in a single time series, a variety of decomposition techniques can be employed to help identify the separate components.

Time series techniques vary significantly according to their level of sophistication. For example, a basic business forecasting technique is the *simple moving average*, in which the average of

n past values of a variable is used as the forecast of the next value. As actual new data emerges, the average is recalculated to incorporate the new information (the number of past values, n, is judgmental and kept constant). Essentially, each new forecast represents an adjustment of the prior forecast in light of the new data that has emerged; the larger the value of n, the smaller the periodic adjustments, resulting in greater "smoothness." Another basic time series technique is *exponential smoothing*, which—in contrast to the simple moving average, which produces a forecast by weighting the n past values equally—applies greater weight to the more recent data, and less weight to the older information. In practice, this takes the form

$$\hat{y}_{t+1} = \alpha y_t + (1 - \alpha)\hat{y}_t$$

where each forecast is considered a weighted average of the most recent data and the previous forecast (which in turn is a function of the prior data).

More generally, time series models can be categorized according to whether the current value of the time series variable is specified as a function of the prior values of the variable, of the prior residuals, or a combination of these two. An *autoregressive* (AR) model of degree n is characterized by the following equation:

$$y_t = b_1 y_{t-1} + b_2 y_{t-2} + \cdots + b_n y_{t-n} + e_t$$

where e_t is an error term. This is a regression equation, but the independent variables are previous values of the dependent variable. A *moving average* (MA) model has the following form:

$$y_t = e_t + c_1 e_{t-1} + c_2 e_{t-2} + \cdots + c_n e_{t-n}$$

where the e_{t-j} terms represent the prior residuals. This model assumes that values of the dependent variable are a function of the time series of error terms. An *autoregressive moving average*

(ARMA) model combines these two time series models:

$$y_t = b_1 y_{t-1} + b_2 y_{t-2} + \cdots + b_n y_{t-n} + e_t + c_1 e_{t-1} + c_2 e_{t-2} + \cdots + c_n e_{t-n}$$

An advanced time series framework that has become very popular is known as the Box–Jenkins approach. While there has been a great deal of development and sophistication in this area, essentially the Box–Jenkins approach involves a multistep process. First, an appropriate model (which could be AR, ARMA, etc.) is tentatively identified. Next, the model is fit to historical data in order to evaluate its adequacy (the model is discarded if found to be inappropriate, and another form is hypothesized). Finally, once an appropriate model has been determined, a forecast is developed.

Econometric Models

Regression and time series forecasting models can be employed at a variety of levels. When a system of multiple equations, involving several interconnected variables, is needed in order to quantify an economic or financial system, the framework may be termed an *econometric model*. In the type of pure multiple regression framework discussed above, each of the independent variables is assumed to be exogenous (originating externally). In an econometric model, economic reality can be served by allowing for the possibility that one or more of the independent variables, in one or more of the multiple equations that comprise the system, is itself endogenous or dependent. As mentioned in Wheelwright and Makridakis (1985), "The basic premise of econometric modeling is that everything in the real world depends upon everything else."

Much of the development of an econometric model is similar to the work performed in a regression analysis. However, the process can be significantly complicated by the fact that the system involves interactions between many variables. For example,

the variable interrelationships must be accounted for when specifying the functional forms of the equations, and the parameters
of each equation must now be estimated simultaneously. The potential size and complexity—both economic and statistical—of
these models has led to the creation of several specialized firms
that provide forecasting services for a fee. Several such firms are
mentioned in the *Data Sources* section later in this chapter.

Dynamic Financial Analysis

Dynamic financial analysis (DFA) is a recent and important extension of planning and forecasting in the insurance industry. In this section, the DFA process is defined and described, and the various risk factors underlying an insurance
company's operations—both underwriting and investment—are
summarized. The end uses of DFA models are also discussed.

Definition and Perspective

DFA can mean very different things to different people. Some
might use the DFA label only when, for example, a simulation
program uses sophisticated interest rate, asset, and liability models, and produces pro forma financial statements; others characterize DFA much more broadly, almost to the point where any
consideration of financial or economic issues in an insurance
context is DFA. Despite these different characterizations, DFA
is actually a process that can be fairly accurately described by its
name. By examining each of the three words "dynamic financial
analysis," we can get a good idea of the essence of DFA.

DFA is "dynamic" in the sense that it recognizes that the various factors to which the insurance process is subject are variable
and stochastic, as opposed to fixed and deterministic. It is important that actuaries go beyond the analysis of "static" processes,
and recognize the stochastic nature of many of the insurer's underlying asset and liability processes. In this way, the uncertainty
inherent in these processes can be recognized.

The word "financial" indicates an important recent development in property/casualty actuarial work: the recognition that *both* the financial and the underwriting operations of an insurer need to be considered. Historically, property/casualty actuaries have placed far greater emphasis on the liability side of the balance sheet and the traditional insurance operations of the insurer. However, an actuary's skills can also be effectively applied to the asset and financial areas, and, in fact, a thorough financial analysis of an insurer must recognize the *interaction* between assets and liabilities. This interaction is, to some degree, a product of underlying economic and financial processes common to both assets and liabilities.

The final word in "DFA," "analysis," indicates that the DFA process involves an examination of the various economic, financial, and insurance relationships, and suggests the development and use of a "model" to perform this examination. A quote from a monograph by William S. Jewell (1983) nicely describes the notion of a model:

> "A model is a set of verifiable mathematical relationships or logical procedures which is used to represent observed, real-world phenomena, to communicate alternative hypotheses about the causes of the phenomena, and to predict future behavior of the phenomena for purposes of decision-making."

This sentence identifies the essence of what actuaries have been attempting in their recent development of DFA models.

A nice summary of DFA is provided in the Casualty Actuarial Society's *Dynamic Financial Analysis Handbook* (Valuation and Financial Analysis Committee, 1996):

> "Dynamic Financial Analysis is the process by which an actuary analyzes the financial condition of an insurance enterprise. Financial condition refers to the ability of the company's capital and surplus to adequately

> support the company's future operations through an unknown future environment.... The process of DFA involves testing a number of adverse and favorable scenarios regarding an insurance company's operations. DFA assesses the reaction of the company's surplus to the various selected scenarios."

Note that, given the reference in this quote to "the company's future operations," DFA recognizes the "going concern" nature of an insurer.

DFA, then, involves evaluating distributions of outcomes resulting from a variety of scenarios. Those outcomes that are classified as "unacceptable"—e.g., the company becomes insolvent, the business is not sufficiently profitable—can then be reviewed to determine the causes of, or primary factors relating to, that particular outcome. If necessary, a change in the operations of the company can be implemented in the model; the analysis can then be performed again, and the impact evaluated.

Placed in a broader perspective, and consistent with the description of the general planning process discussed in a preceding section of this chapter, DFA is a critical component of the overall financial risk management process, the steps of which include the following.

- *Determine the corporation's objectives*—e.g., profitability, solvency

- *Identify the risk exposure*—e.g., interest rate risk, catastrophe potential

- *Quantify the exposure*—e.g., measure volatility

- *Assess the impact of the exposure on the company*—this is the primary role undertaken by DFA

- *Examine alternative financial risk management tools*—e.g., reinsurance, financial and insurance derivatives

- *Select the appropriate tools and approach*

- *Implement and monitor the financial risk management program*

Viewed from this broad perspective, dynamic financial analysis is analogous to similar efforts in other disciplines and industries. Recent articles in the popular press have introduced the public to this emerging brand of quantitative analysis. For example (Valdmanis, 1999):

> "...real option valuation, or ROV, could quickly become the new standard for valuing risky ventures that exist not just in M&A activity, but also in making billion-dollar bets from setting up oil fields in Azerbaijan to developing cancer cures... (ROV is) a 'dynamic road map,' outlining the future risks of big projects and strategic investments and how management might adjust to them."

This description of "real option valuation" sounds analogous to the dynamic financial analysis process that has recently emerged in the property/casualty insurance industry. Actually, DFA does not merely have close relatives in other industries—its predecessors came from another financial service industry. Banks began to develop DFA-type models in response to the U.S. savings and loan crisis, which largely resulted from increases in interest rates during the late 1970s and early 1980s. The objectives of the banking models were to quantify risk and evaluate the impact on S&Ls of various economic events. Later, the essence of this analytical framework spread to other financial services, including insurance.

DFA Modeling

Although its essential goals are straightforward, the implementation of the DFA process can take a variety of forms. Broadly speaking, there are two approaches to DFA from a modeling perspective: scenario testing or stochastic simulation. Scenario testing involves the projection of financial and operating results under certain specified conditions. For example, the impact on the company of a catastrophic loss or a significant movement in interest rate levels can be evaluated, either in isolation or in combinations of events. Such analyses are often used for cash flow or stress testing, and may be required in certain regulatory environments (e.g., New York life insurance regulations). The disadvantages of scenario testing involve the potential incompleteness of the specified scenarios, and the lack of probabilities associated with the scenarios.

These problems can be addressed by incorporating stochastic simulation into the DFA model. In this framework, entire probability distributions are specified, to the extent possible, for each of the stochastic variables underlying an insurance company's results. A large number of outcomes are generated by randomly selecting values from each of these probability distributions, and allowing the model to determine the interactions of the variables. The collection of simulated outcomes is then analyzed to assess the proportion of "acceptable" versus "unacceptable" outcomes. In a good stochastic simulation dynamic financial analysis model, the unacceptable outcomes can then be analyzed to determine the primary cause(s) of those outcomes. Such an analysis might suggest operational changes that the company can consider to alleviate the unacceptable results.

Ultimately, regardless of the specific form, a DFA model must consider and evaluate the types of risks, both underwriting and economic/financial, that can impact the results of an insurance company. There are a variety of ways to classify these risks. For example, risks can be classified on a balance sheet basis, according to whether each risk is associated with assets or with liabilities. On the other hand, risks can be categorized on an operating basis, as relating either to the underwriting operations or to the investment operations of an insurer. Regardless of the classification scheme, there are a number of variables that can impact an insurer's operating situation. Specifically, some of the important variables in a dynamic financial analysis model might include the following.

1. Financial variables

     a. ***Interest rates:*** Interest rates are one of the fundamental variables in the economy. The simulation of future interest rates is critical for a DFA model because of their potential impact on, and correlation with, other financial and underwriting variables. For example, there is a clear and well-established empirical relationship between interest rates and inflation. In addition, interest rate movements can affect stock market performance and other financial variables. But interest rates might also have an impact on some insurance-specific processes, for example the underwriting cycle. Some of the specific interest rate characteristics that a DFA model should consider include:

        i. *Short-term/"risk-free" rate:* The interest rate model employed must consider issues such as possible reversion to a mean level over time (and what that long-run mean level is), as well as the nature of the volatility of the rate.

       ii. *Term structure:* Since insurers invest in bonds of different maturity lengths, it is important to analyze the impact of simulated movements in the yield curve.

      iii. *Default premium:* Different yields apply to financial instruments with different default characteristics. For example, corporate bonds typically offer higher yields than government bonds of the same maturity, because of the additional risk of default. The difference between the yields or interest rates applicable to these two instruments can be termed the "default premium."

b. *Inflation:* General inflation is correlated with interest rates. In turn, claim inflation by line of business is to some degree related to overall inflation, although each line of business has its indigenous characteristics. This variable is important, because it impacts the ultimate costs of future claim payouts.

c. *Equity market performance:* Although most property/casualty insurer assets are invested in bonds, insurers also invest significant monies in the equity markets. Simulations of overall investment performance should thus include an equity market component (which, again, is likely to be related to interest rate movements).

d. *Mortgage prepayment patterns:* The incidence of mortgage prepayments depends largely on the path that interest rates take over time. This variable is important since it affects the values of mortgage-backed securities.

2. **Underwriting variables**

a. *Non-catastrophe losses:* An insurer's future losses and loss adjustment expenses must be simulated, either on an aggregate basis, or as a compound frequency-severity process.

b. *Catastrophe losses:* One of the most significant insurance-specific risk factors in determining insurer results is the incidence of natural catastrophes. Because of their significance, and the fact that such large losses are often treated separately for reinsurance purposes, a DFA model might simulate catastrophes separately from non-catastrophe losses.

c. *Exposures:* The number of exposure units to be insured by the company must be projected. This is an important component of the loss simulations, and will be related to, among other things, the company's growth targets and to overall insurance market conditions.

d. *Expenses:* In addition to losses, the writing of insurance business involves incurring expenses, which may be stochastic to a certain degree.

e. *Underwriting cycle:* The profitability of an insurer depends, in part, on the general economic and industry conditions within which the company does business. The rate level at which the company can write business is a function of the position of the industry along the underwriting cycle. A DFA model could include a variable that simulates the possible future implications of the industry's movement from one point on the underwriting cycle to another.

f. *Loss reserve development:* One of the inputs to a DFA model would be the loss and loss adjustment expense reserves held by the company at the beginning of the time period being simulated. Reserve redundancies or deficiencies in that initial reserve can be simulated according to the run-off of those liabilities.

g. *Jurisdictional risk:* Insurers writing in different jurisdictions are exposed to different judicial and regulatory environments. Jurisdictional risk reflects, for example, the delays in implementing rate increases or decreases, any limitations imposed by the jurisdiction on such rate changes, and possible mandated premium rebates.

h. *Payment patterns:* There is risk associated with the speed with which losses are paid. Payments must be simulated in order to properly project the future cash flows of the insurer.

In addition to these stochastic variables, the following elements of an insurer's operations should be considered by a DFA model.

1. **Rates:** As alluded to above, future rates charged by the insurer will be a function of a number of factors, e.g., historical and emerging loss experience, the position in the underwriting cycle, competitive forces, and the specific jurisdictional and regulatory forces involved.

2. **Ceded reinsurance:** A DFA model should be capable of accommodating common types of reinsurance— proportional, working excess, catastrophe, and aggregate/stop-loss. The specific approach to programming reinsurance recoveries depends upon the manner in which direct losses are simulated, i.e., whether losses are simulated on an individual basis, an aggregate basis, or some combination. In addition, a DFA model should be capable of simulating the degree to which the insurer's ceded reinsurance is unrecoverable, a variable that might be a function of general economic conditions such as the underwriting cycle and interest rates.

3. **Taxes:** In addition to projecting statutory and market values, financial statements consistent with the prevailing tax code also need to be projected by a DFA model, in order to simulate future cash flows associated with taxes properly.

Outputs and Uses of DFA Models

Depending upon the size and sophistication of the model, a variety of useful outputs can be generated by the DFA process. Possible outputs, reflecting simulated results over a multiyear projection period, and for a given operating scenario, include:

- Pro forma balance sheets and income statements (statutory or market value)

FIGURE 10.1

DISTRIBUTION OF 5-YEAR PROJECTED SURPLUS

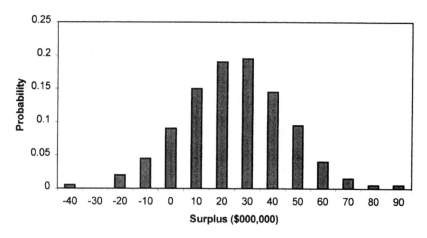

- Loss ratio reports

    — Aggregate versus line of business

    — Direct versus net of reinsurance

- Results of IRIS or other regulatory tests

- Probabilities of ruin at various critical likelihood levels

- Histograms of future surplus (statutory or market value) that display the distribution of the simulated trials

The last type of output is a useful management tool, as it shows graphically the likelihood of unacceptable results. A hypothetical example of such a chart, showing the relative probabilities of various levels of simulated company surplus five years into the future, is shown in Figure 10.1. Comparison of histograms representing simulations under different operating assumptions—e.g., different ceded reinsurance programs—can demonstrate the impact of different management decisions.

The uses of a DFA model and its output include those that can aid internal decision-making, and those that involve parties external to the insurer. Internal uses include general strategic planning, analyzing valuation and merger and acquisition activity, asset-liability management, reinsurance planning, and analyzing competitors' situations. External uses include projecting company ratings, supporting discussions with regulators (e.g., regarding solvency or risk-based capital considerations), and communicating with financial markets.

Insurance Securitization

An understanding of how insurers manage their financial and underwriting risks is becoming critical for actuaries. The potential use of a recent development—securitized insurance products and techniques—should be a consideration with regard to any insurer's operations. In this section, the insurance securitization process is defined, and related to its noninsurance forebears. The evolution of insurance securitization is then presented through a description of the various instruments that have been developed. Examples of the more important types of securitized products are provided, with emphasis on their general structure and format.

Definition of Insurance Securitization

"Insurance securitization" can be considered to involve two elements: the *transformation* of underwriting cash flows into tradable financial securities, and the *transfer* of underwriting risks to the capital markets through the trading of those securities. *Transformation* essentially corresponds to "financial engineering," which basically involves the bundling and/or unbundling of cash flows into new and different financial securities. This has become a common practice in the financial markets— examples include Treasury strips or "zero-coupon bonds" (that essentially involve separating the principal and coupon payments in a Treasury bond, which are then sold as single-cash-flow securities), and collateralized mortgage obligations (involving the unbundling and rebundling of cash flows on mortgages). The second element of insurance securitization, *transfer*, involves the ultimate recipient of the traded risks. Instead of an insurance company transferring its underwriting risk to a reinsurer within the insurance industry, securitized insurance risk is transferred to the broader capital markets (which might well include other insurers and reinsurers, as well as banks, pension funds, and mutual funds, among others). This is typically accomplished by the buying and selling of financial instruments whose cash flows (payoffs) are contingent upon underwriting experience.

Securitization in Historical Perspective

It is instructive to consider "insurance securitization" not in isolation, but rather within the broad context of "financial risk management" (FRM). By understanding the history of securitization in general, and by becoming familiar with FRM concepts and terminology, including the types of derivative securities that have been imported into the insurance industry, actuaries will be better prepared to implement and deal with securitized insurance products in a broad financial and corporate context.

Although securitization first came to the significant attention of the insurance industry in the 1990s, the process has existed in the general financial markets since the late 1970s. The original securitization efforts grew out of a response by the financial markets to a funding shortfall in the home mortgage market. In particular, excess demand for mortgages led the financial markets to explore alternatives for more efficiently moving funds from the suppliers in the capital markets to the mortgage demanders. These efforts resulted in the development of the mortgage securitization industry, in which the interest and principal payments on groups of individual mortgages formed the backing for the cash flows of newly created, tradable, and more liquid securities. The development of these securities and this market facilitated the transferring of funds from investors to borrowers. The first mortgage securitization product was issued in 1977, by the Bank of America. Since that time, the securitization market has grown significantly—with some help from changes in the tax code and improvements in investment technology. Some of the benefits of the securitization process include enhanced *liquidity*, more readily determinable *market values*, and more efficient and *lower cost* ways of moving funds from the capital markets to those entities needing the funds.

The Evolution of Insurance Securitization

Insurance derivatives—specifically, reinsurance futures— were first speculated upon even before the word "securitization" was initially used by the financial markets (Goshay and Sandor (1973)). The later emergence of actual securitized insurance products represented an evolutionary step in the general securitization process. It is interesting, however, to note some of the differences between early insurance securitization efforts and the other prior securitized products. For example, the existence of a "funding shortfall" in the mortgage financing market was the primary motivation for the initial development of securitization. Conversely, insurance securitization initially evolved during a period of time generally characterized by a soft insurance market, in which many kinds of insurance were available and even relatively inexpensive. Another interesting issue involves the types of things that have been securitized. Historically, the assets that have been most successfully securitized have been those involving significant volume and that are in some sense relatively "stable"—e.g., mortgage loans, auto loans, and credit card receivables. Conversely again, the property/casualty insurance industry initially concentrated its securitization efforts primarily upon an extremely volatile and unpredictable process: natural catastrophes.

Although it had been more than two decades since insurance derivatives were first suggested, only in the mid-1990s did a market begin to develop for such products. There appear to have been three primary factors affecting the timing of the insurance securitization industry's emergence:

- The significant *catastrophe losses* in the first half of the 1990s, particularly Hurricane Andrew in 1992 and the Northridge earthquake in 1994, which caused the insurance industry to reassess its exposure to catastrophe risk.

- The *maturation of the capital markets* and the continued development of new financial instruments aimed at achieving high yields and/or additional diversification.

- The changing *structure of the insurance industry* in the 1990s, which involved a number of mergers, acquisitions, and consolidations. This increased the impact of Wall Street and financial considerations on the insurance industry.

These trends led to two commonly accepted reasons for the development of securitized insurance products: (1) *capacity* considerations, which focus on the ability of the capital markets, due to their enormous size, to handle potentially large catastrophic events that might otherwise impair the insurance industry; and (2) *investment* considerations, which suggest that investing in instruments with cash flows related to catastrophe exposures would have diversification benefits, since they are uncorrelated with movements in other capital market instruments. While both of these reasons are arguable, they are commonly given as reasons for the development of the insurance securitization industry.

Types of Securitized Insurance Products

There are several ways to categorize the many types of insurance-related instruments that exist or have been proposed. One approach is as follows:

- Those that *transfer risk*. These techniques include *reinsurance, swaps, catastrophe bonds*, and *exchange-trade derivatives*, and may involve the transfer of risk to either another insurer/reinsurer or to the capital markets.

- Those that provide *contingent funding*. Such techniques include a *line of credit* (which involves the right to borrow), *contingent surplus notes* (which represent an option to borrow contingent upon the occurrence of an event), and *catastrophe equity puts*. Several of these categories of instruments are described in more detail below.

Exchange-Traded Derivatives

During the 1990s, two exchanges attempted to develop and trade insurance derivatives: the Chicago Board of Trade (CBOT) and the Bermuda Commodities Exchange (BCOE). The CBOT derivatives underwent a significant evolutionary process over a period of years [see, for example, D'Arcy, Gorvett, and France (1999)], culminating on September 29, 1995, when catastrophe option spreads were introduced [see Chicago Board of Trade (1995) for extensive and detailed descriptions.] These instruments were European cash options (settled in cash at the expiration of the contract), with either quarterly or annual calendar loss periods, with values based upon estimates of aggregate industry catastrophic losses made daily by *Property Claim Services* (PCS). These estimates were expressed in the form of an index, with each index point being equivalent to $100 million of aggregate industry catastrophe losses and having a cash value (in terms of the settlement value of the option) of $200 per index point. An option had value when the aggregate industry catastrophe losses exceeded the option's "strike value." Nine different geographical instruments were available, allowing a purchaser either to speculate upon or hedge exposures with respect to different geographic catastrophe exposures. Essentially, the CBOT option spreads worked much like excess reinsurance, where the retention and reinsurance limit were expressed in index points and, hence, in terms of aggregate industry catastrophe losses.

An example demonstrates the analogy with excess reinsurance. Suppose a December 30/50 Texas call option spread has been purchased by an insurer that has property exposure in that state. The insurer's purpose might be to hedge the catastrophe risk associated with that property exposure. Essentially, this option spread is analogous to a \$2 billion in excess of \$3 billion layer on fourth-quarter aggregate industry catastrophe losses in Texas, since

$$[50 - 30] \times \$100 \text{ million} = \$2 \text{ billion,} \qquad \text{and}$$

$$30 \times \$100 \text{ million} = \$3 \text{ billion.}$$

(Financially, the excess nature of the spread is accomplished by buying a call option with an exercise price of 30, and selling an option with an exercise price of 50. This buy-sell combination is built into the spread.) If, for example, fourth-quarter Texas catastrophe losses to the industry amount to \$4.5 billion, the company that purchased this option spread would receive \$3,000:

$$[(\$4.5 \text{ billion}/\$100 \text{ million}) - 30] \times \$200 = \$3,000.$$

The Bermuda Commodities Exchange also traded insurance derivatives. Although the basic concept underlying these options was the same as that of the CBOT PCS options, there were some important differences. The BCOE option index values were based on a Guy Carpenter Catastrophe Index [see, for example, Major (1997)], which was in the form of a loss-to-value (or damage) ratio (paid homeowners losses divided by housing values). Values for the index were available as finely as by zip code, and updated quarterly. Three different types of catastrophe options were available: single loss (largest catastrophic event during a period), secondary loss (the second largest event), and aggregate cat. The risk periods underlying the options were semi-annual: either the first-half or the second-half of the calendar year. The BCOE options were "binary options," i.e., the options paid off either \$0 or \$5,000 at expiration; there was no intermediate value possible (as there was with CBOT option spreads).

Risk Exchanges

While there are many forms that a financial "swap" can take, one example of the swap concept in the insurance industry is the risk exchange. Catastrophe Risk Exchange (CATEX) New York is a computer-based exchange that was designed to allow subscribers to swap their catastrophe exposures. Thus, subscribers can adjust their risk distribution profiles—by geographic location and/or by property type—by trading written exposures. Risks available for trade can be "advertised" on the electronic system, where trades can be negotiated and completed. Since its inception, CATEX has expanded into a facilitator for commercial insurance and reinsurance. Another risk exchange is CATEX Bermuda, which is a joint venture between CATEX and the Bermuda Stock Exchange.

Catastrophe Equity Puts

Catastrophe equity puts are a form of contingent financing. A financial put is the right (but not the obligation) to sell an asset at a pre-specified price (the "exercise" price), on a certain date or dates, or during a certain period of time. Catastrophe equity puts are agreements whereby an insurer, in the event of a catastrophe, has the right to sell equity (usually preferred stock) to investors at a pre-specified price. This right to sell equity is triggered by a specified catastrophic event, for example when catastrophe losses exceed a certain threshold (e.g., when the insurer's catastrophe reinsurance protection has been exhausted). This contingent infusion of equity allows the insurer to shore up its balance sheet by replacing equity immediately after a catastrophe.

Catastrophe Bonds

Of the various forms of insurance securitization introduced in the 1990s, perhaps the greatest amount of activity and publicity involved catastrophe bonds. In general, a catastrophe bond is a debt issue by an insurance company. The debt is similar to a traditional corporate bond, except that, in certain circumstances, the insurer is relieved (fully or partially) from the obligation of making interest and/or principal payments to the bondholders. Circumstances providing such relief involve the occurrence of a catastrophic event. Thus, the essential concept is that, in the

event of a catastrophe, one type of debt—payments of catastrophic losses to policyholders—is at least partially offset by the
diminishment of payment obligations by the insurer under the
bond issue.

To a large extent, a securitized product's ability to hedge
catastrophe risk depends on the type of "trigger" used. Here,
"trigger" refers to the "event" that causes an adjustment to the
payoff of the instrument. With a *direct trigger* the contingency
upon which the payoff of the instrument depends is based on the
company's losses. Under an *industry trigger* the payoffs depend
upon overall industry loss experience, as reflected by an index.
Under an *event trigger* the payoffs depend upon the occurrence
of a defined event, such as an earthquake that exceeds a certain
measure on an intensity scale.

A common practice in capital markets is to subdivide a series
of cash flows into different segments, called "tranches." These
tranches differ based upon maturity, riskiness, or other characteristics. A catastrophe bond may have several tranches. From
the standpoint of an investor in such bonds, depending upon the
tranche invested in, there is the risk of losing some or all of the
principal invested, and/or the risk of diminished or lost interest
payments. Very often, there is a tranche in which both principal
and interest is at risk (and the coupon rate on that tranche reflects
this large amount of risk and is, appropriately, relatively high).
In addition, there is often a tranche in which at least part of the
principal is "protected" or "defeased." This means that, when the
bonds are issued, some of the proceeds are placed in a protected
account that funds the repayment of the principal. Often, there is
a provision whereby, in the event of a catastrophe, the protected
principal is repaid over an extended period of time.

The issuance structure underlying the initial catastrophe bonds
has typically involved the insurer setting up a Special Purpose
Vehicle (SPV) to act as an "intermediary" between the company
and the capital markets. Generally, the SPV has been an offshore

reinsurer (this structure is used to maintain favorable tax and accounting treatments). The SPV issues a reinsurance contract to the company; in turn, the company issues bonds to the capital markets through the SPV. The SPV pays the cash flows on the bonds (and funds the reinsurance protection) from the reinsurance premiums paid by the company, and from the invested bond proceeds.

The June 1997 USAA catastrophe bond, one of the earlier of such bonds issued, can be used as an example. This bond was originally intended to be a $150 million offering, but was significantly over-subscribed, and USAA ended up issuing, through a Cayman Islands SPV called Residential Re, $477 million of catastrophe bonds. These one-year bonds were sold to 62 investors; several investment banks were involved in the advising and issuing process. Of the $477 million in proceeds, $400 million represented a reinsurance cover provided by Residential Re; the other $77 million was placed in a defeasance account to fund the principal repayment on tranche A-1 (see below). The reinsurance, in effect, represented a layer equal to 80% of $500 million in excess of $1 billion on USAA's hurricane losses. Thus, the bond involved a "direct" trigger: principal and/or interest payments would be affected in the event of a hurricane loss to the company in excess of $1 billion.

The USAA bond issue involved two tranches: tranche A-1, in which only interest (but not principal) was at risk from the standpoint of the investor; and tranche A-2, in which both principal and interest were at risk. Tranche A-1, which received an investment rating of AAA (the highest available), had its principal protected via a defeasement account. In the event of a catastrophic loss, principal repayment was guaranteed for tranche A-1 investors, but an extension of as much as ten years to repay the principal would be permitted. Tranche A-2, which was rated BB (below investment grade), was exposed to the risk of both lost interest and lost principal, and thus was riskier than tranche A-1. This relative riskiness between the two tranches was reflected in their respective coupon rates. The USAA bonds were floating-rate bonds that paid a specified risk premium in excess of the London Interbank Offer Rate (LIBOR). The risk premium for tranche A-2 was more than twice that for tranche A-1.

Other significant early insurance securitization successes included a Swiss Re (1997) bond involving an industry trigger on a California earthquake, and a Tokio Marine & Fire (1997) bond involving an "event" trigger (based on the Japanese Meteorological Association scale) on a Tokyo earthquake. A review of these and other successful bond offerings reveals certain traits common to many or most of them: they typically involved highly volatile catastrophic risk, relatively high levels of protection, relatively short maturities (except, for example, the Japanese issues), some protection of principal, and high coupon rates. However, with respect to the last trait, subsequent bond issues (e.g., the USAA bond issues in 1998 through 2000) suggested that coupon rates were diminishing, perhaps reflecting growing comfort with the mechanism and a lower "newness premium."

The Outlook for Insurance Securitization

The insurance securitization industry developed quickly during the late 1990s. As the industry and techniques evolve and mature, the future success and development of insurance securitization is a function of a number of issues and questions:

- The *relative costs* of traditional insurance and reinsurance products on the one hand, and of securitized instruments on the other. The former involves the state of the market at any given time, as well as supply-demand pressures stemming from competitive and alternative products. The latter includes, for example, with respect to catastrophe bonds, the costs of setting up a special purpose vehicle, the level of coupon rates, and the like.

- Advances in *technology*, and the acceptance of that technology by both insurers and the capital markets for quantifying risks.

- Potential *efficiencies* in the insurance intermediation process that might be introduced through cooperation with the capital markets.

- The *types of risks* securitized—e.g., catastrophe risks versus more traditional insurance lines.

- The *legal status* of securitized insurance instruments. Each jurisdiction will need to come to terms with the question of whether investors in insurance securitization products are engaging in the business of insurance.

- The *tax and accounting implications* of the various instruments.

What forms will insurer financial risk management take in the future? There is a wide range of techniques available to insurers—e.g., asset hedges, liability hedges, asset-liability management, contingent financing, and post-loss financing and recapitalization. "Insurance securitization" encompasses one group of techniques in a broad rainbow of financial risk management tools available for the insurer's consideration.

REGULATING AN INSURANCE COMPANY

The regulatory environment in which insurance companies operate is rather unique. In the United States, property/casualty insurers are primarily regulated by the individual states (which interact, to a degree, via the National Association of Insurance Commissioners). There are specific reporting requirements, accounting standards, and various rate filing regulations. This section introduces several issues involved in regulating insurance companies and the insurance industry. The property/casualty insurance regulatory process will be described, including an overview of guaranty funds, and the risk-based capital process and calculations will be discussed.

Regulation and Solvency Issues

This section describes the regulatory environment of the property/casualty insurance industry. Several of the important historical court cases and pieces of legislation are summarized, the state-versus-federal issue is discussed, and the NAIC framework is described. Also described are the guaranty fund system and the NAIC early warning (IRIS) tests.

The Property/Casualty Regulatory Environment

Regulation of insurance is a well-established aspect of the industry. Nevertheless, the question can be asked: why should insurance be regulated? Some of the possible reasons that have been offered for the existence of regulation include the following:

- *Solvency/solidity:* Since policyholders have purchased a promise from insurers to provide indemnification in the event of a loss, those policyholders must be protected from possible insurer insolvency. This is done by monitoring the financial conditions of insurers.

- *Asymmetric information:* Consumers have inadequate knowledge of the insurance process, and must be protected.

- *Reasonable rates:* Since the purchase of insurance can be a legal or practical necessity, and because the individual consumer typically has little "power" in the transaction relative to insurance companies, consumers must be protected from unfair pricing practices.

- *Availability:* The insurance market must be kept healthy and competitive, in order to ensure the existence and availability of insurance coverages.

These and other regulatory considerations have been evaluated and discussed over a long period of time—perhaps as far back as the beginnings of insurance regulation itself. In the U.S., states took increasingly active roles in overseeing the insurance industry throughout the 1800s. The responsibilities of chartering, licensing, and taxing insurance companies led to the creation in the various states of departments devoted to regulating the insurance industry. The first state to create a commission specifically devoted to the insurance industry was New Hampshire in 1851.

The first watershed judicial event in the history of U.S. insurance regulation is normally considered to be the *Paul vs. Virginia* case of 1869. This case, which was ultimately decided by the U.S. Supreme Court, involved a New York fire insurance agent named Samuel Paul, who was sued for selling insurance in Virginia without a Virginia license. Paul, claiming he was involved in interstate commerce, contended that Virginia's licensing requirements were unconstitutional. The Court, finding against Paul, held that insurance is *not* commerce, and thus not subject to the commerce clause of the U.S. Constitution. As a result, this case espoused the rights of states, as opposed to the federal government, to regulate insurance. Two years later, this state regulatory framework led to the organization of the National Convention of Insurance Commissioners (later the National Association of Insurance Commissioners, or NAIC), with the goals of enhancing regulatory consistency across states and sharing important information.

The legal position that insurance was not interstate commerce was maintained until 1944, when the U.S. Supreme Court made a contrary ruling in the *United States vs. Southeast Underwriters Association (SEUA)* case. The SEUA was a rating bureau that, the U.S. federal government claimed, violated antitrust laws (in particular, the Sherman Act). Agreeing with the U.S., the Court found the SEUA guilty of price fixing, on the basis that insurance *is* interstate commerce, and thus subject to federal regulation.

The insurance industry and the states responded to the SEUA decision quickly by putting pressure on Congress to address this issue. The very next year, in 1945, Congress passed Public Law 15, better known as the McCarran-Ferguson Act. This law puts the primary responsibility for insurance regulation back into the hands of the states. In particular, except for cases of boycott, intimidation, or coercion, federal antitrust laws do not apply to the insurance industry. However, federal regulation *is* considered appropriate and authorized in the event that state regulation is found to be inadequate.

This regulatory framework has existed into the 21st century. The primary efforts involving regulation of the insurance industry have come from the states, to some degree coordinated by the NAIC. Typical areas of state regulation include licensing, approval or disapproval of rates and policy forms, solvency and market conduct monitoring, and the rehabilitation and liquidation of insurers.

Insurer Insolvencies

During the 1970s and 1980s, insolvencies in the property/casualty insurance industry increased rather alarmingly. A. M. Best (1991) examined 372 U.S. property/casualty insurer insolvencies that occurred between 1969 and 1990; of those, Best's was able to determine primary causes behind 302 of the insolvencies, distributed as follows:

Primary Cause of Insolvency	Percentage of 302 Cases
Deficient loss reserves (inadequate pricing)	28%
Rapid growth	21
Alleged fraud	10
Overstated assets	10
Significant change in business	9
Reinsurance failure	7
Catastrophe losses	6
Miscellaneous	9

Initial indications of potential insurer difficulty can come from a number of sources. Regulatory examinations often provide a warning regarding existing or future problems. Similarly, audit reports, actuarial loss reserve opinions, or consumer complaints can bring coming difficulties to the attention of regulators.

A state insurance department, when it suspects an insurer of being in financial trouble, has a number of options and responsibilities. A typical regulatory process involving an insurer in potential difficulty would begin with an examination of the company to identify and quantify the problem. Financial statements and accounting records are analyzed, and on-site investigations of the company and its operations are made. Following this analysis, the regulator might decide to place the company under *supervision*. This is an administrative action by the regulator, and may or may not involve restrictions on the company's operations. In any case, closer scrutiny is paid by the regulator to the insurer.

If warranted, the regulator might then obtain a court order for *conservation* or *seizure* of the company. Essentially, this places the company under the control of the regulator. Finally, a decision may be made to either *rehabilitate* or *liquidate* the company. Rehabilitation typically involves an inflow of cash, often from a party interested in taking an ownership interest in the insurer. Liquidation occurs when it is decided that rehabilitation is not a viable option; bankruptcy law and guaranty fund regulations then take control of the situation.

Guaranty Funds

When a property/casualty insurer does become insolvent, a mechanism known as a "guaranty fund" responds. Guaranty funds, which exist in each state, essentially guarantee (with certain limitations) the promises made by an insurer to its policyholders. Although the specific parameters of each fund can vary by state, some of the general characteristics of a property/casualty insurance guaranty fund include the following (see Duncan (1984) and Lee, Mayers, and Smith (1997) for details; both articles describe the NAIC model which was adopted in 1969).

- Guaranty funds are involuntary, not-for-profit associations. Each state's fund is comprised of all insurers licensed in the state that write covered lines of insurance.

- Guaranty funds pay policyholders' loss claims that go unful-filled by insurers due to insolvency. They also provide for refunds of unearned premiums in the event of insurer insol-vency. These payments do not necessarily make the policy-holder whole: the insured's policy coverage limits apply, there is a cap on claims paid by the guaranty fund (although the cap does not apply to workers compensation loss claims), and a deductible applies to unearned premium claims.

- Policyholder claims are funded by assessments on the mem-ber insurers of the association. The assessment made on each insurer is proportional to the relative amount of business the insurer writes in the state. Typically, the maximum assessment on an insurer in a given year is 2% of the company's net direct written premium in that state (based on the preceding year's writings). All states assess their companies on a post-insolvency basis, except for New York, which operates as a pre-assessment fund. There is a provision for a company to pass along at least some of those assessments in the form of future rates.

Over the years, net guaranty fund assessments for the property-liability insurance industry have totaled billions of dol-lars. Assessments increased dramatically in the mid-1980s, in line with the increase in the incidence of insolvencies. Through 1992, annual assessments have been as high as nearly 0.5% of industry premiums. [See Klein (1995) for these and other fig-ures.]

Insurance Regulatory Information System

Regulators have developed processes—both quantitative and qualitative—to monitor the performance and financial health of insurers. In a prior section of this chapter, a number of financial ratios were described that can assist analysts in quantifying the financial performance and solidity of companies. Such ratios are based upon information found in a company's financial reports, e.g., balance sheets and income statements. Similar quantitative measures are utilized by insurance regulators, largely based upon information provided in the Annual Statement (discussed further in the "Data Sources" section of the chapter). Such quantitative measures are an important component of the Insurance Regulatory Information System (IRIS), which has been used by the National Association of Insurance Commissioners since 1973.

IRIS is a system that provides a framework for monitoring insurance companies, and for identifying those companies in need of additional attention. The 11 statistical measures that comprise the *IRIS ratios* (at one time, referred to as "Early Warning Tests") represent the first quantitative step in the process of evaluating insurer solvency. The tests are summarized briefly below.

Leverage Tests:	1. Ratio of premium to surplus
	2. Change in premium writings
	3. Ratio of surplus aid to surplus
Profitability Tests:	4. Two-year operating ratio
	5. Investment yield
	6. Change in policyholders' surplus
Liquidity Tests:	7. Ratio of liabilities to liquid assets
	8. Ratio of agents' balances to surplus
Loss Reserving Tests:	9. One-year reserve development to surplus
	10. Two-year reserve development to surplus
	11. Estimated current reserve deficiency to surplus

These tests provide regulators with an initial screen, helping to identify insurers with potential solvency problems. Associated with each ratio is a "normal" industry range, which may be revised periodically to reflect changes in the general economic or industry environment. Consideration is given to the number of "unusual" ratio results a company has—along with a variety of other criteria—when determining what level of priority to assign a company with respect to the need for additional regulatory investigation.

The importance of monitoring insurer solvency has been manifested by the recent development of additional tests and measures. For example, the Financial Analysis and Surveillance Tracking (FAST) system includes 20 financial ratios (some of which are also IRIS ratios). Whereas the result of applying an IRIS ratio is binary (the ratio is either in or out of the normal range), the FAST system assigns point values for different ratio ranges. Another, very significant, development in the regulatory analysis of solvency is risk-based capital.

Risk-Based Capital

Risk-based capital (RBC) is more than a recently implemented regulatory mechanism—it is also a new and important framework for considering, examining, and measuring insurance company value. In this section, the RBC system is discussed, and the relevant formulas are described in general terms.

Traditionally, an insurer's required capital and surplus levels have been determined simplistically, without appropriate consideration given to the riskiness of the company's operations. After the significant number of insolvencies experienced by the industry in the 1980s, regulators began to recognize that traditional measures of required capital were becoming quickly outdated in an increasingly volatile industry and financial environment. Regulators felt that a new approach to quantifying insurer risk was necessary. In the 1990s, this led to the development of the risk-based capital approach.

The NAIC adopted risk-based capital standards for the property-liability insurance industry beginning with the 1994 annual statement. (Life insurance RBC standards had been adopted one year earlier.) The objectives of these requirements are to:

- Promote the financial stability of property/casualty insurance companies,

- Encourage timely corrective regulatory action in the event a company experiences financial difficulties (in some cases within the RBC framework, corrective action by the regulator is mandatory (see below), which potentially removes some of the discretionary and political aspects of the regulator's job in such situations), and

- Minimize the costs of insurer insolvencies through early identification and treatment of potential financial distress.

These objectives are addressed by a regulatory structure that attempts formally to relate a company's surplus requirements to the nature and riskiness of its operations. These risk-based surplus standards are meant to replace prior flat dollar minimum requirements.

The essence of the RBC formula involves the identification of the nature and degree of risk-taking by the insurer [see, for example, Cummins, Harrington, and Niehaus (1995), Cummins, Harrington, and Klein (1995), Feldblum (1996), and Laurenzano (1995) for more details]. In general, risks are categorized according to type, and a "charge" for each element of risk is applied, with the various charges ultimately totaling an amount that is related to the required amount of surplus. The two broad risk categories are:

- *Asset risks.* The charge associated with each risky asset reflects the relative riskiness of the asset. For example, for unaffiliated bonds held in the insurer's asset portfolio, the charge ranges from 0 to 30 percent, depending upon the default risk of the bond. (All RBC charges referenced here are as of this writing; future charges may differ.) Bonds with greater risk receive higher charges, and the NAIC assigns each bond to one of six classes, from Class 1 (bonds of highest quality) to Class 6 (bonds in or near default). Preferred stock is treated similarly to bonds, with slightly different charges. Unaffiliated common stock holdings receive a charge of up to 15 percent. Finally, the charges are adjusted to reflect the degree of asset concentration. In effect, this adjustment provides an incentive for a company to diversify its investment portfolio. Specific asset classifications include subsidiary insurers (R0), fixed income (R1), equity (R2), and credit (R3). The "credit" classification refers to the possibility of unrecoverable reinsurance, and involves a charge to reinsurance recoverables.

- *Underwriting risks.* The focus of this category is the charge for the riskiness of loss and loss adjustment expense reserves. Specific risk classifications include reserves (R4) and net written premium (R5).

After all the risk charges have been applied, a formula provides the "Authorized Control Level" (ACL) risk-based capital. This amount can then be compared with the company's actual capital, and the relationship between the two values determines the result of the RBC process. According to the NAIC Risk-Based Capital Model Law, there are four levels of regulatory activity resulting from the process:

- *Company Action Level:* If an insurer's capital is less than 200% of the ACL, the insurer must submit a plan to the regulator. In this plan, the insurer explains the company's financial situation, and proposes corrective action.

- *Regulatory Action Level:* If an insurer's capital is less than 150% of the ACL, the regulator must examine the company and specify corrective action.

- *Authorized Control Level:* If an insurer's capital is less than 100% of the ACL, the regulator is authorized to rehabilitate, liquidate, or otherwise take control of the company.

- *Mandatory Control Level:* If an insurer's capital is less than 70% of the ACL, the regulator is required to take control of the company.

As insurance enters the 21st century, many regulatory issues are still being debated. The respective positions of state and federal regulation, the place and role of regulation as financial markets converge, and appropriate methods for ensuring continued solvency are among the contested topics. Insurance continues to be one of the most heavily regulated industries in the United States, and an understanding of the regulatory framework in which insurers operate is critical for actuaries.

DATA SOURCES

The insurance industry is a significant producer and user of information, both quantitative and qualitative. Much of the information that insurers generate is a product of regulatory requirements, e.g., financial statements, information in support of rate filings. Actuaries are prime users of such information, whether their specific roles involve regulatory oversight or corporate or consulting actuarial activities. This section describes for the reader several of the many data sources, both internal and external to the insurance industry, that are available to aid the actuary in performing analyses.

Insurance Industry Data

NAIC Annual Statement

The National Association of Insurance Commissioners (NAIC) requires that each insurance company file an Annual Statement with the insurance department of each state within which the company is licensed to do business; the due date for filing is March 1 of the year following the operating year summarized by the company's statement. The Annual Statement is the industry's primary source of regulatory information, and is prepared under statutory accounting rules and procedures. Each year, the NAIC considers, and sometimes approves, changes to the Annual Statement blank. However, the general format of many of the pages, exhibits, and schedules in the document have been essentially the same for many years. The following list summarizes several of the important components of the Annual Statement.

- *Title page (page 1)*. Identifies the company, address, state of domicile, officers, directors, and other administrative information.

- *Balance sheet (pages 2 and 3)*. Lists the assets (page 2) and the liabilities and surplus accounts (page 3) of the insurer, as of the end of the operating (generally calendar) year. Classifications of assets and liabilities at this point are fairly broad; later pages and schedules provide much greater detail regarding year-end accounts.

- *Income statement (page 4)*. Shows the statutory income earned during the year. Premiums, losses, and investment income are identified in broad, general categories.

- *Statement of cash flows (page 5)*. Shows the movements of cash during the year. Cash flows resulting from premiums collected, losses paid, expenses paid, and investment operations are identified.

- *Underwriting and Investment Exhibit*. This multi-part exhibit provides information at greater levels of detail than the preceding pages. Specifically, various parts of the exhibit show detail regarding:

  — Interest, dividends, and real estate income

  — Capital gains

  — Premiums written and earned, by line of business

  — Losses paid and incurred, by line of business

  — Expenses

- *Analysis and Reconciliation of Assets*. Shows the changes in asset categories during the year.

- *Five-Year Historical Data*. Provides historical data for each of the following:

— Gross and net written premiums, by line of business categories

— Underwriting and investment income, policyholder dividends, and taxes

— Various balance sheet items (e.g., admitted assets, losses, unearned premium reserves)

— Asset allocations by investment category

— Capital and surplus accounts

— Gross and net losses paid

— Various operating ratios

— One- and two-year loss development

- *Schedule A.* Shows real estate acquired and sold during the year, as well as real estate owned at the end of the year.

- *Schedule D.* Shows activities in bonds and common stocks during the year, and the holdings in each at the end of the year. Given that nearly two-thirds of the property/casualty insurance industry's assets are typically in bonds, this is an extremely important exhibit, especially for asset-liability management and dynamic financial analysis purposes. Bonds are listed separately, and summarized by type (e.g., governments, political subdivisions, etc.), by quality (classes 1 through 6), and by maturity distribution (five categories: maturing within one year, over one but within five years, over five but within ten years, over ten but within twenty years, and over twenty years).

- *Schedule F.* Shows the amount of ceded reinsurance, by assuming reinsurer. In addition, it documents the sources and amounts of assumed reinsurance, and shows the funds held on account of reinsurance in unauthorized companies.

- *Schedule P.* This is, for actuaries, potentially one of the most useful sections of the Annual Statement. This is the only data in the Statement that is configured on an "accident year" basis. Ten years of information are included for each major line of business category; specific information includes:

— Direct and assumed, ceded, and net earned premiums

— Direct/assumed and ceded loss payments

— Direct/assumed and ceded allocated loss adjustment expense payments

— Salvage and subrogation received

— Unallocated loss adjustment expense payments

— Losses and allocated loss adjustment expenses unpaid

  • On a case basis (direct/assumed and ceded)

  • Bulk and IBNR (direct/assumed and ceded)

— Unallocated loss adjustment expenses unpaid

In addition, various loss development triangles are provided for the major line of business categories. Ten-year triangles (on a net basis) are provided for total incurred losses and allocated loss adjustment expenses, cumulative paid loss and ALAE, and bulk and IBNR reserves. These exhibits can be used to analyze loss development and historical reserve accuracy.

• *Schedule T.* Shows direct premiums and losses by state.

• *Insurance Expense Exhibit.* Shows premiums, losses, and expenses allocated to the statutory lines of business.

One other item associated with the Annual Statement is the "Statement of Actuarial Opinion," which is to be included with the Annual Statement. This is a document in which a qualified actuary, generally appointed by a company's board of directors, opines on the company's loss and loss adjustment expense reserves. A "qualified actuary" is typically considered to be a member in good standing of the Casualty Actuarial Society, although other persons can also qualify if they meet certain conditions.

The opinion statement includes a *scope* paragraph that identifies the subjects being opined upon, an *opinion* paragraph in which the actuary expresses an opinion on those subjects, and possibly one or more *relevant comments* paragraphs that permit the actuary, if necessary, to qualify or explain the opinion. The opinion statement typically includes comments regarding the impact on loss and loss adjustment expense reserves of relevant material issues, e.g., collectibility of reinsurance, discounting. Since loss and loss adjustment expense reserves generally represent the largest liability on a property/casualty insurer's balance sheet, the Statement of Actuarial Opinion is an important piece of information for regulators.

A. M. Best

A. M. Best is a firm that collects, compiles, and publishes significant information with regard to both the property-liability and life insurance industries. Much of this information has its source in the Annual Statements filed by insurers. Based on this information, and both quantitative and qualitative analyses of insurers and the insurance industry, Best also promulgates ratings that reflect its estimate of an insurer's ability to meet its future obligations to its policyholders. (Although this description will focus on A. M. Best, other organizations also analyze and evaluate the solvency of property/casualty insurance companies; such organizations include Weiss, Standard & Poor's, Duff & Phelps, and Moody's.)

A. M. Best produces a number of different statistical compilations and other publications, including:

- *Aggregates and Averages.* This annual publication provides aggregate industry financial values, both current and historical. The information is compiled from Best's database, permits evaluations of historical industry performance, and provides industry aggregate measures against which to compare an individual insurer's financial and operating results. Specific sections of the publication include consolidated industry

information, historical time series of important financial and
operating results, performance measures by line of business,
and summaries of results for the "leading" property/casualty
companies.

- *Insurance Reports.* Another annual publication, this volume
  provides summary reports on property/casualty insurers, with
  current and some historical financial and operating information on both an individual company and a group basis. This
  publication also includes a description of Best's insurer rating
  system, a list of companies by location (city and state), and a
  list of companies that either changed names or retired (voluntarily or involuntarily) recently. The summary report on each
  company includes the rationale for the current Best's rating
  and a five-year history of ratings and key financial indicators,
  a review and description of the company's business and operations, and a summary of recent financial performance.

Best's ratings process results in two distinct ratings: a "Best's
Rating," which reflects Best's opinion—based on both quantitative and qualitative evaluations—of a company's financial
strength, operating performance, and market profile; and a "Financial Performance Rating," which is a financial and operating
evaluation based primarily on a quantitative analysis. Specifically, Best's Rating categories include "secure" ratings (A++
through B+), and "vulnerable" ratings (B and below); specific
Financial Performance Ratings range from FPR 9 (very strong)
to FPR 5 (good) in the "secure" category, and FPR 4 (fair) to
FPR 1 (poor) in the "vulnerable" category.

For both Best's and FPR ratings, the evaluation is with respect to a company's ability to meet its policyholder obligations,
and to its vulnerability to potentially adverse economic and underwriting conditions. According to A. M. Best, "The objective
of Best's rating system is to evaluate the factors affecting the
overall performance of an insurance company in order to provide our opinion of the company's financial strength and ability
to meet its contractual obligations" [A. M. Best (1991), page

63]. Best uses quantitative and qualitative analysis in evaluating the financial and operating condition of a P-L insurance company. The quantitative tests can be categorized into three groups: profitability tests (e.g., combined ratio, operating ratio, change in surplus), leverage tests (e.g., premium-to-surplus ratio, liabilities-to-surplus ratio), and liquidity tests (e.g., net cash flow, agents' balances to surplus). The qualitative evaluation includes the following five areas: spread of risk, adequacy and soundness of reinsurance, quality and estimated market value of assets, adequacy of loss reserves, and management.

Standard & Poor's

Standard & Poor's (S&P), as well as other financial rating organizations, provides evaluations and ratings on the claims-paying ability of property/casualty insurance companies. For each company rated, on a scale of AAA to CCC, S&P provides a corporate summary, including a rationale for the rating, a review of the company's business, a summary of management and corporate strategy, a summary of historical operating performance, and descriptions of the company's underwriting, investments, capital, liquidity, and reinsurance.

Insurance Services Office and the National Council on Compensation Insurance

Insurance Services Office, Inc. (ISO) provides actuarial and statistical services and information to the property/casualty industry. Member companies can subscribe to these services, which might provide, for example, ratemaking information (such as loss costs) for a particular line and in a particular state. In addition, they periodically produce a number of research reports which compile and analyze information with regard to important topics. The subject matter of some of the recent reports produced by ISO includes:

- Risk/return and profitability of the industry
- Projecting and financing catastrophic risks

- Personal auto insurance profitability and costs

- Legal defense costs

- Health care costs

Subscriptions are available to ISO's "ISOnet" Web Site, which provides on-line access to ISO circulars, downloadable spreadsheets and exhibits, policy forms, surveys, and a variety of other services. Loss and premium experience on CD-ROM is also available for certain lines of business.

The National Council on Compensation Insurance (NCCI) is, like the ISO, an insurance advisory organization. Both organizations employ a number of actuaries, and provide information useful for ratemaking and other actuarial processes to their member companies. The NCCI focuses its efforts and services on workers compensation (the primary line of business not addressed by ISO). The NCCI also publishes articles and perspectives on the workers compensation industry and environment.

Reinsurance Association of America

The Reinsurance Association of America (RAA) is a property/casualty reinsurance trade association. In addition to its work with state and federal authorities, the RAA also produces periodic reports regarding reinsurance data. These reports include a historical reinsurance loss development study, and an annual reinsurance underwriting review.

GAAP Financial Statements

Many of the data sources described above are based upon financial information provided by insurers within a statutory accounting framework. In order to record and summarize financial activity for shareholders and other external claimholders, publicly traded insurers are required to file a variety of reports with the Securities and Exchange Commission (SEC). These include an annual report to shareholders, and a yearly Form 10-K. These reports are prepared on a GAAP basis, making them an interesting complement to statutory filings such as the NAIC Annual Statement.

Other Sources of Information

Insurance-specific information has historically provided the foundation for actuarial analyses. However, the property-liability insurance industry evolved significantly during the late 20th century. The operating environment is now multinational, insurer performance is linked to economic and financial conditions, and ratemaking is taking on a total rate of return perspective. Under these circumstances, and consistent with the broad planning perspective provided by dynamic financial analysis, sources of general business and economic information are becoming critical for actuaries. Some such sources include the following.

- *Wall Street Journal.* This newspaper is a source for daily information regarding interest rates, foreign exchange rates, commodity prices, and stock prices (individual and indices). These items can be found in Section C of the paper.

- *Ibbotson Associates.* This is a commercial organization that sells several products, including the *Stocks, Bonds, Bills and Inflation Yearbook.* This book is an annual publication that provides long-run historical information on interest rates, inflation, and equity market performance. These data can be useful for analyzing long-term financial trends and the correlations between financial variables.

- *Commercial forecasting services.* These firms, which provide economic forecasts using econometric and mathematical models, include Chase Econometrics, Data Resources, Inc., and Wharton Econometrics, among others.

- *Academic publications:* Some of the journals that publish research relevant to actuaries include the *Proceedings of the Casualty Actuarial Society*, the *North American Actuarial Journal*, the *Journal of Actuarial Practice*, the *Geneva Papers*, the *Scandinavian Actuarial Journal, Insurance: Mathematics and*

Economics, and the *Journal of Risk and Insurance.* The *Journal of Economic Literature* can also be useful in scanning for relevant articles, as it categorizes and lists recent papers published in a number journals, on a variety of economic and financial subjects.

- *Internet-based sources:* Web-based sources of information are becoming numerous and popular. Some of the sites that actuaries might find useful include the following.

  — The *Casualty Actuarial Society* maintains a Web Site (www.casact.org) with a number of useful pages and links, including an on-line catalog with a large collection of recent and past CAS articles and abstracts.

  — The *Federal Reserve Bank of St. Louis* maintains its *"FRED"* (Federal Reserve Economic Data) database (www.stls.frb.org/fred/), which includes a number of economic and financial time series of value to actuaries, including employment and population data, interest rates, consumer price indices, and monetary information.

  — The *U.S. Census Bureau* (www.census.gov) provides demographic information of importance for personal lines ratemaking and strategic planning.

  — *State insurance department* Web Sites, in addition to consumer information, may have data on consumer complaints, rate comparisons, industry experience, and legislative updates.

*   *   *   *   *

Prior chapters of this book have provided readers with an understanding of the key concepts and techniques traditionally used by property/casualty actuaries. In this chapter, several special and emerging areas have been presented. Actuaries need to not only master the traditional areas of expertise, but also be able to apply those techniques in nontraditional and emerging settings.

ADDITIONAL READINGS AND CITED REFERENCES

Environmental Liabilities

American Academy of Actuaries, *Costs Under Superfund: A Summary of Recent Studies and Comments on Reform*, Washington, DC., 1995.

American Academy of Actuaries, *Reserving for Asbestos, Pollution, and Other Mass Tort Liabilities; A Report on Recent Surveys of Chief Financial Officers, Consulting Actuaries, and State Regulators*, Washington, DC., 1997.

A. M. Best Company, "Environmental/Asbestos Liability Exposures: A P/C Industry Black Hole," *Best Property/Casualty Supplement*, March 1994.

A. M. Best Company, "P/C Industry Begins to Face Environmental and Asbestos Liabilities," *BestWeek Property/Casualty Supplement*, January 1996.

A. M. Best Company, "Footnote 24 Ushers in a New Era of Asbestos, Environmental Disclosure," *BestWeek Property/Casualty Supplement*, July 1996.

A. M. Best Company, "Property/Casualty A&E Losses Plunge, But Concerns Remain for Individual Companies," *BestWeek Property/Casualty Special Report*, September 21, 1998.

Bhagavatula, R., et al., "Estimation of Liabilities Due to Inactive Hazardous Waste Sites," *CAS Forum*, Summer 1994, 301–365.

Bouska, A., and T. McIntyre, "Measurement of U.S. Pollution Liabilities," *CAS Forum*, Summer 1994, 73–160.

Bouska, A., "Pollution: After Reform, Beyond Superfund," *Contingencies*, January/February 1996.

Bouska, A.,"From Disability Income to Mega-Risks; Policy Event Based Loss Estimation," *CAS Forum*, Summer 1996, 291–320.

Brown, B., et al., "Disclosure Requirements for Mass Torts," *CAS Forum*, Summer 1996, 321–348.

Covaleski, J., "Reinsurers Face Onslaught of Pollution Claims," *Best's Review*, August 1996.

Cross, S., and J. Doucette, "Measurement of Asbestos Bodily Injury Liabilities," *Proceedings of the Casualty Actuarial Society*, 1997, 84:187–300.

Humphrey III, H. H., Minnesota Attorney General, *Report on Insurance Recovery Under the Landfill Cleanup Act, presented to the Minnesota Legislative Commission on Waste Management*, January 29, 1996.

Institute of Actuaries of Australia, *Asbestos-Related Diseases— The Insurance Cost*, 1991.

Insurance Services Office, Inc., *Superfund and the Insurance Issues Surrounding Abandoned Hazardous Waste Sites*, ISO Insurance Issues Series, December 1995.

Kazenski, P., "Recognition, Measurement, and Disclosure of Environmental Liabilities," *CAS Forum*, Summer 1994, 367–400.

Kazenski, P., "Reporting Environmental Liabilities," *Contingencies*, September/October 1995.

Miller, P., and A. Bouska, "The Loser and Still Champion," *Emphasis*, No. 2, 1999.

Ollodart, B., "Loss Estimates Using S-Curves; Environmental and Mass Tort Liabilities," *CAS Forum*, Winter 1997, 111–132.

Probst, et al., *Footing the Bill for Superfund Cleanups: Who Pays and How?*, Washington, DC: Brookings Institution, 1995.

Sharma, V., "Long-Term Threats Remain for Property/Casualty Insurers," *Standard and Poor's CreditWeek*, January 28, 1998.

United States General Accounting Office, *Superfund: Estimates of Number of Future Sites Vary*, 1994.

United States General Accounting Office, *Superfund: How States Establish and Apply Environmental Standards When Cleaning Up Sites*, 1996.

United States General Accounting Office, *Superfund: Number of Potentially Responsible Parties at Superfund Sites is Difficult to Determine*, 1996.

United States General Accounting Office, *Superfund: Information on the Program's Funding and Status*, 1999.

United States General Accounting Office, and L. Dyckman, *EPA's Use of Risk Assessments in Cleanup Decisions*, 1995.

"The Asbestos Epidemic: An Emerging Catastrophe," *USA Today*, Four-Part Series on Asbestos Worldwide, February 1999.

Catastrophe Modeling

Davenport, A. G. "What Makes a Structure Wind Sensitive?" In *Wind Effects on Buildings and Structures*. Edited by J. D. Riera and A. G. Davenport. Rotterdam: A. A. Balkema, 1998.

Feld, J., and K. L. Carper. *Construction Failure*. New York: John Wiley & Sons, 1997.

Frankel, A., "Mapping Seismic Hazard in the Central and Eastern United States," *Seism. Res. Lett*, 1995, 66:8–21.

Friedman, D. G. Computer Simulation of the Earthquake Hazard. In *Geologic Hazards and Public Problems Conference Proceedings*. Edited by R. A. Olson and M. Wallace. Washington, D.C.: U.S. Government Printing Office/Office of Emergency Preparedness, Executive Office of the President, 1969, 153–181.

Friedman, D. G., "Insurance and the Natural Hazards," *International Journal for Actuarial Studies in Non-Life Insurance and Risk Theory*, 1972, 7, Pt. 1:4–58.

Friedman, D. G., *Computer Simulation in Natural Hazard Assessment*, Monograph no. NSF-RA-E-75-002, Boulder, Colo.: Institute of Behavioral Science, University of Colorado, 1975.

Friedman, D. G. "A Possible National Simulation Model Using Geographic Coordinates." In *Natural Hazards Data Resources: Uses and Needs*. Monograph no. 27. Edited by S. K. Tubbesing and P. D. Dinney. Boulder, Colo.: Program on Technology, Environment, and Man, Institute of Behavioral Science, University of Colorado, 1979.

Friedman, D. G., "Natural Hazard Risk Assessment for an Insurance Program," *Geneva Papers on Risk and Insurance*, January 1984, 9:57–128.

Friedman, D. G., and J. J. Mangano. Actuarial Approach to the Estimation of Storm Surge Probabilities on an Open Beach in Lee County, Florida. In *Report of Committee on Coastal Flooding from Hurricanes*. Washington, DC: National Research Council, National Academy of Sciences, 1983.

Fujita, T., *The Mystery of Severe Storms*, University of Chicago, 1992.

Georgiou, P. N., A. G. Davenport, and B. J. Vickery, "Design Wind Speeds in Regions Dominated by Tropical Cyclones," *Journal of Wind Engineering and Industrial Aerodynamics*, 1983, 13:139–152.

Gray, W. M., C. W. Landsea, P. W. Mielke, and K. J. Berry, "Predicting Atlantic Seasonal Hurricane Activity 6–11 Months in Advance," *Weather and Forecasting*, 1992, 7:440–445.

Gray, W. M., and C. W. Landsea. Examples of the Large Modification in US East Coast Hurricane Spawned Destruction by Prior Occurring West African Rainfall Conditions. In *Tropical Cyclone Disasters*. Edited by J. Lighthill, et al. Beijing: Peking University Press, 1993.

Ho, F. P., R. W. Schwerdt, and H. V. Goodyear, *Some Climatological Characteristics of Hurricanes and Tropical Storms, Gulf and East Coasts of the United States*, National Oceanic and Atmospheric Administration Technical Report no. NWS 15, Washington, D.C.: U.S. Department of Commerce, National Oceanic and Atmospheric Administration, National Weather Service, 1975.

Ho, F. P., J. C. Su, K. L. Hanevich, R. J. Smith, and F. P. Richards, *Hurricane Climatology for the Atlantic and Gulf Coasts of the United States*, National Oceanic and Atmospheric Administration Technical Report no. NWS 38, Washington, D.C.: U.S. Department of Commerce, National Oceanic and Atmospheric Administration, National Weather Service, 1987.

Holland, G. J., "An Analytical Model of the Wind and Pressure Profile in Hurricanes," *Monthly Weather Review*, 1982, 108:1212–1218.

Holland, G. J., and M. Lander, "The Meandering Nature of Tropical Cyclone Tracks," *J. Atmos. Sci*, 1993, 50:1254–1266.

Jones, C. G., and C. D. Thorncroft, "The Role of El Nino in Atlantic Tropical Cyclone Activity," *Weather*, 1998, 53:324–336.

Landsea, C. W., "A Climatology of Intense (or Major) Atlantic Hurricanes," *Monthly Weather Review*, 1993, 12:1703–1713.

Lowe, S. P., and J. N. Stanard, "An Integrated Dynamic Financial Analysis and Decision Support System for a Property Catastrophe Reinsurer," *ASTIN Colloquium* XXVII, Renaissance Re Publication, 1996.

Major, J. A., and J. J. Mangano, "Selecting Among Rules Induced from a Hurricane Database," *Journal of Intelligent Information Systems*, 1995, 4:39–52.

Major, J. A. Worldwide Natural Catastrophe Issues. In *Natural Disaster Management*. Edited by J. Ingleton. Great Britain: Tudor Rose, 1999.

Pielke, R. A., *Hurricanes*, Chichester: John Wiley & Sons, 1997.

Schwerdt, R. W., F. F. Ho, and R. R. Watkins, *Meteorological Criteria for Standard Project Hurricane and Probable Maximum Hurricane Wind Fields, Gulf and East Coasts of the United States*, National Oceanic and Atmospheric Administration Technical Report no. NWS 23, Washington, D.C.: U.S. Department of Commerce, National Oceanic and Atmospheric Administration, National Weather Service, 1979.

Stiegler, D. J., and T. T. Fujita, "A Detailed Analysis of the San Marcos, Texas, Tornado, Induced by Hurricane Allen on 10 August 1980," *12th Conf. on Severe Local Storms*, Amer. Met. Soc., Boston, MA, 1982.

Twisdale, L. A., P. J. Vickery, and M. B. Hardy. Uncertainties in the Prediction of Hurricane Windspeeds. In *Hurricanes of 1992: Lessons Learned and Implications for the Future.* Edited by R. A. Cook and M. Soltani. New York: American Society of Civil Engineers, 1994.

Woo, G., *The Mathematics of Natural Catastrophes*, London: Imperial College Press, 1999.

Yeats, R. S., K. Sieh, and C. R. Allen, *The Geology of Earthquakes*, Oxford: Oxford University Press, 1997.

Dynamic Financial Analysis

Appel, D., M. Mulvaney, and S. Witcraft, "Dynamic Financial Analysis of a Workers Compensation Insurer," *CAS Forum*, Summer 1997, 2:89–114.

Canadian Institute of Actuaries, *Dynamic Capital Adequacy Testing—Life and Property and Casualty*, Educational note, 1999.

D'Arcy, S., R. Gorvett, J. Herbers, T. Hettinger, S. Lehmann, and M. Miller, "Building a Public-Access PC-Based DFA Model," *CAS Forum*, Summer 1997, 2:1–40.

D'Arcy, S., R. Gorvett, T. Hettinger, and R. Walling, "Building a Dynamic Financial Analysis Model That Flies," *Contingencies*, November/December 1997, 40–45.

D'Arcy, S., R. Gorvett, T. Hettinger, and R. Walling, "Using the Public-Access DFA Model: A Case Study," *CAS Forum*, Summer 1998, 2:53–118.

Feldblum, S., "Forecasting the Future: Stochastic Simulation and Scenario Testing," *CAS Discussion Paper Program*, 1995, 151–177.

Hodes, D., T. Negaiwi, J. D. Cummins, R. Phillips, and S. Feldblum, "The Financial Modeling of Property/Casualty Insurance Companies," *CAS Forum*, Spring 1996, 3–88.

Kirschner, G., and W. Scheel, "Specifying the Functional Parameters of a Corporate Financial Model for Dynamic Financial Analysis," *CAS Forum*, Summer 1997, 2:41–87.

Lowe, S., and J. Stanard, "An Integrated Dynamic Financial Analysis and Decision Support System for a Property Catastrophe Reinsurer," *CAS Forum*, Spring 1996, 89–118.

Valdmanis, T., "Corporate Execs Examine Strategic Tool: A New Way to Assess Risk Arrives," *USA Today*, May 12, 1999.

Valuation and Financial Analysis Committee, "CAS Dynamic Financial Analysis Handbook," *CAS Forum*, Winter 1996, 1–72.

Venter, G., "Modeling the Evolution of Interest Rates: The Key to DFA Asset Models," *CAS Forum*, Summer 1997, 135–163.

Insurance Securitization

Albert, "Is an Insurance Bond or Derivative an Insurance Contract?," *Financing Risk and Reinsurance*, September 1998, 5–7.

Borden, S., and A. Sarkar, "Securitizing Property Catastrophe Risk," *Current Issues*, Federal Reserve Bank of New York, August 1996.

Canter, M. and J. Cole, "The Foundation and Evolution of the Catastrophe Bond Market," *Global Reinsurance*, September 1997.

Canter, M., J. Cole, and R. Sandor, "Insurance Derivatives: A New Asset Class for the Capital Markets and a New Hedging Tool for the Insurance Industry," *Journal of Applied Corporate Finance*, Fall 1997, 10:69–83.

Chicago Board of Trade, *PCS Catastrophe Insurance Options: A User's Guide*, Chicago: Chicago Board of Trade, 1995.

Cox, S., and R. Schwebach, "Insurance Futures and Hedging Insurance Price Risk," *Journal of Risk and Insurance*, 1992, 59:628–644.

Cummins, J. D., and H. Geman, "Pricing Catastrophe Insurance Futures and Call Spreads: An Arbitrage Approach," *Journal of Fixed Income*, March 1996, 46–57.

Doherty, N., "Financial Innovation in the Management of Catastrophe Risk," *Journal of Applied Corporate Finance*, Fall 1997, 10:84–95.

Doherty, N., "Innovations in Managing Catastrophe Risk," *Journal of Risk and Insurance*, 1997, 64:713–718.

D'Arcy, S., and V. France, "Catastrophe Futures: A Better Hedge for Insurers," *Journal of Risk and Insurance*, 1992, 59:575–600.

D'Arcy, S., and V. France, "Catastrophe Insurance Futures," *CPCU Journal*, December 1993, 46:202–213.

D'Arcy, S., V. France, and R. Gorvett, "Pricing Catastrophe Risk: Could the CBOT Derivatives have Coped with Andrew?," *CAS Discussion Paper Program*, 1999, 59–109.

Gorvett, R., "Insurance Securitization: The Development of a New Asset Class," *CAS Discussion Paper Program*, 1999, 133–173.

Goshay and R. Sandor, "An Inquiry into the Feasibility of a Reinsurance Futures Market," *Journal of Business Finance*, 1973, 5:56–66.

Han, L-M., and G. Lai, "An Analysis of Securitization in the Insurance Industry," *Journal of Risk and Insurance*, 1995, 62:286–296.

Harrington, S., "Insurance Derivatives, Tax Policy, and the Future of the Insurance Industry," *Journal of Risk and Insurance*, 1997, 64:719–725.

Jaffee, D., and T. Russell, "Catastrophe Insurance, Capital Markets, and Uninsurable Risks," *Journal of Risk and Insurance*, 1997, 64:205–230.

Koegel, D., "Securitizing Insurance Risk: A Technique for Spreading Catastrophic Exposure," *Best's Review: Property/ Casualty Edition*, January 1996, 44–49.

Litzenberger, R., D. Beaglehole, and C. Reynolds, "Assessing Catastrophe Reinsurance-Linked Securities as a New Asset Class," *Journal of Portfolio Management*, December 1996, 76–86.

Major, J., "A Synthetic History of the Guy Carpenter Catastrophe Index: Methodology, Data, and Analysis," Guy Carpenter & Company, Inc., 1997.

Major, J., "Index Hedge Performance: Insurer Market Penetration and Basis Risk," Guy Carpenter & Company, Inc., 1996.

McDonald, L., "Investing in Risk Gets Real," *Best's Review: Property/Casualty Edition*, April 1998, 35–39.

Niehaus, G., and S. Mann, "The Trading of Underwriting Risk: An Analysis of Insurance Futures Contracts and Reinsurance," *Journal of Risk and Insurance*, 1992, 59:601–627.

Powers, M., and I. Powers, "Seeking the Perfect Catastrophe Index," *Best's Review Property/Casualty Edition*, December 1997, 101–103.

Quinn, L., "Catastrophe Bonding: Reinsurance and Wall Street versus Mother Nature," *Contingencies*, September/October 1998, 20–27.

Ray, "The Pros and Cons of Insurance Futures," *CPCU Journal*, December 1993, 46:197–200.

Other Topics

A. M. Best Company, *Best's Insolvency Study: Property/Casualty Insurers 1969–1990*, Oldwick, New Jersey, 1991.

A. M. Best Company, *Best's Aggregates and Averages*, Oldwick, New Jersey, Various years.

Cummins, J. D., S. Harrington, and R. Klein, "Insolvency Experience, Risk-Based Capital, and Prompt Corrective Action in Property-Liability Insurance," *Journal of Banking and Finance*, 1995, 19:511–527.

Cummins, J. D., S. Harrington, and G. Niehaus. "Risk-Based Capital Requirements for Property-Liability Insurers: A Financial Analysis." Chapter 5 in *The Financial Dynamics of the Insurance Industry* (New York: Irwin Professional Publishing, 1995).

DeAngelo, H., L. DeAngelo, and S. Gilson, "The Collapse of First Executive Corporation: Junk Bonds, Adverse Publicity, and the 'Run on the Bank' Phenomenon," *Journal of Financial Economics*, 1994, 36:287–336.

DeAngelo, H., L. DeAngelo, and S. Gilson, "Perceptions and the Politics of Finance: Junk Bonds and the Regulatory Seizure of First Capital Life," *Journal of Financial Economics*, 1996, 41:475–511.

Duncan, M., "An Appraisal of Property and Casualty Post-Assessment Guaranty Funds," *Journal of Insurance Regulation*, 1984, 2:289–303.

Feldblum, S., "NAIC Property/Casualty Insurance Company Risk-Based Capital Requirements," *Proceedings of the Casualty Actuarial Society*, 1996, 83:297–435.

The Financial Dynamics of the Insurance Industry. Edited by E. P. Altman and I. T. Vanderhoof. New York: Irwin Professional Publishing, 1995.

Ibbotson Associates, *Stocks, Bonds, Bills, and Inflation 1999 Yearbook*, Chicago, IL., 1999.

Kendall and Fishman, *A Primer on Securitization*, Cambridge, MA: The MIT Press, 1996.

Klein, R., "Insurance Regulation in Transition," *Journal of Risk and Insurance*, 1995, 62:363–403.

Klein, R. "Solvency Monitoring of Insurance Companies: Regulators' Role and Future Direction." Chapter 3 in *The Financial Dynamics of the Insurance Industry* (New York: Irwin Professional Publishing, 1995).

Laurenzano, V. "Risk-Based Capital Requirements for Property and Casualty Insurers: Rules and Prospects." Chapter 4 in *The Financial Dynamics of the Insurance Industry* (New York: Irwin Professional Publishing, 1995).

Lee, S-J., D. Mayers, and C. Smith Jr., "Guaranty Funds and Risk-Taking: Evidence from the Insurance Industry," *Journal of Financial Economics*, 1997, 44:3–24.

Santomero, A., and D. Babbel, "Financial Risk Management by Insurers: An Analysis of the Process," *Journal of Risk and Insurance*, 1997, 64:231–270.

Wheelright, S., and S. Makridakis, *Forecasting Methods for Management*, New York: John Wiley & Sons, Inc., 1985.

INDEX